New perspectives on adolescent risk behavior

Leading scholars of adolescent risk behavior present the most recent ideas and findings about the variety of behaviors that can compromise adolescent development. The volume emphasizes new perspectives on development and on person-centered analysis.

The book is divided into six sections. The first section focuses on development, with a comprehensive chapter by Robert Cairns and his colleagues. The second section covers problem behavior (including drug use and risky driving), and the third section focuses on early sexual activity. The fourth section deals with psychopathology, with a chapter on depression, and the fifth section focuses on social role performance (covering school disengagement and adolescent work). In the final section, John Hagan and Rainer Silbereisen provide integrative chapters.

This important volume, providing a broad overview and reflections on the development of the field, is crucial for all professionals involved in the social psychology of adolescent risk behavior.

Richard Jessor is Director of the Institute of Behavioral Science at the University of Colorado, Boulder. His research interests include adolescent and young adult development, the social psychology of problem behavior, and psychosocial aspects of poverty. He has been awarded fellowships by the National Institute of Mental Health, the Social Science Research Council, and the Center for Advanced Study in the Behavioral Sciences at Stanford. His most recent books include *Ethnography and Human Development: Context and Meaning in Social Inquiry* (editor), *Beyond Adolescence: Problem Behavior and Young Adult Development*, and *Perspectives on Behavioral Science: The Colorado Lectures* (editor).

New perspectives on adolescent risk behavior

Edited by
Richard Jessor

CAMBRIDGE UNIVERSITY PRESS

PUBLISHED BY THE PRESS SYNDICATE OF THE UNIVERSITY OF CAMBRIDGE
The Pitt Building, Trumpington Street, Cambridge, CB2 1RP, United Kingdom

CAMBRIDGE UNIVERSITY PRESS
The Edinburgh Building, Cambridge CB2 2RU, UK   http://www.cup.cam.ac.uk
40 West 20th Street, New York, NY 10011-4211, USA   http://www.cup.org
10 Stamford Road, Oakleigh, Melbourne 3166, Australia

First published 1998

Printed in the United States of America

Typeset in Ehrhardt 11/13 pt. in Quark XPress™ [RF]

*A catalog record for this book is available from
the British Library.*

Library of Congress Cataloging-in-Publication Data
New perspectives on adolescent risk behavior / edited by Richard
Jessor.
p.   cm.
"This volume is the outcome of a remarkably stimulating conference
on 'New perspectives on adolescent risk behavior' held in Los
Angeles on June 28–30, 1996" – Preface.
Includes bibliographical references and indexes.
ISBN 0-521-58432-9 (hb.). – ISBN 0-521-58607-0 (pbk.)
1. Risk-taking (Psychology) in adolescence.   2. Adolescent
psychology.   3. Adolescent psychopathology.   I. Jessor, Richard.
RJ506.R57N49   1998
155.5 – dc21   97-49944
                                                          CIP

ISBN 0 521 58432 9 hardback
ISBN 0 521 58607 0 paperback

Contents

Contributors

Shelli Avenevoli, Doctoral Student, Department of Psychology, Temple University

John S. Baer, Research Associate Professor, Department of Psychology, University of Washington, Seattle

Marsha E. Bates, Associate Research Professor, Center of Alcohol Studies, Rutgers University, New Brunswick, NJ

Peter S. Bearman, Professor of Sociology, University of North Carolina, Chapel Hill

Jeanne Brooks-Gunn, Virginia and Leonard Marx Professor of Child Development and Director, Center for Children and Families, Teachers College, Columbia University

Beverley D. Cairns, Director, Social Development Research, Center for Developmental Science, University of North Carolina, Chapel Hill

Robert B. Cairns, Director, Center for Developmental Science, and Cary C. Boshamer Professor of Psychology, University of North Carolina, Chapel Hill

Bruce E. Compas, Professor of Psychology and Director of Clinical Training, Department of Psychology, University of Vermont

Jennifer K. Connor, Doctoral Student in Clinical Psychology, Department of Psychology, University of Vermont

Margaret E. Ensminger, Associate Professor, Department of Health Policy and Management, School of Hygiene and Public Health, The Johns Hopkins University, Baltimore

David P. Farrington, Professor of Psychological Criminology, Institute of Criminology, University of Cambridge, Cambridge, England

Britt R. Galen, Doctoral Student in School Psychology, Teachers College, Columbia University

Julia A. Graber, Associate Director, The Adolescent Study Program, Teachers College, Columbia University

John Hagan, University Professor of Sociology and Law, University of Toronto

Beth R. Hinden, Postdoctoral Fellow, Children's Hospital, Boston

Richard Jessor, Director, Institute of Behavioral Science, and Professor of Psychology, University of Colorado, Boulder

Monica Kirkpatrick Johnson, Doctoral Student, Department of Sociology, University of Minnesota

Hee Soon Juon, Research Associate, Department of Health Policy and Management, School of Hygiene and Public Health, The Johns Hopkins University, Baltimore

Denise B. Kandel, Professor of Sociomedical Sciences, Department of Psychiatry and School of Public Health, College of Physicians and Surgeons, Columbia University

Erich Labouvie, Professor of Psychology, Center of Alcohol Studies and Psychology Department, Rutgers University, New Brunswick, NJ

Rolf Loeber, Professor of Psychiatry, Psychology and Epidemiology, Western Psychiatric Institute and Clinic, School of Medicine, University of Pittsburgh

Michael G. MacLean, Postdoctoral Research Fellow, Department of Psychology, University of Washington, Seattle

G. Alan Marlatt, Director, Addictive Behaviors Research Center, and Professor of Psychology, University of Washington, Seattle

Jeylan T. Mortimer, Director, Life Course Center, and Professor of Sociology, University of Minnesota

Philip Rodkin, Assistant Director, Center for Developmental Science, University of North Carolina, Chapel Hill

Rainer K. Silbereisen, Professor of Developmental Psychology, and Dean, College of Behavioral and Social Sciences, University of Jena, Germany

Laurence Steinberg, Professor of Psychology, Temple University

Magda Stouthamer-Loeber, Associate Professor of Psychiatry and Psychology, Western Psychiatric Institute and Clinic, School of Medicine, University of Pittsburgh

J. Richard Udry, Kenan Professor of Maternal and Child Health and Sociology, Carolina Population Center, University of North Carolina, Chapel Hill

Welmoet B. Van Kammen, Research Scientist, Macro International, Atlanta

Helene Raskin White, Professor of Sociology, Center of Alcohol Studies and Sociology Department, Rutgers University, New Brunswick, NJ

Allan F. Williams, Senior Vice President, Insurance Institute for Highway Safety, Arlington, VA

Hongling Xie, Research Associate, Center for Developmental Science, University of North Carolina, Chapel Hill

Preface

This volume is the outcome of a remarkably stimulating conference on "New Perspectives on Adolescent Risk Behavior" held in Los Angeles on June 28–30, 1996. The conference was an effort to capture and consolidate the pervasive changes that were taking place in the way in which adolescent risk behavior was being studied at the close of the century – changes in conceptualization, in research design, and in analytic methods. The contextualization of risk behavior, its embeddedness in life-span developmental process, and the new explanatory concern with protection as well as risk were only a few of the ways in which contemporary inquiry had been transformed from its earlier orientations.

An interdisciplinary group of distinguished scholars whose own work had contributed to the transformation was assembled for 3 days of presentations and intense interchange. Each scholar had been charged with the tasks of identifying new trends in the field in which he or she was working, considering empirical exemplifications of those trends, and reflecting on their implications for future research. The chapters in this volume, all extensively revised in light of the conference discussions, are the final product. Together they limn the outlines of an agenda for inquiry about adolescent risk behavior at the opening of a new century.

The idea for the conference and for a subsequent volume was conceived during the editor's 1995–1996 tenure as a Fellow at the Center for Advanced Study in the Behavioral Sciences at Stanford. That superb context of intellectual and collegial support facilitated the planning of the conference, and the committed and unstinting assistance of Ms.

Nancy Pinkerton of the Center staff ensured its successful realization. Personal support during the Fellowship year was provided by the William T. Grant Foundation (950 30 128) and the John D. and Catherine T. MacArthur Foundation (8900078), and I am grateful to both. I want also to acknowledge the deep influence on my thinking about adolescent risk behavior that has come from my experience on the Carnegie Council on Adolescent Development and from a decade as chair of the MacArthur Foundation Research Network on Successful Adolescent Development among Youth in High-Risk Settings.

The conference itself was organized with extraordinary grace and efficiency by the Youth Enhancement Service, a division of the Brain Information Service of the University of California at Los Angeles, directed by Professor Michael H. Chase. Funding for the conference was provided to the Youth Enhancement Service by the Anheuser-Busch Foundation, and its support for this endeavor is very much appreciated.

The task of processing draft papers and their revisions into final chapter drafts and, ultimately, into a book manuscript once again fell to Marilyn Sena of the Institute of Behavioral Science here at the University of Colorado. Her dedication and competence in this regard have been celebrated before, but my appreciation and indebtedness grow with each new accomplishment. She has been a long-time, indispensable collaborator.

My hope is that readers of the chapters in this volume, scholars and students alike, will gain a new appreciation of the promise of further work on adolescent risk behavior – and will be spurred to pursue it.

1

New perspectives on adolescent risk behavior

Richard Jessor

Introduction

The past several decades have witnessed a remarkable invigoration of theoretical and empirical work on adolescent risk behaviors – behaviors that can, directly or indirectly, compromise the well-being, the health, and even the life course of young people. Knowledge about risk behavior has expanded almost geometrically in recent years, and it has become far more coherent and systematic than before. Today's conceptualizations encompass a wide array of causal domains, from culture and society on one side to biology and genetics on the other; they also convey, at the same time, a hard-earned awareness of complexity and a renewed respect for developmental processes.

This invigoration and, indeed, transformation of work on adolescent risk behavior is obviously part of larger and more far-reaching trends in social inquiry as a whole, trends that, taken together, have been labeled "developmental science" (Cairns, Elder, & Costello, 1996) or, more narrowly, "developmental behavioral science" (Jessor, 1993). As an emerging paradigm, the trends refer to the multidisciplinary, multivariable, time-extended, process-focused, contextually situated, person-centered kinds of studies increasingly represented in contemporary social problem research. The chapters in this volume reflect, in one way or another, this newer orientation to inquiry, and risk behavior has been one of the arenas of social inquiry in which a developmental behavioral science approach has been most evident.

Most earlier work on adolescent risk behaviors was confined to a particular subset, often termed *problem behaviors,* that involved legal or normative transgression and that usually elicited social sanctions; traditionally, these included delinquency, drug use, alcohol abuse, and early sexual activity. More recent work has not only enlarged the perimeter around problem behavior to include, for example, tobacco use and risky driving, but has also recognized the functional commonality of these problem behaviors with other domains of adolescent activity that also compromise healthy development – inadequate social role performance, such as poor school progress; psychopathology, such as depression; and health-compromising behaviors, such as poor dietary practices or insufficient exercise. Increasingly, scholars have begun to show concern for an expanded repertoire of adolescent risk behavior and, increasingly, they have been exploring the organization and structure of diverse risk behaviors – their covariation, for example – rather than approaching them as unique or separate or isolated actions.

Expansion of the adolescent risk behavior domain has been accompanied by a parallel expansion of explanatory efforts. Single-variable explanations, such as low self-esteem or the absence of positive role models, have given way to well-articulated, multivariate, multilevel accounts that implicate person, context, and their interaction. As Wachs has noted in relation to development as a whole, "causality is best assigned to a complex of covarying multiple influences" (1996, p. 798), and this view seems to capture the current consensus in regard to risk behavior as well.

The concept of risk behavior as behavior that can compromise well-being, health, and the life course has its focus on the potential of such behavior to result in negative outcomes or adverse consequences – drug use can lead to trouble with parents or the law; early sexual activity can lead to unintended childbearing; school dropout can result in chronic unemployment. Risk behaviors can be considered, therefore, as *risk factors* for personally or socially or developmentally undesirable outcomes. Understanding the processes that link risk behaviors to such outcomes – that is, how risk behaviors function as risk factors – is a key task for research in this domain. Obviously, there is considerable uncertainty or variability in the linkage of risk behaviors to adverse outcomes, and that variability presents a critical explanatory challenge.

But the challenge on this outcome or consequence side of engaging in risk behavior is only half of the explanatory challenge. The other half lies on the other side, the side of accounting for why an adolescent engages in risk behavior in the first place. It is in this regard that the search for understanding has articulated a large array of antecedents or risk factors – both proximal and distal – that have been shown to influence engagement in risk behavior, and the explanatory account has progressed far beyond such early dispositional simplifications as "risk-taking" and such contextual simplifications as "poverty." The elaboration of risk factors for engaging in risk behavior has implicated a variety of causal domains, and it has permitted the identification of both direct and indirect pathways of influence. At the same time, however, it has become quite clear that risk factors alone yield a less than exhaustive account of involvement in risk behavior. Just as there is great heterogeneity in the linkage between involvement in risk behaviors and the likelihood of adverse outcomes, as noted earlier, there is also great heterogeneity in the linkage between exposure to risk factors and the likelihood of involvement in risk behavior. In this connection, O'Connor and Rutter have noted that "*variability* in response to risk is as important as the effect of the risk itself" (1996, pp. 787–788).

It is this heterogeneity or variability on both the antecedent and the consequent sides of engaging in risk behavior that has led to an important new focus of inquiry concerning adolescent risk behavior, namely, the identification and assessment of *protective factors*. Conceptually, protective factors have both direct and indirect effects; they lessen the likelihood of engaging in risk behaviors, or of adverse outcomes from having engaged in them, but they also can serve as moderators of or buffers against exposure to risk factors or actual involvement in risk behaviors themselves. Recent research has begun to examine the concept of protective factors in a wide range of studies of adolescent risk behavior and, increasingly, to engage this additional level of complexity in the quest for more exhaustive explanation (Costa, Jessor, & Turbin, in press; Garmezy, 1985; Garmezy & Masten, 1986; Jessor, Turbin, & Costa, under review; in press; Jessor, Van Den Bos, Vanderryn, Costa, & Turbin, 1995; Luthar, 1992; Rutter, 1979, 1990; Stattin, Romelsjö, & Stenbacka, 1997; Werner, 1989).

A recent attempt to capture some of the new trends in thinking about adolescent risk behavior is shown in Figure 1.1. As a generic conceptual framework (Jessor, 1992), it seeks to represent the multilevel domains implicated in current research, their differentiation into multiple risk and protective factors, their linkage to each other, and their joint influ-

Interrelated Conceptual Domains of Risk Factors and Protective Factors

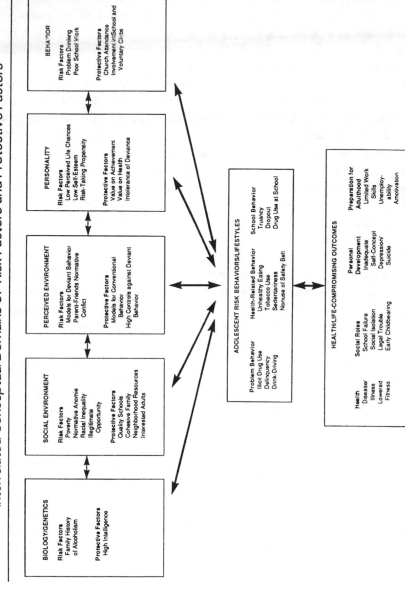

RISK & PROTECTIVE FACTORS

RISK BEHAVIORS

RISK OUTCOMES

RISK & PROTECTIVE FACTORS

BIOLOGY/GENETICS

Risk Factors
Family History
of Alcoholism

Protective Factors
High Intelligence

SOCIAL ENVIRONMENT

Risk Factors
Poverty
Normative Anomie
Racial Inequality
Illegitimate
Opportunity

Protective Factors
Quality Schools
Cohesive Family
Neighborhood Resources
Interested Adults

PERCEIVED ENVIRONMENT

Risk Factors
Models for Deviant Behavior
Parent-Friends Normative
Conflict

Protective Factors
Models for Conventional
Behavior
High Controls against Deviant
Behavior

PERSONALITY

Risk Factors
Low Perceived Life Chances
Low Self-Esteem
Risk-Taking Propensity

Protective Factors
Value on Achievement
Value on Health
Intolerance of Deviance

BEHAVIOR

Risk Factors
Problem Drinking
Poor School Work

Protective Factors
Involvement in School and
Voluntary Clubs
Church Attendance

ADOLESCENT RISK BEHAVIORS/LIFESTYLES

Problem Behavior
Illicit Drug Use
Delinquency
Drink-Driving

Health-Related Behavior
Unhealthy Eating
Tobacco Use
Sedentariness
Nonuse of Safety Belt

School Behavior
Truancy
Dropout
Drug Use at School

HEALTH/LIFE-COMPROMISING OUTCOMES

Health
Disease/
Illness
Lowered
Fitness

Social Roles
School Failure
Social Isolation
Legal Trouble
Early Childbearing

Personal
Development
Inadequate
Self-Concept
Depression/
Suicide

Preparation for
Adulthood
Limited Work
Skills
Unemploy-
ability
Amotivation

ence on adolescent risk behaviors and risky lifestyles. It also illustrates the linkage of risk behaviors and risky lifestyles, in turn, to health-, development-, and life-compromising outcomes. The directional arrows are intended to convey that the framework is really a "web of causation" (MacMahon, Pugh, & Ipsen, 1960, p. 18), an interacting rather than a linear system, and that, in a dynamic system developing and changing over time, what is effect at one point in time may well be cause at another, and vice versa. The particular variables shown in the framework are an illustrative subset, and their location may well be arguable or depend on where the focus is in the ongoing developmental process (e.g., depression in this volume is considered a risk behavior, whereas it is shown as an outcome in Figure 1.1). But the overriding purpose of the framework is to illustrate the magnitude of the explanatory task, the complexity it entails, the need for differentiation of structures of variables, and the importance of articulating lines of both direct and indirect influence. Understanding the linkages in such a framework, and grasping its dynamics of change over time and development, constitute a truly daunting task. That, however, is what appears to be required by the recent trends and the new perspectives on adolescent risk behavior.

The chapters in this volume

In the preparation of this volume, no attempt was made to address every adolescent risk behavior that has drawn research attention in recent years. On the contrary, our primary concern was to articulate and exemplify the major new perspectives. Given the covariation among risk behaviors and the commonality of many of their risk and protective factors, a sampling of risk behavior domains and of the risk behaviors in those domains was deemed adequate. Three major do-

Figure 1.1 A conceptual framework for adolescent risk behavior: risk and protective factors, risk behaviors, and risk outcomes. (From Risk behavior in adolescence: A psychosocial framework for understanding and action (p. 27) by Richard Jessor, 1992, in *Adolescents at risk: Medical and social perspectives*, edited by D. E. Rogers and E. Ginzburg, Boulder, CO: Westview Press, Copyright © 1992 by Westview Press. Reprinted by permission of Westview Press.

mains of adolescent risk behavior are represented by the various chapters: problem behavior, such as drug use, delinquency, early sexual activity, and risky driving; psychopathology, here depression; and inadequate social role performance, such as school failure and work-related difficulties. A fourth domain, that of health behavior – diet, exercise, safety, and so on – was reserved for a later conference and volume and, therefore, was excluded from this one.

Assignment of the various chapters to the different sections is also somewhat arbitrary because many of them transcend those confines. An effort was made to group them according to the salience of their substantive focus and to invite the reader to see them all as interrelated, despite their formal segregation.

Because the task assigned to the authors of the last two chapters in the volume – John Hagan, a sociologist, and Rainer Silbereisen, a psychologist – was to comment on the various contributions and to reflect on their implications for the next phase of research on adolescent risk behavior, only brief introductions to the various chapters need to be made at this point. The chapter by the Cairns and their two colleagues stands somewhat apart as a compelling exegesis on developmental science. It captures the centrality that development and change have assumed in contemporary risk behavior research – reliance on longitudinal design and on a life-span perspective in which the childhood antecedents and the young adult outcomes of adolescent risk behavior are considered an integral part of its investigation. The Cairns' concern for person-centered inquiry is also a theme echoed in later chapters as well. As Abbott has admonished us, "our normal methods . . . attribute causality to the variables . . . rather than to agents; variables do things, not social actors" (1992, p. 428). By way of counterpoint, the Cairns urge that agency be restored to persons in context, and they elaborate methods that are germane to that task.

The chapter by Kandel is a powerful example of the illumination that can be achieved by engaging biological variables in an account of variation in drug abuse. Her chapter makes it clear that biological risk factors can no longer be ignored and that what she terms "the mutual relevance of epidemiology and biology" can be a source of provocative hypotheses for future research. Loeber and associates provide an exhaustive examination of structure and organization among a larger than usual set of diverse risk behaviors and also among their risk factors.

Their establishment of covariation of risk behaviors in these younger age cohorts argues for its robustness over a larger developmental span than adolescence alone. In the chapter by White, Bates, and Labouvie, as in several of the others, the focus is on the other side of adolescence, that is, on young adulthood, and on the long-term outcomes of earlier involvement in risk behavior – for them, adolescent drug use. An application of new, more sophisticated methods in an effort to understand the developmental process, the analysis of individual growth curves turns out to be descriptively enlightening.

Baer, MacLean, and Marlatt make a critical distinction between substance use per se and use-related problems in working toward a harm-reduction approach to treatment. Offering a new perspective on treatment or intervention for substance abuse problems, the authors emphasize the need to tailor treatment to differential trajectories of risk behavior development. Allan Williams brings new attention to a conventionally neglected problem behavior – risky driving. Motor vehicle crashes are the most serious cause of mortality for 16- to 19-year-olds. Williams shows the linkage of risky driving and crashes to other risk behaviors assessed earlier in adolescence.

The chapter by Udry and Bearman describes an extraordinary research endeavor – Add Health – that approaches the study of sexual behavior in a way that includes nearly every aspect of the new perspectives in developmental behavioral science. It involves biology and behavior genetics while assessing multiple social contexts and psychosocial dispositions; it is longitudinal in design; it is unusually comprehensive in the variables measured; and it even permits analyses of friendship pairs as well as of individuals. Clearly an exemplar for future research design, it is already an available resource of exceptional richness for risk behavior researchers and scholars. Adolescent sexual activity as risk behavior is also addressed by Graber, Brooks-Gunn, and Galen. They discuss the important notion of transition-based turning points in characterizing sexual initiation and then elaborate an extensive list of recent reorientations in the study of adolescent sexuality.

The chapter by Compas, Connor, and Hinden is an authoritative appraisal of the current state of research knowledge about adolescent depression, and it provides new perspectives that challenge conventional wisdom in that field. In their conclusion that comorbidity of depression is the rule rather than the exception, there is a challenge to the appropriateness of psychiatric nosological distinctions; and in their conclusion that gender differences are very small in magnitude, there is a challenge to the view of depression as being especially relevant to female adolescent development.

Ensminger and Juon implement a person-centered approach by clustering their now-adult sample on a variety of attributes reflecting successful role performance beyond adolescence, and then examining the differential childhood and adolescent precursors of membership in the various clusters. Illuminating the process of "making it" despite the adversities of the inner-city background common to all the clusters, the analysis also illuminates the role that protective factors, such as a supportive family and strong family supervision, play in that process. The chapter by Steinberg and Avenevoli focuses on school, family, and work as interactive contexts that influence the emergence of risk behavior in adolescence. Using both variable-centered and person-centered analyses and a longitudinal design, they reveal the centrality of role performance in school and the cascade of life-compromising consequences that can follow school disengagement. Their conclusion that "early engagement in school may serve as an important protective factor against subsequent problem behavior" appears to hold true for both boys and girls in their study. Mortimer and Johnson examine the paid work experience of teenagers as a risk behavior in an impressive longitudinal study, with follow-up into young adulthood. Different patterns of work, based on both duration and intensity, can, depending on the pattern, increase the likelihood of involvement in certain problem behaviors or, by contrast, result in higher grades and lower dropout during high school. Paid work experience in high school can also lead to more positive work-related outcomes in young adulthood. The study is, indeed, an instantiation of a rather new perspective in this domain of adolescent risk behavior.

Each of the two commentary chapters goes well beyond discussion of the various chapters to constitute a contribution in its own right. For Hagan, a key challenge is to find a language that can help to unify the various analytic approaches while being sensitive, at the same time, to the fact that young people are differentially advantaged or disadvantaged due to their life circumstances. His exploration of the "language of capitalization" and his conceptualization of "youth development as a capitalization process" are extremely provocative and richly heuristic.

And finally, Silbereisen's summary of "lessons learned" gives salience to and elaborates the key themes emerging from the preceding chapters. But he also reminds us that much still remains to be done; for example, we have not yet succeeded in capturing the phenomenology of adolescence, the meanings that everyday life has for young people, nor have we taken full advantage of the "natural experiments" of rapid social change occurring internationally, contextual changes that directly affect the course and context of youth development. Silbereisen's chapter leaves us with a sobering reminder that the accomplishments represented by the various new perspectives are only one more step along the road to a fully comprehensive understanding of adolescent risk behavior. Much still remains to be done.

References

Abbott, A. (1992). From causes to events: Notes on narrative positivism. *Sociological Methods and Research, 20*, 428–455.

Cairns, R. B., Elder, G. H., Jr., & Costello, J. (Eds.). (1996). *Developmental Science*. New York: Cambridge University Press.

Costa, F. M., Jessor, R., & Turbin, M. S. (in press). Psychosocial risk and protective factors in adolescent problem drinking: A longitudinal approach. *Journal of Studies on Alcohol*.

Garmezy, N. (1985). Stress resistant children: The search for protective factors. In J. Stevenson, Jr. (Ed.), *Recent research in developmental psychopathology* (pp. 213–233). Oxford: Pergamon Press.

Garmezy, N., & Masten, A. S. (1986). Stress, competence, and resilience: Common frontiers for therapist and psychopathologist. *Behavioral Therapy, 17*, 500–521.

Jessor, R. (1992). Risk behavior in adolescence: A psychosocial framework for understanding and action. In D. E. Rogers & E. Ginzburg (Eds.), *Adolescents at risk: Medical and social perspectives* (pp. 19–34). Boulder, CO: Westview Press.

Jessor, R. (1993). Successful adolescent development among youth in high-risk settings. *American Psychologist, 48*, 117–126.

Jessor, R., Turbin, M. S., & Costa, F. M. (under review). Risk and protection in successful outcomes among disadvantaged adolescents. *Applied Developmental Science*.

Jessor, R., Turbin, M. S., & Costa, F. M. (in press). Protective factors in adolescent health behavior. *Journal of Personality and Social Psychology: Personality Processes and Individual Differences*.

Jessor, R., Van Den Bos, J., Vanderryn, J., Costa, F. M., & Turbin, M. S. (1995). Protective factors in adolescent problem behavior; Moderator of fects and developmental change. *Developmental Psychology, 31*, 923–933.

Luthar, S. (1992). Methodological and conceptual issues in research on childhood resilience. *Journal of Child Psychology and Psychiatry, 34*, 441–453.

MacMahon, B., Pugh, T. F., & Ipsen, J. (1960). *Epidemiologic methods.* Boston: Little, Brown,

O'Connor, T. G., & Rutter, M. (1996). Risk mechanisms in development: Some conceptual and methodological considerations. *Developmental Psychology, 32*, 787–795.

Rutter, M. (1979). Protective factors in children's response to stress and disadvantage. In W. M. Kent & J. E. Rolf (Eds.), *Primary prevention of psychopathology* (Vol. 3, pp. 49–74). Hanover, NH: University Press of New England.

Rutter, M. (1990). Psychosocial resilience and protective mechanisms. In J. Rolf, A. S. Masten, D. Cicchetti, K. N. Neuchterlein, & S. Weintraub (Eds.), *Risk and protective factors in the development of psychopathology* (pp. 181–214). Cambridge: Cambridge University Press.

Stattin, H., Romelsjö, A., & Stenbacka, M. (1997). Personal resources as modifiers of the risk for future criminality: An analysis of protective factors in relation to 18-year-old boys. *British Journal of Criminology, 37*, 198–223.

Wachs, T. D. (1996). Known and potential processes underlying developmental trajectories in childhood and adolescence. *Developmental Psychology, 32*, 796–801.

Werner, E. E. (1989). High-risk children in young adulthood: A longitudinal study from birth to 32 years. *American Journal of Orthopsychiatry, 59*, 72–81.

Part I

A focus on development

2

New directions in developmental research: Models and methods

Robert B. Cairns, Beverley D. Cairns,
Philip Rodkin, and Hongling Xie

Developmental research has enjoyed enormous growth in the past two decades. Virtually all gauges of scientific activity – research articles published, funds generated, journals created, volumes released – indicate that the discipline's expansion in the 1980s and 1990s matches the earlier growth spurt of the 1920s and 1930s. The main difference is that contemporary progress is occurring on several fronts simultaneously.[1] Each of the modern domains of developmental research can claim increases in scientific activity and, possibly, in influence.

Epidemiological measures of childhood and adolescent mental health tell a different story, however. They suggest decline rather than progress. During the past two decades, there have been increases in problems that have been targeted for solution by developmental researchers. These include heightened rates of arrests for violence among girls, increased drug use, more sexually transmitted diseases in adolescence, increases in unmarried teen parenthood, and increases in the rate of teenage suicide. To be sure, not all the news is bad. Over the same period, there have been increases in performance on cognitive tests, higher rates of high school graduation, and lower rates of infant mortality for children of teenage parents.

Because commonsense measures of progress in developmental research yield conflicting results, a third perspective seems called for. It is provided by persons who should know the discipline best, namely, a sample of its leading contributors. To this end, a group of senior developmental researchers recently completed an evaluation of the state of the science and its methods (Cairns, Elder, & Costello, 1996). The statement takes stock of where the discipline has been and what appear to be the most promising directions for future conceptual and methodological development (Carolina Consortium on Human Development, 1996) Over an 8-year period, this group addressed the distinctive emphases of developmental concepts and the need to close the gap between developmental concepts and developmental methods. In brief, the Consortium contributors pointed to a need for restructuring the discipline. They wrote:

> Developmental science refers to a fresh synthesis that has been generated to guide research in the social, psychological, and biobehavioral disciplines. It describes a general orientation for linking concepts and findings of hitherto disparate areas of developmental inquiry, and it emphasizes the dynamic interplay of processes across time frames, levels of analysis, and contexts. Time and timing are central to this perspective. The time frames employed are relative to the lifetime of the phenomena to be understood. Units of focus may be as short as milliseconds, seconds, and minutes, or as long as years, decades, and millennia. In this perspective, the phenomena of individual functioning are viewed at multiple levels – from the subsystems of genetics, neurobiology, and hormones to those of families, social networks, communities, and cultures.
>
> We believe that recognizing the complexity of development is the first step toward understanding its coherence and simplicity. On this perspective, patterns of adaptation represent interactions across levels within and without the person. Because the relative weights of these contributors to behavior vary across ontogeny and across domains, longitudinal analyses have particular value in understanding how they are coalesced over development. The pathways of development are relative to time and place; they contribute to – and reflect – temporal changes in culture and society. Developmental investigation focuses attention to the ontogenies of both embryos and ancestors, and to the process by which pathways may be repeated or redirected across successive generations. Toward this end, comparative, cross-cultural, and intergenerational research strategies should be employed in conjunction with standard experimental methods.(p. 1)

In a far-reaching design recommendation, longitudinal designs are seen as necessary for the conduct of developmental research, but they are not sufficient. If the measures adopted and the analyses employed are irrelevant to the developmental concepts that undergird the research, longitudinal designs are gutted of their distinctiveness.

For issues of social development, the Consortium's statement emphasized that several layers of influence must be considered because of the holistic and dynamic nature of behavioral development. Behavioral variables rarely function as independent entities that are separable from the web of influences in which they occur. Characteristics of two or more individuals are necessarily interwoven in the support of social exchanges. Moreover, because of the operation of mutual constraints within a holistic system, variables do not occur in isolation in the person and the environment; they appear in clusters and clumps. In each person, configurations of characteristics become correlated and mutually constrained (Carolina Consortium on Human Development, 1996).

Is a holistic system so complicated that it is beyond the methods of science? The answer depends on which methods of science are employed. If variable-oriented approaches are adopted, where the goal is to identify the separate and distinctive contribution of each variable, identifying new relationships and interactions over time may indeed overwhelm the analysis by adding fresh layers of complexity. But if person-oriented approaches are employed, identifying new relationships and interactions over time helps specify how the system is constrained and, thereby, reduces the range of solutions that are possible (Magnusson, 1988). Too complicated? To the contrary, the Consortium's statement holds that "recognizing the complexity of development is the first step toward understanding its coherence and simplicity" (p. 1).

The Consortium's statement is consistent with other proposals that have been offered on developmental study. Accordingly, Jessor and his colleagues succinctly observed:

Understanding the integrity of the life course, tracing its continuity over large segments of time, distinguishing what is ephemeral from what is lasting, grasping the role that the past plays in shaping the future – all these, and more, are issues that yield only to research that is longitudinal and developmental in design. (Jessor, Donovan, & Costa, 1991, p. 3)

Similarly, in his comments on the relevance of the Consortium's statement for modern methods, Bronfenbrenner (1996) observed:

[T]he defining properties of the emergent model contradict, almost point for point, the now prevailing conceptual and operational strategies of choice in each specialized field of inquiry. (p. ix)

What are the point-for-point contradictions? Four of the more prominent are the following:

1. *Aggregation versus disaggregation.* Prevailing methods frequently begin with a research design that involves sampling persons and aggregating across individuals and contexts. Aggregation across persons into the sample typically occurs at the first stage of the study to obtain estimates of population parameters and to identify the distinctive residual that reflects individual differences. By contrast, a primary goal of developmental methods is to understand the "residual" – those individual processes that contribute to the ontogeny of the child's adaptations in the particular settings of life. Hence, developmental research ultimately seeks description of the person-in-context in terms of a configuration of influences.

2. *Disentangling variables versus integrating variables.* A second goal of prevailing research methods is to identify the unique contribution of a variable in predicting a particular outcome independent of other sources of variance. The statistical dilemma is that higher-order interactions among variables constitute key findings for developmental theory, yet they present formidable problems for analysis (Wahlsten, 1990). By contrast, a major goal of developmental research is to understand how characteristics (i.e., variables) function together to guide, regulate, and constrain actions. This aim leads, in turn, to a focus on the relations among characteristics and how the resultant configurations are associated with later adaptive behaviors.

3. *Eliminating time versus understanding time.* Many of the conventional research and statistical procedures eliminate, control, or mute the effects of time and age. These include the standard use of correlations, z-scores, and the transformations that control for age by attempting to rule out age effects. Once eliminated methodologically, the effects of age tend to be forgotten theoretically. For developmental analyses, however, variations in age and timing are central to understanding effective change and continuity processes. Rather than getting rid of the effects associated with time and timing, researchers can exploit this information in developmental designs to clarify how integration occurs.

4. *Eliminating contexts versus measuring contexts.* Conventional research procedures also tend to hold constant, isolate, or other-

wise eliminate variations in context. This is a research goal for experimental laboratory and medical procedures that try to control for potentially confounding effects (e.g., circadian variations, environmental distractions, and other confounds). Such controls are necessary to bring into focus the effects of the variables of interest.

Developmental analyses, by contrast, view social contexts and the everyday events of life as critical agents of developmental stability and change. Accordingly, attention must be given to identifying units of social context beyond the individual, including the social network in which the person is embedded. Hence social-contextual influences must be assessed and integrated into any analysis of individual prediction, and units of analysis beyond the person become key in modern developmental methods. Moreover, the characteristics of the person and the properties of the environment tend to become correlated. These "correlated constraints" have been assumed to be key to understanding continuity and change over time (Cairns, McGuire, & Gariépy, 1993).

In summary, the methodological implications of developmental concepts extend beyond the need to employ longitudinal designs. Three central issues are:

A.   the need to clarify techniques to disaggregate samples into coherent subgroups and to identify the nature of correlated constraints that operate in individual development;

B.   the need to develop procedures that permit the precise description of change in the social environment, including changes in the child's social networks and interactional patterns; and

C.   the need to devise operations for tracking individual developmental pathways over ontogeny, including ways to integrate information from configurations and social networks.

A. Clusters and configurations

Even though multivariate, multimethod, and multilevel longitudinal investigation is becoming the developmental design of choice, it has certain hazards that can cripple the enterprise. Data tyranny is one of them. The investigator can become overwhelmed by enormous quantities of raw data that are generated over several years of assessment with multiple tests and multiple informants. Although advances in computer memory have helped to solve many problems of data storage, there are inherent limits in the capacity of humans to organize and reflect on the information. In addition, certain stubborn statistical and interpretative issues arise if one attempts to consider multiple variables and multiple levels of interaction simultaneously. To the extent that the bidirectional proposition is correct, it must be assumed that key variables merge, converge, and coalesce, losing their separate identities. Moreover, novel patterns of behavior and constraints are assumed to emerge in the course of development and cannot be anticipated in the original factorial design. These theoretical propositions on the integrated nature of development seem directly at odds with traditional statistical designs whose aim is to capture the distinctive variance attributable to a given variable by holding constant or covarying other variables. Then there are additional pitfalls because of the insensitivity of analysis of variance models to interaction effects (Wahlsten, 1990).

How does one avoid being tyrannized by data? The solution turns out to be less a matter of statistics than one of logic and theory (Bakeman, Cairns, & Appelbaum 1979). In this regard, an assumption about the holistic nature of social development suggests a radically different approach for studying lives over time. The proposition is: *Given the interdependence of characteristics in persons and contexts, it can be assumed that there exists a finite number of patterns of variables that may be linked to meaningful developmental outcomes.* This working assumption, when adopted at the first stage of analysis, helps solve the knotty problem of how to cope with the interaction between multiple layers of variables over time. The goals of the analysis shift. Rather than disentangling the variables and their interactions, the investigator retains them together as a primary unit for analysis. The characteristics of the individual and the environment can be preserved in a small number of subgroups composed of persons who have reasonably similar configuration patterns.

How investigators identify configuration subgroups at the onset of the study can involve strategic, theoretical, or pragmatic decisions. Distinctive subgroups of persons can be determined, for example, on a priori theoretical grounds (e.g., categories of social attachment; Ainsworth, Blehar, Waters, & Wall, 1978). Or categories of persons may be identified by virtue of their being extreme cases or outliers (Kagan, Snidman, & Arcus, 1998). Alternatively, empirical configurations may be identified by splitting groups at the median on two or more variables (Hinde, 1998). Finally, natural categories or clusters of individuals may be identified by the use of standard statistical algorithms, such as configural frequency analysis (CFA) and hierarchical clustering procedures.

Clustering techniques

A number of statistical techniques can isolate the most common configural patterns in ways that preserve intervariable associations. One method is to perform a principal components analysis in which variables and individuals are, respectively, the rows and columns of the data matrix. Each resultant component will group together individuals whose patterns of variable associations are relatively homogeneous. This inverted principal components analysis is desirable when, first, the optimal unit of association is the correlation coefficient and, second, matrix singularity can be avoided by having the number of variables exceed the number of individuals.

Because these requirements are typically too restrictive for application to longitudinal data sets, a common alternative is to employ any one of several cluster analytic algorithms. Clusters can be generated through many measures of association including parametric and nonparametric correlations, distances, and frequencies. Further, problems of matrix singularity do not arise. Cluster analytic algorithms lack the mathematical grounding and comprehensive statistics enjoyed by principal components and factor analyses. One should not be surprised, as factoring has been refined for almost a century since Spearman (1904) invented it as a means for understanding intelligence data. In contrast, clustering methods have evolved from disparate sources that have emphasized different rules of group formation (Aldenderfer & Blashfield, 1984, p. 15). As "closeness" is operationalized differently across methods, irrespective of the index used to measure similarity, the methods can sometimes lead to different results. For this reason, cluster analysis is relatively controversial; Johnson and Wichern (1988, p. 543) deem it "rudimentary," "quite helpful," "important," and "primitive" in the space of two paragraphs.

Clustering methods generally fall into three groups. *Linkage* methods, such as single, complete, and average between and within groups, utilize the distance information between pairs of individuals. *Centering* methods calculate distances from the middle of two clusters. Centroid clustering defines the middle as a mean. Finally, *variance* methods, such as Ward's, examine the sum of squared error deviations from the mean of a cluster. Clustering algorithms also differ in the size and homogeneity of the groups they produce. Variations in clustering schedules, the steps by which the method proceeds from *n* clusters to one cluster, may be conceptualized in terms of Lance and Williams's (1967) "space-contracting" and "space-dilating" distinction: "*Space-contracting* methods affect these relationships [between the points in the multivariate space] by reducing the space between any groups in the data. When new points are encountered . . . they tend to be joined to existing groups rather than to be used to start new clusters. *Space-dilating* linkage forms are the opposite. Clusters here appear to recede on formation; thus smaller, more distinct clusters are formed in that space. This strategy of linkage also tends to create clusters of hyperspherical form and roughly equivalent size." Centroid, median, and single linkage methods are space-contracting; complete linkage and Ward's methods are space-dilating; the average linkage methods are somewhere in between and are called "space-conserving" (Aldenderfer & Blashfield, 1984, pp. 44–45).

When cluster analytic techniques are employed to generate configurations, it is wise to try more than one method on the same data. For instance, one might use a space-conserving linkage method such as the average distance between groups, a space-dilating variance method such as Ward's, and a space-contracting centering method such as median clustering. If all three algorithms yield the same optimal number of clusters and the same people within each cluster, the researcher can have some confidence in the stability of the resultant configurations. On the other hand, configurations that appear, for instance, in Ward's but not in average linkage are less likely to capture accurately the natural co-occurrence between variables. Attention should also be paid to individuals who are placed in one cluster according to one algorithm but in a separate cluster according to another algorithm. These individuals, whose cluster placement is unstable across methods, will overlap with Bergman's (1988) residue. By submitting the same data set to multiple algorithms, it is possible to obtain an intuitive sense of configural stability and a clearer understanding of individuals not well captured by the clustering solution.

All clustering solutions require informed decisions on the part of the investigator. The number and type of subgroups that may be identified at the beginning of a longitudinal investigation depend on such factors as (1) the statistical solution adopted, (2) the closeness of relationship among variables selected to be clustered, (3) the number of variables selected to be clustered, (4) the number and diversity of subjects studied, and (5) the criteria employed to establish within-cluster homogeneity.

Moreover, the range of variables is critical. For instance, if one's objective is to predict school dropout, decisions must be made at the outset on whether to include simply characteristics of the person (e.g., academic competence, aggression, popularity) alone or, in addition, characteristics of the person's environment (e.g., socioeconomic class, neighborhood, social group membership). The range of variables selected is a strategic decision that reflects, among other things, one's hypothesis about the outcomes to be predicted. In addition, in contrast to multiple logistic regression algorithms that allow nonpredictive variables to be dropped early, superfluous measures in cluster analysis are more difficult to detect and can undermine the quality of the solution obtained.

One way to supplement a cluster solution is to perform multidimensional scaling (MDS) and individual differences scaling (INDSCAL) analyses on the same data, and then to superimpose the groupings provided by cluster analysis on the spatial representation provided by MDS (Carroll & Chang, 1970; Kruskal, 1977; Kruskal & Wish, 1978; Seber, 1984). It is comforting if those individuals placed in the same cluster are relatively close to one another in multidimensional space. As in the analysis of multiple clustering algorithms, those individuals whose spatial and cluster locations are discrepant can be flagged for further scrutiny. If there is poor general correspondence between the cluster and spatial locations of individuals, it is likely that a nonoptimal number of cluster or MDS dimensions have been retained.[2]

This strategy of exploring multiple analytic routes, all of which derive from the natural associations between variables, serves the dual purposes of enhancing stability and facilitating knowledge about the individuals who constitute prominent configurations. The strategy avoids arbitrary criteria, such as median splits, and results in a finite number of configurations that researchers can present with confidence.

Assume that we have now arrived at a finite set of configurations. These configurations, which subsume more or fewer of the individuals within a sample, consist of the elevation and form of the variables on which individuals were assessed. Each configuration represents, at one point in time, the natural co-occurrences between variables. Individual profiles within a configuration are relatively homogeneous, and individual profiles between configurations are relatively distinct. But how homogeneous and how distinct? The fact that changes are observed over time invites an analysis of factors responsible for developmental change.

To sum up, a variety of statistical techniques are available to identify natural configurations of variables. This wealth of procedures creates a dilemma of riches. Of course, researchers can avoid the dilemma by ignoring the disaggregation problem. But in longitudinal designs, covering up the problem is usually a radical and an unfortunate choice. It is also unnecessary. In comparisons of various disaggregation solutions in our data sets, procedures that differ markedly in statistical assumptions have proved to yield robust and consistent conclusions.[3] Similar configuration subgroups have been identified using different methods of disaggregation, and these subgroups typically show comparable relations to meaningful developmental outcomes. To be sure, investigators should in all cases determine whether reasonable correspondences exist across solutions. This caution is not unique to disaggregation procedures: It holds for the application of any statistical technique to empirical data. "None of these techniques are automatic avenues to the truth and all can be abused. . . . They are not masters, only tools to be masterfully used" (Bakeman et al., 1979, p. 231).

Applications to longitudinal research

Is there evidence that disaggregation actually helps clarify the interpretation of massive longitudinal data sets?[4] What keeps one from being tyrannized by large numbers of ill-defined and poorly described groups of personal configurations? One of the robust findings to emerge from virtually all cluster solutions is that the solutions are economical. Typically, a small number of common configurations has proved to be sufficient to describe whole samples of persons (see, e.g., Cairns, Cairns, & Neckerman, 1989, and Gustafson & Magnusson, 1991). The economy may reflect the constrained and holistic nature of human nature, or it may reflect the nature of the solutions, the limits of measurements, or a combination of all of these factors.

Are these configurations simply ways to identify types of persons who are expected to remain relatively unchanged in their classification across ontogeny? Not necessarily. If one assumes that the correlations among variables that give rise to the clusters reflect transient and enduring factors in the environment and the person, they will not qualify as "types." The configurations merely constitute a common ground that promotes precise analysis of the factors that contribute to developmental continuity and change. This is the application that we have found most productive and consistent with our concern with the processes of developmental organization and change. But if one assumes that the configurations describe profiles of enduring personality dispositions – whether based on genetic factors or on the effects of early experience – they may be seen as empirical typologies.

Can configurations enhance developmental comparisons?

When employed to establish common starting points in longitudinal study, configurations may be used as control procedures to identify and track those resilient or vulnerable children who defy the group odds, for good or for ill. A focus on the persons who do not conform to the longitudinal pattern of the original configuration – the errors of prediction, whether false positive or false negative – can be especially informative. Specifically, within-configuration comparisons can be made between (1) the persons who conform to the dominant outcome for the configuration and (2) those who do not conform. "Errors" include all persons who were inconsistent with the expectation underlying selection of the original variables and the cluster identification. In conventional analyses, they contribute to the within-group error variance or lower predictive correlations. Configuration analyses promote procedures to determine whether these persons differ from other members of the configuration in their initial state (i.e., errors of classification) or whether they reflect differences that arise during development.

This step toward within-configuration analysis over time is a group-based variant of the matched case-control design. That is, developmental comparisons are made among persons who were presumably roughly equivalent to each other at the beginning of the investigation but who proved to be different in outcomes. Although the designs are not identical (e.g., relative within-group homogeneity is not the same as matched-pair homogeneity), they both attempt to ensure high levels of similarity on variables and their interactions that are presumed to be linked to particular outcomes. Relative to matched control procedures, two features of configuration designs are that (1) they potentially include all subjects (without pruning the sample to persons who are capable of being matched) and (2) they preserve intact natural clusters of characteristics.

How can one determine whether the resilient or vulnerable cases differed in initial condition or differed in turning points in development? If children in the configuration who travel the less well known path relative to others in the same configuration also differ from them on key initial variables, the most parsimonious interpretation is that the original placement was faulty. The slippage may reflect shortcomings in the original cluster solution or in the hypothesis that led to the variables' selection. But what if the individuals did not differ in their original status? This second possibility – that the original within-group differences are modest and inconsistent – is more challenging because it implies differential effects in the course of development. In some important respects, we can learn most about developmental change by studying individuals who do not conform to the dominant trend or pathway.

When this logic is applied to the analysis of longitudinal data sets, it can identify the critical changes over time that are associated with eventual changes in outcomes. For example, we (Xie & Cairns, 1996) reported that "resilient" boys, regardless of their original configuration, seemed to be buffered against early school dropout if they showed a progressive decrease in aggressive behavior in middle school and high school. Conversely, "vulnerable" boys were those who showed a progressive increase in aggressive behavior over the same years of adolescence. Interestingly, the vulnerable and resilient boys were virtually identical to others in their original configurations at the beginning of the investigation.

Related configuration applications

Configurations can be computed at the end of the study rather than at the beginning. Problems of adolescence and early adulthood tend to occur in clusters, not as separate entities (Jessor & Jessor, 1977; Jessor et al., 1991). Accordingly, configurations of outcomes can be identified by clustering persons in terms of the similarity of their profiles on measures associated with problematic developmental outcomes. If end-point configurations are accompanied by longitudinal data extending backward in time, it becomes possible to explore causal hypotheses. This strategy has been employed by Ensminger and Juon (Chapter 11, in this volume) in a 30-year follow-up of children in the Chicago Woodlawn project. She found that there were common behavioral and familial antecedents to patterns of substance use, and that these antecedents differed for males and females. At first, it would appear that the backward tracking involved in the end-point strategy may preclude developmental analyses. To the contrary, the procedures are quite compatible with developmental investigation. For instance, as Ensminger and Juon point out, children who possessed risk antecedents but who did not become substance abusers could emerge as a focus for special developmental studies of resilience.

Another use of configural analysis involves clustering on the basis of characteristics of individuals at each sampling interval and then determining whether the clusters remain stable and, if so, whether membership in the clusters was stable. This method involves an examination of stability of the clusters over time and of individual membership within the clusters over time. In a nice illustration of this method, Gustafson and Magnusson (1991)selected the same measures assessing adolescent girls' intelligence, academic achievement, self-judgments concerning ability, and self-judgments concerning school adaptation to create configurations of girls at 13 and at 16 years of age. They found that clusters with similar profiles (e.g., gifted, high-adapted achievers; low-adapted, normal-ability underachievers; moderately adapted, realistic, low achievers) emerged at both time points but that the discriminative power of particular measures varied at 13 and 16 years of age. Developmental "streams" were identified that indicated the proportion of girls who were placed in the same or different configurations at age 13 and age 16.

Proportions greater than those expected by chance were designated as *types,* and *antitypes* represented developmental streams that were underrepresented relative to chance. More focused analysis of particular developmental streams of interest enabled a further disaggregation of the sample into subconfigurations, analyses of variability among girls within particular configurations and/or developmental streams, and the determination of relationships between developmental streams with background family characteristics. As with other ways of approaching configural analyses, clustering at multiple time intervals and the determination of developmental streams allow for the identification of common change points for individuals within a cluster and of rare (or antitype) streams embarked on by a small proportion of individuals.

Another way to organize longitudinal information has been to identify, for each person in the sample, an individual developmental pathway with respect to study-relevant characteristics. Profile configurations can be employed usefully in conjunction with hierarchical linear modeling (HLM) and latent growth analysis. Examination of commonalities of pathways across different persons typically yields a finite subset of reasonably common or homogeneous patterns over time. In this regard, McCall, Appelbaum, and Hogarty (1973) identified common trajectories of intellectual change in the Fels Institute's longitudinal study. More recently, Mayer and Kellam (personal communication, 1995) used HLM procedures to identify common profiles of change over time in response to a well-defined intervention program. Once the common pathways were identified, Mayer and Kellam employed the information to locate developmental events associated with year-to-year fluctuations within each of the configurations.

To sum up, several designs are now available to study configurations of persons and developmental trajectories. They illustrate the methodological implications of the shift from the goal of disentangling variables to understanding how variables operate together to produce meaningful outcomes. They also indicate that the study of persons-in-context is now available and that the study of individual developmental pathways is within our grasp. To equate configuration analysis or "person-oriented" analysis with a single statistical technique – cluster analysis – is an error. The logic of the configuration procedure is open to a range of statistical and theoretical methods for disaggregating samples into relatively homogeneous subgroups. Once this step is taken, a number of avenues are opened to promote the developmental study of individuals.

B. Social networks: Units of analysis beyond the individual

It has been proposed that conservation in social behavior over time is supported by the correlations between events within and without individuals (e.g., Magnusson & Cairns, 1996). Biological states of individuals are brought into line with the environmental context and social actions, and vice versa. The result is that behavior organization tends to be continuous and conservative over time despite the fluidity and change. In ontogeny, correlated constraints establish the conditions such that (1) variables occur in packages, not as independent elements, (2) similarities evolve among individuals in that only a limited number of configurations of characteristics are possible, and (3) commonalities in developmental pathways will occur, given the parallel constraints that become active over time. A fundamental proposition in this framework is that forces in the social environment – including the social networks of families, friends, and communities – serve as catalysts for continuity.

This concept that individuals are tied together by invisible bonds into networks of relationships has been a recurrent theme over the first 100 years of social and developmental psychology (Baldwin, 1897). Yet it has been difficult to evaluate this insight critically because of unresolved theoretical issues and methodological shortcomings in the developmental investigation of social processes beyond the individual.

One problem in the analytic task is that social relations over the life course do not depict static structures so much as they represent changing, adaptive processes. Over time, specific social relationships among persons and groups may fade into the background or become thrust into the foreground, depending on time and context. To the extent that such dynamic processes are operative in the support and direction of one's behaviors and thoughts, they may be difficult to identify by standard methods of network analysis.

In this regard, Bronfenbrenner and Crouter (1983) have argued that precise identification of the effective social ecology is necessary to clarify how social influences are mediated in the lives of children and adolescents. According to this view, information about an individual's "social address" or social status is not sufficient to understand social processes. To clarify the dynamics of social influence, interactional reciprocity, and group constraints, techniques are required that identify the actual relationships that children form and how they change over time.

Over the life span, persons tend to affiliate with, to influence, and to be influenced by others who share common interests, behaviors, and beliefs. At each developmental stage, this web of social relations provides boundaries, opportunities, and a frame of reference for actions and attitudes. The social groups do not stand alone: They are themselves embedded in larger social units that cohere on the basis of similarities in gender, age, race, time, and space. Accordingly, the individual is enmeshed throughout development in a fabric of influence that includes the immediate dyads and groups with which she or he affiliates and with the social network of which these groups are a part.

One important recent methodological advance is the development of techniques that are effective in tracking social networks and relationships over time. One simple but powerful procedure has been to establish network affiliations on the basis of observations or, alternatively, through the reports of members who are in the social ecology. Once a reliable method has been adopted, it can be used to unravel some of the primary issues concerned with social network development.

When do children develop the ability to establish affiliative structures in relations with peers? Strayer and Santos (1996) note that little attention has been accorded to tracing early developmental changes in peer group size and function. They found that preliminary structures of cohesive social activities occur even among 1-year-old children. Among 3-year-old children, a gradual increase in average clique size is associated with a marked increase in affiliative acts to children who are members of the individual's group. Strayer and Santos conclude that "network analyses of similarity in dyadic associations offer a new view of affiliative organization which differs radically from more classic sociometric procedures" (p. 127).

Space and time may prove to be fundamental in understanding changes in social relations and social groups. In an investigation of the stability of social groups over a 1-year period, Neckerman (1996) discovered a powerful effect of propinquity on the fluidity of social groups. In this longitudinal study of American children and adolescents, 55% of groups were stable when the school promoted classroom as a unit. However, only 6.8% of social groups were stable in schools where the students were not kept together as a unit into the next school year. Distance in space over time seemed to increase distance in social relationships. Neckerman concluded that stable environments promoted stability in relationships and behaviors.

Leung (1996) has identified a critical issue of social group methodology and analysis that may transcend societies. Specifically, he discovered that the self-enhancement bias found in self-reports in social and personality psychology also plays a role in the types of individuals whom children claim as their friends and associates. In self-named groups, the tendency is to accentuate the positive and eliminate the negative. With the shift from childhood to adolescence, Chinese teenagers add peer-relevant concerns to their childhood identification with the traditional values of achievement and cooperation in peer group formation.

One of the conundrums of the recent sociometric status literature has been the finding that children who are identified as rejected, antisocial, or aggressive tend to have as many reciprocal friendships as nonaggressive children and those in the acceptable sociometric categories. How can this dilemma be solved? One of the originators of the social cognitive map procedure, Kindermann (1996), observes that the investigation of peer influences on children's development "rests squarely on appropriate methods to identify individuals who are influential for a given child." He notes that sociometric status procedures – as they have been employed over the past decade – do not identify specific relationships and reciprocal influences.

Schools provide rich opportunities for the construction of social groups and social networks. There is, however, considerable diversity among students in American elementary schools, according to Farmer and Rodkin (1996). These investigators find that school populations can be disaggregated into subsamples that are homogeneous with respect to levels of academic achievement and problem behaviors. The social groups that are formed tend to be composed of other persons similar to oneself, and they promote values and behaviors that can be distinctive to the subsample. For example, aggressive behaviors apparently do not disqualify boys from being central in social networks, on the contrary, aggressiveness may enhance their standing. Just the opposite effect is observed among girls. The broader point is that failure to disaggregate school samples into homogeneous subgroups can lead to spurious and misleading conclusions.

The involvement with deviant friends or groups whose behaviors and values are not normative does not necessarily indicate psychopathology or social rejection. Deviance may reflect the opportunities in one's environment and the impact of the values and behaviors of one's peers. This proposition was explored by Clarke-McLean (1996) in an investigation of seriously delinquent youth incarcerated in a maximum security facility. Clarke-McLean found that these extremely delinquent youth formed reasonably stable social networks within the institution. Moreover, the processes of group formation were similar to those observed in public school. But an ability to form stable relationships and groups does not necessarily reduce the risk. Clarke-McLean observed that their affiliations with other problem teenagers are likely to lead to continued exclusion from conventional institutions.

In sum, the recent deployment of methods indicates that social network procedures consistent with developmental propositions are within our grasp. But certain design requirements must be met to study persons-in-context over time. These include, among other things, the use of saturated samples of whole social units (e.g., schools, neighborhoods, summer camps), the establishment of procedures for tracking groups as well as individuals over time, and the adoption of statistical methods that integrate rather than disentangle variance.

C. Developmental integration and individual pathways

One concern about the developmental proposal is that it may be right, but it is too complicated and beyond disconfirming evidence. That concern would have merit if developmental researchers limited themselves to prevailing research designs and methods. But recognition of the complexity of development may indeed be the first step toward understanding its coherence and simplicity. With appropriate methods, the ideas become more accessible to objective analysis, not less. To close this chapter, we illustrate how these procedures can be employed

(1) to integrate information about personal configurations and social clusters and (2) to plot individual pathways.

Integrating individual configurations and social networks

It is relatively straightforward to combine personal configuration analyses with social network analyses if appropriate data sets are available. In this regard, the Carolina Longitudinal Study (CLS) was designed with such an integration in mind (Cairns & Cairns, 1994). This investigation began in 1981 as an accelerated longitudinal design in which two cohorts of subjects were first seen at a mean of 10 years and 13 years of age. All children of a given age in the school were eligible for participation; hence it was a saturated sample. The samples were sufficiently large ($N = 695$ overall) so that it was possible to employ the methods described for cluster analysis. In brief, the children's status on five variables (aggression, popularity, academic competence, socioeconomic class, and school failure) were clustered separately for males and females and separately for each cohort. This yielded four clusters of children who were relatively homogeneous with respect to the profiles on the variables.

The saturated sampling strategy permitted the identification of social networks by the SCM procedure (i.e., a social cognitive map) and independent assessment of the characteristics of the children in each social group. With information on the children in each group available, it was possible to identify, for all children, the means of the social group members with whom they affiliated.

The next step in the individual-social integration was to identify the nature of the social influence that members of the social group had on the subject. To obtain an estimate of the effect of social embeddedness, the mean scores of children who were in the subject's social group were used to create a new set of peer configurations. Consistent with expectation, virtually the same four solutions were obtained in the peer configuration analysis as were obtained in the individual configuration analysis.

These data permitted the answer to two empirical questions. First, is there evidence for correlated constraints, and does the profile of characteristics of the individual child tend to be similar to the profile of characteristics of the child's peer group? It should be noted that the characteristics of the child, the characteristics of the peers, and the group composition were obtained by independent operations and through independent agents (i.e., peers, teachers, self). The findings indicate strong support for the proposition that the children's pattern of social and school adaptation tend to be matched by the adaptations of their peers. Figure 2.1 shows the results obtained for females in one cohort; the essential findings and patterns were replicated in the other three sex-age cohorts.

The other question has to do with longitudinal prediction. Will the combination of information from individual-configurations and peer configurations do better in long-term prediction than merely one source of information taken alone? Preliminary analyses of the predictions over an 8- to 10-year period indicate that the combination depends on the outcome selected and the gender. For example, the combination of peer and person-configurations provided the best prediction of school drop-out depicted in Figure 2.1. Interestingly, peer group profiles provided the primary predictions of teenage motherhood, with the individual-configurations yielding nonsignificant predictions. A full analysis of these contingencies appears in a separate paper (Xie, Cairns, & Cairns, 1997).

Identifying individual pathways: Prodigal analysis

Disaggregation procedures provide a step toward understanding the development of persons-in-context, but they cannot substitute for the analysis of individual pathways. Because individuals within a configuration are more or less similar, the configuration defines a homogeneous subset of individuals within the sample. When the question "In what respects do otherwise similar individuals differ?" is asked, configural analyses become a means of obtaining a nonexperimental control. In this respect, they are a quantitative counterpart of studies such as that of Bandura and Walters (1959), who wrote:

The sociological approach {emphasizing} the importance of the social environment as a causative factor, however, does not explain why only a minority of children who live in deteriorated areas have police records (Kobrin, 1951), or why one child in a family becomes delinquent when a sibling does not. Nor

Correlated Constraints

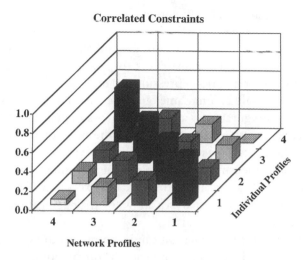

Network Profiles

Figure 2.1 Do adolescents tend to hang around with peers who have similar behavioral profiles? "Individual profiles" refer to the four configurations derived from cluster analysis of the individual's status on measures of aggression, popularity, academic competence, socioeconomic class, and age in grade. "Network profiles" refer to four comparable configurations derived from cluster analysis of the mean scores of persons in the subject's peer group. The height of each cell in the matrix indicates how the adolescents in a given individual profile configuration were distributed across the four network profiles (i.e., 58% of the subjects in the individual profile "1" configuration also had network profile "1" configurations, and so on). Support for the correlated constraints proposal is reflected in the phi coefficient = .50 (p < .001). [Shown here are Cohort II females (N = 248); comparable findings were obtained in the other CLS cohort and gender subgroups.]

can it account for the occurrence of delinquency among children who live in more privileged and more stable neighborhoods . . . a partial explanation is to be found in the psychological development of the individual child. (p. 5)

Bandura and Walters do not deny the importance of poverty or social disintegration for aggression; on the contrary, because they agree that these effects can powerfully influence adolescent aggression, their control of these larger demographic features enables them to detect more subtle influences on their phenomena of interest.

As we noted earlier, the derivation of configurations can be a means for controlling the more global differences between individuals in order to reveal those that are relatively subtle. In this sense, configurations differ importantly from many typologies, such as attachment or psychodiagnostic categories, that emerge from the confluence of multiple variables. It is relatively rare for researchers to peer within categories of insecure attachment or manic-depression to understand why not all manic-depressives are alike. The same outcome variables used to differentiate between configurations may also be associated with people within a cluster in an attempt to understand the individual child. For these analyses, the precautions mentioned in the last section can be of exploratory value in focusing the researcher on individual cases likely, according to Lewin (1935, p. 151), to mark the exceptional or "prodigal" cases. In sum, configural analyses allow for the aggregation as well as the disaggregation of individuals.

Accordingly, subgroup information can be employed to highlight the pathways of the limited number of persons who constitute exceptions to the rule. Depending on the normative pathway of their original subgroup configuration, prodigal cases – individuals whose developmental pathways significantly depart from that of their configuration subgroup – may be viewed as either resilient or vulnerable.

Longitudinal information from the subgroup and the total sample provides the background from which to identify salient individuals who have been deflected from the normative course of development, with the recognition that there are as many normative courses as there are subgroup configurations. A prodigal analysis reverses the typical figure–ground relationship between subgroups and individuals. Rather than being buried in the error term, exceptional pathways of individuals are projected into the foreground. They become candidates for intense analysis of when and how developmental deflections occur and what their consequences are. The remaining members of the subgroup become the background, or the foundation for interpreting individual contrasts.

Although systematic prodigal analysis has been infrequent in psychology, the logic of the design is represented in related sciences. For example, research in astronomy depends on a precise description of phenomena and movement patterns of bodies of matter throughout the universe in order to understand specific exceptions or deflections. Detection of change in, say, orbital pathways or spectral frequencies requires enormous amounts of information about the nature of regularities in these domains.

More generally, prodigal analysis permits investigators to use information from the total longitudinal sample in order to identify individuals who experience significant turning points in their lives. The normal and expected becomes the background for identifying change and deflections. Once recognized, the exceptions can become the focus for intensive study. At this stage, hypotheses with respect to possible turning points can be evaluated in the person and the context on an individual basis. Standard descriptive and statistical procedures can be employed to determine the extent to which there is sufficient replication across individuals to generalize. Depending on the probability of exceptions, medium-sized to large samples (500 to 2,000) may be required in order to identify a sufficient number of prodigal cases for quantitative analysis. Each subgroup may be expected to yield prodigal cases, and these cases may be studied individually or as a special subset in order to yield generations that transcend personal circumstances.

Is prodigal analysis simply another name for the case study method? Although the two procedures have the same goal – to understand individuals over time – they can be distinguished on four counts. First, in prodigal analysis, whole samples of persons are assessed with common measures and procedures over standard intervals. Second, persons qualify for selection by virtue of the exceptionality of their pathways relative to those of the subgroup or total sample. Third, this systematic form of individual analysis relies on advanced statistical procedures to obtain precise accounts of both individual and group pathways. Finally, objective guides are available to classify types of pathways across individual cases in order to clarify the operation of common transitions and turning points.

By contrast, case studies may or may not rely on quantification because the method does not presuppose systematic assessment at standard time intervals by common procedures. Accordingly, it is impossible to know whether a given case is an exemplar of an entire subgroup and a population or an exception to the rule. Although case studies typically emphasize the uniqueness of individuals and the contexts in which they have been observed, they are often used to illustrate general principles. Despite the pitfalls of case studies, one cannot overestimate the value of the intensive analysis of individual children in the concrete realities of their lives. This was the essential message of Barker and Wright (1951) in their classic monograph, *One Boy's Day*. The challenge remains to develop procedures that can capture and quantify such rich descriptions.

In summary, prospective configurations bring organization to medium-sized to large longitudinal data sets by separating persons through disaggregation procedures into natural subgroups. Systematic configuration analyses are guided by hypotheses at each step, from the initial selection of common variables across persons to proposals on what may account for within-cluster variations in pathways. Configurations also provide a refined control for prospective longitudinal comparisons. The intensive study of persons who show deflections from the normative course of the subgroup is assumed to be key in identifying the events that are necessary and sufficient to maintain or change developmental patterns. In prodigal analyses, normative, subgroup, and individual information is available to plot the course of individual development.

Concluding comment

Theoretical and methodological changes in the discipline seem inevitable, like the phenomena of development. Although the Consortium's statement is more a progress report than a finished product, it contains a reasonable plan for progress in the science (Cairns et al., 1996). The ideas and methods that we have focused on in this chapter – configuration analysis, social network integration, correlated constraints, individual pathway analysis – help bridge the gap between models and methods. But they need to be refined and evaluated as longitudinal designs and methods evolve. It is one thing to be critical about the current state of affairs; it is quite another matter to improve on it. To ensure that hard-won gains in empirical rigor and objectivity are not compromised, precise linkages must be established between new recommendations and traditional methods of data organization and statistical analysis. Where differences appear, the reasons for the differences must be carefully explored and their implications monitored (Magnusson & Bergman, 1990). Yet innovations must be welcomed rather than shunned. The models and methods should be described with sufficient precision to challenge the imagination and talents of developmental researchers in the next generation.

Notes

1. They include the development of human personality and social actions; the ontogeny and evolution of the behavioral adaptions in nonhuman animals; the development of perception, movement, and language development in infants and young children; the development of psychopathology and emotional disorders; and the development of cognitive processes in children and older adults.
2. Two other benefits arise from using MDS and INDSCAL in conjunction with cluster analysis. First, a spatial representation of configurations derived from cluster analysis enables researchers to assess quantitatively how configurations differ from one another. Configurations that are relatively close to each other are more similar than configurations that are relatively far apart. If semantic meaning can be assigned to the spatial dimensions, then one may also gain insight into the characteristics that best differentiate configurations. Second, results from INDSCAL provide a numerical measure of the extent to which, and the direction in which, individual configurations depart from the prominent configurations within the sample. In conjunction with an analysis of various clustering algorithms and the comparison of the final cluster solution to the MDS configuration, the statistics provided by INDSCAL facilitate understanding of individual departures from prominent configurations of variables.
3. Cairns, Gariépy, and Kindermann (1989) demonstrate this convergence in the use of these methods to analyze social clusters.
4. See Cairns and Rodkin (1998) for further elaboration of the issues covered in this section and in the later section on prodigal analysis.

References

Ainsworth, M. D. S., Blehar, M., Waters, E., & Wall, S. (1978). *Patterns of attachment: A psychological study of the strange situation*. Hillsdale, NJ: Erlbaum.

Aldenderfer, M. S., & Blashfield, R. K. (1984). *Cluster analysis*. Newbury Park, CA: Sage.

Bakeman, R., Cairns, R. B., & Appelbaum, M. (1979). Note on describing and

analyzing interactional data: Some first steps and common pitfalls. In
R. B. Cairns (Ed.), *The analysis of social interaction. Methods, issues, and
illustrations* (pp. 227–234). Hillsdale, NJ: Erlbaum.

Baldwin, J. M. (1897). *Social and ethical interpretations in mental development:
A study in social psychology.* New York: Macmillan.

Bandura, A., & Walters, R. H. (1959). *Adolescent aggression.* New York: Ronald.

Barker, R. G., & Wright, H. F. (1951). *One boy's day.* New York: Harper.

Bergman, L. R. (1988). You can't classify all of the people all of the time.
Multivariate Behavioral Research, 27, 417–433.

Bronfenbrenner, U. (1996). Foreword. In R. B. Cairns, G. H. Elder, Jr., &
E. J. Costello (Eds.), *Developmental science* (pp. ix – xvii). New York:
Cambridge University Press.

Bronfenbrenner, U., & Crouter, A. C. (1983). The evolution of environmental
models in developmental research. In P. H. Mussen (Ed.), *Handbook of
child psychology, Vol. 1: History, theory, methods* (pp. 357–414). New York:
Wiley.

Cairns, R. B., & Cairns, B. D. (1994). *Lifelines and risks: Pathways of youth in
our time.* New York: Cambridge University Press.

Cairns, R. B., & Rodkin, P. C. (1998). Phenomena regained: From group
configurations to individual pathways. In R. B. Cairns, L. Bergman, & J.
Kagan (Eds.), *Models and methods for studying the individual.* Thousand
Oaks, CA: Sage.

Cairns, R. B., Cairns, B. D., & Neckerman, H. J. (1989). Early school dropout:
Configurations and determinants. *Child Development, 60,* 1437–1452.

Cairns, R. B., Elder, G. H., Jr., & Costello, J. (1996). (Eds.) *Developmental
science.* New York: Cambridge University Press.

Cairns, R. B., McGuire, A. M., & Gariépy, J-L.(1993). Developmental behavior genetics: Fusion, correlated constraints, and timing. In A. Angold &
D. Hay (Eds.), *Precursors and causes in development and psychopathology*
(pp. 87–122). Chichester, UK: Wiley.

Carolina Consortium on Human Development (1996). Developmental science:
A collaborative statement. In R. B. Cairns, G. H. Elder, Jr., & E. J.
Costello (Eds.), *Developmental science* (pp. 1–6). New York: Cambridge
University Press.

Carroll, J. D., & Chang, J. J. (1970). Analysis of individual differences in
multidimensional scaling via an N-way generalization of "Eckart–
Young" decomposition. *Psychometrika, 35,* 283–319.

Clarke-McLean, J. G. (1996). Social networks among incarcerated juvenile
offenders. *Social Development, 5,* 203–217.

Farmer, T. W., & Rodkin, P. C. (1996). Antisocial and prosocial correlates of classroom social positions: The social network centrality perspective. *Social Development, 5,* 174–188.

Gustafson, S., & Magnusson, D. (1991). *The development of female careers: A pattern approach.* Hillsdale, NJ: Erlbaum.

Hinde, R. A. (1998). Through categories towards individuals: Attempting to tease apart the data. In R. B. Cairns, L. Bergman, & J. Kagan (Eds.), *Models and methods for studying the individual.* Thousand Oaks, CA: Sage.

Jessor, R., Donovan, J. E., & Costa, F. M. (1991). *Beyond adolescence: Problem behavior and young adult development.* New York: Cambridge University Press, 1991.

Jessor, R., & Jessor, S. L. (1977). *Problem behavior and psychosocial development: A longitudinal study of youth.* New York: Academic Press.

Johnson, R. A., & Wichern, D. W. (1988). *Applied multivariate statistical analysis.* Englewood Cliffs, NJ: Prentice-Hall.

Kagan, J., Snidman, N., & Arcus, D. (1988). The value of extreme groups. In R. B. Cairns, L. Bergman, & J. Kagan (Eds.), *Models and methods for studying the individual.* Thousand Oaks, CA: Sage.

Kindermann, T. A. (1996). Strategies for the study of individual development within naturally-existing peer groups. *Social Development, 5,* 158–173.

Kruskal, J. B. (1977). The relationship between multidimensional scaling and clustering. In J. Van Rysin (Ed.), *Classification and clustering* (pp. 17–44). New York: Academic Press.

Kruskal, J. B., & Wish, M. (1978). *Multidimensional scaling.* Newbury Park, CA: Sage.

Lance, G., & Williams, W. (1967). A general theory of classificatory sorting strategies. *Computer Journal, 9,* 373–380.

Leung, M.-C. (1996). Social networks and self enhancement in Chinese children: A comparison of self reports and peer reports of group membership. *Social Development, 5,* 146–157.

Lewin, K. (1935). *A dynamic theory of personality: Selected papers.* New York: McGraw-Hill.

McCall, R. B., Appelbaum, M. I., & Hogarty, P. S. (1973). Developmental-changes in mental performance. *Monographs of the Society for Research in Child Development, 38* (Serial No. 150).

Magnusson, D. (1988). *Individual development in paths through life. Vol. 1: A longitudinal study.* Hillsdale, NJ: Erlbaum.

Magnusson, D., & Bergman, L. R. (Eds.). (1990). *Data quality in longitudinal research.* Cambridge: Cambridge University Press.

Magnusson, D., & Cairns, R. B. (1996). Developmental science: Toward a unified framework. In R. B. Cairns, G. H. Elder, Jr., & E. J. Costello

(Eds.), *Developmental science* (pp. 7–30). New York: Cambridge University Press.

Neckerman, H. J. (1996). The stability of social groups in childhood and adolescence. *Social Development, 5,* 131–145.

Seber, G. A. F. (1984). *Multivariate observations.* New York: Wiley.

Spearman, C. (1904). General intelligence objectively determined and measured. *American Journal of Psychology, 15,* 201–293.

Strayer, F. F., & Santos, A. J. (1996). Affiliative structures in preschool groups. *Social Development, 5,* 117–130.

Wahlsten, D. (1990). Insensitivity of the analysis of variance to heredity–environment interaction. *Behavioral and Brain Sciences, 13,* 109–161.

Xie, H., & Cairns, R. B. (1996, August). *The development of aggression: Antecedents and pathways of early school dropout.* Poster presented at the biennial meeting of the International Society for the Study of Behaviour Development (ISSBD), Québec City, Canada.

Xie, H., Cairns, R. B., & Cairns, B. D. (1997). *Predicting teen parenthood: Peer affiliations or individual dispositions?* Unpublished manuscript, University of North Carolina at Chapel Hill.

Part II

A focus on problem behavior

3

Persistent themes and new perspectives on adolescent substance use: A lifespan perspective

Denise B. Kandel

Exactly 20 years ago, I organized a conference that brought together researchers involved in longitudinal studies on drug use and statistical experts in longitudinal data analysis (Kandel, 1978a). My goal was to assess the state of knowledge regarding the predictors and consequences of drug use and the best methods to identify these factors. Richard Jessor was a key participant at the meeting and reported on his classic panel study of drinking, marijuana use, and other problem behaviors among high school and college students (Jessor & Jessor, 1977). The 1970s represented a very exciting period for drug researchers. A number of parallel longitudinal studies had been initiated using comparable samples, methods, and designs. These studies provided unusual opportunities for replication that are all too rare in the social sciences. In an introductory chapter in the volume published after the conference, I summarized in the form of 19 propositions our knowledge regarding the predictors and consequences of drug use (Kandel, 1978b). The title of the chapter, "Convergences in Prospective Longitudinal Surveys of Drug Use in Normal Populations," reflected the commonality of findings that emerged from the various research groups. The chapter provides a useful benchmark from which to assess how the field has progressed in the intervening two decades. In this chapter, I briefly highlight major new advances. Although the emphasis is on studies based on representative adolescent population samples, epidemiological

Support for the research has been provided by research grants DA02867, DA03196, DA04866, and DA09110 and by research scientist award DA00081 from the National Institute on Drug Abuse.

research on adults and animal laboratory research are discussed selectively when this work informs on substance abuse in adolescence. I also discuss issues that need to be addressed in the next phase of the research. I stress at the outset that this is not a systematic review of the literature, but rather my selective reading and interpretations that are perforce influenced by my own work.

Themes in drug research

Research on drug behavior focuses on three basic themes: the natural history, the etiology, and the consequences of drug behavior. Adolescence has been the focus of much of drug research because it is the period in the life cycle when most drug use is initiated. Except for cocaine and selected other illicit drugs, most young people start using cigarettes, alcohol, and marijuana by the age of 20 (Kandel & Logan, 1984). The seven advances identified by Richard Jessor (letter of January 4, 1996) as underlying recent work on problem behaviors apply to drug research, although in varying degrees: (1) increasing theoretical sophistication and inclusiveness; (2) increasing attention to underlying developmental processes; (3) increasing attention both to biological factors and to community and social contexts; (4) increasing attention to protective factors in addition to risk factors; (5) increasing attention to mediational models; (6) increasing diversification of the populations being studied; and (7) use of a broader variety of methods. To this list I would add two issues that are particularly salient with respect to drug research: increasing concern with the definition and measurement of the behaviors being studied and with the validity of these measurements (Harrison & Hughes, 1996).

Over the last two decades, several major reviews of substance use in adolescence have been published, in particular Hawkins, Catalano, and Miller's (1992) and Clayton's (1992) reviews of etiological factors and Petraitis, Flay, and Miller's (1995) review of theoretical frameworks. Jessor (1992) and Elliott (1993) provided integrated formulations that considered substance use as one class of risk behavior that is part of a person's lifestyle. White (1996a) presents updated views of major theoretical frameworks underlying drug research. Hawkins et al.'s (1992) review of risk and protective factors for drug use has been perhaps the most influential and the most often cited of these articles. The inclusion of protective factors in the title of the review reflected the influence of work on psychopathology on drug researchers' thinking about the etiology of substance use. The promise of the title, however, was not realized in the body of the article itself, which still focused almost exclusively on risk factors. Although 17 specific risk factors were identified and discussed across 20 pages, no clear delineation of protective factors appeared in the single page devoted to them. Brook (Brook, Brook, Whiteman, Gordon, & Cohen, 1990) and Jessor (Jessor, Van Den Bos, Vanderryn, Costa, & Turbin, 1995) provided much more extensive discussions of protective factors in the etiology of drug use and other problem behaviors in adolescence. Newcomb and Bentler's (1989) very brief review addressed and succinctly stated views on the future of drug research perhaps better than anyone else: "At this point, effort on understanding the correlates and etiology of drug use would not seem to be an important research priority, except to distinguish the causes of very heavy use or abuse and to distinguish differential etiologies for different substances or different problem behaviors, should these exist" (p. 245). I agree only partially with the first part of this statement because we still have much to learn about the etiology of drug use per se, especially how biological predispositions interact with experiences and environmental conditions to give rise to drug behavior.

However, the two exceptions highlighted by Newcomb and Bentler represent a very ambitious and important agenda that still remains to be fulfilled. We still have not dealt with the issue of understanding heavy use and abuse or dependence, in contrast to use per se. (For a similar point, see White, 1996b.) Furthermore, although there has been increasing interest in documenting the interrelationships among the different problem behaviors that were the focus of the Conference on New Perspectives on Adolescent Risk Behavior, for which this chapter was originally prepared, very little progress has been made in identifying the developmental processes, the pathways, and the common and specific factors that underlie participation in the various behaviors (Kandel, 1989). Very little new work has been added to the basic features of problem behavior theory outlined by Jessor almost 30 years ago (Jessor & Jessor, 1977). Moreover, the etiological factors listed by Newcomb and Bentler (1989) – environmental, behavioral, psychological, and social – omitted biological factors. This omission is all the more questionable in view of the remarkable advances that have recently been made in understanding the biological bases of drug addiction and the impact of drugs of abuse on the brain. As I will illustrate on the basis of my own work, as social scientists we cannot ignore biological factors in the etiology of drug behavior. (See also Tarter et al., in press.) Etiological research, which includes biological factors in addition to social and psychological factors, and research on the transition from drug use to dependence are of high priority.

A major paradigmatic shift is taking place in the current conceptualization of substance abuse, which is viewed as a chronic relapsing brain disorder (Leshner, 1995). This conceptualization will have profound implications for research, prevention, and treatment activities, as well as for the social perceptions of individuals who use and abuse drugs. This conceptualization does not necessarily bring with it a neglect of psychological and social variables, as witness perspectives on heart disease, which is seen to be as much a matter of lifestyle and personality as of physiology.

Issues to be addressed by the field

My own assessment of progress in drug research in light of the seven trends highlighted by Richard Jessor is that theoretical advances in psychosocial research on substance use/abuse in adolescence have lagged behind the accumulation of empirical findings and the application of increasingly sophisticated analytical techniques to data. Several issues, including issues that have confronted the field for a long time, need to be addressed. I would stress the following directions:

1. A shift in emphasis from substance use to substance abuse and dependence with respect to epidemiology, etiology, and consequences. This shift carries with it a strong focus on psychopathology and on underlying biological processes.

2. Developmental studies of the factors underlying progression through the different phases of use of specific drugs (from onset to casual use to dependence) across drugs and across domains of risk behaviors, such as delinquency, early sexual activity, school dropout, and psychological problems. Although there has been increasing interest in documenting the interrelationships among the different problem behaviors that were the focus of this conference, very little progress has been made

in identifying the developmental processes, the pathways, and the common and specific factors that underlie participation in various behaviors.

3. Efforts to include biological markers in nonlaboratory population-based field studies, both to validate self-reports of drug use and to identify susceptibility to drugs of abuse in regard to initiation, increasing involvement, persistence, and desistence.

4. Refinements in the conceptualization and measurement of peer influences. The progress made with respect to family processes has not been paralleled by progress regarding processes underlying peer effects. As I discuss elsewhere (Kandel, 1996a), the assessment of peer influence based on perceptual reports by adolescents of their friends' behaviors in cross-sectional studies may overestimate by a factor of 5 the extent of that influence.

5. Improvements in the measurement and validity of reports of drug use.

6. Attempts to bridge epidemiological and laboratory studies by developing animal models and conducting controlled human studies that would allow a test of hypotheses suggested by epidemiological research.

Each of these questions is important and represents exciting opportunities for new research initiatives. In my own work, I have recently turned to several of these themes. I will illustrate two in particular: the need to include biological factors among the risks for drug involvement, and the importance of examining drug dependence and abuse in addition to use per se.

Although I emphasize individual-level factors, I do not want to imply that contextual factors are unimportant. Individual behaviors are obviously influenced by contextual factors, such as the neighborhood, the community, or the larger society. For instance, I have recently found that although blacks as a group are much more likely than any other ethnic group to become dependent on cocaine once having experimented with it, there are wide variations across six large metropolitan areas in rates of dependence among black cocaine users (Kandel, 1996b). The stress on a systematic investigation of those more distal contextual factors, in conjunction with individual-level variables, constitutes one of the most important new foci of the last decade (Arnett,

1992; Jessor, 1992, 1993). Biologists long ago recognized that the manifestation of a particular phenotype results from an interaction between genotype and environment.

In this chapter, I focus on two of these issues: biology and dependence.

Effects of prenatal smoking on child smoking and conduct problems

I illustrate the importance of considering biological factors in the etiology of adolescent substance use with findings from an ongoing study.

Over the last two decades, a longitudinal cohort that I have followed over 19 years from adolescence to adulthood has been a major focus of my research activities. The New York State Cohort (NYS) represents adolescents formerly enrolled in Grades 10 and 11 in New York State public high schools in 1971–1972. Members of the cohort have been contacted four times: in adolescence (at ages 15–16), in the mid-20s, in the late 20s, and in the mid-30s. In the last wave of data collection, 1,160 men and women were reinterviewed. Over time, the focus of the research has expanded from the determinants to the consequences of drug use. We have elucidated the developmental pathways of involvement in different drug classes, the nature of interpersonal influences affecting drug behavior, and many of the relationships between drug use, health, and participation in social roles at different stages of the life cycle (e.g., Kandel, 1975, 1986; Kandel & Andrews, 1987; Kandel & Davies, 1992, 1992; Kandel, Davies, Karus, & Yamaguchi, 1986; Kandel, Mossel, & Kaestner, 1987; Kandel, Yamaguchi, & Chen, 1992; Yamaguchi & Kandel, 1984, 1985, 1987, 1993).

As members of the cohort reached their late 20s and early 30s, we turned our attention to the intergenerational consequences of drug use. How does parental drug involvement affect family functioning, especially child-rearing practices, and the children's psychosocial adjustment and involvement with drugs (Griesler & Kandel, in press; Kandel, 1990; Kandel & Wu, 1995; Kandel, Wu, & Davies, 1994; Wu & Kandel, 1995)? In order to assess the familial determinants and consequences of drug involvement in adulthood more precisely, we obtained data from spouses or partners, children aged 9–17, and teachers in addition to focal respondents. The last wave of data collection on the

NYS cohort provided direct assessments of the children's psychosocial functioning, with multi-informant assessments of the children's adjustment obtained from the children, their mothers, fathers, and teachers. A sample of mother–father–child triads was available for analysis. Not only did this new wave of data collection allow us to continue our investigation of the natural history of drug involvement and of the consequences of drug use for the individual (including health, economic status, and marital interaction), it also allowed us to investigate the intrafamilial consequences of drug use for family functioning, child rearing, child development, and the child's drug behavior. Thus, the study allowed us to identify intergenerational risk factors in an unselected general population sample.

We found that current and lifetime parental drug involvement had deleterious effects on child development. Drug users reported having less control over their children, and those children, in turn, were seen by their parents as being more aggressive and having more behavior problems (Kandel, 1990). The finding of an effect of parental drug use on the child's behavior is important because conduct problems in childhood and early adolescence are among the most important precursors of adolescent drug use and delinquency.

Parental influences on child smoking

Parents also directly influence the drug behavior of their children. Given our long-term interest in socialization influences on adolescent development, we were particularly interested in assessing the intergenerational transmission of drug use behaviors. Because of their young age, few children had yet used illegal drugs. We focused on the use of cigarettes and alcohol and the respective roles of mothers and fathers as models for their children's smoking. In considering parental influences on children's drug use, we were particularly interested in parental socialization influences. The research has generated a finding that has led me to think in new ways about the etiology of adolescent drug use. It also has blurred in some ways the distinction between risk factors and consequences. Behavior that is defined as a consequence of drug use for one generation constitutes an etiological factor for the next generation.

With rare exceptions, the majority of studies that have examined the

role of parents on the child's smoking are based on the child's perceptions of parental behaviors rather than on parental self-reports. Of more
than 50 studies that we identified, which examined the reflective influences of parental smoking on their child smoking, 6 obtained independent data from both parents. These six studies reported contradictory
results regarding the respective influences of mothers and fathers (Annis, 1974; Banks, Bewley, Bland, Dean, & Pollard, 1978; Hops, Tildesley, Lichtenstein, Ary, & Sherman, 1990; Melby, Conger, Conger, &
Lorenz, 1993; Murray, Kiryluk, & Swan, 1985; Rossow, 1992). This
raised three questions: Is one parent more important than the other? If
so, how is this influence mediated? Does it affect boys and girls equally?

In a sample of 201 mother–father–child triads, we found that the
mother's current smoking was consistently more strongly related than
the father's smoking to smoking by young adolescents, especially
daughters (Kandel & Wu, 1995). More than nine times as many girls
reported smoking in the last year (46.4%) when their mothers currently
smoked at least a pack of cigarettes a day compared with mothers who
never smoked (5.9%), or almost three times as many compared with
those who stopped smoking (11.1%) or smoked less than a pack a day
(10.5%). The comparable percentages for boys were 40.9%, 13.0%,
8.5%, and 11.8%. The association between smoking by fathers and
their children was weaker. The maternal advantage remained with controls for other variables that could potentially account for the differential maternal and paternal influences, including opportunities for modeling parental smoking and parental socialization practices. It was not
clear what other factors could potentially account for the observed differences in parental influences on adolescent smoking. It occurred to us
that the most irreducible difference between mothers and fathers was
that only mothers could bear children and expose them to a direct
prenatal smoking effect.

Effects of prenatal maternal smoking on child smoking

We proceeded to test the hypothesis that maternal smoking during
pregnancy was related to the child's smoking in preadolescence and
that it explained the observed relationship between current maternal
smoking and daughter's smoking. The prenatal effect had to be estimated net of current maternal smoking to remove any confounding due

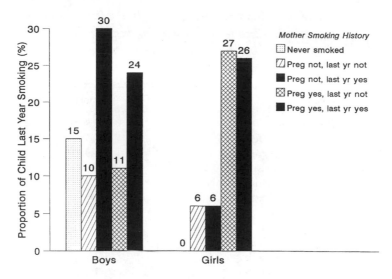

Figure 3.1 Child current smoking by maternal smoking history during pregnancy and afterward (NYS cohort).

to role modeling/socialization and passive smoking effects. There was a significant and dose-related relationship between maternal smoking during pregnancy and daughter's smoking 13 years later (Kandel et al., 1994). The proportion of daughters smoking within the last year was 4.3% when the mother had not smoked during her pregnancy but 24.0% when she had smoked up to half a pack of cigarettes per day and 29.4% when she had smoked a pack or more per day. We classified mothers according to their smoking behavior during pregnancy and within the last year. The joint consideration of maternal smoking during pregnancy and afterward documented the preeminent influence of prenatal smoking (Figure 3.1). Daughters' smoking rates were related to their mothers' pattern of prenatal smoking and were independent of the mothers' current smoking.

We conducted multivariate logistic regressions to estimate the effects of current maternal smoking and smoking during pregnancy on the child's smoking, with controls for other potential predictors of child smoking, including maternal alcohol drinking during pregnancy, child's age and sex, maternal education, and socialization practices (Table 3.1). Maternal smoking during pregnancy was the only maternal smoking

Table 3.1. *Adjusted odds ratios (AOR) from logistic regression predicting child's smoking last year from mother's smoking during and after pregnancy (N — 192 dyads, NYS Cohort)*

Predictors	Smoking AOR[a]
Child's age	1.8***
Child's sex (= female)	1.3
Mother's years of education	.9
Mother closeness to child	.9
Mother monitoring of child	.4
Maternal rule against smoking (vs. no rule)	1.1
Mother smoking during pregnancy (vs. not smoking)	
< 1 pack a day	1.1
≥ 1 pack a day	1.2
Mother smoking after pregnancy (vs. never)	
Not last year	.7
Last year < 1 pack a day	.9
Last year ≥ 1 pack a day	1.2
Interaction: Child sex × mother smoking during pregnancy	
< 1 pack a day	2.7
≥ 1 pack a day	12.3†

[a]Exponentiated unstandardized coefficients.
†$p < .10$; ***$p < .001$.

behavior that retained statistical significance; it had a stronger effect on the child's smoking during the last year than did lifetime smoking. The interaction between gender and maternal smoking during pregnancy was significant at a low level because of the small sample sizes. When mothers smoked at least a pack a day during pregnancy, the odds of the offspring's smoking in the last year were 15.2 for daughters but 1.2 for sons.

The findings were replicated in a large national sample of mother–child dyads from the National Longitudinal Survey of Youth (NLSY). Indeed, we were concerned with the limited evidence based on the small size of our sample and were seeking another data set in which the analyses could be replicated. The NLSY is a nationally representative cohort of young adults who were first contacted in 1979 at ages 14–21 and have been reinterviewed annually since then. Blacks, Hispanics, and disadvantaged whites have been oversampled. I was very familiar with the NLSY, having been responsible for the inclusion of the drug-related questions, including questions about smoking, in the 1984 wave of the study. I was also aware that a tape from the 1990 survey was to be released shortly and would contain data about self-reported smoking by children of the women in the cohort. We decided to attempt a replication of our NYS analyses in the NLSY data set and add specific-ity to the hypothesis because of the increased sample size, even though the data set had certain limitations. A subsample of 797 mother–child pairs, with a child 10 years old or over, was available for analysis. In both cohorts, the adjusted odds ratios of maternal smoking during pregnancy (irrespective of quantities smoked) on daughters' current smoking were almost identical: 4.1 in the NYS sample and 4.1 in the NLSY. A Mantel–Haentzel chi-square test of the common underlying association between mother's and daughter's smoking across the two samples was statistically significant ($p < .01$) (Kandel et al., 1994).

The large size of the NLSY allowed us to test the hypothesis that the effect of maternal prenatal smoking was stronger for daughters' persistence of smoking than for experimentation with cigarettes. We conducted a logistic regression predicting persistent smoking among adolescents who had ever smoked in the NLSY cohort. Maternal smok-ing during pregnancy increased the odds of persistent smoking by daughters more than five times (5.5) but had no effect on sons. The adjusted odds ratios for daughters were statistically significantly differ-ent from those for sons.

An important component of adolescent smoking is familial. Because current maternal smoking was not statistically significant with control for smoking during pregnancy, and because current maternal smoking was more important than paternal smoking, we concluded that the pre-natal maternal effect was stronger than any potential effect of subse-quent exposure to passive smoke. The differential impact of maternal smoking during pregnancy on the child's current (and persistent) smok-ing compared with lifetime smoking is consonant with the existence of a physiological prenatal effect. Furthermore, maternal prenatal smoking may have more pervasive effects than prenatal drinking on the child's subsequent drug behavior. Indeed, we recently completed an analysis parallel to that of prenatal smoking for prenatal drinking (Griesler & Kandel, 1998). Prenatal drinking as well as prenatal smoking has a statistically significant effect on daughters' drinking, although the effect of prenatal drinking is stronger than that of prenatal smoking. By contrast, prenatal drinking has no observable effect on adolescent smoking.

Validity of retrospective reports of maternal drug use during pregnancy

A limitation of our analysis is that in both data sets prenatal smoking and drinking were assessed retrospectively. In the NLSY, these assessments took place within 1 to 3 years of the pregnancy. In the NYS cohort, women were not asked directly whether they had smoked or drunk alcohol during their pregnancies. Instead, we timed the retrospective reports of the use of drugs in any month obtained from drug histories with the pregnancies, taking gestational age of the child into account. On average, the retrospective drug histories were provided 3½ years after the birth of the child. No external criteria, such as physicians' records or independent reports from other informants, were available to validate these reports. As an alternate strategy, we tracked separately the mothers' monthly reported use of each drug (cigarettes and alcohol) prior to, during, and following the pregnancy and compared their drug use to that of two other groups of users over identical 18-month periods. Thus, we identified mothers who smoked in the third month prior to their pregnancy and charted their monthly reported smoking during the 3-month prepregnancy period, the pregnancy, and the 6 months postpartum. Two comparison groups were selected from the larger cohort: women who reported smoking in the same calendar months as the pregnant women 3 months prior to the pregnancies, but who never had children (nonmothers), and men who smoked in the third month prior to their wives' pregnancy. These men were not the husbands of the pregnant women, but rather focal men from our original follow-up cohort for whom we collected the same retrospective drug histories. The same procedure was implemented for the retrospective recall of drinking during pregnancy.

The results are striking. There were sharp declines in self-reported smoking or drinking among women during the first 3 months of their

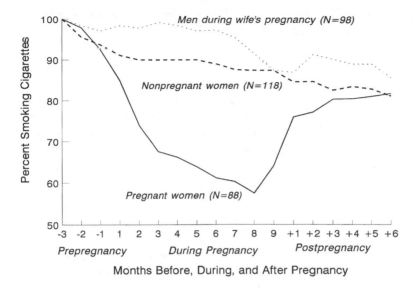

Figure 3.2 Monthly cigarette use over 18 months by pregnant women, non-pregnant women, and men during their wives' pregnancy.

pregnancy, a plateau during the remaining months of the pregnancy, and a sharp increase and resumption of smoking (and drinking) during the postpartum period (Figure 3.2 illustrates the results for smoking). This patterning was not observed among the other two groups. Six months postpartum, the rates for the three groups had converged; the rates for the two groups of women were especially close. Thus, despite probable distortions in recall, the data appear to be valid.

Speculations regarding underlying mechanisms: Latent dependence on nicotine

One mechanism underlying the effect of prenatal maternal smoking might be the impact of nicotine, passing through the placenta, on the fetus's developing brain. The nicotine may act on components of the dopaminergic system that has been implicated in the reinforcing effects of various classes of drugs. Nicotine, which crosses the placental barrier and stimulates the action of these cholinergic neurons, enhances activity in the dopaminergic system. The resulting alterations in the brain could have several consequences. In particular, prenatal exposure might create a latent dependence on nicotine, which would be subsequently activated in adolescence when opportunities to smoke arise. There is now good evidence that the mesolimbic and mesocortical components of the dopaminergic system mediate some motivational consequences of reinforcing stimuli, including the craving of drug dependence (Beitner-Johnston, Guitart, & Nestler, 1992; Corrigall, 1991; Koob, 1992; Mereu et al., 1987; Nestler, 1992). Once dependence on a drug has been established, its withdrawal leads to decreased activity in those components of the dopaminergic system that are manifest clinically in craving, despondency, and anhedonia. Drug seeking restores the rewarding effects of dopamine transmission (Collins, 1990–1991; Hughes, 1986). Addictive drugs, including cocaine, opiates, and perhaps even alcohol and sedatives, enhance the activity of these components of the dopamine system. For example, cocaine inhibits the uptake of dopamine by the dopaminergic presynaptic terminals, thereby prolonging the action of dopamine on their target cells. Cholinergic neurons from the lateral dorsal tegmental nucleus and the pedunculotegmental nucleus connect to and excite the dopaminergic neurons of the nigroventral tegmental region of the brain stem. Nicotine, which crosses the placental barrier, enhances activity in the dopaminergic system (Mereu et al., 1987).

Our findings raise the possibility that, during a critical prenatal period of brain development, nicotine might modify the properties of the dopaminergic system and change the threshold of this system, or of related systems in the brain, to the effects of nicotine later in life. Nicotine might predispose the child, especially if female, not only to smoke but to begin smoking at an early age and to persist in smoking once the child is given the opportunity to smoke. These differences could be reflected in the child's initial response to nicotine and result in persistence of smoking. This suggestion is consistent with the notion (Beitner-Johnston et al., 1992) that nicotine, like other addictive drugs, can alter gene expression and produce long-lasting functional and structural changes in dopaminergic neurons, an effect that might be particularly profound in the developing brain. The findings that nicotine administration to mice during pregnancy increases adenylate cyclase activity in the midbrain and brain stem at postpartum and that the levels of this substance return to normal within 4 weeks, only to recur in adulthood (Slokin, McCook, Lappi, & Seidler, 1992), lend support to this interpretation.

As this line of argument and the studies of cocaine use during pregnancy suggest, the mother's prenatal exposure to drugs can have two types of consequences for the child: immediately manifest consequences, most clearly evident in crack babies or infants with the fetal alcohol syndrome; and latent consequences, as may be the case for smoking, which may require more than a decade to become manifest. This perinatally induced predisposition might be enhanced further by passive smoking after birth, which would increase the child's desire to experiment with cigarettes and potential dependence on tobacco. There may be subtle physiological effects deriving from the child's exposure to prenatal maternal smoking, as well as to postnatal passive smoke, which may create in these children a low level of nicotine dependence without their having ever smoked a cigarette. In our study, we could not measure exposure to passive smoking by other household members. We assumed that the effects of passive smoking would be captured by measures of current maternal smoking. However, because we showed this factor not to retain a unique statistically significant effect, and because we showed that current maternal smoking was more important than paternal smoking, we concluded that the perinatal maternal effect was stronger than the effect of subsequent passive smoke. Our data did not exclude a variety of additional social or physiological effects. Nor did the data exclude the existence of a genetic predisposition to smoking, reflected in differential regulation of brain nicotinic receptor numbers and response to nicotine (Collins, 1990–1991; Hughes, 1986). Such a genetic predisposition might be especially strong among women who continue to smoke during their pregnancies despite the well-advertised hazards of doing so.

Why the prenatal effect should be stronger among female than male children is not clear. Female rats have also been found to be more sensitive than males to intrauterine exposure to cocaine, a stimulant like nicotine (Dow-Edwards, 1989). The sex difference may reflect the distinctive sexual dimorphism of the brain, including hormonal and structural factors, which emerges during fetal development; the release of androgens may protect the male against the priming effect of nicotine. The female-specific effect may also be related to depression in a manner that is not understood. Smoking and depression are correlated in adolescence and adulthood (Breslau, Kilbey, & Andreski, 1993; Kandel & Davies, 1982), adolescent depression predicts continued and heavy smoking in early adulthood (Kandel & Davies, 1982), and depressive disorders are much more prevalent among women than among men (Weissman & Klerman, 1985). Thus, the relationships between mothers' and daughters' smoking may be related to depression and the greater risk of depressive disorders in females than in males. Maternal depression may be related to the increased risk of substance abuse among offspring more generally; it has been found to increase the risk of cocaine and opioid abuse among adult children, especially daughters, as well as alcoholism (Kendler, Health, Neale, Kessler, & Eaves, 1993a; Luthar, Merikangas, & Rounsaville, 1993; Merikangas, Risch, & Weissman, 1994). Kendler (Kendler et al., 1993a, 1993b) speculates that common familiar factors, probably genetic, may underlie depression, smoking, and alcoholism in women, whereas Merikangas (Merikangas & Gelentner, 1990) is more cautious.

Underlying mechanisms: Effects of prenatal smoking on problem behaviors in childhood

An hypothesis complementary to that of a latent dependence on nicotine is that prenatal nicotine exposure induces childhood hyperactivity, aggression, and disruptive behavior problems, and these problems, in turn, lead to deviance and the use of cigarettes during adolescence.

An extensive body of epidemiological and clinical studies has established that the offspring of mothers who smoke during pregnancy are at risk for various developmental problems (Fried, 1989). In addition to the immediate deleterious effects on fetal development and infant birthweight (Abel, 1980; Rantakallio, 1978) and compromised physical and cognitive development in infancy and childhood (Bauman, Flewelling, & LaPrelle, 1991; Fox, Sexton & Hebel, 1990; Olds, Henderson, & Tatelbaum, 1994; Tong & McMichael, 1992), in utero exposure to nicotine is consistently associated with childhood attention problems, hyperactivity (Denson, Nanson, & McWalters, 1975; Nichols & Chen, 1981), and a range of behavioral disturbances, including delinquency (Bagley, 1992), although the latter may be attenuated with controls for socioeconomic resources (Rantakallio, 1983). In two large New Zealand cohorts (Fergusson, Horwood, & Lynskey, 1983; McGee & Stanton, 1994) and in two Dutch studies (Orlebeke, Boomsma, & Verhulst, 1994; Orlebeke, Knol, & Verhulst, 1997), the children of mothers who smoked during pregnancy were more restless and distractable and had more parent- and teacher-reported conduct problems than those not exposed. Similarly, Weitzman, Gortmaker, and Sobol (1992) found, in a national sample of children from the NLSY, that maternal smoking both pre- and postnatally was associated with higher levels of antisocial behavior and hyperactivity. Animal studies have corroborated this pattern of nicotine-induced hyperactivity (Richardson & Tizabi, 1994), suggesting that prenatal biological insults may be one origin of excessive and disregulated behavior during childhood.

The behavioral outcomes associated with maternal prenatal smoking are well-documented risk factors in the development of adolescent conduct problems, delinquency, and substance use (Moffitt, 1993). Child behavior problems, especially early aggression and antisocial patterns, show strong developmental continuity (Kazdin, 1987; Loeber, 1982; Patterson, Reid, & Dishion, 1992) and are associated concurrently and predictively with adolescent and adult substance use (Brook, Whiteman, & Finch, 1992; Ensminger, Brown, & Kellam, 1982; Henry et al., 1993; Kellam, Ensminger, & Simon, 1980; Lochman & Wayland, 1994; Lynskey & Fergusson, 1995; Van Kammen, Loeber, & Stouthamer-Loeber, 1991). Although the majority of these studies have focused on the behavioral precursors and correlates of adolescent alcohol and illicit drug use, few studies, except for that of Ensminger and colleagues (1982), have systematically investigated the role of childhood behavior problems in the prediction of cigarette smoking or have examined this risk factor as a function of gender (Ensminger et al., 1982; Kellam et al., 1980).

We proceeded to test the hypothesis that prenatal smoking increased a child's problematic behaviors in childhood and that these behaviors predicted smoking in adolescence (Griesler & Kandel, in press). Consistent with previous investigations, we found that maternal smoking during pregnancy was associated with behavior problems during childhood. At age 7, as noted earlier, the children of mothers who smoked during pregnancy were perceived by their mothers to be more disobedient, to have more control problems, more negative relationships with their parents, and higher scores for total behavior problems than chil-

Table 3.2. *Adjusted odds ratios (AOR) from logistic regressions predicting high score on child behavior problems[a] as a function of maternal smoking during pregnancy and selected demographic variables for boys and girls (N = 187 dyads, NYS Cohort)*

Predictors	High score on behavior problems AOR[b]
Males (N = 102)	
Child age	1.1
Maternal education	.9
Maternal smoking pregnancy	
Did not smoke	
< 1 pack a day	1.3
≥1 pack a day	2.0
Constant	−.16**
Chi-square	2.97
Females (N = 85)	
Child age	.9
Maternal education	.7
Maternal smoking pregnancy	
Did not smoke	
<1 pack a day	1.7
≥1 pack a day	3.9*
Constant	4.65
Chi-square	8.69†

[a]Top 75th percentile of total behavior problem summary score.
[b]Exponentiated unstandardized coefficients.
†$p \leq .10$; *$p \leq .05$; **$p \leq .01$.

dren whose mothers did not smoke during pregnancy. With the inclusion of demographic covariates in multivariate regression models, the association between parental prenatal smoking and child problem behaviors remained significant and became slightly stronger among females than among males (Table 3.2). The total behavior problems score was dichotomized at the 25th percentile to identify a high-scoring group. Extensive maternal smoking during pregnancy increased the odds of the child's scoring high on the scale, especially females (Table 3.2). The odds were significant only for girls and were twice as high as for boys.

Behavior problems, however, had few direct effects on adolescent smoking. Effects were observed only for girls' lifetime smoking. With control for behavior problems, maternal smoking during pregnancy, particularly smoking a pack or more per day, was still associated with current smoking among female offspring. This effect persisted, with odds of 11.2 ($p < .05$), controlling for mother's current smoking, child behavior problems, and maternal monitoring. These findings suggest a direct biological effect of prenatal maternal smoking on daughters' current smoking. Prenatal maternal smoking may also have an indirect effect on initiation of smoking by adolescent girls via increased behavior problems, which together with other factors (e.g., low levels of maternal monitoring) set the stage for experimentation with smoking, which may be sustained through the activation of a latent biological vulnerability to nicotine.

Indeed, although child behavior problems did not predict current smoking, they were significantly associated with lifetime smoking by adolescent girls. Experimentation with cigarettes may be influenced by social and behavioral factors, as well as by behavior problems for females that may be partially induced by prenatal factors, whereas the continued use of cigarettes, again by females, may have partial and direct origins in early biological processes. The conditions that increase the likelihood of a behavior are not necessarily the same as those associated with its maintenance. Problem behaviors may predict the initiation of cigarette smoking among daughters. Those daughters whose mothers smoked heavily during pregnancy may then be at heightened risk for persisting in smoking and eventually developing biologically induced nicotine dependence.

Implications

Although our sample size is small, the results underscore the importance of examining risk factors by gender. This parallels the findings of Ensminger and colleagues (1982), who reported that different childhood variables predicted adolescent substance use for males and females, and the findings of other researchers, who have emphasized the role of gender-specific risk factors and vulnerabilities in the development of psychopathology (Leadbeater, Blatt, & Quinlan, 1995). Models of risk based largely on samples of males (Lochman & Wayland, 1994; Loeber & Dishion, 1983; Patterson et al., 1992) may not be generalizable to females, and aggregated samples of males and females that do not include gender as an interaction term potentially obscure sex-specific influences in the development of normal and pathological behavior. Furthermore, gender differences may appear at different periods of development. In the Dunedin Multidisciplinary Health and Development Study (McGee & Stanton, 1994), there were no sex differences in the impact of maternal smoking during pregnancy on problem behaviors at age 5. However, by age 9, gender effects emerged: Only female offspring of mothers who smoked during pregnancy showed low IQ and poor reading performance.

Our findings suggest that assumptions concerning risk factors for adolescent smoking, particularly among females, need to be reexamined. Social and proximal modes of influence have been emphasized, including cultural factors, the mass media, familial characteristics, role modeling, smoking among siblings, deviant peer influences, and problem behaviors (Barnes, Farrell, & Cairns, 1986; Chassin, Presson, Sherman, Montello, & McGrew, 1986; Chilcoat, Dishion, & Anthony, 1995; Conrad, Flay, & Hill, 1992; Flay et al., 1994; Pollay et al., 1996; Stanton & Silva, 1992; U.S. Department of Health and Human Services, 1994). Few studies have considered the role of biological risk factors. Although the current findings provide support for the role of early behavior problems in fostering cigarette experimentation and of maternal monitoring in decreasing adolescent smoking, they also suggest that prenatal biological factors may be an important risk factor for smoking among girls, and perhaps other forms of drug behavior as well.

The findings bring us back full circle to the developmental paradigm of stages in drug involvement. The now well-replicated work on stages of drug use indicates that there are well-delineated stages of involvement in drugs. Most young people do not experiment with marijuana unless they have already tried alcohol and/or cigarettes. And almost no one tries cocaine who has not experimented with marijuana (Kandel, 1975; Kandel & Yamaguchi, 1993; Kandel et al., 1992; Yamaguchi & Kandel, 1984). We have consistently found sex differences in the developmental pathways of involvement in drugs, whereby cigarette smoking plays a more important role for women's progression to higher stages of drug use, including the use of medically prescribed drugs, than it does for men (Kandel & Yamaguchi, 1993; Kandel et al., 1992). Thus, cigarette smoking, which plays a particularly important role for women's progression to higher stages of drug use, appears to play a critical role in the intergenerational transmission of smoking from mother to child, especially for daughters.

Very few studies of in utero exposure to licit or illicit drugs have followed offspring into adolescence or early adulthood, especially to consider outcomes other than physical or cognitive development. This research represents an advance in our understanding of the etiology of smoking and illicit drug use in adolescence. Such understanding has important public health implications, not only because of the deleterious long-term health effects of smoking, but also because smoking and drinking in adolescence are precursors of progression to other forms of drug use and because adolescence is the period of highest risk for initiation of smoking and drinking. The earlier the age of onset of legal drug use, the greater the risk of progression to a higher-stage drug and to dependence.

The perinatal effect of maternal smoking suggests novel ways of examining latent and long-term effects of drug consumption during pregnancy. Such consumption may affect brain functioning in utero, both functionally and in ways that do not become apparent until the child has had opportunities to try the relevant substances. The increased liability to nicotine dependence due to intrauterine exposure and its presumed effect on the dopamine system may lead to greater liability to drug dependence more generally. Such exposure might index an endogenous vulnerability factor generalizable to drugs other than cigarettes.

The findings related to the effect of prenatal smoking on child smoking and the interpretations regarding the potential underlying neurophysiological mechanisms stimulated my interest in drug dependence.

The epidemiology of drug dependence

Drug dependence as a crucial area of inquiry

Drug-dependent individuals represent a fraction of the drug-using population, a fraction, as we shall see, that varies across substances. Because drug-dependent individuals constitute the most heavily involved subgroup of users, they represent those with the most severe negative consequences associated with the use of drugs. Whether there is a threshold, such as meeting criteria for dependence, at which these consequences increase sharply or whether the negative consequences increase linearly with increasing involvement is not known. Understanding the epidemiology and etiology of drug dependence is important from a public health perspective. In this section, I describe ongoing activities that I initiated recently as a preliminary step to the initiation of research that needs to be pursued on the etiology of drug dependence and that I hope to pursue.

In 1992, Glanz and Pickens published an important volume on the precursors to drug abuse and dependence based on papers prepared for a conference that they organized on the "Transition from Drug Use to Abuse/Dependence." The conference was cosponsored by the American Psychological Association and the National Institute on Drug Abuse. In my estimation, the volume did not stimulate as much new research as one would have hoped. Understanding how persons move from use to abuse and dependence is a most important issue and one that is in need of much additional research. However, the descriptive basis on which to develop appropriate longitudinal studies is lacking.

As is true of most of drug research conducted on representative community samples, most of my own work to date has focused on patterns of drug use. However, a high priority for the field of drug research is to understand progression to problematic drug use and dependence. I have become increasingly concerned with doing so in my own research. My goal is to bridge research on substance dependence in treated samples, which emphasizes functional impairment to the neglect of patterns of use, and epidemiological research on substance use in the general population, which usually ignores dependence or abuse criteria. It is my strong belief that progress in our understanding of the development of substance use and of problems related to substance use will come about only when these two streams of research are brought more closely together. My immediate goal is to assess the epidemiology and phenomenology of substance use disorders from a comparative and lifespan perspective. In my current work, I examine the phenomenology of substance dependence on different drug classes, including nicotine, in different subgroups of the population, and the correspondence between diagnostic criteria of dependence and abuse and quantity/frequency measures of drug use. My long-term goal is to understand how individuals move from use to dependence and what role nicotine plays in that progression.

These are completely neglected areas of research. Extensive data on patterns of substance use in both adults and adolescents in the U.S. population are available on an ongoing basis (Johnston, O'Malley, & Bachman, 1995; SAMHSA, 1996). By contrast, epidemiological data on the national prevalence of substance use disorders are more seldom collected, especially in the population younger than 18 years old. However, data on adolescents are critical because adolescence is the period in the life cycle when use of different classes of drugs is initiated. Current epidemiological surveys of substance use disorders in the population (Anthony, Warner & Kessler, 1994; Grant, Harford, Dawson, Chou, & Pickering, 1995; Kessler et al., 1994; Warner, Kessler, Hughes, Anthony & Nelson, 1995) have several limitations, although these studies represent improvements over earlier investigations (Robins & Regier, 1991). No data are available for adolescents compared with other age groups because most surveys have sampled persons 18 years old and over. Limited data are provided for nicotine dependence, the most common substance use disorder. No attempt is made to relate patterns of drug use to rates of drug dependence.

A new initiative

My colleagues and I have recently undertaken analyses on the National Household Survey on Drug Abuse (NHSDA), a large national survey of drug use patterns in the general population aged 12 and over (SAMHSA, 1996). The survey constitutes an important and mostly unused source of data for assessing the epidemiology of drug dependence in the United States in adolescence and adulthood. The NHSDA was initiated in 1972, and was conducted every 2 or 3 years until 1988 and annually as of 1990. Although the survey focuses on patterns of use of 12 classes of drugs, starting in 1985 questions have been asked about symptoms of dependence experienced with respect to each drug class. The large sample size of the survey and the oversampling of minorities and individuals in the ages of highest risk for drug use (ages 12–34) permit age, sex, and ethnic subgroup comparisons not otherwise possible in other surveys. The NHSDA makes possible the (approximated) assessment of dependence on and abuse of nicotine and other substances among adolescents for comparison with adults, as well as the assessment of rates in different age and ethnic groups. The opportunity to examine nicotine dependence among adolescents is unique. However, a limitation of the data is that the identification of dependence and abuse allowed by the NHSDA can only be approximated and cannot be as systematic as that based on structured schedules developed specifically to measure psychiatric disorders, such as the Diagnostic Interview Schedule (DIS) (Robins, Helzer, Croughan, Williams, & Spitzer, 1981), the Composite International Diagnostic Interview (CIDI) (Kessler et al., 1994; Robins et al., 1988), and the Alcohol Use Disorder and Associated Disabilities Interview Schedule (AUDADIS) (Grant et al., 1995).

We are currently analyzing three aggregated waves (1991–1993) of the NHSDA ($N = 87,915$). Data on drug-related symptoms of dependence and drug-related problems experienced within the last years have been used to develop approximated DSM-IV diagnostic criteria for last-year substance use disorders (dependence and abuse) involving nicotine, alcohol, marijuana, and cocaine. DSM-IV (American Psychiatric Association, 1994) defines seven diagnostic criteria and associated symptoms (see Table 3.3).

As per the DSM-IV definition, an individual in the NHSDA was defined as being dependent on alcohol, nicotine, marijuana, or cocaine within the last year if he or she met three out of seven approximate criteria for that substance. Prior to carrying our substantive analyses based on the proxy measure of last-year dependence, we assessed the consistency of the prevalence estimates from the NHSDA with DSM-IV last-year rates observed for age ranges 18–54 in two other national surveys that assessed substance use disorders with specially designed instruments (Kandel, Chen, Warner, Kessler, & Grant, 1997). We compared rates across the surveys and the relative ranking of different sociodemographic groups on drug-specific dependence rates for age-matched groups. The correlations across studies were very high and established the usefulness of the NHSDA data.

Prevalence rates of last-year dependence among users of each drug class have been examined for adolescents and adults and as a function of sex and ethnicity. The rates have been calculated *conditional* on use rather than in the total population so as to identify drug-specific liability for dependence without confounding for baseline rates of experi-

Table 3.3. *Comparison of DSM-IV criteria for substance dependence and corresponding questions in the NHSDA*

DSM–IV criteria	Questions in NHSDA
(1) tolerance, as defined by either of the following: (a) a need for markedly increased amount of the substance to achieve intoxication or desired effect (b) markedly diminished effect with continued use of the same amount of the substance	DR–3. *During the past 12 months*, for which drugs have you *needed larger amounts to get the same effect*; that is, for which drugs could you no longer get high on the same amount you used to use?
(2) withdrawal, as defined by either of the following: (a) the characteristic withdrawal syndrome for the substance (b) the same (or a closely related) substance is taken to relieve or avoid withdrawal symptoms	DR–6. For which drugs have you had withdrawal symptoms; that is, you *felt sick because you stopped or cut down* on your use of them *during the past 12 months?*
(3) the substance is often taken in larger amounts or over a longer period than was intended	DR–5. Which drugs have you *felt that you needed* or were dependent on *in the past 12 months?*
(4) there is a persistent desire or unsuccessful efforts to cut down or control substance use	DR–1. *During the past 12 months*, for which drugs have you consciously *tried to cut down* on your use? DR–2. *During the past 12 months*, for which drugs have you *been unable to cut down* on your use, even though you tried?
(5) a great deal of time is spent in activities necessary to obtain the substance (e.g., visiting multiple doctors or driving long distances), use the substance (e.g., chain-smoking), or recover from its effects	Drug-specific pattern of heavy use as follows: ■ Tobacco: smoking 2+ packs daily in the past 30 days ■ Alcohol: drinking 5+ drinks a day for 15+ days in the past 30 days; or "gotten very high or drank" nearly daily (3+ days a week) in the past 12 months

Table 3.3. *(cont.)*

DSM-IV criteria	Questions in NHSDA
	■ Marijuana: used 3+ joints near daily (3+ times a week) in the past 30 days; or 2+ ounces (86+ joints or 43+ grams) in the past 30 days; or traded service for marijuana ■ Cocaine: about 2+ grams (37+ big lines of powder) used in the past 30 days, or traded services for cocaine/crack
(6) important social, occupational, or recreational activities are given up or reduced because of substance use	DP-1. As a result of drug use at any time in your life, did you, in the past 12 months . . . (h) get less work done than usual at school or on the job?
(7) the substance use is continued despite knowledge of having a persistent or recurrent physical or psychological problem that is likely to have been caused or exacerbated by the substance (e.g., current cocaine use despite recognition of cocaine-induced depression, or continued drinking despite recognition that an ulcer was made worse by alcohol consumption)	DP-1. As a result of drug use at any time in your life, did you, in the past 12 months . . . (a) Become depressed or lose interest in things? (b) Have arguments/fights with family and friends? (c) Feel completely alone and isolated? (d) Feel very nervous and anxious? (e) Have health problems? (f) Find it difficult to think clearly? (g) Feel irritable and upset? (i) Feel suspicious and distrustful of people? (j) Find it harder to handle your problems? (k) Have to get emegency medical help? (l) Have someone suggest you seek treatment?[a] *Respondent had any one of the 11 listed problems*

[a]Not asked in the 1991 NHSDA. An additional problem in the NHSDA (1992–1993) list, "Drive unsafely," is a DSM-IV abuse but not a dependence criterion.

mentation with each specific drug class. Degree of drug involvement and thresholds of use at which dependence occurs have been examined to explain group differences (or similarities) in rates of dependence.

Of the four drugs that we have examined, cigarettes are associated with the highest last-year conditional rate of dependence and alcohol with the lowest rate among adolescents who have smoked in the last year; 20% meet criteria for dependence, and 8% of those who have drunk alcohol are dependent. Of those who have used marijuana in the last year, 14% are dependent; of those who have used cocaine, 11% are dependent. Almost twice as many youths are dependent on cigarettes as on cocaine. The prevalence of the rates of conditional dependence does not follow the ranking of the prevalence of the rates of use of these drugs.

Age, gender, and ethnic differences in rates of dependence

Age and gender differences. It is not an exaggeration to emphasize that nothing is known regarding the liability for dependence across the life-span and whether this liability is stronger or weaker in adolescence than in adulthood. The NHSDA allows one to examine rates of dependence from adolescence on because individuals are sampled as of age 12, and the same methodology has been used to assess substance use, dependence, and abuse at all ages.

Five age groups were considered: adolescents 12–17 years old and adults aged 18–25, 26–34, 35–49, and 50 and over (Figure 3.3). There are striking age differences in conditional rates of current (last-year) dependence on different drug classes throughout the life cycle. The differences across drugs are accentuated among adults compared with adolescents. Because the rates are for last-year symptoms conditional on being a last-year user of each substance, the age-related trends can be attributed mainly to maturational processes rather than to cohort differences.

Among males and females, the conditional rates of dependence on cigarettes increase among each successively higher age up to age 50, when the rates decline. Among females, the conditional rates of dependence on alcohol, marijuana, and cocaine are highest in adolescence. Among males, the highest conditional rates of dependence on marijuana also occur in adolescence, but the highest rates of dependence on other

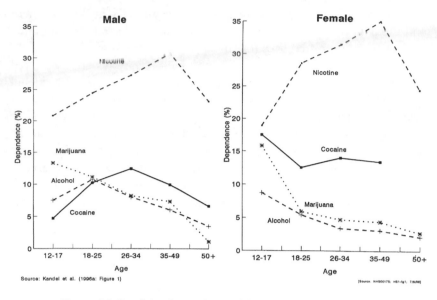

Source: Kandel et al. (1996a: Figure 1)

Figure 3.3 Conditional prevalence of last-year dependence among last-year users of nicotine, alcohol, marijuana, and cocaine in the United States by age and gender (NHSDA, 1991–1993).

substances occur in adulthood (at ages 18–25 for alcohol and at ages 26–34 for cocaine). Among both males and females, the highest rates of dependence on cigarettes occur at ages 35–49, later than for any other drug.

Thus, males and females appear to be differentially susceptible to dependence on different drug classes once they have used these drugs. Furthermore, with the exception of cigarettes, the pattern of sex differences varies with age. Except for cocaine, approximately the same proportions of adolescent boys and girls who have used each class of drugs in the last year are dependent on these drugs. However, more than three times as many adolescent girls are dependent on cocaine than adolescent boys. The higher proportion of girls than boys dependent on marijuana is not statistically significant. In adulthood the overall rates are higher for males than for females for alcohol and marijuana, whereas the reverse sex difference occurs for cigarettes and cocaine (Figure 3.4).

It is important to understand when in adolescence and young adult-

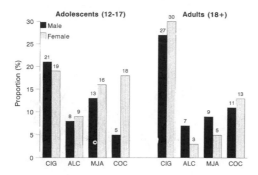

Figure 3.4 Prevalence of conditional dependence among last-year users of cigarettes, alcohol, marijuana, and cocaine by gender among adolescents and adults (NHSDA, 1991–1993).

hood the rates increase and when they peak. The large size of the NHSDA sample allows us to examine in detail the relationship between age and liability to drug dependence. Age-specific conditional dependence rates year by year from age 12 to 30 for alcohol and any illicit drug reveal that no user meets criteria for last-year substance dependence, excluding cigarettes, below the age of 14 (Figure 3.5). The rate increases throughout adolescence and reaches a peak at ages 16 to 19, when it begins to decline. It must be kept in mind that these rates describe age-specific prevalence and not incidence.

Almost identical developmental patterns were observed in another study restricted to a nonrepresentative sample of adolescents 12 to 17 years old and based on sophisticated assessments of substance use disorders (Kandel et al., 1997). In this multisite methodological study of psychiatric disorders in childhood and adolescence (Methods for the Epidemiology of Child and Adolescent Mental Disorders [MECA] Study), the standard instrument for measuring psychiatric disorders among children (Diagnostic Interview Schedule for Children [DISC]) was administered to 1,270 children 9–17 years old and to their caretakers. Nicotine dependence was not assessed. The rates of 6-month substance use disorders focusing on alcohol and any illicit drug were calculated for all adolescents and were not restricted to users. For comparison, the NHSDA rates were recalculated on the total sample of adolescents as well, and took into account abuse as well as dependence criteria to obtain a measure of substance use disorder comparable to

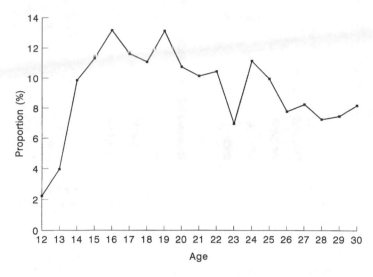

Figure 3.5 Prevalence of conditional dependence on alcohol or any illicit drugs among last-year users by age among 12- to 30-year-olds (NHSDA, 1991–1993).

that used in the MECA study. The age–related trends in overall rates of substance use disorders in adolescence (not restricted to drug users of each respective drug class) were very similar to those in the NHSDA (Kandel et al., 1997) (Figure 3.6).

In both samples, very few adolescents below age 14 met criteria for a substance use disorder. The rates increased sharply at age 16 or 17. As noted earlier, when we examined the rates through age 30 in the NHSDA, peak rates of dependence among users occurred in late adolescence and did not increase further in adulthood.

Ethnic differences. Striking ethnic differences in the conditional prevalence of current substance dependence were observed for cigarettes and cocaine. Once having smoked, whites are more likely than nonwhites to become dependent on cigarettes. By contrast, once having used cocaine, blacks are much more likely than whites or Hispanics to become dependent (Figure 3.7). The highest rates of cocaine dependence are observed among black females. Relatively small ethnic differences are observed for alcohol. As regards marijuana, white and black females are

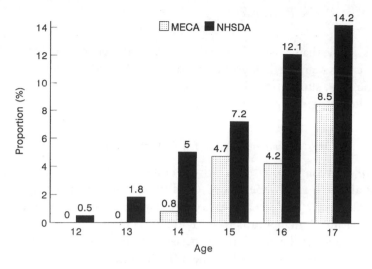

Figure 3.6 Prevalence of any substance use disorder (excluding cigarette use) in the past 6 months (in MECA, 1992) and in the past 12 months (in NHSDA, 1991–1993) by age among 12- to 17-year-olds.

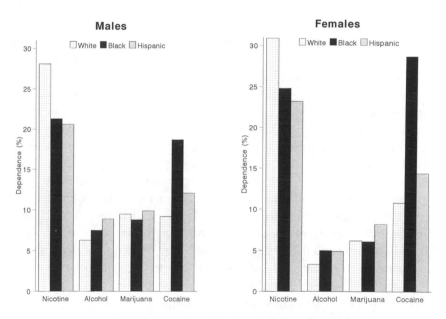

Figure 3.7 Prevalence of conditional dependence among last-year users of alcohol, nicotine, marijuana, and cocaine in the United States by sex and ethnicity (NHSDA, 1991–1993).

less likely than Hispanic females to become dependent. Demographic differences among subgroups in rates of dependence are smallest for cigarettes, supporting the conclusion that nicotine is the most addictive of the four substances we examined.

Drug dependence and extensiveness of drug use

The question of interest is, why do different groups experience differential liability to dependence on different drugs? In particular, what explains why adolescents, especially females, become more dependent on marijuana than adults (see Figure 3.4)? Differences in extensiveness of use and in the relationship between frequency and quantity of use and dependence may explain the different rates of dependence observed among subgroups of users of specific drug classes. Very little research has integrated information on patterns of drug use, such as frequency and quantity, with information on substance use disorders. Most work has focused on alcohol dependence among adults (Grant & Harford, 1990; MacDonald, Barry, & Fleming, 1992). Most assessments of substance dependence focus on clinical criteria of problematic use and do not obtain information about the individual's patterns and levels of use. In the NHSDA, one can examine in detail the relationship between level of use and dependence.

In considering the relationship between intensity of marijuana use and dependence, we were interested in examining adolescents in comparison with adults and males in comparison with females. We examined the relationship between marijuana use and dependence at different levels of frequency and quantity of use by age and by gender (Chen, Kandel, & Davies, 1997). Frequency of marijuana use in the past year and average number of joints smoked in the past 30 days were used to index the intensity of marijuana use. In these analyses, we excluded frequency of use from the definition of dependence so as not to confound the two variables being correlated. The definition of dependence was changed from three out of seven criteria to three out of six criteria. To simplify the analysis and the presentation of the results, all adults aged 18 and over were considered as a group.

Fewer than 10% of users used marijuana on a daily basis; another 7–13% among the various subgroups used it almost daily, that is, four to

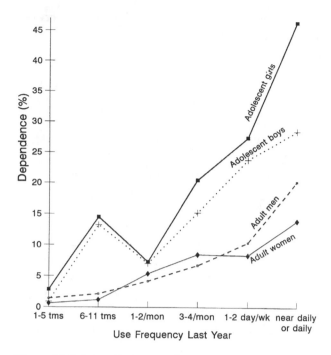

Figure 3.8 Relationship between frequency of marijuana use last year and 12-month dependence among last-year users, by gender, among adolescents and adults (NHSDA, 1991–1993; $N = 9,284$).

six times a week. As a group, adolescents used marijuana less frequently than adults. However, although adolescents were less likely than adults to have used marijuana within the last 30 days, those who did so reported using a higher quantity in that period. Almost half of those who used it within the last 30 days smoked one joint or less on an average day. There were no gender differences in frequency or quantity of marijuana use among adolescents; by contrast, among adults, males used marijuana at higher frequencies and quantities than females.

As expected, there is a strong relationship between extent of marijuana use and dependence for all groups (Figure 3.8): the higher the frequency (or quantity) used, the higher the rate of dependence. The association is stronger for adolescents than for adults; it is also stronger for females than for males in adolescence but stronger for males than for females in adulthood. Thus, there is an interaction between age and gender in the association between intensity of marijuana use and marijuana dependence.

To explain group-specific rates of dependence, intensity of marijuana use (indexed by frequency and/or quantity of use) could be important in several ways. Groups that have *higher rates* of dependence (1) may be using marijuana more heavily, or (2) they may be more sensitive to the effects of marijuana at the same intensity of use, or (3) both processes could be operative. Groups that have *similar rates* of dependence (4) may be using marijuana at different levels of intensity but may be differently responsive to similar doses. Thus, different groups may experience different liability for dependence at the same levels of use.

We carried out a formal test of these hypotheses. We estimated separate logistic regressions predicting dependence from frequency of marijuana use (or quantity used) for all respondents, adolescents, and adults together. Two sets of five hierarchical logistic regressions each were estimated to permit a systematic test of age and gender effects of frequency and quantity of marijuana use separately on dependence. The models included gender, age and gender, and all two-way and three-way interactions between age, gender, and frequency (or quantity smoked) of use. The only significant interaction was the age-by-gender interaction. These regressions provide two parameters of interest for our purpose: a slope and an intercept for each group. The slope indexes the rate of response (i.e., dependence) to increasing levels of use. The intercept indexes the response threshold to the drug. A high intercept reflects a low threshold, that is, a high proportion of persons dependent at low doses. By contrast, a low intercept reflects a high threshold, that is, a low proportion of persons dependent at low doses. We compared through statistical tests (i.e., z-tests of the differences) the regression coefficients from these logit models between pairs of groups to determine whether variations in rates were due to differences in response threshold to the drug (indexed by the intercept), or differences in the rate of response to increasing levels of use (indexed by the slope), or both. Different intercepts would indicate that groups have different threshold responses to marijuana and that the level at which dependence develops is different. Different slopes would indicate that the associations between frequency (or quantity) used and marijuana dependence differ.

Table 3.4. *Schematic summary of group differences in marijuana use behavior and multivariate coefficients by age and age and gender in the NHSDA (1991–1993)*

Group contrasts	Dependence rates	Frequency	Slopes	Intercepts
Female				
Adolescents vs. adults	Adol>adults	Same	Same	Adol>adults
Male				
Adolescents vs. adults	Adol>adults	Adol<adults	Same	Adol>adults
Adolescents				
Males vs. females	M>F?	Same	Same	M<F†
Adults				
Males vs. females	M>F	M>F	Same	M>F†

†$p < .10.$

Table 3.4 summarizes the results of these analyses with respect to frequency of marijuana use. The table also summarizes the group differences in rates of dependence to be explained, as well as group differences in frequency of use. As noted earlier, the prevalence of dependence is higher among adolescent users than among users in any other age group and is higher among adult male users than among female adult users. In adolescence, the gender difference in the rates, which was not statistically significant at the univariate level, becomes significant when intensity of use is controlled. Adolescents, especially adolescent males, use marijuana at lower frequency but at higher quantity than adults. Males and females use it at similar levels in adolescence, whereas males use it at higher levels than females in adulthood.

Frequency and quantity of marijuana use are linearly associated with the probability of becoming dependent on marijuana. As reflected in the slopes, the associations do not vary significantly, either by age or by gender, among adolescents or adults. However, as reflected in the higher intercepts, adolescents of both sexes become dependent at a *lower threshold* of frequency than adults. At low intensity of use, a higher proportion of adolescents than adults become dependent. Similarly, adult males become dependent at a *lower threshold* than adult females. The opposite gender difference obtains in adolescence: Adolescent males become dependent at a *higher threshold* than females, that is, they have a lower rate of dependence than females at low frequency of use.

These results provide insights into the processes that underlie the age and sex differentials observed in the prevalence of marijuana dependence. Once having used marijuana, adolescents appear to experience higher rates of dependence than adults. This is not because they use marijuana more frequently than adults, although they use it in higher quantities. Adolescents experience higher rates of dependence because they appear to be more sensitive to the effects of marijuana: At low intensity of use, adolescents, especially female adolescents, become more dependent than adults. As a result, the tendency to become drug dependent at each level of frequency (and quantity) of use is higher for adolescent girls than for adolescent boys. Although the relative rate of increase, given increasing intensity of use, is the same irrespective of age, at the same levels of frequency or quantity of use, adolescents experience higher rates of dependence than adults because the threshold at which they first become dependent is lower than for adults.

An additional process becomes important in accounting for gender differences in adulthood. Adult males experience higher rates of dependence than adult females because (1) they are more likely than adult females to become drug dependent at the same levels of use but also because (2) they use at higher frequency (and quantity) than females. By contrast, adolescent males experience lower rates of dependence than adolescent females because they are less sensitive to the drug than females and become dependent at higher frequency of use than adolescent females. The frequency of use for males is the same as for females.

Thus, the results provide some understanding of the factors that account for differences in rates of dependence observed among adolescents and adults, and among males and females in adolescence and adulthood. The results also provide some understanding of the extent of problematic use and of need for treatment in the general population represented by specific patterns of drug use. Estimates of needs based on substance dependence criteria for a variety of drugs, and for various age and ethnic groups in the population, are crucial for policy and the planning of services for drug-abusing individuals.

This work, however, is but a first and very simple stage in the investigation of drug dependence in the general population. It provides the beginning descriptive knowledge basis of the epidemiology of substance use disorders, especially in adolescence, which is necessary for planning more sophisticated longitudinal research on the progression of use to dependence. In terms of future directions for research on drug behavior, I consider this area to be crucial.

Epilogue

I also would like to propose that, in addition to their implications for policy, our results illustrate the mutual relevance of epidemiology and biology for understanding addiction and, in particular, how epidemiological studies suggest hypotheses that need to be tested in the laboratory both in humans and in animals. The findings on the effects of prenatal maternal smoking on adolescent smoking, and on gender and age differences in the relationships between patterns of marijuana use and dependence, illustrate how epidemiological data provide new insights and may frame new questions for research into the biological bases of drug dependence and addiction. At present, epidemiological and biological investigations by and large are carried out independently of each other. Yet, much is to be gained by a closer interchange and collaboration between the two disciplines, as has been shown to be the case for lung cancer, the slow viruses of the nervous system, and coronary heart disease. The relevance of biology for the epidemiology of substance use disorders is obvious. Biological factors, not only social and psychological factors, underlie the natural history of drug use and the causes and consequences of using drugs. What is less obvious are the contributions that epidemiology can make in providing novel insights into the biology of addiction and in suggesting new hypotheses to be pursued and tested in the laboratory.

Substance abuse and addiction is a complex behavior. Its understanding can only come from a multidisciplinary perspective in which biological, psychological, and sociological factors are taken into account. Biological risk factors, in addition to social influences, contribute to vulnerability to substance use and dependence among different groups of individuals. Large-scale prospective studies incorporating measures of biological and social risk are necessary to examine such vulnerability issues further.

Postscript

An unanticipated but most exciting consequence of my participation at the conference is the unusual opportunity it created for me to test in the laboratory the basic hypothesis that I proposed regarding the effect of prenatal smoking on female offspring. During a lunch, Richard Udry, a conference participant, mentioned to me that he had access to data that would permit a test of the hypothesis. These data consist of frozen prenatal blood samples collected approximately 35 years earlier on cohorts of more than 450 pregnant women, as well as smoking histories taken from these same women and their daughters when the daughters were 15 years old. The sample would make it possible to examine simultaneously the biological effects of prenatal smoking and the social effects of parental modeling. Richard Udry had analyzed these samples earlier in a study of testosterone influences on gender behavior. We decided to proceed with a study that would test my hypothesis based on an actual biological assay of smoking during pregnancy. Inquiry about the feasibility of analyzing these samples for nicotine indicated that whatever degradation may have taken place in the samples over time would not affect our ability to determine the prenatal smoking status of these women. I obtained a grant supplement from the National Institute on Drug Abuse to carry out the biological assays. As of the writing of this postscript, the assays have been completed and the analyses are ongoing.

This development exemplifies the benefits of the conference in ways that Richard Jessor himself could not have anticipated. This development is important not only for my own professional program of research but also for progress in the field and the approach that I am advocating.

References

Abel, E. L. (1980). Smoking during pregnancy: A review of effects of growth and development of the offspring. *Human Biology, 52,* 593–625.

American Psychiatric Association. (1994). *Diagnostic and statistical manual of mental disorders* (4th ed.). Washington, DC.

Annis, H. M. (1974). Patterns of intra-familial drug use. *British Journal of Addiction, 69,* 361–369.

Anthony, J. C., Warner, L. A., & Kessler, R. C. (1994). Comparative epidemiology of dependence on tobacco, alcohol, controlled substances, and inhalants: Basic findings from the National Comorbidity Survey. *Experimental and Clinical Psychopharmacology, 2,* 244–268.

Arnett, J. (1992). Reckless behavior in adolescence: A developmental perspective. *Developmental Review, 12,* 339–373.

Bagley, C. (1992). Maternal smoking and deviant behaviour in 16-year-olds: A personality hypothesis. *Personality & Individual Differences, 13,* 377–378.

Banks, M. H., Bewley, B. R., Bland, J. R., Dean, S., & Pollard, V. (1978). Long-term study of smoking by secondary schoolchildren. *Archives of Disease in Childhood, 83,* 12–19.

Barnes, G., Farrell, M. P., & Cairns, A. (1986). Parental socialization factors and adolescent drinking behaviors. *Journal of Marriage and the Family, 48,* 27–36.

Bauman, K. E., Flewelling, R. L., & LaPrelle, J. (1991). Parental cigarette smoking and cognitive performance of children. *Health Psychology, 10,* 282–288.

Beitner-Johnson, D., Guitart, X., & Nestler, E. J. (1992). Neurofilament proteins and the mesolimbic dopamine system: Common regulation by chronic morphine and chronic cocaine in the rat ventral tegmental area. *Journal of Neuroscience, 12,* 2165–2175.

Breslau, N., Kilbey, M., & Andreski, P. (1993). Nicotine dependence and major depression. *Archives of General Psychiatry, 50,* 31–35.

Brook, J. S., Brook, D. W., Whiteman, M., Gordon, A. S., & Cohen, P. (1990). The psychosocial etiology of adolescent drug use and abuse. *Genetic, Social and General Psychology Monographs, 116*(2), 111–267.

Brook, J. S., Whiteman, M., & Finch, S. (1992). Childhood aggression, adolescent delinquency, and drug use: A longitudinal study. *Journal of Genetic Psychology, 153,* 369–383.

Chassin, L., Presson, C. C., Sherman, S. J., Montello, D., & McGrew, J. (1986). Changes in peer and parent influence during adolescence: Longitudinal versus cross-sectional perspectives on smoking initiation. *Developmental Psychology, 22,* 327–334.

Chen, K., Kandel, D. B., & Davies, M. (1997). Relationships between frequency and quantity of marijuana use and last year proxy dependence among adolescents and adults in the United States. *Drug and Alcohol Dependence, 46,* 53–67.

Chilcoat, H. D., Dishion, T. J., & Anthony, J. C. (1995). Parent monitoring and the incidence of drug sampling in urban elementary school children. *American Journal of Epidemiology, 141,* 25–31.

Clayton, R. (1992). Transitions in drug use: Risk and protective factors. In

M. D. Glanz & R. W. Pickens (Eds.), *Vulnerability to Drug Abuse* (pp. 15–51). Washington, DC: American Psychological Association.

Collins, A. C. (1990–1991). Genetic influences on tobacco use: A review of human and animal studies. *International Journal of Addictions, 25,* 35–55.

Conrad, K. M., Flay, B. R., & Hill, D. (1992). Why children start smoking cigarettes: Predictors of onset. *British Journal of Addiction, 87,* 1711–1724.

Corrigall, W. A. (1991). Understanding brain mechanisms in nicotine reinforcement. *British Journal of Addiction, 86,* 507–510.

Denson, R., Nanson, J. L., & McWalters, M. A. (1975). Hyperkinesis and maternal smoking. *Canadian Psychiatric Association Journal, 20,* 183–187.

Dow-Edwards, D. L. (1989). Long-term neurochemical and neurobehavioral consequences of cocaine use during pregnancy. *Annals of the New York Academy of Science, 562,* 280–289.

Elliott, D. S. (1993). Health-enhancing and health-compromising lifestyles. In S. G. Millstein, A. C., Petersen, & E. O. Nightingale (Eds.), *Promoting the health of adolescents* (pp. 119–145). New York: Oxford University Press.

Ensminger, M., Brown, C. H., & Kellam, S. (1982). Sex differences in antecedents of substance use among adolescents. *Journal of Social Issues, 38,* 25–42.

Fergusson, D. M., Horwood, L. J., & Lynskey, M. T. (1983). Maternal smoking before and after pregnancy: Effects on behavioral outcomes in middle childhood. *Pediatrics, 92,* 815–822.

Flay, B. R., Hu, F. B., Siddiqui, O., Dau, L. E., Kedeker, D., Petraitis, J., Richardson, J., & Sussman, S. (1994). Differential influence of parental smoking and friends' smoking on adolescent initiation and escalation of smoking. *Journal of Health and Social Behavior, 35,* 248–265.

Fox, N. L., Sexton, M., & Hebel, J. R. (1990). Prenatal exposure to tobacco: I. Effects on physical growth at age three. *International Journal of Epidemiology, 19,* 66–71.

Fried, P. A. (1989). Cigarettes and marijuana: Are there measurable long-term neurobehavioral effects? *Neurotoxicology, 10,* 577–584.

Glanz, M., & Pickens, R. (1992). Vulnerability to drug abuse: Introduction and overview. In M. Glanz & R. Pickens (Eds.), *Vulnerability to drug abuse* (pp. 1–14). Washington, DC: American Psychological Association.

Grant, B. F., & Harford, T. C. (1990). The relationship between ethanol intake and DSM-III-R alcohol dependence. *Journal of Studies on Alcohol, 51,* 448–456.

Grant, B. F., Harford, T. C., Dawson, D. A., Chou, P. S., & Pickering, R. P. (1995). The alcohol use disorder and associated disabilities interview schedule (AUDADIS): Reliability of alcohol and drug modules in a general population sample. *Drug and Alcohol Abuse, 39,* 37–44.

Griesler, P., & Kandel, D. (in press). Maternal smoking in pregnancy, child behavior problems, parenting, and smoking in adolescence. *Journal of Research in Adolescence.*

Griesler, P. and Kandel, D. (1998). The impact of maternal drinking during and after pregnancy on the drinking of adolescent offspring. *Journal of Studies on Alcohol, 59.*

Harrison, L., & Hughes, A. (Eds.). (1997). *The validity of self-reported drug use: Improving the accuracy of survey estimates.* NIDA Research Monograph No. 167. Rockville, MD: National Institute on Drug Abuse.

Hawkins, J. D., Catalano, R. F., & Miller, J. Y. (1992). Risk and protective factors for alcohol and other drug problems in adolescence and early adulthood: Implications for substance abuse prevention. *Psychological Bulletin, 112,* 64–105.

Henry, B., Feehan, M., McGee, R., Stanton, W., Moffitt, T. E., & Silva, P. (1993). The importance of conduct problems and depressive symptoms in predicting adolescent substance use. *Journal of Abnormal Child Psychology, 21,* 469–480.

Hops, H., Tildesley, E., Lichtenstein, E., Ary, D., & Sherman, L. (1990). Parent–adolescent problem-solving interactions and drug use. *American Journal of Drug and Alcohol Abuse, 16,* 239–258.

Hughes, J. R. (1986). Genetics of smoking: A review. *Behavior Therapy, 17,* 335–345.

Jessor, R. (1992). Risk behavior in adolescence: A psychosocial framework for understanding and action. *Developmental Review, 12,* 374–390.

Jessor, R. (1993). Successful adolescent development among youth in high-risk settings. *American Psychologist, 48,* 117–126.

Jessor, R., & Jessor, S. L. (1977). *Problem behavior and psychosocial development: A longitudinal study of youth.* New York: Academic Press.

Jessor, R., Van Den Bos, J., Vanderryn, J., Costa, F. M., & Turbin, M. S. (1995). Protective factors in adolescent problem behavior: Moderator effects and developmental change. *Developmental Psychology, 6,* 923–933.

Johnston, L. D., O'Malley, P. M., & Bachman, J. G. (1995). *National survey results on drug use from the Monitoring the Future Study, 1975–1994: Vol. 1. Secondary Students.* Rockville, MD: National Institute on Drug Abuse.

Kandel, D. B. (1975). Stages in adolescent involvement in drug use. *Science, 190,* 912–914.

Kandel, D. B. (Ed.). (1978a). *Longitudinal research on drug use: Empirical findings and methodological issues.* Washington, DC: Hemisphere-Wiley.

Kandel, D. B. (1978b). Convergences in prospective longitudinal surveys of drug use in normal populations. In D. B. Kandel (Ed.), *Longitudinal research on drug use: Empirical findings and methodological issues* (pp. 3 38). Washington, DC: Hemisphere-Wiley.

Kandel, D. D. (1986). Processes of peer influences in adolescence. In R. K. Silbereisen, K. Eyferth, & G. Rudinger (Eds.), *Development as action in context* (pp. 203–227). New York: Springer-Verlag.

Kandel, D. B. (1989). Issues of sequencing of adolescent drug use and other problem behaviors. *Drugs & Society, 3,* 55–76.

Kandel, D. B. (1990). Parenting styles, drug use and children's adjustment in families of young adults. *Journal of Marriage and the Family, 52,* 183–196.

Kandel, D. B. (1996a). The parental and peer contexts of adolescent deviance: An algebra of interpersonal influences. In H. White (Ed.), Empirical validity of theories of drug abuse. *Journal of Drug Issues, 26,* 289–315.

Kandel, D. B. (1996b). Drug dependence among adolescents and adults in the United States and in selected metropolitan areas. *Epidemiologic trends in drug abuse. Vol. II: Proceedings – June 1996* (pp. 460–467). Rockville, MD: National Institute on Drug Abuse.

Kandel, D. B., & Andrews, K. (1987). Processes of adolescent socialization by parents and by peers. *International Journal of the Addictions, 22,* 319–342.

Kandel, D. B., Chen, K., Warner, L. A., Kessler, R. C., & Grant, B. (1997). Prevalence and demographic correlates of symptoms of last year dependence on alcohol, nicotine, marijuana and cocaine in the U.S. population. *Drug and Alcohol Dependence. 44,* 11–29.

Kandel, D. B., & Davies, M. (1982). Epidemiology of depressive mood in adolescents. *Archives of General Psychiatry, 39,* 1205–1212.

Kandel, D. B., & Davies, M. (1991). Friendship networks, intimacy and illicit drug use in young adulthood: A comparison of two competing theories. *Criminology, 29,* 601–629.

Kandel, D. B., & Davies, M. (1992). Progression to regular marijuana involvement: Phenomenology and risk factors for near-daily use. In M. Glantz & R. Pickens (Eds.), *Vulnerability to drug abuse* (pp. 211–253). Washington, DC: American Psychological Association.

Kandel, D. B., Davies, M., Karus, D., & Yamaguchi, K. (1986). The consequences in young adulthood of adolescent drug involvement: An overview. *Archives of General Psychiatry, 43,* 746–754.

Kandel, D. B., Johnson, J. G., Bird, H. R., Canino, G., Goodman, S. H., Lahey, B., Regier, D. A., & Schwab-Stone, M. (1997). Psychiatric disorders associated with substance use among children and adolescents: Findings from the Methods for the Epidemiology of Child and Adolescent Mental Disorders (MECA) Study. *Journal of Abnormal Child Psychology, 25*, 121–132.

Kandel, D. B., & Logan, J. A. (1984). Patterns of drug use from adolescence to young adulthood – I. Periods of risk for initiation, continued use, and discontinuation. *American Journal of Public Health, 74*, 660–666.

Kandel, D. B., Mossel, P., & Kaestner, R. (1987). Drug use, the transition from school to work and occupational achievement in the United States. *European Journal of Psychology of Education, 2*, 337–363.

Kandel, D. B., & Wu, P. (1995). The contribution of mothers and fathers to the intergenerational transmission of cigarette smoking in adolescence. *Journal of Research on Adolescence, 5*, 225–252.

Kandel, D. B., Wu, P., & Davies, M. (1994). Maternal smoking during pregnancy and smoking by adolescent daughters. *American Journal of Public Health, 84*, 1407–1413.

Kandel, D. B., & Yamaguchi, K. (1993). From beer to crack: Developmental patterns of involvement in drugs. *American Journal of Public Health, 83*, 851–855.

Kandel, D. B., Yamaguchi, K., & Chen, K. (1992). Stages of progression in drug involvement from adolescence to adulthood: Further evidence for the gateway theory. *Journal of Studies on Alcohol, 53*, 447–457.

Kazdin, A. E. (1987). *Conduct disorders in childhood and adolescence.* Newbury Park, CA: Sage.

Kellam, S. G., Ensminger, M. E., & Simon, M. B. (1980). Mental health in first grade and teenage drug, alcohol, and cigarette use. *Drug and Alcohol Dependence, 5*, 273–304.

Kendler, K. S., Heath, A. C., Neale, M. C., Kessler, R. C., & Eaves, L. J. (1993a). Alcoholism and major depression in women. *Archives of General Psychiatry, 50*, 690–698.

Kendler, K. S., Neale, M. C., MacLean, C. J., Heath, A. C., Eaves, L. J., & Kessler, R. C. (1993b). Smoking and major depression. A causal analysis. *Archives of General Psychiatry, 50*, 36–43.

Kessler, R. C., McGonagle, K. A., Zhao, S., Nelson, C. B., Hughes, M., Eshleman, S., Wittchen, H. U., & Kendler, K. S. (1994). Lifetime and 12-month prevalence of DSM-III-R psychiatric disorders in the United States: Results from the National Comorbidity Survey. *Archives of General Psychiatry, 51*, 8–19.

Koob, G. F. (1992). Drugs of abuse: Anatomy, pharmacology and function of reward pathways. *Trends in Pharmacological Sciences, 13*, 177–184.

Leadbeater, B. J., Blatt, S. J., & Quinlan, D. M. (1995). Gender-linked vulnerabilities to depressive symptoms, stress, and problem behaviors in adolescents. *Journal of Research on Adolescence, 5*, 1–29.

Leshner, A. L. (1995, November–December). Broadening the role of NIDA's neuroscience research. *NIDA Notes*, 3–4.

Lochman, J. E., & Wayland, K. K. (1994). Aggression, social acceptance, and race as predictors of negative adolescent outcome. *Journal of the American Academy of Child & Adolescent Psychiatry, 33*, 1026–1035.

Loeber, R. (1982). The stability of antisocial and delinquent child behavior: A review. *Child Development, 53*, 1431–1446.

Loeber, R., & Dishion, T. J. (1983). Early predictors of male delinquency. A review. *Psychological Bulletin, 94*, 68–99.

Luthar, S. S., Merikangas, K. R., & Rounsaville, B. J. (1993). Parental psychopathology and disorders in offspring. *Journal of Nervous and Mental Disease, 181*, 351–357.

Lynskey, M. T., & Fergusson, D. M. (1995). Childhood conduct problems, attention deficit behaviors, and adolescent alcohol, tobacco, and illicit drug use. *Journal of Consulting and Clinical Psychology, 23*, 281–302.

MacDonald, R., Barry, K. L., & Fleming, M. D. (1992). Patterns of substance use among student meeting lifetime DSM-III criteria for alcohol misuse. *International Journal of the Addictions, 27*, 905–915.

McGee, R., & Stanton, W. R. (1994). Smoking in pregnancy and child development to age 9 years. *Journal of Paediatric Child Health, 30*, 263–268.

Melby, J. A., Conger, R. D., Conger, K. J., & Lorenz, F. O. (1993). Effects of parental behavior on tobacco use by young male adolescents. *Journal of Marriage and the Family, 55*, 439–454.

Mereu, G., Yoon, K. W., Boi, V., Gessa, G. L., Naes, L., & Westfall, T. C. (1987). Preferential stimulation of ventral tegmental area dopaminergic neurons by nicotine. *European Journal of Pharmacology, 141*, 395–399.

Merikangas, K. R., & Gelentner, C. S. (1990). Comorbidity for alcoholism and depression. *Psychiatric Clinics of North America, 13*, 613–632.

Merikangas, K. R., Risch, N. J., & Weissman, M. M. (1994). Comorbidity and cotransmission of alcoholism, anxiety and depression. *Psychological Medicine, 24*, 69–80.

Moffitt, T. E. (1993). Adolescence-limited and life-course-persistent antisocial behavior: A developmental taxonomy. *Psychological Review, 100*, 674–701.

Murray, M., Kiryluk, S., & Swan, A. V. (1985). Relation between parents' and children's smoking behavior and attitudes. *Journal of Epidemiology and Community Health, 39*, 169–174.

Nestler, E. J. (1992). Molecular mechanisms of drug addiction. *Journal of Neuroscience, 12*, 2349–2450.

Newcomb, M. D., & Bentler, P. M. (1989). Substance use and abuse among children and teenagers. *American Psychologist, 2*, 242–248.

Nichols, P. J., & Chen, T. C. (1981). *Minimal brain dysfunction: A prospective study*. Hillsdale, NJ: Erlbaum.

Olds, D. L., Henderson, C. R., & Tatelbaum, R. (1994). Intellectual impairment of children of women who smoke cigarettes during pregnancy. *Pediatrics, 93,* 221–227.

Orlebeke, J. F., Boomsma, D. I., & Verhulst, F. C. (1994). *Child behavior problems increased by maternal smoking during pregnancy.* Paper presented at the 13th meeting of the International Society for the Study of Behavioral Development, Amsterdam, Holland. July.

Orlebeke, J. E., Knol, D. L., & Verhulst, F. C. (1997). Increase in child behavior problems resulting from maternal smoking during pregnancy. *Archives of Environmental Health, 52,* 317–321.

Patterson, G. R., Reid, J. B., & Dishion, T. J. (1992). *Antisocial boys.* Eugene, OR: Castalia.

Petraitis, J., Flay, B. R., & Miller, T. Q. (1995). Reviewing theories of adolescent substance use: Organizing pieces in the puzzle. *Psychological Bulletin, 1,* 67–86.

Pollay, R. W., Siddarth, S., Siegel, M., Haddix, A., Merritt, R. K., Giovino, G. A., & Eriksen, M. P. (1996). The last straw? Cigarette advertising and realized market shares among youths and adults, 1979–1993. *Journal of Marketing, 60,* 1–16.

Rantakallio, P. (1978). The effect of maternal smoking on birth weight and the subsequent health of the child. *Early Human Development, 2,* 371–382.

Rantakallio, P. (1983). A follow-up study up to the age of 14 of children whose mothers smoked during pregnancy. *Acta Pediatrica Scandinavica, 72,* 747–753.

Richardson, S. A., & Tizabi, Y. (1994). Hyperactivity in the offspring of nicotine-treated rats: Role of the mesolimbic and nigrostriatal dopaminergic pathways. *Pharmacology, Biochemistry and Behavior, 47,* 331–337.

Robins, L. N., Helzer, J. E., Croughan, J. L., Williams, J. B., W., & Spitzer R. L. (1981). *The NIMH diagnostic interview schedule: Version III.* Washington, DC: Public Health Service (HSS) ADM-T-42-3.

Robins, L. N., & Regier, D. A. (Eds.). (1991). *Psychiatric disorders in America. The epidemiologic catchment area study.* New York: Free Press.

Robins, L. N., Wing, J., Wittchen, H. W., Helzer, J. E., Babor, T. F., Burke, J. D., Farmer, A., Jablenski, A., Pickens, R., Regier, D. A., Sartorius, N., & Towle, L. H. (1988). The composite international diagnostic interview (CIDI): An epidemiologic instrument suitable for use in conjunction with different diagnostic systems and in different cultures. *Archives of General Psychiatry, 45,* 1069–1077.

Rossow, I. (1992). *Addictive and interactional effects of parental health behaviors in adolescence: An empirical study of smoking and alcohol consumption in Norwegian families.* Paper presented at the Youth and Drug Conference, Larkollen, Norway.

Slokin, T. A., McCook, E. C., Lappi, S. E., & Seidler, F. J. (1992). Altered development of basal and forskolin-stimulated adenylate cyclase activity in brain regions of rats exposed to nicotine prenatally. *Developmental Brain Research, 68,* 233–239.

Stanton, W. R., & Silva, P. A. (1992). A longitudinal study of the influence of parents and friends on children's initiation of smoking. *Journal of Applied Developmental Psychology, 13,* 423–434.

Substance Abuse and Mental Health Service Administration (SAMHSA) (1996). *Preliminary estimates from the 1995 National Household Survey on Drug Abuse.* Advance Report No. 18. Rockville, MD: Office of Applied Studies, SAMHSA.

Tarter, R., Moss, H., Blackson, T., Vanyukov, M., Brigham, R., & Loeber, R. (in press). Disaggregating the liability for drug abuse. In C. Wethington & J. Falk (Eds.), *Laboratory behavioral studies of vulnerability to drug abuse.* NIDA Research Monograph Series No. 000. Rockville, MD: National Institute on Drug Abuse.

Tong, S., & McMichael, A. J. (1992). Maternal smoking and neuropsychological development in childhood: A review of the evidence. *Developmental Medicine and Child Neurology, 34,* 191–197.

U.S. Department of Health and Human Services. (1994). *Preventing tobacco use among young people: A report of the Surgeon General.* Atlanta, GA: Centers for Disease Control and Prevention.

Van Kammen, W. B., Loeber, R., & Stouthamer-Loeber, M. (1991). Substance use and its relationship to conduct problems and delinquency in young boys. *Journal of Youth and Adolescence, 20,* 399–413.

Warner, L. A., Kessler, R. C., Hughes, M., Anthony, J. C., & Nelson, C. B. (1995). Prevalence and correlates of drug use and dependence in the United States. *Archives of General Psychiatry, 52,* 219–229.

Weissman, M. M., & Klerman, G. L. (1985). Gender and depression. *Trends in Neuroscience, 8,* 416–420.

Weitzman, M., Gortmaker, S., & Sobol, A. (1992). Maternal smoking and behavior problems of children. *Pediatrics, 90,* 342–349.

White, H. (Ed.). (1996a). Empirical validity of theories of drug abuse. *Journal of Drug Issues,* Special Issue, *26(2),* 279–520.

White, H. (1996b). Empirical validity of theories of drug abuse: Introductory comments. In H. White (Ed.), Empirical validity of theories of drug abuse. *Journal of Drug Issues,* Special Issue, *26,* 279–288.

Wu, P., & Kandel, D. B. (1995). The roles of mothers and fathers in intergenerational behavioral transmission: The case of smoking and delinquency. In H. Kaplan (Ed.), *Longitudinal studies of drugs, crime, and other deviant adaptations* (pp. 106–123). New York: Plenum.

Yamaguchi, K., & Kandel, D. B. (1984). Patterns of drug use from adolescence to young adulthood – II. Sequences of progression. *American Journal of Public Health, 74,* 668–672.

Yamaguchi, K., & Kandel, D. B. (1985). On the resolution of role incompatibility: Life event history analysis of family roles and marijuana use. *American Journal of Sociology, 90,* 1284–1325.

Yamaguchi, K., & Kandel, D. B. (1987). Drug use and other determinants of premarital pregnancy and its outcome: A dynamic analysis of competing life events. *Journal of Marriage and the Family, 49,* 257–270.

Yamaguchi, K., & Kandel, D. B. (1993). Marital homophily on substance use among young adults. *Social Forces, 72(2),* 505–528.

4

Multiple risk factors for multiproblem boys: Co-occurrence of delinquency, substance use, attention deficit, conduct problems, physical aggression, covert behavior, depressed mood, and shy/withdrawn behavior

Rolf Loeber, David P. Farrington, Magda Stouthamer-Loeber, and Welmoet B. Van Kammen

Researchers have not been in agreement about whether to consider all juvenile problem behaviors as sufficiently similar to be covered by a single construct. Some have advocated a general deviance or problem construct (e.g., Donovan, 1996; Donovan, Jessor, & Costa, 1988; Jessor, Donovan, & Costa, 1991; Jessor & Jessor, 1977; Kaplan, 1980; Patterson, Reid, & Dishion, 1992; Robins, 1966), whereas others have advocated a more differentiated approach (e.g., Loeber, 1988; McCord, 1990; McGee & Newcomb, 1992; Osgood, Johnston, O'Malley, & Bachman, 1988). Some have distinguished between types of externalizing problems – for example, covert or property offenses versus overt or person-related offenses (e.g., Frick et al., 1993; Loeber, 1988; Loeber & Schmaling, 1985a), but others have focused on externalizing prob-

The authors are indebted to the staff of the Pittsburgh Youth Study for their assistance in collecting and preparing the data for this chapter and to JoAnn Fraser for compiling the reference list. The chapter was written with financial support of Grants MH 48890 and MH 42529 of the National Institute of Mental Health and Grant No. 86-JN-CX-0009 of the Office of Juvenile Justice and Delinquency Prevention. Points of view or opinions in this document are those of the authors and do not necessarily represent the official position of either agency.

lems or delinquency in general (e.g., Hirschi & Gottfredson, 1983; Patterson, 1982). Some researchers have made a distinction between externalizing problems or delinquency and substance use (Loeber, 1988; White & Labouvie, 1994), but others have maintained that they represent the same underlying construct (e.g., Elliott, Huizinga, & Ageton, 1985; Jessor & Jessor, 1977; Pulkkinen, 1983). Few researchers have investigated the extent to which externalizing, attention deficit/ hyperactivity, and internalizing behaviors (such as depressed mood and shy/withdrawn behavior) can be best captured by a single-problem approach. Also, whereas sociological investigators have ignored attention deficit and hyperactivity as possible components of a general problem syndrome, they have been more strongly stressed by psychiatrists and psychologists (Hinshaw, 1987). Moreover, practically all investigations about problem syndromes have been limited to adolescents; consequently, very little is known about syndrome patterns among elementary school children. Problem behavior in this age group is particularly of interest because of the emergence of early-onset delinquents, who later often become chronic, diversified offenders (Farrington, Loeber, & Van Kammen, 1990).

Whether data fit a single problem theory or different theories for different problem behaviors at different ages can be evaluated according to several criteria, of which we want to stress (1) interrelations between problem behaviors; (2) age shifts in problem behaviors; (3) specific and general risk factors; (4) shifts in risk factors with age; and (5) predictors of multiproblem juveniles. We will briefly address the importance of each of these criteria:

Interrelations between problem behaviors

A single underlying problem syndrome with several manifestations can be best justified when the intercorrelations between the manifestations are similar. However, when the intercorrelations are very different, this provides some evidence that there may be several underlying problem entities. For example, there is a consensus that factor analytic studies have produced separate factors for externalizing and internalizing child problems (Achenbach, 1985; Achenbach, Conners, Quay, Verhulst, & Howell, 1989). Even within the domain of externalizing problems, such studies support factorial distinctions between oppositional behaviors and conduct problems (e.g., Achenbach et al., 1989; Achenbach & Edelbrock, 1979; Frick et al., 1993), and between these disruptive behaviors and hyperactive/inattentive problems (Hinshaw, 1987). Similarly, meta-analytic techniques have suggested distinctions between overt or aggressive problems and covert or sneaky, nonconfrontive problems (Frick et al., 1993; Loeber & Schmaling, 1985a).

Likewise, diagnostic systems of pathology in childhood and adolescence have made distinctions between such diagnoses as oppositional defiant disorder, conduct disorder, and attention-deficit hyperactivity disorder. Also, within the domain of internalizing problems, different diagnoses have been applied, such as anxiety disorders and depressive disorders (American Psychiatric Association, 1987, 1994). In summary, distinctive but interrelated classifications of child problem behaviors have emerged from the fields of psychiatry and psychology.

Moreover, a single problem theory usually does not address the question of whether problem behaviors are interchangeable or whether the direction of effects between problem behaviors is symmetrical or not. For example, we found that physical fighting enhanced the probability of boys' onset of covert conduct problems, but that the onset of covert conduct problems did not enhance the probability of physical fighting (Loeber et al., 1993). As another example, attention deficit and hyperactivity are implicated in the onset of delinquency or conduct problems (Farrington, Loeber, Elliott, et al., 1990; Loeber, Green, Keenan, & Lahey, 1995), but delinquency or conduct problems are not known to affect the onset of attention deficit or hyperactivity. Thus, several types of problem behavior are not equivalent or interchangeable, and their interaction may be asymmetrical in that one problem behavior may influence another but the reverse may not apply.

Age shifts in problem behavior

One of the most characteristic features of problem behavior during childhood and adolescence is that manifestations change. The change pattern varies in terms of severity, frequency, variety, and onset (Loeber, 1982). In general, with age the severity, frequency, and variety of problem behaviors increase. This happens as new problem behaviors emerge: The onset of novel problem behaviors occurs while, as a rule, old problem behaviors are retained (Loeber, 1988). A problem theory should specify age shifts in the configuration of problem behaviors.

Specific and general risk factors

There is increasing evidence that different problem behaviors are associated with distinct risk factors, which is also reflected in distinct diagnoses applicable to mental disorders occurring in childhood and adolescence (American Psychiatric Association, 1987, 1994). For example, the etiology of attention deficit/hyperactivity is very different from the etiology of conduct problems, particularly in terms of age of onset (attention deficit and hyperactivity starting earlier), correlates, and risk factors (discussed later) (Hinshaw, 1987; Loeber, Brinthaupt, & Green, 1990; Loeber, Green, Lahey, Christ, & Frick, 1992).

A single problem theory assumes that the correlates of problem behaviors are equivalent. Thus, according to such a theory, the same factors would influence a child to become aggressive, to steal frequently, or to be hyperactive. Only a few research projects have addressed this issue. For example, aggression and theft were found to have only partly overlapping correlates in at least one study (Loeber & Schmaling, 1985b). Likewise, some studies have found distinctive correlates of attention deficit/hyperactivity and conduct problems (Farrington, Loeber, & Van Kammen, 1990; Loeber et al., 1990).

The issue of specific versus general risk factors is particularly pertinent to the development of multiproblem boys. We know too little to what extent risk factors associated with the development of single deviant outcomes also apply to the development of multiple deviant outcomes.

Age shifts in risk factors

Another criterion for evaluating a problem theory is to examine the extent to which risk factors at one age are the same as those at another age or whether there are risk factors that emerge as children grow up. Examples are risk factors in the realms of peer and school influences that do not clearly apply to the preschool period, or unemployment that does not apply to childhood or most of adolescence. In our eyes, the best theories of problem behavior need to take into account that risk factors may change with age and that such changes need to be incorporated in the theory.

Risk factors for multiproblem juveniles

A final criterion for evaluating a problem theory is the extent to which empirical work supporting such a theory identifies risk factors for juveniles with problem behaviors in multiple domains. On the one hand, there is no doubt that groups of individuals with specific problem behaviors emerge over time (e.g., delinquents with no substance use problems and nondelinquent substance abusers). At the same time, there is a consensus that groups of multiproblem youth develop as well (Loeber, 1988). For example, many aggressive youth eventually may engage in both violent and property crimes in adulthood and may become heavy substance abusers. When a single-problem theory is applied to both single-problem youth and multiproblem youth, it becomes impossible to discover why some individuals' deviance becomes varied, whereas for others deviance remains limited to a single domain. Furthermore, a focus on multiproblem boys is important because these boys constitute a large proportion of the individuals who inflict the most damage on society and consume the most time of treatment professionals, particularly by receiving mental health services, remedial or special education, and referrals to the juvenile court (Farrington & West, 1993; Marttunen, Aro, Henriksson, & Lonnquist, 1994; Wolfgang, Figlio, & Sellin, 1972).

To address these five issues, this chapter investigates the co-occurrence and risk factors in eight domains of problem behaviors in three samples of the Pittsburgh Youth Study. The three samples of participants were assessed in first, fourth, and seventh grades (called the *youngest, middle,* and *oldest samples,* respectively). Screening of the sample produced an overrepresentation of the most deviant boys, which facilitated the study of co-occurring problem behaviors. The eight categories of problem behaviors are delinquency, substance use, attention deficit, conduct problems, physical aggression, covert behavior, depressed mood, and shy/withdrawn behavior. Sexual behavior was measured in the oldest sample, but because of the young age of the boys in the youngest and middle samples, this factor could not be recorded for these boys. Because most analyses concern comparisons between the samples, we decided to concentrate on the problem behaviors measured in all three samples, thereby excluding sexual behavior from the problems in the oldest sample. The present data are based on the initial screening assessment and the first follow-up 6 months later. The chapter examines individual, family, socioeconomic, demographic, and neighborhood risk factors for each of the eight problem behaviors. It addresses key questions about how far each outcome is predicted by the same risk factors and how far each risk factor predicts several different outcomes.

A new approach to the study and understanding of multiple problem behaviors

In this chapter, we attempt to advance the study of juvenile problem behaviors in several ways. First, we stress that the development of problem behavior tends to occur throughout childhood and early adolescence (Loeber, 1985), that the configuration of problem behaviors changes with age (Loeber, 1985; Loeber & Keenan, 1994), and that, therefore, both preadolescent and early adolescent age groups need to be the focus of studies. Second, the range of problem behaviors to be studied should not be limited to the traditional problems of delinquency and substance use but should also include symptoms of attention deficit/hyperactivity disorder, which has an early age of onset and which is known to be associated with both delinquency and substance use. In addition, we advocate including internalizing problems, such as depressed mood and shy/withdrawn behaviors, because many delinquent and substance-abusing youngsters often are depressed and withdrawn (Loeber & Keenan, 1994). Third, we need to examine which risk factors are specific to a certain outcome and which risk factors are shared by multiple outcomes, and whether this pattern varies for different age groups. Fourth, we advocate the study of continuous *variables* representing each problem domain but also include the study of *individuals* displaying problems in multiple domains. The focus on multiproblem boys can help to identify the core problems these boys share and may help to reveal those risk factors that distinguish multiproblem boys from boys with single problems. Information about risk factors that predict several different child problem behaviors is of potential importance for prevention and treatment because targeting these risk factors could have increased benefits in reducing a wide range of child problem behaviors. Fifth, we need to consider more carefully the ecological aspects of problem behaviors and determine which problem behaviors are particularly concentrated in the worst neighborhoods. Finally, we advocate that the study of problem behaviors be advanced by improvements in measurements, such as by using age-appropriate and age-relevant questions to measure each problem domain, and by the use of multiple informants, including parents and teachers in addition to the reports from the boys themselves.

Methods

The Pittsburgh Youth Study

The Pittsburgh Youth Study is a prospective longitudinal survey of the development of problem behaviors in three samples, each of about 500 Pittsburgh boys, totaling 1,517 boys. Girls were not included because the prevalence of delinquency and substance use in boys during late childhood and early adolescence tends to exceed by far the prevalence of these problems in girls. At the time the boys were first contacted in 1987–1988, random samples of first-, fourth-, and seventh-grade boys enrolled in the Pittsburgh public schools were selected. At that time, 72% of all children resident in Pittsburgh attended public schools. In 1990 the city of Pittsburgh covered the inner-city population of about 370,000 out of the Pittsburgh–Beaver Valley Metropolitan Statistical Area of about 2,243,000 (Hoffman, 1991). Many of the assessments in the Pittsburgh Youth Study were designed to be comparable to those used in two other contemporaneous longitudinal surveys conducted in Denver, Colorado (Huizinga, Loeber, & Thornberry, 1993), and Rochester, New York (Thornberry, Lizotte, Krohn, Farnworth, & Jang, 1994).

Out of about 1,000 boys in each grade selected at random for a screening assessment, about 850 (85%) were actually assessed. The boys completed a self-report questionnaire about antisocial behavior and delinquency – the Self-Reported Delinquency Questionnaire (SRD) for the oldest sample and Self-Reported Antisocial Behavior Questionnaire (SRA) for the youngest and middle samples (Loeber, Stouthamer-Loeber, Van Kammen, & Farrington, 1989). The reason for the administration of different questionnaires was that the boys in the youngest and middle samples were deemed to be too young to respond to the SRD. Their primary caretakers completed an extended Child Behavior Checklist (Achenbach & Edelbrock, 1983), and their teachers completed an extended Teacher Report Form (Edelbrock & Achenbach, 1984). We will refer to the primary caretaker as the mother because this was true in 94% of cases. Participants did not differ significantly from the comparable male student population in their scores on the California Achievement Test (CAT) and in their ethnic composition (African American or Caucasian).

From the screening assessment, a risk score was calculated for each boy indicating how many of 21 serious antisocial acts he had ever committed (including types of stealing, running away, fire setting, truancy, vandalism, robbery, gang fighting, attacking with a weapon, joyriding, burglary, liquor use, and marijuana use). Information from the boy, the mother, and the teacher was taken into account. The risk score was used to select the sample for follow-up, consisting of the approximately 250 most antisocial boys in each grade and about 250 boys randomly selected from among the remaining 600. Hence, the screening sample of about 850 per grade was reduced to a follow-up sample of about 500 per grade. The 500 boys in each grade were then assessed every 6 months for 3 years, with data collected from the boy, the mother, and the teacher on each occasion. Regular data collection from the middle sample then ceased, but the oldest and youngest samples are still (in 1998) being followed up at yearly intervals.

Tables 4.1 and 4.2 show characteristics of the samples. The percentage of African American participants in the follow-up sample was not significantly different from the percentage of African American students in the city of Pittsburgh (see Table 4.1). Also, the follow-up sample had CAT reading scores similar to those obtained in the public schools. In Table 4.1, the screening procedure did not significantly alter these aspects of the sample.

Other characteristics of the samples were also not greatly affected by the screening procedure (see Table 4.2). Almost all the boys in the follow-up samples lived in households with their natural mother (92.6%), but only 37.8% of them lived with their natural father. In 43.6% of the households there was no father or acting father. About one fifth (18.5%) of the mothers or acting mothers living with the child had not completed high school, whereas at the other extreme, 6.4%

Table 4.1. *Ethnic representativeness and CAT reading scores of the participants in the follow-up assessment, compared to boys in all public schools in Pittsburgh*

	Youngest sample		Middle sample		Oldest sample	
	Study (%)	School (%)	Study (%)	School (%)	Study (%)	School (%)
African American	57.3	56.5	55.8	54.0	57.5	54.6
>50th percentile in CAT reading score	55.2	56.5	37.6	40.9	36.5	36.7

Note: School denotes boys in all public schools in Pittsburgh.

Table 4.2. *Characteristics of the follow-up samples*

	Sample		
	Youngest	Middle	Oldest
Average age	7.4	10.7	13.8
% living with natural mother	94.0	90.9	93.0
% living with natural father	38.5	40.7	34.1
% not living with (acting) father	45.3	40.5	45.1
% (acting) mother not completed high school	16.9	18.7	19.8
% (acting) mother with college degree	6.3	5.7	7.1
% (acting) father not completed high school	15.4	16.6	19.9
% (acting) father with college degree	12.4	11.4	10.4

had a college degree; for fathers or acting fathers living with the child, 17.3% had not completed high school and 11.4% had a college degree.

A major aim of the Pittsburgh Youth Study was to measure as many factors as possible that were alleged to be causes or correlates of problem behaviors. The first follow-up was much more extensive than the screening assessment. The boys in the middle and oldest samples completed the SRD, and the boys in the youngest sample completed the

SRA. In addition, boys were given the Substance Use Scale (Elliott et al., 1985). The mothers again completed the extended Child Behavior Checklist (CBCL) and the teachers again completed the extended Teacher Report Form (TRF). These questionnaires yielded data not only on antisocial behavior but also on individual factors such as hyperactivity, anxiety, and shyness. In addition, the mothers completed a demographic questionnaire yielding information about adults and children living with the boy, and the Revised Diagnostic Interview Schedule for Children (DISC-P; Costello, Edelbrock, Kalas, Kessler, & Klaric, 1987), which yielded child psychiatric diagnoses such as attention-deficit hyperactivity disorder (ADHD). The boys completed the Recent Mood and Feelings Questionnaire (Costello & Angold, 1988) as a measure of depressed mood. Also, CAT results on reading, language, and mathematics were obtained from the schools.

Various questionnaires were used to assess parental discipline and supervision, parent–child communication, parental attitudes toward child antisocial behavior, parental disharmony (where two parents were present), parental stress, parental anxiety, and parental substance use. Socioeconomic status was assessed using the Hollingshead (1975) index based on parental occupational prestige and educational level. Where two parents were present, the higher score was recorded. Housing quality was assessed by the interviewer based on such features as the structural condition of the house and visible signs of peeling paint. Neighborhood quality was rated by the mother and assessed from census data (e.g., on median family income, percentage unemployed, percentage separated or divorced).

In order to maximize the validity of all variables, information from different sources was combined as far as possible, as was information from the screening and first follow-up assessments. Only brief descriptions of variables are included in this chapter; more extensive descriptions can be found in other works (e.g., Loeber et al., 1989, 1991; Loeber, Farrington, Stouthamer-Loeber, & Van Kammen, 1998; Stouthamer-Loeber, Loeber, & Thomas, 1992; Stouthamer-Loeber et al., 1993; Van Kammen, Loeber, & Stouthamer, 1991).

Child problem behavior

The following measures of child problem behavior were included in the study:

Delinquency (*lifetime*). The delinquency classification categorized the most serious behavior ever committed by a boy. The information was derived from the parent (CBCL, Lifetime Scale), the teacher (TRF), and from the boy himself (SRA or SRD, and for the oldest sample the Youth Self Report YSR) at screening and at follow-up. In order to classify delinquent behaviors according to seriousness, the severity ratings developed by Wolfgang, Figlio, Tracy, and Singer (1985) were used. Most behaviors were measured by one or more questions and one or more respondents. The constructs were made first from the screening and follow-up data separately and then were combined to form the final construct.

Delinquent acts were classified in the following manner: *no delinquency* or minor delinquency at home, such as stealing small amounts of money from a parent's purse or minor vandalism; *minor delinquency* outside the home, including minor forms of theft, such as shoplifting and stealing something worth less than $5, and vandalism and minor fraud, such as not paying for a bus ride; *moderately serious delinquency*, such as any theft of $5 or over, gang fighting, carrying weapons, and joyriding; *serious delinquency*, such as car theft, breaking and entering, strongarming, attacking to seriously hurt or kill, forced sex, or selling drugs.

In order to identify the most serious delinquents within each sample, we dichotomized the delinquency seriousness score. For the middle and oldest samples, we split the score between moderately serious delinquency and serious delinquency, effectively identifying those boys who had committed the most serious crimes during their lifetime (as far as possible, approximately the upper 25%; $N = 140$ and 185, in the middle and oldest samples, respectively). For the youngest sample, however, few boys (51) had engaged in serious delinquency. For that reason, the split was made between minor delinquency and moderately serious delinquency. Thus, for this group, the procedure identified as delinquents boys who had committed moderately or seriously delinquent acts ($N = 140$ or 27.9%).

Substance use (*lifetime*). The substance use classification score measured the boy's self-reported involvement in smoking, drinking beer, wine, and hard liquor (except drinking alcohol at festive occasions with parental knowledge); and using marijuana and other drugs such as LSD and barbiturates (the middle and oldest samples only). For the youngest sample, this involved 5 questions and, for the middle and oldest samples, a maximum of 19 questions. The substance use classification score was computed in the following way: All boys who had never used any substances received a score of 0. Boys who, at the time of follow-up, had ever consumed either beer or wine received a score of 1, and those who had smoked at least once in their life received a score of 2. A score of 3 was given to boys who had used hard liquor, and a score of 4 was given to those who had smoked marijuana. For the middle and oldest samples, a score of 5 was given to boys who had used other drugs, such as LSD or barbiturates. Boys were given the highest score they had achieved.

For the analyses, we dichotomized the substance use construct. For the youngest sample, the dichotomization was between no use (418 boys) and beer/wine or tobacco use (85); for the middle sample, between no use or beer/wine use (432) and tobacco use, liquor use, or illegal drug use (76); and for the oldest sample, between no use or wine, beer or tobacco use (384), and liquor or illegal drug use (122). In each case, the aim was to identify the worst quarter of substance users (approximately).

ADHD score (previous 6 months). The 28 DISC questions to the mother, covering 14 behaviors used in the diagnosis of attention deficit hyperactivity, make up the ADHD symptom score (called here the *ADHD score*). Symptoms were scored as described for the conduct problems symptom score, with a range of 0 to 50. The behaviors fall under the broad categories of restlessness or hyperactivity, attention deficit, and impulsivity.

Conduct problems symptom score (previous 6 months). This construct is based on the DISC questions used in the diagnosis of conduct disorder. The behaviors range from frequent lying to status offenses and delinquent acts. Twenty-five questions in the DISC cover 13 conduct problems. The values of the answers, ranging from 0 = never to 1 = sometimes and 2 = often, were added, and then standardized to range from 0 to 50.

The psychiatric definition of conduct problems partly overlaps with the legal definition of delinquency. We considered whether to pare down the conduct problem list to the nondelinquent items only. Although this was attractive in that such a construct would not overlap with delinquency, the disadvantage was that it would yield a construct that would not be very meaningful for psychiatrists. Therefore, we opted for a construct of conduct problems based on the full list of symptoms of conduct disorder.

Physical aggression (*lifetime*). This construct summarizes the boy's physical aggression, based on screening data, including the lifetime assessment, and at follow-up, using information from the parent (CBCL) and teacher (TRF). The scale consisted of seven items, such as "starts physical fights" and "hits teacher." An endorsement of "sometimes" or "often" by any informant at either screening or follow-up resulted in a score for that behavior.

Covert behavior (*previous year*). This score combines the z-scored values of concealing behaviors, untrustworthiness, and manipulating behaviors based on parent and teacher ratings.

Depressed mood (*previous 2 weeks*). This construct is the total score of the 13 items on the Recent Mood and Feelings Questionnaire at follow-up. The questions cover the symptoms necessary for making a diagnosis of major depression according to DSM III-R criteria.

Shy/withdrawn behavior (*previous year*). This construct combines information from the caretaker (CBCL) and teacher (TRF) at screening and follow-up. It consists of seven items concerning such behaviors as "likes to be alone," "refuses to talk," "shy," and "gets teased."

Risk factors

The key risk factors are divided into three categories: individual, family, and macro (socioeconomic, demographic, and neighborhood). For ease of exposition they will be termed *predictors*, although they are measured at the same time as the child problem behaviors.

Individual predictors. 1. *Lack of Guilt* was measured by one question from caretakers (CBCL) and one question from teachers (TRF) at screening and follow-up. 2. *Academic Achievement:* This construct combines, from screening and follow-up, judgments of caretakers (CBCL), teachers (TRF), and boys (YSR) on how well boys performed on a maximum of seven academic subjects. 3. *CAT Scores:* Reading and math percentile scores from the CAT were obtained for boys who attended local public schools and were combined. 4. *Old for Grade.* The age of the boy at the time of follow-up interview was determined. The cutoff was 7.8, 11, and 14 years of age for the youngest, middle, and oldest samples, respectively. Thus, this construct captures age-inappropriate boys who have been held back for failing a grade. 5. *Hyperactivity-Impulsivity-Attention* (*HIA Problems*) (previous year). This construct is made up of 14 behaviors, represented by ratings on hyperactivity, impulsive behaviors, and attention problems at screening and at follow-up by both parents (CBCL) and teachers (TRF). In contrast to the diagnosis of ADHD, this construct has the advantage of capturing the extent to which HIA behaviors occur in the settings of the home and the school. 6. *Anxiety.* This construct is a measure of the boy's anxiety problems and combines information from nine ratings by the caretakers (CBCL) and teachers (TRF) at screening or follow-up. 7. *Low Organizational Participation* combines information from the caretaker (CBCL) at screening and follow-up on the number of organizations, clubs, and teams the boys belonged to and how active they were in these organizations. For the oldest sample, boys also provided this information. 8. *Few Friends.* This is a combined construct based on the parent's and the boy's information about how many close or special friends the boy has. 9. *Low Jobs/Chores Involvement* uses information from the caretakers (CBCL) from screening and follow-up on the number of jobs and chores the boys had and how well they performed them. For the oldest sample, boys also provided this information. 10. *Low Religiosity* is based, for the youngest and middle samples, on two questions at follow-up about the boys' religious participation; for the oldest sample, three questions were combined.

Family predictors. 1. *Poor Supervision* is based on the boy's and mother's reports (four questions each) and reflects parental knowledge of the boy's whereabouts and activities. 2. *No Set Time Home.* This construct is based on the mother's and the boy's answers to three questions about whether there is a set time for the boy to be home on school or weekend nights and whether the mother would know if the boy did not come home on time. 3. *Low Parental Reinforcement.* This construct is based on the mother's and the boy's information about the frequency of the parent's positive behaviors toward the boy, measured by nine items on the parent questionnaire and seven items on the child questionnaire. 4. *Physical Punishment:* This combined mother–child construct measures the extent of physical punishment used by the mother. 5. *Poor Communication* combines information from the mother (30 items) and the boy (28 items: middle and oldest samples) on the Revised Parent-Adolescent Communication Form (based on Barnes & Olson, 1982) about the boy's communication with parents regarding emotions, disagreements, and problems. 6. *Boy Not Close to Mother.* This construct consists of two questions, asking the boy whether he thinks that his mother feels close to him and how close he feels to his mother (only for the middle and oldest samples). 7. *Boy Not Involved in Family Activities.* This construct is based on four questions to the parent and four questions to the boy about the degree to which he is involved in family activities, such as planning family activities and joining family members on outings. 8. *Disagree on Discipline:* Two questions for the mother and one question for the boy (middle and oldest samples only) measure the agreement between parents on how to discipline the boy. 9. *Unhappy Parents* is an evaluation by the mother of her degree of happiness with her partner. 10. *Parental Stress* is based on 14 items measuring the mother's perceived stress and ability to handle problems. 11. *Parent Antisocial Attitude.* This is a summary construct encompassing 18 questions about the mother's attitude toward antisocial behaviors of the boy, such as whether it is all right to yell, argue, and fight, to be truant, and to choose one's own friends even if they are undesirable. 12. *Parent Anxiety/Depression.* This combines information on the father and mother about whether either of them had ever had problems with anxiety, depression, or suicide. 13. *Father Behavior Problems.* This is based on the mother's report that the father (either living in the house or absent) has ever had behavior problems. 14. *Parent Substance Use Problems.* This combines information on the father and mother about whether either of them has ever had substance use problems (i.e., alcohol or drug problems).

Macro predictors. Macro variables included socioeconomic, demographic, and neighborhood factors. 1. *Socioeconomic Status:* The parents' socioeconomic scores were calculated according to Hollingshead (1975).

If there were two parents in the family, the higher score was selected. 2. *Family on Welfare.* This construct was scored if anyone in the boy's household was on welfare during the year prior to follow-up. 3. *Poor Housing* is based on an assessment by interviewers of the condition of the house. 4. *Small House.* This construct covers the total number of rooms in the boy's residence, including bathrooms and kitchens, as reported by the mother at follow-up. Residences with fewer than six rooms were considered small. 5. *Unemployed Mother/Father.* The total number of weeks of unemployment in the year prior to follow-up was calculated for both parents. For the time period during which parents were homemakers, they were not considered unemployed. 6. *Poorly Educated Mother.* The total number of years of schooling of the mother was assessed at follow-up. Mothers who had not reached Grade 12 were considered to be poorly educated. 7. *Large Family* measured the number of siblings living in the home and was based on the boys' report. 8. *Young Mother* was reported by the mother and measured the age of the mother when the boy was born. Mothers were considered young if they were less than 27, 30, and 33 years of age for the youngest, middle, and oldest samples, respectively. 9. *Broken Family.* Based on the mother's report at follow-up, this construct classified the boy's living condition as living with both biological parents or not living with both biological parents. 10. *African American.* Information on the boy's ethnicity was obtained from the parent at screening. Participants were classified as Caucasian ($N = 652$, which includes 11 Asians) or African American ($N = 865$, which includes 23 of mixed race, 4 Hispanics, and 1 American Indian). 11. *Bad Neighborhood (Parent)* is based on 10 questions to the mother about crime and other problems in her neighborhood. 12. *Bad Neighborhood (Census)* is a combination of the following U.S. Census information from 1980: median household income; proportion of persons who were unemployed in 1979; proportion of families below the poverty level; proportion of juveniles aged 10–14 in the population; proportion of households with children under age 18 headed by a single female; and proportion of separated or divorced persons out of those aged 15 and over.

Methods of analysis

For many analyses, risk factors and outcomes were dichotomized, as far as possible, into the "worst" quarter of boys (e.g., the quarter with low attainment) versus the remainder. This approach makes it possible to focus on the worst boys with extreme scores on risk factors and problem behaviors. A more conservative approach (e.g., dichotomization at the 10th percentile) creates statistical problems. Therefore, we aimed at a cutoff in the 15–35% range.

There are many advantages of dichotomized variables. First, they permit a risk factor approach and make it possible to study the cumulative effects of several risk factors. Second, they make it easy to investigate interactions between variables (interactions between continuous variables are more difficult to study). Hence, they encourage a focus on types of individuals as well as on variables, permitting the investigation of relationships within different subgroups of individuals. Information about individuals is more useful for interventions than information about variables. Third, they make it possible to compare all variables directly by equating sensitivity of measurement. Some variables are inherently dichotomous (e.g., broken family, family on welfare). In many studies, it is difficult to know whether one variable is more closely related to an outcome than another because of differential causal influence.

Fourth, dichotomous data permit the use of the odds ratio (OR) as a measure of strength of relationship, which has many attractions (Fleiss, 1981). It is easily understandable as the increase in risk associated with a risk factor. It is a more realistic measure of predictive efficiency than the percentage of variance explained (Rosenthal & Rubin, 1982). For example, an OR of 2, doubling the risk of delinquency, might correspond to a correlation of about .12, which translates into 1.4% of the variance explained. The percentage of variance explained gives a misleading impression of weak relationships and low predictability. Unlike correlation-based measures, the OR is independent of the prevalence of risk factors and outcome variables and independent of the study design (retrospective or prospective). Nevertheless, because of the mathematical relationship between the logarithm of the OR and the phi correlation (Agresti, 1990, p. 54), conclusions about the relative strengths of associations based on ORs and phi correlations are similar. Also, the OR emerges in logistic regression analyses as a key measure of strength of effect while controlling for other variables.

Fifth, the use of the OR encourages the study of the worst affected individuals. In delinquency research, there is often more interest in predicting extreme cases (e.g., chronic offenders) than the whole range of variation. Some variables are nonlinearly related to delinquency, with a large increase in delinquency in the most extreme category compared with the remainder. Some variables (e.g., self-reported delinquency) often have a highly skewed distribution, causing the product-moment correlation to have a theoretical maximum value considerably below 1 and hence to give a misleadingly low impression of the strength of the relationship.

Although dichotomization is a way of dealing with these various problems, it is often criticized because of loss of information and lower measures of association (Cohen, 1983). However, loss of information is also involved in other commonly used analytic techniques – for example, combining several different aspects of parenting into one composite variable or including only a small subset of measured variables in the analysis. The criticism of lower measures of association has force only if the product-moment (phi) correlation is used with dichotomous data. The use of relative improvement over chance (RIOC) or the tetrachoric correlation does not lead to a lower measure of strength of association in comparison with product-moment correlations and continuous data. Essentially, RIOC corrects phi for its maximum possible value (Farrington & Loeber, 1989), whereas the tetrachoric correlation estimates what the product-moment correlation would have been between two normally distributed, intervally scaled variables that were dichotomized.

In the Pittsburgh Youth Study, there was a great deal of data reduction to produce distinct measures of a relatively small number of key theoretical constructs. The aim was to eliminate redundancy without causing significant loss of information. Only clear risk factors were included as predictive factors. For example, peer delinquency was excluded because it could merely be measuring the boy's own delinquency (as 76% of seriously delinquent acts in the middle sample in Pittsburgh were committed with others). Amdur (1989) pointed out that a common fault in much delinquency research is to include measures of the outcome variable as predictors. If two variables basically measure the same underlying construct, using one as a predictor of the other will artifactually increase the percentage of variance explained, but this is of little practical significance for the explanation of delinquency.

In order to avoid multicollinearity problems in regression analyses, we deleted variables that were highly correlated (phi > .40) with other, conceptually similar variables. Examples from the middle sample are retaining behavior problems of the father in preference to parental substance use (phi = .54), using age of the mother at first birth in preference to age of the mother at the birth of the boy (phi = .45), and using broken family (not living with two biological parents) in preference to living in a single-parent, female-headed household (phi = .59). However, African American ethnicity and bad neighborhood (according to census data) were both retained (phi = .52), as were African American ethnicity and living on welfare (phi = .42) and broken family and living on welfare (phi = .43) because these were judged to be important and distinctly different variables.

Results

Interrelations among child problem behaviors

Table 4.3 summarizes the interrelationships among all child problem behaviors using ORs. Generally, there was no evidence of two separate clusters of externalizing and internalizing problems. Also, there was little tendency for the strength of associations to vary with age because results were replicated across the three samples. The number of ORs of 2.0 or greater was 18 in the oldest sample, 19 in the middle sample, and 18 in the youngest sample (out of 28 in each case).

The majority of all outcomes tended to be significantly related to all other outcomes, but the strength of associations varied greatly between sets of outcomes. For instance, across the three samples, the most interlinked behaviors were a high ADHD score (20 significant ORs out of a possible 21), covert behavior (20), physical aggression (19), conduct problems (19), and delinquency (19). In contrast, the least interconnected behaviors were depressed mood (16), shy/withdrawn behavior (15), and substance use (15), but even these were significantly interrelated in the majority of comparisons. In general, the strength of the associations between internalizing and externalizing behaviors was weaker than that among externalizing behaviors.

Overall, behaviors that were developmentally more proximal to each other tended to show stronger associations than behaviors that were

Table 4.3. *Interrelations among child problem behaviors (ORs)*

Sample	Substance use	High ADHD score	Conduct problems	Physical aggression	Covert behavior	Depressed mood	Shy/ withdrawn
Youngest Sample							
Delinquency	3.4	2.2	4.3	4.6	3.8	2.6	1.5
Substance use		1.6	1.5[a]	1.6	1.2[a]	2.3	1.3[a]
High ADHD score			6.0	4.3	5.1	1.8	2.3
Conduct problems				4.8	6.8	2.1	2.9
Physical aggression					8.4	1.5[a]	2.5
Covert behavior						1.7	3.4
Depressed mood							1.3[a]
Middle Sample							
Delinquency	2.2	2.8	3.1	5.8	4.6	1.8	1.6
Substance use		2.2	2.1	1.8	2.5	1.7	1.3[a]
High ADHD score			7.5	3.9	4.1	2.3	2.5
Conduct problems				4.2	7.4	1.5	2.4
Physical aggression					7.2	1.6	2.5
Covert behavior						1.4[a]	1.9
Depressed mood							
Oldest Sample							
Delinquency	4.2	1.8	2.8	3.6	4.2	1.7	-1.2[a]
Substance use		1.7	1.6	2.0	2.2	1.5[a]	-1.5[a]
High ADHD score			5.2	4.1	5.3	2.3	2.3
Conduct problems				3.1	6.0	1.8	1.4[a]
Physical aggression					4.9	-1.1[a]	1.8
Covert behavior						1.9	2.0
Depressed mood							2.1

[a]Not significant.

developmentally more distal (judging from the magnitudes of the ORs). Thus, across the three samples, a high ADHD score was more strongly related to physical aggression and covert behavior than to delinquency or substance use. As another example, physical aggression and covert behavior were more strongly related to delinquency than to substance use. Also, delinquency was more strongly related to the more proximal substance use than to the more distal high ADHD score.

Specifically, in the youngest sample, the strongest associations were between early externalizing problems, including a high ADHD score, physical aggression, covert behavior, and conduct problems (ORs ranged from 4.3 to 6.8). Note that shy/withdrawn behavior was also related to these behaviors, but at a lower magnitude of strength (ranging from 2.3 to 2.9), and only marginally to delinquency (1.5). Physical aggression, covert behavior, and conduct problems were about equally related to delinquency (ranging from 3.8 to 4.6), and a high ADHD score and shy/withdrawn behavior were also related to delinquency but at a lower magnitude (2.2).

Delinquency at this young age was weakly related to physical aggression (1.6) and, as mentioned, weakly related to a high ADHD score but strongly to substance use (3.4). Alongside these relationships, depressed mood was related to some forms of early externalizing problems (a high ADHD score, 1.8, and covert behavior, 1.7), but not to physical aggression. In addition, depressed mood was related to conduct problems, delinquency, and substance use (2.1, 2.6, and 2.3, respectively).

Thus, for the youngest sample, the results show a network of interrelations between externalizing and internalizing behaviors. Although the two internalizing problems, shy/withdrawn behavior and depressed mood, were not interrelated, each was associated with several externalizing problems. Some differences should also be pointed out: At this early age, depressed mood but not shy/withdrawn behavior was related to substance use. Also, shy/withdrawn behavior but not depressed mood was related to physical aggression.

The pattern of associations between externalizing problems observed for the youngest sample was largely replicated for the middle sample, but the number of significant associations increased. Covert behavior and conduct problems (but not physical aggression) were associated with substance use (2.5, 2.1). As to internalizing problems, shy/withdrawn behavior was associated with depressed mood (1.9).

Finally, the results for the oldest sample largely replicated the results for externalizing problems in the youngest and middle samples. Also, whereas covert behavior remained associated with substance use (2.2), substance use was also associated with physical aggression (2.0). Turning to internalizing problems, shy/withdrawn behavior remained embedded in most of the early manifestations of externalizing problems. Depressed mood, as in the youngest and middle samples, remained associated with a high ADHD score. Shy/withdrawn behavior was associated with depressed mood (2.1).

In summary, across the three samples, the strongest associations were found between externalizing problems, particularly a high ADHD score, covert behavior, physical aggression, and conduct problems, and slightly less strong between delinquency and substance use. Behaviors that tended to be developmentally proximal were more closely interrelated than behaviors that were developmentally more distal. Externalizing problems were consistently related to internalizing problems. It should be noted that across the three samples, depressed mood but not shy/withdrawn behavior was related to substance use.

Factor analysis is one method of investigating the extent to which the child problem behaviors reflect only one underlying construct. Table 4.4 shows the results of a principal component analysis. In agreement with the hypothesis of a single underlying construct, the first factor (A) generally explained about twice as much of the variance as any succeeding factor (31.2% in the youngest sample, 31.5% in the middle sample, 28.8% in the oldest sample). Also, all eight problem behaviors had substantial positive weightings on this first factor. The problems with the lowest weightings were substance use (.25–.38), depressed mood (.25–.41), and shy/withdrawn behavior (.28–.31). This supports the idea of a scale of juvenile multiple problem syndrome.

However, there was some evidence of specificity in the second and third factors. Depressed mood and shy/withdrawn behavior had the highest positive weightings on factor B, whereas delinquency, physical aggression, and substance use (in the oldest sample) had the highest negative weightings. Factor B seems to reflect internalizing versus externalizing behavior. Delinquency, substance use, and depressed mood had the highest positive weightings on factor C, whereas physical aggression, shy/withdrawn behavior, and covert behavior had the highest

Table 4.4. *Principal component analyses of problem behaviors*

Factor Sample	A			B			C		
	Y	M	O	Y	M	O	Y	M	O
Delinquency	.58	.59	.57	−.28	−.22	−.48	.40	.21	.16
Substance use	.25	.32	.38	.13	.17	−.58	.70	.80	.33
High ADHD score	.61	.64	.63	.01	.15	.29	−.17	−.11	−.10
Conduct problems	.69	.68	.64	−.02	−.10	.08	−.12	−.13	−.11
Physical aggression	.68	.68	.60	−.30	−.23	−.05	−.13	−.07	−.44
Covert behavior	.72	.71	.72	−.10	−.25	.04	−.25	−.02	−.11
Depressed mood	.31	.28	.29	.34	.80	.29	.56	.12	.81
Shy/withdrawn	.41	.41	.25	.76	.41	.69	−.30	−.49	.08
% variance	31.2	31.5	28.8	11.1	12.8	15.4	14.7	12.1	12.8

Note: Figures show weightings on factors. Y = youngest sample, M = middle sample, O = oldest sample

negative weightings. Factor C represents a distinction between more serious behavior (delinquency, substance use, and depressed mood) and less serious behavior (physical aggression, shy/withdrawn behavior, and covert behavior). Hence, although the results of the principal component factor analysis are concordant with a general problem behavior theory, there is also evidence of an internalizing–externalizing dimension as well. However, these results are not highly consistent in factors A, B, and C. For that reason, subsequent analyses will consider each problem behavior separately, particularly because the associations varied with age. This strategy has the additional advantages of allowing us to examine differences in the strength of associations between different problem behaviors and how such behaviors are nested among each other, and permits us to identify risk factors that are common to different outcomes and those that are specific to a certain outcome.

Risk factors predicting child problem behaviors

Generalized associations. Table 4.5 summarizes all the relationships (using ORs) between the risk factors and all child problem behaviors. We first focus on risk factors that predict most outcomes. Low academic achievement (based on parent's, boy's, and teacher's ratings) was the only risk factor that was related to all problems in all three samples (ORs 1.6–2.8 for the youngest sample, 1.9–3.2 for the middle sample, and 1.7–3.2 for the oldest sample). HIA problems, which often are associated with poor academic achievement, were also related to most problems, but more strongly to externalizing problems (conduct problems, physical aggression, and covert behavior) than to internalizing problems (depressed mood, shy/withdrawn behavior) or delinquency. Being old for the grade, which is a result of poor academic performance, was associated with almost all problems.

Of the family factors, poor supervision was related to all externalizing and internalizing problems in two of three of the samples. Likewise, poor communication (measured only in the middle and oldest samples) was related to all externalizing problems (most strongly to covert behavior) and internalizing problems. None of the macro factors was consistently related across all outcomes.

Table 4.5. *Risk factors versus child problem behaviors (ORs)*

		Delin-quency	Substance use	High ADHD score	Conduct problems	Physical aggression	Covert behavior	Depressed mood	Shy/withdrawn
Child									
Lack of guilt	Y	3.4	—	5.5	5.5	6.5	4.7	—	2.7
	M	4.7	2.1	4.0	5.1	5.0	6.0	1.6	1.5
	O	3.5	1.6	5.0	2.8	5.9	6.2	—	2.3
Low achievement	Y	1.7	1.6	2.8	2.4	1.9	2.1	2.0	2.2
(PBT)	M	2.6	2.8	3.2	2.4	2.0	2.9	2.2	1.9
	O	2.6	1.8	2.6	3.2	2.0	2.9	1.7	2.8
Low achievement	Y	—	1.8	1.7	—	1.6	—	1.5	—
(CAT)	M	3.0	—	2.0	1.8	2.1	—	2.4	—
	O	1.6	—	1.7	1.9	1.7	—	—	1.9
Old for grade	Y	1.9	1.7	—	—	2.4	1.6	1.9	1.7
	M	2.7	2.2	2.1	1.9	1.5	2.7	1.6	—
	O	2.3	1.5	—	1.7	1.7	1.9	—	1.4
HIA problems	Y	2.1	—	4.0	4.0	5.2	5.4	—	2.5
	M	1.9	1.9	4.0	2.5	4.2	3.7	1.8	2.6
	O	2.7	1.8	3.3	2.5	6.1	5.5	1.6	2.3
Anxiety	Y	—	—	1.9	—	2.0	1.6	NA	NA
	M	—	1.8	2.2	1.6	1.5	1.9	NA	NA
	O	—	—	2.2	1.5	1.6	2.0	NA	NA

Few friends	Y	—	2.0	—	—	—	—	NA	NA
	M	—	—	1.6	1.7	—	—	NA	NA
	O	—	—	—	—	—	—	NA	NA
Low organizational participation	Y	1.5	—	—	—	—	—	—	—
	M	1.6	—	—	1.5	—	—	—	—
	O	—	—	—	—	1.7	—	—	1.8
Low jobs/chores involvement	Y	—	—	—	—	—	—	—	—
	M	—	—	—	—	—	1.6	—	—
	O	—	—	—	—	—	1.5	—	—
Low religiosity	Y	—	—	—	—	—	—	—	—
	M	—	—	—	—	—	—	—	—
	O	—	1.8	—	—	—	-1.8	—	-2.0
Family									
Poor supervision	Y	1.9	1.7	2.2	2.9	2.2	—	—	—
	M	1.5	—	1.8	2.2	1.5	2.0	1.7	1.9
	O	2.6	2.3	1.6	2.1	1.7	3.3	1.6	1.8
No set time home	Y	—	—	—	—	—	—	—	—
	M	—	—	—	—	—	—	—	—
	O	1.5	2.0	—	—	—	—	—	1.7
Low reinforcement	Y	—	—	—	—	—	—	—	—
	M	—	—	2.1	1.9	1.6	2.2	1.6	1.6
	O	—	—	1.8	2.0	2.0	2.4	—	1.8
Physical punishment	Y	1.7	—	—	—	1.5	1.6	2.0	—
	M	2.0	1.8	2.5	2.1	2.0	1.8	2.1	—
	O	1.9	1.7	1.6	1.7	4.6	—	1.9	—

Table 4.5. (cont.)

		Delin-quency	Substance use	High ADHD score	Conduct problems	Physical aggression	Covert behavior	Depressed mood	Shy/withdrawn
Poor communication	Y	—	—	—	—	—	—	—	—
	M	2.4	2.5	3.6	3.4	2.5	3.8	3.3	2.3
	O	1.5	—	3.4	3.2	2.8	4.1	1.9	2.3
Boy not close to mother	M	—	—	1.7	—	—	—	2.5	—
	O	—	—	1.7	1.9	1.6	2.5	1.7	2.2
Boy not involved	Y	1.6	—	—	—	1.5	2.1	—	—
	M	—	—	1.6	1.5	—	1.9	—	—
	O	1.8	1.7	—	1.6	—	1.9	—	—
Disagree on discipline	M	2.1	1.9	2.4	2.2	1.7	1.8	—	—
	O	—	—	1.8	2.5	—	—	—	—
Unhappy parents	Y	2.0	1.9	—	2.3	2.8	—	−2.4	—
	M	—	—	2.3	1.8	1.8	2.1	—	2.1
	O	—	—	1.8	—	—	—	—	—
Parental stress	Y	1.7	—	—	1.8	1.8	2.2	—	1.9
	M	1.9	—	2.8	2.7	2.6	2.5	1.6	1.7
	O	—	—	2.8	3.2	1.9	3.5	—	1.8
Parent antisocial attitude	Y	—	—	1.5	2.1	—	2.3	1.5	—
	M	—	—	—	1.5	—	—	—	1.7
	O	—	—	—	—	—	—	—	—

Parent anxiety/ depression	Y	1.5	—	2.0	2.3	2.1	2.1	1.9	1.7
	M	1.8	—	2.0	1.6	1.8	—	—	—
	O	—	1.6	1.9	2.5	—	2.7	1.5	—
Father behavior problems	Y	—	—	2.3	2.6	1.8	2.3	2.0	—
	M	1.7	—	—	2.8	1.8	1.8	—	—
	O	—	—	—	2.1	—	—	—	—
Parent substance use problems	Y	1.9	—	2.5	2.0	2.0	1.6	—	1.8
	M	1.6	—	2.3	3.4	—	2.1	1.5	—
	O	—	—	—	2.0	—	—	—	—
Macro Low SES	Y	1.5	1.7	—	—	1.9	—	1.6	—
	M	2.2	2.2	1.6	2.0	1.7	1.5	—	—
	O	1.5	—	—	1.5	—	1.8	—	—
Family on welfare	Y	2.1	—	1.7	2.2	1.5	1.6	1.9	—
	M	2.5	1.7	—	1.7	—	1.7	1.7	—
	O	2.4	—	—	1.6	2.1	1.8	—	—
Poor housing	Y	—	—	—	—	—	—	—	—
	M	—	—	—	1.7	—	1.5	—	1.7
	O	1.7	—	1.8	1.6	2.0	1.8	—	1.9
Small house	Y	1.7	—	—	1.5	—	1.5	—	—
	M	—	—	—	—	—	1.5	—	—
	O	1.7	—	—	—	—	—	—	—
Unemployed mother	Y	—	1.8	—	1.5	—	1.9	—	—
	M	1.5	1.9	—	—	—	—	2.7	—
	O	—	—	—	—	1.6	—	—	—
Unemployed father	Y	2.2	—	—	2.2	—	—	1.9	—
	M	2.6	—	—	—	—	—	—	—
	O	—	—	—	—	—	—	—	—

Table 4.5. (cont.)

		Delinquency	Substance use	High ADHD score	Conduct problems	Physical aggression	Covert behavior	Depressed mood	Shy/withdrawn
Poorly educated mother	Y	2.1	1.9	—	1.5	—	—	1.5	—
	M	—	1.7	—	—	—	1.6	—	—
	O	1.9	—	—	2.2	—	2.2	—	—
Large family	Y	1.7	—	—	1.8	1.6	—	—	2.0
	M	—	—	—	—	—	—	—	—
	O	—	—	—	—	—	—	—	—
Young mother	Y	—	—	—	—	—	—	—	—
	M	1.9	—	—	—	—	—	—	—
	O	2.1	—	—	—	—	—	—	—
Broken family	Y	2.0	—	3.1	2.7	2.0	1.9	2.7	—
	M	2.9	—	2.2	2.2	1.7	2.6	—	—
	O	2.8	—	—	2.1	2.2	1.9	—	—
African American	Y	1.9	1.6	—	—	—	—	2.4	1.7
	M	2.5	—	—	—	1.5	1.8	—	—
	O	2.3	—	—	—	—	—	—	—
Bad neighborhood (P)	Y	2.2	—	—	2.1	1.9	—	2.1	—
	M	1.8	—	—	—	—	1.9	—	—
	O	2.0	—	1.6	2.0	2.2	1.7	—	—
Bad neighborhood (C)	Y	2.0	—	—	1.8	—	—	1.7	1.5
	M	1.8	—	—	—	—	—	—	—
	O	2.1	1.7	—	—	—	—	—	—

Note: Y = youngest sample; M = middle sample; O = oldest sample; — = nonsignificant odds ratios; P = parent; B = boy; T = teacher; C = census.

Specific associations. Which risk factors were mostly related to externalizing problems? In each of the three samples, lack of guilt was most strongly related to conduct problems, physical aggression, delinquency, and a high ADHD score; less strongly to shy/withdrawn behavior; and weakly to depressed mood and substance use. Several other risk factors were mostly related to externalizing problems and far less consistently to internalizing problems: broken family, low socioeconomic status, parent substance use problems, father behavior problems, African American ethnicity, and bad neighborhood (parent rating).

A few risk factors were related only to delinquency, including boys' low participation in organizations, African American ethnicity, young mother, and a bad neighborhood (according to census measures). For example, African American ethnicity was significantly related to delinquency in all three samples (ORs = 1.9, 2.5, and 2.3 in the youngest, middle, and oldest samples, respectively) but was not significantly related to any other problem behavior in more than one sample and had only one other strong relationship (with depressed mood in the youngest sample; OR = 2.4). Similarly, a bad neighborhood (according to census measures) was significantly related to delinquency in all three samples (OR = 2.0, 1.8, and 2.1, respectively) but was not significantly related to any other problem (including internalizing problems) in more than one sample and had no other strong relationships. Moreover, the 13 macro variables had 17 strong relationships with delinquency, 10 with conduct problems, and 15 with the other six problems, suggesting a possibly specific link between macro variables and delinquent behavior.

Turning to other specific relationships, three risk factors were primarily related to covert behavior: low involvement in jobs and chores, not involved in family activities, and living in a small house. These findings shed new light on familial interactions by covert boys, which heretofore had been seen as resulting mostly from neglectful parenting (Loeber & Stouthamer-Loeber, 1986). The present findings may indicate that covert boys distance themselves from family matters.

Turning to physical aggression, we did not find risk factors that were related to this problem only; in fact, variables related to physical aggression also tended to be related to delinquency (e.g., shy/withdrawn behavior, low socioeconomic status, bad neighborhood, according to the parent).

Among the family factors, parental stress was particularly associated with externalizing problems, such as conduct problems, physical aggression, covert behavior, and a high ADHD score, but for the two older age groups only. Parental stress was less strongly related to shy/withdrawn behavior and was not related to depressed mood. Bad neighborhood (parent rating) was most consistently related (i.e., across the three samples) to delinquency and physical aggression but much less to substance use, a high ADHD score, covert behavior, and depressed mood and was not related to shy/withdrawn behavior.

Several risk factors discriminated between a high ADHD score and conduct problems. Parental child-rearing practices such as poor supervision, physical punishment, and parental disagreement about discipline were mostly related to conduct problems (but not in all samples). In addition, several parent characteristics were also related mainly to conduct problems (rather than a high ADHD score), including parent anxiety/depression, unhappy parents, family on welfare, parental substance use problems, and a poorly educated mother. Physical punishment and family on welfare were more consistently related to depressed mood than to shy/withdrawn behavior.

Age effects. Table 4.5 allows us to examine the extent to which the *strength* of the association between a risk factor and a problem behavior stays the same or changes across the three grade samples. In most instances, the strength of association between risk factors and problems was quite similar across the three age groups. However, a few exceptions should be noted. For example, physical punishment became increasingly related to physical aggression, particularly between late childhood and adolescence (ORs of 1.9, 2.0, and 4.6, for the youngest, middle, and oldest samples, respectively). Also, poor supervision became increasingly related to covert behavior (ORs of 1.4, 2.0, and 3.3, for the respective samples). However, these increases in strength of association were specific and did not apply to other problems.

In summary, the results showed only a few instances in which the strength of association between a risk factor and a problem behavior changed with age. In most instances, the magnitudes of the relationships were similar across the three grade samples.

Overlap between risk factors predicting different problems

We now review the extent to which diverse problems, such as delinquency and depressed mood, are associated with the same risk factors. Comparisons of risk factors for different problems also can shed light on the extent to which they are unique to some problems or are shared between pairs of problems.

Unique risk factors are shown when the proportion of risk factors for problem A that are also associated with problem B is substantially larger than the proportion of risk factors for problem B that are also associated with problem A. Thus, asymmetry in the relative proportions of risk factors among pairs of problems can indicate unique risk factors that are not shared by the two problems.

Overall, Table 4.6 shows a high degree of symmetrical overlap in the proportions of risk factors shared between most pairs of problems. The table shows the percentage of significant risk factors shared by pairs of problems based on the number of significant ORs as a proportion of the total number of possible ORs. This applied not only to problems that had some similarities, such as delinquency and conduct problems, physical aggression, and covert behavior, but also to problems associated with a high ADHD score.

We now focus on asymmetrical relationships. The first column in Table 4.6 shows the percentage of risk factors associated with each single problem in each of the three samples. For example, in the youngest sample, 22 of the 35 risk factors (63%) were significant predictors of delinquency. The third column in Table 4.6 shows that of these 22 risk factors, 7 (32%) were also significant predictors of substance use. How does this compare when we take substance use as a starting point? The first column in Table 4.6 shows that, overall, 10 of the 35 risk factors (29%) were significant predictors of substance use. Of these 10, 7 (70%) were also significant predictors of delinquency. Thus, for the youngest sample, most risk factors associated with substance use were nested within the risk factors associated with delinquency, but over half of the risk factors associated with delinquency were not predictive of substance use. The results were replicated in the middle and oldest samples. Likewise, Table 4.6 shows that across the three samples, risk factors of shy/withdrawn behavior were a subset of the risk factors of

Table 4.6. *Percentage of significant risk factors shared by different problems (based on significant ORs)*

Problem A		% Sig	Delin-quency	Substance use	High ADHD score	Conduct problems	Physical aggression	Covert behavior	Depressed mood	Shy/ withdrawn
						Problem B				
Delinquency	Y	63	—	32	36	68	73	55	59	45
	M	62	—	43	61	74	61	70	52	26
	O	54	—	45	45	75	65	65	25	40
Substance use	Y	29	70	—	30	50	60	30	78	33
	M	32	83	—	75	83	75	92	73	36
	O	30	82	—	64	82	64	82	45	55
High ADHD score	Y	54	67	25	—	83	92	83	64	45
	M	54	70	45	—	95	80	80	67	44
	O	43	56	44	—	94	81	75	47	67
Conduct problems	Y	51	83	28	56	—	72	61	56	44
	M	65	71	42	79	—	71	79	55	45
	O	62	67	38	62	—	62	75	30	48
Physical aggression	Y	54	84	32	58	68	—	68	61	44
	M	46	82	53	94	100	—	88	62	50
	O	51	68	37	68	79	—	74	33	67

Covert	Y	49	75	19	62	69	81	—	53	47
behavior	M	65	67	46	67	79	67	—	48	39
	O	54	65	45	60	90	70	—	32	58
Depressed	Y	48	81	44	44	62	69	50	—	31
mood	M	40	86	57	86	86	71	79	—	50
	O	20	71	71	100	100	86	86	—	71
Shy/	Y	30	100	30	50	80	80	70	50	—
withdrawn	M	31	55	36	73	91	73	82	64	—
	O	37	62	46	77	85	92	85	38	—

Note: % Sig. is the percentage of risk factors significantly predicting the outcome. Values above the diagonal are the percentage of risk factors for A that are also significant for B. Values below the diagonal are the percentage of risk factors for B that also apply to A. Y = youngest sample; M = middle sample; O = oldest sample.

conduct problems, whereas many of the risk factors of conduct problems were not predictive of shy/withdrawn behavior.

In judging the results in Table 4.6, one should keep in mind that the percentages of risk factors that are shared are generally higher for problems with fewer significant predictors. Inspection of Table 4.6 further shows several other pairs of problem behaviors with asymmetries in the proportion of risk factors. Some of these relationships apply to some but not all samples. For example, in the oldest sample, only 30% of the predictors of conduct problems were also among the predictors of depressed mood. However, the converse percentage was high: 100% of the predictors of depressed mood were among the predictors of conduct problems. This asymmetrical result was replicated in the middle sample (but not in the youngest sample), indicating that, whereas most risk factors applicable to depressed mood were also risk factors for conduct problems, a substantial proportion of risk factors were unique to conduct problems. Further asymmetries were identified between delinquency and covert behavior (two samples) and between shy/withdrawn behavior and conduct problems, delinquency (two samples), physical aggression, and covert behavior. Thus, the results suggest that risk factors for internalizing problems (depressed mood and shy/withdrawn behavior) only partly overlap with risk factors for externalizing behaviors.

There were only two cases in which both percentages were less than 50% in more than one of the samples, indicating symmetrical independence of risk factors. In the youngest sample, only 35% of the predictors of a high ADHD score were also among the predictors of substance use, and only 30% of the predictors of substance use were among the predictors of a high ADHD score. Hence, there was least overlap between the risk factors for a high ADHD score and substance use in that sample (the other example is substance use and covert behavior, also in the youngest sample). Thus, two findings in the youngest sample show considerable separation of risk factors for substance use as distinct from either a high ADHD score or covert behavior. It should be noted that these findings are not obvious from Table 4.3 (the association between different problem behaviors), which shows a significant overlap between a high ADHD score and substance use and nonsignificant overlaps in the case of five other problems.

Risk factors predicting several problems

We now investigate how far each risk factor predicted several problems. A few precautions against confounds should be noted. HIA problems were not studied as predictors of a high ADHD score or conduct problems (which were both derived from the DISC); and anxiety and few friends were not studied as predictors of depressed mood or shy/withdrawn behavior. Hence, for these risk factors, percentages are based on six problem behaviors.

Table 4.7 shows the percentage of problems significantly predicted by each risk factor and the percentage of relatively strong relationships (with ORs of 2.0 or greater). The ordering of variables in Table 4.7 is based on the percentage of problems with ORs of 2.0 or greater. Several risk factors were significantly related to all or nearly all problems, a finding that was replicated in all three samples. This was true for several child variables, including low achievement (based on parent, boy, and teacher ratings), lack of guilt, and HIA problems. Several family factors similarly had a generalized impact, including poor family communication and poor parental supervision.

Overall, the child variables were stronger predictors than the family variables, which in turn were stronger predictors than the macro variables. No macro variable was strongly (OR = 2.0 or greater) related to the majority of problems compared with three child variables and one family variable (poor communication). A broken family was strongly related to half of all problems. Generally, the risk factors that were related to only a few problems tended to be rather weakly related to them and were not significantly related to the same problems in all samples.

Age effects

In some instances, the impact of a risk factor on several problems narrowed with age, as shown by the larger number of associations at a young age compared to the smaller number of associations at an older age. For example, parent deviant behavior and attitudes (parent substance use, father behavior problems, parent antisocial attitude, and, to a lesser extent, parent anxiety/depression) were more related to diverse

Table 4.7. *Percentage of problems significantly predicted by each risk factor*

	Sample					
	Youngest		Middle		Oldest	
	% Sig.	OR = 2+	% Sig.	OR = 2+	% Sig.	OR = 2+
Child						
Low achievement (PBT)	100	63	100	88	100	75
Lack of guilt	75	75	100	75	88	75
HIA problems	67	67	100	50	100	67
Old for grade	75	13	87	50	75	13
Low achievement (CAT)	63	13	75	50	75	13
Anxiety	50	17	67	17	67	33
Few friends	17	17	33	0	0	0
Low organizational participation	25	0	13	0	25	0
Low jobs/chores involvement	0	0	13	0	13	0
Low religiosity	0	0	0	0	13	0
Family						
Poor communication	—	—	100	100	100	63
Poor supervision	63	38	88	25	100	50
Parental stress	63	13	88	50	63	38
Physical punishment	50	13	88	63	75	13
Parent substance use problems	75	38	63	38	13	13
Unhappy parents	50	38	63	38	25	13
Parent anxiety/depression	88	50	50	13	63	25
Disagree on discipline	—	—	75	38	25	13
Father behavior problems	63	50	50	13	13	13
Low reinforcement	0	0	75	25	63	38
Not close to mother	—	—	25	13	75	25
Parent antisocial attitude	50	25	25	0	0	0
Boy not involved	38	13	38	0	50	0
No set time home	0	0	13	0	25	13
Macro						
Broken family	75	63	63	50	50	38
Family on welfare	75	25	63	13	50	38
Bad neighborhood (P)	50	38	25	0	63	38
African American	50	13	25	13	25	13
Low SES	50	0	75	38	38	0
Poorly educated mother	50	13	25	0	38	25

Table 4.7. *(cont.)*

Unemployed father	25	13	25	25	0	0
Bad neighborhood (C)	50	13	13	0	13	13
Poor housing	0	0	38	0	75	13
Unemployed mother	38	0	38	13	13	0
Large family	50	13	0	0	0	0
Young mother	0	0	13	0	13	13
Small house	25	0	13	0	13	0

Notes: Sig = percentage of significant outcomes, usually calculated on the basis of eight outcomes (see text); 2+ = percentage of outcomes with ORs = 2.0 or greater; — = not measured at this age.

problems for the youngest sample, slightly less related for the middle sample, and even less related for the oldest sample. Likewise the percentage of significant associations for unhappy parents was higher for the youngest and middle samples compared with the oldest sample.

Similar age trends were found for several of the macro factors, such as African American ethnicity, bad neighborhood (per the census, but not according to parent report), unemployed mother, and large family. These results strongly indicate the pervasive effect that family psychopathology, ethnicity, and some social handicaps have on diverse child problem behaviors at a young age but not at a later age. In contrast, such age effects were not noted for child risk factors.

In a few instances, the impact of a risk factor on several problems increased with age. For example, the percentage of problems associated with HIA increased from 67% in the youngest sample to 100% in the middle and oldest samples. Similarly, some child-rearing practices, particularly poor supervision and physical punishment, became associated with a higher number of problem behaviors for the middle and oldest samples compared with the youngest sample (poor supervision: 63%, 88%, and 100% in the youngest, middle and oldest samples, respectively; physical punishment: 50%, 88%, 75%).

Identifying multiproblem boys

So far, the analyses in this chapter have summarized associations between one risk factor and one child problem behavior. It is clear from

Table 4.8. *Boys with different numbers of problem behaviors (%)*

Number of problems	Sample					
	(N)	Youngest	(N)	Middle	(N)	Oldest
0	152	(30.2)	153	(30.1)	118	(23.3)
1	114	(22.7)	95	(18.7)	114	(22.5)
2	70	(13.9)	83	(16.3)	89	(17.6)
3	67	(13.3)	63	(12.4)	62	(12.3)
4	48	(9.5)	45	(8.9)	65	(12.8)
5	27	(5.4)	45	(8.9)	34	(6.7)
6	18	(3.6)	18	(3.5)	17	(3.4)
7	4	(.8)	4	(.8)	5	(1.0)
8	3	(.6)	2	(.4)	2	(.4)
4 or more	100	(19.9)	114	(22.4)	123	(24.3)

Note: Total percentage varies due to rounding.

the relations between the different problems that a proportion of boys show multiple problem behaviors. Prior research suggests that multi-problem boys have an early age at onset, show an increasing rate of offending over time, and are at risk for a career of chronic delinquency (Loeber, 1982). Therefore, we need to identify multiproblem boys and investigate which risk factors predict them. We also need to examine how far risk factors for multiproblem boys are quantitatively or qualitatively different from risk factors for less problematic boys.

In order to investigate these questions, each boy was scored according to the number of problems he possessed out of eight problems (delinquency, substance use, a high ADHD score, conduct problems, physical aggression, covert behavior, depressed mood, and shy/withdrawn behavior). Table 4.8 shows the number of boys with each score, ranging from 0 to 8. Where a boy was not known on any problem, his score on the remaining problems was scaled up appropriately. For example, if a boy had 4 out of 7 problems, this fraction (4/7) was multiplied by 8 and rounded up or down to the nearest integer to produce the boy's score. (In this case, (4/7) $\times$ 8 = 4.57, giving a score of 5).

Table 4.8 shows that the number and percentage of boys steadily decreased in each of the three samples with an increasing number of

Table 4.9. *Percentage of boys with each problem who were multiproblem boys*

	Sample								
	Youngest			Middle			Oldest		
Problem	%	(N)	OR	%	(N)	OR	%	(N)	OR
High ADHD score	53.5	(129)	12.7	64.8	(122)	18.4	67.5	(117)	16.3
Physical aggression	59.1	(115)	16.1	56.8	(146)	14.1	61.9	(113)	10.4
Covert behavior	59.2	(125)	19.6	64.1	(128)	19.4	70.5	(122)	22.4
Conduct problems	65.2	(112)	25.2	61.1	(126)	14.7	62.0	(137)	14.2
Delinquency	49.3	(140)	10.4	52.9	(140)	9.2	48.1	(185)	7.8
Substance use	41.2	(85)	3.8	53.9	(76)	5.8	48.4	(122)	4.7
Shy/withdrawn	44.1	(118)	5.5	47.1	(153)	6.6	39.6	(149)	3.0
Depressed mood	39.8	(118)	4.1	41.7	(115)	3.6	48.3	(116)	4.5

problems. We decided to identify the worst 20–25% of the boys in each sample – those with four or more problems out of eight – as the *multiproblem boys*. It can be seen that there were 100 (19.9%) of these boys in the youngest sample, 114 (22.4%) in the middle sample, and 123 (24.3%) in the oldest sample.

Problems of multiproblem boys

Table 4.9 shows the extent to which boys with each problem were multiproblem boys. For example, 140 boys were classified as delinquents in the youngest sample; 69 (49.3%) of them were multiproblem boys, compared with only 31 of the 363 nondelinquents (8.5%), giving an OR of 10.4. The ORs were highest for covert behavior (19.6, 19.4, and 22.4 for the youngest, middle, and oldest samples, respectively), a high ADHD score (12.7, 18.4, 16.3), conduct problems (25.2, 14.7, 14.2), physical aggression (16.1, 14.1, 10.4), and delinquency (10.4, 9.2, 7.8), showing that boys with these externalizing problems were especially likely to be multiproblem boys. Conversely, the multiproblem boys were less likely to be found among substance users (3.8, 5.8, 4.7) or among those showing internalizing behaviors: shy/withdrawn behavior (5.5, 6.6, 3.0) or depressed mood (4.1, 3.6, 4.5).

Risk factors for multiproblem boys

Previous results showed that several risk factors predicted most problem behaviors. It remains to be verified, however, that those risk factors also predict the boys who have multiple problems.

Table 4.10 shows how far the multiproblem boys were predicted by risk factors. The best predictors in all these samples were lack of guilt (ORs = 6.1, 7.3, and 5.8 in the youngest, middle, and oldest samples, respectively) and HIA problems (5.7, 4.9, 5.8). Low achievement (according to parents, boys, and teachers), poor parent–boy communication, parental stress, and a broken family were also strong predictors. Slightly less strongly predictive (but still consistently predictive across the three samples) were old for grade, poor supervision, boy not involved, unhappy parents, parent substance use problems, parent anxiety/depression, father behavior problems, low socioeconomic status, and family on welfare. In addition, several risk factors in the middle and oldest samples were associated with multiproblem boys: anxiety, poor communication, physical punishment, low reinforcement, and parental disagreement about discipline. A few risk factors in the youngest and middle samples were associated with multiproblem boys: low achievement according to CAT scores, unemployed mother, and African American ethnicity.

Regression analyses for multiproblem boys

Because several of the risk factors are intercorrelated, we need to identify those risk factors that predict multiproblem boys independently of other risk factors. Table 4.11 shows the results of hierarchical multiple regression analyses carried out to establish the most important independent predictors of multiproblem boys. In these analyses the child variables were entered first, then the family variables, and finally the macro variables. This order of entry was chosen because we thought that child factors were likely to have the most proximal influence on problems, that family factors were more likely to predict child factors than the reverse, and that macro factors were more likely to predict family factors than the reverse. Table 4.10 also indicates that this was the order of importance of the categories of variables according to ORs.

Lack of guilt and HIA problems proved to be the most important

Table 4.10. ORs for risk factors for multiproblem boys

	Sample		
	Youngest	Middle	Oldest
Child			
Lack of guilt	6.1****	7.3****	5.8****
Low achievement (PBT)	3.0****	3.7****	3.9****
Low achievement (CAT)	1.6*	2.1***	1.3
Old for grade	1.8*	2.3****	1.6*
HIA problems	5.7****	4.9****	5.8****
Anxiety	1.6	3.0****	2.1****
Low jobs/chores involvement	1.0	1.3	1.6*
Family			
Poor supervision	2.2***	2.4****	2.9****
Low reinforcement	1.0	1.8**	2.0***
Physical punishment	1.3	2.3****	2.3***
Poor communication	—	4.4****	4.0****
Boy not close to mother	—	1.3	2.1**
Boy not involved	1.7*	1.6*	1.9**
Disagree on discipline	—	2.4**	1.8*
Unhappy parents	2.7**	2.5**	2.0*
Parental stress	2.0**	3.3****	3.0****
Parent antisocial attitude	2.3***	1.2	−1.1
Parent anxiety/depression	2.7****	2.0**	2.4****
Father behavior problems	3.0****	1.5	2.3***
Parent substance use problems	2.6****	2.0**	1.6*
Macro			
Socioeconomic			
Low SES	2.0**	1.8**	1.7**
Family on welfare	2.4***	1.8**	1.6*
Poor housing	1.0	1.3	2.1***
Unemployed mother	1.9*	1.7*	1.2
Unemployed father	1.4	2.1*	−1.1
Poorly educated mother	1.9**	1.0	2.5****
Demographic			
Large family	1.7*	1.1	1.5*
Broken family	4.0****	2.7****	2.2***
African American	1.6*	1.5*	−1.2
Neighborhood			
Bad neighborhood (P)	2.5****	1.1	2.1***
Bad neighborhood (C)	1.8*	−1.1	1.1

Note: C = census, P = parent, B = boy, CAT = California Achievement Test, T = teacher. *$p < .05$, **$p < .01$, ***$p < .001$, ****$p < .0001$ (one-tailed), based on chi-squared with correction for continuity. No significant relationship: low organizational participation, few friends, low religiosity, no set time home, small house, young mother. — Variable not measured in this sample.

Table 4.11. *Hierarchical multiple regression analysis for multiproblem boys*

	Multiple R	F Change	p
Youngest Sample			
Child			
Lack of guilt	.352	65.01	.0001
HIA problems	.418	27.98	.0001
Low achievement (PBT)	.426	3.89	.025
Family			
Parent anxiety/depression	.457	8.61	.002
Unhappy parents	.473	4.83	.014
Parent antisocial attitude	.482	2.66	.052
Macro			
Bad neighborhood (P)	.500	5.81	.008
Middle Sample			
Child			
Lack of guilt	.410	89.20	.0001
HIA problems	.455	21.87	.0001
Anxiety	.485	16.21	.0001
Low achievement (PBT)	.502	10.04	.0008
Family			
Poor communication	.527	15.54	.0001
Parental stress	.541	9.15	.001
Oldest Sample			
Child			
Lack of guilt	.358	65.28	.0001
HIA problems	.419	25.52	.0001
Low achievement (PBT)	.440	9.94	.0009
Anxiety	.448	3.84	.025
Family			
Poor communication	.491	23.14	.0001
Parent anxiety/depression	.508	10.41	.0007
Physical punishment	.525	10.29	.007
Parental stress	.533	5.41	.011
Macro			
Poorly educated mother	.540	4.32	.019

Note: p values are one-tailed.

predictors in all three samples, followed by low achievement and anxiety (in two samples). The most important family predictors were poor parent–boy communication, parent anxiety/depression, and parental stress (each in two samples). Parent antisocial attitude was predictive in the youngest sample only. With only two exceptions (bad neighborhood in the youngest sample and a poorly educated mother in the oldest sample), the macro factors were not important predictors independent of the child and family factors.

In summary, in the regression analyses three child characteristics – lack of guilt, HIA problems, and low academic achievement – independently predicted multiproblem boys *in each of the samples.* In contrast, family and macro factors varied more across the three samples. For the youngest sample, parent characteristics (deviant behavior and attitudes but not child-rearing practices) contributed most, followed by bad neighborhood. For the middle sample, poor communication and parental stress contributed most, but not neighborhood or other macro factors. For the oldest sample, poor communication, physical punishment, and parental stress contributed most, followed by poor education of the mother. Again, macro factors, including bad neighborhood, did not enter into the equation.

Thus, the three multiple regressions showed consistency in terms of child variables but a shift from the importance of deviant parent behavior and attitude in the youngest sample (antisocial attitude, unhappy parents, parent anxiety/depression) to less than optimal child-rearing practices (such as poor communication and physical punishment) in the older age groups. The second shift was from the presence of neighborhood effects in the youngest sample to the absence of such effects (or most other macro effects) in the older two samples.

Detecting interaction effects for multiproblem boys

A search was carried out for interaction effects between the independently important predictors in each sample. Only one interaction was statistically significant over and above the main effect. The combination of parent anxiety/depression and a poorly educated mother was associated with a very high prevalence of multiproblem boys in the oldest sample (of boys with neither of these problems, 16.6% were multiproblem boys; of boys with parent anxiety/depression only, 26.3% were multiproblem boys; of boys with a poorly educated mother only, 24.7% were multiproblem boys; of boys with both a poorly educated mother and an anxious/depressed parent, 60.0% were multiproblem boys (likelihood ratio chi square = 3.77, p = .052; F change in regression = 4.15, p = .042). Thus, in the oldest sample, a poorly educated mother predicted multiproblem boys especially when parent anxiety/depression also occurred; conversely, parent anxiety/depression predicted multiproblem boys, especially in the presence of a poorly educated mother.

The effect of excluding multiproblem boys

A key issue is whether the relationships between single risk factors and single child problems are greater for multiproblem boys than for less problematic boys, and indeed, whether the relationships are present among less problematic boys. In order to investigate this, the multiproblem boys were excluded from the analyses and the relationships between 14 key risk factors and 8 problems were examined for the remaining boys. The findings showed that the significant relationships generally were attenuated but did not disappear; decreases in ORs were usually marginal.

By far the largest decreases in ORs occurred for the relationships between HIA problems and a high ADHD score in the oldest sample (from 3.3 to 1.3) and between HIA problems and conduct problems in the youngest sample (from 4.0 to 1.2). These decreases probably occurred because most of the boys who had both HIA problems and a high ADHD score, or both HIA problems and conduct problems, were multiproblem boys.

Remarkably, for covert behavior in the oldest sample, the ORs generally increased after excluding the multiproblem boys (for nine predictors, with one unchanged and only four decreasing). The greatest increase was for African American ethnicity (from 1.1 to 3.2), suggesting that the overlap between African American ethnicity and covert behavior was greater among boys who were not in the multiproblem group.

Uniquely, the strength of the relationship between African American ethnicity and delinquency was always greater after excluding the multiproblem boys in all three samples (OR = 1.9–2.3 in youngest sample, 2.5–2.7 in the middle sample, and 2.3–3.9 in the oldest sample). Again, this suggests that the overlap between African American ethnicity and delinquency was greater among boys who did not have multiple problems than among multiproblem boys.

In summary, the results suggest that, to a large extent, the relationships between single risk factors and single problems are similar for multiproblem boys and for boys with fewer problems.

Risk scores versus multiproblem boys

In order to investigate the cumulative effect of risk factors on the prevalence of multiproblem boys, and indeed on the boys with multiple risk factors, we scored all the boys according to their number of independent predictors identified in Table 4.10. For example, because there were seven independent predictors of multiproblem boys in the youngest sample, we scored each boy from 0 to 7 according to how many of them he possessed. (As before, the scores of boys not known on one or more of these predictors were prorated accordingly.) Table 4.12 shows the increasing prevalence of multiproblem boys with increasing risk scores. For example, of boys scoring 4 or more (i.e., with four or more risk factors), 55.2% were multiproblem boys in the youngest sample, 70.7% were multiproblem boys in the middle sample, and 57.7% were multiproblem boys in the oldest sample. The ORs corresponding to the link between multiple risk factor boys and multiproblem boys were 7.3, 12.5, and 7.3, respectively.

Conclusion

Overall, the results lend considerable support to Jessor's problem behavior theory (Jessor & Jessor, 1977; Jessor et al., 1991), with many problem behaviors being associated with many other problem behaviors and with shared risk factors being linked to different manifestations of problem behavior. We expanded the test of the problem behavior theory by focusing on three samples of boys who were studied in middle to late childhood and in early adolescence. In addition, we expanded the usual array of problem behaviors by including attention deficits/ hyperactivity, depressed mood, and shy/withdrawn behavior. We also focused on measurements that not only relied on the boys' reports but also included parents and teachers as informants. Additionally, we examined to what extent risk factors could explain multiproblem boys and whether such risk factors differed from those explaining boys with

Table 4.12. *Percentage of multiproblem boys versus risk score*

	Sample		
Risk score	Youngest	Middle	Oldest
0	0.9 (117)	2.6 (156)	2.2 (89)
1	10.6 (142)	12.9 (147)	7.3 (124)
2	23.8 (105)	29.3 (92)	18.6 (102)
3	30.6 (72)	41.8 (55)	37.9 (87)
4+	55.2 (67)	70.7 (58)	57.7 (104)
	OR = 7.3	OR = 12.5	OR = 7.3

fewer problems. Overall, the robustness of Jessor's problem behavior theory was remarkable, especially since this study focused on much younger age groups than did earlier tests of the theory (e.g., Donovan, 1996; Jessor & Jessor, 1977; Jessor et al., 1991) and relied on improved measurements using multiple informants. At the same time, however, our findings qualify the theory in some important ways and provide directions for future research.

Interrelations among problem behaviors

We showed that the outcomes we studied were interrelated, but with variations in pattern. We interpret these findings to show a basic underlying structure of disruptive and delinquent behavior that cuts across different age groups. Early manifestations of externalizing problems (a high ADHD score, physical aggression, covert behavior and conduct problems) were particularly highly interrelated. Thus, like Jessor (Jessor & Jessor, 1977; Jessor et al., 1991) and others (Martin et al., 1994), we found associations among different externalizing problems (with the understanding that a small part of the intercorrelation in the present study resulted from the few common elements among these outcomes).

However, we go beyond Jessor and Jessor's (1977) formulation by stressing the importance of variations among different domains of problems that are linked to externalizing behaviors. For example, we found that shy/withdrawn behavior, unlike depressed mood, was not related to substance use. We also found that the relationships between early manifestations of externalizing problems (a high ADHD score, physical aggression, covert behavior, and conduct problems) were stronger than those between early and later externalizing problems (e.g., physical aggression, covert problems versus delinquency and substance use). We see attention deficit/hyperactivity as a key element in boys' progression to diverse problem behaviors, being associated with boys' progression to delinquency and substance use and with their vulnerability to internalizing problems (shy/withdrawn behavior and depressed mood). However, in line with other longitudinal studies (e.g., Farrington, Loeber, & Van Kammen, 1990; Loeber et al., 1995), we suggest that boys with ADHD *only* are not at high risk of developing serious delinquency or substance use. Instead, we conceptualize that ADHD leads to serious forms of externalizing problems only when it becomes associated with minor problem behaviors (such as physical fighting and covert behavior).

In addition, we see serious problem behavior of elementary school boys as involving several domains of maladaptation: first, because of the presence of externalizing problems and, second, because of comorbid internalizing problems. In that sense, early serious problem behaviors often occur as a mixture of poor control over acting-out behavior, socially distant and withdrawn behavior, and mood dysregulation.

Age shifts

In a differentiated problem theory we would expect several forms of age shifts: (1) in the manifestations of problem behaviors, (2) in the interrelations among different problem behavior, and (3) in the patterns of risk factors associated with the problem behaviors at different ages.

Age shifts in problem behaviors. Elsewhere (Loeber et al., 1998), we showed that there are major shifts with age in the manifestation of problem behaviors and that age shifts in one domain of problem behaviors do not necessarily mirror those in another domain. For example, we found a sequential pattern of onset, with less serious forms of delinquency occurring first and the most serious forms occurring last. Moreover, the prime time for the emergence of minor and moderate forms of delinquency was in the elementary school age period, whereas the middle school period was the most crucial time for the emergence of more serious forms of delinquency. In addition, the variety of delinquent acts greatly increased with age, basically doubling between Grades 2 and 8, and between middle childhood and adolescence the frequency of delinquent acts increased considerably (we could not measure frequency for the youngest sample). We also found that a proportion of the youth committed both violence and theft. This percentage was clearly smallest for the youngest sample and greatest for the oldest sample (21.6%, 47.1%, and 62.7% in the three respective samples). Thus, versatility in offending increased with age. Conversely, specialized offending was more common among younger boys than among older boys.

Turning to substance use, Loeber et al. (1996) also found that the onset of substance use unfolded gradually over time, with beer or wine use coming first, liquor use coming next, and use of marijuana and other illegal drugs following slightly later (measured in the middle and oldest samples only). For both samples we demonstrated that the magnitude of the onset of substance use during the elementary school period was already substantial, even when only substances used without parental knowledge were included.

In regard to disruptive behavior disorders, we observed a gradual decrease in ADHD across the three age groups but an increase, particularly in the elementary school period, in oppositional defiant disorder and an increase in conduct disorder between the ages of 7 and 10. As to internalizing problems, we found that the average shy/withdrawn score *increased* with age, but that there was a substantial *decrease* in the average depressed mood and anxiety scores.

Age trends in interrelations among problem behaviors. We found that most often the interrelationships among problem behaviors did not vary materially with age. However, several exceptions should be noted. The association between physical aggression and delinquency decreased across the different grade samples, as did the association between substance use and delinquency. We interpret this as meaning that the comorbid association among different early forms of problem behavior is particularly high in elementary school boys. Between that period and adolescence, however, as we know from other research findings (Loe-

ber, 1985, 1988), the associations between physical aggression and delinquency and between substance use and delinquency decreased with
age, largely because of the emergence of a group of less deviant or more
normal delinquents, such as nonaggressive and not seriously substance-
using delinquents. However, over time, a minority of juveniles become
characterized by multiple serious problem behaviors. Longitudinal research is needed to demonstrate to what extent this group emerges from
the young comorbid group spoken of before.

Shifts in risk factors with age. The next criterion for evaluating a problem theory is the extent to which risk factors were similar at different
ages. We found that many risk factors, especially child factors, were
associated with the same variety of outcomes at different ages. However, for several risk factors (shy/withdrawn behavior, old for grade
[reflecting low attainment], low achievement, and having few friends),
the largest variety of associations were observed at a young age and
fewer associations were seen at an older age. All of these factors also
emerged in multivariate analyses, showing that they contributed independently at a young age to outcomes when other variables were taken
into account.

The same conclusion applied to several family factors in that several
forms of parent deviance, including parent substance use problems,
father behavior problems, and, to a lesser extent parent anxiety/depres-
sion, were more strongly associated with a larger variety of outcomes at
a young age than at older ages. Remarkably, with the exception of the
last factor, all of these forms of family deviance contributed independently to multiple problem outcomes in multivariate analyses. The
same was true for unhappy parents. Only in the case of child-rearing
practices did we find trends for the strength of an association between
child-rearing practices and a given outcome to *increase* across the grade
samples. This was the case for physical punishment, which became
increasingly related to physical aggression, particularly between late
childhood and adolescence, and poor supervision, which became increasingly related to covert behavior with age.

Turning to macro factors, several of them were associated with a
larger variety of outcomes in the younger age group compared to the
older age group. This applied to bad neighborhood (according to census
information), unemployed mother, large family, and African American

ethnicity. However, only unemployed mother emerged in the multivariate analyses.

Finally, opposite age effects were observed for a few risk factors. In the case of HIA problems, poor supervision, physical punishment, and high parental stress, the association with multiple outcomes *increased* across the grade samples.

Thus, against a background of findings of risk factors being related to similar sets of outcomes across the three age groups, we found several instances of what we consider important age effects. The fact that several risk factors were associated with an increased diversity of problem behaviors over time speaks to the importance of such factors over and above those factors with an apparently more constant effect.

Specific and general risk factors

To what extent are risk factors associated with one outcome also associated with other outcomes? We calculated this by summarizing relevant tables across the different outcomes in terms of the percentages of significant ORs and magnitudes of ORs. Using the percentage of significant ORs as a criterion, we found that our two measures of attention deficit/impulsivity and hyperactivity (a high ADHD score, and HIA problems) were consistently related to multiple outcomes. This also applied to low achievement (which is often associated with attention problems) and lack of guilt. When the results were narrowed down to those resulting from hierarchical multiple regressions, the following variables contributed independently to multiple outcomes: a high ADHD score, HIA problems, and lack of guilt.

Of the family factors, only poor communication and poor supervision showed a high percentage of significant associations across multiple outcomes. However, in hierarchical multiple regression analyses, only poor communication survived. None of the macro factors was consistently related to multiple outcomes, nor did these factors emerge consistently in the multivariate analyses.

In summary, several risk factors were consistently associated with multiple outcomes in each of the three samples. However, most risk factors, particularly macro factors, were not consistently related to all outcomes.

The magnitude of ORs is another criterion for examining the possible differential effects of risk factors across different outcomes. For several risk factors the magnitudes of ORs remained the same across outcomes (e.g., low achievement and HIA problems). In contrast, several child factors were more related to externalizing behaviors than to other problem behaviors. These included lack of guilt, which was most strongly related to a high ADHD score, conduct problems, physical aggression, and delinquency. Also, several family factors were mostly related to externalizing problems. For instance, poor communication was especially strongly related to externalizing behaviors, including a high ADHD score, conduct problems, and covert behavior. Likewise, poor supervision was mostly related to externalizing problems. In addition, high parental stress was most strongly related to early forms of externalizing problems (a high ADHD score, physical aggression, and covert behavior), and slightly less to delinquency. The results agree with findings reported by Conger, Patterson and Ge (1995) showing that high parental stress affected adolescents' adjustment through parents' depressed mood and their poor disciplinary practices.

Several macro factors, such as a broken family, low socioeconomic status, bad neighborhood, and African American ethnicity, were more strongly related to externalizing rather than internalizing problems. In fact, African American ethnicity was specifically related to delinquency but not to other outcomes. Also, bad neighborhood was especially related to delinquency, physical aggression, and covert behavior. Because African American boys are overrepresented in the worst neighborhoods in inner cities, it is highly plausible that these environments rather than ethnicity are implicated in the development of delinquency. This is borne out by regression analyses (reported in Loeber et al., 1998) showing that ethnicity did not explain delinquency once other child factors, family factors, and neighborhood factors were taken into account. It should be noted that bad neighborhood was less strongly associated with a high ADHD score, covert behavior, substance use, and depressed mood and was not related to shy/withdrawn behavior.

A few risk factors were differentially associated with internalizing problems: Lack of guilt was more related to shy/withdrawn behavior than to depressed mood, whereas the opposite applied to physical punishment, which was related to depressed mood but not to shy/withdrawn behavior.

Another criterion to evaluate a general theory of problem behavior is the degree to which risk factors for pairs of problem behavior were interchangeable or not, suggesting similar forms of influences on several outcomes. The results showed that risk factors for substance use were largely but not fully a subset of the risk factors for delinquency. Similarly, the risk factors for depressed mood (and shy/withdrawn behavior) were largely but not fully a subset of the risk factors for conduct problems, covert behavior (two of the three samples), physical aggression, and a high ADHD score.

On the other hand, risk factors for substance use were largely *different* from risk factors for physical aggression, covert behavior, and conduct problems. There was least overlap between risk factors for substance use and those associated with a high ADHD score. Finally, we found considerable overlap among the risk factors for the following pairs of outcomes: delinquency and conduct problems, delinquency and physical aggression, delinquency and covert behavior, and delinquency and a high ADHD score.

Multiproblem boys

Clinicians, parole officers, and school psychologists rarely base their decisions on relationships between risk factors and outcomes. Instead, they attempt to establish which type of intervention can be best applied to which kinds of youth. They often are particularly concerned about multiproblem youth because of the complexities of the presenting problems and the risk these youth incur for poor outcomes in the long run. Part of the professionals' decisions is influenced by what they know about factors that have shaped these youth in becoming multiproblem children. Certainly, those professionals who are interested in devising preventive interventions want to know what are the most important factors that can explain the emergence of this group among all youth in a particular age group.

We investigated the extent to which risk factors that applied to multiproblem boys also applied to boys with fewer problems, and we summarize the results here. We saw that multiproblem boys were best predicted by sets of risk factors in the domains of child, family, and, to a lesser extent, macro variables. Among the child variables, the most powerful risk factors were lack of guilt, HIA problems, low achievement (based on parent, boy, and teacher ratings or, according to the

CAT score, the youngest and middle samples), poor communication (middle and oldest samples), anxiety (middle and oldest samples), and, slightly less strongly, old for grade. Of these, the following survived in multivariate analyses: lack of guilt and HIA problems (all three samples), followed by low achievement and anxiety (in two samples).

Of the family factors, univariate analyses showed that the following factors were associated with multiproblem boys: poor supervision, boy not involved in family activities, unhappy parents, parent substance use problems, parent anxiety/depression, and father behavior problems. In addition, several risk factors in the middle and oldest samples were associated with multiproblem boys: poor communication, physical punishment, low reinforcement, and parental disagreement about discipline. However, only the following family factors survived in the multivariate analyses: poor parent–boy communication, parent anxiety/depression, and high parental stress (all in two samples). In addition, parent antisocial attitude and bad neighborhood (parent rating) contributed in the youngest sample only.

Finally, only a few macro variables were associated at the bivariate level with multiproblem boys: low socioeconomic status, family on welfare, and African American ethnicity (two samples). With only two exceptions (bad neighborhood in the youngest sample and a poorly educated mother in the oldest sample), the macro factors were not important independently of the child and family factors. Remarkably, most of the factors that accounted for multiproblem boys also accounted for boys with fewer problems.

Directions for further research

The present research was cross-sectional, with age comparisons being limited to comparisons between the three grade samples. There is an obvious need to expand the analyses to include longitudinal data (which in the meantime have become available on these samples). Specifically, we need to know more about the developmental sequencing of problem behaviors as they unfold over time. Three aspects require further study. First, we need to determine whether developmental sequences among problem behaviors occur at rates higher than can be expected by chance alone. Second, we need to explore further which problem behaviors alter the probability of onset *and* the course of other problem behaviors, and whether this pattern applies across different age groups. Examples are the relationship between depressed mood and delinquency or substance use and the relationship between attention deficit/hyperactivity and the emergence of externalizing *and* internalizing problems. Third, since many youth show problem behavior at some time during childhood or adolescence, researchers need to shift their attention away from these "normal" forms of deviancy to focus, instead, on persisting problem behaviors. Longitudinal data are essential for researchers to distinguish between youths with incidental problem behaviors and those whose problems persist or recur over time.

Another neglected area is the interrelationship between risk factors. There is no doubt that many risk factors are correlated, with many youth being exposed to multiple risk factors. More knowledge is required about the concentration of risk factors in the neighborhoods of inner cities. Thus, we see a need for future studies to explore further the contrasting patterns of risk factors in better versus worse neighborhoods and to describe how such patterns accumulate as youth grow up in different settings. In addition, it is essential to understand more clearly protective factors that either prevent youth from escalating to serious, multiple problem behaviors or help account for the apparently temporary nature of the problems.

Knowledge about risk factors that apply to multiple outcomes is relevant for early interventions because the modification of risk factors that predict several outcomes will have a greater impact on child psychopathology and maladjustment than the modification of risk factors that predict only a single outcome. Awareness of risk factors that apply to specific outcomes is important to sharpen interventions in order to make them more applicable to the outcomes of greatest concern.

References

Achenbach, T. M. (1985). *Assessment and taxonomy of child and adolescent psychopathology*. Beverly Hills, CA: Sage.

Achenbach, T. M., Conners, C. K., Quay, H. C., Verhulst, F. C., & Howell, C. T. (1989). Replication of empirically derived syndromes as a basis for taxonomy of child/adolescent psycho-pathology. *Journal of Abnormal Child Psychology, 17*, 299–320.

Achenbach, T. M., & Edelbrock, C. S. (1979). The child behavior profile. II. Boys aged 12–16 and girls aged 6–11 and 12–16. *Journal of Consulting and Clinical Psychology, 47,* 223–233.

Achenbach, T. M., & Edelbrock, C. S. (1983). *Manual for the Child Behavior Checklist and Revised Child Behavior Profile.* Burlington: University of Vermont, Department of Psychiatry.

Agresti, A. (1990). *Categorical data analysis.* New York: Wiley.

Amdur, R. L. (1989). Testing causal models of delinquency: A methodological critique. *Criminal Justice and Behavior, 16,* 35–62.

American Psychiatric Association (1987). *Diagnostic and statistical manual of mental disorders (DSM-III-R).* (3rd ed. revised). Washington, DC: American Psychiatric Association.

American Psychiatric Association (1994). *Diagnostic and statistical manual of mental disorders (DSM-IV).* Washington, DC: American Psychiatric Association.

Barnes, H., & Olson, D. H. (1982). Parent–adolescent communication. In D. H. Olson, H. McCubbin, H. Barnes, A. Larsen, M. Muxen, & W. Wilson (Eds.), *Family inventories* (pp. 55–57). St Paul: University of Minnesota Press.

Cohen, J. (1983). The costs of dichotomization. *Applied Psychological Measurement, 7,* 249–253.

Conger, R. D., Patterson, G. R., and Ge, X. (1995). It takes two to replicate: A mediational model for the impact of parents' stress on adolescent adjustment. *Child Development, 66,* 80–97.

Costello, A., Edelbrock, C., Kalas, R., Kessler, R., & Klaric, S. H. (1987). *The Diagnostic Interview Schedule for Children, Parent Version (revised).* Worcester: University of Massachusetts Medical Center.

Costello, E. J., & Angold, A. (1988). Scales to assess child and adolescent depression: Checklists, screens and nets. *Journal of the American Academy of Child and Adolescent Psychiatry, 27,* 726–737.

Donovan, J. E. (1996). Problem behavior theory and the explanation of adolescent marijuana use. *Journal of Drug Issues, 21,* 379–404.

Donovan, J. E., Jessor, R., & Costa, F. M. (1988). Syndrome of problem behavior in adolescence: A replication. *Journal of Consulting and Clinical Psychology, 56,* 762–765.

Edelbrock, C., & Achenbach, T. (1984). The teacher version of the Child Behavior Profile: I. Boys aged six through eleven. *Journal of Consulting and Clinical Psychology, 52,* 207–217.

Elliott, D. S., Huizinga, D., & Ageton, S. S. (1985) *Explaining delinquency and drug use.* Beverly Hills, CA: Sage.

Farrington, D. P., & Loeber, R. L. (1989). Relative improvement over chance

(RIOC) and phi as measures of predictive efficiency and strength of association in 2 × 2 tables. *Journal of Quantitative Criminology, 5,* 201–213.

Farrington, D. P., Loeber, R., Elliott, D. S., Hawkins, J. D., Kandel, D. B., Klein, M. W., McCord, J., Rowe, D. C., & Tremblay, R. E. (1990). Advancing knowledge about the onset of delinquency and crime. In B. B. Lahey & A. E. Kazdin (Eds.), *Advances in clinical child psychology* (Vol. 13, pp. 283–342). New York: Plenum.

Farrington, D. P., Loeber, R., & Van Kammen, W. B. (1990). Long-term criminal outcomes of hyperactivity-impulsivity-attention deficit and conduct problems in childhood. In L. Robins & M. Rutter (Eds.), *Straight and devious pathways from childhood to adulthood* (pp. 62–81). New York: Cambridge University Press.

Farrington, D. P., & West, D. J. (1993). Criminal, penal and life histories of chronic offenders: Risk and protective factors and early identification. *Criminal Behaviour and Mental Health, 3,* 492–523.

Fleiss, J. L. (1981). *Statistical methods for rates and proportions.* (2nd ed.). New York: Wiley.

Frick, P. J., Lahey, B. B., Loeber, R., Tannenbaum, L., Van Horn, Y., Christ, M. A. G., Hart, E. A., & Hanson, K. (1993). Oppositional defiant disorder and conduct disorder: A meta-analytic review of factor analyses and cross-validation in a clinic sample. *Clinical Psychology Review, 13,* 319–340.

Hinshaw, S. P. (1987). On the distinction between attentional deficit/hyperactivity and conduct problems/aggression in child psychopathology. *Psychological Bulletin, 101,* 443–463.

Hirschi, T., & Gottfredson, M. (1983). Age and the explanation of crime. *American Journal of Sociology, 89,* 552–584.

Hoffman, M. S. (Ed.). (1991). *The world almanac and book of facts, 1992.* New York: Pharos.

Hollingshead, A. B. (1975). *Four factor index of social status.* Unpublished manuscript. New Haven, CT.

Huizinga, D., Loeber, R., & Thornberry, T. (1993). Longitudinal study of delinquency, drug use, sexual activity, and pregnancy among children and youth in three cities. *Public Health Reports: Journal of the U.S. Public Health Service, 108,* Supplement 1, 90–96.

Jessor, R., Donovan, J. E., & Costa, F. M. (1991). *Beyond adolescence. Problem behavior and young adult development.* Cambridge: Cambridge University Press.

Jessor, R., & Jessor, S. L. (1977). *Problem behavior and psychosocial development.* New York: Academic Press.

Kaplan, H. B. (1980). *Deviant behavior in defense of self.* New York: Academic Press.

Loeber, R. (1982). The stability of antisocial and delinquent child behavior. *Child Development, 53,* 1431–1446.

Loeber, R. (1985). Patterns and development of antisocial child behavior. In G. J. Whitehurst (Ed.), *Annals of child development* (Vol. 2, pp. 77–116). Greenwich, CT: JAI Press.

Loeber, R. (1988). Natural histories of conduct problems, delinquency, and associated substance use. In B. B. Lahey & A. E. Kazdin (Eds.), *Advances in clinical child psychology* (Vol. 11, pp. 73–124). New York: Plenum.

Loeber, R., Brinthaupt, V. P., & Green, S. M. (1990). Attention deficits, impulsivity, and hyperactivity with or without conduct problems: Relationship to delinquency and unique contextual factors. In R. J. McMahon & R. DeV. Peters (Eds.), *Behavior disorders of adolescence: Research, intervention, and policy in clinical and school settings* (pp. 39–61). New York: Plenum.

Loeber, R., Farrington, D. P., Stouthamer-Loeber, M., & Van Kammen, W. B. (1998). *Antisocial behavior and mental health problems: Explanatory factors in childhood and adolescence.* Mawhaw, NJ: Erlbaum.

Loeber, R., Green, S. M., Keenan, K., & Lahey, B. B. (1995). Which boys will fare worse? Early predictors of the onset of conduct disorder in a six-year longitudinal study. *Journal of the American Academy of Child and Adolescent Psychiatry, 34,* 499–509.

Loeber, R., Green, S. M., Lahey, B. B., Christ, M. A. G., & Frick, P. J. (1992). Developmental sequences in the age of onset of disruptive child behaviors. *Journal of Child and Family Studies, 1,* 21–41.

Loeber, R., & Keenan, K. (1994). The interaction between conduct disorder and its comorbid conditions: Effects of age and gender. *Clinical Psychology Review, 14,* 497–523.

Loeber, R., & Schmaling, K. (1985a). Empirical evidence for overt and covert patterns of antisocial conduct problems. *Journal of Abnormal Child Psychology, 13,* 337–352.

Loeber, R., & Schmaling, K. (1985b). The utility of differentiating between mixed and pure forms of antisocial child behavior. *Journal of Abnormal Child Psychology, 13,* 315–336.

Loeber, R., & Stouthamer-Loeber, M. (1986). Family factors as correlates and predictors of juvenile conduct problems and delinquency. In N. Morris & M. Tonry (Eds.), *Crime and justice: An annual review of research* (Vol. 7, pp. 29–149). Chicago: University of Chicago Press.

Loeber, R., Stouthamer-Loeber, M., Van Kammen, W. B., & Farrington, D. P. (1989). Development of a new measure of self-reported antisocial behavior for young children: Prevalence and reliability. In M. Klein (Ed.), *Cross-national research in self-reported crime and delinquency* (pp. 203–255). Dordrecht, the Netherlands: Kluwer-Nijhoff.

Loeber, R., Stouthamer-Loeber, M., Van Kammen, W. B., & Farrington, D. P. (1991). Initiation, escalation and desistance in juvenile offending and their correlates. *Journal of Criminal Law and Criminology, 82*, 36–82.

Loeber, R., Wung, P., Keenan, K., Giroux, B., Stouthamer-Loeber, M., & Van Kammen, W. B. (1993). Developmental pathways in disruptive child behavior. *Development and Psychopathology, 5*, 101–132.

McCord, J. (1990). Problem behaviors. In S. S. Feldman & G. R. Elliott (Eds.), *At the threshold: The developing adolescent* (pp. 441–430). Cambridge, MA: Harvard University Press.

McGee, L., & Newcomb, M. D. (1992). General deviance syndrome: Expanded hierarchical evaluations at four ages from early adolescence to adulthood. *Journal of Consulting and Clinical Psychology, 60*, 766–776.

Magnusson, D., & Bergman, L. R. (1988). Individual and variable based approaches to longitudinal research on early risk factors. In M. Rutter (Ed.), *Studies of psychosocial risk* (pp. 45–61). Cambridge: Cambridge University Press.

Martin, C. S., Earleywine, M., Blackson, T. C., Vanyukov, M. M., Moss, H. B., & Tarter, R. E. (1994). Aggressivity, inattention, hyperactivity, and impulsivity in boys at high and low risk for substance abuse. *Journal of Abnormal Child Psychology, 22*, 177–204.

Marttunen, M. J., Aro, H. M., Henriksson, M. M., & Lonnqvist, J. K. (1994). Antisocial behavior in adolescent suicide. *Acta Psychiatrica Scandinavica, 89*, 167–173.

Osgood, D. W., Johnston, L. D., O'Malley, P. M., & Bachman, J. G. (1988). The generality of deviance in late adolescence and early adulthood. *American Sociological Review, 53*, 81–93.

Patterson, G. R. (1982). *A social learning approach, Vol. 3: Coercive family process*. Eugene, OR: Castalia.

Patterson, G. R., Reid, J. B., & Dishion, T. J. (1992). *Antisocial boys*. Eugene, OR: Castalia.

Pulkkinen, L. (1983). Search for alternatives to aggression in Finland. In A. P. Goldstein & M. Segall (Eds.), *Aggression in global perspective* (pp. 104–144). New York: Pergamon.

Robins, L. N. (1966). *Deviant children grown up*. Baltimore: Williams & Wilkins.

Rosenthal, R., & Rubin, D. B. (1982). A simple, general purpose display of magnitude of experimental effect. *Journal of Educational Psychology, 74*, 166–169.

Stouthamer-Loeber, M., Loeber, R., Farrington, D. P., Zhang, Q., Van Kammen, W. B., & Maguin, G. (1993). The double edge of protective and risk factors for delinquency: Interrelations and developmental patterns. *Development and Psychopathology, 5*, 683–701.

Stouthamer-Loeber, M., Loeber, R., & Thomas, C. (1992). Caretakers seeking help for boys with disruptive and delinquent child behavior. *Comprehensive Mental Health Care, 2*, 159–178.

Thornberry, T., Lizotte, A. J., Krohn, M. D., Farnworth, M., & Jang, S. J. (1994). Delinquent peers, beliefs, and delinquent behavior: A longitudinal test of interaction theory. *Criminology, 32*, 601–637.

Van Kammen, W., Loeber, R., & Stouthamer-Loeber, M. (1991). Substance use and its relationship to conduct problems and delinquency in young boys. *Journal of Youth and Adolescence, 20*, 399–414.

White, H. R., & Labouvie, E. W. (1994). Generality versus specificity of problem behavior: Psychological and functional differences. *Journal of Drug Issues, 24*, 55–74.

Wolfgang, M. E., Figlio, R. M., & Sellin, T. (1972). *Delinquency in a birth cohort.* Chicago: University of Chicago Press.

Wolfgang, M., Figlio, R. M., Tracy, P. E., & Singer, S. I. (1985). *The national survey of crime severity.* Washington, DC: U.S. Government Printing Office.

5

Adult outcomes of adolescent drug use: A comparison of process-oriented and incremental analyses

Helene Raskin White, Marsha E. Bates, and Erich Labouvie

Introduction

Many longitudinal studies of drug use began in the 1970s with cohorts of adolescents (Kandel, 1980; White, 1996). Participants in these studies are now adults, allowing researchers to identify the impact of adolescent drug use on adult role functioning and health. Recent work in the area of adolescent substance use and its consequences has begun to focus on developmental processes and recognizes the need to examine long-term outcomes beyond adolescence. Since the emergence of a renewed interest in a lifespan developmental perspective in the 1960s, views of human development have evolved considerably. Earlier descriptions of change patterns as universal, invariant, irreversible, and unidirectional have lost ground to the recognition that there is wide variability in human development throughout the entire life course. This recognition has contributed to a growing interest in individual differences in the paths and trajectories of human development from childhood to adulthood (Campos, Hinden, & Gerhardt, 1995; Magnusson, 1996).

The need to be able to differentiate between the contemporary and cumulative impact of drug use on developmental outcomes has led to the implementation of longitudinal designs that cover extended time periods and incorporate more than two measurement occasions. How-

The writing of this chapter was supported, in part, by grants from the National Institute on Drug Abuse (DA/AA #3395) and the Alcoholic Beverage Medical Research Foundation.

ever, the techniques for analyzing longitudinal data have lagged behind (see Chapter 2 in this volume), and one of the foremost issues confronting researchers today is how to best analyze change (e.g., Collins & Horn, 1991). Because several longitudinal studies have collected data at more than two points in time, it becomes possible to systematically compare traditional techniques with newer ones that are more explicitly focused on intraindividual change (Rogosa, Brandt, & Zimowski, 1982; Rogosa & Willett, 1985). In the past, research on outcomes of drug use was based almost exclusively on an incremental approach that emphasized changes in individual differences rather than differences in intraindividual changes (Francis, Fletcher, Stuebing, Davidson, & Thompson, 1991). There is a growing recognition, however, that greater attention needs to be directed to individual growth curves and to the description and explanation of differences in intraindividual change (Francis et al., 1991; Labouvie & Ruetsch, 1994; Rogosa et al., 1982; Rogosa & Willett, 1985; see also Chapter 2 in this volume). Thus, it is not surprising that process-oriented techniques based on the concept of individual growth curves have gained in popularity, although the extent to which they may contribute to a better understanding of the behavioral outcomes of intraindividual change has not been well established. Therefore, we think it is useful if longitudinal data are used to compare both approaches systematically. In this chapter we attempt to compare and contrast incremental and process-oriented analyses of longitudinal drug use data to obtain information about possible long-term outcomes of adolescent use.

Incremental versus process-oriented analysis of longitudinal data

Whenever a longitudinal study entails the repeated assessment of the same individuals on more than two measurement occasions, it is possible to analyze the resulting data using either an incremental or a process-oriented approach (Francis et al., 1991). The traditional incremental analysis of longitudinal data is consistent with the notion that individual differences in any characteristic or behavior at time T are best predicted by differences in other variables assessed either concurrently or at time $T-1$. Thus, a given series of occasions is used to divide the total time interval spanned by a longitudinal study into a sequence of time segments, and the analysis is aimed at identifying relationships among individual differences within and across adjacent time points. The conceptual basis for this approach offers several advantages. First, it does not require the developmental changes of interest to be quantitative and relatively continuous in nature. Nor does it require that relationships between variables, and therefore the underlying mechanisms, remain relatively constant and homogeneous throughout the total time interval studied. Instead, developmental changes may be qualitative, allowing for the emergence of novel or different behaviors across time, or they may be relatively discontinuous in either level or rate of change. As a consequence, the incremental analysis of longitudinal data is most appropriate when one is studying transitional periods with potential turning points that are likely to generate novel, rapid, or relatively discontinuous changes.

The disadvantages of an incremental approach are most evident when it is applied to the study of change that is quantitative and relatively continuous in both level and rate of change. By dividing the total time interval into a sequence of time segments and identifying relationships between individual differences across adjacent time points, this approach cannot provide a description of individual trajectories across the total time interval. It may also fail to separate shorter-term intraindividual fluctuations from longer-term intraindividual trends. Although the two types of intraindividual change may be governed by different processes and relate differently to a given set of predictors, the empirical relationships identified by an incremental analysis will yield a confounding of rather than a separation of those processes and relationships.

The process-oriented analysis of longitudinal data represents the mirror image of the incremental approach in terms of its advantages and disadvantages. Conceptually, it is based on the notion that the changes of interest are quantitative and relatively continuous in nature. Observations of an individual across several measurement occasions are assumed to represent manifestations of a single growth curve and, thus, provide a description of individual trajectories of change across the total time interval studied. Furthermore, it is possible to decompose trajectories into trends by expressing them, for instance, as a linear combination of orthogonal polynomials (Cohen & Cohen, 1983; Von Eye, 1992). Each polynomial represents a different base trend. The zero-order polynomial delineates the average level across the total time period studied; the first-order polynomial represents the linear trend indicating the rate and direction of change (increases and decreases across the total time period); the second-order polynomial represents the quadratic trend and assesses change in the rate of change (deceleration or acceleration in change); the third-order polynomial represents the cubic trend and indicates changes in deceleration or acceleration, and so on.[1] In general, lower-order trends (i.e., average level, linear trend) are assumed to capture differences in longer-term intraindividual trends. In comparison, higher-order trends (quadratic, cubic, etc.) are more likely to represent differences in shorter-term fluctuations and are, therefore, often ignored.

As one might expect, process-oriented analyses are inconsistent with the notion that the changes of interest are qualitative in nature, leading to the emergence of novel behaviors or characteristics. Disadvantages of this approach also arise when the quantitative changes of interest are nonmonotonic and/or relatively discontinuous in either level or rate of change. In those cases, failure to incorporate higher-order trends into the description and analysis of individual trajectories is likely to yield a misleading and oversimplified picture of the phenomena under study. Before applying the process-oriented and incremental approaches to the study of outcomes of drug use, we review other studies of drug use outcomes.

Longitudinal studies of drug use outcomes in adulthood

Direct intrapersonal consequences of acute drug intoxication are potentially complex but are relatively easy to identify. They can be classified in terms of impairments in cognitive function, biological function, psychomotor skills, affect regulation, and motivational states (Anthony & Petronis, 1991; Grabowski, 1984; Klatsky, 1987). Such consequences and complications of acute intoxication are immediate and visible (e.g., auto accidents, drug-related medical emergencies and arrests, drug overdoses) and, thus, have warranted and received attention. The developmentally subtle and cumulative effects of longer-term use are more difficult to document. Such deficits may result from, but extend beyond, episodes of acute intoxication and may accumulate as the result of either temporarily heavy use or prolonged use that is less intense (Pandina, Labouvie, White, Johnson, & Bates, 1994).

Evidence for deficits in personal and social functioning due to drugs has been derived primarily from clinical and experimental observations of the acute effects of intoxication. Clinical cases, however, represent only a small percentage of the users who have progressed beyond experimental use. Support for the generalization of negative outcomes of drug use to the day-to-day functioning of even relatively chronic and intensive users (in nonclinical populations) remains largely inferred even for widely used substances such as alcohol (e.g., Parsons, 1986). The need to understand both contemporary and cumulative outcomes of different drug use histories on individual development is critical and, at this point, empirical evidence is relatively sparse (Pandina et al., 1994).

Despite methodological limitations, some data have begun to suggest that early and relatively intensive psychoactive substance use, or steady increases in use over time, may affect developmental outcomes by serving to either accelerate or delay entry into adult roles, constrain educational attainments, perpetuate and facilitate the expression of personal and mental health difficulties, impair physical health, and foster the expression of antisocial behavior (Erickson, Adlaf, Murray, & Smart, 1987; Hansell & White, 1991; Kandel, Davies, Karus, & Yamaguchi, 1986a; Kandel & Yamaguchi, 1987; Mensch & Kandel, 1998; Miller, Leonard, & Windle, 1991; Newcomb, 1996; Newcomb & Bentler, 1985, 1986, 1987, 1988; Newcomb, Bentler, & Collins, 1986; Newcomb, Scheier, & Bentler, 1993; Stacy & Newcomb, 1995; Stein, Newcomb, & Bentler, 1987a, 1987b; Temple et al., 1991; Yamaguchi & Kandel, 1985). However, many of the findings from existing studies are contradictory. For example, early drinking problems (Horwitz & White, 1991), as well as early marijuana use (Yamaguchi & Kandel, 1985), can lead to postponement of marriage and/or parenthood as well as marital dissolution. On the other hand, early use of illicit drugs has predicted early marriage and cohabitation (Newcomb & Bentler, 1985) and premarital pregnancy (Mensch & Kandel, 1992; Yamaguchi & Kandel, 1987). In addition, high school drug use has predicted failure to graduate, reduced involvement in continued education, and earlier work force involvement in young adulthood (Newcomb & Bentler, 1985, 1986). Yet, most studies have found no effect of early drug use on later career status (Newcomb & Bentler, 1988; White, Aidala, & Zablocki,

1989), although drug use has been related to job turnover and loss (Kandel & Davies, 1990; Kandel & Yamaguchi, 1987).

Studies that have examined the longitudinal associations between drug use and criminal behavior have also yielded mixed findings. Stacy and Newcomb (1995) found that adolescent drug use predicted adult criminality, whereas Kandel, Simcha-Fagan, and Davies (1986b) found that adolescent drug use predicted adult delinquency only for females. For both sexes, however, drug use in the period between adolescence and young adulthood predicted theft, but not aggressive delinquency, in young adulthood. Conversely, Kaplan and Damphousse (1995) found that early drug use did predict later aggression for both males and females. Similarly, some studies have found that early alcohol use predicts later aggressive behavior (e.g., Dembo et al., 1991), whereas others have not (e.g., White & Hansell, 1996).

Data regarding the effects of drug use on psychological distress in nonclinical samples also have been inconsistent (Castro, Newcomb, & Bentler, 1988; Deykin, Levy, & Wells, 1987; Farrow, Rees, & Worthington-Roberts, 1987; Hansell & White, 1991; Johnson & Kaplan, 1990; Kandel et al., 1986a; Newcomb & Bentler, 1986, 1987, 1988; White, Hansell, & Vali, 1993). Newcomb et al. (1993) identified both positive and negative effects of level of, and linear increases in, adolescent alcohol use on adult mental health. Hansell and White (1991) found that early drug use led to increases in psychological distress in late but not early adolescence, yet White and colleagues (1993) found no increases in psychological distress as a result of early alcohol use from adolescence to young adulthood. A study of high-risk youth reported that marijuana use affected subsequent personal difficulties (Dembo, Williams, Schmeidler, & Wothke, 1993). A reciprocal effect of drug use and psychological distress was reported by Johnson and Kaplan (1990). They found that early psychological problems led to drug use, and drug use then led to subsequent increases in psychological problems.

The physical illnesses associated with chronic, excessive alcohol use are well known (Driver & Swann, 1987; Klatsky, 1987; Kurata & Haile, 1984; Urbano-Marquez et al., 1989). Among adults, prolonged, heavy alcohol use increases the risk of diseases such as cirrhosis and cancer (for a review see Klatsky, Armstrong, & Kipp, 1990). At the same time, other research suggests that moderate levels of alcohol use can have beneficial effects on other health conditions, such as coronary heart disease and stress, even among young adults (Andreasson, Allebeck, & Romelsjo, 1988; DeLabry et al., 1992; Klatsky, 1987; Lange & Kinnunen, 1987; Turner, Bennett, & Hernandez, 1981). A recent examination of a normal population sample of youth indicated that early intensive alcohol use directly predicted subsequent physical impairments (White et al., 1993). On the other hand, Johnson and Kaplan (1990) found no effect of adolescent drug use on later physical health. In another study, drug use in late adolescence was found to have an indirect negative effect on adult health status through its direct effect on unhealthy life-style behaviors later in adolescence and young adulthood and by causing a decrease in physical hardiness during young adulthood (Newcomb & Bentler, 1987). (For summaries of the possible health consequences of adolescent substance use, see Arria, Tarter, & Van Thiel, 1991, for alcohol; Farrow et al., 1987, and Nicholi, 1983, for marijuana; and Nicholi, 1984, and White & Bates, 1993, for cocaine.)

In sum, although several longitudinal studies have begun to address the long-term outcomes of drug use in nonclinical samples, the existing evidence is inconclusive. All of the previously cited studies utilized incremental analyses with outcome levels at some point in adulthood as dependent variables and drug use levels at some point in adolescence as independent variables. Differences between studies in the strength of the observed relationship between dependent and independent variables may, therefore, be due in part to differences in the age/time interval separating the assessment of dependent and independent variables (e.g., Cohen, 1991). In view of the lack of process-oriented analyses of drug use outcomes, the main purpose of this study is to examine the utility of modeling intraindividual trajectories of drug use as predictors of adult outcome levels of physical and mental health, substance abuse, criminal behavior, and marital, parenting, and occupational status, and to compare the results with those obtained with the more traditional incremental approach. In previous studies, growth curves were used to model change in dependent variables (e.g., Bates & Labouvie, 1995; Johnson, Arria, Borges, Ialongo, & Anthony, 1995) and in both independent and dependent variables (e.g., Bates, White, & Hansell, 1995; Francis et al., 1991). In the present study, we examine the utility of characterizing adolescent to adult drug use behaviors as continuous growth curves and using these growth curves as independent variables to predict differences in adult outcomes.

Method

Design and sample

Eligible adolescents were recruited through a random sampling of telephone numbers covering all but the five counties of New Jersey most distant from the test site. The procedure used was designed to take into account unlisted numbers and differences in population densities associated with different telephone interchanges. The procedure was estimated to reach 95% of all households in the specified geographic area. Between 1979 and 1981, successive rounds of telephone calls were made to fill specified quotas of 200–225 males and females aged 12, 15, or 18 years. An initial anonymous telephone interview served to identify households with eligible adolescents and to obtain demographic information. Following the telephone survey, field interviewers visited prospective subjects at their homes to gather additional demographic data, interview parents, obtain informed consent, and enroll adolescents in the study. To ensure equal representation of the sexes within age groups, potential subjects were not contacted by field interviewers once the target number for each age–sex group was reached. Overall, 46% of those asked to participate enrolled in the study. Demographic comparisons of nonparticipants and participants on variables obtained in the initial telephone interview indicated that higher levels of family income and parental education are somewhat overrepresented among the sample of participants compared to refusers. In spite of these initial biases, the sample was heterogeneous and similar to the population of the State of New Jersey at that time in terms of family income and religion (Bureau of the Census, 1981). This sample is most representative of white, working- and middle-class youth living in a metropolitan area of the eastern United States. (For more detail on sample and design, see Pandina, Labouvie, & White, 1984.) Patterns of drug use in this sample are comparable to those reported in national representative samples for same-age peers living in the northeastern region of the United States (Johnston, O'Malley, & Bachman, 1996).

The subjects were tested initially between 1979 and 1981 (Time 1,

T1) at the ages of 12, 15, and 18 ($N = 1,380$). These subjects returned 3 years later in 1982–1984 (Time 2, T2), again in 1985–1987 (Time 3, T3), and finally in 1992–1994 (Time 4, T4). Ninety one percent of the original participants returned at T4. A comparison between the subjects who were retested and those who dropped out indicated minimal differences in the extent of substance use at T1. For the purposes of this study, we used subjects from only the two oldest cohorts, ages 28 and 31 at T4, who were tested on all four measurement occasions ($N = 789$), because the youngest cohort, age 25 at T4, was not old enough to allow assessment of all of the adult outcomes investigated here.

Measures

Drug use intensity. For each of eight substances (marijuana, cocaine, psychedelics, heroin, and nonprescription use of sedatives, tranquilizers, stimulants, and analgesics), we computed the product of typical quantity (8-point scale ranging from no units to more than six units) and frequency within the past year (8-point scale ranging from no use to every day). These eight scales were summed, and the log ($+1$) was then used (in order to reduce skewness) to represent total drug use at each of the four points in time.

Health. Overall level of physical health at T4 was operationalized by summing the presence of 55 illness symptoms in various areas of the body, including the heart, lungs, skin, ears, eyes, nose, and throat, and the skeletal, digestive, urinary, reproductive, and nervous systems (White et al., 1993). Symptoms highly associated with psychological distress, such as sleep problems and eating disorders, were eliminated from the analysis. Participants were asked whether or not each symptom was experienced within the last 3 years.

Psychological distress at T4 was assessed by the Global Severity Index (GSI) from the Johns Hopkins Symptom Checklist (SCL-90-R) (Derogatis, 1977). The GSI is the best single SCL-90-R indicator of current level of psychological distress that combines information on the number and intensity of mental health symptoms across nine primary symptom dimensions: Somatization, Obsession/Compulsion, Interpersonal Sensitivity, Depression, Anxiety, Hostility, Phobic Anxiety, Paranoid Ideation, and Psychoticism. Derogatis (1977) reported high internal consistency across the primary symptom dimensions (mean alpha = .84), and we found similar internal consistency in this sample (alpha = .85).

T4 dependence on alcohol and other drugs was measured by a self-report inventory of negative consequences and symptoms associated with the use of alcohol, marijuana, cocaine, and other drugs. Items were selected that corresponded to the types of problems included in the DSM-IV diagnosis of substance use dependence (American Psychiatric Association, 1994). Negative consequences were assigned to one of the seven criteria used for diagnosis. For each drug, subjects received a score of 0 to 7, depending on the number of criteria they met. For drug dependence, the maximum score for marijuana, cocaine, and other drugs was chosen.

Adult role functioning. At T4, subjects were dichotomized into married (= 1) and not married (single, divorced, separated, and cohabiting) (= 0). (Widowed subjects, $N = 3$ at T4, were excluded from the marital status analyses.) Subjects were also dichotomized into those with any children (= 1) and those with none (= 0). Occupational status at T4 was assessed on a 5-point ordinal scale (unemployed = 0, unskilled labor = 1, skilled labor = 3, clerical and small business = 3, and professional = 4). (Unemployed women with children were eliminated from this analysis.) T4 criminal behavior was measured as the sum of the frequency of engaging in 15 criminal behaviors ranging from evading payment and simple assault to grand theft and armed robbery.

Control variables. Sex (coded 1 for males and 2 for females) and age at T1 (15 and 18 years) were controlled in the analyses. We also controlled for highest grade completed (5-point scale ranging from less than high school to postgraduate degree). In addition, we controlled for alcohol use at T4, which was measured as the log (+ 1) for the sum of quantity times frequency for beer, wine, and hard liquor. Similarly, we controlled for the quantity of cigarettes smoked at T4 in the analyses for physical health outcomes. For the analyses of physical health, psychological distress, criminal behavior, and alcohol and drug dependence, we controlled for the same behavior at T3[2] using the same measure described earlier (except that the criminal behavior scale at T3 had only 9 of the 15 items used at T4). None of the control variables was correlated with each other highly enough to suggest multicollinearity problems (i.e., all $r <$ absolute .35).

Analyses

Growth curve approach. The modeling of individual growth curves was based on the method of orthogonal polynomials (Cohen & Cohen, 1983). Both normative and individual patterns of intraindividual change in drug use intensity were described as composites of: (1) differences in average levels across the full time interval [AL = ((T1 + T2 + T3 + 4) / 4)], (2) differences in linear trends from T1 to T4 [LT = $(-.57*T1) + (-.26*T2) + (.05*T3) + (.78*T4)$], and (3) differences in quadratic trends representing deceleration or acceleration in change in drug use during each test interval [QT = $(.58*T1) + (-.29*T2) + (-.66*T3) + (.37*T4)$].[3] The coefficients for the orthonormalized trends were generated by a General Linear Model (GLM) program for repeated measures analyses of variance (SAS, 1990). These coefficients take into account the unequal spacing of test occasions.[4]

Figure 5.1 presents the three trends in drug use for the whole sample, as well as the average drug frequency score on each measurement occasion. Note that the average trend (AL) is represented as a constant level, the linear trend (LT) is represented by a straight line, and the quadratic trend (QT) is indicated by a U-shaped curve. The linear trend was negative, which indicates that there was a net decline in overall drug use from T1 to T4. The quadratic trend was also negative, and the shape indicates that drug use peaked in the early 20s and then decreased.

A series of hierarchical regressions was used to examine T4 adult role functioning and health outcomes. Step 1 provided statistical tests for all main effects of control variables, and step 2 added the average, linear, and quadratic trends in drug use. Note that the correlations among these three trends were relatively low (absolute $r < .35$); thus, multicollinearity was not a problem.

Incremental approach. To assess incremental effects, we also conducted hierarchical regressions. In the first step, we regressed T4 adult role functioning and health outcomes on the control variables, as noted earlier. In the second step, we entered the total drug use variable at T3.

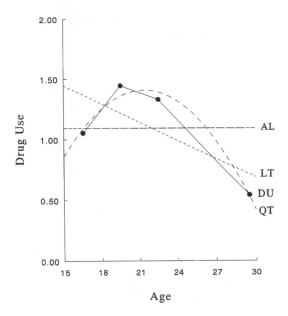

Figure 5.1 Actual drug use (DU) and trends (AL, LT, QT) for the total sample.

Results

Table 5.1 presents the results of two (sex) by two (cohort) analyses of variance for average level, linear trend, quadratic trend, and T3 drug use. Although males reported significantly higher average levels of drug use than females over the 13 years, the trends were the same for both sexes. For both males and females, the linear and quadratic trends were negative.

All the cohort differences in trends were significant. Those subjects who were age 28 compared to 31 at T4 reported lower average levels of use. Figure 5.2 shows cohort differences in linear trends compared to actual use levels. The younger subjects compared to the older subjects reported smaller linear decreases in use over time. However, this difference occurred because data collection began at age 15 for the younger subjects compared to age 18 for the older subjects, and drug use levels were lower at age 15 than at age 18. Therefore, if we had included drug use data for the older subjects at age 15, we would probably have seen

Table 5.1. *Sex, cohort, and sex by cohort interaction effects on average level, linear trend, quadratic trend, and T3 drug use (means presented)*

Drug use	Sex		Cohort		Sex × Cohort			
	Male	Female	Young	Old	YM	OM	YF	OF
AL	5.01	3.78*	3.9	4.91*	4.44	5.68	3.4	4.21
LT	−0.43	−0.54	−0.22	−.79*	−0.07	−0.85	−0.4	−0.74*
QT	−0.54	−0.44	−0.65	−.30*	−0.75	−0.29	−0.6	−0.3
Drug3	0.72	.37*	0.56	0.52	0.78	0.66	0.36	0.38

Note: AL = average level, LT = linear trend, QT = quadratic trend, Drug3 = overall drug use at T3, YM = young males, OM = old males, YF = young females, OF = old females.
*$p < .05$.

similar linear trends for both groups, although absolute levels were higher for the older than for the younger subjects. (See Chapter 2 in this volume for a discussion regarding the importance of timing when beginning a study.) Note that the average levels of drug use at ages 28 or 31 were comparable to those at age 15. The data indicated a larger negative quadratic trend for the younger compared to the older subjects. The shapes of these trends are presented in Figure 5.3. The sharper bend in the curve for the younger compared to the older subjects was again due to the difference in the age at the first measurement occasion.

The sex by cohort interactions were significant only for the linear trend indicating that females decreased drug use more than males in the younger but not the older cohort. Males had significantly higher levels of drug use than females at T3; however, there were no significant cohort main effects or sex by cohort interaction effects for T3 drug use.

Table 5.2 shows the results of the hierarchical regression analyses. Least squares regression analyses were used for all of the dependent variables except marital and parent status. For marital and parent status, we used logistic regression analyses. Significant changes in R^2 values between the nested models were assessed using the F-statistic. Significant improvements in the models for the logistic regression anal-

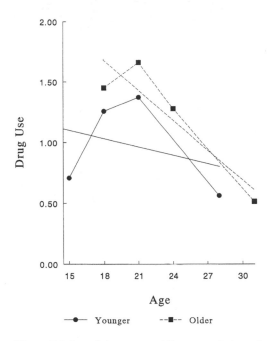

Figure 5.2 Actual drug use and linear trends by cohort.

yses were determined by a chi square test comparing the difference in chi square in relation to the difference in degrees of freedom between the two models.

As can be seen in Table 5.2, the results of the process-oriented approach indicated that drug use patterns over time significantly affected all outcomes except parent and occupational status and physical health symptoms. An examination of the beta weights for the individual predictors (not shown) indicated that the higher the average level of use over time, the greater the psychological distress and criminal behavior, the lower the likelihood of being married, and the higher the alcohol and drug dependence. In addition, smaller decreases in drug use over time (i.e., linear trends) predicted higher levels of psychological distress and criminal behavior, lower rates of marriage, and more alcohol and drug dependence. Finally, a significant, positive effect of quadratic trends was found for psychological health, criminal behavior, and alcohol and drug problems. These effects were consistent with corresponding effects of linear trends and implied that those individuals

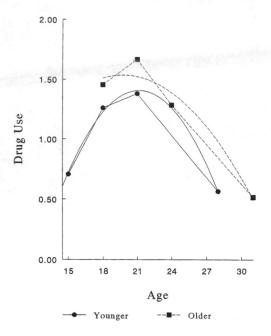

Figure 5.3 Actual drug use and quadratic trends by cohort.

Table 5.2. *Regression results for baseline, process-oriented (T1–T4), and incremental (T3) models (R² values presented)*

Outcomes	Baseline	Process-oriented	Incremental
Physical health	.27	.27	.27
Mental health	.28	.30*	.28
Criminal behavior	.19	.24*	.19
Occupational status	.12	.13	.12
Marital status	54.01	79.96*	58.36*
Parent status	145.87	146.83	145.95
Alcohol dependence	.31	.37*	.33*
Drug dependence	.28	.59*	.31*

Note: For marital and parent status we conducted logistic regressions, and χ^2 values are presented instead of R^2 values.
*$p < .05$.

whose deceleration was slower than the norm were more likely to report higher levels of psychological distress, criminal behavior, and alcohol and drug dependence.

In comparison, when we used the incremental approach, we found that T3 drug use did not significantly predict T4 outcomes except for marital status and alcohol and drug dependence. Those subjects who had higher compared to lower levels of drug use at T3 were less likely to be married and more likely to have alcohol or drug problems at T4. Thus, these two different approaches to analyzing the outcomes of drug use for adult functioning yielded contradictory results. Based on a process-oriented approach, one would conclude that overall patterns and changes in drug use over a relatively long period of time significantly affected marital status, adult criminality, and adult mental health. However, based on the incremental approach, we would conclude that earlier drug use was not significantly related to adult role status, except marriage, or to criminality, physical health, or mental health.

Given the inconsistency of the results, we decided to conduct additional analyses. We suspected that the inclusion of T4 drug use data in the drug use trajectories may have primarily accounted for differences in the results; thus, we reanalyzed the growth curves using only the T1 to T3 drug use data to predict the T4 outcomes. The same baseline model was used, and to it we added a different set of average levels [AL T1 to T3 = ((T1 + T2 + T3)/3)], linear trends [LT T1 to T3 = (T3 − T1)], and quadratic trends [QT T1 to T3 = (T1 + T3) − (2*T2)]. The results of these analyses are presented in the second column of Table 5.3. Here we see that knowledge about levels and trends in drug use from T1 to T3 did not significantly improve any of the models except for alcohol and drug dependence. Thus, these data suggest that the inclusion of the T4 drug use measure in the process-oriented model significantly increased the predictive power of drug use trajectories on outcomes at T4.

As a final test of this hypothesis, we simply used T4 drug use to predict T4 outcomes. These analyses were conducted similarly to those described earlier and the original baseline model was compared to a model that added drug use at T4. These results are shown in the third column of Table 5.3. The findings were virtually identical to those reported in Table 5.2 for the T1–T4 process-oriented model. The T4 drug use models were significant improvements over the baseline model

Table 5.3. *Regression results for baseline, process-oriented (T1–T3), and cross-sectional (T4) models (R^2 values presented)*

Outcomes	Baseline	Process-oriented	Incremental
Physical health	.27	.27	.27
Mental health	.28	.28	.30*
Criminal behavior	.19	.19	.24*
Occupational status	.12	.12	.13*
Marital status	54.01	59.70	79.45*
Parent status	145.87	146.26	146.82
Alcohol dependence	.31	.33*	.37*
Drug dependence	.28	.31*	.59*

Note: For marital and parent status we conducted logistic regressions, and χ^2 values are presented instead of R^2 values.
*$p < .05$.

for all outcomes except parent status and physical health. The R^2 values for the models including the T4 drug use variable were the same as those for the process-oriented model using T1–T4 trends (compare with the second column of Table 5.2). Inspection of the beta weights for T4 drug use (not shown) indicated that higher levels of drug use at T4 were related to greater psychological distress and criminality, not being married, lower occupational status, and higher rates of alcohol and drug dependence.

Summary and Discussion

Long-term outcomes of drug use

A process-oriented approach to individual change was compared to an incremental approach in order to examine the outcomes of longitudinal patterns of drug use in terms of physical and mental health, role functioning, and substance use dependence in adulthood. The findings indicated that selection of the data-analytic strategy clearly affected the results. We found that, regardless of the analysis strategy, drug use was related to a lower likelihood of being married (except with the T1–T3 process-oriented approach) and to higher levels of alcohol and drug dependence. On the other hand, occupational status, criminal behavior, and psychological distress outcomes differed across analyses. When T4 drug use was included as a predictor, either by itself or within the growth curves (not for occupational status), these outcomes were negatively affected by drug use, but when T4 drug use was not included, these outcomes were not affected by drug use. Finally, with none of the analytic techniques did we find significant effects on parent status and physical health.

Lower levels of earlier and current drug use were found among married persons compared to those who were unmarried (i.e., single and divorced/separated). This finding is consistent with other studies (e.g., Yamaguchi & Kandel, 1985). On the other hand, we did not find that drug use affected parent status after controlling for gender, education, and alcohol use. Studies of older adolescents suggest that drug use may lead to early childbearing (e.g., Mensch & Kandel, 1992), yet by adulthood these effects are no longer evident. However, some drug users delay childbearing in adulthood (Labouvie, 1996) and when these subjects are combined with early child bearers who are also drug users, the effects may cancel out each other.

We found that concurrent drug use was related to current levels of criminal behavior, but that earlier drug use without consideration of current use was not. As discussed in the introduction, the findings in the literature are also mixed (e.g., Kandel et al., 1986b; Stacy & Newcomb, 1995). We also found that concurrent drug use predicted current psychological distress, but earlier drug use by itself did not. Again, the literature on drug effects on mental health in nonclinical samples is equivocal (e.g., Newcomb et al., 1993). Given the brief window of the SCL-90 (i.e., symptoms experienced within the last month), we would expect that current compared to earlier drug use would have a much stronger effect. We also found that higher levels of drug use at T4 predicted lower occupational status at T4, but that growth curves from T1 to T4 were not significantly related to occupational status. The fact that the former model was significant and the latter was not reflects the additional two degrees of freedom in the latter model, inasmuch as both nested models increased the R^2 of the baseline model by a modest 1%. Most other research has not found a negative effect of drug use on occupational status (Johnson & White, 1995).

With none of the analytic strategies did we find an effect of drug use, after controlling for alcohol and cigarette use, on physical health symptoms. Given the age of the subjects, this finding is not surprising, and few other studies of young, nonclinical samples have found negative health effects of drugs other than alcohol (e.g., Johnson & Kaplan, 1990; Kandel et al., 1986a). The strongest finding across all four data-analytic techniques and across time was that heavier drug use predicted higher levels of both alcohol and drug dependence in adulthood. This finding was expected given that only users could experience use-related problems, and given the stability of and relatively strong associations between drug use and drug problems (White, 1987).

Implications for future research

Our analyses that used T4 drug use to predict T4 outcomes produced results almost identical to those from the growth curve analyses (T1–T4). Thus, knowledge of contemporary drug involvement allowed statistical prediction of adult outcomes and statuses on par with knowledge of drug use patterns over the full range of the study. Including information regarding more temporarily distal drug use behaviors did not provide any additional or unique information regarding the outcomes of drug use in adulthood. At first glance, this suggests that information about an individual's history of drug use was not pertinent for prediction of the outcomes examined here. However, given that early use predicts later use, knowledge about drug use in adolescence is not irrelevant. That is, individuals who do not use most illicit drugs in adolescence or early adulthood are unlikely to begin to use them in adulthood (Kandel & Logan, 1984). Further, drug use during adolescence may have negative consequences at the time, which also may have implications for the future. For example, young people may miss school while they are high or get into trouble with the police while using drugs, both of which could have serious long-term consequences for adulthood.

At the same time, however, the data suggested that for some adolescents, drug use was time-limited and did not negatively affect the adult outcomes examined here. These results are consistent with Moffitt's (1993) distinction between two types of delinquents, "adolescence-limited" and "life-course-persistent." She argued that some experimentation with delinquency (including drug use) may be normative for adolescents. Hence, both short-term and long-term longitudinal studies are needed to understand the outcomes of adolescent substance use (see Chapter 12 in this volume).

It appears that those individuals who use drugs without serious consequence during adolescence, and stop using them before adulthood, may not be at increased risk for experiencing negative outcomes during adulthood. The analyses presented here cannot directly address this point because we did not compare stoppers with current users. Schulenberg and colleagues (1996) found that individuals who were high in substance use in adolescence but decreased use by adulthood were more likely to be married, to be employed, and to attain higher levels of education than those who were high users in adulthood. Yet, there were no significant differences in adult role status between individuals who were chronically high in substance use from adolescence to adulthood and those who were high only in adulthood.

It should be noted that our study was limited to a sample of primarily middle- and working-class youth with relatively low levels of adolescent drug use. Perhaps, in a sample with higher levels of drug involvement, heavier use levels during adolescence would be associated with more serious consequences in adulthood. In addition, middle-class youth may have the "social capital" to make it through adolescence unscathed even though they experiment with drugs, whereas lower-class youth without social capital may be less able to get involved with drugs without also getting into trouble (see Chapter 14 in this volume). Jessor, Donovan, and Costa (1991) also discussed this concept of social capital as accounting for their failure to find long-term effects of early problem behavior on adult outcomes. Their sample was largely middle-class, with considerable access to opportunities. They suggested that middle-class environments, in contrast to contexts of poverty and social disorganization, may provide more resources for overcoming a history of problem behavior, or make "second chances" more easily available (Jessor et al., 1991, p. 289). Although the present analyses controlled for subject educational level, they did not control for broadly defined social capital. In order to more clearly understand the consequences of adolescent drug use among different groups, it may be useful to examine the interaction of drug use with indicators of social capital, such as socioeconomic status, social support, competency, differential opportunities, and neighborhood stability, in future research.

Similarly, we did not control for or study the effects of other predictor variables on drug use trajectories or outcomes. For example, early childhood misbehavior and school behavior problems may contribute to early drug use, persistence of use, and later adult outcomes. Clearly, drug use trajectories without consideration of other concomitant intra- and extrapersonal factors cannot provide adequate predictive information about adult outcomes. Thus, there is also a need to examine these other factors in future research (see Jessor et al., 1991).

The findings of this study have implications for the direction of future research and prevention. Earlier patterns of drug use predicted alcohol and drug dependence in adulthood, which is an important outcome. However, if individuals stop using drugs before adulthood, then they obviously cannot be dependent on drugs in adulthood. The only other direct effect of early drug use on adult outcomes was on marital status; those who used drugs heavily in adolescence were less likely to be married at T4. It is probable that this effect was not causal; rather, it reflected the fact that both drug use and not getting married are the result of similar factors. Thus, with the preceding caveats in mind, it appears that drug use that is limited to adolescence does not have direct negative effects for any of the adult outcomes studied here.

Our findings are consistent with several other studies (see Jessor et al., 1991). For example, using several data-analytic strategies, Jessor et al. (1991) found that earlier involvement in problem behavior (including heavy marijuana use) was not associated with differential outcomes in other domains of young adult life once adult problem behavior was controlled. Thus, they concluded that problem behavior in youth did not compromise adult role attainment and satisfaction. Similarly, Newcomb and Bentler (1989, pp. 247–248) concluded that "infrequent, intermittent, or occasional use of drugs by a basically healthy teenager probably has few short-term and no long-term negative or adverse consequences."

In light of these findings, it is time to modify the focus of current research and prevention efforts. Most of the research on the etiology of drug use to date has focused on identifying risk factors for adolescent onset or experimental use (see Hawkins, Catalano, & Miller, 1992; Petraitis, Flay, & Miller, 1995). We now need to study transition periods and pay greater attention to late adolescence and early adulthood (see also Chapters 2, 7, 11 and 13 in this volume). Not only should we examine the effects of adolescent risky behaviors on these transitions, we also should examine the impact of these transitions on reduction of risky behavior. Therefore, our research should concentrate on those individuals who do not mature out of drug use during the transition from adolescence to adulthood. It is important to understand the processes that determine desistance compared to persistence, which requires in-depth studies of this phase in the life cycle.

We agree with Kandel (Chapter 3 this volume) that it is time to direct our research efforts toward identifying the predictors of drug abuse rather than onset and experimental use and the factors that sustain drug use from adolescence to adulthood in both community and high-risk populations. Such information can be used to design appropriate prevention programs targeted at specific age groups including older adolescents and young adults (Clayton, 1992; Gorman, 1996; White, 1996). Prevention efforts to date have concentrated primarily on preventing the initiation of drug use in adolescence and, for the most part, have been rather unsuccessful (Gorman, 1996). Although early prevention with children and adolescents may prevent or delay onset of drug use for some youth, in order to prevent problems from developing or increasing, it is also important to target older adolescents who have already tried drugs. (See Chapter 6 in this volume for a discussion of prevention approaches aimed at college students.)

Implications for data analytic strategies

From conceptual and methodological perspectives, the results also have several implications. Growth curve analyses usually include data from all points in time because additional data increase accuracy (Rogosa & Willett, 1985; Rogosa et al., 1982). Yet, it was specifically the inclusion of T4 concurrent behaviors that increased the predictive utility of the T1–T4 process-oriented models. Note that this study was limited to examining trajectories in drug use as independent variables to predict static outcomes at T4. Most studies using process-oriented approaches examine growth curves as dependent variables and then assess correlates or predictors of change (Francis et al., 1991). If growth curves had been the dependent variable, the inclusion of T4 data obviously would not have impacted on variables measured earlier and therefore would not have influenced the results, as was the case in the present analyses.

Hence, issues surrounding the impact of including current status are most relevant when growth curves are used as independent variables. Nevertheless, the impact of including concurrent information in process-oriented approaches needs to be addressed in future studies.

The process-oriented approach, as used here, shares a potential drawback with the incremental one. In the case of a multiple-occasion, longitudinal design, the incremental approach decomposes the total trajectory into a series of time segments. In comparison, the process-oriented approach decomposes the total trajectory into a set of trend components. But it is a decomposition nevertheless, and the conceptual interpretation of findings based on a process-oriented approach may be more difficult, especially if trajectories are nonlinear and/or nonmonotonic, requiring the incorporation of more than just linear trends in one's model.

A process-oriented approach that avoids such decomposition, and one that might prove more useful, would be based on clustering or grouping individuals on the basis of their trajectories into relatively-homogeneous subgroups, each representing a distinct trajectory (c.f. Johnson, White, & Labouvie, 1995; Schulenberg et al., 1996). According to Cairns and Cairns (Chapter 2, this volume), the use of homogeneous groupings is an appropriate strategy for developmental research. Clustering individuals into homogeneous groups may help to identify pathways and transition points, as well as protective factors. Further, clustering allows researchers to study those individuals who depart from normative trajectories, which can be especially instructive in the case of atypically sustained substance use patterns across time. It may thus be useful to group subjects by developmental trajectories or early predictors and then look at outcomes across groups. Alternatively, subjects, can be grouped according to adult outcomes, and then these groups can be compared in terms of early predictors (e.g., Chapter 11 in this volume).

At a more fundamental level, currently popular process-oriented approaches emphasize the level and shape of trajectories as the critical parameters to be considered. However, some developmentalists have argued that timing and duration are alternative parameters of trajectories that may be just as, or even more, important (Wohlwill, 1973; see also Chapters 2 and 9 in this volume). Nonmonotonic temporal patterns, as found here for drug use, suggest that the time period studied represents a transitional period and that, therefore, the underlying processes that generate these patterns are not operating continuously throughout the total time interval that is being studied. As noted earlier, different processes appear likely to be more or less dominant at different segments of that total time period in general population samples. If so, it may be more appropriate to subdivide the total time interval empirically into a series of developmentally relevant time segments, as may be done with an incremental approach (e.g., life event history analysis; see, e.g., Yamaguchi & Kandel, 1985). This perspective suggests that future analyses should also include parameters of timing and duration.

Conclusions

One unsettling aspect of these results, which is probably new to few, is that statistics can be manipulated selectively, depending on the desired outcomes. That is, had we had an agenda to prove that early drug use was "bad," we could have simply presented the results of the process-oriented approach at T1–T4 and concluded that adolescent drug use was consistently related to negative outcomes in adulthood. If, however, we were invested in showing that earlier drug use was not harmful, we could have presented the results of the T1–T3 process-oriented models or the T3 incremental approach. It is obvious that the inconsistent findings in the literature on long-term outcomes of drug use in nonclinical samples have resulted, in part, from differences in conceptualizing change and the resultant data analysis strategies.

It has been argued that an advantage of process-oriented approaches over incremental approaches is that, in the former, the prediction of future events is enhanced by knowledge about past trends, but in the latter, predictions about the future are based primarily on knowledge of the current or most recent status (Labouvie & Ruetsch, 1994). However, in this study, the T4 measure, or current status, was most informative; thus, a cross-sectional approach was just as useful for "prediction" of contemporary outcomes or statuses and was most parsimonious. Other researchers have also found that current rather than past drug use better predicted adult statuses (e.g., Jessor et al., 1991; Schulenberg et al.,

1996). However, that result only highlights the need to identify the pre-dictors of T4 drug use, which requires the study of the factors that pro-mote stability or change in drug use.

At the same time, equivalence of statistical prediction is not the sole criterion to use in evaluating the adequacy of a model. The current study did not include the factors that promote consistency and change in drug use trajectories and, thus, did not address the adequacy of a process-oriented versus incremental approach for understanding the factors that influence intraindividual change. Our results suggest that growth curve approaches, as used in the present study to characterize independent variables in regression models, may be no more useful than traditional incremental approaches for examining the outcomes of adolescent drug use behaviors. This may be true especially when study-ing periods of developmental transitions characterized by nonmonotonic, nonlinear change patterns (Cicchetti, 1993). On the other hand, process-oriented approaches may be best suited for studying risk factors that predict involvement in drug use in adolescence and adulthood and the outcomes of such use, inasmuch as these approaches tell us more about development than does an incremental approach. In sum, more research is needed to compare process-oriented and incremental techniques, as well as other techniques, to determine the best strategies for analyzing developmental data.

Notes

1. The total number of trends that can be examined depends on the number of test occasions (N). The highest order trend is limited to $N - 1$.
2. One could argue that by controlling for outcomes at T3, we may have eliminated the effects of earlier drug use on outcomes prior to T4. The analyses were repeated, controlling for T1 physical symptoms, psycholog-ical distress, and delinquency in the appropriate analyses and without the T3 controls for alcohol and drug dependence. The findings from the hierarchical regression analyses remained unchanged. That is, although baseline R^2 values were somewhat lower, the increments in R^2 values were the same.
3. Due to the difficulty in interpreting the cubic trend, we limited our anal-yses to the first three trends.
4. This type of growth curve analysis is best accomplished when all test occasions are spaced at equal intervals (Labouvie & Ruetsch, 1994). Given

that T1 to T2 and T2 to T3 had 3-year spans between them and T3 to T4 had a 7-year span, we obtained the weights from the GLM output. These orthogonal polynomials provide a decomposition of temporal patterns into trends using a system of coefficients. Alternatively, we could have eliminated T2 data and used only T1, T3, and T4 data, which are at almost equal intervals (6 and 7 years, respectively). However, we would have lost important T2 drug use data, which may have represented the subjects' peak use given that they were either 18 or 21 years old at T2. We calculated the growth curves using this alternative approach, and both the average level and linear trends correlated .97 with the ones used in this chapter. The quadratic trend correlated .65 with the quadratic trend used in this chapter. This correlation was lower than for the other trends because T2 provided an additional measurement occasion that affected the shape of the trajectory.

References

American Psychiatric Association. (1994). *Diagnostic and statistical manual of mental disorders* (4th ed.) (*DSM-IV*). Washington, DC: American Psychiatric Association.

Andreasson, S., Allebeck, P., & Romelsjo, A. (1988). Alcohol and mortality among young men: Longitudinal study of Swedish conscripts. *British Medical Journal, 296*, 1021–1025.

Anthony, J. C., & Petronis, K. R. (1991). Epidemiologic evidence on suspected associations between cocaine use and psychiatric disturbances. In S. Schober & C. Schade (Eds.), *The epidemiology of cocaine use and abuse* (pp. 71–94). Rockville, MD: National Institute on Drug Abuse.

Arria, A. M., Tarter, R. E., & Van Thiel, D. H. (1991). The effects of alcohol abuse on the health of adolescents. *Alcohol Health and Research World, 15*, 52–57.

Bates, M. E., & Labouvie, E. W. (1995). Personality–environment constellations and alcohol use: A process-oriented study of intraindividual change during adolescence. *Psychology of Addictive-Behaviors, 9*, 23–35.

Bates, M. E., White, H. R., & Hansell, S. (1995, November). *Health consequences of alcohol use patterns over 13 years*. Paper presented at the International Conference on Social and Health Effects of Different Drinking Patterns, Toronto.

Bureau of the Census. (1981). *Current population survey: Money, income and poverty status of families and persons in the United States, 1980*. Current population reports, Series P-60, No. 127. Washington, DC: U.S. Government Printing Office.

Campas, B. E., Hinden, B. R., & Gerhardt, C. A. (1995). Adolescent development: Pathways and processes of risk and resilience. *Annual Review of Psychology, 46,* 265–293.

Castro, F. G., Newcomb, M. D., & Bentler, P. M. (1988). Depression and poor health as antecedents and consequences of cocaine use. *Psychology and Health, 2,* 157–186.

Cicchetti, D. (1993) Developmental psychopathology: Reactions, reflections, projections. *Developmental Review, 13,* 471–502.

Clayton, R. R. (1992). Transitions in drug use: Risk and protective factors. In M. Glantz & R. Pickens (Eds.), *Vulnerability to drug abuse* (pp. 15–51). Washington, DC: American Psychological Association.

Cohen, J., & Cohen, P. (1983). *Applied multiple regression/correlation analysis for the behavioral sciences* (2nd ed.). New York: Erlbaum.

Cohen, P. (1991) A source of bias in longitudinal investigations of change. In L. M. Collins & J. L. Horn (Eds.), *Best methods for analysis of change* (pp. 18–25). Washington, DC: American Psychological Association.

Collins, L. M., & Horn, J. L. (Eds.). (1991). *Best methods for the analysis of change.* Washington, DC: American Psychological Association.

DeLabry, L. O., Glynn, R. J., Levenson, M. R., Hermos, J. A., LoCastro, J. S., & Vokonas, P. S. (1992). Alcohol consumption and mortality in an American male population: Recovering the U-shaped curve – Findings from normative aging study. *Journal of Studies on Alcohol, 53,* 25–32.

Dembo, R. Williams, L., Getreu, A., Genung, L., Schmeidler, J., Berry, E., Wish, E. D., & La Voie, L. (1991). A longitudinal study of the relationships among marijuana/hashish use, cocaine use, and delinquency in a cohort of high risk youths. *Journal of Drug Issues, 21,* 271–312.

Dembo, R., Williams, L., Schmeidler, J., & Wothke, W. (1993). A longitudinal study of the predictors of the adverse effects of alcohol and marijuana/hashish use among a cohort of high risk youth. *International Journal of the Addictions, 28,* 1045–1083.

Derogatis, L. R. (1977). SCL-90-R (questionnaire form). *Administration, scoring and procedures manual,* Vol. 1, Baltimore: Johns Hopkins University, School of Medicine.

Deykin, E. Y., Levy, J. C., & Wells, V. (1987). Adolescent depression, alcohol and drug use. *American Journal of Public Health, 77,* 178–182.

Driver, H. E., & Swann, P. F. (1987). Alcohol and human cancer (review). *Anticancer Researche, 7,* 309–320.

Erickson, P. G., Adlaf, E. M., Murray, G. F., & Smart, R. G. (1987). *The steel drug: Cocaine in perspective.* Lexington, MA: Lexington Books.

Farrow, J. A., Rees, J. M., & Worthington-Roberts, B. S. (1987). Health, developmental and nutritional status of adolescent alcohol and marijuana abusers. *Pediatrics, 79,* 218–223.

Francis, D. J., Fletcher, J. M., Stuebing, K. K., Davidson, K. C., & Thompson, N. M. (1991). Analysis of change: Modeling individual growth curves. *Journal of Consulting and Clinical Psychology, 59,* 27–37.

Gorman, D. M. (1996). Etiological theories and the primary prevention of drug use. *Journal of Drug Issues, 26,* 505–520.

Grabowski, J. (Ed.). (1984). *Cocaine: Pharmacology, effects, and treatment of abuse* (Research Monograph 50, DHHS Pub. No. ADM84-1326). Rockville, MD: National Institute on Drug Abuse.

Hansell, S., & White, H. R. (1991). Adolescent drug use, psychological distress, and physical symptoms, *Journal of Health and Social Behavior, 32,* 288–301.

Hawkins, J. D., Catalano, R. F., & Miller, J. Y. (1992). Risk and protective factors for alcohol and other drug problems in adolescence and early adulthood: Implications for substance abuse prevention. *Psychological Bulletin, 112,* 64–105.

Horwitz, A. V., & White, H. R. (1991). Becoming married, depression, and alcohol problems among young adults. *Journal of Health and Social Behavior, 32,* 221–237.

Jessor, R., Donovan, J. E., & Costa, F. M. 1991. *Beyond adolescence: Problem behavior and young adult development.* New York: Cambridge University Press.

Johnson, E. O., Arria, A. M., Borges, G., Ialongo, N., & Anthony, J. C. (1995). The growth of conduct problem behaviors from middle childhood to early adolescence: Sex differences and the suspected influence of early alcohol use. *Journal of Studies on Alcohol, 56,* 661–671.

Johnson, R. J., & Kaplan, H. B. (1990). Stability of psychological symptoms: Drug use consequences and intervening processes. *Journal of Health and Social Behavior, 31,* 277–291.

Johnson, V., & White, H. R. (1995). The relationship between work-specific and generalized stress and alcohol and marijuana use among recent entrants to the labor force. *Journal of Drug Issues, 25,* 237–251.

Johnson, V., White, H. R., & Labouvie, E. W. (1995, August). *Developmental outcomes in adulthood as differentiated by longitudinal drug use trajectories.* Paper presented at the annual meeting of the American Sociological Association, Washington, DC.

Johnston, L. D., O'Malley, P. M., & Bachman, J. G. (1996). *National survey results on drug use. Vol. 1.* Rockville, MD: National Institute on Drug Abuse.

Kandel, D. B. (1980). Drug and drinking behavior among youth. *American Sociological Review, 6,* 235–285.

Kandel, D. B. & Davies, M. (1990). Labor force experiences of a national sample of young adult men: The role of drug involvement. *Youth and Society, 21,* 441–445.

Kandel, D. B., Davies, M., Karus, D., & Yamaguchi, K. (1986a). The consequences in young adulthood of adolescent drug involvement. *Archives of General Psychiatry, 43,* 746–754.

Kandel, D. B., & Logan, J. A. (1984). Patterns of drug use from adolescence to young adulthood: I. Periods of risk for initiation, continued use, and discontinuation. *American Journal of Public Health, 74,* 660–666.

Kandel, D. B., Simcha-Fagan, O., & Davies, M. (1986b). Risk factors for delinquency and illicit drug use from adolescence to young adulthood. *Journal of Drug Issues, 16,* 67–90.

Kandel, D. B., & Yamaguchi, K. (1987). Job mobility and drug use: An event history analysis. *The American Journal of Sociology, 92,* 836–878.

Kaplan, H. B., & Damphousse, K. R. (1995). Self-attitudes and antisocial personality as moderators of the drug–violence relationship. In H. B. Kaplan (Ed.), *Drugs, crime, and other deviant adaptations: Longitudinal studies* (pp. 187–210). New York: Plenum.

Klatsky, A. L. (1987). The cardiovascular effects of alcohol. *Alcohol 22 (Suppl. 1),* 117–124.

Kurata, J. H., & Haile, B. M. (1984). Epidemiology of peptic ulcer disease. *Clinics in Gastroenterology, 13,* 289–307.

Labouvie, E. (1996). Maturing out of substance use: Selection and Self-correction. *Journal of Drug Issues, 26,* 457–476.

Labouvie, E., & Ruetsch, C. (1994, February). *Hierarchical structural equation modeling: A process-oriented analysis of normative and differential change.* Paper presented at the 5th biennial meeting of the Society for Research on Adolescence, San Diego, CA.

Lange, L. G., & Kinnunen, P. M. (1987). Cardiovascular effects of alcohol. *Advances in Alcohol and Substance Abuse, 6,* 47–52.

Lieber, C. S. (1984). Alcohol and the liver. *Hepatology, 4,* 1243–1260.

Magnusson, D. (Ed.). (1996). *The lifespan development of individuals: Behavioral, neurobiological, and psychosocial perspectives.* New York: Cambridge University Press.

Mensch, B. S., & Kandel, D. B. (1988). Dropping out of high school and drug involvement. *Sociology of Education, 61,* 95–113.

Mensch, B. S., & Kandel, D. B. (1992). Drug use as a risk factor for premarital teen pregnancy and abortion in a national sample of young white women. *Demography, 29,* 409–429.

Miller, C. T., Leonard, K. E., & Windle, M. (1991). Marriage and alcohol use: A longitudinal study of "maturing out." *Journal of Studies on Alcohol, 52,* 434–440.

Moffitt, T. E. (1993). Adolescence-limited and life-course-persistent anti-social behavior: A developmental taxonomy. *Psychology Review, 100,* 674–701.

Newcomb, M. D. (1996). Pseudomaturity among adolescents: Construct validation, gender differences, and associations in adulthood. *Journal of Drug Issues, 26,* 477–504.

Newcomb, M. D., & Bentler, P. M. (1985). The impact of high school substance use on choice of young adult living environment and career direction. *Journal of Drug Education, 15,* 253–261.

Newcomb, M. D., & Bentler, P. M. (1986). Cocaine use among adolescents: Longitudinal associations with social context, psychopathology, and use of other substances. *Addictive Behaviors, 11,* 263–273.

Newcomb, M. D., & Bentler, P. M. (1987). The impact of late adolescent substance use on young adult health status and utilization of health care services: A structural equation model over four years. *Social Science and Medicine, 24,* 71–82.

Newcomb, M. D., & Bentler, P. M. (1988). *Consequences of adolescent drug use.* Newbury Park, CA: Sage.

Newcomb, M. D., & Bentler, P. M. (1989). Substance use and abuse among children and teenagers. *American Psychologist, 44,* 242–248.

Newcomb, M. D., Bentler, P. M., & Collins, C. (1986). Alcohol use and dissatisfaction with self and life: A longitudinal analysis of young adults. *Journal of Drug Issues, 16,* 479–494.

Newcomb, M. D., Scheier, L. M., & Bentler, P. M. (1993). Effects of adolescent drug use on adult mental health: A prospective study of a community sample. *Experimental and Clinical Psychopharmacology, 1,* 215–241.

Nicholi, A. M. (1983). The college student and marijuana: Research findings concerning adverse biological and psychological effects. *Journal of American College Health, 32,* 73–77.

Nicholi, A. M. (1984). Cocaine use among the college age group: Biological and psychological effects; clinical and laboratory research findings. *Journal of American College Health, 32,* 258–261.

Pandina, R. J., Labouvie, E. W., & White, H. R. (1984). Potential contributions of the life span developmental approach to the study of adolescent alcohol and drug use: The Rutgers Health and Human Development Project, a working model. *Journal of Drug Issues, 14,* 253–268.

Pandina, R. J., Labouvie, E. W., White, H. R., Johnson, V., & Bates, M. (1994). *Vulnerability to the consequences of drug abuse in adulthood.* (Research proposal submitted to NIDA.) New Brunswick, NJ: Rutgers Center of Alcohol Studies.

Parsons, O. (1986). Cognitive functioning in sober social drinkers. A review and critique. *Journal of Studies on Alcohol, 47*, 101–114.

Petraitis, J., Flay, B. R., & Miller, T. Q. (1995). Reviewing theories of adolescent substance use; organizing pieces of the puzzle. *Psychological Bulletin, 117*, 67–86

Rogosa, D. R., Brandt, D., & Zimowski, M. (1982). A youth curve approach to the measurement of change. *Psychological Bulletin, 90*, 726–748.

Rogosa, D. R., & Willett, J. B. (1985). Understanding correlates of change by modeling individual differences in youth. *Psychometrica, 50*, 203–228.

SAS (1990). *SAS/STAT user's guide* (Version 6, Vol. 1, 4th ed.). Cary, NC: SAS Institute.

Schulenberg, J., O'Malley, P. M., Bachman, J. G., Wadsworth, K. N., & Johnston, L. D. (1996). Getting drunk and growing up: Trajectories of frequent binge drinking during the transition to young adulthood. *Journal of Studies on Alcohol, 57*, 289–304.

Stacy, A. W., & Newcomb, M. D. (1995). Long-term social-psychological influences on deviant attitudes and criminal behavior. In H. B. Kaplan (Ed.), *Drugs, crime, and other deviant adaptations: Longitudinal studies* (pp. 99–127). New York: Plenum.

Stein, J. A., Newcomb, M. D., & Bentler, P. M. (1987a). An 8-year study of multiple influences of drug use and drug use consequences. Special issue: Integrating personality and social psychology. *Journal of Personality and Social Psychology, 53*, 1094–1105.

Stein, J. A., Newcomb, M. D., & Bentler, P. M. (1987b). Structure of drug use behaviors and consequences among young adults: Multitrait-multimethod assessment of frequency, quantity, work site, and problem substance use. *Journal of Applied Psychology, 4*, 595–605.

Temple, M. T., Fillmore, K. M., Hartka, E., Johnstone, B., Leino, E. V., & Motoyoshi, M. (1991). The collaborative alcohol-related longitudinal project: A meta-analysis of change in marital and employment status as predictors of alcohol consumption on a typical occasion. *British Journal of Addictions, 86*, 1269–1281.

Turner, T. B., Bennett, V. L., & Hernandez, H. (1981). The beneficial side of moderate alcohol use. *The Johns Hopkins Medical Journal, 148*, 53–63.

Urbano-Marquez, A., Estrugh, R., Navarro-Lopez, F., Grau, J. M., Mont, L., & Rubin, E. (1989). The effects of alcoholism on skeletal and cardiac muscle. *New England Journal of Medicine, 320*, 409–415.

Von Eye, A. (1992). Going beyond correlations: Parameter specificity of stability and change. In J. B. Asendorpf & J. Valsiner (Eds.), *Stability and change in development* (pp. 150–154). Newbury Park, CA: Sage.

White, H. R. (1987). Longitudinal stability and dimensional structure of problem drinking in adolescence. *Journal of Studies on Alcohol, 48,* 541–550.

White, H. R. (1996). The empirical validity of theories of drug abuse: Introductory comments. *Journal of Drug Issues, 26,* 279–288.

White, H. R., Aidala, A., & Zablocki, B. (1989). A longitudinal investigation of drug use and work patterns among white, middle-class adults. *Journal of Applied and Behavioral Sciences, 24,* 455–469.

White, H. R., & Bates, M. E. (1993). Self-attributed consequences of cocaine use. *The International Journal of the Addictions, 28,* 187–209.

White, H. R., & Hansell, S. (1996). The moderating effects of gender and hostility on the alcohol–aggression relationship. *Journal of Research on Crime and Delinquency, 33,* 451–472.

White, H. R., Hansell, S., & Vali, F. (1993, June). *A longitudinal investigation of alcohol use, psychological distress, and health.* Paper presented at the annual meeting of the Research Society on Alcoholism, San Antonio, TX.

Wohlwill, J. F. (1973). *The study of behavioral development.* New York: Academic Press.

Yamaguchi, K., & Kandel, D. (1985). On the resolution of role incompatibility: A life event history analysis of family roles and marijuana use. *American Journal of Sociology, 90,* 1284–1325.

Yamaguchi, K., & Kandel, D. (1987). Drug use and other determinants of premarital pregnancy and its outcome: A dynamic analysis of competing life events. *Journal of Marriage and the Family, 49,* 257–270.

6

Linking etiology and treatment for adolescent substance abuse: Toward a better match

John S. Baer, Michael G. MacLean, and G. Alan Marlatt

Introduction

In this chapter we examine the relationship between the etiology and course of substance use problems among adolescents and our societal responses to those problems. A thorough review of this topic is a large task, one that could fill several volumes if completed comprehensively. Our review is selective. We argue that the treatment of adolescents with substance abuse problems must be sensitive to, if not specifically designed for, the psychological and social contexts of adolescent lifestyles. Unfortunately, many current treatment efforts are based on methods and rationales developed with adult populations. A new perspective on the treatment of adolescent substance abuse would begin with an understanding of the manner, rates, and predictive factors for adolescent substance abuse. Further, a new perspective would go beyond refining a model originating in adult psychopathology to developing a new model based on the specific developmental challenges of adolescence. For this effort, the assessment of variability in developmental trajectories of substance use is critical. Variability of substance use course suggests that not all adolescent use is problematic and that problematic use among adolescents is not often chronic. Different psychological factors are associated with different trajectories, suggesting the need for treatment of comorbid conditions as well. Essentially, we argue for a version of patient–treatment matching, but one that is sensitive to developmental issues in adolescents.

To make this case, we first describe the specific nature of adolescent substance use and related problems. Distinguishing between use and use-related problems is a key theme, as are distinctions between adult and adolescent substance use and associated problems. Some use during adolescence is normative, not all use is problematic, and problems that occur do so in a manner different from that of adults. Research pertaining to the etiology and course of substance use is reviewed next. Developmental trajectories, some continuous into adulthood and some limited to adolescence, can characterize the variability of adolescents' substance use problems. Using the college campus as one environmental context, we present data from a longitudinal study that examines risk factors for continuity of alcohol problems. Next, we turn our attention to current treatment approaches and critically examine their underlying assumptions. Few treatment programs have been evaluated, and most draw heavily from models based on adult substance dependence. Finally, we present a harm reduction model of treatment services and argue that such an approach provides a fit with extant data. Again using the college campus as an example, we present data from a harm reduction program for high-risk drinkers. We suggest that different forms of adolescent substance use and substance-related problems require different forms of prevention and treatment.

It is important to state from the outset that although we are sometimes critical of current treatment practices, we have considerable concern about adolescent substance abuse. Clearly, as will be described in the following section, alcohol and drug use by adolescents poses a significant public and personal health risk. We offer this review with a critical eye, seeking to improve prevention and treatment effectiveness.

Epidemiology and prevalence: Substance use among adolescents is normative

Use of psychoactive substances is the norm for adolescents. In the nationwide school sample of the Monitoring the Future study, 73% of high school seniors reported consuming alcohol in the past year, with 52% reporting getting drunk (Johnston, O'Malley, & Bachman, 1995). Well over half (62%) had tried cigarettes, with 19% reporting daily use. Almost half (49%) had tried some type of illicit drug, including inhalants, with 23% reporting use in the past month. Many adolescents start substance use at a young age. The same survey found that 56% of eighth graders had already tried alcohol, 46% had tried cigarettes, and 35% had tried some type of illicit drug. These estimates are based on school populations and are most likely conservative if extended to the adolescent population as a whole (Oetting & Beauvais, 1990).

Responses to the high school survey, however, suggest that the use of many of the psychoactive substances is experimental or episodic in nature. For example, the proportion of 12th graders reporting having ever used various types of hard drugs, but reporting no use in the past year, was 55% for inhalants, 50% for heroin, 37% for crack cocaine, and 20% for marijuana (Johnston et al., 1995). Alcohol had a substantially lower noncontinuation rate (9%), suggesting that drinking is not only prevalent but is also a more recurrent behavior for many adolescents. This pattern of intermittent use among many adolescents is consistent with the categorization of most users as "infrequent" (88%; Gutierres, Molof, & Ungerleider, 1994), "experimental" (50%; Shedler & Block, 1990), or "non-problem" (85%; Donovan & Jessor, 1978).

The spectrum of negative consequences that adolescents experience related to substance use is rather broad. In a community sample of New Jersey adolescents aged 12 to 18, rates ranged from 37% saying they had neglected responsibilities because of drinking at least once over the past year to 5% reporting feeling physically or psychologically dependent (White & Labouvie, 1989). In a school sample of 13- to 19-year-old Ontario youths in 1991, 20% had driven within an hour of drinking two or more drinks, and 6% reported having been arrested or warned because of drinking in the past year (Smart, Adlaf, & Walsh, 1994). Addressing similar use-related consequences of alcohol use, Donovan and Jessor (1978) found that 13.9% of adolescents who were at least moderate drinkers had experienced a minimum of three negative consequences dispersed over at least two types of problems.

In general, then, alcohol and drug use is prevalent enough among adolescents to be considered normative. A relatively small minority of adolescents are heavy users and suffer negative consequences related to use. Nevertheless, the extent of the negative consequences by this subgroup is extensive enough to warrant further investigation of abuse-specific risk factors and intervention programs.

Defining problem use of alcohol and other drugs among adolescents

The incidence and harmfulness of substance use–related consequences, of course, vary, depending on how the terms are defined. How best to distinguish alcohol abuse and dependence from nonproblem use at any age is not straightforward. Difficulty with definitions has been attributed to such factors as the vast heterogeneity of drinking patterns, cultural drinking norms, and the variety of types of negative consequences that can result. Many of the inherent difficulties in defining problem use in adults are magnified when considering problem use among adolescents. For example, cultural relativity can be especially pertinent, as the laws, norms, and consequences surrounding adolescent use can be quite different from those surrounding adults.

Several authors (Bailey & Rachal, 1993; Kilty, 1990) point to important ways that adolescent drinking differs from that of adults: (1) they engage in different patterns of drinking, with adolescents drinking more episodically; (2) the alcohol-related problems experienced by adolescents are not those associated with chronic conditions of adult alcohol dependence; and (3) the type of drinking patterns that relate to problems are different for adolescents and adults. Recently, in an application of DSM-IV criteria to an adolescent sample, Martin, Kaczynski, Maisto, Bukstein, and Moss (1995) found that several diagnostic criteria did not apply well to even the heaviest adolescent drinkers (e.g., physical problems, withdrawal), that at least one criterion did not differentiate problem from nonproblem drinkers (tolerance), and that factors not included in the criteria may be helpful when diagnosing adolescents (e.g., cravings). Clearly, adolescent problem drinking is different from adult problem drinking in important ways, and simply applying adult definitions and conceptualizations may not be appropriate or useful.

Despite a great deal of research on adolescent drinking levels, there remains no consensus on how best to define adolescent problem drinking. A "zero tolerance" or "any drinking is problem drinking" perspective has been the most prominent, especially among those active in prevention (Chng, 1981; Dusenbury & Botvin, 1992; Engs & Fors, 1988) and treatment (Newcomb & Bentler, 1989). One result of this philosophy is that possession of alcohol can result in punitive consequences that would not occur for adults engaged in the same behavior. Such "status offenses" can mean that adolescents' reports of getting into trouble related to drinking can be a reflection of rule-breaking behavior rather than the intoxication-related trouble usually reported by adults. It is not clear if such rule-breaking behavior is necessarily related to other psychosocial or substance use–related difficulties.

A *normative-developmental* perspective, advocated here, holds that some degree of drinking is a normal part of adolescent exploration of adult behaviors (Dusenbury & Botvin, 1992; Hillman & Sawilowsky, 1992) and that occasional substance use can be a normal aspect of the experimentation and rebelliousness that are part of identity formation (Baumrind & Moselle, 1985; Newcomb & Bentler 1988; Shedler & Block, 1990). From a normative-developmental perspective, problems associated with substance use are evaluated along a continuum from none to moderate to severe. Existing research supports the position that adolescent alcohol use is not synonymous with alcohol abuse or dependence. The correlation of adolescent alcohol use intensity with various types of drinking–related consequences has varied from .30 (Chassin, Mann, & Sher, 1988; White, 1989) to .60 (White, 1987; White & Labouvie, 1989), with most findings falling somewhere in between (Bailey & Rachal, 1993; Donovan & Jessor, 1978; Moberg, 1983; Rooney, 1982–1983; Smith, McCarthy, & Goldman, 1995). Using confirmatory factor analysis, White (1987) tested four different models of how various elements of adolescent drinking were interrelated. Keeping drinking level and problems as two separate dimensions fit White's data much better than a model that combined the two as a single factor (see also Smith et al., 1995).

In summary, it appears that a wide range of substance use–related problems are possible in adolescents, but, as noted earlier, these problems occur infrequently and across a range of severity. To date, formal diagnostic criteria for adolescent substance abuse and dependence have not been developed separately from adult criteria. Further, knowing that an adolescent drinks or drinks heavily may not be informative about the presence or absence of negative consequences or problems. A distinction between adolescent substance use and related problems is validated by differential risk correlates, reviewed next.

Adolescent drinking levels and drinking problems associated with different etiologic factors

The research literature addressing the factors associated with adolescent alcohol and substance use rates or level is quite large and has already been extensively reviewed elsewhere (e.g., Braucht, 1982; Bucholz, 1990; Chassin, 1984; Hawkins, Catalano, & Miller, 1992; Kandel, 1980; Newcomb & Bentler, 1989; Radosevich, Lanza-Kaduce, Akers, & Krohn, 1980; Swaim, 1991). Two factors that have emerged as particularly strongly related to adolescent drinking are peer variables and deviant behavior. Reviewers have consistently concluded that peer variables are among the strongest predictors of adolescent alcohol use in particular (Bucholz, 1990; Kandel, 1980; Radosevich et al., 1980) and substance use in general (Hawkins et al., 1992; Newcomb & Bentler, 1989). Drinking level has also been linked to problem behavior, deviance, and low levels of conventionality and conformity to social norms (Donovan & Jessor, 1978; Farrell, Danish, & Howard, 1992; McGee & Newcomb, 1992).

Adolescents' drinking levels are also associated with parents' level of alcohol use, parental attitudes toward their own use (see Barnes, 1990, for review), parental control and emotional support, and the quality of the parent–child relationship (Barnes, 1990; Bucholz, 1990; Hawkins et al., 1992). Factors such as self-esteem and alienation have been noted *not* to be linked to substance use level (e.g., Baumrind, 1985), and a relationship with negative affect is found in some studies but not in others (Braucht, 1982; Bucholz, 1990; Swaim, 1991). Intrapersonal characteristics that have been found to be strongly related to drinking level are personal expectancies related to drinking and the motives underlying drinking. In particular, the expectancy that drinking facilitates social functioning has been a consistent predictor of drinking level (e.g., Christiansen & Goldman, 1983), as has drinking in order to regulate affect (e.g., Cooper, 1994).

As noted earlier, although research has shown that adolescent use and problems are best considered as two separate but related dimensions, research on differences in risk factors for use versus harmful consequences of use has only recently began to emerge. For example, in some contrast to the research findings on drinking level, the effects of parental alcohol use and related norms on adolescent drinking-related problems have not been well established. In a multivariate analysis, parental alcohol use was a significantly stronger predictor of adolescent drinking level than of drinking-related problems (MacLean, 1995). Interestingly, Christiansen and Goldman (1983) found that along with adolescents with heavy-drinking parents, adolescents with nondrinking parents scored higher on the problem drinking scale than adolescents with occasional- and moderate-drinking parents. This suggests that lack of parental modeling of moderate alcohol use may be a risk factor in the development of problem drinking in adolescence and that linear tests might not detect such curvilinear relationships. Parents' norms concerning drinking have not been found to be strong predictors of adolescent drinking problems (Bailey & Rachal, 1993; Dielman, Butchart, Shope, & Miller, 1990–1991; Rooney, 1982, 1982–1983). Examination of general parenting behaviors, however, has consistently found that adolescent problem drinkers experience a more aversive familial environment than nonproblem drinkers (Baumrind, 1991; Colder & Chassin, 1992).

Adolescent problem drinkers associate with peers who drink and use drugs more frequently than do adolescent nonproblem drinkers (Colder & Chassin, 1992; Donovan & Jessor, 1978; Hover & Gaffney, 1991). Furthermore, these peers tend to have more influence on the problem drinkers relative to parental influence than is the case with nonproblem drinkers. However, association with peers who drink and who approve of drinking has been found to be more closely associated with drinking level than with alcohol-related problems (Adlaf & Kohn, 1989; Bailey & Rachal, 1993; MacLean, 1995).

A greater tendency toward an undercontrolled behavioral style has consistently been found for adolescent problem drinkers when compared directly with nonproblem drinkers. Problem drinkers have been found to be higher in externalizing behavior and impulsiveness and lower in frustration tolerance and self-control (Mayer, 1988; see also Baumrind, 1991; Colder & Chassin, 1992). This behavioral style is coupled with lower attachment to social norms (Mayer, 1988), resulting in higher rates of deviance (Baumrind, 1991; Donovan & Jessor, 1978).

Adolescent problem drinkers have been found to experience a greater degree of negative affect and maladjustment relative to nonproblem drinkers. Adolescent problem drinkers experience more stress (Colder & Chassin, 1992; Mitic, McGuire, & Neumann, 1987), anxiety, and depression (Colder & Chassin, 1992). They have been found lower in competence, tend to have a more negative view of themselves (Mayer, 1988), and expect less of themselves (Donovan & Jessor, 1978). They report higher levels of alienation from others (Baumrind, 1991), perhaps related to their greater social immaturity (Mayer, 1988) and their poorer social skills (Hover & Gaffney, 1991).

Like drinking level, drinking expectancies and motivational factors have been demonstrated to be strong predictors of drinking-related problems. But the expectancies and motives that have been the strongest predictors have differed for the two drinking dimensions. The expectancy that "alcohol can enhance or impede social functioning" was the best predictor of frequent drinking, but the expectancy that "alcohol improves one's cognitive and motor functioning" was the best predictor of problem drinking (Christiansen & Goldman, 1983; Christiansen, Smith, Roehling, & Goldman, 1989). Similarly, different reasons for drinking are predictive of problem and nonproblem drinking. Drinking to alleviate negative affect has been found to be a stronger predictor of drinking-related problems (Cooper, Frone, Russell, & Mudar, 1995; MacLean, 1995). Furthermore, the tendency to cope with problems by using substances has been found to be a significantly stronger predictor of drinking-related problems (MacLean, 1995). Conversely, drinking to enhance positive affect has been found to be a stronger predictor of drinking level (Cooper et al., 1995; MacLean, 1995). Although this line of research is still developing, motivational factors and drinking expectancies show potential in helping to differentiate those who experience problems related to their drinking from those who do not.

The research just reviewed is based almost exclusively on alcohol use; we know of no data comparing differences between problem and nonproblem use of other substances by adolescents. Although this research is far from conclusive, some general themes seem to be emerging. From a dimension-centered perspective, drinking level seems to be tied more closely to peer factors, whereas drinking-related problems may be tied more closely to familial and psychological factors. In comparison with drinking level, drinking-related problems may be associated with different reasons (negative affect abatement rather than positive affect enhancement) and with different expectancies (cognitive and motor functioning improvement rather than enhanced social functioning). From a person-centered perspective, problem drinkers have been found to differ significantly from nonproblem drinkers even at similar levels of consumption. Adolescents who experience problems come from more aversive familial environments, associate with deviant, heavy-drinking peers, have an undercontrolled behavioral style, are more heavily engaged in deviant behaviors, experience more negative affect, and are more poorly adjusted than those who drink but do not experience problems.

The longitudinal perspective: Etiology and course

Many of those investigating substance use and abuse have noted the importance of placing the behavior within a developmental framework (e.g., Newcomb & Bentler, 1988; Tarter & Vanyukov, 1994, Zucker, 1987), especially when focusing on adolescents (e.g., Baumrind & Moselle, 1985; Kandel, 1985). The developmental history of the individual, as well as current developmental challenges, can define the function of adolescent substance use. Further, longitudinal research linking adolescence to both childhood and young adulthood identifies both precursors and consequences of substance use.

In their review of studies that followed participants from early childhood through adolescence, Zucker, Fitzgerald, and Moses (1995) examined six childhood factors found to be predictive of adolescent behavior considered at risk for future alcohol problems. Consistent across studies (i.e., at least two supporting studies, with no discrepant findings) were childhood antisocial behavior and aggression, childhood achievement problems, poor childhood interpersonal relationships, hyperactivity, lower levels of parental contact and parenting quality, and higher levels of parent psychopathology, including alcoholism. These conclusions are consistent with those of earlier reviews (Hawkins et al., 1992; Swaim, 1991). It appears, then, that higher levels of drinking are more likely in those adolescents who experienced a difficult familial environment as children and who demonstrated problematic behaviors at an early age. These longitudinal data, then, are consistent with data reviewed earlier associating substance use–related problems with conflicted family environments and deviant peers. It is also noteworthy that the most extreme cases often account for the significance of longitudinal prediction of problems between childhood and adolescence (Baumrind, 1991).

A longitudinal perspective also considers if adolescent use leads to problems later in life. Adolescent substance use and related problems could lead to addiction to substances in adulthood (adolescent use is the first stage of addiction) and/or generalized poor psychological and social adjustment (adolescent substance use sets people on a life trajectory of low achievement). Research on the longitudinal course of adolescent substance use is fairly limited, perhaps due in part to the cost and time necessary to gather such information. Several data sets have been developed and analyzed, however, including those by Jessor and colleagues (Jessor, Donovan, & Costa, 1991), Newcomb, Bentler, and colleagues (Newcomb & Bentler, 1988), Temple and Fillmore (1986), Kandel and associates (Chen & Kandel, 1995), and Johnston, O'Malley, and Bachman, (1995). Our review highlights what we see as general themes across studies.

First, levels of alcohol and substance use peak in adolescence and young adulthood and tend to decline, on average, in the 20s. This general pattern of reduction over time was documented over 20 years ago by Cahalan and Room (1974) and more recently by Temple and Fillmore (1986), Chen and Kandel (1995), and the Monitoring the Future studies (Johnston et al., 1995). Fillmore and colleagues have noted that drinking of younger individuals is less consistent and predictable, that is, less stable over time, than is drinking of older individuals (Fillmore, 1987; Fillmore & Midanik, 1984; see also Donovan, Jessor, & Jessor, 1983). Theoretical writings have usually implicated adult role demands, such as marriage, parenthood, and employment, as central in a natural process toward moderation of drinking among young people (Cahalan & Room, 1974; Jessor, 1985; Yamaguchi & Kandel, 1985a, 1985b).

Second, despite a large average decline in substance use with the transition to young adulthood, levels of substance use during adolescence are the single best predictor of adult substance use. For example, in multivariate analyses completed by Stein, Newcomb, and Bentler (1987), levels of adolescent substance use are the strongest predictors of levels of substance use in young adulthood. It appears that some lifestyle habits are developed in adolescence and continue into young adulthood.

The prediction of drug use–related *problems* in adulthood, however, presents a different picture. Multivariate analysis of the 8-year longitudinal study by Stein et al. (1987) suggests that a measure of adolescent social conformity was the best predictor of problems with drug use in young adulthood (social conformity did not provide an independent prediction of drug use level). Similarly, in Jessor et al.'s (1991) longitudinal analyses, the best predictor of problem behavior in young adulthood, which includes problematic substance use, was problem behavior during adolescence. Zucker and Gomberg's (1986) review of six longitudinal studies that examined childhood characteristics in the prediction of adult alcohol problems revealed several consistencies as well. The most common linkage was that of childhood antisocial behavior, which was noted in five studies. Children who would develop alcohol problems in adulthood were also described as having difficulties in achievement and were loosely connected interpersonally. The families of these children were marked by marital conflict, parental psychopathology, and lack of contact between children and parents.

Other possible consequences of adolescent substance use are more general adjustment problems in young adulthood (independent of substance use in adulthood). Here the data are not consistent. In Jessor et al.'s (1991) 8-year follow-up study, adolescent problem behavior was generally unrelated to adult satisfaction with family, work, and friends. Data from Newcomb and Bentler's (1988) study, however, suggest that adolescent substance use is associated with early family creation, relationship dissatisfaction, drug crimes, stealing, high school dropout, and job instability. This pattern of results is described as consistent with a model of pseudoemancipation (Baumrind & Moselle, 1985) in which adolescents adopt adult behaviors before they have sufficient life skills to succeed. The effects noted by Newcomb and Bentler, although statistically significant, may be accounted for by a subgroup of individuals most involved with illicit drug use. It is also noteworthy that in Newcomb and Bentler's study, adolescent alcohol use was associated with some positive outcomes in young adulthood (i.e., enhanced social functioning), although a general factor of substance use (that included alcohol) was not.

In summary, longitudinal data reveal two consistent patterns of substance use over time. First, alcohol use and substance use begin in adolescence and decline significantly with the transition to young adulthood. Such general declines suggest that, at least in part, some adolescent substance use patterns are stage (adolescent) specific. Use of substances is only moderately related to psychosocial problems. Psychological process of marriage and employment are associated with declines in substance use in the 20s. Second, some continuities in behavior do exist across developmental stages, and there are risks for adult adjustment based on adolescent behavior. Data are inconsistent with respect to the long-term risks of adolescent substance use for adult adjustment. It does appear, however, that substance use problems, as well as general adjustment in young adulthood, are predicted by adolescent problem behavior and nonconformity rather than level of use per se.

Multiple addictions with multiple developmental paths?

The development of addictive patterns of use (at any point in life) is thought to be multidetermined, encompassing biological differences in reactions to substances, temperament and personality, psychological processes of tolerance and expectancies about drug effects, and social processes involving modeling and reinforcement (see Marlatt, Baer, Donovan, & Kivlahan, 1988; Sher, 1991; Tarter & Vanyukov, 1994). Clinical presentations of addictive problems vary as well, causing generations of researchers to posit typologies (see Babor & Lauerman, 1986; Hesselbrock, 1995). Alcoholics have been grouped by a host of factors, including heredity, patterns of use, severity, and psychological factors. Babor and colleagues (1992) have recently completed a comprehensive review and integration of this line of research and propose two primary types of alcohol problems: those associated with sociopathy and those associated with negative affect (depression and anxiety) syndromes. These two types differ in terms of typical onset (earlier among sociopaths), course (more chronic among sociopaths), family history of alcoholism (greater among sociopaths), and degree of comorbid psychopathology (greater among sociopaths).

For the purpose of this review, our interest lies in the linkage of adolescent substance use to different types of adult addiction problems. Robert Zucker and colleagues (Zucker, 1987, 1994; Zucker et al., 1995) have added a developmental component to the understanding of alcoholism subtypes, suggesting that different types of "alcoholisms" follow different developmental trajectories. Three central developmental paths are proposed to account for common courses. Consistent with the longitudinal data reviewed earlier, Zucker posits first a "sociopathic alcoholism," characterized by early onset, high sociopathy, criminality, and very severe drinking problems. A pattern of "developmentally limited" alcohol problems is also proposed, consistent with the epidemiological data reviewed earlier showing that heavy drinking in adolescents is associated with other delinquent behaviors but is commonly limited in time, diminishing significantly on the transition to young adulthood. "Negative affect alcoholism," consisting of alcohol problems related to depressive and anxious symptomatology, is a third developmental path, proposed to develop more slowly and to be less associated with adolescence in general and delinquent behavior in particular. Note that these different paths are suggested to be associated with somewhat different developmental or etiological processes and risk factors. Zucker et al. (1995) suggest that in each case environmental (stress, lack of essential parenting) and/or biological (temperament, physiological sensitivity) processes facilitate the development of problems (see also Tarter & Vanyukov, 1994). Zucker et al. (1995) also propose three paths to alcohol problems that lack initial continuity or comorbidity: "developmentally cumulative," "episodic," and "isolated."

Models of multiple development paths to alcohol problems are remarkably similar to recent etiological models of adolescent conduct disorder. In a recent review, Moffitt (1993; Moffitt, Caspi, Dickson, Silva, & Stanton 1996) proposes two developmental trajectories for adolescent conduct disorder: *Life Course Persistent* (*LCP*) and *Adolescent Limited* (*AL*). Moffitt suggests that LCP conduct problems are characterized by difficult early temperament, early onset of antisocial acts, aggressive tendencies, and a chronic life course. In addition, LCP individuals are more likely to become ensnared in the negative consequences of their actions, such as incarceration, school dropout, social isolation, and injuries. These consequences further perpetuate antisocial behavior. Importantly, Moffitt notes that discriminating among LCP and AL trajectories is difficult if they are evaluated only on the basis of adolescent behavior. However, when developmental history is examined, particularly age of onset and degree of aggressiveness, reliable differences among subgroups emerge.

Models of developmental paths or trajectories provide a potential integration of much of the data reviewed earlier. Most adolescents use substances, but only a few do so in a manner that creates significant psychosocial problems. Much adolescent substance use remits over time, even use associated with psychosocial problems. Substance use that does not remit is associated with early developmental problems. Problems related to use, both cross-sectionally and longitudinally, are often associated with generalized family conflict and deviant behavior. Adolescents with a significant risk of long-standing problems report different motivations and expectancies for drug effects. Those with the most severe substance use problems may represent a different developmental process (associated with different etiological factors and showing different courses) from those with mild to moderate problems, who may nevertheless use heavily at times. Clearly, such an integration is speculative. The research to be described provides one example of the type of information needed to develop such a model further.

College graduation: An example of research on developmental paths

A model of multiple developmental paths suggests the need to develop assessment procedures to identify individuals at risk for particular substance use–related problems, as well as greater understanding of the processes involved in facilitating (or limiting) different developmental trajectories. Trajectories are assumed to be context specific. The Transitions Project, an ongoing study at the University of Washington, is described here briefly as an example of one study testing assumptions about differential developmental paths to alcohol problems between late adolescence and young adulthood within a specific subgroup. In this study, graduation from college was selected as an important developmental transition. College students represent one population of late adolescents who commonly abuse alcohol and who are targeted as a special population for early intervention (Institute of Medicine, 1990; Wechsler, Davenport, Dowdall, Moeyken, & Castillo, 1994). Nevertheless, most college students seem well adjusted while in college, and many reduce their drinking in the years after college (Donovan et al., 1983). Not all heavy-drinking college students remit in the years following college, however (Donovan et al., 1983; Johnston, O'Malley, & Bachman, 1994).

The Transitions Project assessed young people prior to and after college graduation. A variety of assessment domains were included in order to develop prediction of change based on biological, psychological, and social measures. Given that the greatest continuity of alcohol problems has been associated with sociopathic personality and behavioral styles, it was anticipated that young people with a family history of alcoholism, a personal history of conduct problems, impulsive personality patterns, and a reduced response to alcohol would show continuity of alcohol problems across this developmental transition. In addition, it was anticipated that persons showing continuity of problems would continue group-based collegelike living arrangements and continue to socialize with college peers.

Graduating seniors from the University of Washington were recruited for a 3-year longitudinal study of the transition from college ($n = 294$). Heavy drinkers were selected on the basis of self-reports of regular drinking to intoxication (a blood alcohol content [BAC] of .12% twice monthly). Subjects reported drinking an average of 2.81 (sd = 1.31) times per week, consuming an average of 6.44 (sd = 2.67) standard drinks per drinking occasion. The estimated peak BAC averaged .15%. Subjects participated in a comprehensive interview and completed questionnaires measuring family history of alcohol problems and a host of personality and behavior dimensions and beliefs about alcohol and drinking. They also completed a laboratory alcohol challenge in which alcohol sensitivity and stress reactivity when sober and intoxicated were assessed.

Preliminary results from the study reveal two general trends consistent with those of the longitudinal studies described earlier. First, subjects reported marked reductions in drinking patterns roughly 1 year after graduation from college. Significant reductions were found on all measures, with the largest decrease occurring in the number of drinks per drinking occasion. Prior to graduation, 23% of the sample reported three or more DSM-III-R alcohol dependence symptoms; 1 year later, only 4.9 % reported this level of symptoms. It is also noteworthy that, despite large general effects, the change was variable; based on Alcohol Dependence Scale cut scores (Ross, Gavin, & Skinner, 1990), 46 individuals (17%) moved from above to below the cutoff over the 1-year period, and 14 (5.3%) moved from below to above the cutoff.

Some continuity in alcohol use and related problems was also evident. Consistent with studies of young adolescents, prospective analyses suggest different predictive models for drinking levels and drinking problems. Prediction of drinking level appears to be a function of previous drinking level and social network drinking level. Measures of laboratory stress response, perceived intoxication, gender, family history, and psychiatric symptomatology were not associated with course of drinking level.

Prediction of alcohol-related problems, however, appears to be a function of previous problems, drinking frequency (but not quantity) at baseline, neuroticism and anxious and depressive symptomatology. Thus, contrary to expectations, a general pattern of psychological distress is related prospectively to continuity of alcohol problems. These relationships were also noted in cross-sectional analyses of data from the 1-year follow-up. Those reporting continued alcohol problems were less successful and less satisfied with their employment.

Results from the Transitions Project provide tentative directions for prevention and treatment of heavy drinking on college campuses. They inform us about different courses of risk for different individuals and suggest developmental processes that may contribute to long-term risk. For otherwise well-adjusted college students, one can expect drinking problems to remit. Programming can be directed at ensuring safety during the college years. Concern about later addiction should be modest at best. In contrast, the risk of continuity of alcohol problems appears to be associated with psychiatric comorbidity. Programming to limit longer-term alcohol problems could target heavy drinkers with anxious and depressive symptoms and potentially could target treatment of coexisting conditions. Further, programs could be developed to facilitate adjustment after college graduation. Continued follow-up of the Transitions Project sample can evaluate if this poor adjustment is time-limited or more chronic in course.

These types of analyses and treatment recommendations follow from the examination of multiple developmental paths to addiction problems within specific populations. Before applying this type of analysis to the complex picture of adolescent substance use problems, we describe typical existing treatments.

Current approaches to the prevention and treatment of substance abuse in adolescents

Literature describing adolescent prevention and treatment programs reveals a mixed picture, particularly in identifying successful approaches. As will be documented, although a variety of theories have been developed and related intervention strategies have been implemented, no one approach to either prevention or treatment of alcohol or substance abuse problems in adolescents appears to be uniformly successful. Of course, the development of effective prevention of alcohol and other drug problems in adolescents is hampered by the lack of consensus on a conceptual goal of primary prevention efforts (see the earlier discussion; see also Bukstein, 1995). Targets for prevention may include any of the following: prevent onset of substance abuse, prevent the consequences of use, prevent or reduce risk factors for use/abuse, and increase protective factors that reduce the risk of use/abuse. As a further complication, types of prevention programs designed for adolescents include a wide range of efforts, including legal proscription; public disapproval, scare tactics; education and information designed to affect attitudes, values, and decision making, programs to enhance social competency skills; family-focused interventions, community-based comprehensive approaches, and early psychiatric/mental health interventions (Bukstein, 1995).

As a group, prevention programs can be distinguished in terms of whether they target individuals (e.g., through processes of socialization) or the larger environment (e.g., through mechanisms of social control; Howard, 1993). In this way, the prevention of alcohol and drug problems is similar in goals and methods to how our society currently works with adolescents to prevent driving accidents. In both cases, programs can be developed that focus either on the individual (e.g., driver-training programs and manuals) or on environmental and community-based conditions (e.g., seat belt requirements, speed limits, and impaired-driving sanctions). Prevention of alcohol problems often involves parallel processes. Alcohol information programs, like driver-training programs, often are designed to provide the individual with the knowledge and skills to avoid alcohol and drug problems (primary prevention) or to minimize the harm of ongoing use (secondary prevention). Environmental or community-based programs, on the other hand, support policy changes that have a global impact on all members of the target group. Community-based policies for the prevention of alcohol and substance problems in adolescents include enacting lower blood-alcohol limits for young drivers (Hingson, 1993), changing the alcohol price policy (Grossman, Chalupka, Saffer, & Laixuthai, 1995), and mobilizing community resources.

Proponents of the community approach have noted the limited impact of educational programs targeted for individuals:

Changing beliefs and perceptions about alcohol through such programs have little long-term effect because social structures, public policies, drinking models, and other antecedent dimensions of the environment are typically left unchanged. (Wagenaar & Perry, 1995, p. 206)

Primary or universal prevention programs based on the educational model applied to individuals, often in the school setting, have not proven to be effective (Ennett, Tobler, Ringwalt, & Flewelling, 1994; Gorman, 1995, 1996; Mandell, 1992; Moscowitz, 1989; Tobler, 1986). Although recent school-based prevention studies demonstrate that psychosocial and educational approaches may delay the onset of alcohol and marijuana use (Botvin, Baker, Dusenbury, Tortu, & Botvin, 1990; Pentz et al., 1989), the effectiveness of such programs to produce significant and sustained changes in drinking or drug use has been questioned, as reported effects have often been minimal and short-lived (Ellickson, Bell, & McGuigan, 1993; Gorman, 1995, 1996).

One limitation of primary prevention programs that teach "refusal skills," that is, socially adroit ways to avoid alcohol or drug experimentation (Botvin, 1986), is that alcohol consumption has become a largely normative behavior in adolescent development. In this sense, alcohol consumption may be different from consumption of other substances (tobacco, illicit drugs), for which lifelong abstinence is the preferred goal of prevention efforts. Although alcohol use is illegal for all American adolescents because of the age-21 national drinking age law, drinking is often encouraged and glamorized in the wider culture, thereby enhancing its value as a rite-of-passage symbol of freedom. Most alcohol and substance abuse prevention programs for adolescents retain the "just say no" message, even when the targeted individuals have broken the taboo and are actively drinking or experimenting with drugs. Prevention messages may be disregarded when adolescents witness their peers not experiencing the negative consequences associated with use. Furthermore, prevention programs aimed at stopping initiation of use are often based on risk factors associated with level of use (e.g., peers) but may not directly address use-related problems associated with different risk factors (see also Gorman, 1992). Thus, prevention programs may have little impact on precisely those adolescents most likely to be experiencing problems. Secondary prevention, designed to minimize the harmful consequences for those adolescents who are currently drinking or using, has been limited to a few harm reduction studies with older adolescents and young adults, such as college students (see the later discussion).

Unlike prevention, there is relatively little research on the effectiveness of treatment for adolescent alcohol and substance abuse. The outcome studies that have been conducted suggest weak results at best. There is no shortage of recommended treatment approaches, however, as documented in several recent texts on the topic (Boyd, Howard, & Zucker, 1995; Bukstein, 1995; Lawson & Lawson, 1992; Ross, 1993). The Center for Substance Abuse Treatment (CSAT) has also published a Treatment Improvement Protocol (TIP) specifically for the treatment of adolescent substance abuse (U.S. DHHS, 1993a). Treatment programs for adolescent substance abuse include inpatient, hospital-based treatment (Brock, 1992), family-based treatment (Liddle et al., 1992), peer counseling (Covert & Wangberg, 1992), therapeutic communities (Jainchill, Bhattacharya, & Yagelka, 1995), and pharmacotherapy (Kaminer, 1995).

As noted earlier, there is little agreement in the research field about what constitutes an adolescent substance use problem. Not surprisingly, descriptions of adolescent treatment programs vary in the degree to which the diagnostic syndrome of adolescent substance abuse is assessed and defined. For example, CSAT (U.S. DHHS 1993a) suggests the use of a comprehensive continuum of treatment services for adolescents based on six diagnostic criteria (i.e., withdrawal, medical complications, inter- and intrapersonal problems) but does not provide specific assessments or cut scores for clinical placements. The CSAT publication on assessment of adolescent substance abuse (U.S. DHHS 1993b) provides a wealth of assessment options but not clinical cut scores or treatment recommendations. In this publication the DSM-III-R diagnostic criteria are provided in an appendix, with a footnote that the criteria were developed based on adults and should be used "primarily as a frame of reference in addressing adolescent AOD problems" (p. 119). It is not unusual for treatment programs to propose treatment for low-level problems. For example, Ross (1993) recommends outpatient treatment for adolescents who have used substances one to five times with no interference with psychosocial functioning (p. 31) and inpatient treatment for adolescents with problem use without psychological or physical dependence (p. 32). (For a noteworthy exception, see Del Boca, Babor, & McLaney, 1995.)

Most traditional adolescent treatment programs for alcohol and substance abuse are based on an extension of the adult "chemical dependency" model originally developed for adult addiction treatment (Ross, 1993). These programs are usually rooted in the 12-step tradition of Alcoholics Anonymous (Lawson, 1992). Programs support identification of the patient as an "addict" or "alcoholic," acceptance of a belief that life has become unmanageable due to addiction, and acceptance of a "higher power" to return oneself to sanity. Concerns about psychological denial of problems can limit the flexibility of treatment strategies. As one proponent of this approach states:

> The issue of a creator being, a higher power, or God is extremely important and needs to be addressed at some point in the treatment of a chemically dependent adolescent. . . . One method used to help recovering teenagers begin to confront this important issue is to challenge openly their denial of God's existence by asserting that they do, indeed, believe in God. Many will vehemently argue they do not believe in God. After patiently listening to their protests, calmly remind them that they do believe in God. . . . As effective therapists, it is important not to sidestep the issue of a higher power when questioned by recovering teenagers. (Ross, 1993, pp. 48–49)

Unfortunately, the data on treatment outcome fail to support the overall effectiveness of traditional chemical-dependency programs designed for adolescents. Brown and her colleagues (Brown, Vik, & Creamer, 1989) assessed the relapse rates of adolescents; 56% of the adolescents returned to regular use in the first 6 months following treatment. Lapse rates showed that 64% of the adolescents used at least once during the first 3 months following completion of primary treatment, and 70% used at least once during the first 6 months posttreatment. Similar findings are reported by Spear and Skala (1995), whose treatment outcome study showed that 92% of the adolescent participants had at least one isolated use incident during the first year after completion of residential treatment, with 42% using drugs at least once within the first month. In addition, 76% of the clients used at least monthly by the end of the first year, and 62% had returned to weekly or multiweekly use. As the authors conclude:

> Most programs for adolescents see total abstinence as the objective of treatment. Nevertheless, the relapse data suggest that nearly all adolescents have

some level of drug use following primary treatment. The relapse rates indicate that total abstinence may be an unrealistic objective and from a research perspective may lead to treatment outcome measures that are insensitive to real though not absolute changes in drug use behaviors. (p. 345)

Although some reviewers note that treatment may have some beneficial effect for adolescent substance abusers, there is no evidence to date to support the superiority of any one general or specific approach (Catalano, Hawkins, Wells, Miller, & Brewer, 1991). However, most adolescent treatment programs are still based on adult treatment ideology. Because there is so little research, it is unclear how acceptable the basic tenets of the 12-step approach are for many adolescents.

Treatment based on etiology

Given the different development paths to substance abuse and the wide range of treatment strategies that have been implemented with little systematic success, a new approach is warranted. Prevention and treatment developed for adolescents (rather than adjusted from adult models) should begin with basic questions: "What kind of treatment, with what kind of treatment goal, for what kind of individual?" Note that different individuals may require different treatment approaches. The existence of multiple developmental contexts for adolescent substance use suggests that treatment should seek to match individuals on developmental paths to developmentally appropriate and individualized goals. Based on the literature reviewed earlier, there appear to be two general trends in adolescent substance use, each requiring different prevention and treatment goals and strategies.

Users characterized by a developmental trajectory associated with conduct disorder and eventual sociopathy, Zucker's "sociopathic alcoholism," present a considerable challenge to mental health and substance use professionals. Recall that some individuals show remarkable consistency in behavior from early childhood through adolescence to adulthood. Indeed, an early-onset chronic trajectory pattern has been proposed for conduct disorder as well (Moffitt, 1993). Given the chronicity of severe conduct problems, it is unlikely that individuals with long-standing sociopathic behaviors will respond to treatments designed to focus on one particular manifestation of their antisocial behavior: substance use and abuse. Nor is it clear that prevention programs seeking to delay drug experimentation or limit use are effective with a group of children with multiple psychosocial problems.

This is not to say that substance abuse problems should be ignored in those with the greatest adjustment problems. Rather, substance use should be one part of a multifaceted treatment aimed at minimizing conduct-disordered behavior. Treatment for conduct disorder should begin early in life. As Moffitt et al. (1996) state, "practitioners must be prepared to wage a vigorous extended battle against a formidable adversary" (p. 422). Conduct-disordered youth have typically been described as at high risk for adult sociopathy. Several targeted prevention programs have been developed and tested (Catalano, Haggerty, Gainey, Hope, & Brewer, in press). Large treatment effects for conduct disorder, particularly for adolescents as opposed to younger children, are not the norm (see McMahon & Wells, 1989). Integrated treatment efforts often focus on assisting parents and teachers in providing structure and on the systematic consequences of delinquent behavior (Moffitt et al., 1996). Such programming usually includes family therapy, parent training for younger children, and community and school programs. In some cases, social skills training can be helpful (Kazdin, 1995). Given the risk of long-standing addictive problems for these individuals, the goal of a substance abuse component of multifaceted treatment should be to reduce and eventually eliminate substance use. Attention to the broader constellation of behavior problems may alter a life trajectory of sociopathy and reduce the likelihood of relapse to associated substance abuse.

Treatment of adolescents with substance abuse related to comorbid depressive and anxious symptomatology remains largely unexplored. Although it is still unclear whether a separate developmental trajectory is defined by negative affect features (Zucker et al., 1995, propose that this tends to occur later in life), stress, depression, and family conflict are associated with substance use problems. For youths with such comorbidity, a comprehensive treatment plan would best be augmented by including existing effective treatments for anxiety and depression (e.g., see Kendall, 1993, for an overview). The resulting treatment plan might be quite different from that for a youth on the sociopathic trajectory.

It is possible that some adolescents experience alcohol or drug problems without coexisting conduct or depressive problems, what we might term *simple* or *noncomorbid* addiction. This pattern could be due to biological differences in drug responsivity. Although conceivable, we assume this clinical presentation to be least common. It is perhaps only for such a path that the programs focusing almost exclusively on substance use are most appropriate. However, the currently common approach of treating all adolescents as if they were simply addicted, without serious attention to developmental pathways and comorbid problems, seems unlikely to be effective for most.

A treatment-matching approach, of course, can rely on many different dimensions of individual differences when designing treatments. Adolescents who use drugs are more likely to engage in high-risk sexual behavior that puts them at risk for acquired immunodeficiency syndrome (AIDS); treatment programs need to include AIDS prevention for this reason (Steel, 1995). In terms of gender differences, female adolescents may need a specialized treatment approach that differs from programs designed largely for males (Waite-O'Brien, 1992). Similarly, adolescents from various ethnic minority groups may also benefit from treatment programs that are culturally matched, such as specialized programs for young Native Americans (Young, 1992) and African Americans (Copeland, 1992).

Yet the most common developmental path for adolescent substance abuse is one limited to the period of adolescence. Substance use levels are associated with social processes (peers). The risks and problems associated with this pattern of use are variable, ranging from status offenses to mild symptoms of dependence, but nevertheless are restricted in time. Epidemiological data indicate that many if not most adolescents will reduce substance use and related problems with the transition to young adulthood. Long-term negative consequences are few. A pragmatic rather than an ideological approach would focus on limiting or reducing harms associated with use until the window of risk has passed. Thus, in designing societal responses, harm reduction goals and strategies seem logical (cf. Jessor, 1982).

Harm reduction is actually an umbrella term, encompassing both clinical and social policy approaches to health problems (Des-Jarlais, 1995; Duncan, Nicholson, Clifford, Hawkins, & Petosa, 1994; Marlatt & Tapert, 1993). Harm reduction, as a conceptual model and as a set of strategies, evaluates the "by-products" of substance use, that is, the health and psychological consequences of use along a continuum, and seeks to move individuals along the continuum to a position of reduced risk. A number of clinical and strategic features follow from this basic assumption. Clinical or prevention programs should have low thresholds for treatment entry, attempting to engage as many individuals as possible in some change effort. Goals for behavior change are not preordained and can include nonabstinence. Further, small change efforts are seen as preliminary to large change efforts. Ultimately, to facilitate contact with those in need, social services should be perceived as supportive and nonjudgmental.

A harm reduction approach to adolescent substance use follows logically from the natural history of adolescent substance abuse reviewed earlier. Use is normative. Many of the problems associated with substance use do not come from those who are addicted in a traditional sense, but rather from those who intermittently use heavily. The label "alcoholic" or "addict" does not apply to such individuals, who most likely do not feel that their lives have become unmanageable because of substance use. A harm reduction approach can be used to minimize labeling. It seems unreasonable to attach a lifelong label to a time-limited problem. Harm reduction models also allow for a variety of treatment goals. Thus, one does not need to insist on abstinence from a group unlikely to accept it (and unlikely to need it once the window of risk has passed). Several substance abuse prevention and treatment strategies are consistent with a harm reduction approach. Certainly, delaying the onset of use, minimizing use, restricting access, changing norms, and creating safer contexts associated with use might lead to reduced health risks during a high-risk period. As noted earlier, however, it is not clear that many prevention and treatment programs are successful in reducing the harms associated with substance use. Recall that level of use and problems associated with use are only moderately correlated. A focus solely on level of use addresses harms indirectly.

The Lifestyles project is one example of a harm reduction approach for heavy drinking on college campuses and is presented here illustratively. Clearly, there are large differences between the substance use of young adolescents who drop out of high school and that of older adolescents who enter college. Yet our thesis is that etiology and treatment must be considered within the social and psychological contexts wherein young people live. The college campus is thus one specific setting where harm reduction approaches have been studied. The Lifestyles project represents a test of a brief motivational intervention to reduce harm. Results and further description of this project have been reported with varying degrees of detail in Baer, Kivlahan, and Marlatt (1992, 1994), Baer (1993), and Marlatt, Baer, and Larimer (1995). A complete report of the study is in press (Marlatt et al., in press).

A brief intervention provided in the winter term of the first year of college (January–March) was based on our prior research with brief interventions with college students (see Baer, Marlatt, Kivlahan, & Frome, 1992) and motivational interviewing more generally (Miller & Rollnick, 1991). Students were provided with alcohol consumption monitoring cards and asked to keep track of their drinking on a daily basis for 2 weeks prior to their scheduled interview. In the feedback session, interviewers met individually with students, reviewed their alcohol self-monitoring cards, and gave them concrete, individualized feedback about their drinking patterns, risks, and beliefs about alcohol effects. Subjects' self-reported drinking rates were compared to college averages, and risks for current and future problems (low grades, blackouts, accidents) were identified. Beliefs about real and imagined alcohol effects were addressed through discussions of placebo effects and the nonspecific effects of alcohol on social behavior. Biphasic effects of alcohol (stimulation followed by depression) were described, and the students were encouraged to question the "more alcohol is better" assumption. Suggestions for risk reduction were outlined.

The style of the interview was based on techniques of motivational interviewing (Miller & Rollnick, 1991). The purpose of the intervention was to facilitate motivation or stimulate "contemplation" for change (Prochaska, DiClemente, & Norcross, 1992). Confrontational communications such as "You have a problem and you are in denial" (thought to create a defensive response in the student) were specifically avoided. Risk factors, such as a family history of alcohol problems or conduct disorder, were explored with students to determine their own experiences and their impressions of risk. The specific goals of behavior change were left to the student and were not directed or demanded by the interviewer.

The results of this project are encouraging. Summarizing through 2-year follow-up assessments, students who received the motivational intervention and follow-up graphic feedback reported significantly less drinking quantity, less drinking frequency, and fewer alcohol-related problems at each assessment compared to those in the control condition. The effects on alcohol-related problems and dependence scores reveal the largest changes. For example, using a cutoff score of 11 on the ADS (Ross, G., et al., 1990), only 16 of 145 (11.0%) of those in the motivational intervention group were classified as showing mild dependence at the 2-year assessment compared to 42 of 156 (26.9%) of those in the control condition. It is noteworthy that this harm reduction effect was noted in comparison to that of a control group whose drinking and related problems were declining over time. Thus, the intervention seemed to accelerate a natural moderation process and served to reduce risks during a developmental period where drinking risks were extreme.

The Lifestyles project, although suggesting a technique and a context in which harm reduction can be helpful, does not yet provide the type of data that would validate the treatment-matching approach advocated here. In fact, through a series of analyses, we have been unable to show that our harm reduction approach was differentially effective within our sample of high-risk drinkers. Theoretically, those college students with the greatest problems, those perhaps on a more chronic and severe developmental trajectory, should be least responsive to our brief intervention. Our analyses indicate that those with a history of conduct-disordered behavior do, in fact, report more drinking-related problems, but they are as responsive to our clinical program as are others. It is possible that we do not have a sufficient range of adjustment problems represented within the sample to assess fairly those with a high risk of chronic drinking problems. Many of these individuals may not be successful enough to enter a competitive 4-year college. Nevertheless, it is this type of analysis that is needed to provide validation for a developmental matching model.

Finally, it is important to note that harm reduction approaches are not without critics (see Califano, 1994, and Huber, 1994). Primary concerns about harm reduction, particularly with adolescents and young adults, surround the implicit acceptance of alcohol and substance use (which is often illegal). It is sometimes suggested that programs designed to minimize the consequences of use, but not use itself, might unwittingly promote experimentation. To date there are little clear data to resolve these issues, although some preliminary data with high school students suggest that open discussion of risk reduction does not lead to increased use (Somers, 1995).

Summary and research recommendations

We end this review by making recommendations for research pertaining to the link between etiology and treatment of adolescents with substance use problems. In essence, we are proposing a *matching hypothesis* stating that prevention and treatments approaches may be differentially effective for different individuals. This is an approach popular in the treatment of adult addictive behavior (see the *Journal of Studies on Alcohol,* supplement 12, 1994). When treatment matching is applied to adolescents, models of development assume an important role in defining individual differences and in focusing treatment content. In addition, different developmental trajectories raise questions about the most appropriate and most effective prevention and treatment goals.

Our review of the literature on adolescent substance use suggests that there are important individual differences, not only in its causes but also in its course and consequences. Thus, an initial and critical step is to develop assessment technologies that reliably distinguish individuals who can be characterized as following different developmental trajectories. Such assessment, of course, assumes that different developmental trajectories exist. Distinctions in risk factors between use and abuse, differences in associated expectancies and drinking motivations, and linkages over time between substance problems and conduct problems support this conceptualization. Much research is needed, however, to confirm the predictability of these paths and eventually to develop clinical assessments. For example, sociopathic alcoholism could constitute the extreme end of a continuum rather than a different developmental trajectory. Moffitt's (1993) work in the area of conduct disorders is an excellent model to follow. It is possible, for example, that early childhood temperament and conduct problems can be used to identify adolescent substance abusers who are more likely to show continuity of substance problems. Similarly, Moffitt's concept of young people becoming "ensnared" by the consequences of their acts has implications for the development of substance abuse problems as well as addiction.

Following Martin et al. (1995), much more research is needed to understand how concepts of dependence apply to adolescents. Growth modeling procedures may be useful in predicting different patterns of change related to individual differences.

If risk profiles are reliably established, research is needed to examine how individuals with different profiles respond to preventive programs and treatment strategies. It is possible that those most at risk for drug-related problems are least affected by prevention and treatment programs. For example, we need to know the impact of primary prevention programs on individuals who already have begun to drink or experiment with drugs. We have suggested that harm reduction approaches could be added to the list of strategies for working with adolescents. Harm reduction also provides a conceptual umbrella that can integrate a variety of intervention strategies. For example, a stepped care treatment scheme increases the intensity of intervention based on the response (or lack of response) to earlier interventions. At this time, we do not know if this approach is differentially effective for adolescents with different risk profiles.

There are also a host of pragmatic and logistical challenges in tailoring interventions to subsets of youth with different risk profiles. How does one keep them physically separate? For example, in a junior high school, how would one conduct a prevention program for only those youths most at risk? Could they be separated without labeling or social ostracism? Would harm reduction messages for the larger group create a social norm for the acceptance of use, which in turn would undermine intensive programming for those with high-risk profiles?

Research is also needed to evaluate integrated mental health and substance abuse treatment. Both substance abuse treatments and mental health treatments have much to offer adolescents who are at highest risk of developing ongoing problems. Given the multiple and etiological factors associated with sociopathy and their persistence over time, it seems shortsighted to treat these young people as if they had only an addiction, without addressing long-standing conduct-disordered behavior or comorbid depression and anxiety. Similarly, to the extent that substance dependence has developed, mental health interventions would benefit from integration with substance abuse treatment. It is not clear if the current 12-step philosophies are particularly useful in this context. Nevertheless, specified identification, targeting, and behavioral contracting about substance use within an integrated treatment program seem necessary.

When we embarked on this review, one of our goals was to evaluate what worked in the treatment of adolescent substance use problems. Unfortunately, few treatment outcome studies have been conducted. At this stage of treatment development, no one knows what is most effective. We have attempted to argue that an approach based on developmental definitions of alcohol-related problems and the minimization of harms makes sense in the treatment of adolescents who drink and use substances problematically. We conclude with the relatively straightforward recommendation that adolescent substance abuse treatments be subjected to the same rigorous scientific evaluations that are the standard in other forms of health care.

References

Adlaf, E. M., & Kohn, P. M. (1989). Alcohol advertising, consumption and abuse: A covariance-structural modeling look at Strickland's data. *British Journal of Addiction, 84*, 749–757.

Babor, T. F., Hofmann, M., DelBoca, F. K., Hesselbrock, V. M., Meyer, R. E., Dolinsky, Z. S., & Rounsaville, B. (1992). Types of alcoholics: I. Evidence for an empirically-derived typology based on indicators of vulnerability and severity. *Archives of General Psychiatry, 49*, 599–608.

Babor, T., & Lauerman, R. (1986). Classification and forms of inebriety: Historical antecedents of alcoholic typologies. In M. Galanter (Ed.), *Recent developments in alcoholism* (vol. 4, pp. 113–144). New York: Plenum Press.

Baer, J. S. (1993). Etiology and secondary prevention of alcohol problems with young adults. In J. S. Baer, G. A. Marlatt, R. J. McMahnon. (Eds.), *Addictive behaviors across the lifespan* (pp. 111–137). Newbury Park, CA: Sage.

Baer, J. S., Kivlahan, D. R., & Marlatt, G. A. (1992). Feedback and advice with high-risk college freshmen reduces drinking rates at three-month follow-up. *Alcoholism: Clinical and Experimental Research, 16*, 403.

Baer, J. S., Kivlahan, D. R., & Marlatt, G. A. (1994). Drinking risk reduction based on feedback and advice with college students: Two-year follow-up. *Alcoholism: Clinical and Experimental Research, 18*(2), 466.

Baer, J. S., Marlatt, G. A., Kivlahan, D. R., & Fromme, K. (1992). An experimental test of three methods of alcohol risk reduction with young adults. *Journal of Consulting & Clinical Psychology, 60* (6), 974–979.

Bailey, S. L., & Rachal, J. V. (1993). Dimensions of adolescent problem drinking. *Journal of Studies on Alcohol, 54,* 555–565.

Barnes, G. M. (1990). Impact of the family on adolescent drinking patterns. In R. L. Collins, K. E. Leonard, & J. S. Searles (Eds.), *Alcohol and the family: Research and clinical perspectives* (pp. 137–161). New York: Guilford Press.

Baumrind, D. (1985). Familial antecedents of adolescent drug use: A developmental perspective. In C. L. Jones & R. J. Battjes (Eds.), *Etiology of drug abuse: Implications for prevention.* NIDA Research Monograph No. 56. DHHS Publ. No. (ADM) 85–1335. Rockville, MD: National Institute on Drug Abuse.

Baumrind, D. (1991). The influence of parenting style on adolescent competence and substance use. *Journal of Early Adolescence, 11,* 56–95.

Baumrind, D., & Moselle, K. A. (1985). A developmental perspective on adolescent drug abuse. *Advances in Alcohol and Substance Abuse, 4,* 41–67.

Botvin, G. J. (1986). Substance abuse prevention research: Recent developments and future directions. *Journal of School Health, 56,* 369–374.

Botvin, G. J., Baker, E., Dusenbury, L., Tortu, S., & Botvin, E. M. (1990). Preventing adolescent drug abuse through a multimodal cognitive-behavioral approach: Results of a 3-year study. *Journal of Consulting and Clinical Psychology, 58,* 437–446.

Boyd, G. M., Howard, J., & Zucker, R. A. (1995). *Alcohol problems among adolescents: Current directions in prevention research.* Northvale, NJ: Erlbaum.

Braucht, G. N. (1982). Problem drinking among adolescents: A review and analysis of psychological research. *Alcohol and health monograph no. 4: Special population issues* (pp. 143–162). Rockville, MD: National Institute of Alcohol Abuse and Alcoholism.

Brown, S. A., Vik, P. W., & Creamer, V. A. (1989) Characteristics of relapse following adolescent substance abuse treatment. *Addictive Behaviors, 14,* 291–300.

Bucholz, K. K. (1990). A review of correlates of alcohol use and alcohol problems in adolescence. In M. Galanter (Ed.), *Recent developments in alcoholism* (Vol. 8, pp. 111–123). New York: Plenum Press.

Bukstein, O. G. (1995). *Adolescent substance abuse.* New York: Wiley.

Cahalan, D., & Room, R. (1974). *Problem drinking among American men.* New Brunswick, NJ: Rutgers Center for Alcohol Studies.

Califano, J. A. (1994). *Radical surgery: What's next for America's health care?* New York: Times Books.

Catalano, R. F., Haggerty, K. P., Gainey, R. R., Hope, M. J., & Brewer, D. (in press). Effectiveness of primary prevention interventions with high-risk youth. In W. J. Bukoski & R. I. Evans (Eds.), *Cost benefit/cost effectiveness research of drug abuse prevention: Implications for programming and policy*. Nida Research Monograph Series. Rockville, MD: National Institute on Drug Abuse.

Catalano, R. F., Hawkins, J. D., Wells, E. A., Miller, J., & Brewer, D. (1991). Evaluation of the effectiveness of adolescent drug abuse treatment, assessment of risks for relapse, and promising approaches for relapse prevention. *International Journal of the Addictions, 25*, 1085–1140.

Chassin, L. (1984). Adolescent substance use and abuse. In P. Karoly & J. J. Steffan (Eds.), *Adolescent behavior disorders: Foundations and contemporary concerns* (pp. 99–152). Lexington, MA: D. C. Heath.

Chassin, L., Mann, L. M., & Sher, K. J. (1988). Self-awareness theory, family history of alcoholism, and adolescent alcohol involvement. *Journal of Abnormal Psychology, 97*, 206–217.

Chen, K., & Kandel, D. B. (1995). The natural history of drug use from adolescence to the mid-thirties in a general population sample. *American Journal of Public Health, 85*, 41–47.

Chng, C. L. (1981). The goal of abstinence: Implications for drug education. *Journal of Drug Education, 11*, 13–18.

Christiansen, B. A., & Goldman, M. S. (1983). Alcohol-related expectancies versus demographic/background variables in the prediction of adolescent drinking. *Journal of Consulting and Clinical Psychology, 51*, 249–257.

Christiansen, B. A., Smith, G. T., Roehling, P. V., & Goldman, M. S. (1989). Using alcohol expectancies to predict adolescent drinking behavior after one year. *Journal of Consulting and Clinical Psychology, 57*, 93–99.

Colder, C. R., & Chassin, L. (1992, August). *Differentiating "substance use" from "problem substance use" in adolescents: Data from a study of adolescents at risk.* Paper presented at the annual meeting of the American Psychological Association, Washington, DC.

Cooper, M. L. (1994). Motivations for alcohol use among adolescents: Development and validation of a four-factor model. *Psychological Assessment, 6*, 117–128.

Cooper, M. L., Frone, M. R., Russell, M., & Mudar, P. (1995). Drinking to regulate positive and negative emotions: A motivational model of alcohol use. *Journal of Personality and Social Psychology, 69*, 990–1005.

Copeland, P. (1992). Prevention of alcoholism in black youth. In G. W. Lawson & A. W. Lawson (Eds.), *Adolescent substance abuse: Etiology, treatment and prevention* (pp. 507–515). Gaithersburg, MD: Aspen.

Covert, J., & Wangberg, D. (1992). Peer counseling: Positive peer pressure. In

G. W. Lawson & A. W. Lawson (Eds.), *Adolescent substance abuse: Etiology, treatment and prevention* (pp. 131–139). Gaithersburg, MD: Aspen.

Del Boca, F. K , Babor, T. F., & McLaney, M. A. (1995). Youth evaluation services (YES): Assessment, systems of referral, and treatment effects. In E. Rahdert & D. Czechowicz (Eds.), *Adolescent drug abuse: Clinical assessment and therapeutic interventions* (pp. 325–340). NIDA Research Monograph 156. Rockville, MD: National Institute on Drug Abuse.

Des-Jarlais, D. C. (1995). Harm reduction: A framework for incorporating science into drug policy. *American Journal of Public Health, 85*(1), 10–12.

Dielman, T. E., Butchart, A. T., Shope, J. T., & Miller, M. (1990–1991). Environmental correlates of adolescent substance use and misuse: Implications for prevention programs. *International Journal of the Addictions, 25*, 855–880.

Donovan, J. E., & Jessor, R. (1978). Adolescent problem drinking: Psychosocial correlates in a national sample study. *Journal of Studies on Alcohol, 39*, 1500–1524.

Donovan, J. E., Jessor, R., & Jessor, L. (1983). Problem drinking in adolescence and young adulthood. *Journal of Studies on Alcohol, 44*, 109–137.

Duncan, D. F., Nicholson, T., Clifford P., Hawkins, W., & Petosa (1994). Harm reduction: An emerging new paradigm for drug education. *Journal of Drug Education, 24*(4), 281–290.

Dusenbury, L., & Botvin, G. J. (1992). Applying the competency enhancement model to substance abuse prevention. In M. Kessler, S. E. Goldston, & J. M. Joffe (Eds.), *The present and future of prevention: In honor of George W. Albee* (pp. 182–195). Newbury Park, CA: Sage.

Ellickson, P. L., Bell, R. M., & McGuigan, K. (1993). Preventing adolescent drug use: Long-term results of a junior high program. *American Journal of Public Health, 83*, 856–861.

Engs, R. C., & Fors, S. W. (1988). Drug abuse hysteria: The challenge of keeping perspective. *Journal of School Health, 58*, 26–28.

Ennett, S. T., Tobler, N. S., Ringwalt, C. L., & Flewelling, R. L. (1994). How effective is drug abuse resistance education? A meta-analysis of project DARE outcome evaluations. *American Journal of Public Health, 84*, 1394–1401.

Farrell, A. D., Danish, S. J., & Howard, C. W. (1992). Relationship between drug use and other problem behaviors in urban adolescents. *Journal of Consulting and Clinical Psychology, 60*, 705–712.

Fillmore, K. M. (1987). Prevalence, incidence and chronicity of drinking patterns and problems among men as a function of age: A longitudinal and cohort analysis. *British Journal of Addiction, 82*, 77–83.

Fillmore, K. M., & Midanik, L. (1984). Chronicity of drinking problems among men: A longitudinal study. *Journal of Studies on Alcohol, 45,* 228–236.

Gorman, D. M. (1992). Using theory and basic research to target primary prevention programs. Recent developments and future prospects. *Alcohol and Alcoholism, 27,* 583–594.

Gorman, D. M. (1995). Are school-based resistance skills training programs effective in preventing alcohol misuse? *Journal of Alcohol and Drug Education, 41,* 74–98.

Gorman, D. M. (1996). Do school-based social skills training programs prevent alcohol use among young people? *Addiction Research, 4,* 191–210.

Grossman, M., Chaloupka, F. J., Saffer, H., & Laixuthai, A. (1995). Effects of alcohol price policy on youth: A summary of economic research. In G. Boyd, J. Howard, & R. Zucker (Eds.), *Alcohol problems among adolescents* (pp. 225–242). Hillsdale, NJ: Erlbaum.

Gutierres, S. E., Molof, M., & Ungerleider, S. (1994). Relationship of "risk" factors to teen substance use: A comparison of abstainers, infrequent users, and frequent users. *International Journal of Addictions, 29,* 1559–1579.

Hawkins, J. D., Catalano, R. F., & Miller, J. Y. (1992). Risk and protective factors for alcohol and other drug problems in adolescence and early adulthood: Implications for substance abuse prevention. *Psychological Bulletin, 112,* 64–105.

Hesselbrock, M. N. (1995). Genetic determinants of alcoholic subtypes. In H. Begleiter & B. Kissin, *The genetics of alcoholism* (pp. 40–69). New York: Oxford University Press.

Hillman, S. B., & Sawilowsky, S. S. (1992). A comparison of two grouping methods in distinguishing levels of substance use. *Journal of Clinical Child Psychology, 21,* 348–353.

Hingson, R. (1993). Prevention of alcohol-impaired driving. *Alcohol Health and Research World, 17,* 28–34.

Hover, S., & Gaffney, L. R. (1991). The relationship between social skills and adolescent drinking. *Alcohol & Alcoholism, 26,* 207–214.

Howard, J. (1993). Alcohol prevention research: Concepts, phases, and tasks at hand. *Alcohol Health and Research World, 17,* 5–9.

Huber, C. (1994). Needle park: What can we learn from the Zurich experience? *Addiction, 89*(5), 513–516.

Institute of Medicine. (1990). *Broadening the base of treatment for alcohol problems.* Washington, DC: National Academy Press.

Jainchill, N., Bhattacharya, G., & Yagelka, J. (1995). Therapeutic communities for adolescents. In E. Rahdert & D. Czechowicz, (Eds.), *Adolescent drug abuse: Clinical assessment and therapeutic interventions* (pp. 190–217). NIDA Research Monograph 156. Rockville, MD: National Institute on Drug Abuse.

Jessor, R. (1982). Problem behavior and developmental transition in adolescence. *Journal of School Health, 52,* 295–300.

Jessor, R. (1985). Adolescent problem drinking: Psychosocial aspects and developmental outcomes. In L. H. Towle (Ed.), *Proceedings: NIAAAA WHO Collaborating Center designation meeting and alcohol research seminar.* DHHS Pub. No. (ADM) 85-2370. Washington, DC: U.S. Government Printing Office

Jessor, R., Donovan, J. E., & Costa, F. M. (1991). *Beyond adolescence: Problem behavior and young adult development.* Cambridge: Cambridge University Press.

Johnston, L. D., O'Malley, P. M., & Bachman, J. G. (1994). *National survey results on drug use from the Monitoring the Future study, 1975–1993.* NIH Pub. No. 94-3810. Rockville, MD: National Institute on Drug Abuse.

Johnston, L. D., O'Malley, P. M., & Bachman, J. G. (1995). *National survey results on drug use from the Monitoring the Future study, 1975–1994, Vol. 1: Secondary school students.* NIH Pub. No. 95-4026. Washington, DC: U.S. Department of Health and Human Services.

Kaminer, Y. (1995). Pharmacotherapy for adolescents with psychoactive substance use disorders. In E. Rahdert & D. Czechowicz (Eds.), *Adolescent drug abuse: Clinical assesment and therapeutic interventions* (pp. 291–324). NIDA Research Monograph 156. Rockville, MD: National Institute on Drug Abuse.

Kandel, D. B. (1980). Drug and drinking behavior among youth. *Annual Review of Sociology, 6,* 235–285.

Kandel, D. B. (1985). On processes of peer influences in adolescent drug use: A developmental perspective. *Advances in Alcohol and Substance Abuse, 4,* 139–163.

Kazdin, A. E. (1995). *Conduct disorders in childhood and adolescence.* (2nd ed.). Thousand Oaks, CA: Sage.

Kendall, P. C. (1993). Cognitive-behavioral therapies with youth: Guiding theory, current status, and emerging developments. *Journal of Consulting and Clinical Psychology, 61,* 235–247.

Kilty, K. M. (1990). Drinking styles of adolescents and young adults. *Journal of Studies on Alcohol, 51,* 556–564

Lawson, G. W. (1992). Twelve-step programs and the treatment of adolescent substance abuse. In G. W. Lawson & A. W. Lawson (Eds.), *Adolescent substance abuse: Etiology, treatment and prevention* (pp. 219–230). Gaithersburg, MD: Aspen.

Lawson, G. W., & Lawson, A. W. (1992). *Adolescent substance abuse; Etiology, treatment and prevention.* Gaithersburg, MD: Aspen.

Liddle, H. A., Dakot, G., Diamond, G., Holt, M., Aroyo, J., & Watson, M. (1992). The adolescent module in multidimensional family therapy. In G. W. Lawson & A. W. Lawson (Eds.), *Adolescent substance abuse: Etiology, treatment and prevention* (pp. 165–186). Gaithersburg, MD: Aspen.

McGee, L., & Newcomb, M. D. (1992). General deviance syndrome: Expanded hierarchical evaluations at four ages from early adolescence to adulthood. *Journal of Consulting and Clinical Psychology, 60,* 766–776.

MacLean, M. G. (1995). *Distinguishing between problem and non-problem drinking in adolescence.* Unpublished doctoral dissertation, Arizona State University, Tempe.

McMahon, R. J., & Wells, K. C. (1989). Conduct disorders. In E. J. Mash & R. A. Barkley (Eds.), *Treatment of childhood disorders* (pp. 73–132). New York: Guilford Press.

Mandell, M. F. (1992). Primary prevention of alcoholism: Public school programs. In G. W. Lawson & A. W. Lawson (Eds.), *Adolescent substance abuse: Etiology, treatment and prevention.* (pp. 451–462). Gaithersburg, MD: Aspen.

Marlatt, G. A., Baer, J. S., Donovan, D. M., & Kivlahan, D. R. (1988). Addictive behaviors: Etiology and treatment. *Annual Review of Psychology, 39,* 223–252.

Marlatt, G. A., Baer, J. S. & Larimer, M. E. (1995). Preventing alcohol abuse in college students: A harm-reduction approach. In G. M. Boyd, J. Howard, & R. Zucker *Alcohol problems among adolescents: Current directions in prevention research* (pp. 147–172). Northvale, NJ: Erlbaum.

Marlatt, G. A., & Tapert, S. (1993). Harm reduction: Reducing the risks of addictive behaviors. In J. S. Baer, G. A. Marlatt, & R. J. McMahnon, (Eds.), *Addictive behaviors across the lifespan* (pp. 243–273). Newbury Park, CA: Sage.

Martin, C. S., Kaczynski, N. A., Maisto, S. A., Bukstein, O. M., & Moss, H. B. (1995) Patterns of DSM-IV alcohol abuse and dependence symptoms in adolescent drinkers. *Journal of Studies of Alcohol, 56,* 672–680.

Mayer, J. E. (1988). The personality characteristics of adolescents who use and misuse alcohol. *Adolescence, 23,* 383–404.

Miller, W. R., & Rollnick, S. (1991). *Motivational interviewing: Preparing people for change.* New York: Guilford Press.

Mitic, W. R., McGuire, D. P., & Neumann, B. (1987). Adolescent problem drinking and perceived stress. *Journal of Alcohol and Drug Education, 33,* 45–54.

Moberg, D. P. (1983). Identifying adolescents with alcohol problems: A field test of the Adolescent Alcohol Involvement Scale. *Journal of Studies on Alcohol, 44*, 701–721.

Moffitt, T. E. (1993). "Life-course-persistent" and "adolescent-limited" anti-social behavior: A developmental taxonomy. *Psychological Review, 100*, 674–701.

Moffitt, T. E., Caspi, A., Dickson, N., Silva, P., & Stanton, W. (1996). Child-hood-onset versus adolescent-onset antisocial conduct problems in males: Natural history from ages 3 to 18 years. *Development and Psychopathology, 8*, 399–424.

Moscowitz, J. M. (1989). The primary prevention of alcohol problems: A critical review of the research literature. *Journal of Studies on Alcohol, 1989, 50*, 54–88.

Newcomb, M. D., & Bentler, P. M. (1988). *Consequences of adolescent drug use.* Newbury Park, CA: Sage.

Newcomb, M. D., & Bentler, P. M. (1989). Substance use and abuse among children and teenagers. *American Psychologist, 44*, 242–248.

Oetting, E. R., & Beauvais, F. (1990). Adolescent drug use: Findings of na-tional and local surveys. *Journal of Consulting and Clinical Psychology, 58*, 385–394.

Pentz, M. A., Dwyer, J. H., MacKinnon, D. P., Flay, B. R., Hansen, W. B., Wang, E. Y., & Johnson, C. A. (1989). A multi-community trial for primary prevention of adolescent drug abuse: Effects on drug use preva-lence. *Journal of the American Medical Association, 261*, 3259–3266.

Prochaska, J. O., DiClemente, C. C., & Norcross, J. C. (1992). In search of how people change: Applications to addictive behaviors. *American Psy-chologist, 47*(9), 1102–1114.

Radosevich, M., Lanza-Kaduce, L., Akers, R. L., & Krohn, M. D. (1980). The sociology of adolescent drug and drinking behavior: A review of the state of the field: Part II. *Deviant Behavior, 1*, 145–169.

Rooney, J. F. (1982). Perceived differences of standards for alcohol use among American youth. *Journal of Studies on Alcohol, 43*, 1069–1083.

Rooney, J. F. (1982–1983). The influence of informal control sources upon adolescent alcohol use and problems. *American Journal of Drug and Alco-hol Abuse, 9*, 233–245.

Ross, G. R. (1993). *Treating adolescent substance abuse.* Boston: Allyn & Bacon, 1993.

Ross, H. E., Gavin, D. R., & Skinner, H. A. (1990). Diagnostic validity of the MAST and the Alcohol Dependence Scale in the assessment of DSM-III alcohol disorders. *Journal of Studies on Alcohol, 51*(6), 506–513.

Sher, K. J. (1991). *Children of alcoholics: A critical appraisal of theory and research.* Chicago: University of Chicago Press.

Smart, R. G., Adlaf, E. M., & Walsh, G. W. (1994). The relationships between declines in drinking and alcohol problems among Ontario students: 1979–1991. *Journal of Studies on Alcohol, 55,* 338–341.

Smith, G. T., McCarthy, D. M., & Goldman, M. S. (1995). Self-reported drinking and alcohol-related problems among early adolescents: Dimensionality and validity over 24 months. *Journal of Studies on Alcohol, 56,* 383–394.

Somers, J. M. (1995). *Harm reduction and the prevention of alcohol problems among secondary school students.* Unpublished doctoral dissertation, University of Washington.

Spear, S. F., & Skala, S. Y. (1995). Posttreatment services for chemically dependent adolescents. In E. Rahdert & D. Czechowicz (Eds.), *Adolescent drug abuse: Clinical assessment and therapeutic interventions* (pp. 341–364). NIDA Research Monograph 156. Rockville, MD: National Institute on Drug Abuse.

Steel, E. (1995). AIDS, drugs, and the adolescent. In E. Rahdert & D. Czechowicz (Eds.), *Adolescent drug abuse: Clinical assessment and therapeutic interventions* (pp. 130–145). Rockville, MD: NIDA Research Monograph 156.

Stein, J. A., Newcomb, M. D., & Bentler, P. M. (1987). An 8-year study of multiple influences on drug use and drug use consequences. *Journal of Personality and Social Psychology, 53,* 1094–1105.

Swaim, R. C. (1991). Childhood risk factors and adolescent drug and alcohol abuse. *Educational Psychology Review, 3,* 363–398.

Tarter, R. E., & Vanyukov, M. (1994). Alcoholism: A developmental disorder. *Journal of Consulting and Clinical Psychology, 62,* 1096–1107.

Temple, M. T., & Fillmore, K. M. (1986). The variability of drinking patterns and problems among young men, age 16–31: A longitudinal study. *The International Journal of the Addictions, 20,* 1595–1620.

Tobler, N. S. (1986). Meta-analysis of 143 adolescent drug prevention programs: Quantitative outcome results of program participants compared to control or comparison group. *Journal of Drug Issues, 16,* 537–567.

U.S. Department of Health and Human Services. (1993a). *Guidelines for the treatment of alcohol- and other drug-abusing adolescents: Treatment improvement protocol #4.* DHHS Pub No. 93-2010. Public Health Service, Substance Abuse and Mental Health Services Administration, Center for Substance Abuse Treatment.

U.S. Department of Health and Human Services. (1993b). *Screening and assessment of alcohol- and other drug-abusing adolescents: Treatment improvement protocol #3.* DHHS Pub No. 93-2009. Public Health Service, Substance Abuse and Mental Health Services Administration, Center for Substance Abuse Treatment.

Wagenaar, A. C. & Perry, C. L. (1995). Community strategies for the reduction of youth drinking: Theory and application. In G. Boyd, J. Howard, & R. Zucker (Eds.), *Alcohol problems among adolescents* (pp 197–224). Hillsdale, NJ: Erlbaum.

Waite-O'Brien, N. (1992). Alcohol and drug abuse among female adolescents. In G. W. Lawson & A. W. Lawson (Eds.), *Adolescent substance abuse: Etiology, treatment and prevention* (pp. 367–380). Gaithersburg, MD: Aspen.

Wechsler, H., Davenport, A., Dowdall, G., Moeyken, B., & Castillo, S. (1994). Health and behavioral consequences of binge drinking in college. A national survey of students at 140 campuses. *Journal of the American Medical Association, 272*(21), 1672–1677.

White, H. R. (1987). Longitudinal stability and dimensional structure of problem drinking in adolescence. *Journal of Studies on Alcohol, 48,* 541–550.

White, H. R. (1989). Relationship between heavy drug and alcohol use and problem use among adolescents. In S. Einstein (Ed.), *Drug and alcohol use: Issues and factors* (pp. 61–71). New York: Plenum Press.

White, H. R., & Labouvie, E. W. (1989). Toward the assessment of adolescent problem drinking. *Journal of Studies on Alcohol, 50,* 30–37.

Yamaguchi, K., & Kandel, D. B. (1985a). On the resolution of role incompatibility: A life event history analysis of family roles and marijuana use. *American Journal of Sociology, 90,* 1284–1325.

Yamaguchi, K., & Kandel, D. B. (1985b). Dynamic relationships between premarital cohabitation and illicit drug use: An event-history analysis of role selection and role socialization. *American Sociological Review, 50,* 530–546.

Young, T. J. (1992). Substance abuse among Native American youth. In G. W. Lawson & A. W. Lawson (Eds.), *Adolescent substance abuse: Etiology, treatment and prevention* (pp. 381–390). Gaithersburg, MD: Aspen.

Zucker, R. A. (1987). The four alcoholisms: A developmental account of the etiologic process. In P. C. Rivers (Ed.), *Nebraska symposium of motivation, Vol. 34. Alcohol and addictive behaviors* (pp. 27–83). Lincoln: University of Nebraska Press.

Zucker, R. A. (1994). Pathways to alcohol problems and alcoholism: A developmental account of the evidence for multiple alcoholisms and for contextual contributions to risk. In R. Zucker (Ed.), *The development of alcohol problems: Exploring the biopsychosocial matrix of risk.* Research Monograph No. 26. Rockville, MD: U.S. Department of Health and Human Services.

Zucker, R. A., Fitzgerald, H. E., & Moses, H. D. (1995). Emergence of alcohol problems and the several alcoholisms: A developmental perspective on etiologic theory and life course trajectory. In D. Cicchetti & D. J. Cohen (Eds.), *Developmental psychopathology* (Vol. 2, pp. 677–711). New York: Wiley.

Zucker, R. A., & Comberg, E.S.L. (1986). Etiology of alcoholism reconsidered: The case for a biopsychosocial process. *American Psychologist, 41,* 783–793.

7

Risky driving behavior among adolescents

Allan F. Williams

It is well known that many young people have driving styles that heighten their risk of being in a motor vehicle crash. Compared with older people, young drivers are more likely to drive fast, follow too closely, overtake in a risky manner, allow too little time to merge, and fail to yield to pedestrians (Bergeron, 1995; Jonah, 1986; Romanowicz & Gebers, 1990; Saibel, Salzberg, & Thurston, 1996). When these factors combine with young people's lack of driving experience – especially their reduced ability to recognize and respond to hazardous situations – the result is a greatly elevated crash involvement rate, particularly among the youngest drivers (Williams, 1996). The elevated crash rate of young beginners per mile driven is illustrated in Figure 7.1. Teenagers have a higher crash risk than older drivers; within the teenage years, 16-year-olds (43 crashes per million miles) and 17-year-olds (30) have particularly high crash rates compared with 18- to 19-year-olds (15). Deaths from motor vehicle crashes represent the largest health problem among 16- to 19-year-olds, accounting for about one-third of all their deaths in the United States. Thus, in terms of behaviors that compromise the health of adolescents, motor vehicle use is a major contributor.

Overview and new perspectives

Despite the importance of motor vehicle use in contributing to health problems among adolescents, the highway safety field has existed largely outside the broader public health field. Because most people drive cars and were once young drivers, the risky driving style of many

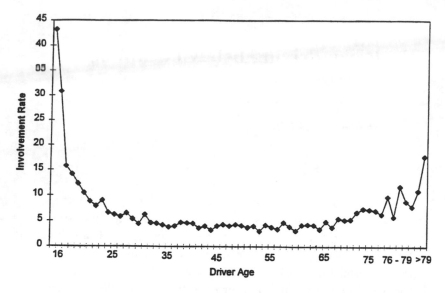

Figure 7.1 All crash involvement per million miles by driver age, 1990.

adolescents has wide recognition and has been a focus of prevention programs. Speeding is a factor often associated with young driver crashes, and emphasis has been placed on controlling this behavior through enforcement and punishment rather than trying to understand what of factors in adolescent development promote and support risky behaviors of this type. There has been a tendency to focus on single behaviors, especially alcohol use and driving, in isolation from other related problem behaviors related to crash involvement. Cross-sectional studies have predominated. Licensing systems have traditionally concentrated on the risky behaviors themselves and have been designed to identify and punish wrongdoers. Basically, the traditional approach has been to provide formal driver education courses to teach young people how to drive and to single out and punish those who get into trouble while doing so.

Newer perspectives on this problem include more sophisticated approaches to both understanding and reducing it. There is increasing recognition of the importance of lifestyle factors contributing to adolescent driving practices. There is new awareness that youthful driving should be viewed in the more general context of adolescent development. It is also recognized that those most likely to display risky driving practices engage in a variety of other problematic and health-compromising behaviors. This link is important for understanding and potentially modifying both risky driving and the other behaviors. In addition, the twin contributions of driving inexperience and immaturity, and their interactive role in producing the young driver problem, are now increasingly recognized. These perspectives have been furthered by studies following young people over time as they traverse the developmental stage. These studies are yielding more through understanding of the development and course of risky driving styles among young people and indicating how lifestyle factors might be modified to reduce the motor vehicle injury problem.

Licensing systems also are becoming more sophisticated. Graduated licensing systems, now being considered in many jurisdictions, address both inexperience and risky driving by encouraging the accumulation of beginning on-road driving experience in situations in which risky driving is less likely to occur, thereby extending the licensing process over time so that some maturity may be gained prior to receiving an unrestricted license. In constructing effective licensing systems, it is important to follow young people over time – before, during, and after they leave the graduated system – to determine how those differing in risk tendencies react to the restrictions and other provisions. In this chapter these new approaches are discussed, as well as other approaches to understanding and dealing with the risky driving syndrome of many adolescents.

This chapter presents primarily an applied perspective, focusing mainly on the safety consequences of early licensing and risky driving and how the problem can be reduced. Getting a license and access to a motor vehicle are, however, key events in adolescent development, with all sorts of lifestyle ramifications. Although highway safety professionals typically have not embraced the broader public health field, it is also the case that social scientists studying adolescent development have largely neglected the area of motor vehicle use by young people. This is unfortunate, both because of the developmental importance of this behavior and because it relates importantly to many of the behaviors they do study and that are addressed in this volume.

Are all adolescents risky drivers?

Questions about the origins and meaning of risky driving practices among youth are important both for understanding the phenomena and for providing clues as to how to deal with them in ways that reduce crash involvement. For example, we know that young people as a group are more likely to drive in risky ways, but is it all young people or primarily a subgroup that we should be concerned about? In the highway safety literature, there is scant discussion of what biological and psychosocial factors might contribute to youthful driving practices or the extent to which risky driving is a developmental phenomenon, an adaptive behavior to be expected of normal adolescents (see Lavery, Siegel, Cousins, & Rubovits, 1993). However, most researchers in the field read the data that have attempted to sort out the separate contributions to crashes of age and driving experience as indicating that young drivers as a group are more of a problem than older drivers, not just because of inexperience but also because of some age-related factors (Mayhew & Simpson, 1990). Obviously, not all young drivers display a risky driving style, but from this perspective, risky driving and other contributing factors are attributed nonspecifically to "immaturity associated with youthful age," and until people "mature out" of this behavior they may be subject, as a group, to special attention. At the same time, we have known for a long time that there is a subgroup of special interest – a problem group – that is particularly likely to have a risky driving style and contribute to the motor vehicle crash problem. So this group is an important one to consider.

Thrill-seeking or inexperience?

What has received some attention in the highway safety literature is how to interpret the risky driving style. This style is risky in that it increases the likelihood of a crash, but is this deliberate risk-taking – sensation or thrill-seeking – or something else? Certainly, some young people are rewarded for high-risk behavior through feelings of power, esteem and independence, peer recognition, and the satisfaction that comes from mastering risk (Simpson, 1996). Alternatively, it may be that some risky driving behaviors are not motivated by risk-taking, but rather that drivers are unaware or unappreciative of the potential consequences. Some have argued that what appears to be risk-taking is primarily a reflection of inexperience in terms of car placement, speed adjustments, and so on. For example, according to Macdonald (1994), "it needs to be recognized that behavior such as excessive speeding or following too closely, which are objectively risky, might be due at least in part to a failure to identify all the potential hazards and associated risks of such behavior. From this point of view, the behavior might be due not so much to deliberate risk taking or risk acceptance, as to lack of skill in hazard perception and cognition" (p. 26).

The circumstances of some of the crashes of young people appear to reflect primarily thrill-seeking (more likely among the problem sub-group but not restricted to them), although some crashes that initially appear to be related to risk-taking (whether deliberate or not) probably are related, on closer inspection, primarily to inexperience. Many crashes combine risk-taking and inexperience, such as getting into trouble because of driving too fast around a curve and then overcorrecting. How one decodes the meaning of risky driving shapes one's approach to how to reduce this behavior. Do we try to teach young people risk awareness or hazard perception techniques through some form of driver training or alternatively try to find ways to persuade young drivers to modify their risky driving style? This question is posed in an either-or fashion, but clearly inexperience and immaturity factors that result in driving that heightens the risk of crashing are interactive, and both need to be addressed.

The problem group

Much of the study of risky driving among adolescents has focused on the subgroup most likely to display this driving style. It has been known for a long time that there is such a subgroup (e.g., see Cohen, 1955; McClelland, Wanner, & Vanneman, 1972; McFarland & Moore, 1960; Sobel & Underhill, 1976). Various studies have noted the inter-relationship among certain personality traits (rebelliousness, alienation, independence, defiance of authority), risky driving practices (speeding, drinking and driving), reduced parental influence, and crashes and vi-olations. It is in this subgroup that thrill-seeking is an important motive for risky driving. Deviant driving and crash involvement also have been found to be related to a syndrome of problem behavior including marijuana use, heavy alcohol use, smoking, trouble with the law, and various other delinquent behaviors (see also Beirness & Simpson, 1988; Wilson & Jonah, 1988).

Early studies of risky driving merely noted its relationship to other characteristics of young people and did not develop a coherent framework for understanding the interrelationships further. An important advance occurred when Jessor (1987) extended problem-behavior theory to risky driving as another example of adolescent problem behavior, which in turn is an aspect of a more general lifestyle, and demonstrated that the psychosocial risk factors in problem-behavior theory account for a substantial portion of the variance in adolescent risky driving behavior.

Interventions targeting risky driving

The subgroup of problem drivers is a natural target for intervention because of their elevated crash rate within a group that as a whole already has a very high crash rate. Jessor (1987) noted that the embeddedness of risky driving in the same set of personality, perceived environment, and behavior variables as other adolescent problem behaviors suggests that intervention should be focused at the level of lifestyle rather than restricted to risky driving by itself. Recognition that how a young person drives is a reflection of other lifestyle characteristics, and that lifestyle changes may hold the key to reducing motor vehicle injuries, represents an important shift in focus in dealing with the young driver problem. At the same time, the traits, values, and peer associations of this high-risk subgroup make it a hard-to-reach group, difficult to influence through educational or persuasive efforts.

One notable attempt to modify risky driving was undertaken in the late 1960s by Schuman, McConochie, and Pelz (1971), who conducted an extensive program for a group of high school seniors. Drivers in the treatment group participated in seven 2-hour sessions dealing with the effects of anger, frustration, and competition on driving; situational factors in driving and how to deal with them; traffic incidents (collisions, close calls, etc.) experienced by the participants; and examination of personal driving styles – their strengths and weaknesses and what changes might be needed. Discussions were facilitated by "trigger films" that depicted potentially dangerous driving situations aggravated by emotional factors and by films of real traffic situations. Personalized letters were sent to each participant 6 and 12 months after the workshops, congratulating the drivers if they had recorded no crashes or expressing concern if they had been in a crash. Crash rates of participants in the pilot phase were lower, but not significantly so, than those of a comparison group over the subsequent 2-year period. A follow-up, larger-scale program, somewhat less intense than the pilot program (e.g., 6 hours of discussion rather than 14) did not find similar positive effects on crashes (Pelz & Williams, 1974).

A recently instituted driver education curriculum in Germany has similar program elements, focusing on driving situations that can trigger emotional responses, such as self-assertion when driving with other teenagers and dealing with impatience and traffic pressures (Heinrich, 1993). This program has not been formally evaluated.

Studies of young people over time

Fuller understanding of the risky driving syndrome and the target subgroup is being developed from studies that follow young driver populations over time. This represents an important advance both in the understanding of this behavior and in the possibilities for intervention. In a 4-year longitudinal cohort study of young people, variables from problem-behavior theory were particularly useful in distinguishing between young people who subsequently became involved in a crash and those who did not, and these differences were evident up to 3 years prior to crash involvement. As Beirness, Simpson, and Mayhew (1993) pointed out, "Early intervention – as early as age 13 or 14 – seems warranted" (p. 890) and "While grade school traffic programs may have some merit, broader benefits may be achieved through programs that target the psychosocial correlates of problem behavior – e.g., self confidence and self esteem" (p. 890). This longitudinal study tracked precursors of the development of risky driving practices. In a complementary study, Jessor, Turbin, and Costa (1997) traced the developmental course of risky driving over time based on a three-wave annual survey of licensed drivers aged 18–25. This study found that change in behavioral conventionality among men (e.g., decreased tolerance of deviance, increased religiosity) predicted maturing out of risky driving, whereas among women the significant predictors were changes in social role status (getting married, getting a job). According to the authors, "The changes in social roles and in conventionality appear to reflect a developmental process that involves the adoption of more conventional attitudes, values, beliefs, and behaviors with the approach to and entry into young adulthood" (p. 14). In terms of reducing the motor vehicle crash problem, the authors noted, "Since it is very likely that risky driving is a significant cause of crashes, changes in lifestyle – in social roles and in psychosocial and behavioral conventionality – may be important targets for intervention to reduce the morbidity and mortality associated with youthful driving" (p. 15).

These recent studies that follow young people over time provide important information about the type and timing of applicable interventions. On the one hand, one might try to intervene early in the teenage years because behaviors that are associated with driving problems are identifiable well before any driving has taken place. Alternatively, one might try to speed up the maturity process, making young people more like older drivers in terms of decision making and responsibility. Presently, the development of such programs that would be effective and applicable on a widespread basis seems unlikely. Part of the issue is our lack of thorough understanding of why risky driving occurs. As Simpson (1996) notes, "The current state of knowledge provides little information about how the developmental process and motivational factors influence young people to engage in risky driving behaviors" (p. 15). However, lifestyle behaviors, by their nature, are not easy to affect through intervention programs that are, inevitably, short-term efforts. Attempting to enlighten young people through group discussion or other techniques demonstrating how lifestyle influences driving, indicating that they themselves are at high risk, and providing them with protective strategies is likely to have a short-term effect at most.

Because risky driving is associated with other problem behaviors, it is instructive to examine how modification of such behaviors has been approached. Sophisticated education programs based on social learning and communication theory principles have been applied to alcohol use, including drinking and driving, but these ventures have had limited success. Interestingly, there are no known examples of current lifestyle influence programs in the United States that have tried to modify risky driving not involving alcohol use. In recent years, programs utilizing techniques such as social skills/peer pressure resistance, decision making training, and so on have been applied, with very limited success, to alcohol use, other drug use, and smoking, but risky driving practices have not been addressed in this manner (see, e.g., Dielman, Shope, Leech, & Butchart, 1989; Ellickson, Bell, & McGuigan, 1993; Hansen, Malotte, & Fielding, 1988). There has been discussion in the driver education field about developing advanced programs that would attempt to reduce risky driving by teaching safe driving skills, decision-making techniques, awareness of personal risk, and so on (Gregerson, 1995; Lonero & Clinton, 1996; U.S. Department of Transportation, 1994). Such programs have yet to be developed and tested.

Licensing systems targeting problem drivers

Licensing systems are obligated to deal with all young people as they become old enough to begin the licensing process. Licensing and testing systems traditionally have not addressed lifestyle factors; the risky driving style of young people is taken as a given. Licensing regulations in the United States traditionally have been based on treatment or punishment of those who incur traffic violations or crashes. That is, the focus has been on the risky behaviors themselves, behaviors proximal to crashes or the risk of crashing such as speeding, without attention to what factors in the lives of young people promote and support risky driving. States typically allow full driving privileges on licensure but keep young beginners in a probationary phase, using the threat of punishment – license suspension and/or extension of the probationary period – to encourage safe driving. Many states have regulations that allow license penalties to be applied to young beginners at an earlier stage than older drivers, and the penalties may be more severe. Probationary licensing systems basically are a way to try to deal with youthful problem drivers, but there are serious limitations in the ability to identify the relevant population through driver records (see Williams, 1985), and probationary systems have not been very effective in achieving crash reductions (Mayhew & Simpson, 1990).

Graduated licensing

In recent years there has been a shift in focus from the problem driver population to all young drivers as a group, based primarily on the fact that all such drivers are inexperienced. Graduated licensing systems are intended to provide the opportunity to obtain initial on-road driving experience in lower-risk settings so that young beginners and others they encounter on the roads are protected. Most licensing systems in the United States allow quick and easy access to full-privilege driving at a young age, but in graduated licensing the path to full licensure is lengthened. A period allowing for supervised driving must take place, with a learner's permit held for a specified minimum period. After the student passes the driving test, there initially are prohibitions against high-risk situations, such as nighttime recreational driving, driving after any alcohol use, and driving with other teenagers and no adults in the car. Completion of this period without incurring crashes or moving violations allows graduation to full-privilege driving.

Graduated licensing systems address the risky driving syndrome by restricting driving in situations where risky behavior is most likely to be manifested. Crashes associated with risky driving practices such as speeding typify young drivers in general but are most characteristic of the very youngest drivers – 16-year-olds – and decrease with age (Williams Preusser, Ulmer, & Weinstein, 1995). Delaying full-privilege driving through graduated licensing also means that this privilege does not come until a later age, allowing young people time to begin to mature out of risky practices. Graduated licensing, when applied to young people, takes into account that they are passing through a developmental stage in which they are highly vulnerable to motor vehicle injury. The goal is to get them through this stage safely without undue mobility restrictions.

Graduated licensing systems deal with the issue of inexperience by providing the opportunity for on-road driving experience in protective settings. There is considerable discussion about "second-stage" driver education programs that would attempt to develop skills such as hazard perception or risk awareness as a way of dealing with driver inexperience (U.S. Department of Transportation, 1994). It is an operating assumption of graduated licensing that these perceptual skills develop through the accumulation of on-road experience over time. Accelerated development of these skills through special training obviously would benefit the graduated licensing process.

Present licensing systems

U.S. states vary considerably in their present licensing systems (Williams, Weinberg, Fields, & Ferguson, 1996). Although no state has bona fide graduated licensing, some states have elements of it, and state systems vary in other ways that affect both licensing and crash rates. This has been illustrated in four northeastern states with widely different licensing requirements. Delaware and Connecticut allow rapid progress to a full-privilege driver's license at a young age, whereas New York has a strong night driving curfew for 16-year-old licensed drivers, and New Jersey is the one state that licenses at age 17 and allows only supervised driving starting at age 16. Studies have shown that crash involvement rates are substantially lower for 16-year-old drivers in New York and New Jersey than for those in Delaware and Connecticut (Ferguson, Leaf, Williams, & Preusser, 1996).

Interaction of licensing systems and individual characteristics

Thus, we know from previous work that both individual characteristics reflecting lifestyle factors and licensing system differences are predictive of future crash likelihood, but we know little about the interaction of these factors in the development of driving experience and crash involvement. Several U.S. states are considering graduated licensing, and it is expected that some will adopt versions of these systems. In structuring a graduated licensing system, it would be useful to know more about how state systems with elements of graduated licensing shape early driving behavior among problem drivers and young drivers in general. This is an especially pertinent question given the early findings on the crash reduction effects of graduated licensing systems. New Zealand instituted graduated licensing in 1987 and has a model system with nighttime, passenger, and alcohol restrictions. Yet it has produced only a modest crash reduction of about 7% (Langley, Wagenaar, & Begg, 1994), mainly due to reduced exposure. If the system worked as intended, a more positive effect would be anticipated.

The key to graduated licensing is management of the quantity and quality of the early driving experience. To the extent that the provisions are violated, positive effects are lessened. That is, driving prior to obtaining a learner's permit, unsupervised driving in the learner stage, and driving in prohibited high-risk conditions do provide on-road experience but subvert the intended functioning of graduated licensing. It is clear that any graduated licensing system will have some amount of illegal driving and that it is the problem group – the high crash risk group – who are the most likely violators. So a key question is how the problem group reacts to the restrictions and other provisions. That is, to what extent is graduated licensing an effective way to curb risky driving practices that combine with driving inexperience to produce a high crash rate?

Four-state longitudinal study

The best way to study this interaction is to track young people over time so that their progress through the system can be monitored. Such a study has now been done in the four northeastern states with varying licensing systems, allowing study of how individuals who differ in risky driving propensities react to easy licensing systems and to systems with elements of graduated licensing. For example, how do the amount and type of legal and illegal driving (and crash involvement) during the beginning driving years differ? How does the problem subgroup respond to New York's 9 p.m. driving curfew, New Jersey's 17-year-old licensing age, and learner's permit requirements? A longitudinal study based on telephone interviews is limited in terms of the depth and richness of information it can provide, but it is an opportunity to examine the interaction of lifestyle factors and licensing requirements over the course of a developmental stage in which major biological and psychosocial changes are occurring.

About 1,000 young people in the four states were interviewed by telephone twice a year starting when they were high school freshmen, whether or not they remained in school. The last wave of data collection took place in April–May 1996, and initial results from the study are now available.

During the fall of their freshman year, study participants completed a questionnaire that asked about various problem behaviors. One such behavior – trouble with the law – illustrates the relationship of problem behavior to later driving behaviors and other characteristics of the students when they were seniors. Table 7.1 presents data based on the

Table 7.1. *Characteristics of high school seniors who reported, when freshmen, that they had been in trouble with the law*

Senior year status	In trouble with law, freshman year (%)	
	Yes	No
Problem behaviors		
Use alcohol ≥2–4 times/month	60	41
Have used illegal drugs	29	13
Smoked >1–5 cigarettes last month	48	24
Drove after drinking last month	25	13
Academic achievement		
Average grade A or B	49	78
Parental influence		
Parents impose curfew	38	49
Parents require seat belt use	52	66
Driving attitudes and behavior		
Rate driving skill much better than average	22	11
Have driven in excess of 90 mph	43	18
Driving record		
Have had one or more crashes	38	25
Have had one or more moving violations	31	20

Note: All comparisons $p < .01$, chi square test.

1,003 students who remained in the study and completed the final telephone interview. In the four states combined, 16% of the freshmen acknowledged having been in trouble with the law (not involving motor vehicle use). This was associated, as expected, with problem behaviors evident in their senior year involving alcohol, illegal drug use, and smoking. Those reporting trouble with the law as freshmen had lower academic achievement, less parental influence on their driving practices, overconfidence in their driving ability, and evidence of risky driving practices. They also had more traffic violations and crashes than those who said they had not been in trouble with the law. Thus, problem behavior evident at ages 13–14 relates to subsequent problem driving.

Table 7.2 provides an example of the relationships anticipated between problem behavior and licensing regulations. In the easy licensing states (Delaware and Connecticut), young people get licensed earlier.

Table 7.2. *Mean ages for first driving and licensure in relation to state licensing requirements and whether respondent, when a high school freshman, had ever been in trouble with the law*

	Minimum age				Trouble with law						
					First drove				Obtained license			
	Permit		License		Yes		No		Yes		No	
State	Yrs	Mos	Yrs	Mos	Yrs	Mos	Yrs	Mos	Yrs	Mos	Yrs	Mos
Delaware	15	10	16	0	14	6	15	3	16	4	16	3
Connecticut	16	0	16	0	15	2	15	8	16	7	16	7
New York	16	0	16	0	15	2	15	8	16	8	16	8
New Jersey	16	0	17	0	15	0	15	11	17	1	17	1

In all states, young people start driving at substantially earlier ages than allowed; this trend was more pronounced in Delaware, the easiest state in which to get a license. Those who had been in trouble with the law were licensed at about the same ages as those not in trouble, but these two groups differed substantially in when they started to drive. Those in trouble with the law reported starting to drive substantially earlier than those not in trouble. These findings indicate that the problem group is much more likely to engage in early illegal driving and support the notion that studies of the development of driving and driving styles should begin at an early age.

The longitudinal survey allows investigation of the development of driving and driving styles in detail close to the time driving is taking place. Further analyses will relate this development over a 4-year period to lifestyle factors and licensing system requirements. As graduated licensing systems are adopted by states, with additional restrictions and delays in full-privilege driving, it will be important to track young people as they progress in order to deepen our understanding of the development and course of driving practices and to provide guidance on how to optimize graduated licensing provisions. Graduated licensing systems will also result in significant lifestyle changes that will affect social and work activities and adolescent development in general, and these changes and their effects are worthy of study in their own right. The importance of motor vehicle use in the lives of adolescents makes its inclusion necessary in the study of adolescent development, and the origins and course of risky driving behavior should be a key concern in research and theory about adolescent risk behavior.

References

Beirness, D. J., & Simpson, H. M. (1988). Lifestyle correlates of risky driving and accident involvement among youth. *Alcohol, Drugs and Driving, 4* (3–4), 193–204.

Beirness, D. J., Simpson, H. M., & Mayhew, D. R. (1993). Predicting crash involvement among young drivers. *Proceedings of the 12th International Conference on Alcohol, Drugs, and Traffic Safety, 2,* 885–890 (Cologne, Germany).

Bergeron, J. (1995, June 8–11). *Behavioral, attitudinal and physiological characteristics of young drivers in simulated driving tasks as a function of past accidents and violations.* Paper presented at the symposium New to the Road, Halifax, Nova Scotia.

Cohen, A. (1955). *Delinquent boys: The culture of the gang.* Glencoe, IL: Free Press.

Dielman, T. E., Shope, J. T., Leech, S. L., & Butchart, A. T. (1989). Differential effectiveness of an elementary school-based alcohol misuse prevention program. *Journal of School Health, 59,* 255–263.

Ellickson, P. L., Bell, R. M., & McGuigan, K. (1993). Preventing adolescent drug use: Long-term results of a junior high program. *American Journal of Public Health, 83*(6), 856–861.

Ferguson, S. A., Leaf, W. A., Williams, A. F., & Preusser, D. F. (1996). Differences in young driver crash involvement in states with varying licensure practices. *Accident Analysis and Prevention, 28,* 171–180.

Gregerson, N. P. (1995). *Prevention of road accidents among young novice car drivers.* Linkoping University Medical Dissertations No. 444. Department of Community Medicine, Faculty of Health Sciences, and Swedish Road and Transport Research Institute, Linkoping, Sweden.

Hansen, W. B., Malotte, C. K., & Fielding, J. E. (1988). Evaluation of tobacco and alcohol abuse prevention curriculum for adolescents. *Health Education Quarterly, 15* (1), 93–114.

Heinrich, H. Ch. (1993, April 22–23). *Some features of a new novice driver curriculum.* Paper presented at the Working Conference on Novice Driver Education, University of Alberta, Edmonton, Alberta, Canada.

Jessor, R. (1987). Risky driving and adolescent problem behavior: An extension of problem-behavior theory. *Alcohol, Drugs and Driving, 3,* 1–12.

Jessor, R., Turbin, M. S., & Costa, F. M. (1997). Predicting developmental change in risky driving. The transition to young adulthood. *Applied Developmental Science, 1*(1), 4–16.

Jonah, B. A. (1986). Accident risk and risk-taking behavior among young drivers. *Accident Analysis and Prevention, 18:* 255–271.

Langley, J. D., Wagenaar, A. C., & Begg, D. J. (1994). The New Zealand graduated driver licensing: Has it worked? University of Otago Medical School, Dunedin, New Zealand.

Lavery, B., Siegel, A. W., Cousins, J. H., & Rubovits, D. S. (1993). Adolescent risk-taking: An analysis of problem behaviors in problem children. *Journal of Experimental Child Psychology, 55,* 277–294.

Lonero, L. P., & Clinton, K. M. (1996). Driver education and graduated licensing: How should they fit together? *Graduated licensing: Past experiences and future status.* Transportation Research Circular No. 458 (pp. 40–43). Washington, DC: National Research Council.

McClelland, D. C., Wanner, E., & Vanneman, R. (1972). Drinking in the wider context of restrained and unrestrained assertive thoughts and acts. *The drinking man; Alcohol and human motivation* (pp. 162–197). New York: Free Press.

Macdonald, W. A. (1994). *Young driver research—a review of information on young driver performance characteristics and capabilities.* Victoria, Australia: Monash University, Accident Research Centre.

McFarland, R. A., & Moore, R. C. (1960). *Youth and the automobile.* New York: Association for the Aid of Crippled Children.

Mayhew, D. R., & Simpson, H. M. (1990). *New to the road, young drivers and novice drivers: Similar problems and solutions?* Ottawa, Ontario: Traffic Injury Research Foundation of Canada.

Pelz, D. C., & Williams, P. A. (1974). *Countermeasures for young drivers: Comparison among experimental groups over 24 months following treatment.* Ann Arbor, MI: Highway Safety Research Institute, University of Michigan.

Romanowicz, P. A., & Gebers, M. A. (1990). *Teen and senior drivers.* Sacramento: California Department of Motor Vehicles.

Saibel, C., Salzberg, P., & Thurston, R. (1996). *Observational survey of driver compliance with the pedestrian crosswalk law, 1995.* Olympia, WA: Washington Traffic Safety Commission.

Schuman, S. H., McConochie, R., & Pelz, D. C. (1971). Reduction of young driver crashes in a controlled pilot study. *Journal of the American Medical Association, 218*(2), 233–237.

Simpson, H. (1996). Summary of key findings. In H. Simpson (Ed.), *New to the road: Reducing the risks for young motorists* (pp. 1–17). Proceedings of the First Annual International Symposium of the Youth Enhancement Service. Los Angeles: University of California Press.

Sobel, R., & Underhill, R. (1976). Family disorganization and teenage auto accidents. *Journal of Safety Research, 8*, 8–18.

U.S. Department of Transportation. (1994). *Research agenda for an improved novice driver education program.* Report to Congress. Washington, DC: National Highway Traffic Safety Administration.

Williams, A. F. (1985). Laws and regulations applicable to teenagers or new drivers: Their potential for reducing motor vehicle injuries. *Young driver accidents: In search of solutions* (pp. 43–62). Ottawa: Traffic Injury Research Foundation of Canada.

Williams, A. F. (1996). Magnitude and characteristics of the young driver crash problem in the United States. H. Simpson (Ed.), *New to the road: Reducing the risks for young motorists* (pp. 19–25). Proceedings of the First Annual International Symposium of the Youth Enhancement Service. Los Angeles: University of California Press.

Williams, A. F., Preusser, D. F., Ulmer, R. G., & Weinstein, H. B. (1995). Characteristics of fatal crashes of 16-year-old drivers: Implications for licensure policies. *Journal of Public Health Policy, 16*(3), 347–390.

Williams, A. F., Weinberg, K., Fields, M., & Ferguson, S. A. (1996). Current requirements for getting a driver's license in the United States. *Journal of Safety Research, 27*, 93–101.

Wilson, R. J., & Jonah, B. (1988). The application of problem-behavior theory to the understanding of risky driving. *Alcohol, Drugs and Driving, 4*(3–4), 173–191.

Part III

A focus on sexual activity

8

New methods for new research on adolescent sexual behavior

J. Richard Udry and Peter S. Bearman

Sexual behavior is always included in the list of "problem behaviors" and "risk behaviors" of adolescence, although it is considered a normal and acceptable behavior among adults.

As the study of adolescent sexual behavior has become established in the social science disciplines, we now apply to it the same new perspectives that we apply to other behaviors, both problem and nonproblem, that we are trying to explain. As new perspectives are applied to understanding the sexual behavior of adolescents, we need new research designs to illuminate these perspectives. In this chapter we show how these new perspectives have shaped the research design of a new study, the National Longitudinal Study of Adolescent Health (hereafter, Add

Thanks to Karen Carver and Jim Moody for contributing data analysis.

This chapter is based on data from Add Health, a program project designed by J. Richard Udry (PI) and Peter Bearman and funded by Grant HD31921 from the National Institute of Child Health and Human Development to the Carolina Population Center, University of North Carolina at Chapel Hill, with cooperative funding participation by the following agencies: The National Cancer Institute; The National Institute of Alcohol Abuse and Alcoholism; The National Institute on Deafness and Other Communication Disorders; The National Institute of Drug Abuse; The National Institute of General Medical Sciences; The National Institute of Mental Health; The National Institute of Nursing Research; The Office of AIDS Research, National Institutes of Health (NIH); The Office of Behavior and Social Science Research, NIH; The Office of the Director, NIH; The Office of Research on Women's Health, NIH; The Office of Population Affairs, Department of Health and Human Services (DHHS); The National Center for Health Statistics, Centers for Disease Control and Prevention, DHHS; The Office of Minority Health, Centers for Disease Control and Prevention, DHHS; The Office of Minority Health, Office of Public Health and Science, DHHS; The Office of the Assistant Secretary for Planning and Evaluation, DHHS; The National Science Foundation.

Health). Add Health provides the data to allow many kinds of adolescent behavior to be examined in ways that have not been possible before, at least on a national scale. Although Add Health is a broad study of adolescent health, it provides special opportunities to study sexual behavior.

This chapter explores how Add Health provides new opportunities to study sexual behavior from three perspectives: contextual (here network) effects, behavior genetics, and behavior of couples. The first section lays out the research design features of Add Health that implement the three perspectives. The three following sections illustrate how Add Health can be used to analyze sexual behavior from each new perspective.

The design of Add Health

Add Health is a study of a nationally representative sample of adolescents in Grades 7 through 12 in the United States. It is designed to help explain the causes of adolescent health and health behavior, with special emphasis on the effects of the multiple contexts of adolescent life. Add Health was mandated to the National Institutes of Child Health and Human Development (NICHD) by action of the U.S. Congress (1993), and is funded by NICHD and 18 other federal agencies as a program project. The first author is the principal investigator. We have a nationwide group of adolescent health researchers as coinvestigators. An important feature of the project is that the data from the study are now available for public use.

Add Health provides coverage of all the main health conditions and health behaviors of current concern. Figure 8.1 reports the aspects of health that we cover. Because the main determinants of poor health among adolescents are the result of their behaviors, in contrast to the determinants of health status among other age groups, Add Health focuses much of its effort on risk behaviors. These range from not wearing helmets while riding bicycles to engaging in unprotected sex. When we say we focus on the effect of context, we cover the following contexts in the study: community, neighborhood, school, peer group, family, friends, and romantic partners. Unlike many other "contextual" studies in which measures of context are derived from respondents' self-report, Add Health collects data from individuals who make up the relevant contexts of an adolescent's life. Thus contextual data about the

Diet and Nutrition	Eating Disorders	Depression	Violent Behavior	Intentional Injury
Unintentional Injury	Suicidal Thoughts and Suicide Attempts	Exercise and Physical Activity	Health Service Use	Health Insurance Coverage
Drug Use	Sex and Contraception	Alcohol Use	Tobacco Use	Weapon Use
Hereditary Conditions of Health	Physical Disabilities	Obesity	Mental Health	Other Health Conditions
Sleep Problems	Safe Vehicle Use	Chronic Health Problems	Viral and Bacterial Infections	Dental Health

Figure 8.1 Add Health coverage.

family are derived from interviews with parents and siblings, data on schools are derived from interviews with all the other students and school administrators, and data on partnerships and friendships are derived from partners and friends.

From a scientific perspective, Add Health is unusual in the degree to which the major theoretical issues of the study are articulated in the features of the research design. Three general theoretical postulates are embedded in the research design. These are that the differential health of adolescents emerges from (1) differential environments, (2) differential behaviors on the part of adolescents exposed to the same environment, and (3) differential health vulnerabilities and strengths of adolescents exposed to the same environments. Our central interest is in interactions among these three sources of differential health. Because adolescents, like all humans, not only are affected by the contexts in which they are embedded but also select and shape the environments they are exposed to, Add Health has a longitudinal design. Figure 8.2 provides an image of our sampling design. Our primary sampling frame is a list of all high schools in the United States. From this frame we selected a stratified sample of 80 high schools, with probability propor-

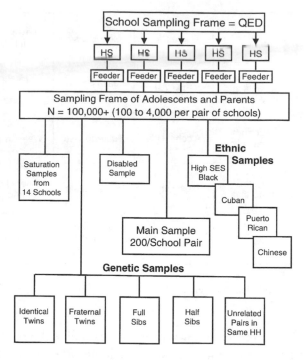

Figure 8.2 Sampling structure for Add Health.

tional to size. For each high school we selected one of its feeder schools with probability proportional to its student contribution to the high school. We then gave a self–administered op–scan questionnaire simultaneously to everyone who attended each school on a particular day of administration. In most schools, over 90% of all students enrolled participated in the in–school phase of the survey. Some schools did not let us do a school administration. We have administered more than 90,000 in–school questionnaires.

The purposes of the in–school questionnaire were (1) to measure school context variables, (2) to obtain friendship networks, (3) to measure a variety of health conditions, and (4) to obtain data on the basis of which to select special samples of individuals in rare but theoretically crucial categories. No sensitive questions were asked in the in–school interview. A school administrator also completed a half–hour self–administered questionnaire on characteristics of the school.

We also obtained a roster of students enrolled in each school. From the rosters, we selected a random sample of 16,000 for a 1½-hour in-home interview. Approximately 200 students were selected from each school pair as part of the core in-home sample, irrespective of size. This creates a self-weighting sample. Whether or not the student was included in the school administration does not affect inclusion in the main home sample. A parent of each respondent received a half-hour interview; over 85% of the parents participated in the survey. The adolescent in-home interview was laptop computer administered. Half of the interview was conducted by the interviewer and half was self-administered on the laptop, with an earphone audio component. All sensitive data were collected using the audio computer-assisted, self-interview technology, thereby reducing potential sources of interviewer effects on crucial risk-behavior data.

In 2 large schools and 12 small schools we attempted to interview all students on the roster. This allowed us to get a complete view of the effects of friend pairs on health and health behaviors.

From the in-school questionnaires, we selected the following special samples: high-education blacks (one parent has a college degree), $N = 1,500$; Puerto Ricans, $N = 500$; Cubans, $N = 500$; Chinese, $N = 400$; and physically disabled (limb disabilities), $N = 500$. In most cases the sample exhausts those available in the school administration.

We also selected a genetic sample using the in-school questionnaire information. In most categories the sample exhausts the cases available in the school administration. The categories of pairs of adolescents in the genetic sample are as follows: identical twins, fraternal twins, full-sib pairs, half-sib pairs, and unrelated pairs in the same household. The sample design yields the full range of genetic relationships within households, from complete similarity (identical twins) to no shared genes (unrelated adolescents).

The genetic sample can be used for many different types of analysis. For the social scientist uninterested in genetic aspects, the sample can be used for analysis that distinguishes variance due to shared parental environment from environmental variance from other sources. It is especially useful for identifying "family effects" as usually defined by social scientists, but it can also provide a measure of family effects purged of genetic variance.

The first wave of in-home interviews was completed in 1995. In

- School Adolescent Questionnaire   N = 90,000

- School Administrator Questionnaire   N = ~140

- In-Home Adolescent Questionnaire—Wave I   N = ~20,000

- In-Home Adolescent Questionnaire—Wave II   N = ~14,000

- Parental Questionnaire—Wave I   N = ~18,000

Figure 8.3 Add Health questionnaires.

- Schools: School Administrator Questionnaire, aggregated
  questionnaire data

- Neighborhoods: Census data

- Communities: Census data, other published sources

- Families: Questionnaire responses of parents and siblings

- Peer relationship: Friendship *nominations* and matches

Figure 8.4 Sources of contextual data.

1996, those originally in Grades 7–11 were followed up with a second interview. Over 88% of those interviewed in Wave I completed Wave II interviews. This enabled us to follow changes in behavior over the year. Figure 8.3 lists the five questionnaires used in the study and the approximate number of completes for each questionnaire.

We can now examine how design features map onto the measurement of contextual effects. Figure 8.4 gives the sources of data used for each level of context in the design.

We have 80 communities. For each community, one of our investigators prepared a list of attributes of communities from public data. Neighborhoods were specified for each in-home respondent, and neighborhood attributes were assembled from public data. School attributes can be aggregated from in-school questionnaires, administrator questionnaires, and in-home questionnaires. Peer groups are constructed and friends matched from in-school and in-home questionnaires. Family characteristics are obtained from parental and sibling questionnaires. The highly clustered sample design creates the possibility of estimating these contextual effects. This direct estimation of context from others' reports is crucial for our assessment of risk. Consider some simple examples. Unprotected sexual intercourse is always risky, but more so if one's partners are embedded in long chains of prior relationships characterized by unprotected sex. Driving drunk is always risky, but more so if all of one's peers do so. Taking drugs may be attractive only if the high-status adolescents within one's peer group are drug users. Analysis of these kinds of direct risks, missed in self-report data, is possible with the Add Health clustered sampling design.

Confidentiality

Add Health sets a new standard in the protection of confidentiality. This is most important because of the highly contextualized research design. We are not going to try to spell out the security features of the design. The design makes it possible to match questionnaires where needed and, at the same time, makes it impossible for anyone – even us – to match any respondent's identity with a questionnaire response. The main feature that makes this possible is a third-party contract with a security manager.

Because of the problems of deductive disclosure involved in providing contextual data, access to various types of data has different restrictions. But for the basic data sets, off-the-shelf unrestricted data sets have been prepared. Our object is to make as much data as possible available as soon as possible and with the minimum restrictions necessary to control deductive disclosure of identities. See the Appendix for further information on data availability.

Almost all the parts of the in-home questionnaire that collected information on sexual behavior were contained in the self-administered section of the laptop questionnaire, so that the respondent was entering responses directly into the computer. The advantage of this procedure is that neither the interviewer nor others in the room heard any questions asked or heard any responses. The disadvantage is that adolescent respondents didn't always follow instructions exactly. But, of course, skip patterns are all automatic, and respondents did not even see questions that were skipped. For example, if a respondent said she had never had sexual intercourse, she never saw any questions about contraception. There was no printed questionnaire at the interview scene.

Contextual factors in adolescent sexual behavior

Contextual analysis is the most sociological form of analysis because it embodies the fundamental sociological principle that the attributes of the collectivities in which people live shape their individual behavior. Beginning more than a decade ago, researchers began using multilevel models to examine contextual factors affecting adolescent sexual behavior. Most of these models rely on the effects on respondent sexual behavior of attributes of populations living in the county or census tract of the respondent's residence. Often these models first use tract data (e.g., percentage of women divorced) to account for an individual's mediating attributes (such as permissive sexual attitudes), which then account for the variance in individual sexual behavior. Such analysis is necessarily restricted to the data available for counties and census tracts in existing census or administrative data. Add Health has census block group data for each individual. Some respondent locations and addresses could not be matched with block groups by available computerized program services. For these the interviewers used Global Position System hand-held devices to ascertain the longitude and latitude of households with precision. These data were then matched with census data to the lowest level of aggregate released by the U.S. Census Bureau.

But because Add Health uses a school-based sampling frame, many aggregate characteristics of the school (based on the in-school questionnaire) can be used as contextual data. Because most schools had 100 or more respondents on the in-home questionnaire, aggregate attributes on sensitive characteristics (such as proportion using illegal drugs) can be prepared. Because most respondents' mothers also completed an in-home questionnaire, even sensitive attributes of the mothers can be used as aggregate characteristics in contextual models. For example, schools' levels of the restrictiveness of parental control can be estimated and used as a contextual variable to explain the sexual behavior of students at the school.

For each school, Add Health has a half-hour questionnaire filled out by a school administrator on policies, rules of behavior, health services offered, and so on. These school administrator questionnaires provide another level of contextual data for each adolescent in the study.

On the in-school adolescent questionnaire, each student identified up to five friends of each sex. More than 80% of the students in schools completed these questions, including identification of each friend by a code from a school directory that each respondent had in hand while completing the in-school questionnaire. We have therefore constructed school networks for each school, and have computed the standard network characteristics of the student body (such as density and centralization) and of individual students (such as reach and centrality). These network attributes become part of our data set and can be used as contextual factors in predicting the behavior of respondents. Finally, the aggregate attributes of friends and others closely connected in the network become contextual variables whose effects on sexual (and any other risk) behavior can be examined. Because the study collected three rounds of data on each respondent at approximately yearly intervals, it is possible to use prior contextual attributes to predict subsequent individual behavior or behavior change.

The data for contextual analysis are so rich and come from so many sources that contextual explanatory models are restricted less by the available data than by the relatively crude contextual theories we have to guide the analysis. We will therefore hardly criticize analysts of the data if they initially follow exploratory strategies to determine the proper level on which to expect effects. But many analysts will be tempted to build two or more levels of hierarchic contextual effects when using Add Health data. For example, a first level of context variables might be community or block group attributes, and school-level context variables might then be added hierarchically to a model explaining the risk behavior of adolescents.

Here we report just one contextual finding as an illustration of the sorts of analyses that are possible. Our example does not concern sexual behavior. Rather, we focus on the determinants of adolescents' perceived closeness (or cohesion) to their school community. Both individual-level effects and school-level effects can be found, each accounting for roughly 15% of the variance in perceived cohesion. But neither alone is sufficient to account for the differences between adolescents. Most critical are how school-level contexts activate individual-level characteristics and make them salient. Figure 8.5 summarizes the relationship between perceived cohesion (the feeling of closeness to the school community) and school size and the percentage of black students in each school. The plot is the combined outcome of two separate

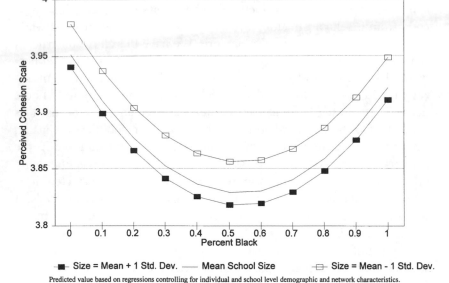

Figure 8.5 The effect of school size on the relationship between percentage of black students and closeness to the school (predicted values by school size).

regressions, one at the individual level and one at the school level. At the individual level, we first model cohesion as a function of grade (as adolescents grow older, they become less engaged), gender (girls feel less close to school than boys), race, social network position, and the number of school activities adolescents participate in. For the second regression at the school level, the intercept from the individual-level analysis is used as the dependent variable. Here we ask what accounts for the differences in the mean level of perceived cohesion by school, net of the individual level variables.

In Figure 8.5, we show the effect of shifting network size and the percentage of black students on perceived cohesion, holding all other demographic and network characteristics at their mean. This is just one of the many interactions that emerge from this kind of multilevel analysis. Note that school size is negatively associated with cohesion. Independent of the racial composition of schools, smaller schools always have higher mean cohesion levels than larger schools. This is to be expected. But the interaction with race is fascinating, for cohesion is uniformly lower in integrated schools than it is in segregated schools, independent of school size. For both blacks and whites, the racial composition of the school activates race as a salient determinant of perceived cohesion. In this sense, context acts on individual characteristics and directs their effects in often unanticipated ways.

The innovative potential of the Add Health data for contextual analysis derives from highly clustered sample designs. All other nationally representative surveys of adolescent sexual behavior derive from area sample random designs that pluck respondents at random from the social landscape. Rarely does any individual know anyone else in the survey (unless it is someone from his or her own family). Add Health respondents know one another in large numbers and share a school, a community, and the same groups of friends. Their mothers know one another. Real groups of people who interact with one another are the fabric of Add Health. This fabric provides a powerful weave of social forces impinging on the adolescent that offers a broad improvement over self-description of isolated individuals.

Psychosocial characteristics of individuals and contexts

Add Health collected many measures of psychosocial, demographic, and other descriptive attributes of the respondents. Illustrative lists of these variables are provided in Tables 8.1 and 8.2. For many purposes, these can be considered the independent variables in models predicting risk behaviors. For example, the analyst can examine the relationship between individual feelings of self-efficacy and reporting a romantic relationship or having a nonromantic sex partner. Because of the highly contextualized design, the interaction of school context with that relationship can be examined. For example, does self-efficacy have a stronger relationship to partner acquisition in schools where most of the students are low in self-efficacy than in schools where most of the students are high?

Behavior genetics in Add Health

Contemporary social science is based on the fundamental postulates that social behavior is learned through social experience, that the most influential learning environment is the family, and that the biological

Table 8.1. *Selected contents of Add Health questionnaires: Psychosocial and descriptive attributes obtained from adolescents*

Health conditions and risk behaviors (listed in Figure 8.1)	Physical development (puberty)
Daily activities	Height and weight
Educational aspirations	Religious behavior and beliefs
Courses taken and grades	Occupational aspirations
Personal feelings	Employment, earnings, allowance
Self-efficacy	Relations with siblings
Parent–child relations	Personality traits
Joint activities with friends	Perception of neighborhood
Joint activities with mother	Pregnancy history
Joint activities with father	Attributes of parents
Knowledge of reproduction and contraception	Parental rules and supervision
Peabody Picture Vocabulary Test	School activity participation
Ideal romantic relationships	Household composition
Contraceptive behavior	Perceived parental attitudes
Romantic relationships	Suicidal thoughts
Motivations for birth control	Future life chances
	Trouble in school
	Race, ethnicity, nativity

and genetic attributes of individuals contribute nothing (or almost nothing) to the variance among individuals, nations, or cultures. We social scientists did not discover this set of postulates through their empirical research because we never doubted its truth. Not doubting its truth, we never developed research designs that allowed taking it as problematic.

It has fallen to a smaller tribe of scholars – the behavior geneticists – to develop the research designs and statistical methods that allow transformation of the basic social science postulates into a program of empirical research. Behavior genetics research designs take advantage of the known degrees of genetic relationships among individuals in the population. Behavior genetics sample designs include sampling units of at least pairs of individuals, and at least two known and different degrees of genetic relationship to one another and a known degree of shared family environment. Adoption designs contain parent–child pairs in which the children are biological offspring in one group and adopted offspring in the other. Twin designs contain pairs of identical

Table 8.2. *Selected contents of the parental questionnaire*

Child's health conditions and risk behaviors (included in Figure 8.1)	Alcohol and smoking
	Attributes of current partner
Parental race, ethnicity, nativity, demographic characteristics	Biological and legal relationship to child
Marital and relationship history	Years mother and father lived with child
Current dating for separated or nonmarried	Support from nonresident father of child
Education	
Employment	Parents' knowledge of child's friends/romantic partners
Public assistance	
Religious affiliation	Child's birth weight
Religious behavior and beliefs	Child's breast-feeding history
Membership in voluntary organizations	Family disease history
	Contact with child's school
Reasons for living in present neighborhood	Evaluation of child's school
	Risk behaviors of the child
Neighborhood relationships	Evaluation of child for disabilities
Household income and income sources	Child's recent residential history

twins and pairs of household members sharing other degrees of relationship, such as fraternal twins. When behavior genetic sample designs are used, it is possible to decompose variance in behavior into genetic and environmental components, and to decompose the environmental component into shared variance (associated with living in the same household) and nonshared variance (whose sources are not shared by persons living in the same household). Other types of genetic designs are also available, such as pedigree designs, and the simplest and most difficult to obtain, samples of identical twins reared apart.

More than 30 years of behavior genetic research is now available. It is generally quite consistent in its findings. Almost all behaviors contain genetic variance, from very little to almost complete. When a behavior contains environmental variance, it is usually found to be mostly nonshared variance (variance not associated with growing up in the same household). Most of the similarity of siblings is genetic in origin (Rowe, 1994). These consistent findings directly contradict the fundamental postulates of the social science paradigm. Either the social science paradigm or the behavior genetics paradigm must be fundamentally flawed, or else something is happening that none of us understands.

The use of behavior genetic designs to study risk behaviors in adolescence dates only to the 1980s. An influential and important paper was that of Rowe and Osgood (1984), which showed that much of what commonly passed for the influence of adolescents on one another's delinquent behavior could be shown in genetic designs to be due to selection of friends on the basis of genetically determined propensities for delinquency. Other risk behaviors were examined in subsequent adolescent studies, showing other risk behaviors to have biological variance (Udry, 1990, 1991).

Traditional area sample surveys and other nongenetic sampling designs contain a few households that can be segregated and treated in a behavior genetic design if pairs with different relationships are picked up. But the numbers are seldom sufficient in even the largest surveys. The research design of Add Health starts with a large enough base sample from the schools (about 100,000) that a suitable behavior genetic sample can be obtained.

The Add Health research design calls for all twins, half-sib pairs, unrelated adolescents sharing a household, a sample of full sibs, and nontwin sibs of twins. Information was obtained from the in-school questionnaire to identify respondents who are part of such a pair. Some twins were picked up from nonparticipants in the school survey by screening the school directories for same-grade enrollees with identical surnames and living at the same address. Several hundred pairs are in our genetic samples. We attempted to include these genetic pairs so identified in our in-home interview sample. Although the information provided by the in-school questionnaire was quite fallible with respect to accurate self-identification, we were successful in completing the design to allow a fully articulated behavior genetic analysis. Identical twins are distinguished from fraternal twins by DNA analysis from mouthwashes in cases where questionnaire responses were not definitive.

The beauty of the Add Health design is that it gives some real purchase on resolution of the contradictions between traditional social science and the behavior genetic paradigm. The reason is that the representative (main) sample of adolescents is basically drawn from the same sampling frame as the behavior genetic sample and uses the same questionnaires. This provides the opportunity to compare model types. It also allows the direct transformation of the two environmental variance components into specifically measured variables.

There is very little behavior genetic research concerning sexual behavior and even less on adolescents. Yet there is a broad nongenetic literature on the biology of sexual behavior. The first author has spent much of the past decade exploring the relationship between biological and social bases of adolescent sexual behavior and the interaction between biological and sociological factors. To summarize this line of research on adolescents, male hormones play an identifiable role in shaping the sexual behavior of adolescents, both boys and girls (Halpern, Udry, & Suchindran 1997; Udry, Billy, Morris, Groff, & Raj, 1985). Furthermore, the physiology of pubertal development itself is related to adolescent sexuality. Although only a few pieces of this line of work have used genetic designs, there is enough to tell us that the variance in hormone levels has a substantial genetic component and that the timing of puberty has genetic roots. If there is any human behavior for which social scientists might grudgingly grant the possibility of some biological basis, it is sexual behavior.

Of course, the behavior genetic design incorporated into Add Health can be used to explore the genetic sources of variance in many other behaviors (e.g., cigarette smoking) and in various health conditions. But the use of the behavior genetic component for understanding sexual behavior seems particularly promising. For the social scientist who doesn't care about the genetic components of behavior, there are two special attractions in the use of the genetic samples of Add Health. The first is that if the genetic samples are used, the genetic components of variance can be "trashed" and the remainder of the variance can be examined without worrying too much about coming to wrong conclusions on the basis of unidentified genetic variance. In social science analysis, the genetic variance generally masquerades as shared environmental variance (coming from living in the same household). This confusion can be avoided by using the genetic samples. Equally important for the improvement of social science understanding, behavior genetic analysis allows the segregation of shared and nonshared environmental variance. We social scientists are confident that we can tell them apart. For example, we think that the influence of friends on respondents must be nonshared environmental variance. But is this where the effects

of friends show up in the genetic decomposition? Not necessarily. Rowe
and Osgood showed that adolescents select friends on the basis of similarity in problem behaviors and that the variance in problem behaviors
is substantially genetic (Rowe & Osgood, 1984). The ability to distinguish shared from nonshared sources of behavior variance might just
be the most important contribution of genetic samples for the analysis
of the workaday social scientist.

The possibilities of exploring sexual relationships in behavior genetic
samples have hardly been tapped because genetic samples have almost
never been asked about their sexual behavior. (This oversight is being
corrected by other studies as well as by Add Health.) The essence of
the exploration is comparing the similarity of the sexual experience of
pairs with different degrees of genetic relationships. One of the simplest
and most interesting questions is how genetic similarity affects similarity of romantic partners. This has been explored for spouse selection
and adolescent friendship selection, but we can now open adolescent
erotic partnerships to examination. The sexual content of relationships
can be similarly examined, combining genetic sample analysis with romantic relationship analysis, discussed in the next section.

Romantic relationships

Sexual partnerships can easily be studied in adults as the behavior of a
pair because the most common form of partnership is marriage: a public
relationship of long duration. Surprisingly, surveys of adult sexual behavior seldom include the partners of respondents. In adolescence, romantic pairs are often ephemeral, and their sexual behavior cannot be
taken for granted. Furthermore, unlike married pairs, adolescent sex
partners' sex is not normative. Consequently, studies of adolescent sex
rarely include the study of actual sexual partnerships. The design of
Add Health explicitly includes pairs of partners.

A feature of Add Health that is specifically targeted to understanding
adolescent sexual behavior is the romantic and sexual relationship history. In the romantic relationship section, the respondent is asked to
identify up to three "special romantic relationships" in the last 18
months. The romantic partner can be either of the same sex or the opposite sex. Respondent is also asked to identify persons whom the respondent had kissed on the mouth, held hands with, and told he or

she likes or loves, but who were not listed as romantic partners. This eliminates relationships with no erotic content at all. Each partner is temporarily identified with dummy initials. The behavioral content of each relationship is elicited, which may or may not include sexual behavior. The questions asked identify the extent to which the relationship is embedded in a context of other social relations. If the relationship includes coitus, a contraceptive history of the relationship is solicited. Questions are then asked about nonromantic sexual relationships.

When this section of the history is completed, the respondent is asked to call up the student directory of his or her school, and for those partners who are enrolled in the same school, to find their names, highlight them, and enter them into the computer. Each computer contains a complete directory of students by sex and grade. When the highlighted name is entered, a code is registered that creates a link between the names of the two partners. The same process is repeated on the next wave of in-home interviews a year later.

The name links work the same way as the links created by the friendship nominations, present in the in-school questionnaire and both in-home questionnaires. With these links in place, identified romantic and sexual partners have their questionnaires linked. Emerging from this set of links is a broad array of research opportunities never before available in a national survey. In the 14 saturated schools, where all respondents are included in the in-home sample, nearly all same-school partners' questionnaires will be linked. In other schools, the probability of a link is substantial as an inverse function of school size. In all schools, most romantic nominations can be linked to the partners' in-school questionnaires.

Illustrative analyses

We now present some early analyses of the data to show what romantic relationships are like.

Duration of relationships

How long do romantic relationships last? Figure 8.6 shows the cumulative survival curves for romantic relationships of four sex compositions. This graph shows how long relationships lasted. Data are based

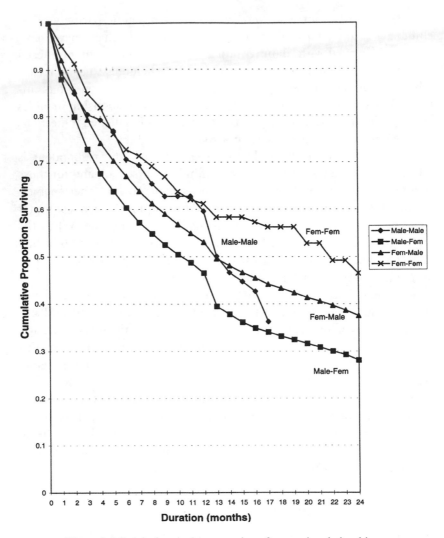

Figure 8.6 Survival curve by sex typing of romantic relationships.

on nominator reports only. The median length of relationships differs by sex composition. Female–female relationships last longer than relationships with other sex compositions. Relationships identified by both partners last no longer or shorter than those identified by one partner only (not shown).

Same-sex partnerships

What are the comparative ages of partners in the two types of same-sex relationships? Eighty-six percent of the female nominations were of females older than the nominator, and 71% of the male nominations were of males older than the nominator. The nominated partners average 2 or 3 years older than the nominators for either sex. Clearly, this type of relationship is seldom perceived by the older partner as romantic.

Do those who identify same-sex romantic and sex partners also identify partners of the opposite sex? Most respondents identified only a single romantic relationship in the 18-month window we allowed. Of those males who identified at least one male partner (either romantic or nonromantic sexual), 4 in 10 also identified at least one female partner. Of those females who identified at least one female partner, 4 in 10 also identified at least one male partner. The adolescents who identify same-sex partners of either type are only a small percentage of the total, but nearly half of them also identify opposite-sex partners.

Although we cannot exhaust the unusual research opportunities created by romantic partner data, we highlight three other possibilities: validity studies, linked sex histories of sex partners, and two-sex prediction models.

Validity of sex histories

Consider that Barbara nominates Burt as a romantic partner. If Burt does not nominate her, we have a mass of data and many theories from which we can build predictive models of nonconfirmed nominations. Of all possible reciprocated nominations, two-thirds were actually reciprocated. Remember that these nominations are not sociometric choices but reports of a relationship with behavior content. If Burt also nominates Barbara, we can see the extent to which they each confirm the relationship content reported by the other. If Burt says they had coitus but Barbara says not, we can build explanatory models. If both say yes, we can compare their contraceptive reports on the sexual relationship. So we derive not only validity measures from these matches, but also predictive models of the report validity.

Sex histories of sex partners

Because we have sex histories for nearly everyone in the saturated schools and for a sample in the nonsaturated schools, we can build sex histories of sex partners and partial sexual networks encompassing the entire student body. These are the data needed for assessing transmission networks for sexually transmitted diseases. Of course, the part missing is sex histories of the sex partners outside the school. But we are not bereft of information on them: We have reports on their attributes from our respondents. And, of course, we can overlay the friendship networks and the romantic/sexual networks. We can identify friends with common sex partners, sex partners with common friends, and even sex partners with common sex partners.

Cross-sex friends and cross-sex romantic partners

For estimating the significance of risk behaviors like sexual behavior, interconnections between adolescents in interacting populations are absolutely critical. We know very little about the structure of adolescent sexual or romantic networks and how these networks shape the risks that adolescents experience within partnerships. What do adolescent romantic relationship networks look like? How do they compare to more standard friendship networks? Do they show the same structure or are they different in systematic ways? Are the individuals whom adolescents identify as romantic partners also identified as friends? Simple questions as these, previously impossible to answer, can now be easily explored with the data collected in the Add Health survey. Here we provide just one example of a romantic partnership network, drawn from adolescents in a single small school in our sample.

Recall that adolescents were asked to nominate five best same-sex and five best opposite-sex friends from school rosters during the in-school phase of the survey. During the in-home phase of the survey, adolescents used the same school rosters to identify both friendships and romantic partners. If partners attended school with the respondent, we asked adolescents to identify them. If partners or friends did not attend school with the respondent, they were assigned a generic identification number. Thus, here we are restricted to analyzing partnerships and friendships only within the school.

Looking first at the overlap between friendship nominations and romantic partnership nominations, we discover that less than half of the romantic partners that adolescents nominate are identified as a friend from either the in-school or in-home friendship nomination modules. This lack of overlap is largely insensitive to characteristics of schools (their size, racial composition, grade range) and characteristics of individuals (age, gender, race, achievement in school, and so on). For many adolescents, partners are not people they identify as friends.

Despite this, the structure of the friendship networks is similar to the structure of the romantic relationship networks. To illustrate this, Figure 8.7 graphically presents the pattern of cross-sex friendships in a small school, composed of 150–200 students, in Grades 7 to 12. Students are represented by symbols, and cross-sex friendships are indicated by a line connecting two symbols. Lines may refer to reciprocal or asymmetric friendship nominations – they are not directed. The sociogram shows that friendship choices are strongly conditioned by grade for younger students and less so for older students. For example, 7th graders are three times more likely to select another 7th grader as a friend than someone from another grade, whereas only 30% of 10th-grade students' cross sex friends are in the 10th grade and fewer than 25% of 11th-grade students' cross-sex friends are in the 11th grade. Juniors and seniors have numerous ties to one another, yielding a dense cluster of interconnected older students whose cross-sex friendship choices cut across grade.

In Figure 8.8, we display the structure of special romantic relations for the same school. As expected, the density of ties is much lower. Although the overlap between students nominated as friends and students nominated as romantic partners is low, we observe a similar structure. As with friendship, grade is highly salient for seventh graders, who are far more likely to select partners from their own grade (88%) than from other grades (12%). Among 11th graders, 76.2% of their cross-sex friends are in another grade and 77.8% of their romantic partnerships are with students in another grade. We again observe a relatively densely knit pattern of association linking juniors and seniors, comparable to that observed from the cross-sex friendship nominations. There are differences, of course. None of the 8th-grade students and none of the 10th-grade students select partners from their own grade. Overall, we find that friendship choices and romantic relationships

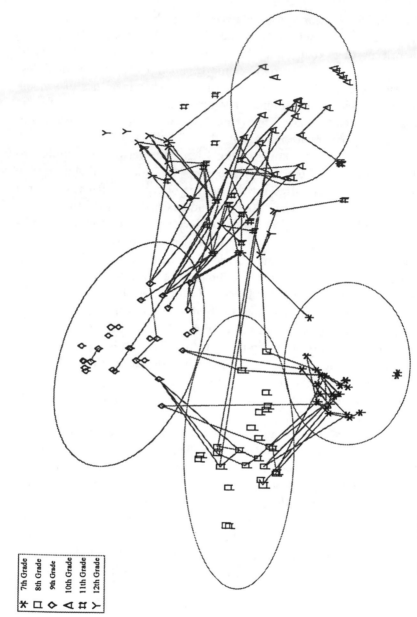

7th Grade
8th Grade
9th Grade
10th Grade
11th Grade
12th Grade

Figure 8.7 Cross–sex friends.

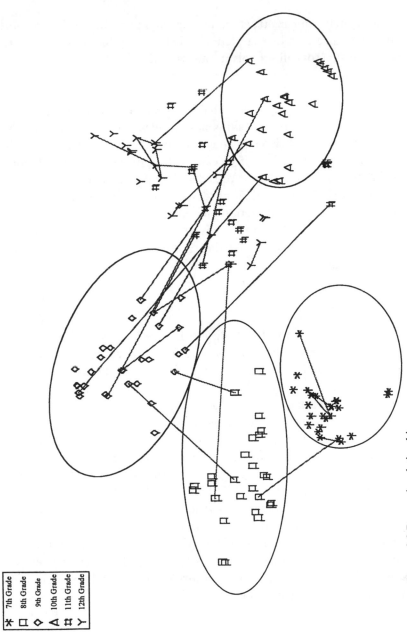

Figure 8.8 Romantic relationships.

share a vaguely similar structure among younger students but a quite similar structure for older students. It is too early to know if this pattern is robust across all schools in our sample.

For such a small school, relatively long chains of interconnected individuals may be observed. One chain involves eight partnerships across four grades, and a second chain involves four partnerships across three grades. If these relationships have a sexual content, the individuals in them and the behaviors they are engaged in will emerge as the critical elements in models of disease diffusion. The unique relational data that we have collected in Add Health make possible the analysis of sexual networks in ways that have not been possible before. These analyses will point new directions for epidemic modeling and increase our understanding of how the behavior of pairs within partnerships is shaped by the partnerships that they are tied to by friendship, sexual, or romantic relations.

Two-sex prediction models

The beauty of the Add Health design for studying sexual behavior is that Add Health sexual behavior is specific to particular pairs, and these pairs are embedded in a broad context of other social relationships that are also comprehended within the study. In Add Health we can build two-sex prediction models of sexual behavior for pairs.

Researchers have already demonstrated the utility of two-sex models in predicting fertility events in married couples. In these models, attributes, attitudes, and plans of both husband and wife are used to predict whether a couple will have a pregnancy during some specific time span in the future (Fried & Udry, 1979). In Add Health, we can use attributes and attitudes of romantic partners who are not yet sex partners to predict whether they will have sex in the future, and if they do, what their contraceptive behavior will be. One of the most useful sets of information for our couple prediction models will be the previous sex histories of the partners. Our opportunity to understand sexual decision making will make a quantum leap.

Ideal versus actual romantic relationships

As part of the romantic relationship section, each respondent is given a set of cards containing events that sometimes happen in relationships.

Respondents are told, "Please imagine your ideal romantic relationship in the next year. Go through this deck of cards and give me any that describe things that would NOT happen in this perfect relationship. Now look through the remaining cards and put them in the order in which you think things should happen in your perfect relationship."

The cards contain the following events:

- We would go out together in a group.
- I would meet my partner's parents.
- I would tell other people that we were a couple.
- I would see less of my other friends so that I could spend more time with my partner.
- We would go out together alone.
- We would hold hands.
- I would give my partner a present.
- I would tell my partner that I loved him (her).
- My partner would tell me that he loved me.
- We would think of ourselves as a couple.
- We would talk about contraception or sexually transmitted diseases.
- We would kiss.
- We would touch each other under our clothing or with no clothes on.
- We would have sex.
- My partner would get pregnant.
- We would get married.

After this is done, respondents describe their actual romantic relationships by using the same technique, once for each romantic relationship. Comparisons of the events and the order selected can be made between the ideal relationships of partners, between ideal and real relationships of individual respondents, between real relationships of the same respondent, and, of course, between the reported events in real partnerships.

On the contextual level, the ideal and real orders of different schools can be compared, as well as the orders within friendships and other groups. The consequences of different orders (e.g., for contraception, pregnancy, relationship violence) for individual relationships can be determined.

In the instructions for romantic relationships, respondents of both sexes are told that the romantic partners they list can be either boys or girls. About 2% of the relationships listed are same-sex. Two percent comes to about 400 relationships that can be analyzed. So there is a good opportunity to learn about the similarities and differences in the context of same-sex and opposite sex romantic relationships.

Nonromantic sex partners

Another section of the questionnaire identifies sex partners who do not meet the romantic screen. (If in this section a relationship meets the romantic screen, it is transferred to the romantic section. Therefore, relationships that remain in this section involve sex, but not hand holding, professions of love, or kissing.) Respondents could provide up to three. Our Wave I respondents listed over 3,000 such relationships. These sex partners were also looked up on the directory if they were schoolmates, and their IDs were linked to those of the respondent as nonromantic sex partners.

Multilevel models extended

It is easy to conceptualize the question "How do different attributes of the social context affect the ways in which sexual relationships develop?" Theoretical models can be developed that propose what kinds of communities with what kinds of schools encourage romantic relationships that are embedded in a broad social matrix, with sex coming late in the sequence, whereas other contexts encourage relationships that are socially isolated, with sex occurring early in the sequence.

Conclusion

The study of adolescent sex as a risk behavior has entered a new era. New perspectives on contextual effects, behavior genetics, and two-person models of behavior promise to transform our understanding of sexual behavior. In order to exploit these new perspectives, we need new research designs and new methods.

Progress in understanding the effect of social contexts on adolescent sexual behavior is now poised for a new leap to maturity. The Add Health project opens opportunities for the study of contextual effects never before available on the levels of community, block group data, school composition, and friendship networks. These contextual data allow exploration of how the relationship between psychosocial characteristics and sexual behaviu differs in different social settings.

The introduction of behavior genetic designs to the study of risk behavior has the potential to allow us to take apart our current models and put them back together in a different order. We can illuminate a picture of adolescents as selectors of social environments that fit their natural propensities. We can put environmental effects of families on sexual behavior into a more balanced perspective compared to other sources of effects. We can even explore how genetic influences on behavior are activated or suppressed by different environments. Add Health is the first nationally representative data set to provide behavior genetic samples for the study of adolescent risk behaviors.

Sexual behavior is the only traditional problem behavior that requires pairs for enactment. We have always known that we needed to study pairs of actors, but we had no research design to make it possible. Add Health provides the design that elicits the first data set of adolescent romantic and sex partners. From these data we can study the validity of reports, trace out the sex partners of sex partners, and build two-partner models to predict the course of sexual relationships. We can see how social context affects the course of the behavior of partners and examine the contribution of genetic differences to understanding paired sexual behavior.

In this chapter, we have been able to give only a few empirical illustrations of the new analyses made possible by the combination of new perspectives with new methods. Because these data are available to other researchers, readers will find new possibilities in the data not dreamed of by their creators.

Appendix: Availability of Add Health data

All Add Health data are available to researchers under varying degrees of restricted use. The restrictions are necessary in the case of Add Health because of the sensitive nature of the data collected and the opportunities for deductive disclosure in the data sets. This is an especially high risk in Add Health because of the clustered nature of the samples and the fact that so many respondents are linked to others by the nature of the data presented. It is surprisingly easy, once you know that a particular person is in the study and you know a little about that person, to find his or her responses. It is in the nature of the school-based sample that innumerable people, both in the study and in the communities studied but not in the study, actually know the identity of many Add Health respondents. This is not the case in typical area sample national studies, where single respondents are plucked out of context and few people know who is interviewed. It is even easy for the parent with a computer to find his or her son or daughter in Add Health. The study contains multiple mechanisms for making direct identification impossible, but these mechanisms do little to control deductive identification based on known respondent characteristics.

Because of these risks, Add Health has a hierarchical system of data availability. Unrestricted public use data for half of the core sample is available from Sociometrics, Inc. These unrestricted data do not contain information allowing identification of those who attend the same school. No linking of romantic partners will be available for unrestricted use. Special samples will not be included. But all other contextual variables will be provided, including constructed network variables.

Researchers who require data not included in the unrestricted public use release will need to meet a set of security conditions for data use, post a deposit to be forfeited in the case of violation of security conditions or release of the data to unauthorized persons, and meet certain other conditions. Those who require all the data from Add Health have to come to the Carolina Population Center. There the users work under supervised data access conditions. Those who work under these conditions pay a flat fee and a per diem fee to defray the costs of the host institution. Our object (indeed, our mandate) is to encourage the wide use of the data, and Add Health takes this seriously. But we cannot risk violation of the confidentiality we promised our respondents.

References

Fried, E. S., & Udry, J. R. (1979). Wives' and husbands' expected costs and benefits of childbearing as predictors of pregnancy. *Social Biology, 26,* 265–274.

Halpern, C. T., Udry, J. R., & Suchindran, C. (1997). Testosterone predicts initiation of coitus in adolescent females. *Psychosomatic Medicine, 59,* 161–171.

Rowe, D. C. (1994). *The limits of family influence.* New York: Guilford Press.

Rowe, D. C., & Osgood, D. W. (1984). Sociological theories of delinquency and heredity: A reconsideration. *American Sociological Review, 49,* 526–540.

Udry, J. R. (1990). Biosocial models of adolescent problem behaviors. *Social Biology, 37* (1–2), 1–10.

Udry, J. R. (1991). Predicting alcohol use by adolescent males. *Journal of Biosocial Science, 23,* 381–386.

Udry, J. R., Billy, J. O. G., Morris, N. M., Groff, T. R., & Raj, M. H. (1985). Serum androgenic hormones motivate sexual behavior in adolescent boys. *Fertility and Sterility, 43* (1), 90–94.

U.S. Congress. (1993). NIH Revitalization Act of 1993 (Public Law 1-03-43, Title X, Subtitle D, Section 1031).

9

Betwixt and between: Sexuality in the context of adolescent transitions

Julia A. Graber, Jeanne Brooks-Gunn, and Britt R. Galen

Research on adolescent development has focused largely on the transitions that define and shape the experiences of adolescents. Historically, the period of adolescence was referred to as the transition from childhood to adulthood, suggesting that the period itself was a single (albeit potentially long) transition period. Whereas the entrance into adolescence has been defined by both biological markers, specifically puberty, and by culturally defined transitional events such as the exit from elementary school and the entrance into middle school, the exit from adolescence has been more varied in its markers. The transition to adulthood has been influenced by the economy and the societal structure of each historical era (Modell & Goodman, 1990; Paige, 1983). For example, the most common markers for entry into adulthood have been those that define an aspect of the adult role, such as finishing one's full-time education, entering the work force, living on one's own, marrying, and having a child. In the past, young adults did not move out of their parents' home until they married, and men did not marry until they had finished their education and had begun to establish themselves in a career (Modell & Goodman, 1990). Thus, many of these transitions were closely linked in their timing. In recent years, the time between living on one's own and marrying has greatly increased, as has the age of marriage for women.

The authors were supported by grants from the National Institute of Child Health and Development (NICHD). We would also like to acknowledge the support of the NICHD Research Network on Child and Family Well-Being, the National Institute of Mental Health Family Research Consortium, and the W. T. Grant Foundation Consortium on Depression in Childhood and Adolescence.

The role of sexual behavior as a defining feature of adulthood has undergone historical change as well. Until the 1960s, social norms strongly enforced the notion that intercourse was confined to married couples and hence was not separated from the attainment of adult roles. Although it may have been accepted that men might engage in this behavior premaritally, often it was still not considered appropriate behavior (Smith, 1994). In contrast, pressures for women to confine sexual activity to marriage were always stronger than for men.

Historical changes in the 1960s resulted in greater acceptance of premarital sex for adults and the start of the decrease in the age of first intercourse (Alan Guttmacher Institute [AGI], 1994; Smith, 1994). Thus, for recent cohorts of adolescents, most individuals will have had intercourse by 17–18 years of age. Given that sexual behaviors often begin much earlier than intercourse, forming a sexual identity and navigating the emotional and physical challenges of sexual behavior have clearly become part of the series of events that occur during the transitional periods of adolescence.

Along with the historical, cultural, or economic context of the period of adolescence, adolescent transitions are shaped by a range of contextual influences (Bronfenbrenner, 1977, 1979; Lewin, 1939). That is, changes occurring during adolescence are inherently defined by an individual's social context and by the roles and expectations for behavior based on an individual's identification or membership in a social group. We have used the phrase "betwixt and between" to indicate the ambiguous status that adolescents experience, as they are not fully members of the adult world but at the same time are more competent and independent than children. Adolescents' experiences, as they develop a sexual identity or a sense of self as a sexual being, clearly fit the notion of "betwixt and between," as adolescents' behavior frequently does not match the expectations for their behavior as expressed by parents and other adults.

In this chapter, we focus on several themes that have been prevalent in the study of adolescent sexuality and, to a lesser extent, in the study of teenage pregnancy (inasmuch as the two fields have been related). The importance of understanding role transitions occurring in adolescence is embedded in the historical course of the research to date on adolescent sexuality, but it may also be of particular importance in determining future directions in this field. Thus, it is important to review briefly the concept of role transitions and their potential importance in the life course.

Role transitions and behavioral change

Current approaches to studying adolescent behavior frequently consider the multiple transitions within the second decade of life, the precursors and outcomes of a variety of events occurring during transitional periods, the constellation of events that define a transition period, and the timing or sequencing of events that occur within a more circumscribed transition period (Graber, Brooks-Gunn, & Petersen, 1996; Lerner et al., 1996). As indicated, puberty and school events are frequently studied as key aspects of the transition to adulthood, as these events signal the entry into adolescence and the beginning of the development of adult roles; less frequently studied, but perhaps just as salient, are transitions such as the onset of sexual behavior (in particular, intercourse). Although puberty and entrance into middle school define the early adolescent period and have been linked to increased sexual interest via biological and social pathways (e.g., Udry, 1988; Udry & Campbell, 1994), most research on sexual behavior focuses on the middle or late adolescent years (Brooks-Gunn & Paikoff, 1993, 1997; Katchadourian, 1990). Certainly, most adolescents make the transition from being a virgin to a nonvirgin during the middle or late adolescent period (AGI, 1994), but it is more likely that the development of a sexual identity or self (i.e., role transition) and the engagement in sexual behaviors is itself a process that potentially involves a series of interlinked transitions spanning the adolescent decade and most likely the life course. *Thus, development of a sexual sense of self occurs prior to first intercourse as well as after this event; furthermore, the potential for the redefinition of self and the role that sexuality plays in it exists throughout the life course.*

The importance of transitional periods (e.g., entry into adulthood) or processes (e.g., puberty) as defining features of adolescent development has led to the testing of developmental models in relation to concepts involving transitions (e.g., Brooks-Gunn, Graber, & Paikoff, 1994; Elder, 1985; Lerner et al., 1996; Pickles & Rutter, 1991). Transition periods or processes have been distinguished from life events in that transitions require reorganization at either the structural or functional level (Kagan, 1984; Rutter, 1994). Clearly, pubertal events at the entry to adolescence and role changes at the entry to adulthood fit the criteria for a reorganization of function or behavior. The same might be true of the onset of sexual intercourse, although virtually no research has taken this viewpoint when examining sexual behavior (see Buzwell & Rosenthal, 1996, as an exception).

Structural or functional reorganization does not necessarily translate into major discontinuities in behavior. Even if reorganization occurs, behavioral discontinuities need not occur for all individuals during transitions but rather may occur for some individuals at some transitions. Pickles and Rutter (1991; Rutter, 1994) have begun to examine individual courses of development under the framework of "turning points" in development; that is, quite simply, events have the potential to alter behavior, affect, cognition, or context, all of which could result in lifelong change. We have elaborated on this construct, focusing on turning points that occur during transitional periods; the term "transition-linked turning points" refers to this extension of Rutter's work (Graber & Brooks-Gunn, 1996). Of relevance to understanding the development of sexual behavior and attitudes during adolescence is the extent to which particular behaviors, such as a first date, first kiss, or first intercourse experience, may actually be transitions resulting in reorganization of roles and subsequent behavioral change. It is also important to consider for whom such events are actually transitional; that is, it is important to determine during which experiences, and for whom, significant role transitions may occur.

We and others have noted that individual differences in the experience or negotiation of behaviors associated with a transition are linked with a variety of conditions, including development prior to the transition, timing of the transition for an individual, the individual's experience of the transition, and the context in which the transition occurs (Graber et al., 1996; Rutter, 1989). It is these conditions that serve as mechanisms that determine whether a transitional experience results in behavioral change. Transitions and the contextual demands occurring at the time of the transition may result in the following types of behavioral change: the emergence of new behaviors, the discontinuation of behaviors, the alteration of behaviors, and the repatterning of behaviors (Graber & Brooks-Gunn, 1996). (1) The emergence of new behaviors is often studied in connection with reproductive transitions and changes in school context during the transition to adolescence. In the case of school changes at early adolescence, new behaviors may be expected in the new school environment (i.e., middle school versus elementary school). Whereas sexual behaviors are not expected of adolescents at school, at least by school officials, such behaviors may occur after the change to middle school because the behaviors are more likely to be exhibited by adolescents in that environment (Dornbusch et al., 1981; Garguilo, Attie, Brooks-Gunn, & Warren, 1987). Similarly, sexual behaviors emerge after puberty due partially to biological stimulation (to be discussed) and partially to the perception that sexual activity is now appropriate for someone who is more adultlike in appearance and reproductive capacity. (2) Behaviors may also be discontinued as the result of a role transition. Pickles and Rutter (1991) find that, depending on the choice of partner, marriage may serve as a time to turn away from a pattern of deviant behavior and poor mental health. Similarly, marriage has been linked with decreases in drug use for young adults (Bachman, Johnston, O'Malley, & Schulenberg, 1996). The onset of sexual behavior during the early adolescent years may signal a change in same-sex friendships and in parental relationships, as well as in other-gender relationships (Paikoff & Brooks-Gunn, 1991). Thus the redefinition of self that results from the events occurring during the transition to adolescence results in beginning to see oneself as a sexual being, giving this role more importance, and subsequently changing behaviors that are affected by this emerging self definition. (3) Behaviors may be altered by the transition experience. For example, the incidence of sexual intercourse is rare prior to the transition to puberty (AGI, 1994) and relatively rare prior to the entry into middle school. Whereas sexual arousal and some behaviors (most often masturbation) occur prior to puberty (Westney, Jenkins, & Benjamin, 1983), the experience of feelings of sexual arousal and related activities increases in early adolescence for many adolescents (AGI, 1994; Hofferth & Hayes, 1987; Katchadourian, 1990). (4) Behaviors may also repattern or cluster differently as a result of a transition. For example, the onset of sexual intercourse seems to be more closely linked with smoking cigarettes, as well as with alcohol use, when sex is initiated earlier than later in the adolescent years (AGI, 1994; Donovan & Jessor, 1985; Donovan, Jessor, & Costa, 1988; Mott & Haurin, 1988). As is apparent, role transitions may affect sexual behaviors, and having made a particular sexual transition may affect engagement in other behaviors. In addition, the experience of a particular transition may alter different behaviors in different directions. In order to understand which individuals are affected by transitions and how transitions are navigated, we have argued for the need for more comparative, model-driven research (Brooks-Gunn et al., 1994; Graber & Brooks-Gunn, 1996).

New perspectives in the study of adolescent sexuality

Sexuality has not been seen as a transition or period of reorganization of roles but rather as a series of behaviors such as intercourse or contraception use. As such, adolescent sexuality is often studied but, in a sense, is not well studied. Perhaps thousands of studies that have been conducted over the past 25 years touch on adolescent sexuality. These studies are conducted within numerous disciplines including demography, economics, sociology, psychology, and public health. Because there are a multitude of studies, methods, and disciplines that comprise this field of research, it is difficult to summarize findings across studies, let alone the perspectives taken in studying sexuality. Consequently, several lines of inquiry have been followed, with little attention to integration among them. Our suggestion that adolescent sexuality is not well understood stems from the failure to specify general or unifying themes in the literature and the paucity of attention to links among findings derived from different approaches. That is, whereas the literature may be multidisciplinary in that it encompasses work from various disciplines, specific studies frequently are not multidisciplinary in content or design.

In examining the study of adolescent sexuality in more recent years (i.e., the past 15), several opposing viewpoints have been pervasive in the literature both implicitly and explicitly. These viewpoints have influenced the type of research conducted, the perspectives taken, and the interpretation of findings. From these varying approaches, we have identified nine perspectives that have emerged when a more developmental viewpoint has been applied to the study of adolescent sexuality. The nine are:

- viewing adolescent sexuality as a normative adolescent transition;

- portraying adolescent sexuality as more than a singular transition (i.e., just sexual behavior) and embedding sexuality within adolescent development;
- conceptualizing the timing of sexual transitions as a contextualized dimension (i.e., timing is relative, timing changes historically, timing encompasses different processes);
- viewing sexuality as a series of events (potentially resulting in a transition) involving multiple behaviors and feelings (rather than focusing only on intercourse);
- framing sexual behaviors as the interaction of biological and social influences;
- examining the development of sexuality as being dependent on the multiple contexts in which youth live, work, and play;
- taking nuanced and complex views of the desires and behaviors of girls and boys (rather than concentrating on gender differences in sexual behavior);
- stressing the promotion of healthy sexual behavior, not just the prevention of sexual behavior;
- conceptualizing adolescent sexual behavior in terms of the potential opportunity cost (i.e., considering the cascade of effects that might occur following certain sexual behaviors).

In opposition to parental, adult, and more general societal desires to regulate adolescent sexuality are the developmental experiences of adolescents that result in this period of life being particularly important in the formation of a sexual identity and the sense of self (Katchadourian, 1990). No matter how much adults might like to ignore it, sex has great meaning in the lives of youth, whether or not they have had any sexual experience (Brooks-Gunn & Furstenberg, 1989). Although sexuality, in terms of both desires and identity, is a part of earlier phases of life, these issues become particularly salient in the adolescent years for several reasons: Identity development in adolescence includes the formation of a sexual identity; sexual exploration (be it kissing, intercourse, or just dreaming) occurs during the adolescent years; and the negotiation of autonomy and intimacy takes place within sexual situations.

Thus, mastering emerging sexual feelings and forming a sense of oneself as a sexual being is a multifaceted set of tasks. These tasks include learning to manage feelings of sexual arousal, developing new forms of intimacy and autonomy, experiencing interpersonal relation-ships with others that may include both physical and emotional inti-macy, and developing the skills to control the consequences of sexual behavior. In addition, forming a sexual identity involves more than sexual behavior; it also includes the integration of behaviors into the construction of the concept one has of oneself (Brooks-Gunn & Paikoff, 1993). On perhaps a more cautionary note, youth also have to recognize situations in which sexual behavior is more difficult to control: in which others may use coercion or pressure to obtain sex; in which (one or both) partners may want intimacy but get sex instead; and in which their choices may not be accepted by their peer group (either to have or not to have sex).

Adolescent sexuality as normative

Whereas our conceptualization of sexuality (one that includes a range of behaviors, feelings, and tasks to be mastered) places sexuality in the domain of normative adolescent experiences, pressures to control ado-lescent sexuality have, in contrast, resulted in the view that sexuality is not an appropriate part of adolescent development; that is, it is nonnor-mative for adolescents. Viewing adolescent sexuality as normative im-plies that the sexual behaviors and feelings that may result in a role transition are part of the normative challenges of life and are of interest for understanding how individuals negotiate or meet such challenges. This perspective has been used with other role transitions but not with sexuality. Furthermore, this perspective has not been adopted by all or many scholars; thus, it is not being used to frame most studies in this area. The normative challenge perspective is lacking in part because groups within our society disagree about whether or not adolescent sexuality is, or should be, a normative event. At the same time, how-ever, this perspective has been applied to adolescent parenthood, an-other life transition that is not considered normative by many. For example, research on the birth of a child, vis-à-vis changes in self-related information seeking, roles within and outside the home, and self-definitions as well as alterations in depression, marital satisfaction and discord, and division of labor between mothers and fathers, has been conducted on older (i.e., nonteen) first-time mothers (Belsky, 1984; Cowan & Cowan, 1992; Deutsch, Ruble, Fleming, Brooks-Gunn,

& Stangor, 1988; Parke, 1988). How such constructs might apply to younger mothers has been considered by Brooks-Gunn and Chase-Lansdale (1995) but remains less fully studied.

A similar approach could be applied to the onset of sexual behavior, although little has been done on *adult* sexual transitions (e.g., onset of sexual intercourse) as a normative life transition necessitating changes in self-definitions, roles, or relationships with others. Consequently, there is little adult work from which to extrapolate or speculate about adolescent sexuality. (See the work of Brooks-Gunn & Paikoff, 1997, Buzwell & Rosenthal, 1996, and Rossi, 1994, as exceptions.)

As indicated, historical perspectives and behavioral norms for sexuality have changed for adults and adolescents over the past century, with more rapid changes occurring in the past 20–30 years. Historical changes also influence how much adherence to societal norms is seen (as well as the range of norms) across subgroups in a society. The synchrony between sexual transitions and marriage, as we have noted, has varied, depending on historical and economic contexts (Modell & Goodman, 1990). Ceasing to live with one's parents was commensurate with marrying and setting up a home of one's own for many young adults at the beginning of the twentieth century. Trends toward younger ages at marriage that were observed into the middle of this century suggested that young adults sought marriage as a mechanism for obtaining self-sufficiency and full adult status (Modell & Goodman, 1990; U.S. Bureau of the Census, 1991). Implicit in this type of attainment of adult status was the notion that the onset of intercourse occurred at about the time of marriage, with reproduction occurring shortly thereafter. Over time, the span between attaining other adult roles, such as working to support oneself and marrying, has been greatly increased; that is, the age of first marriage has increased (U.S. Bureau of the Census, 1991). In most Western societies, marriage is no longer a marker for the transition to adulthood. In addition, presumably due in part to advances in methods of birth control, societal acceptance of premarital intercourse has increased, at least for adults (Smith, 1994).

Permissiveness toward sexuality has been steadily on the rise for several decades (Zelnik & Kantner, 1980), and the percentage of teenagers having sex has been rising, for both boys and girls, over the past 40 years. Using age at first intercourse as an indicator of behavioral trends, it is clear that the trend toward earlier age at first intercourse became notable in the 1970s (Hopkins, 1977; Zelnik & Kantner, 1980). By the end of the 1980s, three-quarters of boys and almost three-fifths of girls reported having intercourse by age 18 (AGI, 1994). Additionally, among those youth who are sexually active, teenage intercourse is occurring earlier. For example 22% of 14-year-olds, 30% of 15-year-olds, 43% of 16-year-olds and 58% of 17-year-olds are sexually active (based on 1988 data; AGI, 1994). Although boys on average have intercourse earlier than girls, gender disparities have decreased over recent decades (AGI, 1994; Chilman, 1980; Hopkins, 1977; Oliver & Hyde, 1993). Becoming a sexual being, as evidenced by sexual intercourse, is now normative for middle to late adolescents, with most making this transition prior to finishing school and well before the attainment of independent living.

Thus, sexuality is no longer relegated to adulthood by cultural definition and is clearly part of adolescent behavior; yet, at the same time, increases in both teen pregnancy and sexually transmitted diseases observed with the lowering of the age of first intercourse have led to continued reluctance to accept sexual behavior in adolescents. A focus on the problem aspects of sexuality has long been cited as a limitation of the study of adolescent sexuality (Jessor & Jessor, 1977; Weddle, McKenry, & Leigh, 1988); less attention is given to the range of behaviors that may encompass normative sexual behaviors and feelings. The fact that parents and other adults are reluctant to view sexuality, especially intercourse, as part of normative development for adolescents not only involves protecting their children from harm but also falls within the domain of moral development. Although popular press information indicates that societal norms have become increasingly permissive toward premarital sex, about 30–40% of adults polled in the late 1980s report that it is always or almost always wrong for a man and woman to have premarital intercourse (Smith, 1994). Perhaps more important, about twice as many adults report that it is always wrong for adolescents to have intercourse. Smith (1994) has examined responses to these questions over time and by cohort and draws the conclusion that trends toward permissiveness seemed to begin to reverse, or at least stop increasing, in the 1980s. Of note is that the generation gap in beliefs about premarital sex appears to be decreasing; in the most recent surveys, the youngest age cohort is somewhat more conservative than prior same-age cohorts, and the oldest age cohort has become more liberal on this topic. Both consistent beliefs about the morality of premarital sex and beliefs about the appropriateness of these behaviors for adoles cents lead to the majority of adults being opposed to adolescents engaging in intercourse. Desire on the part of adults to control adolescent sexuality perpetuates dichotomous approaches to understanding and interpreting adolescent sexual behaviors. Most parents do, in fact, allow their children to date during adolescence and accept their children's sexual explorations up to a point. However, intercourse as a behavior, although normative in terms of rates, is nonnormative by adult standards.

Adolescents themselves seem to hold incongruent attitudes toward sexuality. In particular, stereotypes about gender-appropriate behavior are still prevalent. Surveys of attitudes toward premarital intercourse conducted in the 1930s and 1950s consistently showed disapproval for this behavior for women and men. However, it is commonly held that women have been penalized more by parents and peers if they engaged in this behavior. Hopkins (1977) anticipated that with a converging incidence of intercourse for boys and girls at younger ages, the sexual double standard would be reduced, even if it did not disappear. Since this time, age norms for intercourse by gender have seemed to converge, but it has not been clear that trends in permissiveness toward premarital sex have also converged to reduce the double standard for behavior. The persistence of the double standard for evaluating behavior was exemplified in the recent book *School Girls* (Orenstein, 1994). Although not a controlled study or systematic survey of adolescents, the book is effective in documenting some of the experiences of middle school children in two communities in California. Both girls' reports of social norms and observations in classrooms demonstrate the risk to girls of being identified as sexually active, regardless of the accuracy of the identification. Specifically, both boys and girls seemed to classify girls by whether or not they were "sluts." Orenstein asserts that the appearance, through dress and demeanor, of being willing to have sex may confer this label on girls. Such labels result in teasing and ostracism by both girls and boys. As would be expected from stereotypes of prior generations, such labels, if similar words were ever applied to boys, are compliments rather than taunts.

Disparities between the rates of behavior and social acceptance of the behavior, either by adults or by peers, continue to predispose adolescent girls to unique challenges in forming a sexual sense of self and integrating sexuality into their overall self-image. This supposition is not meant to disregard the challenges that understanding and regulating sexual feelings may pose for boys as well as girls. It merely highlights the necessity of continuing to consider gender and gender stereotypes for behavior when studying adolescent sexuality. Disparities between what is considered acceptable and the rates of actual behavior have also led to intense disagreement over strategies for combating the problem behavior segment of sexual behavior, that is, pregnancy and threats to health (e.g., promoting abstinence versus distributing condoms). The inability of adolescents, parents, and often researchers to come to terms with the incongruence of behaviors and attitudes in determining the normativeness of adolescent sexuality is often related to the narrowness with which sexuality is viewed both developmentally and behaviorally. Both issues are addressed under subsequent headings.

Adolescent sexuality as embedded within development

In the past, adolescent sexuality was often divorced from the literature on or models of adolescent development. Recent work has sought to embed sexuality within development, in part by examining the extent to which sexuality or aspects of it may be one of the transitions of adolescence. The majority of studies on adolescent sexuality are essentially descriptions of behaviors – dating, petting, intercourse, masturbation, contraceptive use. These pictures of what adolescents do and do not do sexually are almost completely divorced from what we know about the adolescent life phase. This chasm is surprising given the explosion of work on the experiences of adolescents, the contexts in which they live, the challenges they face, and the biological, cognitive, and social changes with which they must cope (e.g., Adams, Montemayor, & Gullotta, 1989–1993; Feldman & Elliott, 1990; Graber et al., 1996; Gunnar & Collins, 1988; Lerner & Foch, 1987; Levine & McAnarney, 1988; Schulenberg, Maggs, & Hurrelmann, 1997).

As has been commonly observed in nearly all recent descriptions of adolescence, this period is one of pervasive change. Only in infancy is physical growth as dramatic; by the end of puberty, adult form and reproductive capacity are attained. Early adolescence is also shaped by school change, with most individuals making the change from an elementary to a middle or junior high school environment. Along with physical and school changes, adolescents experience alterations in their interpersonal relationships with peers and family members. Although pursuance of intimate relationships with peers rather than family members usually begins in childhood, the development of intimate, romantic, and sexual relationships greatly advances during adolescence, changing the role that same- and other-gender peers play in adolescents' lives. At the same time that adolescents pursue and develop interpersonal relationships outside of the family, they are also renegotiating their role within the family, seeking greater independence and autonomy in determining and regulating their own behavior (e.g., Hill, 1987; Montemayor, 1983; Smetana, 1988). Alterations in interpersonal relationships are connected in part to the cognitive advances also occurring at this time. Early adolescents experience significant increases in their cognitive reasoning skills (Graber & Petersen, 1991; Keating, 1990), which in some sense provides them with the tools, if not the experience, for greater autonomy in decision making in this domain. As is apparent, cognitive, physical, and social changes are interconnected and combine in their influence on sexual behavior and development of identity, both globally and in terms of sexuality.

The literature on adolescent sexuality often seems devoid of context or texture and is to some extent impoverished in this area. It is impossible to construct a whole person, let alone part of a person, from much of this work. What we are suggesting is that the other features of youth are ignored, as are the developmental changes that occur over the second decade of life, and as are the contextual influences that frame life experiences such as sexual experiences.

What are the reasons that more nuanced views of sexual behavior as embedded in the adolescent experience are not more common, or at least have not been until recently? Several reasons are apparent. First, sexuality has not been viewed as normative for adolescents, as described in the prior section. Second, impediments to research have been prevalent, again due in part to perceived cultural norms and attitudes. In particular, it is often difficult to get permission from school administrators and parents to ask youth about sexuality (Brooks-Gunn, 1990). Hence, many developmentally rich investigations have not included sexuality as a domain of study. Third, youth are perceived as being unwilling to talk about sexual feelings or behaviors; this perception is particularly true of younger teens. Finally, we suspect that many scholars who investigate the period of adolescence do not believe that sexual behaviors and feelings are particularly important. Our impression is that if the importance of various adolescent challenges were ranked, sexuality would be very low on the list; that is, the experience is not important or does not result in reorganization of self-definitions, behaviors, or roles. One belief is that the only important aspect of sexuality is the onset of intercourse; this assumption is frequently coupled with the belief that retrospective report of this event is sufficient for understanding its impact on the lives of adolescents and young adults.

Timing as a contextualized dimension of sexuality

Related to the issue of adolescent transitions and viewing sexuality as normative is the notion that the timing of transitions is important in the developmental course. It has frequently been suggested that the timing of a developmental transition may influence the behavioral outcomes of that transition, as well as the experience of the transition (Brooks-Gunn, Petersen, & Eichorn, 1985; Graber & Brooks-Gunn, 1996; Rutter, 1989). The importance of the timing of a transition has been considered frequently in the case of the pubertal transition but may be relevant for a range of developmental transitions. The onset of sexuality (or at least certain forms of sexuality or sexual behaviors) is often characterized by its timing. The timing of role transitions is an often used perspective, especially for understanding the entry into and exit from adolescence (e.g., Elder, 1974; Graber et al., 1996). However, this perspective has been applied to the consequences of youthful sexuality, with a focus on pregnancy and parenthood (e.g., Cohler & Musick, 1996), much more often than to the onset of sexuality. At least three aspects of the timing of role transitions have been identified by sociologists and others: individual, familial, and historical timing. The first refers to a person's life course – in this case, the adolescent's life course. The second refers to the intersection of life courses by individuals in a family; in this case, the adolescent's experience of transitions occurs in one time frame, the parents' transitional experiences occur in a different time frame, and the position of adolescents or parents on their own time lines may influence the others' development. The third, historical timing, views the timing of transitions in a historical and societal context – in this case, comparisons of the timing of sexual transitions at different decades, at different points in time, or within various subgroups (Elder, 1974, 1985; Hagestad, 1986; Hareven, 1977; Modell, Furstenberg, & Hershberg, 1976).

These three dimensions of timing are not always aligned within or across dimensions. For example, although individuals experience multiple transitions, these transitions do not always occur in a regular sequence for each individual. An individual's transition to sexuality may occur at different times in a parent's life course (e.g., when a divorced or single parent is starting a new relationship with a partner at the same time that his or her adolescent is initiating sexual behavior with a partner). Furthermore, an individual's transitions occur in a context such that timing is always relative to the historical and societal norms.

Prior research has often examined age of intercourse as important to understanding developmental outcomes, both emotional and reproductive. However, a more thorough understanding of the effects of the timing of this transition is needed. The timing of sexual intercourse is studied by demographers, but there is little understanding of what it means to be off-time in making this transition with regard to one's peer group. Furthermore, it is apparent from the limited studies of perceptions of peer behaviors that perceptions of peer group norms may not be very accurate in comparison with actual behavior (Wilcox & Udry, 1986). (See the recent Adolescent Health Survey being conducted at the University of North Carolina, which provides much needed data on peer behaviors.) As indicated, only about one-fifth of all youth do not have sex during their teenage years (AGI, 1994). However, the timing of the onset of sexual behavior differs tremendously across subgroups, such that adolescent sexual intercourse at age 15 may be normative for some groups, whereas intercourse at age 18 may be normative for other groups (e.g., AGI, 1994; Furstenberg, Morgan, Moore, & Petersen, 1987; Paikoff, 1995).

For some developmental transitions, the normative time for making the transition may be determined by biological conditions rather than social norms. This is true to some extent for intercourse in that there are strong social constraints against making this transition prior to pubertal development and often there is less physical desire to do so until after pubertal development. Regardless of how the normative time for making a transition is set, being earlier or later than one's peers has an impact on adolescents' adjustment to the transition. Rutter (1989) noted that the timing of a transition might result in different behavioral or psychological effects of the transition via biological, psychological, or social processes.

The importance of the individual's level of maturity from a biological perspective at the time of initiating sexual behavior, in particular intercourse, has been of concern for teenage childbearing. For example, maternal age at the time of the birth of a child has been linked to the physical condition of the infant and to complications in childbearing for the mother (AGI, 1994; Ketterlinus, Henderson, & Lamb, 1990). In studies of white adolescent girls and women, a curvilinear pattern is found such that lower birth weight and poorer infant health are observed in the youngest and oldest mothers, with peak health seen in infants of women in their 20s (Cogswell & Yip, 1995), at least for women in industrialized countries. Thus, from the standpoint of reproductive health, immature and older reproductive systems appear not to be ideal for childbearing, lending support to the idea that level of biological development prior to this transition is important for mother and child outcomes.

Although biological bases may exist for the regulation of the timing of childbearing, a broad span of years for this transition is feasible. In addition, the timing of sexual transitions, as links to childbearing have diminished, need not be tied to biological precursors or outcomes. That is, there is little to suggest that the biological impact of making the transition to sexual behaviors differs, depending on whether the individual has initial intercourse at age 15 or age 25. It is, however, feasible to suggest that early sexual activity may alter biological development. Initial evidence suggests that prepubertal sexual abuse may accelerate pubertal development (Trickett & Putnam, 1993). Biological influences of sexual activity in the prepubertal years may have little to do with sex per se and more to do with the effect of abuse on the reproductive endocrine system via links with the hormonal systems that control stress responses (Graber & Brooks-Gunn, 1996; McEwen, 1994).

In contrast to biological effects, the timing of sexual transitions may have more social and psychological correlates. Via either path, making transitions off-time might be a risk for subsequent development. The timing of a transition may be important from a developmental or psychological perspective because timing may affect the amount or level of development that each person has attained prior to entering the transition. The *stage termination* hypothesis would further suggest that making a transition earlier than the normative time would place an individual at risk, as that individual may not have developed the necessary coping skills or competencies for dealing with the transition (Brooks-Gunn et al., 1985; Petersen & Taylor, 1980; Simmons & Blyth, 1987). A related hypothesis that has also been applied frequently to the pubertal transition is the *deviancy* hypothesis. In this case, negative effects of making a transition off-time are due to the violation of social norms. That is, normative standards are set by peers or others for when a person should make the transition, and doing so earlier or later than average would be considered deviant.

In either approach, the off-time sexual transition that has garnered the most attention is having intercourse at an early age. Zabin and Hayward (1993) and others (AGI, 1994; Centers for Disease Control, 1992; Durbin, DiClemente, Siegel, & Krasnovsky, 1993; Hofferth, 1987) have noted that earlier ages at first intercourse are a point of concern for several reasons. First, the younger the age at first intercourse, the longer the exposure to risks associated with intercourse and thus the greater the likelihood that adverse outcomes such as disease or early pregnancy will be experienced (Zabin & Hayward, 1993). For example, in their survey of junior high school students, Durbin and colleagues (1993) found that adolescents who experienced an early sexual debut (i.e., before age 13) were nine times more likely to report having three or more partners than adolescents who initiated intercourse at age 15 or 16. Second, younger ages at intercourse are associated with lower rates of contraceptive use (AGI, 1994; Centers for Disease Control, 1991; Zabin & Hayward, 1993). Finally, Zabin and Hayward suggest that younger adolescents may be less responsive to interventions targeting sexual risks due to less advanced cognitive and social cognitive development. In fact, adherence to health regimens in general may be particularly challenging for younger adolescents, as they are often in the process of developing decision-making skills and an understanding of the long-term consequences of behavioral choices (Brooks-Gunn & Graber, 1994; Keating, 1990).

Again, much of this discussion has focused on the timing of intercourse, with less attention to the timing of other aspects of sexuality. It may be that individuals who engage in intercourse earlier or later than peers may have experienced other sexual behaviors and feelings earlier or later than peers. Given that there is some evidence of a progression of sexual behaviors from initial exploration with kissing and touching to intercourse, with this pattern most often having been documented for white, middle-class adolescents (Smith & Udry, 1985; Westney et al., 1983), it is likely that off-time adolescents are experiencing most of these activities out of synchrony with the majority of their peers. In contrast, some adolescents who are later than peers in losing their virginity may have begun other activities earlier or at the same time as peers but may have had more internal and external pressures to delay intercourse. In fact, youth who would be considered late in having intercourse in comparison with their peers may have extensive social supports that reward this decision. Parents and religious groups frequently endorse such decisions. The extent to which adolescents may shape their social environment by seeking out contact with supportive peers or those who hold similar values may determine the extent to which they feel pressure to adhere to social norms and have intercourse. Again, little is known about the psychological effects of the timing of intercourse, especially being late in comparison to peers.

The timing of initiation of sexual behaviors may also be determined in part by the timing of other associated transitions. For example, it has been suggested that earlier pubertal maturation may be a risk factor for earlier sexual activity (Udry & Billy, 1987). Presumably, having a more adultlike physical appearance signals to others, as well as to oneself, that the individual is ready for more adult behaviors such as intercourse. However, support for links between timing of puberty and timing of intercourse has been mixed, and if such behavioral patterns exist, it is only for some groups of adolescents but not all. That is, earlier pubertal development has been linked to earlier ages of intercourse for African American adolescent girls (Udry & Billy, 1987). In contrast, in a study of upper-middle-class white adolescent girls, we found no association between pubertal timing and age of first intercourse (Graber & Brooks-Gunn, 1996); a similar lack of association has also been reported for other groups of adolescents (Udry & Campbell, 1994). Thus, the influence of the timing of the pubertal transition varies by context and may be heightened or lessened by other factors that exert forces on sexual behavior. Factors that protect girls from pressures for earlier sexual experiences are probably more often present for girls in our study than for girls from other economic backgrounds. Alternatively, recent studies have documented pubertal timing differences by race, such that African American girls are more likely to mature earlier than white girls after accounting for demographic differences (Herman-Giddens & MacMillan, 1991; National Heart, Lung, and Blood Institute [NHLBI] Research Group, 1992). Thus, African American girls may be exposed to sexual pressures due to their advanced development more often than girls of other races. At this time, very little research has addressed the pubertal experiences of African American girls; links to earlier sexual initiation and the commensurate links with this behavior clearly indicate that further research is needed in this area.

Sexuality as a series of events and more than just intercourse

Much of the literature to date has focused almost exclusively on first intercourse or behaviors commensurate with intercourse (i.e., safe sex practices). This approach has obviously left several aspects of sexuality unexamined or examined in only the most rudimentary forms. However, such behaviors as dating, sexual identity development, and non-coital sexual behaviors have long been considered part of adolescent development (Weddle et al., 1988). Although we have noted the necessity to incorporate a broader range of behaviors and feelings into the study of sexuality in previous sections, it is worthwhile to discuss some of the exemplars of research that have moved away from the narrower view, as well as the shortcomings of focusing on intercourse in isolation from other activities (and sometimes partners).

The focus on intercourse, and often first intercourse, is in some sense not surprising. It is, as we have indicated, fairly easy to measure retrospectively, although the wording of questions tapping this experience will greatly influence reporting on it. Use of explicit language is preferred to vaguer phrases such as "sexually active" (Rodgers, 1996). In addition, having intercourse for the first time is likely to be one of the more personally salient sexual experiences for an adolescent or young adult (Jessor, Costa, Jessor, & Donovan, 1983; Katchadourian, 1990). In fact, although we would argue that the formation of a sexual identity may be a transition period or process, first intercourse may actually be the culmination of this process when role change and reorganization actually occurs, at least for some adolescents.

One criticism of the study of adolescent sexuality, and the focus on intercourse specifically, is the heterocentric nature of much of this work (Savin-Williams, 1995). Of note is that recent progress in the study of the development of sexual orientation and identity has led to significant shifts from narrower to broader views of sexual behavior. Like the study of sexuality in heterosexual adolescents, the study of sexuality in bisexual, lesbian, and gay youth has frequently focused on problem behaviors and risks, with less emphasis on developmental processes (Savin-Williams, 1995). Savin-Williams examined retrospective reports of sexual activity in a group of college-age gay men. Interestingly, over half of these young men indicated that they had had heterosexual sex, with a mean age of 15.5 at first heterosexual intercourse. Thus, heterosexual sex was certainly part of the sexual experiences of these young men, but it also occurred somewhat earlier than average in comparison to other demographically similar heterosexual men (white middle- to upper-middle-class youth in college). This sexual experience also occurred on average about a year after their first homosexual sex. Even though intercourse was an experience for many of these young men, the relative importance of the event is not clear.

In fact, the descriptive information about sexual activity that is perhaps most striking from Savin-Williams's (1995) study is the pervasiveness of masturbation as part of the daily life of these men when they were adolescents. About 40% indicate having daily orgasms in junior high school, with 50% reporting this occurring in senior high school; orgasms most often occurred through masturbation. Such reports appear to be in line with the experiences of heterosexual youth, at least for boys; for heterosexual youth, fewer studies have examined frequency of masturbation, but instead have focused on questions that tap whether the individual has ever masturbated (Coles & Stokes, 1985; Udry, Billy, Morris, Groff, & Raj, 1985). Coles and Stokes (1985) reported that by age 18, 60% of boys indicate that they have masturbated; however, boys also commonly reported that frequent masturbation held some stigma and would not be admitted to readily. For such activities retrospective reports may be more accurate, although it is difficult to test the accuracy of reporting for socially stigmatized behaviors. The gay men in Savin-Williams's study may be more open about their sexual experiences, as they have been forced to reflect more on their sexual desires and behaviors than have heterosexual youth.

Descriptive studies indicate that adolescents seem to follow a progression in their initiation of behaviors, beginning with sexual feelings or masturbation, which may occur in childhood; debate exists as to whether childhood behaviors that demonstrate affection or intimacy, such as hand holding (most commonly occurring in same-sex relationships), would be classified as sexual (Westney et al., 1983). Childhood displays of intimacy have most often been thought of as precursors to subsequent sexual behaviors, with these experiences being useful in developing skills for behaving in sexual contexts (Spanier, 1977; Sullivan, 1953). By early adolescence (ages 13–14), most individuals will have had their first kiss (Coles & Stokes, 1985) and will have begun to engage in dating-type activities such as going out in mixed-gender groups (Spreadbury, 1982). Adolescents quickly move on to noncoital and coital petting behaviors then to intercourse. (See Katchadourian, 1990, and Westney et al., 1983, for reviews.)

Almost as early as such behavioral progressions were catalogued, it became apparent that individuals and groups of individuals varied in the extent to which they followed this progression (Smith & Udry, 1985). Smith and Udry examined the progression of behaviors in a sample of white and African American young adolescents. White adolescents more often followed the commonly described progression of behaviors from kissing to intercourse, as would be expected given that the studies establishing this behavioral pattern examined only white adolescents. In contrast, African American adolescents did not follow the same behavioral patterns but moved quickly to coital behaviors. In some cases, certain intermediate behaviors were skipped entirely. These differences likely explain the race difference in age of intercourse in that white adolescents spend more time engaging in noncoital behaviors before progressing to intercourse.

Whereas first intercourse may be a major life event, and potentially a transition, for some youth, other sexual activities, such as masturbation and fantasy, more likely define the daily or more common sexual experiences of most youth and many adults (Michael, Gagnon, Laumann, & Kolata, 1994). How adolescents learn to regulate these feelings and activities is relatively unstudied. Development of emotion regulation has been studied more commonly in early childhood, with less focus on the potential need to regulate new emotions that may be emerging for the first time at later phases of life. In addition, research on group differences in sexual behaviors (e.g., Smith & Udry, 1985) and their timing indicates that some behaviors may not be particularly important for some youth, depending on contextual and individual difference factors that have not been fully determined.

Framing sexuality as an interaction of biological and social influences

Early studies of the biological bases of sexual behavior most often looked for direct effects of hormones on behavior. In contrast, the majority of studies of predictors (or even correlates) of adolescent sexual behavior have examined family influences such as maternal education or family structure (Inazu & Fox, 1980; Miller & Bingham, 1989; Zelnick, Kantner, & Ford, 1981) and social contexts or values such as religiosity (Devaney & Hubley, 1981; Zelnick et al., 1981). Predicting sexual behavior has, as we have indicated, focused heavily on initiation of intercourse but has also extended to precursors to intercourse in some studies. In addition to family antecedents and correlates of the timing of intercourse, peer influences have frequently been cited as important in this area. Earlier reviews (Brooks-Gunn & Paikoff, 1993; Hofferth & Hayes, 1987) have noted that despite the assumption that peers influence the sexual behavior of an adolescent (most obviously as potential partners), less research has documented the extent and nature of this influence. Studies of peer choice suggest that sexual behavior may predict friendship choices more often than the reverse (Brooks-Gunn & Furstenberg, 1989) and that adolescents' perceptions of the normative behaviors in their peer groups may be more predictive of sexual behavior than the actual behaviors exhibited by peers (Cvetkovich & Grote, 1980).

Recent studies have considered more sophisticated statistical modeling of the social environment in predicting peer influences on intercourse and on moving from one stage of activity (e.g., kissing) to another (e.g., light petting). Rodgers and Rowe (1993; Rodgers, 1996) have applied the Epidemic Modeling of the Onset of Social Activities (EMOSA) to sexuality; the set of EMOSA models have commonly been termed *contagion models* of behavior, as it is hypothesized that some behaviors become epidemic (or prevalent) as they spread through a population of adolescents. In the case of sexual behavior, the model predicts those individuals most likely to move to more advanced stages of sexuality based on the nature of their social environment (e.g., the number of adolescents in their environment who engage in that behavior and thus would spread it) and physical development (Rodgers & Rowe, 1993).

Other research has examined interactive models that incorporate arousal with social controls and consider potential biologically based influences on sexual behavior that may or may not be via hormonal effects on sexual arousal (Udry & Campbell, 1994). Initial investigations of the hormonal stimulation of sexuality were based on the adult literature suggesting that testosterone is directly associated with sexual interest or drive in men, that is, that men with abnormally low sexual interest increase their sexual activity on receiving testosterone supplements (Kwan, Greenleaf, Mann, Crapo, & Davidson, 1983). (See Udry and Campbell, 1994, for a review of this literature.) Udry and colleagues (1985) conceptualized adolescents as being in the low-testosterone state and expected them to respond to the normatively occurring increase in testosterone with increased sexual activity (across a range of behaviors) until they reached adult hormonal levels.

Initial examinations of this model appeared to find support for direct hormonal effects on sexual behavior, at least for boys (Udry et al., 1985). In their cross-sectional study of young adolescent boys, testosterone was positively correlated with engaging in more advanced sexual behaviors (i.e., coital behaviors). However, it was immediately apparent that the same direct link between hormones and behavior was not present for girls (Udry, Talbert, & Morris, 1986). In order to explain the sexual activity of comparably aged girls, the addition of social factors needed to be included in the models. Androgen effects were found on noncoital behaviors such as kissing, but engagement in coital behaviors was better explained by variables tapping social controls. In this case, Udry and colleagues (1986) asserted that girls received greater pressure by parents, friends, and the culture at large to inhibit sexual activity, with greater constraints on opportunity for intercourse.

Thus, for the past 10 years, it has been commonly held that (1) direct hormonal effect models are appropriate for predicting boys' initiation of intercourse and (2) interactive models accounting for initial hormonal effects curtailed or controlled by social factors best explain initiation of intercourse for girls. However, subsequent longitudinal examination of hormonal and behavioral links suggested that the direct-effect model did not, in fact, apply to boys (Udry & Campbell, 1994). Specifically, extensive analysis of longitudinal models did not find that testosterone levels were associated with behavior over time; only initial level was associated with individual differences in sexual behavior. Instead of a testosterone effect, it is more likely that a high level of testosterone in young adolescent boys was actually a marker for earlier pubertal development, and that earlier puberty set some boys on what Udry and Campbell (1994) refer to as a "growth trajectory" that resulted in earlier sexual behavior for these boys in comparison to on-time and later-maturing boys.

Again, findings for girls were more complicated. In their most recent study of young adolescent girls (beginning at age 13), Udry and Campbell (1994) found that level of pubertal development was associated with sexual activity via what they term an "attractiveness" effect. More advanced sexual behaviors (i.e., coital) did not occur until girls had reached more advanced levels of development, suggesting that physical signs of maturity attract attention from boys and perhaps signal that sexual behavior is more appropriate for someone at this level of development. Of note is that in recent studies of girls' health and development (Herman-Giddens & MacMillan, 1991; NHLBI Research Group, 1992) and the study reported on by Udry and Campbell, African American girls have been found to begin puberty earlier than white girls, resulting in their maturing earlier, on average, than white girls and being more advanced in pubertal development than same-age white girls at any given time in the span of pubertal development. The race difference in pubertal timing, coupled with the pubertal development effects on sexual activity reported by Udry and Campbell, may be important in understanding race differences in age of first intercourse, at least for girls.

It is also important to emphasize that the pubertal development or timing of development effects found in the most recent work at Udry's lab are probably not biologically based or at least not through direct effects of hormones on behavior. Certainly, pubertal hormones are responsible for the changes in secondary sexual characteristics that are visibly observable to adolescents and those around them, and it is likely that the experience of development in this social context is linked to behavior (Brooks-Gunn & Reiter, 1990). In addition, consideration of the interaction of biological and social processes should not be limited to the study of testosterone or related androgens. In fact, drawing on Udry and Campbell (1994) as exemplary work in this field, it has also been suggested that personality factors (e.g., temperament) may have genetic bases that are linked to the timing of initiation of intercourse. Again, it is likely that such temperamental characteristics interact with a set of environment conditions that promote expression of earlier or later sexual behavior.

Examining sexuality within the multiple contexts of adolescents' lives

This perspective considers adolescent sexuality as developing in multiple interconnected contexts, including the adolescent's family, peer group, and neighborhood. This perspective can be seen in the literature on teenage parenthood. Potentially, early parenthood has implications for the life courses of all family members – the new baby, the teenage mother, the teen's own parents, and the teen's siblings (Bachrach, 1984; Chase-Lansdale, Brooks-Gunn, & Zamsky, 1994; Furstenberg, Brooks-Gunn, & Morgan, 1987; Miller & Moore, 1990). Additionally, some family-oriented research examines the *intersections* among consequences for various family members, as exemplified by the work on teenage mothers and their children (Furstenberg et al., 1987; Horwitz, Klerman, Kuo, & Jekel, 1991). Finally, family system approaches would also fit under this rubric. Again, using the teenage parenthood literature for examples, developmental scholars have been studying interactions among family members with a multigenerational focus, observing teenage mothers, their children, and the children's grandmothers or grandmother figures simultaneously and in subsets of interactions (Burton, 1994; Chase-Lansdale et al., 1994; Wakschlag, Chase-Lansdale, & Brooks-Gunn, 1997; Ward & Carlson, 1995).

Again, sexual transitions have not been studied extensively using a family perspective. However, interesting new work is looking at family discussions of sexual issues, as well as parental monitoring and supervision of extrafamilial relationships and activities (Paikoff, 1995; Vera, Reese, Paikoff, & Jarrett, 1996). Conflict between parents and adolescents has been examined in several studies (e.g., Smetana, 1988, 1989), with results suggesting that many parent–adolescent conflict situations center on dating and time spent with peers in the absence of adult supervision (Brooks-Gunn & Zahaykevich, 1989). In other studies, youth are being interviewed about their relationships with parents during the time that these relationships are being altered by role transitions such as initiation of sexual behavior (Powers & Welsh, in press; Turner & Feldman, 1994).

This perspective also considers adolescent sexuality in the context of the peer environment. This approach highlights the importance of peer influences on the onset of sexual behaviors but also considers the multiple contexts that affect adolescents' sexual behaviors. Interestingly, over time more attention has been paid to how peers and families influence sexual behavior. Despite an interest or a belief in the influence of peers on sexual behavior, nearly all research on adolescent sexuality has focused on the individual, with little attention to the partner. Although many consider factors about partners to be important in predicting reproductive and health risks (e.g., Santelli & Beilenson, 1992), there is a noticeable deficit in this area of research.

Most recently, larger contexts such as neighborhoods have been found to impact norms for the timing of sexual behavior and teen pregnancy (Brewster, Billy, & Grady, 1993; Brooks-Gunn, Duncan, Klebanov, & Sealand, 1993; Burton, 1990; Burton, Allison, & Obeidallah, 1995; Hogan & Kitagawa, 1985). Such research considers several aspects of the neighborhood in which an adolescent lives and the influence this may have on adolescent behavior above and beyond the immediate influence of the adolescent's family. Under this perspective, both contagion and socialization models have been posited for how neighborhoods might influence a range of behaviors (Mayer & Jencks, 1989; Wilson, 1991), with subsequent work applying these models to teen pregnancy (Brooks-Gunn et al., 1993). Of note is that rates of teen pregnancy appear to be reduced by the presence of more affluent neighbors and ones with more prestigious jobs, although the impact of neighborhoods differed for white and African American adolescents (Brooks-Gunn et al., 1993). Processes such as socialization and contagion for adolescent sexuality are beginning to be examined, with a focus on broader peer contexts (Rodgers, 1996) and intergenerational influences (Burton, 1990; Burton et al., 1995); further specification of neighborhood influences on sexuality is necessary.

Nuanced views of gender and sexuality

Another dimension on which family, peers, and societal norms shape the development of sexuality is gender and expectations for behavior based on gender. The role of gender in the development of sexuality has been viewed almost exclusively from a gender differences perspective. Oliver and Hyde (1993) conducted a meta-analysis of 177 articles that have examined gender differences in sexuality and the size of differences over the recent historical period. Although gender differences in age of first intercourse and number of partners are smaller in recent cohorts than in prior cohorts, differences persist. Interestingly, in the recent National Health and Social Life Survey of adult sexual behaviors, preferences, and attitudes (Michael et al., 1994), frequency of intercourse did not differ by gender. Instead, frequency of intercourse varied by marital status and age, with older adults (aged 50–59) and unmarried adults having the least frequent sex. In contrast, frequency of thinking about sex differed dramatically by gender, as did frequency of masturbation. Documentation of gender differences in behaviors or activities does not address questions about the extent to which sexuality is experienced differentially or similarly by gender (Brooks-Gunn & Paikoff, 1993).

Part of understanding the role that gender plays in motivation, feelings, and development of a sense of oneself as a sexual being is understanding how sexual roles are determined by societal norms for boys and girls. As we have discussed, adolescent girls who pursue their sexual interests still risk negative peer labels such as "slut," whereas boys are expected to be more openly sexual (Orenstein, 1994). Orenstein's observational accounts of the categorization of adolescents by one another further support the persistence in society of gender-based social constraints on sexual behavior.

A contrasting stereotype (to the notion of girls as sluts or prudes) often held by researchers and parents is that girls are victims of sexual pressures exerted by boys. Although this stereotype is still prevalent, it has become more nuanced as girls have begun to be viewed as agentic. Oddly, both views on the interactions of boys and girls seem to coexist in schools throughout the United States. In surveys of behavior that occurred at school, sexual harassment encompassing physical actions such as grabbing or being flashed, and verbal comments and gestures, is experienced by over 80% of girls across racial and ethnic groups (American Association of University Women [AAUW] Educational Foundation, 1993). Again, the observations of Orenstein (1994) add graphic examples of the pervasiveness and depth of the negativity that characterizes the interactions of young adolescent boys and girls and are recommended as a companion to survey findings. Perhaps more important for the development of a healthy sexual identity is the fact that the negative language and physical aggression observed in mixed-gender situations are sexual in content. Of note is that 70–80% of boys also report experiencing sexual harassment at school (AAUW Educational Foundation, 1993). It is not clear whether the incidents reported are experienced similarly by boys and girls. For example, when a boy pinches a girl in a hallway or classroom at school, is it interpreted by the boy, the girl, their peers, or school officials who may witness the act in the same way as when a girl pinches a boy? It seems likely that the two situations receive very different responses by the participants and those around them.

Although the "boys as predators and girls as victims" stereotype may in some sense be supported, additional contextual factors need to be accounted for in understanding what may place girls at increased risk in sexual situations. Research on teen pregnancy suggests that the age of girls and their partners – in this case, the fathers of their children – is important in the extent to which the interaction fits a victim–predator model. Of adolescent girls between the ages of 16 and 19 who give birth to a child, 15–20% report that the father is 6 or more years older than the mother (Landry & Forrest, 1995). This rate increases to 30% for girls who are 15 when they give birth. Thus, adolescent boys may be less likely to be predators than young men. Societal views about relationships between adolescent girls and adult men appear to be conflicted; in most states these relationships are technically illegal, but prohibitive laws (i.e., concerning statutory rape) are rarely enforced.

What certainly merits further attention is the lack of information on these older male partners of adolescent girls. Most adolescents report that their first sexual partner was about 1.5 to 3 years older than they were at the time (Rodgers, 1996). Hence, the difference in age of 6 or more years between a sizable percentage of teen mothers and the fathers of their children would indicate that girls with much older partners are

more likely to get pregnant than adolescent girls with same-age partners. It may be that because the partners are older, they are better able
to provide for a family; however, initial investigations do not find that
these older men are actually supporting these girls or that these girls
and their babies less often receive Aid to Families with Dependent
Children. Rather, it may be that young (or older) adult men who seek
adolescent girls for sex or relationships are less competent or less mature than other same-age men.

Adolescent–adolescent sexual relationships may be quite different
than adolescent–adult sexual relationships. At this time, both require
more nuanced research to understand the nature and effect of these
different relationship and interaction patterns on girls and boys.

Stressing health promotion rather than prevention of intercourse

Although we have tried to emphasize that the development of adolescent sexuality is not limited to intercourse or the negative outcomes
that may be associated with it, this approach is not meant to minimize
the impact that teen pregnancy or the experience of sexually transmitted disease may have on adolescents. The Alan Guttmacher Institute
(1994) estimates that 25% of sexually experienced adolescents will become infected with a sexually transmitted disease each year (or about
13% of all youth between the ages of 13 and 19). Also, among sexually
experienced adolescents, about 20% become pregnant each year, with
lower rates for younger adolescents and the highest rate for 18- to 19-
year olds (AGI, 1994). At the same time, trends indicate that adolescents have greatly improved their contraceptive use in recent years. In
fact, teenage girls are, on average, about as able as young adult women
to avoid unintended pregnancy and to use contraceptives appropriately.
Two points are apparent from these findings. First, young adults and
adolescents are not perfect contraceptive users, and improvement is
certainly warranted for individuals in both age groups. Second, some
adolescents are able to manage their sexual activity and minimize their
health risks, whereas others are less successful.

The increased use of contraceptives is probably due to successes in
prevention, intervention, and health promotion programs targeting
risky sexual behavior that have been conducted over the past several
years. However, despite trends indicating that knowledge and behavior

have improved, it is often unclear how such changes have been manifested and which strategies might best reach those adolescents who have not been responsive to present approaches (Brooks-Gunn & Paikoff, 1993). In particular, initial work in this area has focused on the prevention of specific outcomes (e.g., pregnancy) rather than on health promotion as a comprehensive endeavor. (See Brooks-Gunn & Paikoff, 1993, for a review of the program evaluation literature in this area.) Using a public health model, prevention or intervention programming has also frequently focused on single risks as antecedents for the behavior being targeted (Felner & Felner, 1989). In contrast, health promotion programs have conceptualized behavior as multidetermined and interrelated across domains (Brooks-Gunn & Paikoff, 1993). Health promotion as a method for improving the lives of adolescents has begun across several domains (Millstein, Petersen, & Nightingale, 1993). This approach is in line with the conceptualization of adolescent sexuality as involving physical, cognitive, and social development in order for a healthy sexual self to develop. Hence, programs that have included feelings about sexuality, decision-making skills, and managing and negotiating risky situations may benefit a broader group of adolescents, including those who have had intercourse and those who have not. Notably, to date, fewer programs have taken this approach. Specific evaluation of the effectiveness of programs or of how programs achieve results is not pervasive; additional evaluation research is necessary in this field.

The divergent approaches to curbing sexual activity, or the health risks associated with it, grew out of divergent perspectives on sexuality as a risk behavior versus part of a cluster of behaviors that must be viewed together. Initial research often considered adolescent sexuality (i.e., usually intercourse) as a problem behavior in isolation from other behaviors. Models of adolescent risk behavior, in contrast, have considered sexual behavior and its timing as part of a constellation of behaviors (Irwin & Millstein, 1986; Jessor, 1992; Jessor & Jessor, 1977). More specifically, sexual behavior may or may not be a problem behavior or a risk for adverse life outcomes when it is examined in isolation. Rather, particular problems that have been identified as associated with morbidity and poorer life outcomes (e.g., school dropout, subsequent unemployment) appear to cluster together in what Jessor (1992) has termed a *lifestyle*. Engagement in behaviors is not the only determinant of an unhealthy lifestyle; age of onset of engagement in such behaviors is also important, with earlier involvement being more often associated with unhealthy practices. For example, most youth will drink alcohol at some point during adolescence and, as has been stated, many will have intercourse. However, engaging in these behaviors at earlier ages is more often associated with adverse outcomes, especially when coupled with engagement in other behaviors such as smoking or drug use. Jessor (1992) also emphasizes the role played by protective factors in the individual's life; many youth in high-risk environments who engage in health-compromising behaviors may overcome risks via involvement with protective factors (e.g., church organizations, parental supervision).

Again, the conceptual view of sexuality as a singular problem behavior versus part of a cluster of behaviors is directly related to the tension previously discussed between targeting sexual activity through prevention and intervention programs versus health promotion programs addressing overall skills to develop health and well-being. It is surprising that single-behavior intervention programs have been so popular given that sexual activity, at least the timing of the onset of intercourse, has been identified as part of a behavioral cluster for at least two decades (Jessor & Jessor, 1977). The incorporation of protective factors into models for understanding these behaviors and their outcomes has been instrumental in programming for youth that has emphasized helping youth build skills to offset engagement in health-compromising behaviors (Botvin & Botvin, 1992; Botvin & Dusenbury, 1992; Dusenbury & Botvin, 1992). Botvin (1995) has also suggested, given the similar etiologies of substance abuse and sexual activity, that the skill-based interventions that have proven effective in reducing substance use should be considered in addressing adolescent sexual activity.

Adolescent sexuality as a potential opportunity cost

Much of the work based on skill-building models for health promotion begins with the premise that individual differences in skills exist among adolescents but that all youth benefit from learning and practicing appropriate skills. Skills thought to be necessary to offset unhealthy behaviors include decision-making ability, ability to understand and evaluate consequences, conflict resolution, and negotiating strategies

(Botvin & Botvin, 1992; Brooks-Gunn, 1993; Dusenbury & Botvin, 1992). These skills again apply to a range of behaviors but are pertinent to making decisions about sexual behavior.

Adolescent decision making about sexual behavior has often been framed in the context of whether adolescents can weigh the cost of sexual decisions accurately. That is, do they see the loss in future opportunities if they become pregnant? In a recent review of the literature on adolescent decision making across outcomes, Beyth-Marom and Fischhoff (1997) conclude that adolescents frequently perform about as well as adults in identifying the consequences of behaviors and assessing the probability that negative or positive outcomes will occur. Of note was that teens from high-risk environments who were exposed to drugs and alcohol were less often correct than middle-class youth on items tapping knowledge about the effects of drugs and alcohol on the body; at the same time, youth from high-risk environments were much more confident than other youth that their answers were correct (cf. Beyth-Marom & Fischhoff, 1997). Exposure appeared to give these adolescents a false sense of knowledge or expertise. Alternately, drawing upon Vygotskian approaches to cognitive development, experiences and contexts may promote (rather than detract from) better decision-making skills via exposure to and interactions with healthier choices. For example, Western European countries have created multiple contexts in which contraceptive use is promoted to youth and adults; the result is a substantially lower teen pregnancy rate for these countries than in the U.S.

Along with potential bias in the metacognitive aspects of decision making, it is commonly noted that decisions, identification of consequences, and the probability of outcomes are ultimately affected by the value that a certain outcome has. Furthermore, the value placed on a particular outcome is subjective and develops out of the individual's beliefs and environmental context. Differential assessment of behaviors and outcomes by adults and adolescents is due in part to the extent to which adults and adolescents perceive the costs and benefits of particular actions differently (Beyth-Marom & Fischhoff, 1997; Brooks-Gunn, 1993). Most adults perceive teen pregnancy to have substantial costs to future life opportunities. Recent work by Geronimus (1994, 1996) has suggested that some groups of adolescents may perceive benefits from earlier childbearing, especially when they assess the possible costs of later childbearing. Specifically, Geronimus (1996) has examined longevity and indicators of the health of rural and urban African American and white women. African American women, especially those in low-income urban environments, experience serious health difficulties (e.g., hypertension, diabetes) at earlier ages and at higher rates than same-age white women. Interviews conducted with pregnant African American adolescent girls about childbearing and about when a woman is too old to have children revealed that these girls seemed aware of the higher rates of morbidity and mortality experienced by women (like themselves) as they aged (Geronimus, 1996). That is, a majority of these girls (67%) reported an age between 26 and 35 years as the oldest a woman should be when she has a child; only 25% of a comparison sample gave ages in this range, instead selecting older ages more often. Girls' reasons for their answers included experiential knowledge of women dying at younger ages; thus, if a woman did not have children earlier, she might not live to see them grow up. Also, girls weighed in their assessments the likelihood that their male partners would be alive to father or raise a child at later ages. High rates of unemployment and mortality among urban African American male youth (Blake & Darling, 1994; National Center for Health Statistics, 1991) would again verify that these girls are incorporating real concerns into their decision-making processes. These assessments are confined to the experiences of African American girls from lower-income and poor families living in urban environments. The value attached to the timing of childbearing or sexual activities varies for other youth not growing up in these environments.

Future directions

Interest in and concern about the sexual behavior of adolescents have grown out of the need in most societies to control their sexuality. Across historical periods and societies, success in controlling adolescent sexuality has varied greatly. Variations in the salience of parental control, peer groups, societal norms, and neighborhood composition exist both across and within societies. Such controls and influences have been thought to be necessary in prior historical periods for controlling the timing and context of childbearing (Paige & Paige, 1985). Certainly, controlling childbearing is still a concern for present societies, but along with this concern is the added threat to physical health via sexually transmitted diseases that have become more prevalent among adolescents in some societies (Brooks–Gunn & Paikoff, 1997). Regulation of sexual activity also protects adolescents psychologically from experiences for which they are emotionally unprepared. In particular, concern is raised about adolescents' ability to engage in sexual intercourse in a way that respects both individuals, such that neither is being manipulated or coerced (Brooks–Gunn & Paikoff, 1993, 1997).

In reviewing the perspectives on research on adolescent sexuality, it is clear that many of these areas overlap and are interconnected in that assumptions about one aspect are associated with conclusions drawn about another aspect of this field. In the identification of future directions across perspectives, some issues have already been discussed, and others can be drawn from our discussion of the perspectives in research on adolescent sexuality. Throughout this chapter, we have tried to note new and innovative approaches to examining adolescent sexuality, especially those that embed sexuality in development and multiple social contexts. For example, the work of Rodgers and Rowe (1993) using contagion or epidemic models will likely be helpful in understanding adolescent sexuality. Future work should expand on these or similar models in order to understand how social forces shape adolescent behavior.

As we have emphasized, adolescent sexuality encompasses a range of feelings and behaviors, some of which may put adolescents at risk for pregnancy or sexually transmitted diseases but many of which are part of normative development and the integration of sexuality into one's sense of self. Thus, limiting research to the risks of sexual behaviors will not be fruitful in understanding sexuality or adolescent development. Recent work in this area by Buzwell and Rosenthal (1996) appears to be particularly promising for understanding sexual behavior. In their approach, Buzwell and Rosenthal have developed a multifaceted model of sexual identity that includes sexual self-esteem, self-efficacy, and attitudes. Based on this multifaceted assessment, adolescents in their study were classified into several clusters or sexual identities, which in turn predicted the propensity to engage in risky sexual behaviors. Although sexual orientation was included in the assessment, the identities that emerged were more encompassing than simple differentiations of homosexual or heterosexual preferences, including factors such as feelings about one's body, interest in sexual exploration, and views on commitment – dimensions of sexual identity that apply to all adolescents, if not all humans. This initial work has been cross-sectional, and it remains to be seen through longitudinal investigations whether the identity typologies are actually stages or steps through which some adolescents pass on their way to a final identity or whether they are final steps for other adolescents. Certainly, this study and prior work by this group (Buzwell & Rosenthal, 1996; Moore & Rosenthal, 1993) demonstrate the value of understanding sexual identity and defining it more broadly.

Whereas the Buzwell–Rosenthal typologies construct sexual identity from a range of feelings and behaviors, the concept of behavioral lifestyles embeds sexual behavior and identity within a larger framework of behavioral choices; both approaches merit further exploration as means for better understanding adolescent sexuality and the role it may play in the life course. For example, sexual identity and self-acceptance may be related to effective contraceptive use. Adolescents, at least girls, who develop greater sexual self-acceptance are more likely to communicate with their sexual partners about contraception; and those adolescents who communicate with their partners may demonstrate more effective contraceptive use (Tschann & Adler, 1997). A related issue is how and to what extent types of sexual identities or behavioral lifestyles, as identified by Jessor (1992), ultimately result in behavioral trajectories into young adulthood and perhaps beyond.

Across domains of study in the area of adolescence, a focal issue has been whether and to what extent the navigation of the transitions and experiences of the adolescent decade shape the navigation of the remainder of the life course. As yet, few studies have addressed long-term outcomes. We have noted that Stattin and Magnusson (1990), in their longitudinal study of girls' development from adolescence to midlife, may document the long-term effects of an adolescent lifestyle on adult attainments. In this case, girls who went through puberty earlier than their peers and socialized with older peers engaged in alcohol use at earlier ages and began to disengage from academic activities at earlier phases in life. One consequence of this lifestyle was that these girls had less prestigious careers in adulthood. Of note is that entry into this lifestyle was based in part on the experience of an adolescent transition, in this case the timing of puberty (Graber & Brooks-Gunn, 1996). Part of this lifestyle was earlier engagement in heterosocial activities (and intercourse), along with other behaviors commonly labeled as problem behaviors (Stattin & Magnusson, 1990).

In addition to the importance of the Stattin and Magnusson study and related work by Jessor in identifying potential behavioral trajectories, these findings highlight the fact that there is an absence of meaningful information about the sexual and romantic partners of adolescents. As demonstrated by both the Swedish study (Stattin & Magnusson, 1990) and investigations of teenage pregnancy discussed previously (Landry & Forrest, 1995), older boys or men may have a very negative influence on adolescent girls, with these relationships having lifelong consequences (e.g., early childbearing, lower educational attainments). Better information about these men and the relationships they are having with girls may be helpful in planning prevention and health promotion programs that would help girls understand these relationships and better avoid men who are predators rather than partners. Such investigations may also inform policy debates on whether or not to utilize legal interventions in these situations.

The investigation of sexual partners is important not only to offset unhealthy relationships but also from a larger developmental perspective. Partners, including sexual and/or romantic ones, are likely to have a large influence on an adolescent's life, yet very little is known about these relationships in terms of either sexuality or the development of intimacy (Furman, Feiring, & Brown, in press). In general, there is a need for a better understanding of the negotiation strategies adolescents use in making decisions about sexual behaviors. Some of these negotiations happen in the context of romantic relationships, whereas others occur between friends, acquaintances, or strangers. These skills are at the heart of building healthy relationships or sexual identities. It is commonly believed, at least in the health promotion field, that all adolescents would benefit from developing better negotiation strategies and building more effective decision-making skills; it is unlikely that this is any less important for skills that apply to sexual behavior. In fact, similar skills are probably needed to navigate many different situations that involve health-compromising or risk behaviors (Botvin, 1995). If anything, practice in applying effective strategies to sexual situations is particularly necessary, as these are often situations in which adolescents (and adults) may have difficulty balancing physical arousal and pleasure with emotional needs and desires.

In conclusion, these avenues of research seem to hold promise for moving toward a better understanding of sexual behavior, by others and by adolescents themselves. Certainly, we have not generated an exhaustive list of such avenues. Inasmuch as adolescent sexuality and the development of a sexual identity are multifaceted processes and potentially a primary transition of adolescence, it is our hope that future studies will incorporate some of this diversity of experience and process in the investigation of this aspect of development.

References

Adams, G. R., Montemayor, R., & Gullotta T. (Eds.). (1989–1993). *Advances in adolescent development, Vols. 1–5*. Newbury Park, CA: Sage.

Alan Guttmacher Institute. (1994). *Sex and America's teenagers*. New York: Author.

American Association of University Women Educational Foundation. (1993). *Hostile hallways: The AAUW survey on sexual harassment in America's schools*. Washington, DC: American Association of University Women.

Bachman, J. G., Johnston, L. D., O'Malley, P. M., & Schulenberg, J. (1996). Transitions in drug use during late adolescence and young adulthood. In J. A. Graber, J. Brooks-Gunn, & A. C. Petersen (Eds.), *Transitions through adolescence: Interpersonal domains and context* (pp. 111–140). Mahwah, NJ: Erlbaum.

Bachrach, C. A. (1984). Contraceptive practice among American women, 1973–1982. *Family Planning Perspectives, 16*(6), 253–259.

Belsky, J. (1984). The determinants of parenting: A process model. *Child Development, 55*(1), 83–96.

Beyth-Marom, R., & Fischhoff, B. (1997). Adolescents' decisions about risks: A cognitive perspective. In J. Schulenberg, J. L. Maggs, & K. Hurrelmann (Eds.), *Health risks and developmental transitions during adolescence* (pp. 110–135). Cambridge, MA: Harvard University Press.

Blake, W. M., & Darling, C. A. (1994). The dilemmas of the African American male. *Journal of Black Studies, 24*, 402–415.

Botvin, G. J. (1995). School-based health promotion: Substance abuse and sexual behavior. *Applied and Preventive Psychology, 4*(3), 167–184.

Botvin, G. J., & Botvin, E. M. (1992). Adolescent tobacco, alcohol, and drug abuse: Prevention strategies, empirical findings, and assessment issues. *Journal of Developmental and Behavioral Pediatrics, 13*(4), 290–301.

Botvin, G. J., & Dusenbury, L. (1992). Substance abuse prevention: Implications for reducing risk of HIV infection. *Psychology of Addictive Behaviors, 6*(2), 70–80.

Brewster, K. L., Billy, J. O. G., & Grady, W. R. (1993). Social context and adolescent behavior: The impact of community on the transition to sexual activity. *Social Forces, 71*(3), 713–740.

Bronfenbrenner, U. (1977). Toward an experimental ecology of human development. *American Psychologist, 32,* 513–531.

Bronfenbrenner, U. (1979). *The ecology of human development.* Cambridge, MA: Harvard University Press.

Brooks-Gunn, J. (1990). Overcoming barriers to adolescent research on pubertal and reproductive development. *Journal of Youth and Adolescence, 19*(5), 425–440.

Brooks-Gunn, J., & Chase-Lansdale, P. L. (1995). Adolescent parenthood. In M. H. Bornstein (Ed.), *Handbook of parenting: Vol. 3. Status and social conditions of parenting* (pp. 113–149). Mahwah, NJ: Erlbaum.

Brooks-Gunn, J., Duncan, G., Klebanov, P. K., & Sealand, N. (1993). Do neighborhoods influence child and adolescent development? *American Journal of Sociology, 99,* 353–395.

Brooks-Gunn, J., & Furstenberg, F. F. (1989). Adolescent sexual behavior. *American Psychologist, 44*(2), 249–257.

Brooks-Gunn, J., & Graber, J. A. (1994). Puberty as a biological and social event: Implications for research on pharmacology. *Journal of Adolescent Health, 15*(8), 663–671.

Brooks-Gunn, J., Graber, J. A., & Paikoff, R. L. (1994). Studying links between hormones and negative affect: Models and measures. *Journal of Research on Adolescence, 4*(4), 469–486.

Brooks-Gunn, J., & Paikoff, R. L. (1993). "Sex is a gamble, kissing is a game": Adolescent sexuality and health promotion. In S. G. Millstein, A. C. Petersen, & E. O. Nightingale (Eds.), *Promoting the health of adolescents: New directions for the twenty-first century* (pp. 180–208). New York: Oxford University Press.

Brooks-Gunn, J., & Paikoff, R. L. (1997). Sexuality and developmental transitions during adolescence. In J. Schulenberg, J. Maggs, & K. Hurrelmann (Eds.), *Health risks and developmental transitions during adolescence* (pp. 190–219). New York: Cambridge University Press.

Brooks-Gunn, J., Petersen, A. C., & Eichorn, D. (1985). The study of maturational timing effects in adolescence. *Journal of Youth and Adolescence, 14*(3), 149–161.

Brooks-Gunn, J., & Reiter, E. O. (1990). The role of pubertal processes. In S. Feldman & G. Elliot (Eds.), *At the threshold: The developing adolescent* (pp. 16–53). Cambridge, MA: Harvard University Press.

Brooks-Gunn, J., & Zahaykevich, M. (1989). Parent–daughter relationships in early adolescence: A developmental perspective. In K. Kreppner &

R. M. Lerner (Eds.), *Family systems and life-span development* (pp. 223–246). Hillsdale, NJ: Erlbaum.

Burton, L. M. (1990). Teenage childbearing as an alternative life-course strategy in multigeneration black families. *Human Nature, 1*(2), 123–143.

Burton, L. M. (1994). Intergenerational legacies and intimate relationships: Perspectives on adolescent mothers and fathers. *ISSPR Bulletin, 10*(2), 1–3.

Burton, L. M., Allison, K. W., & Obeidallah, D. (1995). Social context and adolescence: Perspectives on development among inner-city African-American teens. In L. J. Crockett & A. C. Crouter (Eds.), *Pathways through adolescence: Individual development in relation to social contexts* (pp. 119–138). Mahwah, NJ: Erlbaum.

Buzwell, S., & Rosenthal, D. (1996). Constructing a sexual self: Adolescents' sexual self-perceptions and sexual risk-taking. *Journal of Research on Adolescence, 6*(4), 489–513.

Centers for Disease Control. (1991). Current trends: Premarital sexual experience among adolescent women – United States, 1970–1988. *Morbidity and Mortality Weekly Report, 39*(51–52), 929–932.

Centers for Disease Control. (1992). Selected behaviors that increase risk for HIV infection among high school students – United States, 1990. *Morbidity and Mortality Weekly Report, 41*(14), 231–240.

Chase-Lansdale, P. L., Brooks-Gunn, J., & Zamsky, E. S. (1994). Young African-American multigenerational families in poverty: Quality of mothering and grandmothering. *Child Development, 65*(2), 373–393.

Chilman, C. S. (1980). *Adolescent pregnancy and childbearing: Findings from research.* Washington, DC: National Institutes of Health.

Cogswell, M. E., & Yip, R. (1995). The influence of fetal and maternal factors on the distribution of birthweight. *Seminars in Perinatology, 19*(3), 222–240.

Cohler, B. J., & Musick, J. S. (1996). Adolescent parenthood and the transition to adulthood. In J. A. Graber, J. Brooks-Gunn, & A. C. Petersen (Eds.), *Transitions through adolescence: Interpersonal domains and context* (pp. 201–231). Mahwah, NJ: Erlbaum.

Coles, R., & Stokes, G. (1985). *Sex and the American teenager.* New York: Harper & Row.

Cowan, C. P., & Cowan, P. A. (1992). *When partners become parents: The big life change for couples.* New York: Basic Books.

Cvetkovitch, G., & Grote, B. (1980). Psychological development and the social problem of teenage illegitimacy. In C. Chilman (Ed.), *Adolescent pregnancy and childbearing: Findings from research* (pp. 15–41). Washington, DC: U.S. Department of Health and Human Services.

Deutsch, F. M., Ruble, D. N., Fleming, A., Brooks-Gunn, J., & Stangor, C. (1988). Information-seeking and self-definition during the transition to motherhood. *Journal of Personality and Social Psychology, 55*(3), 420–431.

Devaney, B. L., & Hubley, K. S. (1981). *The determinants of adolescent pregnancy and childbearing.* Final report to the National Institute of Child Health and Human Development. Washington, DC: Mathmetica Policy Research.

Donovan, J. E., & Jessor, R. (1985). Structure of problem behavior in adolescence and young adulthood. *Journal of Consulting and Clinical Psychology, 53,* 890–904.

Donovan, J. E., Jessor, R., & Costa, F. M. (1988). Syndrome of problem behavior in adolescence: A replication. *Journal of Consulting and Clinical Psychology, 56*(5), 762–765.

Dornbusch, S. M., Carlsmith, J. M., Gross, R. T., Martin, J. A., Jennings, D., Rosenberg, A., & Duke, P. (1981). Sexual development, age, and dating: A comparison of biological and social influences upon one set of behaviors. *Child Development, 52,* 179–185.

Durbin, M., DiClemente, R. J., Siegel, D., & Krasnovsky, F. (1993). Factors associated with multiple sex partners among junior high school students. *Journal of Adolescent Health, 14*(3), 202–207.

Dusenbury, L., & Botvin, G. J. (1992). Substance abuse prevention: Competence enhancement and the development of positive life options. *Journal of Addictive Diseases, 11*(3), 29–45.

Elder, G. H., Jr. (1974). *Children of the great depression: Social change in life experience.* Chicago: University of Chicago Press.

Elder, G. H., Jr. (1985). Perspectives on the life course. In G. H. Elder, Jr. (Ed.), *Life course dynamics: Trajectories and transitions, 1968–1980* (pp. 23–49). Ithaca, NY: Cornell University Press.

Feldman, S., & Elliott, G. (Eds.). (1990). *At the threshold: The developing adolescent.* Cambridge, MA: Harvard University Press.

Felner, R. D., & Felner, T. Y. (1989). Primary prevention programs in the educational context: A transactional-ecological framework and analysis. In L. A. Bond & B. E. Compass (Eds.), *Primary prevention and promotion in the schools. Primary prevention of psychopathology* (Vol. 12, pp. 13–49). Newbury Park, CA: Sage.

Furman, W., Feiring, C., & Brown, B. B. (in press). *Contemporary perspectives on adolescent relationships.* New York: Cambridge University Press.

Furstenberg, F. F., Jr., Brooks-Gunn, J., & Morgan, P. (1987). *Adolescent mothers in later life.* New York: Cambridge University Press.

Furstenberg, F. F., Jr., Morgan, S. P., Moore, K. A., & Petersen, J. L. (1987).

Race differences in the timing of adolescents' intercourse. *American Sociological Review, 52,* 511–518.

Garguilo, J., Attie, I., Brooks-Gunn, J., & Warren, M. P. (1987) Girls' dating behavior as a function of social context and maturation. *Developmental Psychology, 23*(5), 730–737.

Geronimus, A. T. (1994). The weathering hypothesis and the health of African-American women and infants: Implications for reproductive strategies and policy analysis. In G. Sen & R. Snow (Eds.), *Power and decision: The social control of reproduction* (pp. 75–100). Cambridge, MA: Harvard University Press.

Geronimus, A. T. (1996). What teen mothers know. *Human Nature, 7*(4), 323–352.

Graber, J. A., & Brooks-Gunn, J. (1996). Transitions and turning points: Navigating the passage from childhood through adolescence. *Developmental Psychology, 32*(4), 768–776.

Graber, J. A., Brooks-Gunn, J., & Petersen, A. C. (1996). Adolescent transitions in context. In J. A. Graber, J. Brooks-Gunn, & A. C. Petersen (Eds.), *Transitions through adolescence: Interpersonal domains and context* (pp. 369–383). Mahwah, NJ: Erlbaum.

Graber, J. A., & Petersen, A. C. (1991). Cognitive changes at adolescence: Biological perspectives. In K. Gibson & A. C. Petersen (Eds.), *Brain maturation and cognitive development: Comparative and cross-cultural perspectives* (pp. 253–279). New York: Aldine.

Gunnar, M., & Collins, W. A. (Eds.). (1988). *Development during transition to adolescence: Minnesota symposia on child psychology,* Vol. 21. Hillsdale, NJ: Erlbaum.

Hagestad, G. O. (1986). Dimensions of time and the family. *American Behavioral Scientist, 29*(6), 679–694.

Hareven, T. K. (1977). Family time and historical time. *Daedalus, 106,* 57–70.

Herman-Giddens, M. E., & MacMillan, J. P. (1991). Prevalence of secondary sexual characteristics in a population of North Carolina girls ages 3 to 10. *Adolescent Pediatrics and Gynecology, 2,* 21–26.

Hill, J. P. (1987). Research on adolescents and their families: Past and prospect. In C. E. Irwin (Ed.), *Adolescent social behavior and health: Vol. 37, New directions for child development* (pp. 13–31). San Francisco: Jossey-Bass.

Hofferth, S. L. (1987). Influences on early sexual and fertility behavior. In S. L. Hofferth & C. D. Hayes (Eds.), *Risking the future: Adolescent sexuality, pregnancy, and childbearing* (pp. 7–35). Washington, DC: National Academy Press.

Hofferth, S. L., & Hayes, C. D. (1987) *Risking the future: Adolescent sexuality, pregnancy, and childbearing.* Washington, DC: National Academy Press.

Hogan, D. P., & Kitagawa, E. M. (1985). The impact of social status, family structure, and neighborhood on the fertility of black adolescents. *American Journal of Sociology, 90,* 825–855.

Hopkins, J. R. (1977). Sexual behavior in adolescence. *Journal of Social Issues, 33*(2), 67–85.

Horwitz, S. M., Klerman, L. V., Kuo, H. S., & Jekel, J. F. (1991). School-age mothers: Predictors of long-term educational and economic outcomes. *Pediatrics, 87*(6), 862–867.

Inazu, J. K., & Fox, G. L. (1980). Maternal influences on the sexual behavior of teenage daughters. *Journal of Family Issues, 1,* 81–102.

Irwin, C. E., & Millstein, S. G. (1986). Biopsychosocial correlates of risk-taking behaviors during adolescence: Can the physician intervene? *Journal of Adolescent Health Care, 7*(6, supplement), 82–96.

Jessor, R. (1992). Risk behavior in adolescence: A psychosocial framework for understanding and action. In D. E. Rogers & E. Ginzberg (Eds.), *Adolescents at risk: Medical and social perspectives* (pp. 19–34). Boulder, CO: Westview.

Jessor, R., Costa, F., Jessor, L., & Donovan, J. E. (1983). The time of first intercourse: A prospective study. *Journal of Personality and Social Psychology, 44,* 608–626.

Jessor, S. L., & Jessor, R. (1977). *Problem behavior and psychosocial development: A longitudinal study of youth.* New York: Academic Press.

Kagan, J. (1984). *The nature of the child.* New York: Basic Books.

Katchadourian, H. (1990). Sexuality. In S. Feldman & G. Elliot (Eds.), *At the threshold: The developing adolescent* (pp. 330–351). Cambridge, MA: Harvard University Press.

Keating, D. P. (1990). Adolescent thinking. In S. Feldman & G. Elliot (Eds.), *At the threshold: The developing adolescent* (pp. 54–90). Cambridge, MA: Harvard University Press.

Ketterlinus, R. D., Henderson, S. H., & Lamb, M. E. (1990). Maternal age, sociodemographics, prenatal health and behavior: Influences on neonatal risk status. *Journal of Adolescent Health Care, 11*(5), 423–431.

Kwan, M., Greenleaf, W. J., Mann, J., Crapo, L., & Davidson, J. M. (1983). The nature of androgen action on male sexuality: A combined laboratory and self-report study in hypogonadal men. *Journal of Clinical Endocrinology and Metabolism, 57,* 557–562.

Landry, D. J., & Forrest, J. D. (1995). How old are U.S. fathers? *Family Planning Perspectives, 27*(4), 159–161, 165.

Lerner, R. M., & Foch, T. T. (Eds.). (1987). *Biological–psychosocial interactions in early adolescence.* Hillsdale, NJ: Erlbaum.

Lerner, R. M., Lerner, J. V., von Eye, A., Ostrum, C. W., Nitz, K , Talwar-Soni, R., & Tubman, J. (1996). Continuity and discontinuity across the transition of early adolescence: A developmental contextual perspective. In J. A. Graber, J. Brooks-Gunn, & A. C. Petersen (Eds.), *Transitions through adolescence: Interpersonal domains and context* (pp. 3–22). Mahwah, NJ: Erlbaum.

Levine, M., & McAnarney, E. R. (Eds.). (1988). *Early adolescent transitions.* Lexington, MA: D.C. Heath.

Lewin, K. (1939). The field theory approach to adolescence. *American Journal of Sociology, 44,* 868–897.

McEwen, B. S. (1994). How do sex and stress hormones affect nerve cells? *Annals of the New York Academy of Sciences, 743,* 1–18.

Mayer, S. E., & Jencks, C. (1989). Growing up in poor neighborhoods: How much does it matter? *Sciences, 243*(4897), 1441–1445.

Michael, R. T, Gagnon, J. H., Laumann, E. O., & Kolata, G. (1994). *Sex in America: A definitive survey.* Boston: Warner Books.

Miller, B. C., & Bingham, C. R. (1989). Family configuration in relation to the sexual behavior of female adolescents. *Journal of Marriage and the Family, 51,* 499–506.

Miller, B. C., & Moore, K. A. (1990). Adolescent sexual behavior, pregnancy, and parenting: Research through the 1980s. *Journal of Marriage and the Family, 52,* 1025–1044.

Millstein, S. G., Petersen, A. C., & Nightingale, E. O. (1993). *Promoting the health of adolescents: New directions for the twenty-first century.* New York: Oxford University Press.

Modell, J., Furstenberg, F. F., Jr., & Hershberg, T. (1976). Transitions to adulthood in historical perspective. *Journal of Family History, 1,* 7–32.

Modell, J., & Goodman, M. (1990). Historical perspectives. In S. Feldman & G. Elliott (Eds.), *At the threshold: The developing adolescent* (pp. 93–122). Cambridge, MA: Harvard University Press.

Montemayor, R. (1983). Parents and adolescents in conflict: All families some of the time and some families most of the time. *Journal of Early Adolescence, 3,* 83–103.

Moore, S., & Rosenthal, D. (1993). *Sexuality in adolescence.* New York: Routledge.

Mott, F. L., & Haurin, R. J. (1988). Linkages between sexual activity and alcohol and drug use among American adolescents. *Family Planning Perspectives, 20,* 129–136.

National Center for Health Statistics. (1991). *Vital statistics of the United*

States, 1988. Volume II – Mortality, Part A. Washington, DC: U.S. Government Printing Office.

National Heart, Lung, and Blood Institute Growth and Health Study Research Group. (1992). Obesity and cardiovascular disease risk factors in black and white girls: The NHLBI growth and health study. *American Journal of Public Health, 82,* 1613–1620.

Ohannessian, C. M., & Crockett, L. J. (1993). A longitudinal investigation of the relationship between educational investment and adolescent sexual activity. *Journal of Adolescent Research, 8*(2), 167–182.

Oliver, M. B., & Hyde, J. S. (1993). Gender differences in sexuality: A meta-analysis. *Psychological Bulletin, 114*(1), 29–51.

Orenstein, P. (1994). *School girls: Young women, self-esteem, and the confidence gap.* New York: Doubleday.

Paige, K. E. (1983). A bargaining theory of menarcheal responses in preindustrial cultures. In J. Brooks-Gunn & A. C. Petersen (Eds.), *Girls at puberty: Biological and psychosocial perspectives* (pp. 301–322). New York: Plenum Press.

Paige, K. E., & Paige, J. M. (1985). *Politics and reproductive rituals.* Berkeley: University of California Press.

Paikoff, R. L. (1995). Early heterosexual debut: Situations of sexual possibility during the transition to adolescence. *American Journal of Orthopsychiatry, 65*(3), 389–401.

Paikoff, R. L., & Brooks-Gunn, J. (1991). Do parent–child relationships change during puberty? *Psychological Bulletin, 110,* 47–66.

Parke, R. D. (1988). Families in life-span perspective: A multilevel developmental approach. In E. M. Hetherington, R. M. Lerner, & M. Perlmutter (Eds.), *Child development in life-span perspective* (pp. 159–190). Hillsdale, NJ: Erlbaum.

Petersen, A. C., & Taylor, B. (1980). The biological approach to adolescence: Biological change and psychological adaptation. In J. Adelson (Ed.), *Handbook of adolescent psychology* (pp. 117–155). New York: Wiley.

Pickles, A., & Rutter, M. (1991). Statistical and conceptual models of "turning points" in developmental processes. In D. Magnusson, L. R. Bergman, G. Rudinger, & B. Torestad (Eds.), *Problems and methods in longitudinal research: Stability and change* (pp. 133–165). Cambridge, England: Cambridge University Press.

Powers, S. I., & Welsh, D. P. (in press). Mother–daughter interactions and adolescent girls' depression. In M. Cox & J. Brooks-Gunn (Eds.), *Conflict and cohesion in families: causes and consequences.* Mahwah, NJ: Erlbaum.

Rodgers, J. L. (1996). Sexual transitions in adolescence. In J. A. Graber, J.

Brooks-Gunn, & A. C. Petersen (Eds.), *Transitions through adolescence: Interpersonal domains and context* (pp. 85–110). Mahwah, NJ: Erlbaum.

Rodgers, J. L., & Rowe, D. C. (1993). Social contagion and adolescent sexual behavior: A developmental and EMOSA model. *Psychological Review, 100*(3), 479–510.

Rossi, A. S. (1994). Eros and caritas: A biopsychosocial approach to human sexuality and reproduction. In A. S. Rossi (Ed.), *Sexuality across the life course* (pp. 3–36). Chicago: University of Chicago Press.

Rutter, M. (1989). Pathways from childhood to adult life. *Journal of Child Psychology and Psychiatry and Applied Disciplines, 30*, 23–51.

Rutter, M. (1994). Continuities, transitions and turning points in development. In M. Rutter & D. F. Hay (Eds.), *Development through life: A handbook for clinicians* (pp. 1–25). London: Blackwell Scientific.

Santelli, J. S., & Beilenson, P. (1992). Risk factors for adolescent sexual behavior, fertility, and sexually transmitted diseases. *Journal of School Health, 62*(7), 271–279.

Savin-Williams, R. C. (1995). An exploratory study of pubertal maturation timing and self-esteem among gay and bisexual male youths. *Developmental Psychology, 31*(1), 56–64.

Schulenberg, J., Maggs, J. L., & Hurrelmann, K. (Eds.). (1997). *Health risks and developmental transitions during adolescence.* Cambridge, MA: Harvard University Press.

Simmons, R. G., & Blyth, D. A. (1987). *Moving into adolescence: The impact of pubertal change and school context.* New York: Aldine.

Smetana, J. G. (1988). Concepts and social convention: Adolescents' and parents' reasoning about hypothetical and actual family conflicts. In M. R. Gunnar & W. A. Collins (Eds.), *21st Minnesota symposium on child psychology: Development during the transition to adolescence* (pp. 79–122). Hillsdale, NJ: Erlbaum.

Smetana, J. G. (1989). Adolescents' and parents' reasoning about actual family conflict. *Child Development, 60*, 1052–1067.

Smith, E. A., & Udry, J. R. (1985). Coital and non-coital sexual behaviors of white and black adolescents. *American Journal of Public Health, 75*, 1200–1203.

Smith, T. W. (1994). Attitudes toward sexual permissiveness: Trends, correlates, and behavioral connections. In A. S. Rossi (Ed.), *Sexuality across the life course* (pp. 63–97). Chicago: University of Chicago Press.

Spanier, G. B. (1977). Sources of sex information and premarital sexual behavior. *Journal of Sex Research, 13*(2), 73–88.

Spreadbury, C. L. (1982). First date. *Journal of Early Adolescence, 2*(1), 83–89.

Staltin, H., & Magnusson, D. (1990). *Paths through life: Vol. 2. Pubertal maturation in female development.* Hillsdale, NJ: Erlbaum.

Sullivan, H. S. (1953). *The interpersonal theory of psychiatry.* New York: Norton.

Trickett, P. K., & Putnam, F. W. (1993). Impact of child sexual abuse on females: Toward a developmental, psychobiological integration. *Psychological Science, 4*(2), 81–87.

Tschann, J. M., & Adler, N. E. (1997). Sexual self-acceptance, communication with partner, and contraceptive use among adolescent females: A longitudinal study. *Journal of Research on Adolescence, 7*(4), 413–430.

Turner, R., & Feldman, S. S. (1994). *The functions of sex in everyday life.* Unpublished manuscript.

Udry, J. R. (1988). Biological predispositions and social control in adolescent sexual behavior. *American Sociological Review, 53,* 709–722.

Udry, J. R., & Billy, J. O. G. (1987). Initiation of coitus in early adolescence. *American Sociological Review, 58,* 210–232.

Udry, J. R., Billy, J. O., Morris, N. M., Groff, T. R., & Raj, M. S. (1985). Serum androgenic hormones motivate sexual behavior in adolescent boys. *Fertility and Sterility, 43*(1), 90–94.

Udry, J. R., & Campbell, B. C. (1994). Getting started on sexual behavior. In A. S. Rossi (Ed.), *Sexuality across the life course* (pp. 187–207). Chicago: University of Chicago Press.

Udry, J. R., Talbert, L., & Morris, N. M. (1986). Biosocial foundations for adolescent female sexuality. *Demography, 23*(2), 217–227.

U.S. Bureau of the Census. (1991). Marital status and living arrangements: March, 1990. *Current Population Reports,* Series P-20, No. 450. Washington, DC: U.S. Government Printing Office.

Vera, E. M., Reese, L. E., Paikoff, R. L., & Jarrett, R. L. (1996). Contextual factors of sexual risk-taking in urban African American preadolescent children. In B. J. R. Leadbeater & N. Way (Eds.), *Urban girls: Resisting stereotypes, creating identities* (pp. 291–304). New York: New York University Press.

Wakschlag, L. S., Chase-Landsdale, P. L., & Brooks-Gunn, J. (1997). Not just "Ghosts in the Nursery": Contemporaneous intergenerational relationships and parenting in young African American families. *Child Development, 67*(5), 2131–2147.

Ward, M. J., & Carlson, E. A. (1995). Associations among adult attachment representations, maternal sensitivity, and infant–mother attachment in a sample of adolescent mothers. *Child Development, 66*(1), 69–79.

Weddle, K. D., McKenry, P. C., & Leigh, G. K. (1988). Adolescent sexual behavior: Trends and issues in research. *Journal of Adolescent Research,* *3*(3–4), 245–257.

Westney, O. E., Jenkins, R. R., & Benjamin, C. A. (1983). Sociosexual development of preadolescents. In J. Brooks-Gunn & A. C. Petersen (Eds.), *Girls at puberty: Biological and psychosocial perspectives* (pp. 273–300). New York: Plenum Press.

Wilcox, S., & Udry, J. R. (1986). Autism and accuracy in adolescent perceptions of friends' sexual attitudes and behavior. *Journal of Applied School Psychology, 16,* 361–374.

Wilson, W. J. (1991). Studying inner-city social dislocations: The challenge of public agenda research. *American Sociological Review, 56*(1), 1–14.

Zabin, L. S., & Hayward, S.C. (1993). *Adolescent sexual behavior and childbearing.* Newbury Park, CA: Sage.

Zelnik, M., & Kanter, J. F. (1980). Sexual and contraceptive experience of young unmarried women in the United States, 1976 and 1971. In C. S. Chilman (Ed.), *Adolescent pregnancy and childbearing: Findings from research* (pp. 43–81). Washington, DC: National Institutes of Health.

Zelnik, M., Kanter, J. F., & Ford, K. (1981). *Sex and pregnancy in adolescence.* Beverly Hills, CA: Sage.

Part IV

A focus on psychopathology

10

New perspectives on depression during adolescence

Bruce E. Compas, Jennifer K. Connor, and Beth R. Hinden

Perhaps more than any for other form of psychopathology, the past several decades have witnessed enormous changes in the recognition of depression as a problem of adolescence. Perspectives have changed from an initial view that depression could not occur in children and adolescents to the acknowledgment of depression as a major mental health concern among young people. We are now witnessing a third phase in the changing perspectives on depression in adolescence. The new perspectives that are emerging are important not only for understanding this disorder but, more broadly, for understanding other forms of psychopathology during adolescence.

The earliest perspective on depression during adolescence was that depression could not occur during this period of development or, if it did occur, it would be masked by other problems or disorders (Poznanski & Mokros, 1994). This belief was based on the theoretical position, derived from psychoanalytic theory, that depression was impossible in children or adolescents because of inadequate development of the superego. If depression could occur, it was assumed that it would be overshadowed by other characteristics or problem behaviors. For example, depression was often assumed to be masked by disruptive behavior disorders. Both of these issues have now been thoroughly dispelled by research verifying that children and adolescents do indeed experience and present clinically with depression (Carlson & Cantwell, 1980; Hammen & Compas, 1994).

During the 1970s and 1980s, these early views gave way to the recognition that young people do indeed suffer from symptoms of depression in a manner similar to that of adults. This perspective shift led to a flood of research on the nature, course, and consequences of depression in adolescence. Research has demonstrated that children and adolescents experience a constellation of affective, cognitive, and behavioral symptoms that reflect Major Depressive Disorder (MDD), as defined by the *Diagnostic and Statistical Manual* (DSM-IV) of the American Psychiatric Association (APA, 1994). Research during this second phase has also suggested that both symptoms of depression and rates of MDD increase from childhood to adolescence, and that rates of depression among girls exceed those among boys during adolescence (Leadbeater, Blatt, & Quinlan, 1995; Nolen-Hoeksema & Girgus, 1994). Therefore, adolescence has come to be seen as the pivotal developmental period during which overall rates and gender differences in depression begin to emerge and become stable into adulthood.

We are now in the midst of a third, and equally important, change in perspectives on depression during adolescence. This transition involves several elements. First, significant changes are occurring in the conceptualization of depression. Both categorical and dimensional approaches are now applied to depression during adolescence, and the interplay between these two taxonomic models has been examined. Second, perspectives on the developmental course of depression during adolescence are changing to recognize that increases in depression from childhood to adolescence and the differences between males and females in rates of depression may be less pronounced in the general population than was previously assumed and may be limited to subgroups of high-risk adolescents. Third, it is now widely recognized that depression during adolescence has a pervasive tendency to co-occur with other disorders, including internalizing problems (e.g., anxiety) and externalizing (e.g., aggression) problems. However, the consequences of co-occurring problems or comorbid disorders are just now beginning to be understood. Depression may place adolescents at risk for a number of other problems, including impairment in social and academic functioning, suicide, and recurrent episodes of depression in adulthood. The degree of risk may depend, however, on the number and types of problems that co-occur with depression. These emerging perspectives on depression during adolescence will be considered in light of recent research findings, and directions for future research will be outlined.

Nature of depression in young people

Conceptualizations of depression

Defining and understanding depression during adolescence is depend ent on the paradigms one uses for the *assessment* and *taxonomy* of psychopathology. Broadly defined, assessment is concerned with the identification of distinguishing features of individual cases, whereas taxonomy is concerned with the grouping of cases according to their distinguishing features (Achenbach, 1985, 1993). Assessment and taxonomy are linked to one another in that the grouping of cases in a taxonomic system should be based on clearly defined criteria and procedures for identifying the central features that distinguish between cases. Similarly, assessment procedures should reflect certain basic assumptions of the underlying system for classifying the phenomena of interest.

One of the major challenges facing researchers and clinicians concerned with depression during childhood and adolescence involves operationally defining and measuring this construct. Researchers and clinicians have drawn on different definitions of depression and different taxonomic systems, including a focus on (1) depressed mood, (2) empirically derived syndromes that include depressive symptoms, and (3) symptoms that meet diagnostic criteria for a categorical disorder (Angold, 1988; Cantwell & Baker, 1991; Compas, Ey, & Grant, 1993; Kovacs, 1989). These three approaches to depressive phenomena during childhood and adolescence have all been included under the general label of *depression,* leading to confusion and miscommunication. The accompanying debate about the most appropriate way to conceptualize depression (and other forms of psychopathology) has often been reflected in polarized views on the nature of this problem (e.g., Coyne & Downey, 1991). Unfortunately, this polarization of views has diverted attention from a richer understanding of the relationship between depressive symptoms on a continuum and a categorical diagnosis of depression (e.g., Jensen et al., 1996). In addition to confusion regarding taxonomic issues, the assessment of depression during adolescence has been fraught with problems. A wide variety of assessment and diagnostic tools has been used in the measurement of adolescent depression.

These measures have varied in the breadth versus specificity of the symptoms that are assessed, in their source of information (children/ adolescents, parents, teachers, clinicians), and in their psychometric quality.

Heterogeneity in the conceptualization and measurement of depression during childhood and adolescence has resulted in a fragmentation of research efforts and has impeded determination of the prevalence of depressive phenomena, understanding of the developmental course of depression, and identification of etiological factors. Therefore, clarifying the relations among the three taxonomic approaches is the first step toward understanding the nature of depression in childhood and adolescence.

The study of *depressed mood* during childhood and adolescence has emerged from developmental research in which depressive emotions are studied along with other features of biological, cognitive, and social development (e.g., Kandel & Davies, 1982; Petersen, Sarigiani, & Kennedy, 1991). The depressed mood approach is concerned with depression as a symptom or an emotional state and refers to the presence of sadness, unhappiness, or blue feelings for an unspecified period of time. No assumptions are made regarding the presence or absence of other symptoms (e.g., poor appetite, insomnia).

The second approach, the study of a *depressive syndrome*, is concerned with depression as a constellation of behaviors and emotions identified empirically through the reports of children/adolescents and other informants (e.g., parents, teachers). This strategy involves the use of multivariate statistical methods in the assessment and taxonomy of child and adolescent psychopathology, represented by the empirically based taxonomy of Achenbach (1985, 1993). Within this approach, depression refers to a set of emotions and behaviors that have been found statistically to occur together in an identifiable pattern at a rate that exceeds chance, without implying any particular model for the nature of causes of these associated symptoms. Differences between individuals are viewed in terms of quantitative deviations in levels of symptoms. An empirically derived syndrome of depressive symptoms is best represented in the research of Achenbach and colleagues (e.g., Achenbach, 1993). Most pertinent here is the syndrome labeled Anxious Depressed, composed of symptoms reflecting a mixture of anxiety and depression (see Table 10.1). The syndrome has been replicated in large samples in

Table 10.1. *Symptoms of the anxious/depressed syndrome based on parent (CBCL) and adolescent (YSR) reports*

Parent report	Adolescent report
Complains of loneliness	I feel lonely
Cries a lot	I cry a lot
Fears the possibility of doing something bad	I am afraid I might think or do something bad
Feels the need to be perfect	
Feels or complains that no one loves him or her	I feel that no one loves me
Feels others are out to get him or her	I feel that others are out to get me
Feels worthless or inferior	I feel worthless or inferior
Nervous, highstrung, or tense	I am nervous or tense
Too fearful or anxious	I am too fearful or anxious
Feels too guilty	I feel too guilty
Self-conscious or easily embarrassed	I am self-conscious or easily embarrassed
Suspicious	I am suspicious
Unhappy, sad, or depressed	I am unhappy, sad, or depressed
Worrying	I worry a lot
	I deliberately try to hurt or kill myself
	I think about killing myself

both the United States and the Netherlands (Achenbach, Verhulst, Baron, & Akkerhuis, 1987). A more "pure" depressive syndrome did not emerge in the reports of parents, teachers, and adolescents, despite the availability of items reflecting all but one of the symptoms (anhedonia) of major depression.

The *categorical/diagnostic* approach is based on assumptions of a disease or disorder model of psychopathology, as reflected in the categorical diagnostic system of the DSM-IV (American Psychiatric Association, 1994) and the International Classification of Diseases and Health Related Problems (ICD-10) of the World Health Organization (1990). This approach views depression as a psychiatric disorder that includes the presence of an identifiable set of symptoms associated with significant levels of current distress or disability and with increased risk for impairment in the individual's current functioning (American Psychiatric Association, 1994). Depressive disorders are classified under the broad category of Mood Disorders. Within the Mood Disorders, depression is divided into two categories: Bipolar Disorders and Depressive Disorders. In distinguishing between them, Bipolar Disorders are defined by the presence of manic or hypomanic symptoms that may alternate with depression. As this chapter is concerned with Depressive Disorders without manic or hypomanic episodes, the reader is referred to the DSM-IV for more information regarding Bipolar Disorders (see also Carlson, 1994). Differences between individuals are considered in terms of quantitative and qualitative differences in the pattern, severity, and duration of symptoms. With only a few exceptions, child/adolescent depression is diagnosed according to the same DSM-IV criteria as adult depression.

To meet the criteria for MDD, the child or adolescent must have experienced *five or more* of the specified symptoms for *at least 2 weeks* at a level that differs from prior functioning, and at least one of the symptoms includes either (1) depressed or irritable mood or (2) anhedonia (see Table 10.2). Irritable mood may be observed in lieu of depressed mood in children/adolescents and is believed to be more common in this age group than in adults. A range of mild, moderate, and severe diagnoses with or without psychotic features is applied. The criteria for diagnosis of Dysthymic Disorder (DY) in childhood and adolescence are that for at least 1 year (compared to 2 years for adults), an individual must display a depressed or irritable mood for more days than not, without being symptom free for more than 2 months, along with additional symptoms specified in Table 10.2.

Integration of depressed mood, syndromes, and disorders

These three approaches appear to be at odds with one another, as depression is conceptualized and measured in different ways for each approach, with checklist measures used to assess depressed mood and depressive syndromes and diagnostic interviews to assess depression as a disorder. One perspective on this problem is represented by Coyne and colleagues, who argue that self-report measures of depressive symptoms reflect generalized psychological distress and not clinical depression (e.g., Coyne & Downey, 1991; Fechner-Bates, Coyne, & Schwenk, 1994). Self-report measures with adults have only moderate to poor correspondence with diagnostic interviews for depression, as

Table 10.2. *DSM-IV Criteria for major depressive episode and dysthymic disorder*

Major Depressive Episode

A. Five (or more) of the following symptoms during the same 2-week period; at least one of the symptoms is depressed mood or loss of interest or pleasure.
   (1) depressed mood most of the day, nearly every day as indicated by subjective report or observation by others. Note: In children and adolescents, can be irritable mood.
   (2) markedly diminished interest or pleasure in all or almost all activities most of the day, nearly every day as indicated by subjective account or observation by others.
   (3) significant weight loss when not dieting or weight gain (e.g., a change of more than 5% body weight in a month), or decrease or increase in appetite nearly every day. Note: In children consider failure to make expected weight gains.
   (4) insomnia or hypersomnia nearly every day.
   (5) psychomotor agitation or retardation nearly everyday (observable by others)
   (6) fatigue or loss of energy nearly every day.
   (7) feelings of worthlessness or excessive or inappropriate guilt nearly every day.
   (8) diminished ability to think or concentrate, or indecisiveness, nearly every day (either subjective or observed by others).
   (9) recurrent thoughts of death (not just fear of dying), recurrent suicidal ideation without a specific plan, or a suicide attempt or a specific plan for committing suicide.

Major Depressive Episode (unipolar) can be further specified as mild, moderate, severe (based on functional impairment and severity of symptoms), with or without psychotic features, with or without melancholic features, whether or not recurrent, or chronic.

Dysthymic Disorder

A. Depressed mood for most of the day, for more days than not, as indicated either by subjective account or observation by others, for at least 2 years. Note: In children and adolescents, mood can be irritable and duration must be at least 1 year.
B. Presence, while depressed, of two or more of the following:
   (1) poor appetite or overeating
   (2) insomnia or hypersomnia
   (3) low energy or fatigue
   (4) low self-esteem
   (5) poor concentration or difficulty making decisions
C. During period of depression, the person has never been without symptoms A or B for more than 2 months at a time. Also, the disturbance must not be accounted for by chronic Major Depressive Disorder (or Major Depressive Disorder in partial remission)—i.e., no Major Depressive Disorder in the first 2 years of the disturbance (1 year for children and adolescents).

reflected in moderate specificity (true positives) but low sensitivity (true negatives). For example, in a study of primary medical care patients who completed the Center for Epidemiologic Studies of Depression Scale (CES-D) and a structured interview to assess DSM-III-R symptoms of MDD, most subjects who scored high on the CES-D did not meet diagnostic criteria for MDD, a fifth of the patients with MDD had low scores on the CES-D, and the CES-D performed as well in detecting anxiety as in detecting depression (Fechner-Bates et al., 1994). Furthermore, the psychosocial factors that correlate with self-report measures in adults differ from the correlates of major depression (Coyne & Downey, 1991). Whether these same patterns are evident with children and adolescents is a central issue in understanding the nature of depression in young people.

Empirical studies of self-report questionnaires, behavior checklists, and diagnostic interviews. Correspondence among the three approaches to measuring child/adolescent depression has been examined by using diagnostic interviews to assign DSM-III-R or DSM-IV diagnoses of MDD and by obtaining questionnaire or behavior checklist data on the same sample of individuals. This method has been applied in several studies using self-report inventories of depressive symptoms and diagnostic interviews (Garrison, Addy, Jackson, McKeown, & Waller, 1991; Gotlib, Lewinsohn, & Seeley, 1995; Kazdin, Esveldt-Dawson, Unis, & Rancurello, 1983; Roberts, Lewinsohn, & Seeley, 1991) and studies in which behavior checklists and diagnostic interviews or other measures of DSM criteria were examined (Edelbrock & Costello, 1988; Gerhardt, Compas, Connor, & Achenbach, 1996; Rey & Morris-Yates, 1991, 1992; Weinstein, Noam, Grimes, Stone, & Schwab-Stone, 1990). Each study provides some evidence for the convergence of these different approaches.

In a study of inpatient children, Kazdin et al. (1983) examined the correspondence of child and parent reports on the Children's Depression Inventory (CDI) with interviews to assess depression. Within-informant responses on the CDI and the interview were moderately correlated ($r = .62$ for children, .71 for mothers, and .54 for fathers). Correspondence of the CDI and interview across informants was low, however, with mother–child and father–child correlations ($r = .16$ and .33, respectively) being lower than mother–father correspondence

(r = .65). Both Roberts et al. (1991) and Garrison et al. (1991) examined the relation between self-report inventories of depressive symptoms and diagnoses of depressive disorders based on clinical interviews in large community samples of children and adolescents. Garrison et al. examined the CES-D and the Schedule for Schizophrenia and Affective Disorders, Child Version (K-SADS); Roberts et al. examined both the CES-D and the Beck Depression Inventory (BDI), along with the K-SADS. Both studies found that these scales served as useful screening instruments for diagnoses of MDD and DD, but that both the BDI and the CES-D produced substantial rates of false positives. That is, most adolescents who received a diagnosis of MDD or DY also reported elevated scores on the CES-D or BDI, but large numbers of individuals with elevated scores on the symptom measures were not judged to be clinically depressed on the basis of interview data.

A recent study by Gotlib et al. (1995) provides the most comprehensive information on the association of self-report questionnaires and diagnostic interviews. In addition to examining the sensitivity and specificity of the CES-D and the K-SADS in a large community sample of adolescents, they carefully examined the characteristics of the false positives within the sample (i.e., those with high CES-D scores who did not meet diagnostic criteria for MDD). Adolescents classified as false positive manifested higher levels of current and future psychopathology than did true negatives (those who scored low on the CES-D and did not meet criteria for MDD), and false positives were at least twice as likely as true negatives to develop a psychiatric disorder over the course of the study. Furthermore, false-positive participants did not differ significantly from true-positive participants on a wide range of measures of psychosocial dysfunction. The authors concluded that scoring high on a self-report measure of depressive symptoms without meeting diagnostic criteria for MDD is far from benign; false-positive individuals experience significant distress and impairment in psychosocial functioning (Gotlib et al., 1995).

Two studies including diagnostic interviews with parents and parent reports on the Child Behavior Checklist (CBCL; Achenbach, 1991) have found considerable correspondence between the two approaches. Edelbrock and Costello (1988), in a study of clinically referred children and adolescents (ages 6–16 years), found that scores on the Depressed Withdrawal scale of the CBCL (derived from the initial version of the

CBCL profile) for girls aged 12–16 correlated significantly with diagnoses of MDD and DY, and that scores on the Uncommunicative scale of the CBCL for boys aged 6–16 correlated with diagnoses of Overanxious Disorder, MDD, and DY. The broad-band Internalizing and Externalizing scales of the CBCL were also correlated with diagnoses of MDD (.31, $p < .001$, and .14, $p < .01$, respectively) and DY (.43, $p < .001$, and .22, $p < .001$, respectively). They also found that scores on a CBCL Depression scale for children aged 6–11 were linearly related to the probability of receiving a diagnosis of either MDD or DY. This finding suggests that there was no specific threshold score of symptoms on the Depression scale above which children received a depressive diagnosis and below which they did not.

In a study of 667 clinically referred Australian adolescents, Rey and Morris-Yates (1991) generated DSM-III diagnoses on the basis of clinical interviews and calculated scores on a Depression scale of the CBCL identified by Nurcombe et al. (1989). To examine the correspondence between diagnoses and CBCL scale scores, these authors used receiver operating characteristic (ROC) techniques to determine the cutpoint on the CBCL scale that would produce the greatest sensitivity and specificity in predicting DSM-III diagnoses. Individuals with a diagnosis of MDD ($n = 23$) were compared to individuals with a diagnosis of DY ($n = 62$), individuals with a diagnosis of Separation Anxiety ($n = 57$), and individuals with all other diagnoses ($n = 634$). Cases with a diagnosis of MDD scored significantly higher on the CBCL Depression scales than any of the other diagnostic groups. Furthermore, ROC analyses indicated that the CBCL scale functioned at a level better than chance in discriminating the MDD group from each of the other three diagnostic groups. Rates of sensitivity (83%) and specificity (55%) were better in distinguishing MDD from all other diagnoses than in distinguishing MDD from DY or Separation Anxiety Disorder. Additional analyses of this sample compared the sensitivity and specificity of six depression scales extracted from the CBCL and the YSR (Rey & Morris-Yates, 1992). All of the scales performed at a level better than chance in ROC analyses discriminating adolescents with MDD diagnoses from those without them.

Using adolescents' self-reports on the Youth Self-Report (YSR) and the Diagnostic Interview schedule for Children – Current (DISC-C), Weinstein et al. (1990) also found evidence of a significant positive association between DSM-III diagnoses of affective disorders and scores on the YSR Depressed scale. However, adolescents who were diagnosed with MDD and/or DY scored higher than those without an affective disorder diagnosis on all narrow-band scales on the YSR (Depressed, Unpopular, Somatic Complaints, Aggressive, Delinquent, Thought Disorder) and on the broader scales of Internalizing and Externalizing problems.

Finally, Gerhardt et al. (1996) examined the correspondence between the Anxious/Depressed syndrome and an analogue measure of MDD in parent and adolescent reports on the CBCL and YSR. Adolescents' self-reports on the YSR and parents' reports on the CBCL showed similar patterns. Of those who met the criteria for the analogue of MDD, 78–94% were also in the clinical range on the Anxious/Depressed syndrome; of those who were in the clinical range on the Anxious/Depressed syndrome, 11–14% met the criteria for the analogue of MDD. Relative risk odds ratios indicated that youth who met criteria for the Anxious/Depressed syndrome at one assessment were 31.2 times more likely, based on parents' reports, and 11.6 times more likely, based on adolescents' self-reports, to meet criteria on the analogue of MDD 3 years later (Gerhardt et al., 1996). Thus, the Anxious/Depressed syndrome identified a larger group of children and youth, a subset of whom also met criteria for clinical depression. Similar to the findings of Gotlib et al. (1995), adolescents who were above the clinical cutoff on the Anxious/Depressed syndrome but who did not meet criteria for the analogue of MDD had lower social competence and higher problem scores on other syndrome scales than adolescents who were not classified as depressed on either measure.

Toward an integrative framework on depression during adolescence

These studies indicate that diagnoses of MDD and DY derived from clinical interviews are related, albeit imperfectly, to both scores on self-report inventories of depressive symptoms (including depressed mood) and depressive syndrome scores from multivariate checklists. Compas et al. (1993) have proposed a hierarchical and sequential model to describe the association among depressed mood (as measured by self-report questionnaires), depressive syndromes (as measured by behavior checklists), and depressive disorders (as measured by diagnostic interviews). Each of these three levels of depressive phenomena is hypothesized to reflect a more severe manifestation of depressive problems, with depressed mood functioning as a risk factor for the development of the syndrome and the syndrome functioning as a risk factor for the disorder. The data presented earlier are generally consistent with this model, although the overlap of the three levels of depressive problems is imperfect. Moreover, it is important to recognize that children/adolescents who obtain high depressive symptom scores on self-report questionnaires, who score in the clinical range on the Anxious/Depressed syndrome, or who meet DSM-IV criteria for MDD or DY all experience significant clinical problems. That is, all of these groups experience significant levels of emotional distress and substantial levels of impairment in social functioning (Gerhardt et al., 1996; Gotlib et al., 1995).

Several explanations for the relationship between the empirically derived Anxious/Depressed syndrome and a categorical diagnosis of MDD are plausible. First, anxiety and depression may be less well differentiated in children and adolescents than in adults. Categorical diagnoses, such as Attention Deficit Hyperactivity Disorder (ADHD), that have been derived specifically for children and adolescents show close correspondence with empirically derived syndromes. The empirically derived syndrome Attention Problems, which reflects symptoms of ADHD, has shown excellent sensitivity and specificity with regard to a diagnosis of ADHD (Chen, Faraone, Biederman, & Tsuang, 1994). In contrast, MDD is based on criteria derived for adults and may be less representative of disorders in adolescents. Second, the measures used to derive the empirically based syndromes may be less sensitive to important variations in the onset, duration, and severity of symptoms. Third, base rates of MDD may be so low that they are difficult to detect using multivariate statistical methods even in relatively large samples of clinic-referred youth. Fourth, there may be subtypes of MDD among adolescents, with one subtype developing out of a syndrome of mixed anxiety and depression symptoms and a second that follows a different etiological course that is qualitatively distinct from the first subtype. Future research is needed to continue to explore the nature and implications of the association between the Anxious/Depressed syndrome and diagnoses of MDD or DY.

Reconsidering age and gender in depression in adolescence

Depressed mood, the Anxious/Depressed syndrome, and MDD are best considered in light of normative developmental data on the base rates of these problems during adolescence. Early to middle adolescence is widely believed to be the developmental period when significant increases occur in depression and when girls begin to experience significantly more depression than boys (e.g., Angold & Rutter, 1992; Nolen-Hoeksema & Girgus, 1994; Petersen et al., 1991). Two reviews of the research on adolescent depression reveal that despite the increasing theoretical and empirical work devoted to explaining age and gender differences in depression during adolescence, these differences may not be as robust as is widely assumed (Leadbeater et al., 1995; Petersen et al., 1993). Specifically, many studies of depression during adolescence have not examined age and gender differences, and among the studies that have examined such differences, the findings have been inconsistent with respect to the main effects of age and gender and, most important, their interaction. For example, Petersen et al. (1992) reviewed 30 studies of "depressed affect" published between 1975 and 1991. Of the eight studies that tested age effects, six reported no main effects for age. Of the 13 studies that tested gender effects, 11 reported higher rates for girls and 2 found no gender differences. In a more recent review, Leadbeater et al. (1995) reported that 14 out of 21 studies found more depressive symptoms among girls than boys, 6 studies found no gender differences, and 1 study found higher rates for working-class boys than girls. Neither Petersen et al. (1992) nor Leadbeater et al. (1995) reported findings with respect to age by gender interactions.

Evidence of a significant interaction of age and gender among a sample of children and adolescents would demonstrate that gender differences in depressive symptoms *emerge* during adolescence. That is, an age by gender interaction would reflect an increase in depressive symptoms among girls *relative to* boys as both grow older. Statistical interactions, however, are often unreliable and difficult to detect (McClelland & Judd, 1993). Thus, if gender differences in depressive symptoms emerge gradually over the course of the adolescent decade as opposed to emerging at a particular point in time, the interaction of age and gender may be difficult to document and may result in inconsistent findings. These discrepancies may be resolved by careful consideration of four methodological issues relevant to the study of developmental processes in depressive symptoms: (1) the ways in which depression is operationally defined, (2) sampling characteristics, (3) informant effects, and (4) research design.

Conceptualization of depression

It is possible that age and gender differences unfold differently across different conceptualizations of depression and that inconsistencies in the literature reflect inadequate attention to these distinctions. Research on adolescent depression has relied heavily on measures of depressed mood or affect. For example, a recent study of depressed mood among a community sample of children and adolescents revealed a significant age by gender interaction when data were examined cross-sectionally, with girls showing higher levels of depressive symptoms than boys after the age of 13 (Ge, Lorenz, Conger, Elder, & Simons, 1994). Latent growth-curve analyses of longitudinal trajectories for the same sample also revealed significantly different trajectories for girls than for boys, with girls showing higher initial levels of depressed mood and greater increases over time. However, despite these significantly different trajectories, the longitudinal age by gender interaction did not attain significance. Petersen et al. (1991) examined age and gender effects on depressed mood in a longitudinal sample of children followed from the 6th to the 12th grade. Gender differences were nonsignificant at assessments during the 6th and 8th grades but were significant by the 12th grade. The interaction of age and gender was not reported, however, and it was unclear when gender differences emerged because the sample was not assessed between the 8th and 12th grades.

Studies of age and gender differences in diagnoses of MDD and DY have yielded similarly mixed results. Point prevalence estimates have been provided by Lewinsohn and colleagues from a large community sample of adolescents (Lewinsohn, Rohde, Seeley, & Hops, 1991; Rohde, Lewinsohn, & Seeley, 1991). Based on diagnostic interviews with the K–SADS, 2.9% of a sample of 1,710 adolescents received a current diagnosis of either MDD, DY, or comorbid MDD and DY;

the lifetime prevalence of depressive disorders was 20% (Lewinsohn et al., 1991). In further analyses with this sample, Lewinsohn, Hops, Roberts, Seeley, and Andrews (1993) found significant gender differences in point prevalence at the initial data collection, with girls qualifying for diagnosis more often than boys. However, at follow-up 1 year later, gender differences were nonsignificant. Gender differences for lifetime prevalence rates were significant, with girls showing higher rates than boys. Age effects and the interaction of age and gender were nonsignificant, although older adolescents were more likely to be diagnosed with DY. Consecutive reports from analyses of the Dunedin, New Zealand, longitudinal sample also showed an emergence of gender differences during adolescence. Girls were four times *less* likely than boys to be diagnosed with MDD at age 13 (Kashani et al., 1987); however, when examined 2 years later at age 15, girls were 1.8 times *more* likely to receive this diagnosis than boys (McGee et al., 1990). Similarly, using retrospective reports of 18-year-old high school students, Giaconia et al. (1993) found that a diagnosis of MDD was most likely to occur between the ages of 14 and 17, and that girls were at much greater risk for diagnosis during this high-risk period than were boys.

In a study comparing depressed mood, syndrome, and disorder in the same sample, Angold and Rutter (1992) examined retrospective chart data on hospitalized 8- to 16-year-olds. Results indicated that age and gender effects were significant for all three conceptualizations of depression. The age by gender interaction, however, was significant for depressed mood only, with girls being 1.12 times more likely to experience depressed mood than boys for each additional year of age. It is noteworthy that the syndrome and diagnostic groups contained small numbers of subjects, and the lack of age by gender interactions in these groups may have reflected insufficient power to detect these effects (Angold & Rutter, 1992).

Sampling effects

Research on adolescent depression has featured both clinical samples of adolescents referred for treatment for psychological problems and community samples of adolescents residing in the community who may or may not exhibit emotional or behavioral problems and may or may not have been referred for treatment. Whether clinical samples represent a qualitatively distinct group of adolescents or simply the upper end of a quantitative continuum is subject to debate

It is important to document the extensiveness of gender differences in depressive problems in community samples to determine their role in overall models of adolescent development. First, if boys and girls in the general population differ in symptoms of depression, then this difference may represent a pervasive feature of normative adolescent development. Data are needed from nationally representative community samples to determine if the emergence of gender differences during adolescence is a pervasive developmental trend. Alternatively, if gender differences in these symptoms are limited to clinically referred youth, they may reflect processes that characterize only a subgroup of high-risk adolescents, suggesting that adolescence is not intrinsically associated with differences in depressive symptoms. Second, research to determine the processes that contribute to gender differences in depressive symptoms (Nolen-Hoeksema & Girgus, 1994) will be advanced by data on the pervasiveness and magnitude of such differences. If gender differences in the general population are small, process-oriented research will need to focus on samples of high-risk or clinically referred adolescents to achieve sufficient statistical power. Third, patterns of gender differences in community versus clinical samples have important implications for prevention and treatment of depressive problems. Prevention and treatment programs may need to be tailored differently for boys and girls, depending on the nature and scope of gender differences in the general population as opposed to selected high-risk subgroups.

Prior studies of age and gender differences in depressive symptoms have typically relied on moderately sized community samples that often reflect a particular geographic or socioeconomic population (e.g., Ge et al., 1994; Giaconia et al., 1993), a limited age range (Leadbeater et al., 1995), or clinical samples (e.g., Angold & Rutter, 1992). However, large samples may be particularly important to the detection of interaction effects that mark this emergence of gender differences during adolescence, as large samples are more sensitive to small effects and are therefore more likely to reveal interactions. Prior studies have failed to address issues of statistical power or effect sizes of ages, gender, and their interaction. Large samples that traverse the entire adolescent decade allow the examination of age and gender differences both across the adolescent decade and separately by age cohort. The division of adolescent samples into age cohorts may be particularly important in detecting interaction effects that are associated specifically with a particular period of adolescence and that are obscured by examinations of a sample as a whole.

Research on gender differences in psychological characteristics has highlighted the need to attend not only to the statistical significance of female–male differences but also to the size of these effects (e.g., Eagly, 1995). Most gender differences that have been found in psychological research are small to moderate in magnitude, and are greater for characteristics that involve social interactions than for purely individual traits or qualities (Eagly, 1995; Maccoby, 1990). Although several studies have reported statistically significant differences in depressive symptoms between adolescent males and females, most have not considered the magnitude of these effects (see Leadbeater et al., 1995, and Petersen et al., 1992, for reviews). An examination of the few studies that have provided sufficient information to determine effect sizes suggests that adolescent males and females differ in symptoms of depression, as well as in the prevalence of depressive disorders, but these gender effects are typically small in magnitude (e.g., Clarke, Lewinsohn, Hops, & Seely, 1992; Hinden et al., 1997; Petersen et al., 1991).

Informant differences

The measurement of child and adolescent psychopathology is characterized by differences across informants such as parents, teachers, and youth (Achenbach, McConaughy, & Howell, 1987). This effect has been found for depressive symptoms as well, where self-reports generally yield higher rates of symptoms than reports by parents or teachers (Kazdin, 1994). Different informants may perceive and report depressive symptoms differently, offering discrepant pictures of developmental trajectories. Age and gender differences in depressive symptoms as a function of informant have not yet been examined, however, as research on adolescent depression has relied primarily on self-report assessments. It is generally assumed that parents are less sensitive informants of internalizing problems than adolescents themselves and, as a consequence, may be less sensitive to gender differences in these symptoms in their children. Thus, gender differences would be expected to be smaller in parents' reports than in adolescents' self-reports. Alternatively, gender stereotypes may be stronger in parents' perceptions of adolescents' symptoms of depression, leading to more pronounced gender differences in parents' reports than in adolescents' self-reports. Regardless of the direction of such differences, it is important to compare parents' and adolescents' reports directly within clinically referred and nonreferred samples because parents are an important source of referral for mental health services for their children.

Cross-sectional versus longitudinal research design

Research design is another central methodological issue in the examination of age and gender differences in depression. Cross-sectional samples of children and adolescents of different ages can be used to test age *differences* in levels of depressive symptoms across different children at one point in time. By contrast, longitudinal designs can be used to test age *changes* in depression for the same individuals over time. Although cross-sectional designs can generate hypotheses regarding potential developmental and etiological processes in the epidemiology of depression, longitudinal designs are necessary to test these hypotheses (Ge et al., 1994; Stanger, Achenbach, & Verhulst, 1994).

Cross-sectional and longitudinal studies have yielded inconsistent findings on the effects of age, gender, and age by gender interaction effects (e.g., Ge et al., 1994; Giaconia et al., 1993; Lewinsohn et al., 1993). Most notably, in their examination of both cross-sectional and longitudinal effects within the same sample, Ge et al. (1994) demonstrated that although both designs revealed expected effects, cross-sectional age and gender differences in depressive symptoms differed from those found in longitudinal analyses with the same sample. Specifically, cross-sectional analyses showed a steady linear increase in girls' depressive symptoms after age 13 until age 16, whereas longitudinal analyses revealed a V-shaped pattern for most cohorts, reflecting an initial decrease followed by increases over time. If the emergence of gender differences in depression is truly a developmental phenomenon, it would be more likely to be observed and more accurately documented in longitudinal studies that follow the development of particular individuals, where sampling errors and cohort differences would be reduced.

Recent research on age and gender effects

Two recent studies by our research group have provided a somewhat different perspective on the nature and extent of age and gender differences in depression during adolescence. In a nationally representative sample, Hinden et al. (1996) examined parents' and adolescents' reports of depressed mood, the Anxious/Depressed syndrome, and an analogue measure of MDD in both cross-sectional and longitudinal analyses. In contrast with most prior studies, we explicitly examined the interaction of age and gender to determine if the gender difference in depressive symptoms emerged during adolescence, compared the reports of adolescents and parents, and compared cross-sectional and longitudinal analyses. In a second study (Compas et al., 1997) we further explored these issues in nationally representative samples of clinically referred and nonreferred adolescents.

In analyses of the national community sample, significant gender differences were found, with considerable consistency in both adolescents' and parents' reports of depressed mood and the Anxious/Depressed syndrome, in both cross-sectional and longitudinal analyses. In every instance, depressive symptoms were greater for girls than for boys. In contrast, significant main effects for age were rare and were limited primarily to longitudinal analyses of parents' reports, indicating that there is no overall increase in rates of depressive symptoms over the course of adolescence. This pattern of strong evidence of gender differences but little evidence of main effects for age is consistent with several previous studies (e.g., Petersen et al., 1991).

Examination of age and gender differences in both cross-sectional and longitudinal analyses suggested that the difference between boys and girls in depressive symptoms emerged during the transition from early to middle adolescence, roughly at ages 11 to 13. Cross-sectional analyses of adolescents' reports of depressed mood in the 11- to 16-year-old cohort revealed an age by gender interaction, as did longitudinal analyses of both adolescents' and parents' reports of depressed mood and the Anxious/Depressed syndrome in the 11- to 13-year-old cohort. With the exception of parents' longitudinal reports of the Anxious/Depressed syndrome for 18- to 22-year olds, no significant age by gender interactions were found in the older cohorts, whereas gender differences were relatively consistent, suggesting that early adolescence is the period when girls' depressive symptoms increase significantly relative to those of boys, and that this difference is sustained throughout the adolescent decade. This is consistent with recent findings of Ge et al. (1994), in which gender differences in depressed mood emerged and peaked between the ages of 13 and 16 years. Moreover, although Ge et al. (1994) found this interaction in cross-sectional but not longitudinal analyses, the effect was significant in both analyses in this study.

Despite these significant age by gender interactions, perhaps the most powerful message of these findings is that in this nationally representative sample of youth, the effects of age and gender and the interaction of age and gender were very small in magnitude, typically accounting for less than 1% of the variance in depressive symptoms (Hinden et al., 1996). Thus, despite the consistency of gender differences, the magnitude of these differences was small, ranging from less than 1% to 5% of the variance in adolescents' self-reports of depressed mood and syndrome. Effects were even smaller for parents' reports, with only one effect size accounting for more than 1% of the variance. Most important to the focus of the present discussion, all age by gender interactions accounted for less than 1% of the variance. Thus, a predictable interaction of age and gender can be located in early adolescent development, and this effect is experienced by adolescents themselves and is observable to their parents, but it is a small effect. The inconsistency observed in previous studies is most likely the result of the use of small samples with insufficient power to detect these small effects.

With respect to conceptualization of depression, the current results underscore both the similarities and differences across operational definitions of depression (Hinden et al., 1996). The interaction of age and gender was observed more consistently for depressed mood than for the Anxious/Depressed syndrome; that is, three of the interaction effects were significant for mood but not for syndrome. Thus, reports of sad, unhappy, or depressed mood were somewhat more sensitive to age and age by gender effects than were reports of the syndrome of mixed symptoms of anxiety and depression. These findings are consistent with those of Angold and Rutter (1992), in which the interaction of age and gender was significant for their measure of depressed mood but not for depressive syndromes or disorder. Relatively consistent gender differences also were found on the Anxious/Depressed syndrome, and the interaction of age and gender was significant for the syndrome in longitudinal analyses of the 11- to 13-year-old cohort in both parents' and adolescents' reports.

Although the responses of both parents and youth were sensitive to expected gender differences across conceptualizations of depression, the pattern of results in this study also differed somewhat as a function of informant (Hinden et al., 1996). Evidence of gender differences was more limited in the longitudinal analyses of parents' reports, where significant gender differences were not found until middle adolescence (cohorts who were 14–17 years old at the first data collection and 17–20 years old at follow-up). Adolescents' reports were also more sensitive to the emergence of gender differences, as evidenced by significant age by gender interaction terms for depressed mood among the entire sample and for the cohort of 11- to 16-year-olds in cross-sectional analyses. However, in spite of the possibility that parents may not have ready access to adolescents' experiences of depressed mood and related symptoms, the significant age by gender interactions for early adolescent cohorts in the longitudinal analyses of both parent and adolescent reports of depressed mood and syndrome suggest that parents were sensitive to differences between boys and girls in the rates of these symptoms during this important developmental period.

Research design and sampling also proved to be important to detection of the emergence of gender differences in depressive symptoms. Cross-sectional and longitudinal analyses revealed that the emergence of gender differences was most pronounced during the transition from late childhood to middle adolescence, represented by the 11- to 16-year-old cohorts in these analyses. The emergence of gender differences in depression was more readily observed in the cohort analyses of age *changes* than in analyses of age *differences.* Specifically, although cross-sectional analyses were inconsistent for age by gender interaction effects, longitudinal analyses revealed that these effects were most readily detectable during the transition from early to middle adolescence. The use of separate analyses for age cohorts within adolescence was important in determining when the gender difference in depression emerged. These results indicate that developmental changes in depression within the same individuals over time are more reliable than differences in depression between different individuals at the same point in time.

Three general impressions can be drawn from these data (Hinden et al., 1996). First, gender differences in adolescence were ubiquitous, appearing across conceptualization of depression in the reports of parents and adolescents in both the cross-sectional and longitudinal analyses. These consistent gender differences were all small in magnitude, however, suggesting that girls express only slightly more depressive symptoms than boys throughout adolescence. Second, gender differences in depressive phenomena do increase in early adolescence. It is important to recognize again, however, that these differences are not large in magnitude. The data indicate, therefore, that normal adolescent development is not characterized by dramatic increases in depressed mood (or other depressive symptoms) for girls or boys, or for girls relative to boys. Third, parents and adolescents are in agreement in their perceptions of this process during early adolescence. Thus, as researchers pursue the task of explaining gender and developmental differences in depressive phenomena (e.g., Leadbeater et al., 1995; Nolen-Hoeksema & Girgus, 1994; Nolen-Hoeksema, Girgus, & Seligman, 1992), it will be important to acknowledge that these effects on the general population are small and that pathways of risk and resilience will be difficult to detect.

It is quite possible, however, that age and gender differences may be more pronounced among high-risk and/or clinically referred adolescents, and that future research on explanatory models may be most illuminating with these samples. We examined this possibility in a second study comparing demographically matched national samples of referred and nonreferred youth (Compas et al., 1997). Gender differences in depressed mood, the Anxious/Depressed syndrome, and symptoms of an analogue of major depression were either nonsignificant or very small in magnitude in a nationally representative sample of adolescents with no history of referral for mental health services. In contrast, gender differences were significant and produced moderate effects in a matched sample of youth who had been referred for mental health services. These data provide further evidence that adolescence is not characterized by pervasive gender differences in depressive symptoms in the general population. Rather, these differences are limited to adolescents who have been referred for mental health services, with referred girls consistently highest in depressive symptoms.

These findings suggest that most adolescent girls and boys do not differ substantially in the amount of sadness, fear, and anxiety that they experience. When the simple effects of gender were examined separately from referral status, nonreferred males and females did not differ in parents' ratings of mood, syndrome, or analogue or in adolescents' ratings of an analogue of major depression (Compas et al., 1997). The only significant gender differences in nonreferred youth occurred in adolescents' self-reports of depressed mood and the mixed Anxious/Depressed syndrome. This is consistent with the findings reported by Silverstein, Caceres, Perdue, and Cimarolli (1995) in a community sample of adolescents in which significant gender differences were found for self-reports of mixed symptoms of anxiety and depression but not for a more pure index of symptoms of major depression. This suggests that the largest gender differences occur in symptoms of affective distress (depressed and anxious mood), and smaller differences exist in other symptoms of depression (e.g., sleep and appetite disruption, concentration problems).

In contrast with the small and typically nonsignificant gender differences in nonreferred youth, there were significant and substantial differences between clinically referred males and females (Compas et al., 1997). The overall effects of referral status were large, accounting for 5–15% of the variance, with Cohen's d values (the difference between the means expressed in standard deviation units) ranging from .7 to more than 1. Both boys and girls who were referred for mental health services scored higher than nonreferred youth in adolescents' self-reports and in parents' reports. However, clinically referred girls were consistently higher than referred boys in all three forms of depressive symptoms. In self-reports of depressed mood and the Anxious/Depressed syndrome, the effects for gender in the referred sample were three to four times greater than in the nonreferred sample. The referred girls comprise a particularly high-risk subgroup of adolescents who may differ from the general population in important but still unidentified ways. These findings are consistent with evidence of a greater proportion of adolescent girls than boys meeting DSM criteria for a major depressive disorder (e.g., McGee et al., 1990), as those girls who meet diagnostic criteria may be more likely to be referred for mental health services.

Surprisingly few effects were found for age in this sample, and none accounted for as much as 1% of the variance (Compas et al., 1997). Furthermore, the lack of interactions between age and gender indicated that the differences between boys and girls were similar throughout adolescence. These findings differ from those found in general population samples of adolescents in which the gender difference in depressive symptoms appears to emerge during early adolescence (e.g., Ge et al., 1994; Hinden et al., 1996). Samples representative of the general population include adolescents who have and have not received mental health services. For example, the Hinden et al. (1996) nationally representative sample included a small percentage of youth who had received mental health services in the past 12 months. Findings of Compas et al. (1997) suggest that gender differences observed in community samples may be the result of differences in a subgroup of youth referred for mental health services. Closer examination of previous studies also suggests that the interaction of age and gender may be more readily detected in longitudinal analyses of age changes than in cross-sectional analyses of age differences (Hinden et al., 1996).

These findings suggest that studies restricted to adolescents who are not receiving mental health services or who are at low risk for depressive symptoms are unlikely to reveal the reasons for gender differences. The gender differences in nonreferred samples are likely to be too small to detect processes that distinguish between boys and girls even in very large samples. Community samples are likely to reflect processes that contribute to internalizing problems in both girls and boys rather than factors that distinguish between them. For example, in a longitudinal study of a community sample from childhood to early adolescence, Nolen-Hoeksema et al. (1992) found that attributional style and stressful events predicted depressive symptoms. Yet, they did not find gender differences in these factors as predictors of depressive symptoms. Cognitive and interpersonal factors may contribute to gender differences in depressive symptoms, but only among the most distressed adolescents. Therefore, research is needed to identify the processes that contribute to the high levels of depressive symptoms in a subgroup of adolescent girls who are eventually referred for mental health services.

The pronounced gender differences in depressive symptoms among referred adolescents suggest that greater attention needs to be paid to gender in interventions for the treatment of these problems. In previous controlled treatment trials, samples typically were too small to test carefully for gender differences in the impact of treatment or to tailor interventions to the distinctive needs and concerns of boys and girls. This should be a focus of future research efforts.

Reconsidering correlates, consequences, and comorbidity

What are the correlates and consequences of depression during adolescence? Researchers have examined both the short- and long-term sequelae of depressed affect, the Anxious/Depressed syndrome, and MDD. The outcomes that have been examined include the occurrence of other forms of psychopathology, impairment in academic and social functioning, recurrence of depression, and suicide. These all need to be considered in the context of syndromes that co-occur and disorders that are comorbid with depression in adolescence.

Comorbidity

Symptoms, syndromes, or disorders rarely occur alone during childhood and adolescence. Nowhere is this phenomenon, referred to as the *covariation* or *co-occurrence of symptoms* and the *comorbidity of disorders*, more evident than for depressive problems in children and youth (Angold & Costello, 1993; Compas & Hammen, 1994). This is true across all three levels of depressive problems discussed earlier; depressed mood covaries with other negative emotions, the Anxious/Depressed syndrome covaries with other empirically derived syndromes, and MDD is highly comorbid with other disorders.

A series of studies have shown that during childhood and adolescence, as in adulthood, depressed mood is closely related to other negative emotions. First, monomethod studies (i.e., studies relying on a single method, such as child/adolescent self-reports) have failed to distinguish depressed mood (and other symptoms of depression) from other negative emotions including anxiety, anger, and hostility. For example, Saylor, Finch, Spirito, and Bennett (1984) found that children and adolescents classified as high or low in depressive symptoms on the CDI also differed significantly on self-reported anxiety. Further, multitrait–multimethod validity studies examining reports from different informants (e.g., children/adolescents, teachers, parents) of various negative emotions (depression, anxiety, anger) have found that strong associations between child/adolescents' depressed mood and other negative emotions, especially anxiety, are not limited to child/adolescents' self-reports of emotions. These findings are consistent with the results of principal components analyses of the CBCL, YSR, and Teacher Report Form (TRF) that revealed the syndrome of mixed anxiety and depression symptoms discussed earlier. That is, reports of child/adolescent depressed mood by each informant are correlated more highly with reports of other negative emotions by that same informant than with reports of depressed mood obtained by other informants (e.g., Wolfe et al., 1987).

It is noteworthy that parent and teacher reports of child/adolescents' emotions and behaviors also show considerable covariance in levels of depressed and anxious mood (Finch, Lipovsky, & Casat, 1989). Thus, the association of depressed mood with other elements of the broader construct of negative affectivity is not the result of a simple bias in child/adolescents' reports about their internal emotional states. Finch et al. suggest that anxiety and depression are not separable in children and adolescents and that the distinction between these two forms of negative affect should be eliminated. These findings must be interpreted with caution, however, as there is some degree of item contamination between measures of depressed and anxious mood. For example, Brady and Kendall (1992) identified several items that are included on the CDI and standard self-report scales of anxiety. The extent to which item similarity on these measures accounts for the degree of association between the scales has not been clarified.

Concerns about confounding of measures notwithstanding, these findings can be understood by considering them within the broader framework of theories of emotion (e.g., Watson & Tellegen, 1985). Extensive evidence from studies of the structure of emotions in children, adolescents, college students, and adults indicates that self-rated mood is dominated by two broad factors: *negative affect,* composed of negative emotions and distress, and *positive affect* made up of positive emotions (King, Ollendick, & Gullone, 1991; Watson & Tellegen, 1985). Depressed and anxious mood are components of the broader construct of *negative affectivity*, whereas positive emotions are important in distinguishing among subtypes of negative emotion (Watson & Clark, 1984).

Research with adults indicates that although depressed mood is strongly correlated with other negative emotions, it appears to be distinguishable from anxiety, if not other forms of negative affect, on the basis of its association with positive emotion (e.g., happiness, excitement, pride, contentment). Specifically, whereas anxiety is uncorrelated with positive affect, depressed mood shows a consistent inverse relationship with positive mood (Watson & Kendall, 1989). Thus, highly anxious individuals may be low, moderate, or high in positive affect, as anxiety and positive emotions can co-occur. In contrast, highly depressed individuals are likely to experience low levels of positive emotion (i.e., anhedonia). The relation between positive affect and depressed mood during adolescence warrants further research. In general, research suggests that sad or depressed mood is a phenomenologically distinct emotional state that, although closely related to the experience of other forms of negative affect, is distinguished by its relation to positive emotion (Watson & Clark, 1992).

In addition to the strong relationship between anxiety and depression, the correlations of the Anxious/Depressed core syndrome with the other core syndromes identified in an empirically derived taxonomy also indicate substantial covariation. These correlations have been reported separately for the CBCL, TRF, and YSR for clinically referred and nonreferred adolescent boys and girls (Achenbach, 1991). Although these correlations vary substantially, ranging from $r = .27$ (with Delinquent for referred boys on the YSR) to $r = .80$ (with Self-Destructive for referred boys on the YSR), the overall mean correlation of the Anxious/Depressed syndrome with the other core syndromes is $r = .51$, indicating substantial covariance. Furthermore, the Anxious/Depressed syndrome correlated highly with both internalizing syndromes (Withdrawn, Somatic Complaints) and externalizing syndromes (Aggressive, Attention Problems). Thus, the degree of covariation of the Anxious/Depressed syndrome with other syndromes is substantial. The covariation of the Anxious/Depressed syndrome with other syndromes remains high even after controlling for measurement factors (Hinden, Compas, Achenbach, & Howell, 1997). That is, the Anxious/Depressed syndrome was highly correlated with other syndromes even after factoring out variance attributable to informant effects (Hinden et al., 1997). Further research is needed to understand the implications of this high degree of covariation for the etiology, course, treatment, and prevention of depressive syndromes (Compas & Hammen, 1994).

The comorbidity of MDD with other psychiatric diagnoses has been examined in epidemiological studies of nonreferred samples of children/adolescents in the community. Community samples rather than clinical samples are necessary to determine true rates of comorbidity, as rates of comorbidity in clinical samples are disproportionately high as result of referral bias and other factors (Caron & Rutter, 1991). Comorbidity appears to be the rule for child/adolescent depression (see Angold & Costello, 1993, Brady & Kendall, 1992, and Compas & Hammen, 1994, for reviews). The recent community studies by Lewinsohn and colleagues described earlier are illustrative in this regard (Lewinsohn et al., 1991; Rohde et al., 1991). The current comorbidity rate for MDD and DY was 20 times greater than that expected by chance, and the lifetime comorbidity rate was three times greater than chance (Lewinsohn et al., 1991). Levels of comorbidity with nonmood disorders were also high, as 43% of adolescents with a depressive disorder received at least one additional diagnosis, a rate that was 9.5 times greater than chance (Rohde et al., 1991). Current comorbidity was highest with anxiety disorders (18%), substance abuse disorders (14%), and disruptive behavior disorders (8%).

Similarly high rates of comorbidity of MDD have been found in the National Comorbidity Study, an epidemiological study of the rates of psychiatric comorbidity in a large national sample of adolescents and adults (Kessler et al., 1996). Seventy-five percent of individuals who had experienced an episode of major depression in their lifetime had experienced at least one other psychiatric disorder. It is also noteworthy that the majority (62%) of episodes of depression followed another disorder; the depressive diagnosis was secondary to the other disorder.

In summary, research drawing on both the categorical diagnostic and the quantitative dimensional approaches has highlighted the significant degree of comorbidity and covariation of depression with other problems and disorders in children and youth (Angold & Costello, 1993; Compas & Hammen, 1994). Depressive syndromes and disorders have been shown to co-occur with other internalizing problems (e.g., anxiety, social withdrawal, somatic problems, eating disorders), as well as with disruptive behavior disorders (e.g., conduct disorder, aggression, oppositional behavior, substance abuse). The evidence is clear that comorbidity of depression is the rule rather than the exception in young people and in adults.

Having established the pervasiveness of syndrome covariation and diagnostic comorbidity, researchers have now turned to an even more pressing question: What are the consequences of covariation and comorbidity? That is, when depression occurs along with another syndrome or disorder, does the presence of depression contribute to worse outcomes? The clinical consequences of comorbid conditions are significant in terms of utilization of mental health services, associated school problems, and global functioning (Lewinsohn, Rohde, & Seeley, 1995).

A recent study by our research group indicates both that there are significant consequences of covariation/comorbidity and that these consequences differ for adolescent boys and girls (Hinden, 1998). Adolescents who are in the clinical range on the Anxious/Depressed syndrome and are also in the clinical range on an externalizing syndrome (Aggressive Behavior or Delinquent Behavior) have significantly greater impairment and higher levels of other psychopathology than adolescents who are in the clinical range on the Anxious/Depressed syndrome but not on externalizing problems, those who are in the clinical range on an externalizing syndrome but not on the Anxious/Depressed syndrome, or those who are not in the clinical range on either syndrome. This pattern was found on both parents' reports on the CBCL and adolescents' reports on the YSR for social and academic competence, as well as other internalizing and externalizing syndromes. The presence of significant symptoms of anxiety and depression along with externalizing problems was clearly associated with poorer overall functioning than the presence of either type of problem alone.

Comorbidity also showed an intriguing association with gender in this sample (Hinden, 1997). Comorbidity of the Anxious/Depressed syndrome and externalizing problems was associated with greater gender differences for adolescent girls and boys. Differences between boys and girls were greater in the comorbid group than in the groups who were in the clinical range only on the Anxious/Depressed syndrome or only on an externalizing syndrome, but the pattern of gender differences was different for parent reports and adolescents' self-reports. In parents' reports on the CBCL, comorbid boys scored higher than comorbid girls on internalizing, externalizing, and total behavior problems. In self-reports on the YSR, comorbid girls scored higher than boys on the Anxious/Depressed and Somatic Complaints scales, and comorbid boys scored higher on the Aggressive and Delinquent Behavior scales. Comorbid boys scored higher than comorbid girls in social competence, whereas girls scored higher than boys in the groups that were in the clinical range only on the Anxious/Depressed syndrome or only on externalizing problems.

Thus, impaired functioning and other symptoms of psychopathology are associated with clinical deviations on either externalizing problems or the Anxious/Depressed syndrome when they occur alone. However, depressive symptoms added to the risk of impairment and psychopathology above the risk associated with externalizing behavior problems. Furthermore, gender differences are more pronounced in adolescents with comorbid depressive problems than in those with depressive problems or externalizing problems alone. These findings suggest that it is important for research concerned with gender differences in depression in adolescence to take into account comorbid problems associated with depression.

Research on comorbidity suggests that it has implications for treatment and prevention, and yet most interventions do not provide clear guidelines or strategies for dealing with comorbid difficulties. Furthermore, most empirically evaluated treatments for depression in children and adolescents have been based on community samples of children and youth with elevated depression scores on scales who may be less comorbid than clinically referred children and adolescents. Depressed youngsters who seek treatment in facilities are likely to have much higher rates of comorbid conditions than the participants in previous intervention research (Caron & Rutter, 1991).

Consequences of depression

Social impairment and disrupted development. A substantial body of data confirms that depressed adults evidence impairment in terms of work, marital and family functioning, and health outcomes for both clinically diagnosed depressions and subsyndromal depression (e.g., Gotlib & Hammen, 1992; Hammen, 1991; Hays, Wells, Sherbourne, Rogers, & Spritzer, 1995). Similar impairments in school behavior and academic functioning, as well as in social and family functioning, also are apparent in children and adolescents with major depression and depressive symptoms (e.g., reviewed in Anderson & Hammen, 1993; Hammen & Rudolph, 1996; Kaslow & Racusin, 1990). Elevated symptoms not sufficient to meet diagnostic criteria clearly are associated with significant psychosocial impairment, as in the Oregon community study of adolescents (Gotlib et al., 1995) and other investigations (e.g., Forehand, Brody, Long, & Fauber, 1988; Rudolph, Hammen, & Burge, 1994). Impairments in interpersonal functioning persist even after remission of a depressive episode (e.g., Puig-Antich et al., 1985). For example, in a longitudinal study of a large community sample of adolescents, Aseltine, Gore, and Colton (1994) examined emotional responsiveness to family members and friends in previously depressed youths and nondepressed youths (based on scores on the CES-D). Adolescents who experienced chronically high levels of depressive symptoms were unresponsive to family problems but were highly reactive to peer relations. Among previously asymptomatic youths, family relations exerted greater effects on depressed mood than did relations with peers.

Achenbach and colleagues examined the 3- and 6-year consequences of symptoms on the Anxious/Depressed syndrome (Achenbach, Howell, McConaughy, & Stanger, 1995; Stanger, Achenbach, & McConaughy, 1993). It is noteworthy that the Anxious/Depressed syndrome was not a strong predictor of six "signs of disturbance" (e.g., academic problems, school behavior problems, referral for mental health services, suicidal behavior, police contacts). Symptoms of anxiety/depression predicted only girls' referral for mental health services at the 3-year follow-up (Stanger, McConaughy, & Achenbach, 1993) and boys' referral for mental health services at the 6-year follow-up (Achenbach et al., 1995).

It is highly likely that impaired academic, family, and social functioning associated with depression interfere with the mastery of important developmental tasks, leaving children to face challenges beyond their abilities for mastery and lacking access to sources of self-esteem and perceived competence. To the extent that depression results, in part, from perceived lack of competence (e.g., Cole, 1991), a recurring cycle of symptoms and failure describes a potentially self-perpetuating disorder. Moreover, to the extent that incompetencies and impairments in developmentally important areas foster depressive reactions, it may be possible to identify youngsters at risk for whom preventive interventions might forestall the development of the depressive cycle.

Adolescent depression and future depressive episodes

Given the high rates of concurrent comorbid psychopathology and depression, it is reasonable to expect that depression during adolescence may be associated with a subsequent risk of psychopathology. The data confirm this expectation, as depression during childhood and adolescence is associated with depression in adolescence and adulthood.

There are three significant concerns about the course of depression in childhood and adolescence. First, recurrence of episodes is common among young people with major depression, as it is with adults. Lewinsohn et al. (1993) noted that 18% of their largely untreated community sample had a recurrence of a major depressive episode within 1 year, and McCauley et al. (1993) reported 25% relapse within a year (and 54% within 3 years). Kovacs et al. (1984) reported that among an outpatient sample, 26% had a new episode within 1 year of recovery, 40% within 2 years, and 72% within 5 years. Asarnow et al. (1988) found that 45% of their hospitalized sample were rehospitalized within 2 years.

A second concern is that although most youngsters recover within a year, a sizable minority remain depressed – approximately 20% at the 1-year follow-up and 10% at the 2-year follow-up (Keller et al., 1988; McCauley et al., 1993; Strober, Lampert, Schmidt, & Morrell, 1993). Kovacs et al. (1984) reported that 41% of their outpatient sample was still depressed after 1 year and 8% after 2 years. Chronic depression, of course, occurs in children and adolescents and portends a particularly pernicious course, including greater recurrence of major depressive episodes (e.g., Kovacs, Akiskal, Gatsonis, & Parrone, 1994; Kovacs et al., 1984). Studies of youth scoring high on self-report measures of depressive symptoms, typically indicating subclinical depression, also suggest considerable stability of depressive symptoms over repeated testing (e.g., Achenbach et al., 1995; Cole, Martin, Powers, & Truglio, 1996; Garrison, Jackson, Marstellar, McKeown, & Addy, 1990; Stanger et al., 1992; Verhulst & van der Ende, 1992).

A third issue is continuity between childhood/adolescent depression and adult depression. Although less information is available on this topic than on recurrence or chronicity during childhood and adolescence, available data do indeed indicate that those who have been depressed as youngsters are likely to have recurrent episodes or continuing symptoms in adulthood (Harrington, Fudge, Rutter, Pickles, & Hill, 1990; Kandel & Davies, 1986; Lewinsohn, Hoberman, & Rosenbaum, 1988). The adage that the best predictor of depression is past depression is alarmingly true for children and adolescents.

Adolescent depression and suicide

Special attention has been given to the link between depressive symptoms and disorder and suicidal ideation, attempted suicide, and completed suicide among adolescents. This is because of the finality of suicide, heightened public concern about adolescent suicide due to the increase in the number of attempted and completed suicides, and the widely assumed link between depression and suicide. Research has established a clear link between depression, whether measured as elevated symptoms or a diagnosis, and subsequent suicide attempts. As with research on the more general consequences of depression, however, the risk of attempted suicide increases dramatically when co-occurring symptoms or comorbid disorders are taken into account.

Lewinsohn and colleagues (1996) have provided extensive data on the association between depression and attempted suicide from the Oregon longitudinal study. They examined comorbidity among adolescent suicide attempters in the community and found higher rates of suicide attempts among adolescents with major depression plus substance abuse compared with the rates of suicide attempts among those with any single diagnosis alone. They also found that comorbid major depression with conduct disorder posed a higher risk of suicide attempts than conduct disorder alone, but not compared with major depression alone. Comorbidity with anxiety, substance use, and disruptive behavior was associated with increased percentages of youth who received treatment, with poor global functioning (except comorbid anxiety), with increased percentages who attempted suicide (only for substance use), and with increased percentages with academic problems (except anxiety). Rates of attempted suicide for pure disorders were 19% for MDD, 2% for anxiety, 9.3% for substance use, 4.7% for disruptive behavior, 22.4% with MDD comorbid with anxiety, 34.6%

with MDD comorbid with substance abuse, and 38.9% with MDD comorbid with disruptive behavior. Thus, a diagnosis of depression was a significant risk factor for attempted suicide, but the risk increases even more with the presence of a comorbid disruptive behavior disorder or substance abuse.

Similarly, in a study of a large community sample of adolescents, Wagner, Cole, and Schwartzman (1996) found an association between depressive symptoms and attempted suicide. Depression alone, conduct disorder alone, alcohol abuse alone, and drug abuse alone all related to a higher risk of a suicide attempt; depression combined with each of the other problems related to a higher suicide risk. Adolescents reporting high levels of depression along with either alcohol abuse or conduct problems were more likely to have made a suicide attempt than were adolescents reporting only one of these disorders. Adolescents reporting comorbid drug abuse plus either depression or conduct problems were more likely to have made a suicide attempt than those reporting only depression or conduct problems without drug abuse.

Directions for future research

The recent changes in perspectives on depression in adolescence, not surprisingly, have generated a new set of questions and challenges for researchers in this field. The three emerging perspectives on depression during adolescence that have been outlined here provide a framework for future research.

Reconciling different conceptualizations of depression

A high priority for researchers concerned with depression during adolescence continues to be the reconciliation and integration of the conceptualizations of depression as an emotion, a syndrome, and a disorder. Among the more pressing questions are: Is MDD a more severe manifestation of depressive problems than manifestations that involve depressed mood or a syndrome of mixed anxiety/depression? Alternatively, is MDD a qualitatively distinct disorder that is unrelated to less severe manifestations involving mood or mixed anxiety/depression? Is MDD a heterogeneous disorder, encompassing several different subtypes with distinct etiologies and courses? What is the clinical significance of depressed mood and the Anxious/Depressed syndrome in comparison with the significance of MDD?

The research summarized in this chapter clearly indicates that adolescents who receive a diagnosis of MDD are a subgroup of a larger group of adolescents who are experiencing depressed mood or symptoms of the Anxious/Depressed syndrome. Furthermore, in longitudinal analyses the Anxious/Depressed syndrome was a strong predictor of meeting criteria for MDD (Gerhardt et al., 1996). Gains in our understanding in this area will be achieved only by research that examines multiple levels of depressive problems. Focusing exclusively on a single conceptualization of depression and discounting the significance of other manifestations of depressive problems will clearly result in a stilted and misleading picture.

Reconciling age and gender effects

Recent research continues to support the impression that adolescence is a period in which males and females diverge in their experience of depressive symptoms and disorders. The recent evidence is also clear, however, in suggesting that these differences are not large or pervasive features of adolescent development. Gender differences and age-related changes are quite small in magnitude in the general population. As a result, they are very difficult to detect in community samples of youth. Gender, but not age, differences are more pronounced among adolescents who have been referred for mental health services. Therefore, a high priority for future research is to clarify the risk processes and mechanisms that contribute to gender differences in high-risk samples – that is, the risk processes that lead some adolescent girls, rather than adolescent girls in general, to experience high levels of depressive symptoms or to meet criteria for MDD. These processes are likely to be distinct from those that contribute to the small gender effects found among nonreferred samples of youth. Moreover, the changing rates of depression and other mental health problems highlight the importance of attending to cohort differences in the effects of both age and gender.

Contending with comorbidity and the consequences of depression

Depressive symptoms, syndromes, and disorders all have a strong tendency to co-occur with other problems. Although general patterns of co-occurrence and comorbidity have been well documented, the etiology and implications of these patterns are less well understood. A high priority for future research continues to be enhanced understanding of the nature of comorbidity of depression during adolescence. For example, it appears that depression most often follows rather than precedes other disorders. This appears to have significant implications for understanding the etiology of depression, yet the etiological processes have not been well defined. Similarly, patterns of comorbidity will be important to consider in interventions designed for the prevention and treatment of depression. Few intervention studies, however, have addressed comorbid disorders or co-occurring symptoms in their samples.

Research on the consequences of depression during adolescence must make the investigation of comorbidity the highest priority. Evidence clearly indicates that depressive symptoms and disorders that are accompanied by other problems, most notably disruptive behavior problems and substance abuse, have a much worse course than depressive symptoms and disorders that occur alone. Future research is needed to continue to evaluate the relative contribution of depression as opposed to other comorbid conditions to these negative outcomes. Continued investigation of the relative contributions of depression and other problems to suicidal behavior in adolescence is a high priority, as depression appears to play a central but certainly not an exclusive role in increasing the risk of attempted suicide.

References

Achenbach, T. M. (1985). *Assessment and taxonomy of child and adolescent psychopathology.* Newbury Park, CA: Sage.

Achenbach, T. M. (1991). *Integrative guide for the 1991 CBCL/4-18, YSR, and TRF profiles.* Burlington: University of Vermont, Department of Psychiatry.

Achenbach, T. M. (1993). *Empirically based taxonomy.* Burlington: University of Vermont, Department of Psychiatry.

Achenbach, T. M., Howell, C. T., McConaughy, S. H., & Stanger, C. T. (1995). Six-year predictors of problems in a national sample of children and youth: I. Cross-informant syndromes. *Journal of the American Academy of Child and Adolescent Psychiatry, 34,* 336–347.

Achenbach, T. M., McConaughy, S. H., & Howell, C. T. (1987). Child/adolescent behavioral and emotional problems: Implications of cross-informant correlations for situational specificity. *Psychological Bulletin, 101*, 213–232.

Achenbach, T. M., Verhulst, F. C., Baron, G. G., & Akkerhuis, G. W. (1987). Epidemiological comparisons of American and Dutch children: I. Behavioral/emotional problems and competencies reported by parents for ages 4 to 16. *Journal of the American Academy for Child and Adolescent Psychology, 26*, 317–325.

American Psychiatric Association. (1994). *Diagnostic and statistical manual of mental disorders* (4th ed.). Washington, DC: American Psychiatric Association.

Anderson, C. A., & Hammen, C. L. (1993). Psychosocial outcomes of children of unipolar depressed, bipolar, medically ill, and normal women: A longitudinal study. *Journal of Consulting & Clinical Psychology, 61*, 448–454.

Angold, A. (1988). Childhood and adolescent depression I. Epidemiological and aetiological aspects. *British Journal of Psychiatry, 152*, 601–617.

Angold, A., & Costello, E. J. (1993). Depressive comorbidity in children and adolescents: Empirical, theoretical, and methodological issues. *American Journal of Psychiatry, 150*, 1779–1791.

Angold, A., & Rutter, M. (1992). Effects of age and pubertal status on depression in a large clinical sample. *Development & Psychopathology, 4*, 5–28.

Asarnow, J., Goldstein, M., Carlson, G., Perdue, S., Bates, S., & Keller, J. (1988). Childhood-onset depressive disorders: A follow-up study of rates of rehospitalization and out-of-home placement among child psychiatric inpatients. *Journal of Affective Disorders, 15*, 245–253.

Aseltine, R. H., Gore, S., & Colton, M. E. (1994). Depression and the social developmental context of adolescence. *Journal of Personality and Social Psychology, 67*, 252–263.

Brady, E., & Kendall, P. (1992). Comorbidity of anxiety and depression in children and adolescents. *Psychological Bulletin, 111*, 244–255.

Cantwell, D. P., & Baker, L. (1991). Manifestations of depressive affect in adolescence. *Journal of Youth and Adolescence, 20*, 121–133.

Carlson, G. A. (1994). Adolescent bipolar disorder: Phenomenology and treatment implications. In W. M. Reynolds & H. F. Johnston (Eds.), *Handbook of depression in children and adolescents* (pp. 41–60). New York: Plenum Press.

Carlson, G. A., & Cantwell, D. P. (1980). Unmasking masked depression in children and adolescents. *American Journal of Psychiatry, 137*, 445–449.

Caron, C., & Rutter, M. (1991). Comorbidity in child psychopathology: Concepts, issues and research strategies. *Journal of Child Psychology and Psychiatry, 32*, 1063–1080.

Chen, W. J., Faraone, S. V., Biederman, J., & Tsuang, M. T. (1994). Diagnostic accuracy of the Child Behavior Checklist scales for Attention-Deficit Hyperactivity Disorder: A receiver-operating characteristic analysis. *Journal of Consulting and Clinical Psychology, 62,* 1017–1025.

Clarke, G. N., Lewinsohn, P. M., Hops, H., & Seeley, J. R. (1992). A self- and parent-report measure of adolescent depression: The Child Behavior Checklist Depression scale. *Behavioral Assessment, 14,* 443–463.

Cole, D. A. (1991). Preliminary support for a competency-based model of depression in children. *Journal of Abnormal Psychology, 100,* 181–190.

Cole, D. A., Martin, J., Powers, B., & Truglio, R. (1996). Modeling causal relations between academic and social competence and depression: A multitrait-multimethod longitudinal study of children. *Journal of Abnormal Psychology, 105,* 258–270.

Compas, B. E., Ey, S., & Grant, K. E. (1993). Taxonomy and assessment of depression during adolescence. *Psychological Bulletin, 114,* 323–344.

Compas, B. E., & Hammen, C. L. (1994). Child and adolescent depression: Covariation and comorbidity in development. In R. J. Haggerty, L. R. Sherrod, N. Garmezy, & M. Rutter (Eds.), *Stress, risk, and resilience in children and adolescents: Processes, mechanisms, and interventions* (pp. 225–267). New York: Cambridge University Press.

Compas, B. E., Oppedisano, G., Connor, J. K., Gerhardt, C. A., Hinden, B., Achenbach, T. M., & Hammen, C. (1997). Gender differences in depressive symptoms in adolescence: Comparison of national samples of clinically-referred and non-referred youth. *Journal of Consulting and Clinical Psychology, 65,* 617–626.

Coyne, J. C., & Downey, G. (1991). Social factors and psychopathology: Stress, social support, and coping processes. *Annual Review of Psychology, 42,* 401–425.

Eagly, A. H. (1995). The science and politics of comparing women and men. *American Psychologist, 50,* 145–158.

Edelbrock, C., & Costello, A. J. (1988). Convergence between statistically derived behavior problem syndromes and child psychiatric diagnoses. *Journal of Abnormal Child Psychology, 16,* 219–231.

Fechner-Bates, S., Coyne, J. C., & Schwenk, T. L. (1994). The relationship of self-reported distress to depressive disorders and other psychopathology. *Journal of Consulting and Clinical Psychology, 62,* 550–559.

Finch, A. J., Lipovsky, J. A., & Casat, C. D. (1989). Anxiety and depression in children and adolescents: Negative affectivity or separate constructs? In P. C. Kendall & D. Watson (Eds.), *Anxiety and depression: Distinctive and overlapping features* (pp. 171–202). New York: Academic Press.

Forehand, R., Brody, G. H., Long, N., & Fauber, R. (1988). The interactive influence of adolescent and maternal depression on adolescent social and cognitive functioning. *Cognitive Therapy and Research, 12,* 341–350.

Garrison C. Z., Addy, C. L., Jackson, K. L., McKeown, R. E., & Waller, J. (1991). The CES-D as a screen for depression and other psychiatric disorders in adolescents. *Journal of the American Academy of child and Adolescent Psychiatry, 30,* 636–641.

Garrison, C. Z., Jackson, K. L., Marstellar, F., McKeown, R. E., & Addy, C. (1990). A longitudinal study of depressive symptomatology in young adolescents. *Journal of the American Academy of Child and Adolescent Psychiatry, 29,* 581–585.

Ge, X., Lorenz, F. O., Conger, R. D., Elder, G. H., & Simons, R. L. (1994). Trajectories of stressful life events and depressive symptoms during adolescence. *Developmental Psychology, 30,* 467–483.

Gerhardt, C., Compas, B. E., Connor, J., & Achenbach, T. M. (1997). *Understanding the nature of adolescent depression: Relations among mood, syndrome, and diagnosis.* Manuscript submitted for publication.

Giaconia, R. M., Reinherz, H. Z., Silverman, A. B., Pakiz, B., Frost, A. K., & Cohen, E. (1993). Ages of onset of psychiatric disorders in a community population of older adolescents. *Journal of the American Academy of Child and Adolescent Psychiatry, 33,* 706–717.

Gotlib, I. H., & Hammen, C. L. (1992). *Psychological aspects of depression: Toward a cognitive-interpersonal integration.* London: Wiley.

Gotlib, I. H., Lewinsohn, P. M., & Seeley, J. R. (1995). Symptoms versus a diagnosis of depression: Differences in psychosocial functioning. *Journal of Consulting and Clinical Psychology, 65,* 90–100.

Hammen, C. L. (1991). *Depression runs in families: The social context of risk and resilience in children of depressed mothers.* New York: Springer-Verlag.

Hammen, C. L., & Compas, B. E. (1994). Unmasking unmasked depression in children and adolescents: The problem of comorbidity. *Clinical Psychology Review, 14,* 585–603.

Hammen, C. L., & Rudolph, K. (1996). Childhood depression. In E. J. Mash & R. A. Barkley (Eds.), *Child psychopathology* (pp. 153–195). New York: Guilford Press.

Harrington, R., Fudge, H., Rutter, M., Pickles, A., & Hill, J. (1990). Adult outcomes of childhood and adolescent depression: Psychiatric status. *Archives of General Psychiatry, 47,* 465–473.

Hays, R. D., Wells, K. B., Sherbourne, C. D., Rogers, W., & Spritzer, K. (1995). Functioning and well-being outcomes of patients with depression compared with chronic general medical illnesses. *Archives of General Psychiatry, 52,* 11–19.

Hinden, B. (1998). *Comorbidity of the anxious depressed syndrome with disruptive behavior disorders: Correlates and consequences.* Unpublished doctoral dissertation, University of Vermont.

Hinden, B., Compas, B. E., Achenbach, T. M., Hammen, C., Oppedisano, G., Connor, J. K., & Gerhardt, C. A. (1997). *Charting the course of depressive symptoms during adolescence: Do we have the right map?* Manuscript submitted for publication.

Hinden, B., Compas, B. E., Achenbach, T. M., & Howell, D. C. (1997). Comorbidity of depression during adolescence: Separating fact from artifact. *Journal of Consulting and Clinical Psychology, 65,* 6–14.

Jensen, P. S., Watanabe, H. K., Richters, J. E., Roper, M., Hibbs, E. D., Salzberg, A. D., & Liu, S. (1996). Scales, diagnoses, and child psychopathology: II. Comparing the CBCL and DISC against external validators. *Journal of Abnormal Child Psychology, 24,* 151–168.

Kandel, D. B., & Davies, M. (1982) Epidemiology of depressive mood in adolescents. *Archives of General Psychiatry, 39,* 1205–1212.

Kandel, D. B., & Davies, M. (1986). Adult sequelae of adolescent depressive symptoms. *Archives of General Psychiatry, 43,* 255–262.

Kashani, J. H., Carlson, G. A., Beck, N. C., Hoeper, E. W., Corcoran, C. M., McAllister, J. A., Fallahi, C., Rosenberg, T. K., & Reid, J. C. (1987). Depression, depressive symptoms, and depressed mood among a community sample of adolescents. *American Journal of Psychiatry, 144,* 931–934.

Kaslow, N. J., & Racusin, G. R. (1990). Childhood depression: Current status and future directions. In A. S. Bellack, M. Hersen, & A. E. Kazdin (Eds.), *International handbook of behavior modification and therapy* (2nd. ed., pp. 649–668). New York: Plenum Press.

Kazdin, A. E., Esveldt-Dawson, K., Unis, A. S., & Rancurello, M. D. (1983). Child and parent evaluations of depression and aggression in psychiatric inpatient children. *Journal of Abnormal Child Psychology, 11,* 401–413.

Kazdin, A. E. (1994). Informant variability in the assessment of childhood depression. In W. M. Reynolds & H. F. Johnston (Eds.), *Handbook of depression in children and adolescents* (pp. 249–271). New York: Plenum Press.

Keller, M. B., Beardslee, W., Lavori, P. W., Wunder, J., Dorer, D. L., & Samuelson, H. (1988). Course of major depression in non-referred adolescents: A retrospective study. *Journal of Affective Disorders, 15,* 235–243.

Kessler, R. C., Nelson, C. B., McGonagle, K. A., Liu, J., Swartz, M., & Blazer, D. G. (1996). Comorbidity of DSM-III-R major depressive disorder in the general population: Results from the U.S. National Comorbidity Survey. *British Journal of Psychiatry, 168,* 17–30.

King, N. J., Ollendick, T. H., & Gullone, E. (1991). Negative affectivity in children and adolescents: Relations between anxiety and depression. *Clinical Psychology Review, 11*, 441–460.

Kovacs, M. (1989). Affective disorders in children and adolescents. *American Psychologist, 44*, 209–215.

Kovacs, M., Akiskal, H. S., Gatsonis, C., & Parrone, P. L. (1994). Childhood-onset dysthymic disorder: Clinical features and prospective naturalistic outcome. *Archives of General Psychiatry, 51*, 365–374.

Kovacs, M., Feinberg, T. L., Crouse-Novak, M. A., Paulauskas, S. L., & Finkelstein, R. (1984). Depressive disorders in childhood: I. A longitudinal prospective study of characteristics and recovery. *Archives of General Psychiatry, 41*, 229–237.

Leadbeater, B. J., Blatt, S. J., & Quinlan, D. M. (1995). Gender-linked vulnerabilities to depressive symptoms, stress, and problem behaviors in adolescents. *Journal of Research on Adolescence, 5*, 1–29.

Lewinsohn, P. M., Hoberman, H. B., & Rosenbaum, M. (1988). A prospective study of risk factors for unipolar depression. *Journal of Abnormal Psychology, 97*, 251–264.

Lewinsohn, P. M., Hops, H., Roberts, R. E., Seeley, J. R., & Andrews, J. A. (1993). Adolescent psychopathology: I. Prevalence and incidence of depression and other DSM-III-R disorders in high school students. *Journal of Abnormal Psychology, 102*, 133–144.

Lewinsohn, P. M., Rohde, P., & Seeley, J. R. (1995). Adolescent psychopathology: III. The clinical consequences of comorbidity. *Journal of the American Academy of Child & Adolescent Psychiatry, 34*, 510–519.

Lewinsohn, P. M., Rohde, P., & Seeley, J. R. (1996). Adolescent suicidal ideation and attempts: Prevalence, risk factors, and implications. *Clinical Psychology: Science and Practice, 3*, 25–46.

Lewinsohn, P. M., Rohde, P., Seeley, J. R., & Hops, H. (1991). Comorbidity of unipolar depression: I. Major depression with dysthymia. *Journal of Abnormal Psychology, 100*, 205–213.

McCauley, E., Myers, K., Mitchell, J., Calderon, R., Schloredt, K., & Treder, R. (1993). Depression in young people: Initial presentation and clinical course. *Journal of the American Academy of Child and Adolescent Psychiatry, 32*, 714–722.

McClelland, G. H., & Judd, C. M. (1993). Statistical difficulties of detecting interactions and moderator effects. *Psychological Bulletin, 114*, 376–390.

McGee, R., Feehan, M., Williams, S., Partridge, F., Silva, P., & Kelly, J. (1990). DSM-III disorders in a large sample of adolescents. *Journal of the American Academy of Child and Adolescent Psychiatry, 29*, 611–619.

Maccoby, E. E. (1990). Gender and relationships: A developmental account. *American Psychologist, 45,* 513–520.

Nolen-Hoeksema, S. N., & Girgus, J. S. (1994). The emergence of gender differences in depression during adolescence. *Psychological Bulletin, 115,* 424–443.

Nolen-Hoeksema, S., Girgus, J. S., & Seligman, M. E. P. (1992). Predictors and consequences of childhood depressive symptoms: A 5-year longitudinal study. *Journal of Abnormal Psychology, 101,* 405–422.

Nurcombe, B., Seifer, R., Scioli, A., Tramontana, M. G., Grapentine, W. L., & Beauchesne, H. C. (1989). Is major depressive disorder in adolescence a distinct entity? *Journal of the American Academy of Child and Adolescent Psychiatry, 28,* 333–342.

Petersen, A. C., Compas, B. E., Brooks-Gunn, J., Stemmler, M., Ey, S., & Grant, K. E. (1993). Depression in adolescence. *American Psychologist, 48,* 155–168.

Petersen, A. C., Sarigiani, P. A., & Kennedy, R. E. (1991). Adolescent depression: Why more girls? *Journal of Youth and Adolescence, 20,* 247–271.

Poznanski, E. O., & Mokros, H. B. (1994). Phenomenology and epidemiology of mood disorders in children and adolescents. In W. M. Reynolds & H. F. Johnston (Eds.), *Handbook of depression in children and adolescents* (pp. 19–40). New York: Plenum Press.

Puig-Antich, J., Lukens, E., Davies, M., Goetz, D., Brennan-Quattrock, J., & Todak, G. (1985). Psychosocial functioning in prepubertal major depressive disorders: II. Interpersonal relationships after sustained recovery from affective episodes. *Archives of General Psychiatry, 42,* 511–517.

Rey, J. M., & Morris-Yates, A. (1991). Adolescent depression and the Child Behavior Checklist. *Journal of the American Academy of Child and Adolescent Psychiatry, 30,* 423–427.

Rey, J. M., & Morris-Yates, A. (1992). Diagnostic accuracy in adolescents of several depression rating scales extracted from a general purpose behavior checklist. *Journal of Affective Disorders, 30,* 423–427.

Roberts, R. E., Lewinsohn, P. M., & Seeley, J. R. (1991). Screening for adolescent depression: A comparison of depression scales. *Journal of the American Academy of Child and Adolescent Psychiatry, 30,* 58–66.

Rohde, P., Lewinsohn, P. M., & Seeley, J. R. (1991). Comorbidity of unipolar depression: II. Comorbidity with other mental disorders in adolescents and adults. *Journal of Abnormal Psychology, 54,* 653–660.

Rudolph, K. D., Hammen, C., & Burge, D. (1994). Interpersonal functioning and depressive symptoms in childhood: Addressing the issues of specificity and comorbidity. *Journal of Abnormal Child Psychology, 22,* 355–371.

Saylor, C. F., Finch, A. J., Spirito, A., & Bennett, B. (1984). The Children's

Depression Inventory: A systematic evaluation of psychometric properties. *Journal of Consulting & Clinical Psychology, 52,* 955–967.

Silverstein, B., Caceres, J., Perdue, L., & Cimarolli, V. (1995). Gender differences in depressive symptomatology: The role played by "anxious somatic depression" associated with gender-related achievement concerns. *Sex Roles, 33,* 621–636.

Stanger, C., Achenbach, T. M., & Verhulst, F. C. (1994). Accelerating longitudinal research on child psychopathology: A practical example. *Psychological Assessment, 6,* 102–107.

Stanger, C., Achenbach, T. M., & McConaughy, S. H. (1993). Three-year course of behavioral/emotional problems in a national sample of 4- to 16-year-olds: II. Predictors of syndromes. *Journal of the American Academy of Child and Adolescent Psychiatry, 31,* 941–950.

Strober, M., Lampert, C., Schmidt, S., & Morrell, W. (1993). The course of major depressive disorder in adolescents. I. Recovery and risk of manic switching in a follow-up of psychotic and non-psychotic subtypes. *Journal of the American Academy of Child and Adolescent Psychiatry, 32,* 34–42.

Verhulst, F. C., & van der Ende, J. (1992). Six-year developmental course of internalizing and externalizing problem behaviors. *Journal of the American Academy of Child and Adolescent Psychiatry, 31,* 924–931.

Wagner, B. M., Cole, R. E., & Schwartzman, P. (1996). Comorbidity of symptoms among junior and senior high school suicide attempters. *Suicide and Life-Threatening Behavior, 26,* 300–307.

Watson, D., & Clark, L. (1984). Negative affectivity: The disposition to experience aversive emotional states. *Psychological Bulletin, 96,* 465–490.

Watson, D., & Clark, L. A. (1992). Affects separable and inseparable: On the hierarchical arrangement of the negative affects. *Journal of Personality and Social Psychology, 62,* 489–505.

Watson, D., & Kendall, P. C. (1989). Common and differentiating features of anxiety and depression: Current findings and future directions. In P. C. Kendall & D. Watson (Eds.), *Anxiety and depression: Distinctive and overlapping features* (pp. 493–508). New York: Academic Press.

Watson, D., & Tellegen, A. (1985). Toward a consensual structure of mood. *Psychological Bulletin, 98,* 219–235.

Weinstein, S. R., Noam, G. G., Grimes, K., Stone, K., & Schwab-Stone, M. (1990). Convergence of DSM-III diagnoses and self-reported symptoms in child and adolescent inpatients. *Journal of the American Academy of Child and Adolescent Psychiatry, 29,* 627–634.

Wolfe, V. V., Finch, A. J., Saylor, C. F., Blount, R. L., Pallmeyer, T. P., & Carek, D. J. (1987). Negative affectivity in children: A multitrait-multimethod investigation. *Journal of Consulting & Clinical Psychology,* 55(2), 245–250.

World Health Organization. (1990). *International classification of diseases and health related problems (ICD-10).* Geneva: Author.

Part V

A focus on social role performance

11

Transition to adulthood among high-risk youth

Margaret E. Ensminger and Hee Soon Juon

Introduction

A recent report by the National Research Council (1993) on high-risk adolescents concludes that research should focus on those who are most at risk for not making a successful transition to young adulthood, that is, those who grow up in poor communities, attend underfunded schools, and live in families that lack the social and economic resources to support their children's socialization process appropriately. In addition, the panel specifically suggested that research should move beyond the sole emphasis on measuring youth problems (such as drug use, pregnancy, arrest) and accomplishments (graduation, employment) to include assessment of the individual and community attributes (alienation, responsibility, attachment, emotional health) that underlie the "status" outcomes (p. 248).

The conceptual issues and empirical results that we present in this chapter are organized around childhood and adolescent social role performance and psychological well-being, which seem to lead to successful adult role performance among a cohort of inner-city children. As Jessor (1993) states, the field of adolescence has been invigorated by a more comprehensive theory, more attention to development, increased awareness of the importance of biology and genetics on the one hand and the social and cultural contexts on the other, a more inclusive focus on previously ignored populations of adolescents, notably ethnic minorities and those living in poverty, and a broader range of research and statistical methods. We attempt to reflect these trends and to address heir implications for future research and program development.

This research is supported by National Institute of Drug Abuse RO1-DA06630. We acknowledge helpful suggestions made by the participants in the meeting on "New Perspectives on Adolescent Risk Behavior."

We focus on a cohort of adults who have been followed since they were in first grade in a poor urban neighborhood in Chicago to try to understand processes that both enhanced and inhibited their growth and development. A recent follow-up has suggested that although they began their schooling in an urban neighborhood with many social problems, such as high crime and gang activity, high rates of infant mortality, high unemployment, and many families with only a single adult in the household to raise the children, there has been great variation in how the cohort members have made the transition to adulthood. At age 32, two-thirds have jobs, 80% have a high school diploma, and rates of drug use are not much higher than those in a comparable nationally representative population of the United States. Nevertheless, problems do exist. Between first grade and age 32, 3.5% of the cohort had died, and more than half had experience with the criminal justice system.

The overall aim of this longitudinal research project is to examine the pathways from childhood through adolescence and young adulthood to drug use, crime, other problem behaviors, and pathways to successful transitions such as employment and marriage. Individuals who engage in the same behavior (e.g., drug use or interpersonal aggression) may vary on the relationship of that behavior to antecedents or co-occurrences of that behavior. The behavior, then, needs to be considered in the context of other aspects of the persons' lives, such as their social class, family situation, interpersonal aggression, and psychological status. The risk of drug use may vary by these social contexts and individual risks. Problem behavior theory focuses on the overlap of different problem behaviors with each other; that is, those individuals who are heavy substance users are also more likely to participate in other antisocial activities, as well as to have distinct personality and contextual characteristics. The pattern approach we explore builds on problem behavior theory to consider the different constellations of characteristics that may accompany drug use (or other problem behaviors). One's family situation and social status may influence the patterning of the problem behaviors that occur.

Although substance use and interpersonal aggression have been frequently examined in terms of their risk factors and early antecedents, there has been less examination of how these behaviors are embedded in other aspects of life. Several studies have confirmed that adolescents with more problem behaviors are more likely to have problem behaviors as adults (Donovan, Jessor, & Jessor 1983; Farrington, 1983; Kandel, Simcha-Fagan, & Davies, 1986), but we do not know how these problem behaviors are embedded in other aspects of adults' lives or how the other aspects of adolescents' lives contribute to the later patterning of behaviors. In this chapter, then, we examine the following questions:

1. What is the patterning among poverty, socioeconomic status (SES), having children, substance use, interpersonal aggression, and anxiety of young adults who began their schooling in an inner-city neighborhood?.
2. How do adolescent problem behaviors such as substance use and interpersonal aggression relate to these later patterns among adults? Is there specificity in the relationships of one kind of problem behavior with another?
3. How do social bonds in adolescence relate to later patterns of behavior?
4. How do early family social origins influence the patterns that develop? Are those with high social origins less likely to be in clusters that have high problem behaviors as adults?
5. How do the transitions to adulthood relate to these patterns?

Methods

Description of the study setting

The Woodlawn longitudinal study of children provides an opportunity to examine how adolescent problem behaviors, social bonds, and family circumstances influence the life course into adulthood. Woodlawn is a neighborhood on the South Side of Chicago. Most of its residents are African American. In 1963, a partnership of community residents, the City of Chicago, and mental health professionals founded the Woodlawn Mental Health Center. Concerned about the future of their young people, the community specified that the Center's first project should focus on Woodlawn's children (Kellam, Branch, Agrawal, & Ensminger, 1975).

In the mental health epidemiological and longitudinal study that resulted, all first-grade children attending Woodlawn's nine public and three parochial schools in 1966–1967 were assessed by their teachers.

Mothers were interviewed about the child's family life. Psychologists observed and rated the children. Ten years later, in 1975–1976, these children and their mothers were reassessed. In 1992–1993, the young adults (age 32–33) were interviewed again.

When the children first were seen in 1966–1967, they all lived within the Woodlawn community. At the follow-up in 1975–1976 during adolescence, two-thirds of those reinterviewed had moved to other neighborhoods; one-third still lived within Woodlawn. During the time of this study, Woodlawn was a poor community. According to 1970 census data, 97% of its residents were African American. In 1965, a year before the study children started school, Woodlawn was substantially overcrowded, with 90,000 people living in an urban area built to house 45,000 (deVise, 1967). Since that time, the population has declined dramatically. The 1970 census indicated a total population of about 54,000 and the 1980 census a population of about 36,000. According to 1965 data, Woodlawn was a community of low median income and high unemployment, ranking among the most impoverished neighborhoods in Chicago (deVise, 1967). It has remained poor. In 1970, about 27% of Woodlawn families were below the poverty level; in 1980, about 32%. In the City of Chicago the comparable figures were 12% in 1970 and 18% in 1980. Given the decline in the population of Woodlawn from 1970 to 1980, it is not surprising that over the 10 years of the first follow-up period of the study, two-thirds of the population moved to other areas within Chicago, mostly on the South Side. Although the study began in the Woodlawn community, from first grade to ages 15–16 the population had moved to 46 of the 76 Chicago community areas.

In 1965, Woodlawn was not an economically homogeneous community. Because residential segregation restricted African Americans to certain neighborhoods, Woodlawn was the home of working-class and middle-class as well as welfare families. Some areas within Woodlawn had median incomes similar to Chicago's median income and a high proportion of home ownership. According to 1980 census data, this diversity remained.

Description of the study

The children ($N = 1,242$) were assessed three times in 1966–1967 by their first-grade teachers and again at the end of third grade. In the spring of 1967, the mothers or mother surrogates of the children who were in first grade were interviewed (Kellam, Ensminger, & Turner, 1977). In 1975–1976, when the children were teenagers, they and their mothers were reinterviewed. About 75% ($N = 939$) of the original population of mothers or mother surrogates were reinterviewed. Twelve percent could not be located, another 6% had moved away from Chicago, and 6% refused to be interviewed. Seventy-five percent ($N = 705$) of the interviewed mothers' children were also reassessed. Of the population not reassessed, about 7% had moved from Chicago, about 9% refused, and 6% of the teenagers were not assessed because data collection efforts ended prematurely due to lack of funds. In 1992–1993, 953 (77%) of the 1,242 members of the original cohort were reinterviewed: 39 (3.1%) refused, 46 (3.7%) had died ($N = 43$) or were incapacitated ($N = 3$), and 204 (16.4%) were not located.

In order to discover any possible bias resulting from sample attrition in 1976, the reinterviewed mothers were compared with those lost to follow-up, using early information available for both groups. The comparisons were made either by analysis of variance tests or by chi square tests. The mothers who could not be reinterviewed were more likely to have started childbearing in adolescence; they had been more mobile before and during the child's first-grade year, and their children were more likely to have been in parochial schools for first grade. (The centralized records of the Chicago public schools were very helpful in locating those who had moved.) The mothers did not differ in 1967 in their self-reports of sadness or nervousness, family income, welfare status, or number or types of adults at home.

We found no statistically significant differences between the children reinterviewed and those not reinterviewed on the first-grade social adaptational status, as assessed by teachers (these ratings are described in further detail later), or mothers' ratings of the children's psychological symptoms, as rated on Connors's (1970) symptom inventory. Nor were differences revealed by the mothers' reports of their teenagers' delinquency, alcohol and drug use, social contact, acceptance of authority, cognitive achievement, concentration, and seriousness about school. Maternal ratings of the teenagers' self-esteem and psychological symptoms did not differentiate those who were reinterviewed from those who were not. Mothers of the teenagers who were not reassessed rated their children as more immature. The reports of family and background characteristics showed no differences. However, mothers of reassessed teenagers reported that their families were more likely to express anger (Kellam, Simon, & Ensminger, 1983).

The best predictor of being found in the young adult follow-up was whether the family and the adolescent had been located in 1975–1976. There were few other differences. Those who were below the poverty line in first grade were slightly less likely to have been interviewed as a young adult. Those who were living with both parents in first grade were slightly more likely to have been interviewed.

Measures

Family origins. Family type, mother's education, participation in welfare, and whether the mother began childbearing as a teenager were included as measures of social origins. These were obtained from the mother in 1967 in a home interview.

School behavior and performance. School adaptational status in first grade was measured by both academic grades and teachers' ratings of children. Woodlawn first-grade teachers rated each child regarding adaptation along dimensions of shy behavior, aggressive behavior, and other classroom behaviors. Earlier, teachers had listed adaptive behaviors in these areas as necessary for children to be successful in accomplishing the tasks of first grade. They have also been shown in past research to be a good predictor of later problem behaviors for adolescent males, as well as for school dropout (Cairns, Cairns, & Neckerman, 1989; Ensminger 1990; Ensminger & Slusarcick 1992; Kellam, Ensminger, & Simon, 1980).

School grades, as given by the teachers at the end of first grade, are used as the measure of school achievement. Reading and arithmetic grades represent the central academic tasks of first grade. These two grades were highly correlated ($r = .75$); we chose the arithmetic grade as the indicator of early school progress.

Adolescent problem behavior. This refers to physical assault behaviors and marijuana and hard liquor use as a teenager. These were self-reported by the adolescents in an audio and visual questionnaire presentation (Petersen & Kellam, 1977). The physical assault items were 6 items from a 23-item delinquency scale and were summed together to make an assault scale (Cronbach alpha = .76 for males and .68 for females). Teenagers were asked about their frequency of drinking liquor and of using marijuana during their lifetimes. The rates they reported were comparable to those in other reports of adolescent drug use studied at the same time (Ensminger, 1990; Kellam, Ensminger, & Simon, 1980).

Adolescent social bonds. Much of the literature on how family characteristics influence teenage behaviors has been concerned with *parental supervision* and monitoring (Abrahamse, Morrison, & Waite, 1988; Loeber & Loeber 1986; Patterson, 1982). Parental supervision was measured by asking the adolescents what rules their parents had regarding drug use, time expected home on week nights, and schoolwork.

According to social control theory, attachment to important social institutions such as school and family is important in controlling deviant behavior (Hirschi, 1969). The more attached individuals feel to these institutions, the less likely they are to participate in deviant activities. *Attachment to school* was measured by asking the adolescents how important doing well in school was to them, how far they would like to go in school, how far they think they will go, how their teachers think they are doing, and how satisfied they are with their teachers' opinion (alpha = .68). *Attachment to mother* was measured by how close the adolescents said they felt to their mothers, how much they wanted to be like their mothers, and whether they confided in them (alpha = .58) (Ensminger, Brown, & Kellam, 1983).

Transitions to adulthood. The acquisition and time of entry into adult social roles are key developmental life events and are thought to play a role in several key outcomes in adulthood (Marini, 1987). For example, being married is thought to be protective in terms of drug use or participation in criminal activities (Knight, Osborn, & West, 1977; Sampson & Laub, 1993). It is also strongly associated with psychological well-being. Early role transitions may also impact later adult outcomes. Beginning childbearing as a teenager or leaving home before finishing school or becoming financially independent may also influence later trajectories to adulthood (Hogan & Astone, 1986). Although it has been examined less thoroughly, returning to the parental home after initially leaving may also reflect on the transition to adulthood.

Adult problem behaviors. During the adult interview, respondents were asked about the frequency and quantity of their use of 13 different substances. We made a 5-point measure of drugs ranging from never used a substance (= 1) to frequent use within the last year (= 5). In the analyses reported here, we examine the use of three drugs: alcohol, marijuana, and cocaine. Interpersonal aggression was measured by self-reports based on the frequency of aggressive acts toward others within the past year, such as carried gun or other weapon, got into a serious fight, used a weapon in a fight, purposely injured someone physically, engaged in a gang fight, used threats to get someone to give them something (alpha = .76). This involved a 6-point scale.

Adult social status. The poverty status of each person was determined according to criteria established by the government based on income and number of persons in the household. We used a 4-point scale to indicate the percentage of the respondents' poverty level, with 1 indicating at poverty and 4 indicating being at 200% of the poverty level. A Hollingshead scale that combined education with occupation was also used to indicate social status. This scale ranged from 1 to 5, with 1 being the highest level and 5 the lowest.

Anxiety. Anxiety was measured by summing seven 6-point Likert items asking respondents how they usually feel (nervous, feel under pressure, feel tense, my hands sometimes shake, new situations make me tense, feel tight inside or startle easily) (alpha = .85). Scores ranged from 1 to 6.

Number of children. The number of children of the respondents was intended to give some indication of the family circumstances of the respondents. The number of children ranged from zero to seven. Those who had four or more children were categorized as 4.

Data-analytic procedure

Our analytic strategy used information gathered in the adult follow-up at ages 31–33 (1992–1993) to construct homogeneous subgroups of individuals who had similar socioeconomic, behavioral, and psychological profiles at the most recent follow-up. Following Magnussen and Bergman (1988) and Cairns et al. (1989), males and females were grouped separately into seven clusters using a standard agglomerative clustering procedure. We describe the clusters and then examine the childhood and adolescent family, social, behavioral, and psychological antecedents to these clusters. We are interested primarily in identifying those early childhood and adolescent characteristics that put individuals at risk, as well as those that are protective.

We used the two steps of cluster analysis. The first step in a cluster analysis is the determination of the number of distinct groups. Hierarchical cluster analysis with agglomerative procedures (Aldenderfer & Blashfield, 1984) begins by placing each individual in a separate cluster. The two closest individuals are then combined to form a larger group. This step is repeated until a further merge results in significant loss of information. One mathematical value, the coefficient, was used to determine when to halt the merging process. Small coefficients indicate that fairly homogeneous clusters are being merged, whereas large coefficients indicate that clusters containing quite dissimilar members are being combined. There is a fairly large increase in the value of the distance measure from a seven-cluster to an eight-cluster solution. Thus, a seven-cluster solution was chosen to represent the data.

Following preliminary cluster analyses by hierarchical methods to identify the number of clusters, K-means cluster analysis with nearest centroid sorting (Anderberg, 1973) was used to determine cluster membership. This is calculated iteratively (Hawkins, Muller, & Kroden, 1982). That is, a case is grouped into the cluster with the closest center, and the cluster centers are recomputed. This procedure tends to produce fairly large clusters with widely separated centers. Eight variables were used in the clustering procedures to group individuals based on their similarities: poverty level (1–4), SES based on the Hollingshead index (1–5), number of children in the household (0–4), alcohol use (1–5), marijuana use (1–5), cocaine use (1–5), interpersonal aggression (1–

6), and anxious feelings (1–6). See Table 11.1 for the frequencies of these clustering variables.

Results

Cluster analysis used information on the population found in young adulthood to construct homogeneous subgroups, that is, statistical clusters of persons who had similar patterns in their drug use, interpersonal aggression, number of children, poverty, social status, and anxiety as adults aged 32–33. Males and females were grouped separately into seven clusters by employing a standard agglomerative hierarchical clustering procedure. A cluster analysis was completed for 497 females and 456 males.

Description of clusters

We describe the clusters of males first. The mean scores for the number of children, poverty level, and Hollingshead social status, and the standardized mean scores (mean of 0 and standard deviation of 1) for drug use, interpersonal aggression, and anxiety are shown in Table 11.2. The first three clusters are all low in the problem behaviors. They differ in other ways. Cluster 1 (18.6%, $N = 85$) is composed of males who are high in terms of economic and social resources. This cluster also has lower rates of drug use and interpersonal aggression than any other cluster (high SES, low problems). Cluster 2 (12.5%, $N = 57$) is differentiated from other clusters in terms of the number of children present in the households of these cluster members. There was a mean number of 2.79 children; the next highest mean number of children for any of the clusters was .92, and all the others were below .50. It was high middle in terms of SES, and had low drug use and interpersonal aggression (middle SES, high number of children, low problem behavior).

Cluster 3 (15.8%, $N = 72$) was composed of males who were poor – their mean poverty level was only slightly higher than their actual poverty level; however, their rates of substance use were below the mean level for all three substances (low SES, low problem behavior). Cluster 4 (22.4%, $N = 102$), the most frequent of the seven clusters, was similar in SES to cluster 1 but had higher alcohol use than average (high SES, high alcohol).

Table 11.1. *Cluster analysis variables (N = 953)*

	Response level	Percent
Poverty index	<100%	35.6
	<150%	9.9
	<200%	7.8
	>200%	46.8
SES status	I (high)	3.9
	II	13.2
	III	37.4
	IV	33.9
	V	11.6
Number of children	0	44.6
in household	1	19.3
	2	20.0
	3	10.3
	4+	5.8
Alcohol use	Never	5.9
	Used, not year	35.2
	Light, last year	7.3
	Mod, last year	26.2
	Heavy, last year	25.4
Marijuana use	Never	42.6
	Used, not year	37.6
	Light, last year	6.7
	Mod, last year	8.0
	Heavy, last year	5.1
Cocaine use	Never	74.8
	Used, not year	15.5
	Light, last year	4.0
	Mod, last year	2.5
	Heavy, last year	3.1
Interpersonal aggression	None	79.7
(times in past year)	1–2	6.1
	3–6	3.8
	7–14	2.4
	15	5.7
	16+	2.3
Anxious feelings	1	21.3
	2	48.2
	3	21.8
	4	5.7
	5	2.1
	6	0.9

Table 11.2. *Woodlawn male clusters, ages 32–33 (rank)*

Cluster[a] % (N)	No. of Child	Poverty	SES	Alcohol	Marij	Cocaine	Aggress	Anxiety
1 18.6% (85)	0.39	3.85	3.13	−1.01	−0.69	−0.47	−0.83	−0.38
Hi SES, lo PB	(4)[b]	(1)	(1)	(1)	(1)	(1)	(1)	(1)
2 12,5% (57)	2.79	2.81	3.19	−0.31	−0.44	−0.46	−0.48	−0.20
Mid SES, hi Child, lo PB	(7)	(3)	(3)	(3)	(3)	(3)	(3)	(2)
3 15.8% (72)	0.24	1.17	3.86	−0.34	−0.49	−0.46	−0.62	0.08
Lo SES, lo PB	(2)	(7)	(5)	(2)	(2)	(2.5)	(2)	(4)
4 22.4% (102)	0.25	3.80	3.11	0.65	0.02	0.00	0.04	−0.05
Hi SES, hi alc	(3)	(2)	(2)	(6)	(4)	(5)	(5)	(3)
5 10.5% (48)	0.48	1.48	4.04	0.62	1.54	0.84	−0.08	0.12
Lo SES, hi drug	(5)	(6)	(6)	(5)	(7)	(6)	(4)	(5)
6 14.5% (66)	0.92	2.06	3.73	0.20	0.05	−0.15	1.48	0.16
Lo SES, hi agg	(6)	(5)	(4)	(4)	(5)	(4)	(6)	(6)
7 5.7% (26)	0.23	2.19	4.15	0.75	1.52	2.64	1.69	1.04
Lo SES, hi PB, hi anx	(1)	(4)	(7)	(7)	(6)	(7)	(7)	(7)
Total mean (456)	0.71	2.68	3.49	0.00	0.00	0.00	0.00	0.00
(s.d.)	(1.13)	(1.36)	(0.99)	(1.00)	(1.00)	(1.00)	(1.00)	(1.00)

[a]SES = socioeconomic status; PB = problem behavior (drug use and interpersonal aggression); agg = interpersonal aggression; anx = anxiety.
[b]Rank 1 = fewest children, lowest poverty, highest SES, lowest use of substances, lowest interpersonal aggression, and lowest anxiety.

Cluster 5 (10.5%, $N = 48$) was composed of poor males; these males were high on substance use but not on interpersonal aggression (low SES, high drug use). The males in cluster 6 (14.5%, $N = 66$) were most noteworthy in their high mean of interpersonal aggression (low SES, high aggression). It is important to note that this cluster does not have elevated rates of substance use. Cluster 7 (5.7%, $N = 26$) included those males who had the highest cocaine use; they were also high in marijuana use and in interpersonal aggression, and they reported the highest level of anxiety (low SES, high problem behavior). Cluster 7 perhaps represents the stereotype portrayed in the media (and in some scientific publications as well) of the African American male who grows up in the inner city: high substance use and high interpersonal aggression. In this regard, it is important to point out that this is the least frequent of the clusters, with only 5.7% of the males included.

Table 11.3. *Woodlawn male clusters by adolescent problem behaviors (ranks)*

	% heavy marij	% heavy liquor	% high assault
1 (49)	20%	12%	23%
Hi SES, lo PB	(3)	(3.5)	(1)
2 (36)	17%	6%	34%
Mid SES, hi child, lo PB	(1)	(1)	(5)
3 (43)	19%	12%	31%
Lo SES, lo PB	(2)	(3.5)	(4)
4 (65)	31%	13%	29%
Hi SES, hi alc	(4)	(5)	(3)
5 (37)	36%	11%	24%
Lo SES, hi drug	(5)	(2)	(2)
6 (42)	41%	27%	60%
Lo SES, hi agg	(6)	(6)	(6)
7 (16)	56%	25%	67%
Lo SES, hi PB, hi anx	(7)	(7)	(7)
Total (286)	29.0%	14.0%	34.9%
	$p < .02$	NS	$p < .002$

SES = socioeconomic status; PB = problem behavior (drug use and interpersonal aggression); agg = interpersonal aggression; anx = anxiety.
Rank 1 = lowest percentage.

The cluster analysis differentiated the males by their socioeconomic resources and their problem behaviors. In terms of problem behaviors, one cluster (7) had high levels of both substance use and interpersonal aggression; one cluster (6) had high rates of interpersonal aggression but not substance use; and one cluster (5) had high rates of substance use but average rates of interpersonal aggression. These three clusters were all relatively poor and lower in status. Only one of the three relatively upper-status male clusters had high levels of one of the problem behaviors (4): alcohol use.

The question becomes whether these clusters differed in their adolescent problem behaviors, in their social control during adolescence, or in their transition to adulthood. Problem behaviors during adolescence are shown in Table 11.3 for the males. In general, the relationship between adolescent problem behavior status and later problems is consistent across time. Clusters 6 and 7 were the highest in adolescent problem behaviors. In general, Clusters 1–5 did not differ dramatically in their adolescent behaviors but did differ from Clusters 6 and 7. For example, the percentage of males who had self-reports of high assault as adolescents ranged from 23% to 34% in clusters 1–5, whereas Clusters 6 and 7 had 60% and 67%, respectively, who reported high assault behaviors as adolescents. This same pattern existed for adolescent heavy use of hard liquor and, to a lesser extent, for heavy use of marijuana. Those adults who reported high interpersonal aggression as adults but were not high in substance use (Cluster 6) were similar in their adolescent substance use behaviors to those adults who reported high substance use and high interpersonal aggression (Cluster 7). On the other hand, those adults who reported high substance use (Cluster 5) as adults but not high interpersonal aggression were more similar to Clusters 1–4 in their adolescent behaviors than to those clusters high in interpersonal aggression (6 and 7).

Next, we examine the family origins of the clusters. In the interviews with the mothers in first grade and during adolescence, we asked the mothers about their education, whether they were on welfare, the age at which they had begun childbearing, the frequency with which they moved, and the adult composition of the family. Using this information, we then examined the clusters of males. The adult clusters were differentiated by mothers' education, receipt of welfare, and the frequency with which the families had moved between first grade and adolescence. See Table 11.4.

The males in Clusters 1 and 4 who had the highest SES ratings as adults also had the highest percentage of mothers who had graduated from high school, the lowest percentage who had received welfare, and the lowest frequency of moving. Males in Cluster 3 who had the lowest SES as adults also had the lowest SES family origins; their mothers were least likely to have graduated from high school, most likely to have received welfare, and most likely to have moved frequently. Males in Cluster 2 who as adults had high SES scores did not come from families with high SES origins. They were in the middle in terms of their mothers' education, a high percentage of their mothers had received welfare, and a high percentage had moved frequently. Cluster 2, then, had relatively low social origins but as adults had relatively high SES ratings.

We examined the clusters by adolescent measures of family supervi-

Table 11.4. *Woodlawn male clusters by family origins (ranks)*

	% on welfare	% mother not HS grad	% moved frequently
1 (85)	41%	54%	37%
Hi SES, lo PB	(2)	(2)	(2)
2 (57)	60%	63%	54%
Mid SES, hi child, lo PB	(5)	(4)	(6)
3 (72)	66%	74%	61%
Lo SES, lo PB	(7)	(7)	(7)
4 (102)	40%	48%	33%
Hi SES, hi alc	(1)	(1)	(1)
5 (48)	57%	65%	52%
Lo SES, hi drug	(4)	(5)	(5)
6 (66)	61%	61%	46%
Lo SES, hi agg	(6)	(3)	(3)
7 (26)	50%	69%	48%
Lo SES, hi PB, hi anx	(3)	(6)	(4)
Total (456)	52%	60%	45.9%
	p < .02	*p* < .02	*p* < .02

SES = socioeconomic status; PB = problem behavior (drug use and interpersonal aggression); agg = interpersonal aggression; anx = anxiety.
Rank 1 = lowest percentage.

sion, family attachment, and school bonds. These were reported by the respondents when they were adolescents. Having stricter drug rules, stricter curfew rules, and stronger bonds to school were related to cluster membership as adults. See Table 11.5. Males in Clusters 1 and 2 reported stricter supervision by parents and stronger bonds to school than other males. This is particularly noteworthy for Cluster 2 males who came from family backgrounds with few social resources. Males in Clusters 6 and 7 as adolescents reported less parental supervision.

We also examined markers of the transition to adulthood by cluster membership: the age at which one left the parental home, whether the men were married, and whether they had ever rejoined the household of their parents after leaving home. Although current incarceration was not a marker of the transition to adulthood, we also examined this factor by the clusters. See Table 11.6. Cluster 2 stands out; only 9% of the males in this cluster were not married – compared to the next

Table 11.5 *Woodlawn male clusters by adolescent social bonds (ranks)*

	% strict drug rules	% strict curfew	% strong school bonds
1 (49)	35%	35%	47%
Hi SES, lo PB	(5.5)	(7)	(6)
2 (36)	44%	33%	61%
Mid SES, hi child, lo PB	(7)	(6)	(7)
3 (43)	28%	19%	23%
Lo SES, lo PB	(4)	(3)	(3)
4 (65)	35%	32%	37%
Hi SES, hi alc	(5.5)	(4.5)	(4)
5 (37)	19%	32%	19%
Lo SES, hi drug	(2.5)	(4.5)	(1)
6 (42)	19%	10%	21%
Lo SES, hi agg	(2.5)	(1)	(2)
7 (16)	13%	13%	44%
Lo SES, hi PB, hi anx	(1)	(2)	(5)
Total (286)	30%	27%	35%
	$p < .07$	$p < .03$	$p < .005$

SES = socioeconomic status; PB = problem behavior (drug use and interpersonal aggression); agg = interpersonal aggression; anx = anxiety.
Rank 1 = lowest percentage.

highest proportion of 65%. None of the males in Cluster 2 were incarcerated. They also had the lowest percentage who had left home before age 16 and the lowest percentage who had rejoined the households of their parents. Cluster 1 had the next "best" rank in terms of these transition indicators. Clusters 3–7 varied in their rankings on these indicators. Cluster 6 (low SES, high interpersonal aggression) had by far the highest percentage of those who were incarcerated – over one-fifth. Cluster 3, which ranked low in both substance use and interpersonal aggression but had the lowest SES, had the next highest group who were incarcerated.

When we go back to earlier stages in the life course – first grade – we also find differences among the clusters. Aggressive behavior, as rated by teachers in first grade, differentiated among the clusters. The proportion of aggressive children in Clusters 3, 6, and 7 (46–49%) was higher than in the other clusters. Cluster 1 had the lowest proportion

Table 11.6 *Woodlawn male clusters by adolescent transitions (ranks)*

	% left home before 16	% rejoined mother's house	% not married	% incarcerated
1 (85)	9%	39%	65%	2.4%
Hi SES, lo PB	(2)	(2)	(2)	(2)
2 (57)	4%	37%	9%	0%
Mid SES, hi child, lo PB	(1)	(1)	(1)	(1)
3 (72)	16%	61%	94%	8.3%
Lo SES, lo PB	(4)	(4)	(7)	(6)
4 (102)	14%	65%	72%	4.9%
Hi SES, hi alc	(3)	(6)	(4)	(5)
5 (48)	17%	67%	85%	4.2%
Lo SES, hi drug	(5)	(7)	(5)	(4)
6 (66)	22%	62%	67%	22.7%
Lo SES, hi agg	(6)	(5)	(3)	(7)
7 (26)	23%	50%	88%	3.8%
Lo SES, hi PB, hi anx	(7)	(3)	(6)	(3)
Total (456)	14%	55%	68%	6.8%
	$p < .005$	$p < .000$	$p < .000$	$p < .000$

SES = socioeconomic status; PB = problem behavior (drug use and interpersonal aggression); agg = interpersonal aggression; anx = anxiety.
Rank 1 = Lowest percentage.

who were rated as aggressive by their first-grade teachers (22%). (These data are not shown.) First-grade arithmetic grades did not differentiate among the clusters.

Next, we turn to the females. The cluster analysis clearly differentiated the females by social and economic resources and by number of children. Table 11.7 shows these results. Clusters 1, 3, and 5 were all high in terms of their economic resources and a lower mean number of children. Clusters 2, 4, 6, and 7 were all low in socioeconomic resources; three of the four clusters had a large number of children (cluster 7 is the exception). Clusters 1 (27.1%, $N = 135$) and 2 (17.9%, $N = 89$) both had low substance use and low levels of aggression; they differed from one another in SES. These two clusters together represent 45% of the total population of females.

Clusters 3 (16.5%, $N = 82$) and 4 (16.7%, $N = 83$) both had relatively high levels of alcohol use and low levels of aggression but

Table 11.7. *Woodlawn female clusters, ages 32–33 (rank)*

Cluster (N)[a]	No. of Child	Poverty	SES	Alcohol	Marij	Cocaine	Aggress	Anxiety
1 27.1% (135)	1.23	3.86	2.83	−0.88	−0.43	−0.40	−0.43	−0.28
Hi SES, lo PB	(3)[b]	(2)	(2)	(6)	(1)	(17)	(3)	(1)
2 17.9% (89)	1.85	1.25	3.57	−0.92	−0.34	−0.23	−0.47	−0.10
Lo SES, lo PB	(6)	(6)	(5)	(1)	(2)	(2)	(2)	(2)
3 16.5% (82)	1.13	3.88	2.82	0.88	0.02	−0.16	−0.52	0.11
Hi SES, hi alc	(2)	(1)	(4)	(6)	(5)	(3)	(1)	(5.5)
4 16.7% (83)	2.27	1.20	3.77	1.07	0.35	−0.03	−0.24	−0.08
Lo SES, hi alc	(7)	(7)	(6)	(7)	(6)	(5)	(4)	(3)
5 9.9% (49)	0.98	3.71	2.80	0.58	−0.05	0.05	1.23	0.11
Hi SES, hi agg	(1)	(3)	(1)	(5)	(3)	(6)	(5)	(5.5)
6 5.6% (28)	1.75	1.29	3.54	−0.22	−0.02	−0.12	1.99	0.69
Lo SES, hi agg	(5)	(5)	(4)	(3)	(4)	(4)	(7)	(7)
7 6.2% (31)	1.48	1.35	4.29	0.54	1.95	2.95	1.51	0.63
Lo SES, hi PB	(4)	(4)	(7)	(4)	(7)	(7)	(6)	(6)
Total mean (497)	1.52	2.64	3.25	0.00	0.00	0.00	0.00	0.00
(s.d.)	(1.23)	(1.37)	(0.95)	(1.00)	(1.00)	(1.00)	(1.00)	(1.00)

[a]SES = socioeconomic status; PB = problem behavior (drug use and interpersonal aggression); agg = interpersonal aggression; anx = anxiety.
[b]Rank 1 = fewest children, lowest poverty, highest SES, lowest use of substances, lowest interpersonal aggression, and lowest anxiety.

differed in SES. Clusters 5 (9.9%, $N = 49$) and 6 (6.2%, $N = 28$) had relatively high levels of aggression and moderate to low levels of substance use; they differed in terms of SES. Cluster 7 (6.2%, $N = 31$) had high levels of both interpersonal aggression and substance use. As for the males, problem behaviors in adolescence were related to cluster membership as adults. See Table 11.8. Clusters 5, 6, and 7 reported having the most problem behaviors as adolescents. The proportion who had reported high assault was at least twice as high in Cluster 7 as in any of the other clusters. Cluster 6, which reported high levels of interpersonal aggression as adults, did not report especially high levels of assault as adolescents.

All the social origin indicators reported by mothers in 1967 or 1975 differentiated among the female clusters. See Table 11.9. Cluster 6 had the lowest origins; it had the highest proportion of mother-headed fam-

Table 11.8. *Woodlawn female clusters by adolescent problem behaviors (ranks)*

	% heavy marij	% heavy liquor	% high assault
1 (88)	2%	1%	8%
Hi SES, lo PB	(1)	(1)	(3.5)
2 (59)	13%	2%	16%
Lo SES, lo PB	(3)	(2.5)	(5)
3 (52)	4%	6%	0%
Hi SES, hi alc	(2)	(4)	(1)
4 (47)	17%	2%	4%
Lo SES, hi alc	(5)	(2.5)	(2)
5 (27)	15%	22%	19%
Hi SES, hi agg	(4)	(7)	(6)
6 (16)	25%	19%	8%
Lo SES, hi agg	(6)	(6)	(3.5)
7 (21)	33%	14%	37%
Lo SES, hi PB	(7)	(5)	(7)
Total (310)	11.2%	5.8%	10.3%
	$p < .000$	$p < .000$	$p < .000$

SES = socioeconomic status; PB = problem behavior (drug use and interpersonal aggression); agg = interpersonal aggression; anx = anxiety.
Rank 1 = lowest percentage.

ilies, teenage mothers, and mothers without a high school education and the next highest proportion of mothers who had received welfare. The three clusters with the highest social origins were not those with the lowest levels of problem behaviors as adults; Clusters 3, 5, and 7 had the highest social origins as children but had either high alcohol use, high aggression, or high scores on both as adults. Clusters 1 and 2, which had the lowest rates of adult problem behaviors, were in the middle range in social origin.

In terms of their social bonds as adolescents, school bonds, attachment to mother, and supervision regarding drugs differentiated among the female clusters. See Table 11.10. The proportion of Cluster 7 who reported strict supervision regarding drug use was one-half that of any other cluster – 14% compared to 34%. Those in Cluster 7 were over twice as likely to report low attachment to their mothers as the next closest cluster (45% compared to 21%) (not shown in the table; it

Table 11.9. *Woodlawn female clusters by family origin (ranks)*

	% mother alone	% teen mother	% on welfare	% mother not HS grad
1 (135)	33%	41%	44%	54%
Hi SES, lo PB	(4)	(3)	(3)	(4)
2 (89)	37%	51%	57%	61%
Lo SES, lo PB	(5)	(6)	(5)	(5)
3 (82)	28%	40%	29%	52%
Hi SES, hi alc	(1)	(2)	(1)	(2.5)
4 (83)	41%	49%	64%	68%
Lo SES, hi alc	(6)	(5)	(7)	(6)
5 (49)	29%	39%	48%	37%
Hi SES, hi agg	(3)	(1)	(4)	(1)
6 (28)	46%	74%	59%	71%
Lo SES, hi agg	(7)	(7)	(6)	(7)
7 (31)	29%	48%	33%	52%
Lo SES, hi PB	(2)	(4)	(2)	(2.5)
Total (497)	34.2%	45.9%	47.6%	56.4%
	$p < .02$	$p < .05$	$p < .01$	$p < .005$

SES = socioeconomic status; PB = problem behavior (drug use and interpersonal aggression); agg = interpersonal aggression; anx = anxiety.
Rank 1 = lowest percentage.

shows high attachment rather than low). Females in Clusters 1 and 3 were particularly likely to report strong bonds to school as adolescents – 60% and 52%, respectively, compared to 38% for the next highest cluster.

Cluster membership was also strongly related to adult transitions for the females. Those in Clusters 1 and 3 were less likely to have become pregnant or left home before age 16, less likely to have rejoined the households of their parents, and more likely to have married. See Table 11.11. Those in Clusters 4, 6, and 7 were at the other end of the scale on these indicators.

First-grade aggressive behavior did not differentiate among the clusters, although arithmetic grades did. (These data are not shown.) The proportion receiving A's or B's in arithmetic in first grade was particularly high in Cluster 3 (64%) and low in Clusters 2 (38%) and 6 (31%).

Table 11.10. *Woodlawn female clusters by adolescent social bonds (ranks)*

	% strict drug rules	% strong school bonds	% high attachment to mother
1 (89)	51%	60%	45%
Hi SES, lo PB	(7)	(7)	(5)
2 (60)	38%	37%	61%
Lo SES, lo PB	(3)	(4)	(7)
3 (52)	40%	52%	47%
Hi SES, hi alc	(4)	(6)	(6)
4 (47)	34%	26%	31%
Lo SES, hi alc	(2)	(1)	(1)
5 (27)	44%	30%	34%
Hi SES, hi agg	(5)	(2)	(2)
6 (16)	50%	38%	44%
Lo SES, hi agg	(6)	(5)	(4)
7 (21)	14%	33%	35%
Lo SES, hi PB	(1)	(3)	(3)
Total (312)	41%	43.4%	44.5%
	$p < .08$	$p < .02$	$p < .02$

SES = socioeconomic status; PB = problem behavior (drug use and interpersonal aggression); agg = interpersonal aggression.

Summary of results

Problem behaviors (*adult*). These cluster analyses indicate that the patterning of problem behaviors varies. One cluster shows the overlapping of substance use and interpersonal aggression for both males and females, but other clusters show high levels of one problem behavior but not of the other.

Socioeconomic status (*adult*). Although in general, for the males, those clusters that had high levels of problem behaviors tended to be lower in SES and poorer, there were upper-status clusters that had higher than average alcohol use. In the case of males, none of the three clusters with high aggression or high cocaine use were upper status. However, the reverse was not true; the cluster with the highest mean poverty ranked low in all the problem behaviors. For the females, the clusters

Table 11.11. *Woodlawn female clusters by adolescent transitions (ranks)*

	% left home before 16	% rejoined mother's house	% not married	% pregnant, age 11–16
1 (135)	2%	45%	59%	8%
Hi SES, lo PB	(1)	(1)	(1)	(1)
2 (89)	11%	51%	85%	28%
Lo SES, lo PB	(3)	(3)	(4)	(4)
3 (82)	7%	47%	71%	16%
Hi SES, hi alc	(2)	(2)	(3)	(2)
4 (83)	19%	68%	89%	42%
Lo SES, hi alc	(6)	(6.5)	(5)	(6)
5 (49)	14%	67%	67%	25%
Hi SES, hi agg	(4)	(4.5)	(2)	(3)
6 (28)	18%	67%	93%	46%
Lo SES, hi agg	(5)	(4.5)	(6.5)	(7)
7 (31)	29%	68%	93%	32%
Lo SES, hi PB	(7)	(6.5)	(6.5)	(5)
Total (497)	10.9%	55.5%	73.7%	24%
	$p < .000$	$p < .001$	$p < .000$	$p < .000$

SES = socioeconomic status; PB = problem behavior (drug use and interpersonal aggression); agg = interpersonal aggression; anx = anxiety.
Rank 1 = lowest percentage.

showed a higher and a lower status cluster for similar problem behavior rankings. For example, there was a higher-status, high-aggression cluster (5) and a lower-status, high-aggression cluster (6).

Adolescent problem behaviors. Adolescent males who reported high problem behaviors were more likely to report such behaviors as adults. This correspondence tended to occur among the females, but it was not as consistent as for the males. For example, the two female clusters that reported high alcohol use as adults (3, 4) ranked relatively low in their self-reports of alcohol use as adolescents.

Family origins. In general, family origins in childhood and adolescence related to the relative rankings of SES as adults for both males and females. There were some important exceptions. One male cluster (2) had relatively low social origins, but as adults their mean poverty and

SES ratings were hardly distinguishable from those of the highest clusters. For the females, Cluster 7 started with relatively high social origins, but as adults ranked as one of the poorest clusters, with low SES ratings. This cluster also had high problem behaviors. We have examples, then, of both upward and downward social mobility in the clusters.

Adolescent social bonds. For both males and females, the social bonds evidenced during adolescence related to how these people did as adults. For the males in Cluster 2 who, based on their early social origins, were not likely to have successful outcomes as adults, a clear protective factor was their attachment to school and parental supervision as adolescents. For both the males and females, those who ended up with high problem behaviors were likely to be less attached to family and school as adolescents.

Adolescent transitions. For the males, the timing and occurrence of the transition to adulthood were clearly related to adult status. Although not leaving home before the age of 16 predicted being in a higher-status, lower-problem behavior cluster, rejoining the parental household after leaving it was related to higher problem behaviors and lower social status as adults for both the males and females. Early pregnancy and marriage seemed more related to the social status rankings than to the problem behaviors for the females.

Conclusions

What do we conclude from these results? First, analyzing these longitudinal data by grouping individuals based on their responses to a variety of variables, rather than by examining the variances of variables, informs us about the patterns of these events in the lives of individuals. Although one cluster scored high on all of the problem behaviors we examined, there were also individuals who were high on substance use but not interpersonal aggression or vice versa. Although these variables (substance use and interpersonal aggression) are highly correlated, the results show that there are substantial proportions of both males and females who are high on one but not the other.

In this population, which began their schooling in a poor neighborhood, social and economic resources were related to problem behaviors, but those with the lowest social origins were not necessarily those at highest risk. There were clusters that were very low in resources but also very low in problem behaviors. For the males, most of the clusters that were high in at least one of the problem behaviors were also low in resources. This was not the case for the females. Those with the lowest problems were in the middle in social origin.

Clearly, the clusters in adulthood were related to adolescent problem behaviors and social bonds. What was apparent was the protectiveness of high social bonds and low problem behaviors for males who had lower social origins (those in Cluster 2). Although in general higher social origins seemed related to higher social bonding in adolescence, those adolescents with higher social origins who had problem behaviors as adults seemed to have few social bonds as adolescents. They had lower school attachment and less parental supervision. This seemed to put them at risk.

Cluster 2 males were quite distinct, having a large number of children, high rates of marriage, low rates of incarceration, and low adult problem behaviors. These males did not have high social origins as children and adolescents. Protective factors seemed to be present in the families of these males and in their school attachment; they reported very high parental supervision as adolescents and higher bonds to school than any of the other clusters. It is interesting to contrast this cluster with another cluster of males who also reported low problem behaviors as adults in spite of having very low social origins as children and adolescents. These males, even though they had low problem behaviors as adults, showed no SES advantage as adults; they had the lowest SES ranks and were least likely to be married. This cluster was the second highest in incarceration rates. So, although they might be evaluated as successful if we were examining only their self-reports of substance use or interpersonal aggression, in terms of other indicators they would not rank high. They did not have the advantage of having high parental supervision as adolescents. Although they did not report high problem behaviors as adolescents, they also did not report having high bonds to school. As adolescents, they had the highest proportion of any cluster who reported high psychological symptoms. The two clusters contrasted quite strongly on marriage, with over 90% of Cluster 2 being married compared to 4% of Cluster 3. Marriage is likely to have been the result of earlier adaptation and family involvement, as well as perhaps being protective and advantageous with regard to later social resources.

The small cluster of males who reported the highest involvement in problem behaviors as adults were not those with the lowest SES origins, but they were the ones with the highest rates of problem behaviors as adolescents and high rates of aggressive behavior in first grade. They reported the lowest parental supervision as adolescents.

The findings presented here provide some understanding of the process by which young people from disadvantaged circumstances may begin to avoid problematic outcomes and improve their social circumstances after growing up in an inner-city community with few opportunities and racial discrimination. Having a supportive family seems to be a key factor. Those with strong family supervision and involvement seem to be protected in terms of both adult problem behaviors and adult social resources. The findings indicate that those at risk of having problematic adult outcomes can be identified relatively early; some indications were notable as early as first grade. During adolescence, risk factors and protective factors were identified that could be used to suggest interventions.

Importantly, the pattern-oriented approach illustrated what many have been calling for in the adolescent literature – an approach that examines people both in terms of their social context and in terms of their behavior patterns. This approach led us to focus not on specific individual risk factors but on combinations of characteristics of individuals that would lead to a better understanding of how behavior and social contexts are integrated into developmental trends. We hope this approach has helped to begin to fill the gap in our knowledge about young people who grow up in disadvantaged circumstances, and to illustrate the advantage of trying to examine the complexity of human behavior by focusing on patterns that exist in people's lives.

References

Abrahamse, A. F., Morrison, P. A., & Waite, L. J. (1988). *Beyond stereotypes: Who becomes a single teenage mother?* Santa Monica, CA: Rand.

Aldenderfer, M. A., & Blashfield, R. K. (1984). *Cluster analysis.* Beverly Hills, CA: Sage.

390   *Margaret E. Ensminger and Hee Soon Juon*

Anderberg, M. R. (1973). *Cluster analysis for applications.* New York: Academic Press.

Cairns, R. B., Cairns, B. D., & Neckerman, H. J. (1989). Early school dropout: Configurations and determinants. *Child Development, 60,* 1437–1452.

Connors, C. K. (1970). Symptom patterns in hyperkinetic, neurotic and normal children. *Child Development, 41,* 667–682.

DeVise. P. (1967). *Chicago's widening color gap.* Interuniversity School Research Committee Report No. 2. Chicago: Chicago Regional Hospital Study.

Donovan, J. E., Jessor, R., & Jessor, L. (1983). Problem drinking in adolescence and young adulthood. A follow-up study. *Journal of Studies on Alcohol, 44*(1), 109–137.

Ensminger, M. E. (1990). Sexual activity and problem behaviors among black, urban adolescents. *Child Development, 61,* 2032–2046.

Ensminger, M. E., & Slusarcick, A. L. (1992). Pathways to high school graduation or dropout: A longitudinal study of a first grade cohort. *Sociology of Education, 65,* 95–113.

Farrington, D. P. (1983). Offending from 10 to 25 years of age. In K. T. VanDusen & S. A. Mednick (Eds.), *Prospective studies of crime and delinquency* (pp. 73–97). Boston: Kluwer-Nijoff.

Hawkins, D., Muller, M., & Kroden, J. (1982). Cluster analysis. In D. Hawkins (Ed.), *Topics in applied multivariate analysis* (pp. 301–351). Cambridge: Cambridge University Press.

Hirschi, T. (1969). *Causes of delinquency.* Berkeley: University of California Press.

Hogan, D. P., & Astone, N. M. (1986). The transition to adulthood. *Annual Review of Sociology, 12,* 109–130.

Jessor, R. (1993). Successful adolescent development among youth in high-risk settings. *American Psychologist, 48*(2), 117–126.

Kandel, D. B., Simcha-Fagan, O., & Davies, M. (1986). Risk factors for delinquency and illicit drug use from adolescence to young adulthood. *Journal of Drug Issues, 16,* 67–90.

Kellam, S. G., Branch, J. D., Agrawal, K. C., & Ensminger, M. E. (1975). *Mental health and going to school: The Woodlawn program of assessment, early intervention, and evaluation.* Chicago: University of Chicago Press.

Kellam, S. G., Ensminger, M. E., & Simon, M. B. (1980). Mental health in first grade and teenage drug, alcohol, and cigarette use. *Drug and Alcohol Dependence, 5,* 273–304.

Kellam, S. G., Ensminger, M. E., & Turner, R. J. (1977). Family structure and the mental health of children. *Archives of General Psychiatry 34,* 1012–1022.

Kellam, S. G., Simon, M. B., & Ensminger, M. E. (1983). Antecedents in first grade of teenage drug use and psychological well-being: A ten year community-wide prospective study. In D. F. Ricks & B. S. Dohrenwend (Eds.), *Origins of psychopathology: Research and public policy* (pp. 17–42). New York: Cambridge University Press.

Knight, F. J., Osborn, S. G., & West, D. J. (1977). Early marriage and criminal tendency in males. *British Journal of Criminology, 17,* 348–360.

Loeber, R., & Loeber, M. S. (1986). Family factors as correlates and predictors of juvenile conduct problems and delinquency. In M. Tonry & N. Morris (Eds.), *Crime and justice* (pp. 29–149). Chicago: University of Chicago Press.

Magnusson, D., & Bergman, L. R. (1988). Individual and variable-based approaches to longitudinal research on early risk factors. In M. Rutter (Ed.), *Studies of psychosocial risk: The power of longitudinal data* (pp. 45–61). Cambridge: Cambridge University Press.

Marini, M. M. (1987). Measuring the process of role change during the transition to adulthood. *Social Science Research, 16,* 1–38.

National Research Council. (1993). *Losing generations: Adolescents in high risk settings.* Washington, DC: National Academy Press.

Patterson, G. R. (1982). *Coercive family processes.* Eugene, OR: Castalia.

Petersen, A. C., & Kellam, S. G. (1977). Measurement of the psychological well-being of adolescents: The psychometric properties and assessment procedures of the How I Feel. *Journal of Youth and Adolescence, 6,* 229–247.

Sampson, R. J., & Laub, J. H. (1993). *Crime in the making: Pathways and turning points through life.* Cambridge, MA: Harvard University Press.

12

Disengagement from school and problem behavior in adolescence: A developmental-contextual analysis of the influences of family and part-time work

Laurence Steinberg and Shelli Avenevoli

The study of adolescent risk behavior has developed through several distinct stages in its relatively brief history. Prior to the mid-1970s, various problem behaviors, such as substance use, delinquent activity, aggression, school failure, depression, and sexual precocity, were studied mainly as isolated phenomena, independent of each other; researchers studied drug use *or* delinquency, sexual precocity *or* academic failure, aggression *or* depression. Few, if any, studies took a developmental approach; more often than not, adolescents who were categorized as having a particular problem (e.g., delinquency) were compared to their peers who did not, with little attention devoted to understanding the processes through which problem behaviors emerged, accelerated, or disappeared over time. And few, if any, researchers attempted to understand adolescent problem behavior within a contextual framework. With the exception of a small number of sociological studies of delinquency, few writers located the causes of problem behavior within the context in which adolescents lived; more typically, problem behaviors

Preparation of this manuscript was supported by grants to the first author from the William T. Grant Foundation and from the MacArthur Foundation Research Network on Psychopathology and Development. The study on which this report is based was supported by grants to Laurence Steinberg and B. Bradford Brown from the U.S. Department of Education, through the National Center on Effective Secondary Schools at the University of Wisconsin-Madison, and to Sanford M. Dornbusch and P. Herbert Leiderman of the Stanford University Center for Families, Children, and Youth, from the Spencer Foundation.

were studied in relation to the individual characteristics – personality, intelligence, attitudes – of the troubled adolescents.

The past two decades have ushered in remarkable conceptual advances in the ways in which researchers and theorists think about adolescent problem behavior and risk-taking, however. Three themes, in particular, have emerged that have had a profound influence on research in the area. First, it has become apparent that there exists substantial covariation within and across different domains of problem behavior and, accordingly, that studies of problem behavior must be informed by a holistic perspective that combines person-centered with variable-centered approaches. Second, it has become evident that the emergence and consolidation of problem behavior is often patterned in a way that follows a predictable developmental trajectory or pathway; as a consequence, that problem behavior must be studied over time. Finally, it is clear that the development of problem behavior during adolescence must be viewed not only in terms of characteristics of the individual adolescent but also as a function of an interaction between the adolescent and the context in which he or she lives; not only are there risk-prone adolescents, there are also risk-prone contexts. Let us examine each of these themes briefly and consider their implications for the scientific study of adolescent problem behavior among contemporary social scientists.

The recognition that there is considerable covariation among adolescent problem behaviors sparked the development of several different frameworks aimed at describing and explaining the nature of the linkages among different types of adolescent problems. Why is it the case that adolescents who violate the law are more likely than their peers to have problems in school? Why is it that drug use and sexual precocity appear to be significantly correlated? One set of explanations, perhaps best exemplified by Jessor's problem behavior theory (Jessor & Jessor, 1977), emphasizes the underlying personality characteristics of risk takers as the psychological force that accounts for the co-occurrence of different types of problems. Within problem behavior theory, the underlying cause of externalizing problems in adolescence is *unconventionality*, both in the adolescent's personality and in his or her social environment. According to this model, unconventional individuals (i.e., those who are tolerant of deviance, extremely liberal in their social views, and not connected to schools or religious institutions) in unconventional environments (i.e., contexts in which a large number of individuals are unconventional) are far more likely to engage in risk-taking.

Although not all scholars agree with the basic tenets of problem behavior theory (e.g., McCord, 1990; Osgood, Johnston, O'Malley, & Bachman, 1988), the evidence that there is covariation in adolescent behavior problems, at least within the broad bands of *externalizing* and *internalizing* problems, is considerable, especially among populations of white middle-class youngsters. (Less is known about the covariation of problem behaviors in other populations, but some studies suggest that the contemporaneous patterning of problems observed by Jessor and his colleagues is not as strong or consistent in nonwhite, non-middle-class samples.) One important implication that derives from past research on the covariation of adolescent problems is that a thorough assessment of adolescent risk-taking and problem behavior should include multiple indicators of adolescent dysfunction that examine problems both within (e.g., different types of antisocial behavior) and across domains or categories (e.g., antisocial behavior, school failure, drug use). It may be the case that covariation is less consistently observed than has been suggested, but this possibility cannot be examined unless multiple domains of problems are studied simultaneously.

A second dominant theme in the modern study of adolescent problem behavior concerns the notion of the developmental trajectory. This idea, taken from the life-course perspective on human development, suggests that it is possible to identify over-time patterns in the ways in which problem behaviors emerge, consolidate, progress, or remit. Rather than viewing adolescence as a separate period in the lifespan, the developmental trajectory approach encourages us to look at the connections between problem behaviors displayed during adolescence and their preadolescent antecedents and adulthood sequelae, and, as well, at the ways in which problem behaviors develop and change within the adolescent period itself. The developmental trajectory approach to the study of adolescent problem behavior has revealed, for example, that many so-called adolescent problems have identifiable antecedents in early and middle childhood (Block, Block, & Keyes, 1988; Moffitt, 1993).

To date, studies of the developmental trajectories of problem behavior have focused mainly on within-domain analyses of the development and progression of different types of problems. These studies include

Kandel's seminal work on the over-time development of drug and alcohol use (e.g., Kandel & Logan, 1984), Cairns and Cairns's research on the development of aggression in childhood and adolescence (e.g., Cairns, Cairns, Neckerman, Ferguson, & Gariepy, 1989); and the work of several investigators who have attempted to bring a life-course approach to the study of crime and delinquency, including Loeber (Loeber et al., 1993), Moffitt (1993), and Farrington (e.g., Farrington & West, 1991). Less is known, however, about the developmental progression of other domains of problems that have received the attention of scholars interested in adolescence, including depression, early sexual behavior, and academic disengagement. It is important to begin to apply the very good life-course models we now have of various types of antisocial behavior to other domains of adolescent problem behavior as well.

The methodological implications of research on developmental trajectories are clear enough. Most important, these studies suggest that problem behavior in adolescence must be studied as a dynamic process that unfolds over time, not as a static event or condition that is measured at one single point. This requires both short- and long-term longitudinal studies that examine periods before and after adolescence, as well as subperiods within adolescence itself. Long-term studies are necessary in order to examine the developmental antecedents and sequelae of problems that are observed in adolescence. Short-term studies are necessary in order to examine the proximal processes and mechanisms of influence through which problem behaviors emerge, consolidate, progress, or remit. Such short-term studies require multiple assessments over relatively short intervals.

The third dominant theme in recent research on adolescent problem behavior concerns the study of context. Although contextual factors have long played a starring role in sociological theories of adolescent problem behavior – especially in studies of crime and delinquency – developmental and clinical psychologists have been slow to incorporate context into their models. Yet it is clear that, from a sociological viewpoint, the underlying causes of adolescent problem behavior inhere mainly in their relations with social institutions, such as the family, school, the labor force, and places of worship. The most familiar of these viewpoints is social control theory, which asserts that individuals who are only weakly attached to society's institutions are more likely to develop unconventional attitudes and affiliate with unconventional in-

dividuals (Hirschi, 1969). More recently, Bronfenbrenner's (1979) ecological perspective on human development has stimulated research on
multiple contexts (both proximal and distal) and their independent and
joint impact on adolescent problem behavior.

Although there are elements of this sort of contextual approach in
the covariation and trajectory models described earlier, it is fair to say
that theorists who have attempted to map the comorbidity and developmental trajectories of various problem behaviors in adolescence have
emphasized psychological rather than sociological accounts of both covariation and over-time progression. That is, the covariation of adolescent problems has been seen as due mainly to underlying characteristics
of individuals (rather than contexts), and the developmental pathways
of problematic behavior have been viewed as deriving from continuity
in individual development rather than continuity in contextual exposure.

Adopting a contextual approach to the study of problem behavior in
adolescence also requires some methodological adaptation. First and
perhaps most obvious, the approach requires that researchers examine
environments as well as persons. Studies that merely correlate individual characteristics of adolescents without also measuring features of
their environments, either at one point in time (in order to examine
covariation) or longitudinally (in order to chart developmental trajectories), cannot determine whether any observed coherence is due to
continuity of personal characteristics, continuity of environmental characteristics, or both. Second, studies of contextual influence on problem
behavior should include assessments of multiple settings (e.g., families
and peer groups, schools *and* work settings) so that hypotheses concerning the additive and interactive impact of different contexts can be
tested.

Although the notions of covariation, trajectory, and context have
come to be widely accepted among scholars of adolescent problem behavior and risk-taking, there have been, in our view, insufficient attempts to integrate these ideas into a theoretical perspective that is
simultaneously holistic, developmental, and contextual. With a few exceptions, for instance, the models derived from problem behavior theory and its kin generally have not posited a temporal sequence in which
the various problems emerge developmentally; that is, most research
has focused on predictions about the contemporaneous co-occurrence

of different sorts of problems, due to their common origins, rather than on the over-time relations among them or, more important, the specific processes that link them across time and space. That is, although there exist many studies of covariation among problems in adolescence (e.g., Attie & Brooks-Gunn, 1989; Cantwell & Baker, 1991; Elliott, Huizinga, & Menard, 1989; McGee & Newcomb, 1992), few of these studies have examined the ways in which patterns of covariation emerge and develop over time.

Similarly, although there exist a number of excellent studies of the developmental trajectories, this research tends to have been conducted mainly *within* specific problem behavior domains (e.g., there exist studies of the developmental trajectories of antisocial behavior [e.g., Farrington & West, 1991; Loeber et al. 1993] or drug use [e.g., Kandel & Logan, 1984]). Far less attention has been paid to the ways in which relations *across* different problem domains (e.g., antisocial behavior *and* school alienation, drug use *and* sexual behavior) might develop and change over time. Given the excellent documentation of covariation and comorbidity in adolescent problems, it would seem prudent to extend the developmental trajectory framework to studies of across-domain relations.

Finally, studies of context have tended to ignore the research literatures on both covariation and developmental trajectories. Most studies of contextual influence on adolescent problem behavior look at one outcome at a time and therefore do not inform questions about how contextual influences affect patterns of problematic behavior. Similarly, most studies of context employ single measures of context that do not allow one to examine how multiple contextual influences exert additive or interactive effects on problem behavior.

In our view, these are unfortunate limitations, for several reasons. From a theoretical standpoint, although it has been exceedingly important to recognize the covariation in adolescent problems, it seems to us that it is essential for the field to move beyond the simple view that "all bad things correlate" and begin to ask whether engagement in certain problems is likely to precede or even precipitate involvement in others. Understanding the sequencing of multiple risky behaviors over time will help illuminate the processes through which problem behaviors develop, consolidate, and dissipate. Moreover, from the point of view of prevention, it is important to understand whether there are certain targets of opportunity for intervention that are likely to prevent the development of future difficulties. In some cases, the most sensible means of preventing one type of problem may involve an earlier intervention in an entirely different domain. Knowing, for example, that the development of drinking problems among late adolescent females is often preceded by the presence of an anxiety disorder in early adolescence (Kessler et al., 1994) suggests that one possible approach to the prevention of alcohol-related problems in adult females would be an intervention aimed at anxious female preadolescents. Similarly, knowing that a high proportion of adolescent boys with conduct problems had earlier histories of attention deficit disorder (Offord et al., 1992) suggests that early intervention aimed at young boys with attentional difficulties may deter later conduct disorders. We may also find, for example, that the best way to prevent adolescent pregnancy is not through sexuality-based interventions but through preventive efforts designed to head off school disengagement or early experimentation with drugs.

In this chapter, we extend and integrate the principles of covariation, trajectory, and context in an examination of the short-term, over-time relations among adolescent deviance (drug use and minor delinquency), school disengagement, parental permissiveness, and extensive part-time employment in a sample of American high school students. We do not present these analyses as definitive studies of the over-time influences on either problem behavior or school disengagement, but instead, and in the spirit of this volume, use them to illustrate how investigators might employ new perspectives in examining the over-time interrelations between risky behavior and risky contexts. Certainly there are other contexts that warrant inclusion in a comprehensive model of adolescent risk behavior (e.g., the peer group, the school, the neighborhood) and other aspects of adolescent risk behavior that could be investigated alongside school disengagement and problem behavior (e.g., sexual precocity, aggression, depression).

The first two of the variables we examine – problem behavior and school disengagement – represent two aspects of adolescent risk behavior that have been widely studied independently of one another, but that have been less systematically studied jointly and seldom studied jointly over time. That is, although it has been established that disengagement from school is correlated with a wide array of problem behaviors (Steinberg, Brown, & Dornbusch, 1996), it is not known whether school disengagement is an antecedent, a correlate, or a consequence of adolescent deviance.

The second two of the variables in our model – parental permissiveness and intensive part-time employment – represent contextual factors that have been shown repeatedly to elevate the risk of both poor school performance and adolescent problem behavior (DeBaryshe, Patterson, & Capaldi, 1993; Steinberg, Fegley, & Dornbusch, 1993). Although each of these contextual factors has been studied in relation to both school disengagement and problem behavior independently, they have not, to our knowledge, been examined in one overall model that takes into account their interrelations over time. For example, although several studies have suggested that intensive part-time employment (i.e., work for more than 20 hours weekly) is associated with disengagement from school, greater involvement in drug and alcohol use and in minor delinquent activity, it has been difficult to determine whether problem behavior is an antecedent, a correlate, or a consequence of intensive involvement in the part-time labor force. In addition, few studies have examined the interrelations among school engagement, deviance, part-time employment, and parental permissiveness, leaving open many questions about the over-time processes through which these phenomena may be connected.

Based on our own previous research and the findings of other investigators, we hypothesize that the following concurrent relations will be observed:

1. Adolescent deviance (drug use, alcohol use, and minor delinquency) will be associated with parental permissiveness.
2. Adolescent deviance will be associated with intensive part-time employment.
3. Disengagement from school will be associated with parental permissiveness.
4. Disengagement from school will be associated with intensive part-time employment.
5. Disengagement from school will be associated with adolescent deviance.
6. Parental permissiveness will be associated with intensive part-time employment.

It is more difficult to offer hypotheses regarding the over-time links among these four variables. Based on the results of the few studies that have examined these linkages longitudinally, we offer the following hypotheses:

7. Parental permissiveness will lead to increased school disengagement rather than the reverse.
8. Parental permissiveness will lead to increased deviance rather than the reverse.
9. School disengagement will both lead to, and follow from, intensive part-time employment.
10. Adolescent deviance will follow from, but *not* lead to, intensive part-time employment.

Method

Sample

Our sample is drawn from the student bodies of nine high schools in Wisconsin and Northern California. The schools were selected to yield a sample of students from different socioeconomic brackets, a variety of ethnic backgrounds, and different types of communities (urban, suburban, and rural). Data for the present analyses were collected during the 1987–1988, 1988–1989, and 1989–1990 school years via self-report surveys filled out by the students on 2 days of survey administration each school year. (Because of its length, the survey was divided into two equal parts and administered on two separate testing days each year.)

Procedure

Recent reports suggest that the use of *active consent* procedures in research on adolescents and their families (i.e., procedures requiring active parental written consent for their adolescents to participate in the research) may result in sampling biases that overrepresent well-functioning teenagers and families (e.g., Weinberger, Tublin, Ford, & Feldman, 1990). Although groups of participants and nonparticipants generated through such consent procedures may be comparable demographically (the dimension along which investigators typically look for evidence of selective participation), the procedure screens out a disproportionate number of adolescents who have adjustment problems and/or family difficulties. Because we were interested in studying adolescents with lax parents, as well as those with relatively more vigilant parents, we were concerned that employing the standard active consent procedure (in which *both* parents and adolescents are asked to return signed consent forms to their child's school) would bias our sample toward families who were more engaged in school and exclude the substantial number of parents who were relatively poor monitors of their youngsters' behavior.

After considering the age of our respondents and their ability to provide informed consent, and with the support of the administrators of our participating schools, the school districts' research review committees, representatives of the U.S. Department of Education (our chief funding agent), and our own institutions' human subjects committees, we decided to employ a consent procedure that requested active informed consent from the adolescents but passive informed consent from their parents. All parents in the participating schools were informed, by first-class mail, of the date and nature of our study well in advance of the scheduled questionnaire administration. (We provided schools with letters in stamped, unaddressed envelopes to be mailed by school officials in order to protect the privacy of the families.) Parents were asked to call or write to their child's school or our research office if they did *not* want their child to participate in the study. Fewer than 1% of the adolescents in each of the target schools had their participation withheld by their parents.

All of the students in attendance on each day of testing were explained the purposes of the study and asked to complete the questionnaires. Informed consent was obtained from all participating students. For each questionnaire administration, out of the total school populations, approximately 5% of the students chose not to participate (or had their participation withheld by parents), approximately 15% were absent from school on the day of the initial questionnaire administration (this figure is comparable to national figures on daily school attendance), and approximately 80% provided completed questionnaires. Each year, approximately 11,000 students responded to the survey, although the sample for whom we have complete longitudinal data is considerably smaller, owing primarily to graduation (we did not follow students once they completed high school) and movement out of the school district. Pairwise deletion was used to deal with the problem of missing data.

The sample is quite diverse with respect to other demographic variables: More than 40% of the respondents are from an ethnic minority group; nearly one-third are from single-parent households or stepfamilies; and nearly one-third come from homes in which the parents have not attended school beyond the 12th grade.

Measures

Of interest in the present analyses are our measures of school engagement, problem behavior, parental permissiveness, and part-time employment.

School engagement. The construct of school engagement was indexed by two scales, one measuring school orientation and the other measuring bonding to teachers. These two scales were derived by factor analyzing a set of items that assesses students' feelings of attachment to school (Wehlage, Rutter, Smith, Lesko, & Fernandez, 1989). Responses to these items were on a 4-point scale, from "Strongly Agree" to "Strongly Disagree." *Bonding to teachers* (5 items, $\alpha = .75$) assesses the student's attachment to his or her teachers. A sample item is "I care what most of my teachers think of me." *School orientation* (6 items, $\alpha = .69$) measures students' valuing of and commitment to school. A sample item is "I feel satisfied with school because I'm learning a lot." Measures of school engagement have been shown to be significantly predictive of school performance (Steinberg et al., 1996).

Problem behavior. Two measures were used to index behavior problems. First, respondents provided information on their frequency of cigarette, alcohol, marijuana, and other drug use, which was used to form an index of *drug and alcohol use* ($\alpha = .86$; Greenberger, Steinberg, & Vaux, 1981). Second, respondents reported on their frequency of involvement in such delinquent activities as theft, carrying a weapon, vandalism, and using a phony I.D., used to form an index of *delinquent activity* ($\alpha = .82$; Gold, 1970).

Parental permissiveness. Parental permissiveness was indexed by two scales, one assessing permissive decision making (Steinberg, Elmen, & Mounts, 1989) and the other assessing lax parental monitoring (Patterson & Stouthamer-Loeber, 1984). Students reported on the frequency of joint, unilateral adolescent, and unilateral parental decision making across 13 topics (e.g., choice of classes, choice of friends, curfew). *Permissive decision making* was operationalized as the proportion of decisions made unilaterally by the adolescent. Students also reported on the extent to which their parents know about various aspects of their activities, including where they spend their free time, how they spend their money, and who their friends are; students' responses to this were used to create an index of *lax monitoring*.

Employment intensity. Each year, students completed questions asking whether they were employed in a "regular paying part-time job" (volunteer work was not counted as employment, nor was occasional work) and, if so, the type of job held, the weekly hours worked, and the monthly earnings from the job (Steinberg et al., 1993). As in previous surveys, the vast majority of the working adolescents in this sample were employed in the service industry, with a significant number working in restaurants and retail stores. Based on previous work indicating significant relations between hours of employment and adolescent adjustment and behavior, *hours of employment* was measured on a 4-point scale: low (not employed or employed fewer than 10 hours weekly), moderate (employment of 11–20 hours), substantial (employment of 21–25 hours), and very high (more than 25 hours weekly).

Plan of analyses

Latent-variable structural equation models were derived theoretically to examine over-time relations among school disengagement, intensive part-time employment, risk-taking behavior, and parental permissiveness during adolescence. Models were conceived to assess the relations among variables over the course of the high school years (9th, 10th, 11th, and 12th grades). However, because each cohort sampled in the present study was followed for a maximum of 3 years, no covariances could be estimated for 9th- to 12th-grade variables (and, consequently, these variables could not be assessed in the same models). Therefore, for each examination of relations among variables, we tested separate models for 9th- through 11th-grade variables and for 10th- through 12th-grade variables. In the Results and Discussion sections, corresponding models are discussed in pairs.

AMOS version 3.50 (Arbuckle, 1995) was used to test the fit of models and to derive path coefficients. We employed pairwise deletion to deal with the problem of missing data To test proposed relations among the latent variables of interest, we first examined "mini" models of the relations between pairs of latent variables (e.g., school engagement and risk-taking behavior) and then examined "grand" models that incorporated multiple latent variables. Because we know from previous research that concurrent relations among our variables are significant and strong – that is, at any one point in time, risky behavior will be significantly correlated with parental permissiveness, extensive part-time employment, and school disengagement – we take into account concurrent relations among variables in all models presented.

Because of the large sample size employed in the present study, there were more than enough cases to estimate all parameters sufficiently (Bollen, 1989). However, due to the large size of the sample, the chi-square statistic is not a good index of model fit. This is the case because the chi-square statistic is a badness-of-fit index such that the larger the sample size, the greater the likelihood that the model will be rejected as a good fit of the data. Thus, in all analyses presented in this chapter, we report other indices of fit, including the comparative fit index (CFI), goodness-of-fit index (GFI), and root mean square error of approximation (RMSEA). The CFI is an index of fit that is based on the comparison of proposed models to other baseline models. In general, CFI values range from 0 to 1 (one represents a perfect fit), and a value greater than .90 represents a close-fitting model. The GFI is a goodness-of-fit index; a value greater than .90 represents a close fit of the model to the data. The RMSEA is a measure based on population discrepancy (estimated correlation matrix vs. matrix implied by the model) that takes into account the complexity of the proposed model. In general, a RMSEA value of .05 or less indicates a close fit of the model, and values greater than .05 and less than .08 represent a reasonable fit (e.g., Browne & Cudeck, 1993).

Table 12.1 contains the correlations, means, and standard deviations for all variables used in testing the structural equation models.

Results

Let us look first at the links between the two different indicators of problem behavior included in our analyses: school disengagement (rep-

Table 12.1. *Correlation coefficients, means, and standard deviations (SD) of observed variables.*

	1	2	3	4	5	6	7	8	9	10	11	12	13	14	15	16
1. drug9	1.00															
2. drug10	.64	1.00														
3. drug11	.50	.68	1.00													
4. drug12	.	.60	.74	1.00												
5. delinq9	.54	.29	.16	.	1.00											
6. delinq10	.23	.53	.23	.24	.39	1.00										
7. delinq11	.17	.28	.52	.28	.25	.36	1.00									
8. delinq12	.	.25	.30	.53	.	.26	.30	1.00								
9. bndtr9	-.23	-.19	-.22	.	-.27	-.15	-.16	.	1.00							
10. bndtr10	-.15	-.23	-.20	-.17	-.16	-.23	-.16	-.14	.51	1.00						
11. bndtr11	-.06	-.13	-.20	-.14	-.11	-.15	-.22	-.14	.45	.45	1.00					
12. bndtr12	.	-.14	-.13	-.19	.	-.13	-.11	-.23	.	.44	.48	1.00				
13. valsch9	-.29	-.26	-.27	-.27	-.30	-.20	-.21	-.16	.48	.38	.35	.	1.00			
14. valsch10	-.22	-.32	-.27	-.24	-.25	-.29	-.20	-.21	.35	.46	.29	.29	.55	1.00		
15. valsch11	-.16	-.21	-.30	-.27	-.19	-.18	-.29	-.28	.30	.29	.46	.32	.44	.52	1.00	
16. valsch12	.	-.18	-.21	-.30	.	-.14	-.15	.	.	.31	.34	.45	.	.45	.57	1.00
17. work9	.09	.09	.02	.02	.11	.09	.01	.01	-.05	-.07	-.10	-.04	-.08	-.05	-.02	.
18. work10	.07	.08	.09	.14	.09	.12	.12	.12	-.06	-.08	-.05	-.09	-.09	-.10	-.13	.02
19. work11	.13	.10	.10	.14	.07	.10	.08	.08	-.04	-.06	-.06	-.07	-.07	-.13	-.10	-.09
20. work12	.	-.08	.14	.	.	.08	.07	.07	.	-.04	-.05	-.06	.	-.09	-.10	-.08
21. montr9	-.07	-.08	-.04	.00	-.13	-.11	-.11	.09	.16	.13	.11	.07	.14	.13	.12	.07
22. montr10	-.10	-.09	-.04	-.04	-.15	-.06	-.06	.00	.18	.16	.15	.12	.16	.13	.07	.07
23. montr11	-.11	-.10	-.07	-.03	-.16	-.12	-.09	.00	.18	.17	.17	.12	.14	.13	.10	.11
24. montr12	.	-.10	-.09	-.05	.	-.10	-.10	.11	.	.14	.19	.14	.	.13	.11	.10
25. dec9	.21	.22	.16	.	.15	.14	.08	.09	-.16	-.15	-.09	-.13	-.18	-.16	-.13	-.15
26. dec10	.21	.23	.23	.17	.14	.15	.12	.12	-.20	-.20	-.14	-.21	-.21	-.20	-.15	-.11
27. dec11	.21	.19	.20	.17	.14	.10	.11	.09	-.15	-.16	-.15	-.12	-.19	-.17	-.18	-.11
28. dec12	.	.12	.18	.18	.	.02	.07	.11	.	-.16	-.17	-.15	.	-.18	-.17	-.14
Mean	1.31	1.47	1.55	1.69	1.16	1.17	1.16	1.18	2.89	2.90	2.94	2.97	2.82	2.79	2.77	2.72
SD	.56	.70	.73	.79	.34	.38	.37	.40	.54	.54	.52	.51	.50	.50	.51	.50

Note: Asterisk (*) represents nonsignificant correlations.

Table 12.1. (cont.)

	17	18	19	20	21	22	23	24	25	26	27	28
17. work9	1.00											
18. work10	.29	1.00										
19. work11	.28	.37	1.00									
20. work12	.	.22	.42	1.00								
21. montr9	-.03	-.03	-.03	.	1.00							
22. montr10	-.02	-.01	-.01	.03	.48	1.00						
23. montr11	-.02	-.02	.00	.00	.39	.54	1.00					
24. montr12	.	-.07	-.02	-.02	.	.40	.56	1.00				
25. dec9	.04	.03	.10	.	-.33	-.30	-.28	.	1.00			
26. dec10	.01	.06	.07	.09	-.26	-.34	-.30	-.23	.50	1.00		
27. dec11	.09	.09	.09	.11	-.18	-.27	-.38	-.34	.42	.52	1.00	
28. dec12	.	.11	.12	.11	.	-.23	-.33	-.39	.	.43	.55	1.00
Mean	.59	1.02	1.65	2.30	2.33	2.31	2.30	2.23	.36	.41	.46	.52
SD	1.37	1.75	2.08	2.28	.47	.49	.50	.52	.25	.26	.27	.27

Note: Asterisk (*) represents nonsignificant correlations.

resented by the construct labeled "School Engage" in the accompanying figures) and deviance (represented by the construct labeled "Risky"). According to structural equation analyses, both models were good fits of the data, as indicated by CFIs and GFIs greater than .90 (9th- through 11th-grade model: CFI = .983, GFI = .987; 10th-through 12th-grade model: CFI = .975, GFI = .981). In addition, the RMSEA index indicated that the 9th- through 11th-grade model was a close fit of the data (RMSEA = .048), and that the 10th- through 12th-grade model fit the data reasonably well (RMSEA = .060).

As Figures 12.1 and 12.2 indicate, although the links between these two problem behaviors are bidirectional, it appears that the impact of school disengagement on problem behavior is generally stronger than the reverse (note: school engagement is coded so that lower scores reflect greater disengagement). In other words, our analyses suggest that, in general, disengagement from school precedes involvement in drug and alcohol use and minor delinquency, especially during the earlier years of high school. Curiously, the models also indicate that engagement in risky behavior has a small but *positive* effect on school engagement 1 year later. This finding is likely an artifact of the reality that most American students, even students who are committed to their education, participate in minor delinquency or drug use to some degree (Elliott, Huizinga, & Ageton, 1985). Further, we believe that this effect is most pronounced between the 11th and 12th grades because many of the most troubled adolescents (i.e., low engaged students who engage in a high degree of risky behavior) either have dropped out of school or have "matured" in their orientation toward school. It is also important to note, from these analyses, the extraordinarily high over-time stability of school engagement across the high school years: Students who begin their high school careers interested in and committed to school tend to remain so.

Next, we turn to the over-time links between adolescent deviance and the two different contextual risk factors examined here: parental permissiveness and intensive part-time employment. Results of the model testing indicated that the proposed models fit the data well (CFIs = .990, .978, .979, .979; GFIs = .993, .985, .988, .988; RMSEAs = .035, .054, .056, .058 for the four models examined [two models for each cohort]). Two interesting patterns are revealed in Figures 12.3 through 12.6. First, and consistent with our hypothesis, we see that

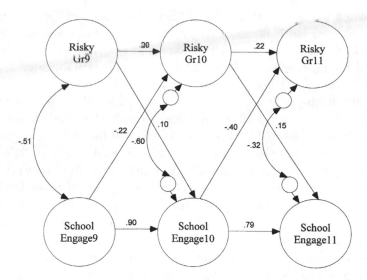

Figure 12.1 The relation between school engagement and problem behavior from Grade 9 to Grade 11. All standardized regression weights are significant at the .05 alpha level.

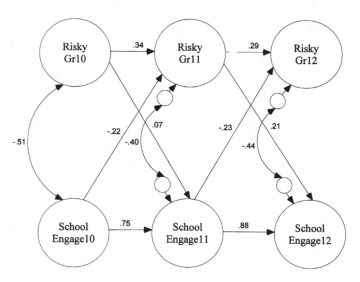

Figure 12.2 The relation between school engagement and problem behavior from Grade 10 to Grade 12. All standardized weights are significant at the .05 alpha level.

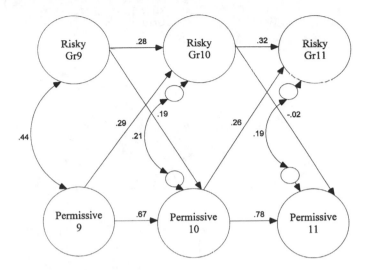

Figure 12.3 The relation between problem behavior and permissive parenting from Grade 9 to Grade 11. Standardized weights greater than .02 are significant at the .05 alpha level.

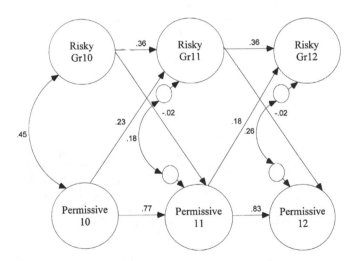

Figure 12.4 The relation between problem behavior and permissive parenting from Grade 10 to Grade 12. Standardized weights greater than .02 are significant at the .05 alpha level.

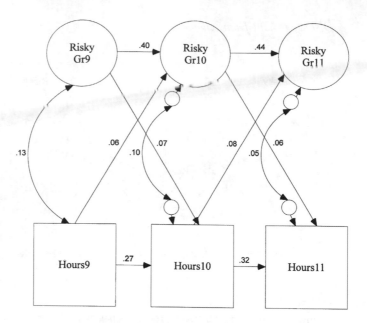

Figure 12.5 The relation between problem behavior and part-time employment from Grade 9 to Grade 11. All standardized regression weights are significant at the .05 alpha level.

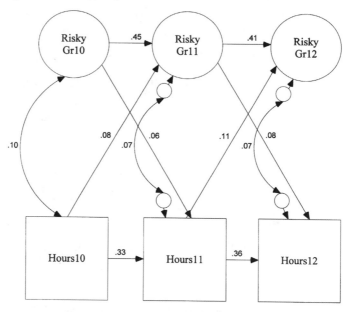

Figure 12.6 The relation between problem behavior and part-time employment from Grade 10 to Grade 12. All standardized regression weights are significant at the .05 alpha level.

parental permissiveness generally leads to increases in deviance, rather than the reverse. (However, the effect is fairly bidirectional in the earliest years of high school.) Second, it appears that the relation between deviance and intensive part-time employment is modest and bidirectional at all points in the high school career: That is, working long hours at a part-time job increases adolescent drug and alcohol use and involvement in minor delinquency, but involvement in these problem behaviors appears to increase the likelihood that adolescents will work longer hours at a job.

Where does school disengagement fit into this overall pattern? Tests of models incorporating these variables suggest that models are close fits of the data, as indicated by CFI and GFI values greater than .90 and RMSEA values less than .075. As Figures 12.7, 12.8, 12.9, and 12.10 indicate, it appears that school disengagement is driving a good deal of the action. Consistent with previous research, disengagement from school is a moderate predictor of intensive part-time employment; interestingly, the impact of employment on school disengagement 1 year later is not substantial, according to our data. And, to our surprise, the impact of school disengagement on parental permissiveness is generally much more considerable than the reverse (except between the 10th and 11th grades in the first cohort only). That is, contrary to our hypothesis that parental permissiveness will lead to increased disengagement from school, we find that adolescents' disengagement from school leads to less vigilant monitoring and more permissive decision making on the part of their parents.

When we look simultaneously at school disengagement, parental permissiveness, part-time employment, and adolescent deviance, the story becomes clearer (see Figures 12.11 and 12.12). Disengagement from school affects adolescent deviance both directly and indirectly through the impact of school disengagement on parental permissiveness and, to a lesser extent, on part-time employment. That is, when youngsters disengage from school, they spend more time working at part-time jobs and are less closely supervised by their parents, and both of these conditions increase the risk of drug and alcohol use and delinquency on top of whatever risk is posed by disengagement alone. These findings make the over-time stability of school engagement all the more important because they suggest that early engagement in school may serve as an important protective factor against subsequent problem behavior.

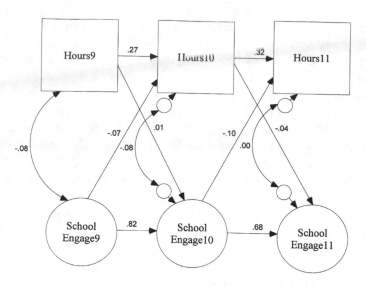

Figure 12.7 The relation between school engagement and part-time employ-ment from Grade 9 to Grade 11. Standardized weights greater than .01 are significant at the .05 alpha level.

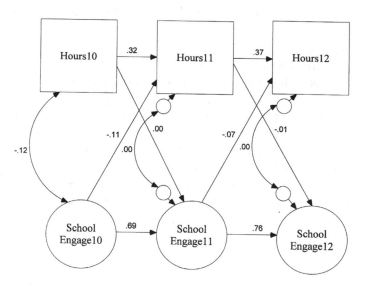

Figure 12.8 The relation between school engagement and part-time employ-ment from Grade 10 to Grade 11. Standardized weights greater than .01 are significant at the .05 alpha level.

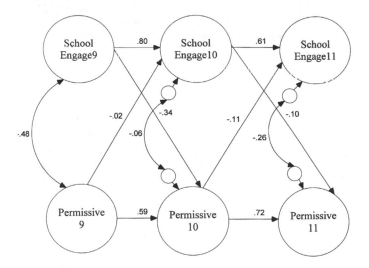

Figure 12.9 The relation between school engagement and parental permissiveness from Grade 9 to Grade 11. Standardized weights greater than .02 are significant at the .05 alpha level.

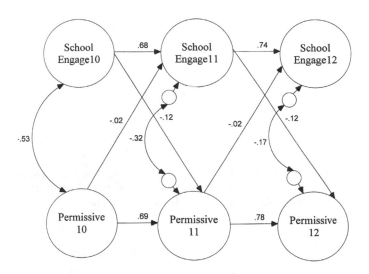

Figure 12.10 The relation between school engagement and parental permissiveness from Grade 10 to Grade 12. Standardized weights greater than .02 are significant at the .05 alpha level.

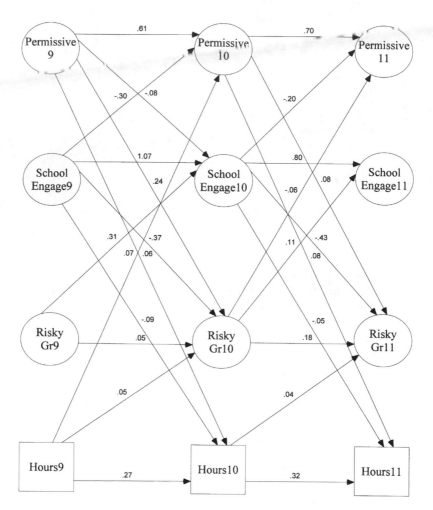

Figure 12.11 The relations among school engagement, problem behavior, parental permissiveness, and part-time employment from Grade 9 to Grade 11. Only significant paths are included in this figure.

Sex differences in patterns of over-time relations

We also looked to see whether there were sex differences in these patterns of over-time relations among school engagement, risky behavior, parental permissiveness, and part-time work. When we compare models

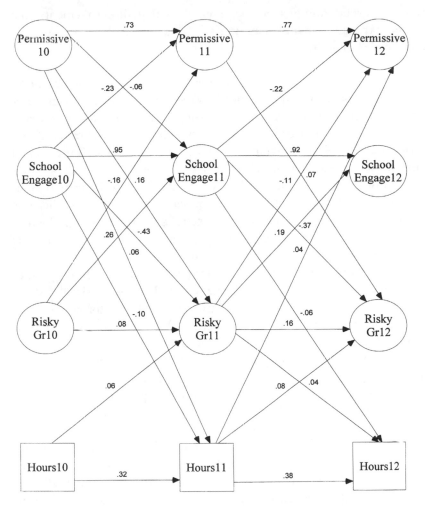

Figure 12.12 The relations among school engagement, problem behavior, parental permissiveness, and part-time employment from Grade 10 to Grade 12. Only significant paths are included in this figure.

generated for males versus females, we see that some of the findings remain the same across both sexes, but others change, and in important ways.

First, it is clear that school disengagement is a strong risk factor for both boys and girls, pretty consistently over time. Thus, one of the most important findings of our research – that disengagement from school may lead to involvement in risky behavior – holds true for males and females, more or less at all points in the high school career.

Second, parental permissiveness has a much more consistently adverse effect on girls than on boys. For boys, it is a risk factor during the early years of high school, but it wanes in importance during later years. For girls, it is a risk factor throughout the high school years, both directly and indirectly (permissiveness not only predicts risky behavior, but school disengagement and work hours as well). This general pattern is consistent with what we have reported in some previous publications (e.g., Steinberg, Fletcher, & Darling, 1994), namely, that girls are more responsive to parental influence than boys. Whether this is because of sex differences in youngsters' susceptibility to influence, or instead to differences between the parents of girls versus boys, is something we cannot determine from our data.

Third, and in contrast, part-time employment is a significant predictor of risky behavior among boys but not at all among girls. We think that this may have something to do with parental monitoring and with gender differences in patterns of spending. With respect to the first, if girls are (1) monitored more closely than boys (we know this from other research) and (2) more responsive to parental monitoring than boys, any other contextual influence (in this case, working long hours) may be moderated by parental monitoring. With respect to the second, we know from other research that much of the impact of part-time employment on risky behavior is mediated through earnings – it's the money, not the work per se, that accounts for most of the relation (Greenberger & Steinberg, 1986). We also know that boys are more likely to spend their work earnings on things that can potentially get them into trouble (cars, which provide for even more autonomy from parents) and recreation (which may include drugs and alcohol); girls use their money mainly for clothing. For this reason, part-time employment may be linked to problem behavior among boys but not girls (unless one considers excessive shopping to be a problem).

Person-centered analyses

In addition to interpreting structural equation models, we examined the data from a more person-centered approach in order to examine the developmental trajectories of students who varied in their degree of engagement in school. We began by dividing the ninth-grade students in our sample into three groups, according to students' level of engagement in school during ninth grade. (Engagement in school was indexed by the school orientation and bonding to teacher scales.) The low engaged group consisted of students whose engagement scores fell in the lowest tertile; the moderately engaged group consisted of students whose scores fell in the middle tertile; the high-engaged group consisted of students whose scores fell in the upper tertile. Next, in order to determine whether the three groups of students differed in their levels of drug use and minor delinquency across the 9th through 11th grades, we performed two Repeated Measures ANOVAs, each with one Between-Subjects Factor (Engagement Group) and one Within-Subjects Factor (Grade in School). (Only those subjects who were present for all three waves of data collection were included in these analyses.)

With drug use as the dependent variable, the repeated-measures ANOVA indicated a significant main effect for group ($F = 27.63$, $p <$ .001). Low-engaged adolescents reported the highest overall level of drug use, and high-engaged adolescents reported the lowest level of drug use. In addition, the within-subject main effect for grade level was significant ($p < .001$). Further interpretation revealed that only the increase between the 9th and 11th grades was significant. Most important, however, we found a significant group by grade interaction ($p <$ .001); this suggests that the pattern of drug use over the course of high school varies with the level of initial engagement in school. As seen in Figure 12.13, low-engaged students reported the highest levels of drug use at all grade levels, high-engaged students reported the lowest levels of drug use at all grade levels, and moderately engaged students reported levels that fall between the low- and high-engaged groups. Moreover, although all groups increased their levels of drug use across the first 3 years of high school, the low-engaged group had the most profound increase in drug use over time, even after taking into account their relatively higher initial level of drug use.

When we examined minor delinquency as the dependent variable, the repeated-measures ANOVA yielded findings similar to those for drug use (see Figure 12.14). At all grade levels, low-engaged students reported the highest overall level of delinquency and high-engaged stu-

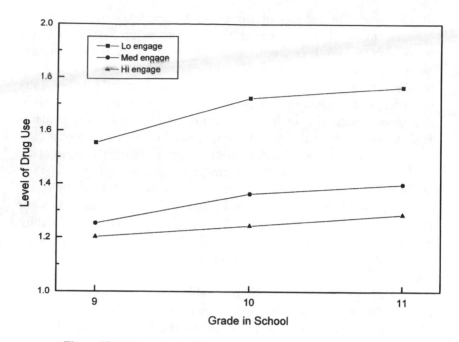

Figure 12.13 Mean level of drug use of high- , medium- , and low-engaged students from Grade 9 to Grade 11.

dents reported the lowest overall level. In addition, we observed a significant increase in minor delinquent acts between the 9th and 11th grades. Most important, the significant group by grade interaction indicated that low-engaged students had a more profound increase in reported levels of delinquency across time than did students who were either moderately or highly engaged in school during ninth grade.

Discussion

In this chapter, we have attempted to illustrate how risky behaviors and risky contexts are interwoven over the course of the high school years. We examined two problem behaviors in particular – deviance and school disengagement – and two contextual factors believed to elevate the risk of each. As expected, we have found that these different variables are linked together in a complex, dynamic, reciprocal pattern that unfolds over time.

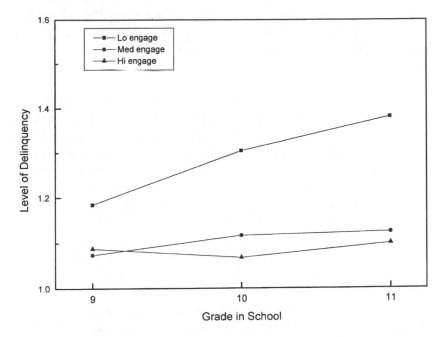

Figure 12.14 Mean level of minor delinquency of high- , medium- , and low-engaged students from Grade 9 to Grade 11.

Many of the results of our analyses replicate findings from previous work on adolescent problem behavior. Specifically, we find that parental permissiveness and extensive part-time employment both increase the probability that an adolescent will experiment with drugs and alcohol and dabble in minor delinquency. Our findings suggest that social policies and programs designed to increase parental vigilance and to limit youngsters' school-year employment to fewer than 20 hours weekly may have a significant deterrent impact on adolescent drug and alcohol use and delinquency.

Our results also indicate, however, that disengagement from school may play a surprisingly strong, and perhaps precipitating, role in the process through which problem behavior arises during the high school years. Youngsters who are less attached to school are, not unexpectedly, more likely to use drugs and alcohol and commit acts of minor delinquency – a finding consistent with predictions from problem behavior theory. But it appears that disengagement from school may increase the risk of, rather than just accompany, deviant behavior. That is, youngsters who reported a relatively fragile orientation toward school and a weak attachment to their teachers early in their high school careers are, over time, significantly more likely to use drugs and alcohol and to be involved in minor delinquency such as theft and vandalism.

Our findings may also suggest a slightly different interpretation – that engagement in school serves as a protective factor against involvement in problem behavior. Youth who are engaged in school likely spend much of their time and focus much of their attention on school-related activities, including coursework and extracurricular activities, thereby allowing little time for or interest in deviant behavior. These youngsters also tend to associate with peers who are similarly engaged in school, further limiting their exposure to disengaged, deviant peer groups and problem behavior. Moreover, in accordance with the basic tenets of social control theory, engaged students' strong bond to school (a conventional institution) serves to maintain conventional behavior and inhibit deviant behavior by increasing the costs of deviance (e.g., suspension or expulsion from school). In other words, students who are engaged in school have more to lose (e.g., a good education, entrance into college, a job) if they become involved in deviant behavior. For these reasons, school engagement may be an important domain for delinquency prevention.

More surprising than the effect of disengagement on problem behavior, perhaps, were the over-time links between school disengagement and the two indicators of contextual risk examined here – parental permissiveness and intensive part-time employment. Interestingly enough, our findings suggest that disengagement from school may lead to both increases in parental permissiveness and intensive involvement in the workplace. Indeed, during the high school year, school disengagement was more likely to predict both parental permissiveness and intensive part-time employment than the reverse. Because permissiveness and intensive employment, in turn, lead to an increase in adolescent deviance, school disengagement appears to increase the risk of other problem behaviors not only directly but indirectly, through its impact on youngsters' experiences in other settings.

Although the observation that disengaged students may be more likely to seek jobs and work long hours is neither surprising nor new (see Steinberg & Cauffman, 1995), the notion that parental permissiveness may be a reaction to, rather than a cause of, school disengagement is both provocative and perplexing. At least two possible explanations come to mind. First, parents may adjust their levels of control in reaction to their children's outward behavior, and in this case, parents may be more likely to "check out" if they perceive their child to be less invested in conventional pursuits. That is, instead of tightening the reins in response to the child's waning commitment to school, parents may withdraw and retreat out of frustration. Second, school disengagement may be a proxy for some other personality or behavioral characteristic that itself may push parents toward less vigilant monitoring and more permissive parenting. Among the likely contenders for this proxy variable are rebelliousness or oppositionalism, both of which conceivably could lead the adolescent to disengage from school and the adolescent's parents to disengage from parenting.

Our data track youngsters only during the high school years. Because our measures do not predate age 14, it is difficult to say with any confidence whether disengagement from school does in fact emerge before other aspects of other problem behaviors. That is, there is no reason to assume that the developmental trajectory one sees during the high school years specifically is identical to what one might observe had one studied younger individuals. It may be the case, for instance, that during middle adolescence disengagement from school leads to parental permissiveness, but that in earlier developmental periods that causal pathway is reversed. By the same token, although our data suggest that school disengagement precedes drug and alcohol use and delinquency, we cannot be certain that this is the case during preadolescence or early adolescence.

Although our results point to disengagement from school as a central part of the process through which problem behavior develops in adolescence (or, conversely, to engagement in school as an important protective factor), it is not clear from our analysis what our measure of this construct is genuinely tapping. We cannot tell whether, for example, it is an early marker for later problems, a causal agent in the developmental process through which subsequent problem behaviors arise, or a proxy for some other, unmeasured factor whose appearance precedes or provokes both disengagement from school and a range of other problems. Without experimental data, it is impossible to draw confident conclusions about cause and effect, and evidence of temporal precedence is a necessary, but not a sufficient, basis for establishing something as a risk factor (Kraemer et al., 1997). From the point of view of social control theory, however, it certainly makes sense to suggest that when youngsters' connections to institutions such as school are weakened, a pattern of problematic behavior may result.

What *is* clear from these analyses is that longitudinal research that begins before adolescence itself is necessary to understand the processes through which problem behaviors emerge and progress during adolescence. As indicated by the developmental-contextual perspective we have illustrated in this chapter, such longitudinal research should examine risky behaviors and risky contexts as they influence each other over time. And such analyses should look carefully at the ways in which youngsters' commitment to school plays a role in this process.

References

Arbuckle, J. L. (1995). Amos (Version 3.50) [Computer software]. Chicago: SmallWaters Corporation.

Attie, I., & Brooks-Gunn, J. (1989). The development of eating problems in adolescent girls: A longitudinal study. *Developmental Psychology, 25,* 70–79.

Block, J., Block, J., & Keyes, S. (1988). Longitudinally foretelling drug usage in adolescence: Early childhood personality and environmental precursors. *Child Development, 59,* 336–355.

Bollen, K. A. (1989). *Structural equations with latent variables.* New York: Wiley.

Bronfenbrenner, U. (1979). *The ecology of human development: Experiments by nature and design.* Cambridge, MA: Harvard University Press.

Browne, M. W., & Cudeck, R. (1993). Alternative ways of assessing model fit. In K. A. Bollen & J. S. Long (Eds.), *Testing structural equation models* (pp. 111–135). Beverly Hills, CA: Sage.

Cairns, R., Cairns, B., Neckerman, H., Ferguson, L., & Gariepy, J. (1989). Growth and aggression: 1. Childhood to early adolescence. *Development Psychology, 25,* 320–330.

Cantwell, D., & Baker, L. (1991). Manifestations of depressive affect in adolescence. *Journal of Youth and Adolescence, 20,* 121–134.

DeBaryshe, B., Patterson, G., & Capaldi, D. (1993). A performance model for academic achievement in early adolescent boys. *Developmental Psychology, 29,* 795–804.

Elliott D., Huizinga, D., & Ageton, S. S. (1985). *Explaining delinquency and drug use.* Beverly Hills, CA: Sage.

Elliott, D., Huizinga, D., & Menard, S. (1989). *Multiple problem youth: Delinquency, substance abuse, and mental health problems.* New York: Springer-Verlag.

Farrington, D., & West, D. (1991). The Cambridge Study in Delinquent Development: A long-term follow-up of 411 London males. In H. Kerner & G. Kaiser (Eds.), *Criminality: Personality, behavior, and life history* (pp. 115–138). New York: Springer-Verlag.

Gold, M. (1970). *Delinquent behavior in an American city.* Belmont, CA: Brooks/Cole.

Greenberger, E., & Steinberg, L. (1986). *When teenagers work: The psychological and social costs of adolescent employment.* New York: Basic Books.

Greenberger, E., Steinberg, L., & Vaux, A. (1981). Adolescents who work: Health and behavioral consequences of job stress. *Developmental Psychology, 17,* 691–703.

Hirschi, T. (1969). *Causes of delinquency.* Berkeley: University of California Press.

Jessor, R., & Jessor, S. (1977). *Problem behavior and psychosocial development: A longitudinal study of youth.* New York: Academic Press.

Kandel, D., & Logan, J. A. (1984). Patterns of drug use from adolescence to young adulthood: I. Periods of risk for initiation, continued use, and discontinuation. *American Journal of Public Health, 74,* 660–666.

Kessler, R. C., McGonagle, K. A., Shanyang, Z., Nelson, C. B., Hughes, M., Eshelman, S., Wittchen, H. U., & Kendler, K. S. (1994). Lifetime and 12-month prevalence of DSM-III-R psychiatric disorders in the United States: Results from the National Comorbidity Study. *Archives of General Psychiatry, 51,* 8–19.

Kraemer, H. C., Kazdin, A. E., Offord, D. R., Kessler, R. C., Jensen, P. S., & Kupfer, D. J. (1997). Coming to terms with the terms of risk. *Archives of General Psychiatry, 54,* 337–343.

Loeber, R., Wung, P., Keenan, K., Girouz, B., Stouthamer-Loever, M., Van Kammen, W., & Maughan, B. (1993). Developmental pathways in disruptive child behavior. *Development and Psychopathology, 5,* 103–133.

McCord, J. (1990). Problem behaviors. In S. Feldman & G. Elliot (Eds.), *At the threshold: The developing adolescent* (pp. 414–430). Cambridge, MA: Harvard University Press.

McGee, L., & Newcomb, M. (1992). General deviance syndrome: Expanded hierarchical evaluations at four ages from early adolescence to adulthood. *Journal of Consulting and Clinical Psychology, 60,* 766–776.

Moffitt, T. E. (1993). Adolescence-limited and life-course-persistent anti-social behavior: A developmental taxonomy. *Psychological Review, 100,* 674–701.

Offord, D, R , Boyle, M. H., Racine, Y. A., Fleming, J. E., Cadman, D. T., Blum, H. M., Byrne, C., Links, P. S., Lipman, E. L., MacMillan, H. L., Grant, N. I. R., Sanford, M. N., Szatmari, P., Thomas, H., & Woodward, C. A. (1992). Outcome, prognosis, and risk in a longitudinal follow-up study. *Journal of the American Academy of Child and Adolescent Psychiatry, 31,* 916–923.

Osgood, D. W., Johnston, L., O'Malley, P., & Bachman, J. (1988). The generality of deviance in late adolescence and early adulthood. *American Sociological Review, 53,* 81–93.

Patterson, G., & Stouthamer-Loeber, M. (1984). The correlation of family management practices and delinquency. *Child Development, 55,* 1299–1307.

Steinberg, L., Brown, B., & Dornbusch, S. (1996). *Beyond the classroom.* New York: Simon & Schuster.

Steinberg, L., & Cauffman, B. (1995). The impact of school-year employment on adolescent development. In R. Vasta (Ed.), *Annals of child development* (Vol. 11, pp. 131–166). London: Jessica Kingsley.

Steinberg, L., Elmen, J., & Mounts, N. (1989). Authoritative parenting, psychosocial maturity, and academic success among adolescents. *Child Development, 60,* 1424–1436.

Steinberg, L., Fegley, S., & Dornbusch, S. (1993). Negative impact of part-time work on adolescent adjustment: Evidence from a longitudinal study. *Developmental Psychology, 29,* 171–180.

Steinberg, L., Fletcher, A., & Darling, N. (1994). Parental monitoring and peer influences on adolescent substance use. *Pediatrics, 93* (6), 1060–1064.

Wehlage, G., Rutter, R., Smith, G., Lesko, N., & Fernandez, R. (1989). *Reducing the risk: Schools as communities of support.* London: Falmer Press.

Weinberger, D., Tublin, S., Ford, M., & Feldman, S. (1990). Preadolescents' social-emotional adjustment and selective attrition in family research. *Child Development, 61,* 1374–1386.

13

New perspectives on adolescent work and the transition to adulthood

Jeylan T. Mortimer and
Monica Kirkpatrick Johnson

This chapter concerns an activity, teen employment, which is not typically dealt with in studies of adolescent risk behavior. Certain behaviors, such as drinking and smoking, acting out in school, unprotected sex, and various forms of deviance, obviously pose clear risks to the healthy development of youth. They have therefore been given considerable attention in the scientific literature and are well represented in the present volume. It is widely believed that, unlike these behaviors, employment during the high school years is a good thing for youth, as it introduces them to an exceedingly important adult social role. If youthwork has such a preparatory function, it might even be considered protective, reducing the likelihood of problematic early life course trajectories and promoting such desirable outcomes as continued schooling and finding employment after leaving high school.

But despite widespread public approval, some have questioned whether early labor force participation might pose risks to teenagers if it draws them away from more valuable activities, such as schoolwork or extracurricular involvements. Employment itself may be risky if it exposes youth to workplace hazards or stressors at a time when requisite coping mechanisms have not yet been adequately developed. Thus, because we are examining a phenomenon that has heretofore been given relatively little attention, this chapter represents a new perspective on adolescent risk behavior. We assess the conditions under which teenage work may be enhancing as well as compromising to healthy develop-

This research was supported by the National Institute of Mental Health (MH42843), "Work Experience and Mental Health: A Panel Study of Youth."

ment. Moreover, unlike most other researchers on this topic, we apply a more differentiated approach to adolescent employment and examine work behavior longitudinally The pattern of employment through-out the high school years, rather than employment at any particular time, is the focus of attention; outcomes are measured in the post-secondary period when youth are beginning to make the transition to adulthood.

In the United States, almost all adolescents work in paid jobs some-time during high school (Manning, 1990). The amount of time that young people invest in employment is substantial. Bachman and Schu-lenberg's (1993) study of 71,863 high school seniors in the annual Mon-itoring the Future surveys showed that 75% of the employed boys, and 38% of the employed girls worked more than 20 hours per week. Most research that has been conducted on this subject is concerned with contemporaneous risks – for example, with whether youth who do more paid work do more poorly in school than other young people or engage in more problem behaviors, such as delinquency, smoking, and drug use (Bachman, Bare, & Frankie, 1986; Bachman & Schulenberg, 1993; Greenberger, 1984; Greenberger & Steinberg, 1986; Steinberg & Dorn-busch, 1991; Steinberg, Greenberger, Garduque, Ruggiero, & Vaux, 1982). Based on such research, some investigators have concluded that employment is an experience that does, in fact, place adolescents at substantial risk and should therefore be limited in scope (Greenberger, 1988; Steinberg, Fegley, & Dornbusch, 1993).

Social scientists have thus far given relatively little attention to the longer-term consequences of paid employment during adolescence. Un-derstanding such lagged effects is greatly hindered by the absence of appropriate data. Because much of the research is based on cross-sectional studies, it is impossible to discern longer-term consequences or the direction of effect (Bachman & Schulenberg, 1993; Greenberger & Steinberg, 1986; Steinberg & Dornbusch, 1991). The few longitudi-nal studies of this topic are plagued by sample selection problems (e.g., Greenberger & Steinberg's [1986] small longitudinal component), low retention rates (Steinberg et al., 1993), or a restricted range of depend-ent variables (Carr, Wright, & Brody, 1996).

In this chapter, we examine teenage work experience as a risk behav-ior with potential consequences beyond high school. We believe that there is a sound basis for expecting that employment in adolescence will influence adolescent mental health and adjustment, as well as the timing of important markers of the transition to adulthood. Our expectations regarding the long-term consequences of adolescent work are grounded in the conceptual foundations of life course analysis, identity theory in social psychology, and the status attainment literature. Adolescent work experience can be characterized as a significant transition in the early life course, linking adolescent and early adult role trajectories. Principles of identity formation in social psychology, particularly with respect to the development of competence and formulations about the possible self, are highly relevant to our analysis. Finally, our hypotheses about the effects of adolescent work on early labor market outcomes are consistent with models of status attainment in sociology. We assess whether youthwork experience enhances the development of human and social capital or detracts from early adult well-being by curtailing postsecondary schooling, lessening attainment prospects, and hastening the transition to adult roles. Based on conceptualizations drawn from these literatures, as well as empirical evidence from our own and other studies, we find it plausible to assume that adolescent work experience, under certain conditions, can be protective, having positive implications for what happens shortly after high school, as well as for early adult role adaptation. Under other conditions, it may pose significant risks, lessening the likelihood of positive transitional behaviors.

Adolescent work as a transition in the early life course trajectory

In modern societies, the central "business" of the child's life is going to school; it is in the role of student that young people acquire literacy, numeracy, basic knowledge, general technical skills, and achievement-related orientations and behaviors that facilitate adaptation to future occupational as well as other adult roles (Dreeben, 1968). Because of the importance of schooling in childhood and adolescence, year-round, full-time employment has become a prerogative of adulthood. Working part-time during adolescence may be seen as a transitional role (Allen & van de Vliert, 1984); the young person is no longer entirely out of the labor force but is still not a full-time worker whose economic livelihood, social status, and identity depend on the job. As such, youth jobs may be seen as constituting a bridge between the two major institutional realms of education and work.

As noted by Graber, Brooks-Gunn, and Galen in Chapter 9 of this volume, transitions require structural and/or functional reorganization. Though schooling prepares young people for their future adult work roles in many ways, the student role is fundamentally different from the role of worker. Despite considerable variation across educational levels and institutional settings, as well as across jobs, the student role is generally more dependent and childlike than the role of a worker, who is more often called upon to make independent decisions. Moreover, the individualistic achievement model, followed in most contemporary U.S. educational settings, yields learning tasks and achievements that are often more solitary than those performed in work settings. Workers more frequently work in teams, and are expected to contribute to one another's task performance.

Implicit in much of the discussion of adolescent employment is the notion that teenage work is a crucial experience, establishing important work habits, attitudes, and values that set the stage for future successful or unsuccessful work adaptation. For example, even the most inexperienced adolescent workers are often given great responsibility, handling cash register receipts, monitoring inventory, and opening and closing up retail and service establishments. It is pertinent to note that adolescents obtain jobs of greater complexity and responsibility as they grow older (Mortimer, Finch, Dennehy, Lee, & Beebe, 1994). Jobs obtained later in high school, in comparison to earlier jobs, involve more complicated tasks, more training, and greater likelihood of supervising other workers, and encompass a wider range of job types than those held in earlier years.

If, in fact, adolescence is a critical period in which the young person is developmentally ready for the crystallization of attitudes and values about work and for the development of achievement-relevant habits of behavior, then part-time jobs held at this time of life may be of great subsequent import. There is substantial evidence, in fact, that early occupational experiences are consequential for the formation of orientations toward work, including job satisfaction (Mortimer, Finch, & Maruyama, 1988), work involvement (Lorence & Mortimer, 1985), and work values (Mortimer & Lorence, 1979). Attitudes toward the job, and toward working in general, tend to become more stable as people acquire more work experience and grow older.

Acquisition and successful maintenance of the work role are, of course, central markers of the transition to adulthood. Failure to obtain employment puts the young adult at risk with respect to standard of living, susceptibility to deviant (even criminal) lifestyles, and the ability to make other life transitions (especially to marriage) successfully. Accordingly, much of the concern about minority youth unemployment is based on the assumption that the absence of opportunities for work in adolescence and early adulthood sets the stage for weak attachment to adult work roles and deviance. Sampson and Laub's (1993) research demonstrates the importance of adult work (as well as family roles) as a turning point with respect to the desistance of adolescent delinquent activity.

Work and adolescent identity formation

Given that the work role is a major aspect of the identity of most adults (Erikson, 1963), the role of future worker is likely to be a key component of the adolescent's future possible self (Markus, Cross, & Wurf, 1990). Because of its perceived connection to valued adult identities and roles, working in adolescence may be a particularly salient experience. Exposure to the work environment is likely to encourage thinking about the self with respect to future occupational goals. The employed adolescent may attend to the following kinds of questions: What do I like to do and what don't I want to do in my jobs as an adult? What credentials do I need to achieve my career objectives? What kinds of rewards (and problems) do people typically confront in the job I now have and in other kinds of work, and what can I do to optimize my future work conditions?

Indeed, the very experience of employment may encourage the kind of thought processes that Clausen (1993) calls "planful competence," involving serious thinking about one's opportunities and options, and making life choices that are congruent with individual abilities and interests. The transition to part-time work could signify progress in becoming an adult if it clarifies issues of vocational identity, including personal interests and job-related preferences.

Moreover, the adolescent typically acquires skills on the job that, although seemingly mundane from the standpoint of the adult worker, could be highly salient for the young person's developing work-related confidence: for example, the knowledge that one is able to find a job; meet supervisors' expectations; accept responsibility; relate to supervisors, coworkers, and customers; manage money; and be on time. The ability to function in the work world could signal to the adolescent an immediate capacity to control important outcomes, as well as to "make it" in the future.

Employed adolescents may learn to manage their time better so as to juggle more effectively the many activities associated with being a worker, student, friend, and family member. Interestingly, though employment is often thought to draw youth away from school, Mihalic and Elliott (1995) report that both employment and hours of work are *positively* related to involvement in school activities. The benefits of multiple roles in adulthood, given that they provide access to social contacts and support, diverse activities, and opportunities to cope with challenging problems, are well known (Thoits, 1983, 1986). The experience of successfully combining schooling and working could promote a self-image in the adolescent of one who is able to meet the challenges of multiple adult roles (Elder & Caspi, 1990).

Consistent with these considerations, Greenberger and Steinberg's (1986) study of students in four California high schools found that teenage employment was associated with self-reported punctuality, dependability, personal responsibility (Greenberger, 1984; Steinberg, Greenberger, Garduque, Ruggiero & McAuliffe, 1982), and girls' self-reliance (Greenberger, 1984). Several longitudinal studies have concluded that adolescent planfulness, responsibility, and future orientation do, in fact, have major consequences for adult adaptation (Clausen, 1991, 1993; Elder, 1969; Jordan & Super, 1974; Laub & Sampson, 1996; Mainquist & Eichorn, 1989).

In predicting the consequences of adolescent work, the broad meaning and social context of working must be taken into account. Marsh (1991) reports positive effects of adolescent employment on grades, but only when the worker is saving earnings for college. This connection of employment to a valued future possible self as a college student apparently transforms its meaning. It is noteworthy, in this regard, that the majority of seniors who plan to complete college save at least some of their earnings from paid work for this purpose (Bachman, 1983).

Alternatively, paid work may be responsive to family need and its consequences related to other family members' gratitude for the adolescent's contribution to the family's economic well-being. Depression-era adolescents who contributed to their families through paid work gained a sense of confidence and efficacy from helping at a time of crisis (Elder & Rockwell, 1979). Similarly, in economically hard-pressed farm settings of rural Iowa, relationships with parents improve with the son's higher earnings (Shanahan & Elder, 1993).

Taking a less salutary perspective, Bachman and Schulenberg (1993) suggest that youth employment is one component of a syndrome of "precocious development" that precipitates a hastened transition to adulthood. Just as early family responsibilities encourage the perception of oneself as adult and foster a take-charge attitude (Burton, Obeidallah & Allison, 1996), working adolescents may come to think of themselves as adults, given access to adultlike responsibilities on the job and a degree of economic independence. Such adolescent precocity may be linked to a state of "premature affluence" in which the young person has considerable discretionary income (Bachman, 1983). This syndrome (Bachman & Schulenberg, 1993) includes early involvement in dating (Mihalic & Elliott, 1995), adultlike leisure behaviors such as drinking and smoking, and withdrawal from the more dependent, preadultlike student role.

It is reasonable to suppose that adolescent employment would enhance economic and/or emotional independence from parents over the longer term. However, little is known about whether contemporary youth who have had greater investment in early work do, in fact, grow up faster, leaving school and moving into adultlike family/residential arrangements (leaving the parental home, cohabitation, marriage, and parenthood) and work roles (acquiring full-time work) more rapidly than other youth.

Adolescent work and the attainment process

Adolescence clearly constitutes the initial stage of a status attainment process that continues throughout adult life. The potential for occupational and income attainments in adulthood depends strongly on the groundwork established in earlier years. Adolescents must make highly consequential decisions regarding school courses and curricular tracks while, at the same time, institutional "gatekeepers," including counselors, teachers, and admissions officers, are screening and evaluating them for future learning and credentialing experiences.

Given that adolescents' perceptions of their own abilities, as well as the evaluations of others, are largely dependent on the grades they achieve, much of the concern about teenage work has focused on its implications for achievement in high school. Whereas some research has found negative associations between work hours and grades (Finch & Mortimer, 1985; Marsh, 1991; Mortimer & Finch, 1986; Steinberg & Dornbusch, 1991; Steinberg et al., 1993), under certain conditions working has been found to have positive academic consequences. Mortimer, Finch, et al. (1996) found that high school seniors who worked at low intensity (20 hours or less per week) obtained grades that are significantly *higher* than the grades of students who worked more hours and those of students who did not work at all. This pattern persisted even when background variables and prior grade point average were controlled. Similarly, D'Amico's (1994) analysis of the National Longitudinal Study (NLS) youth data showed that employment at low intensity (less than 20 hours per week) lessened high school dropout rates.

Carr et al. (1996) found that in an earlier cohort, National Longitudinal Study of Youth (NLSY) youth who were ages 16–19 in 1979, more hours of work during high school predicted a small decrement in educational attainment by the ages of 28–31 in 1991. But with respect to early socioeconomic attainments, adolescent part-time work has repeatedly been shown to have positive consequences for employment and income in the years immediately following high school (Marsh, 1991; Mihalic & Elliott, 1995; Mortimer & Finch, 1986; Steel, 1991; Stern & Nakata, 1989). Although some have expressed concern that these may be very short-term gains, Carr et al. (1996) report that they persist up to a decade following high school. With educational attainment controlled, employment in high school had positive effects on employment and wages 10 years later.

Prior anticipatory socialization, providing an opportunity to learn and to practice future roles, is generally a good predictor of successful role adaptation (Mortimer & Simmons, 1978). But we have little knowledge about whether the transition to part-time work in adolescence constitutes a valuable or necessary anticipatory socialization experience with respect to performance in the future adult work role. The answer to this question may depend on the quality of the work, as suggested by Stern and Nakata's (1989) finding that skill utilization in adolescent work predicts success in the job market during the first 3 years after high school graduation. Moreover, Schulenberg and Bachman (1993) find that students suffer when they work for long periods of time in low-quality jobs that do not make use of their talents, are unconnected to anticipated future jobs, and are being done only for the money. Moreover, they report many direct benefits of high-quality jobs with respect to reduced substance use and other salutary outcomes.

Although a vast social science literature examines the effects of experiences in childhood and adolescence on adult attainment – including the accumulation of human capital through education, work, and job training and the acquisition of social capital through the formation of social ties – the potential implications of adolescents' work experiences for these outcomes have been almost entirely overlooked. Some commentary suggests that adolescent involvement in the paid labor force signals a breakdown of human capital investment, mainly because of the negative association between hours of work and grades. However, there is reason to believe that the increasing prevalence of adolescent paid work is often accompanied by the acquisition of new forms of personal and social resources that facilitate future attainment, including competence and resilience. Moreover, working in adolescence may set the stage for continued simultaneity of work and educational investment such that adolescents who work during high school continue to combine the two roles effectively as they go through college and other postsecondary educational institutions, enhancing their human capital development through educational attainment.

In this chapter we are primarily concerned with the consequences of adolescent investment in employment, as measured by the amount and patterning of paid work. Though we are also very interested in the quality of adolescent work, the dimensions of work experience will be considered in subsequent reports. Here we examine several outcomes of adolescent work investment, including indicators of self-concept formation and mental health – self-esteem, self-efficacy, and depressive affect. We also examine high school achievement (grade point average), behavioral adjustment (drinking, smoking, and school problem behavior), educational aspirations and plans, and the adolescent's anticipated age of marriage.

We assess three transitional attainments, each of which is expected to have a strong influence on achievements later in adulthood: (1) educational attendance during the 4 years following high school; (2) postsecondary work experience; and (3) family/residential arrangements and status. Educational attainment is the most significant form of human capital development during the transition to adulthood, with critical implications for the trajectory of early occupational attainment (Sewell & Hauser, 1975). It is therefore especially important to determine whether employment during high school, net of family background characteristics, diminishes or fosters postsecondary educational investment. We also examine the extent to which high school employment predicts the acquisition of human capital through full- and part-time labor force participation during the transition to adulthood.

Finally, we examine whether greater investment in employment during high school leads to earlier movement through critical family-related markers of the transition to adulthood. For example, do adolescents who exhibit different patterns of employment during high school grow up faster, as evidenced by less time living at home in subsequent years and by more rapid movement into independent living arrangements, cohabitation, marriage, or parenthood? Early marriage and parenthood may have negative implications for the accumulation of human capital through schooling and work experience. Based on earlier studies, we expect the consequences of early marriage and childbearing to be more deleterious for young women than for young men, curtailing their human capital investment in education, as well as work experience, and diminishing their earnings (Marini, 1984, 1987; Marini, Shin, & Raymond, 1989).

Data source

To address these questions, we use data from the Youth Development Study (YDS), a prospective longitudinal study of a community sample of adolescents and their parents. A panel of 1,000 adolescents, chosen randomly from among students registered in the St. Paul, Minnesota, public school district, was surveyed annually from the 9th (1988) to the 12th (1991) grades in high school, with excellent panel retention (93%) over the 4-year period. Yearly questionnaires, administered in the schools, included a large battery of items concerning experiences in work, family, school, and peer group, as well as indicators of mental health, achievement, and adjustment. The surveys were mailed to students who were not present for either of two school administrations. To understand parental perspectives on teenage employment, mothers and fathers were also surveyed by mail in the first and fourth years of the study.

In the 3 years following high school (1992, 1993, and 1994), the respondents were mailed a brief "life history calendar" (Freedman, Thornton, Camburn, Alwin, & Young-DeMarco, 1988), on which they indicated various activities and family status changes during the previous year (school, work, military service, living arrangements, parenthood, etc.) in monthly units.

In the spring of 1995, approximately 4 years after most adolescents' graduation from high school (when most were 21–22 years of age), an extensive survey was conducted including the life history calendar, as well as measures of educational and occupational attainment, sociobehavioral adjustment, and mental health. Almost 78% of the original participants were retained through the 1995 survey. The study design and retention rates through the eighth wave of data collection are shown in Table 13.1.

Self-esteem is measured by the Rosenberg Self-Esteem Scale (Rosenberg, 1965), self-efficacy by the Pearlin Mastery Scale (Pearlin, Lieberman, Menaghan, & Mullan, 1981), and depressive affect by the General Well-Being Scale of the Current Health Insurance Study Mental Health Battery (see Ware, Johnston, Davies-Avery, & Brook, 1979). The unstandardized loadings for each construct, derived from a confirmatory factor analysis using LISREL 7, were used as item weights (see Appendix A). Indicators of self-concept, mental health, and adjustment (drinking and smoking) were measured both during high school and 4 years thereafter. The measures are shown in Appendix A.

Table 13.1. *Youth Development Study (Jeylan T. Mortimer, principal investigator; Michael D. Finch, coinvestigator)*

Administration	Administration in school Full survey				Mail survey Life history calendar, tracking			Full survey
Grade level	9	10	11	12				
Age	14–15	15–16	16–17	17–18	18–19	19–20	20–21	21–22
Year	1988	1989	1990	1991	1992	1993	1994	1995
No. of adolescent respondents	1,000[a]	964	957	933	816	782	799	780
Retention rate	—	96.2%	95.4%	92.8%	81.3%	77.7%	79.6%	77.6%
No. of mothers responding	924	—	—	690	—	—	—	
No. of fathers responding	649	—	—	440	—	—	—	
Percentage of respondents with at least one parent responding	95.9%	—	—	79.1%	—	—	—	

Note: This research was funded by the National Institute of Mental Health, "Work Experience and Mental Health: A Panel Study of Youth" (MH42843).
[a] A total of 1,010 consented to participate in fall 1987.

Prior Findings of the YDS relevant to the transition to adulthood

Prevalence and intensity of adolescent work

Like national samples of youth, the vast majority of YDS adolescents worked while school was in session during their high school years; 58% of boys and 70% of girls reported having paid employment in their senior year (40% and 63%, respectively, were employed in the 9th grade). With the panel data, we constructed continuous monthly work histories over the 4-year period of high school. Only 7% of the panel reported having no paid work at any time while school was in session during these 4 years. However, minority youth were consistently less likely to be employed than white youth; for example, during the senior year, 70% of whites were employed but only 47% of nonwhites. The students' involvement in work grew from a mean of 11 hours per week in the 9th grade to approximately 20 hours per week by the senior year.

During the high school years, adolescent work increasingly occurred in formal settings outside of private households (of those who were employed, 97% of senior boys and 94% of senior girls worked in formal settings). We also found that the character of adolescents' jobs changed over time, with informal work prominent in Year 1, concentration in restaurant work in Years 2 and 3, and then greater dispersion across various types of employment in Year 4. As noted earlier, youthwork also became more complex (as indicated by *Dictionary of Occupational Titles* [1977, 1986] ratings), required more training, and involved greater supervisory responsibility as the young people moved through high school (Mortimer, Finch, Dennehy, Lee, & Beebe, 1994).

We found virtually no differences, at any wave, between students who worked and those who did not, on a wide range of outcomes. Moreover, the intensity of employment (hours spent working per week) bore no consistent relation to indicators of adolescent mental health (self-esteem, self-efficacy, depressive affect, self-derogation, and well-being), time spent doing homework, academic achievement (grade point average), the closeness of relationships with parents and peers (Mortimer, Finch, et al., 1996; Mortimer & Shanahan, 1991, 1994; Mortimer, Shanahan, & Ryu, 1993), or occupational values (Mortimer, Pimentel, Ryu, Nash, & Lee, 1996).

However, evidence from the data collected during high school supports our conjecture that youth who are more heavily involved in their jobs may grow up faster and perhaps embark on a more rapid transition to adulthood. For example, youth who worked more hours per week became more independent of their parents (Mortimer & Shanahan, 1994), a trend that parents viewed as very good (Phillips & Sandstrom, 1990) but that some critics of youthwork view with alarm. Moreover, consistent with Bachman and Schulenberg's notion of "precocious development," we found significant positive associations between work intensity and alcohol use, which occurred irrespective of the particular operationalization of hours of work (Mortimer, Finch, Ryu, Shanahan, & Call, 1996). Controlling socioeconomic background, race, family composition, and gender, as well as the lagged outcome (alcohol use measured one year previously), 10th- and 11th-grade students who worked at higher intensity engaged in more frequent (contemporaneous) alcohol use. Considering the congruence of these findings and those of other studies (Bachman & Schulenberg, 1993; Mihalic & Elliott, 1995; Steinberg & Dornbusch, 1991; Steinberg et al., 1993), the linkage between working long hours and the use of alcohol appears to be one of the most robust findings on this subject.

Quality of adolescent work

Contrary to much recent commentary, we find that most of our job quality indicators are positively skewed (Mortimer, Finch, et al., 1994). For the most part, the adolescents' jobs did provide them with a chance to learn new things and posed challenges. Only a minority of the panel members indicated that they experienced stressors at work, such as time pressure or role conflict. Most of the employed young people agreed that it is "somewhat" or "very true" that the job "gives me a chance to be helpful to others" and said that they were "never" or "rarely" held responsible for things outside their control. The vast majority believed that they could keep their jobs as long as they wanted. Overall, the respondents' reports did not indicate pronounced dissatisfaction with their jobs or widespread exposure to detrimental work environments.

Still, variations in the quality of adolescent work have significant consequences for outcomes that may be considered highly relevant for future adaptations. For example, the sense of self-efficacy of employed adolescents increased over a 1-year period when they reported that they had opportunities for advancement, perceived little conflict between school and work, and felt they were paid well (Finch, Shanahan, Mortimer, & Ryu, 1991). Employed girls with opportunities to help others on the job also manifested a stronger sense of self-efficacy over time (Call, Mortimer, & Shanahan, 1995).

Using data collected both during and 2 years following high school, we find that a sense of self-efficacy distinguishes adolescents who were able to fulfill their senior-year plans for postsecondary educational attainment and residential independence from parents (Pimentel, 1996). Coupled with the fact that efficacy is influenced by the quality of adolescent work experiences (Finch et al., 1991), these findings provide a substantial indication that early work experience may be consequential for the subsequent transition to adulthood. Other orientations that we have found to be responsive to adolescent work experiences – changes in occupational values (Mortimer, Pimentel, et al., 1996) and depressive affect (Shanahan, Finch, Mortimer, & Ryu, 1991) – may likewise influence early attainment processes (Mortimer, 1994).

We find that adolescent work quality has significant consequences for occupational value formation. Occupational values play a major role in occupational choice and career development. Employed adolescents with the opportunity to learn skills on the job became more aware of the variety of rewards that work has to offer, fostering both intrinsic and extrinsic occupational value dimensions (Mortimer, Pimentel, et al., 1996). Moreover, when boys had work that enabled them to learn new skills, the quality of their relationships with both their parents and their peers improved over time (Mortimer & Shanahan, 1991, 1994). Finally, large proportions of working adolescents used their earnings in ways that fostered the attainment of future goals. Thus, adolescent work may be conceived as an instrumental activity directed to the achievement of future objectives, such as paying for school-related expenses and saving for college (Call, 1996).

The findings obtained thus far in the YDS, as well as a review of other relevant studies, lead us to believe that it is the quality, social meaning, and context of adolescent work that are most important for contemporaneous outcomes (Finch, Mortimer, & Ryu, 1997). These immediate consequences, though measured in adolescence, may be exceedingly important for future development and attainment. If the quality of work is indeed critical, it is reassuring to note that most adolescents describe their jobs in a quite salutary manner.

Reports of parents

The data acquired from the parents in the fourth year of the YDS enabled an intergenerational comparison of adolescent paid work (Aronson, Mortimer, Zierman, & Macker, 1996) and an examination of parents' retrospective assessments of the impact of work experience during adolescence on their own lives. The parents believed that working enabled them to develop confidence and resilience, as well as aspects of human and social capital that are rarely considered in sociologists' and economists' operationalizations of the outcomes of adolescent work (which are generally confined to educational achievement, employment, and income).

The parents reported that working in adolescence fostered a greater sense of responsibility, instilled the work ethic, and led to the acquisition of money management skills, confidence, and self-esteem. Working helped the parents to understand their own work preferences, to identify their job-related skills, and to prepare them for their occupational careers. Parents also reported that their ability to get along with other people was strengthened on the job and that the workplace was a source of friends. Interpersonal skills and friendship are key elements in the development of social capital, with important consequences for subsequent opportunities and attainments. In general, we find striking similarities in views about the benefits of youth employment when we compare the reports of parents, measured retrospectively, and those of their children, measured contemporaneously. The advantages of work are perceived as far outweighing any drawbacks in both parents' and children's reports.

Patterns of adolescent employment during high school

Prior studies generally assessed youth investment in work at a single time (D'Amico, 1984; Schill, McCartin, & Meyer, 1985; Steinberg & Dornbusch, 1991) or on two occasions, measured serially (Steinberg et al., 1993). Such studies do not capture the degree of work involvement over a period of time; work intensity at any single time may be a fallible indicator of involvement over a longer duration. In this chapter, we examine the pattern of work investment during high school and its relation to various contemporaneously measured attributes that we consider relevant to future adjustment and attainment, as well as its effects on key markers of the transition to adulthood.

Though work investment may appear to be a relatively simple phenomenon, there are multiple plausible operationalizations of the concept. That is, in any given week or month, an adolescent can be employed or not. Adolescents may work during more or fewer months in any given year. Furthermore, some adolescents spend relatively few hours on work during the period in which they are employed, whereas others work for many hours. We feel that it is useful to distinguish between the duration of adolescent work – operationalized here as the length of employment, in months, and its intensity – measured as the average number of hours of work per week during the total period of employment.

Work history data were collected each year during high school; current employment as well as that occurring in the previous year were registered. In annual surveys commencing in February of the 9th, 10th, 11th, and 12th grades, we asked students for a detailed list of their jobs throughout the previous year. For each job held, the students indicated the month and year the job started and, if applicable, the month and year it ended. They also reported the number of hours that they typically worked on each job per week. On the basis of these data, we computed each student's total months of paid work during high school (the duration of work), as well as each student's work intensity, or average number of hours spent working per week during the entire period of paid employment (the student's total cumulative hours of work divided by the total weeks of work). The present analysis does not include summer employment.

To examine the patterns of work activity, we constructed a typology based on experiences during 24 months of high school, including the full 10th-grade and 11th-grade academic years of 9 months each, and the first 6 months of 12th grade, up to the senior-year survey conducted in March 1995. We omitted ninth-grade employment because so much paid work at this time is informal (Mortimer et al., 1994), such as babysitting for girls and yardwork for boys. A five-category typology was formed by cross-classifying the two temporal dimensions of duration and intensity and including a fifth nonworking group (those who did not work at all while school was in session).

Duration of employment was registered by a dichotomy consisting of those who were employed more and those who were employed less than the median number of months (which was 18 for the total panel). Intensity was likewise dichotomized: Respondents whose *own* cumulative hours of work divided by their *own* cumulative weeks of work was greater than 20 were considered high-intensity workers; those whose cumulative hours of work divided by their weeks of work was 20 or less were considered low-intensity workers. Thus, this typology reflects the feature of adolescent work that has been the focus of so much attention and concern – employment for more than 20 hours per week.

Table 13.2. *Patterns of labor force participation, grades 10–12*

	Percentage distribution		Mean months of work		Mean hours of work	
	Boys	Girls	Boys	Girls	Boys	Girls
Not working	9.9	4.6	0.0	0.0	0	0
Low duration, low intensity	23.2	24.1	9.8	11.7	578	650
Low duration, high intensity	23.2	14.3	10.4	11.8	1,216	1,376
High duration, low intensity	18.2	30.6	22.0	22.0	1,263	1,328
High duration, high intensity	25.6	26.4	21.9	22.2	2,678	2,587
Total	100.0	100.0				
N	406	481				

Inspection of the data illustrates the five different work patterns. The distribution of students in these categories, and their actual mean months and hours of work are shown in Table 13.2. The first, very small group of students does not work at all during this period of high school. The second group works less than half the available months when school is in session at low intensity – on average, 20 or fewer hours per week. A third group works for a relatively brief period at high intensity, or more than 20 hours a week. The fourth group works for a long duration with more limited hours of work. It is especially noteworthy that although the cutoff point used to form the duration dichotomy was set at 18 months (the median number of months of employment in the panel as a whole), the actual mean months of work for those who worked at high duration – approximately 22 for both boys and girls – was close to the total number of available months of observation, 24. Finally, there are those who work for a relatively long duration at high intensity.

It is especially interesting to note that although youth in the low-duration, high-intensity category and those in the high-duration, low-intensity category register about the same number of total hours of work, the pattern of this employment is very different. Those who work at high intensity for a long period of time accumulate the greatest number of paid hours of work during high school.

As indicated by this typology, we believe that neither duration nor intensity, considered independently, tells the whole story about teenage work involvement. The adolescent's total investment in work may be more accurately represented by the combination of these variables. Moreover, these combinations of duration and intensity may be especially suggestive of student lifestyles and orientations to the future. For example, the student who works at low intensity for a long period of time may be consciously limiting her work hours to balance employment and studying appropriately, in an effort to maintain grades that are high enough to enable college admission while still accruing sufficient earnings to finance (or help finance) postsecondary education. In contrast, low-duration, high-intensity employment may be indicative of fluctuating life patterns and goals; students whose employment is characterized by this pattern move into the labor force at high intensity and then out again over relatively brief periods of time.

Consistent with these speculations, we do find that the work history patterns, based on employment in Grades 10–12, are significantly (as indicated by simple chi-square tests, $p < .05$) related to a number of orientations and behaviors measured in 9th grade. For example, the high-duration, high-intensity work history category was associated with more ninth-grade school problem behavior, drinking, smoking, and time spent with friends. Those who subsequently worked fairly continuously at low intensity had higher ninth-grade educational plans and aspirations. Low-intensity employment was also associated with higher intrinsic motivation toward schoolwork, higher academic self-esteem, and higher grade point average. Because of these relations, it is important to control these prior variables when examining the consequences of employment during high school.

Furthermore, the high school employment patterns are significantly related to student background characteristics measured in Wave 1 (see Table 13.3). For example, those who are employed at low intensity have higher parental education and higher family incomes than high-intensity workers. Young people who do not work at all are more likely to be foreign born. Girls (but not boys) in the nonemployed category have relatively high parental education and family incomes. Because of these and other differences, it is also important to control background characteristics in all assessments of the contemporaneous or long-term impacts of the duration and intensity of adolescent work. Whereas it is plausible to assume that youth employment will have different effects

Table 13.3. *Work pattern and social background*

	Boys				
	Parents' education	Family income	% white	% native born	% with two parents
Not working	3.22	4.95	.61	.82	.58
Low duration, low intensity	3.79[a]	6.01	.73	.89	.66
High duration, low intensity	3.53[a]	6.30	.84	.92	.80
Low duration, high intensity	2.97[b]	5.82	.76	.97	.78
High duration, high intensity	2.61[a,b]	5.64	.82	.94	.69
F-ratio	7.35***	2.42*	2.58*	2.44*	2.49*

[a] Low-duration, low-intensity workers were significantly higher than high-duration, low-intensity workers and high-duration, high-intensity workers.
[b] Low-duration, high-intensity workers were significantly higher than high-duration, high-intensity workers.
*$p < .05$ **$p < .01$ ***$p < .001$

	Girls				
	Parents' education	Family income	% white	% native born	% with two parents
Not working	4.00[a]	6.09	.67	.77[d]	.77
Low duration, low intensity	3.39[a]	5.95	.74	.92	.61
High duration, low intensity	3.47[a]	6.48[b]	.86[c]	.96[d]	.78
Low duration, high intensity	2.87	5.32[b]	.61[c]	.98[d]	.71
High duration, high intensity	2.69[a]	5.81	.75	.94[d]	.70
F-ratio	6.67***	3.02*	4.26**	3.85**	2.31†

[a] High-duration, high-intensity workers were significantly lower than nonworkers, low-duration, low-intensity workers, and high-duration, low-intensity workers.
[b] Low-duration, high-intensity workers were significantly lower than high-duration, low-intensity workers.
[c] Low-duration, high-intensity workers were significantly lower than high-duration, low-intensity workers.
[d] Nonworkers were significantly lower than high-duration, low-intensity workers, low-duration, high-intensity workers, and high-duration, high-intensity workers.
†$p < .01$, *$p < .05$, **$p < .01$, ***$p < .001$.

on both contemporaneous and lagged outcomes, depending on family socioeconomic background, we find virtually no evidence that this is the case. The work pattern was more strongly associated with some outcomes under consideration for children of college-educated parents; however, there were relatively few significant interactions.

Markers of the transition to adulthood

The monthly life history calendars (W5–W8) cover a 4-year time span after high school and include human capital investments in education, full-time work, and part-time work. They also include indicators of the youth's residential independence and living arrangements – living with parents, living with roommates, living alone, and cohabiting. For the present analysis, we computed mean months of time spent in each transition-related status each year – for example, mean months of living with parents, as measured in Wave 5, the first year following high school. Finally, we examine whether the youth had married and/or become parents by each wave of data collection.

Before examining the relationships between high school employment dimensions and activities during the post–high school period, it is instructive to observe the aggregate distribution of these activities, shown in Table 13.4. The percentage of students attending school, including 4-year colleges, community colleges, and technical-vocational schools, declines precipitously during the 4-year period. Still, approximately half of the males and females in Wave 8 report some school attendance during the preceding year,[1] and those who do attend school spend over 8 months of the year in this activity.

Over the years, the percentage of students who have part-time work declines, paralleling the decline in schooling. Again, however, the length of involvement in part-time work is substantial for those who report this activity. With greater time out of high school, full-time work becomes more prevalent, as well as the time spent doing it. In Wave 8, two-thirds of the males and 60% of the females report having had full-time jobs. Among those who report full-time work, the months spent engaged in it also increase over time. It is noteworthy that girls are more likely than boys each year to be doing part-time work and less likely to have full-time jobs.

More than one-fourth of the panel spends some time unemployed in

Table 13.4. *Aggregate distributions of students in states: Life history calendar*

	Males				Females			
	W5	W6	W7	W8	W5	W6	W7	W8
% Any time in school	73.8	53.7	52.6	48.2	78.2	63.9	58.3	53.8
Mean months in school – total sample	5.60	4.39	4.39	4.27	5.87	5.26	4.85	4.53
Mean months in school – if attended school	7.58	8.18	8.35	8.86	7.51	8.23	8.33	8.41
% Any time in part-time work	68.4	55.5	52.9	52.1	74.6	66.7	62.2	55.9
Mean months in part-time work – total sample	5.17	4.43	4.23	4.35	6.20	5.61	5.35	5.08
Mean months in part-time work – if worked pt	7.56	7.97	8.00	8.35	8.31	8.40	8.61	9.09
% Any time in full-time work	48.5	62.1	66.4	65.7	39.4	50.8	55.0	60.1
Mean months in full-time work – total sample	3.35	4.83	5.78	5.68	2.44	3.59	4.39	4.94
Mean months in full-time work – if worked ft	6.90	7.77	8.71	8.65	6.20	7.07	7.98	8.22
% Any time unemployed	27.2	17.5	12.7	15.4	25.8	19.9	13.1	10.1
Mean months unemployed – total sample	1.41	0.96	0.53	0.60	1.37	0.92	0.57	0.51
Mean months unemployed – if unemployed	5.16	5.47	4.15	3.88	5.30	4.61	4.33	5.04
% Cohabiting	5.7	12.4	16.5	17.5	14.0	18.7	28.7	28.8
Mean months cohabiting – total sample	0.39	0.79	1.19	1.40	0.90	1.41	2.37	2.39
Mean months cohabiting – if cohabiting	6.86	6.34	7.20	8.00	6.41	7.54	8.28	8.31
% Married by a given wave	1.6	3.4	8.3	9.9	2.0	3.3	3.0	15.2
% Parents by a given wave	4.1	6.8	8.3	13.5	12.5	17.8	23.4	31.8

Wave 5, the first year following high school; this decreases to 15% of the males and 10% of the females 3 years later. For those who reported any unemployment, by Wave 8 the amount of time spent in this state is about 4 months for males and 5 months for females. Though these figures may be somewhat exaggerated, given that students were instructed to check the life history calendar for each month that they experienced any unemployment (not necessarily lasting for the whole month), the data suggest initial difficulties for many of the panel members in finding and/or maintaining work.

With respect to the establishment of intimate and familial relationships, cohabiting increases from 5.7% to 17.5% of the males from Wave 5 to Wave 8; for females the percentages are greater each year, increasing from 14% in Wave 5 to almost 29% in Wave 8. As judged by the mean months of cohabitation registered each year for each gender, the cohabiting state lasts for approximately 8 months of the year (in Wave 8). (However, we cannot presume that cohabiting partners remain the same during these periods.) Fewer men than women are married 4 years after high school (9.9% of the men and 15% of the women). It is interesting to observe how many more women report that they are parents than report being married. In fact, by Wave 8, fully 32% of the women have had one or more children; this is true of only 13.5% of the men.

These activities during the transition to adulthood are, of course, interrelated (see Table 13.5). For both males and females, months of schooling in Wave 8 are positively related to months of *part-time* work. Because part-time work is a means of supporting oneself in college, this positive relationship is to be expected. In contrast, months of schooling is negatively related to *full-time* employment, which is difficult to combine with school. Those who spend more time cohabiting spend less time in school, and this inverse relationship is especially pronounced for females ($r = -.32$ for females, $r = -.16$ for males; for both, $p < .01$). Those who cohabit are more likely to do full-time work and less likely to work part-time (the latter relationship is statistically significant only among girls). Among girls but not boys, months of schooling and months of part-time work are positively related to living alone. Moreover, months of full-time work among males, but not females, is positively associated with living with parents.

Table 13.6 presents mean months spent in school and in part- and

Table 13.5. *Correlation matrix of life activities, wave 8*

Boys

	School	Full-time work	Part-time work	Cohabiting	Living alone	Living with parents	Living with roommates
School	1.00						
Full-time work	−.42**	1.00					
Part-time work	.40**	−.55**	1.00				
Cohabiting	−.16**	.20**	−.09	1.00			
Living alone	.02	−.04	.06	−.09	1.00		
Living with parents	−.05	.14*	.01	−.29**	−.26**	1.00	
Living with roommates	.18**	−.30**	.09	−.16**	−.15**	−.56**	1.00

Girls

	School	Full-time work	Part-time work	Cohabiting	Living alone	Living with parents	Living with roommates
School	1.00						
Full-time work	−.41**	1.00					
Part-time work	.45**	−.48**	1.00				
Cohabiting	−.32**	.21**	−.21**	1.00			
Living alone	.19**	−.03	.12*	−.16**	1.00		
Living with parents	.08	.03	.10*	−.29**	−.20**	1.00	
Living with roommates	.34**	−.12*	.21**	−.18**	−.09	−.32**	1.00

$* p < .05$, $** p < .01$, $*** p < .001$.

Table 13.6. *Education and work activities by marriage and parenthood,*
wave 8

	Boys			
	Married	Not married	Parent	Not parent
Mean months school	4.22	4.86	2.08***	5.02
Mean months part-time work	3.52	4.90	2.38**	5.05
Mean months full-time work	6.70	5.40	8.49***	5.18

**$p < .01$, ***$p < .001$.

	Girls			
	Married	Not married	Parent	Not parent
Mean months school	1.88***	5.29	1.75***	5.80
Mean months part-time work	3.14***	5.87	2.77***	6.45
Mean months full-time work	5.61	4.73	3.77**	5.29

**$p < .01$, ***$p < .001$.

full-time employment by marriage and parenthood status in Wave 8.
Here we see the costs of these early family involvements for human
capital investment. For females, both marriage and parenthood are associated with the curtailment of schooling and part-time work. For
males, these outcomes are associated only with parenthood. That is,
young men who are married and those who are not married report
similar levels of investment in school and in both part- and full-time
work. It is especially noteworthy that parenthood has very different
implications for the full-time labor force participation of men and
women. At this relatively early stage in adult life, mothers but not
fathers are likely to curtail their full-time labor force participation, limiting their human capital investment through work. Whereas men who
have become parents spend significantly more time in full-time jobs
(8.5 vs. 5.2 months for male parents and nonparents, respectively),
women who have become parents are less likely to spend time in full-
time work (3.8 months for female parents, on average, and 5.3 months
for nonparents).

Hypotheses

Based on expectations drawn from prior theoretical and empirical literature, as well as prior findings from the YDS, we hypothesize that students who engage in low-intensity work will have more positive contemporaneous and transitional outcomes. The critics of teenage employment have been concerned mainly about the deleterious effects of high-intensity work, not employment that is limited to 20 or fewer hours per week, which, as noted earlier, has been found to have positive consequences for academic achievement (Mortimer, Finch, et al., 1996) and school retention (D'Amico, 1984).

Those who limit their hours of work have likely achieved a better balance between school and employment because low-intensity employment means less interference with homework and extracurricular activities in school. Moreover, it is high-intensity, not low-intensity, work that is strongly implicated in adolescent alcohol use and smoking; low-intensity employment was found to be protective with respect to the same problem behaviors in the YDS high school data (Mortimer, Finch, et al., 1996). We therefore expect that a pattern of high-intensity employment during high school will be associated with the more negative contemporaneous outcomes measured at the end of the senior year of high school: poorer self-concept, greater depressive affect, lower grade point average, lower educational aspirations, more problem behavior in school, and more frequent drinking and drug use.

Furthermore, high-intensity work is more adultlike in character; it also yields greater monetary returns, increasing the youth's purchasing power and, perhaps, the feeling of economic independence. We therefore expect that youth who work at high-intensity during high school will plan to marry at an earlier age. We also anticipate that they will sooner relinquish the more childlike role of student and more rapidly acquire full-time employment after leaving high school. If they are "precocious" in their social development, as Bachman and Schulenberg (1993) suggest, high-intensity adolescent workers may also move more quickly away from the parental home, gaining earlier residential independence; they may also spend more time living alone, living with roommates, and cohabiting during the years immediately following high school. Finally, the "precocious maturity" argument would lead to the prediction that adolescents who work at higher intensity would marry and have children more quickly after leaving high school.

These predictions address the hours adolescents spend working per week. But given the cumulative character of our data, we are also able to consider work's duration – the period of time the student has been engaging in relatively high- or low-intensity employment. It is reasonable to assume that whatever benefits may be derived from employment may be less evident for those with a relatively short duration of work experience during high school. Moreover, work of long duration, which in our panel signifies working practically all (22 of 24) months while school is in session, implies an ability to maintain employment and to coordinate work and other activities effectively. This pattern may therefore bode well for early adult outcomes. In contrast, employment of short cumulative duration (which here connotes working fewer than half of the available months of observation) could imply difficulties in finding employment, or early failure to maintain the work role over substantial periods of time.

Admittedly, because we lack information about reasons for leaving jobs, much of this discussion is speculative. However, in view of the widespread approval of adolescent employment and the prevalence of teenage work, the approximately one-forth of boys and girls who engage in relatively little paid work activity, as well as those who report no employment at all (10% of boys and 5% of girls), may be deviant, not only statistically but also in terms of widely held social definitions of what constitutes appropriate behavior during the teenage years.

Analytic strategy

In the analyses that follow, we examined mean differences in outcomes for each category of the employment typology, using Multiple Classification Analysis included in the ANOVA program in the SPSS for Windows software package (1993). We then examined differences in adjusted means, controlling parental education, family income, race (coded 1 if white), nativity (coded 1 if born in the United States), family composition (coded 1 if a two-parent family), and a selection to the sample hazard rate to control for differential attrition (Heckman, 1976, 1979).[2] Finally, we added controls for relevant lagged behavioral and attitudinal variables. In the analysis of the psychological variables, we controlled the same constructs measured in Grade 9. In examining problem behaviors, we controlled ninth-grade problem behaviors and an indicator of peer orientation (school problems, smoking, drinking, and time spent with friends). For the achievement-related outcomes (education, work), we controlled intrinsic motivation toward school, an index of educational goals (combining aspirations and plans), and grade point average. The results of these final models are depicted in the figures. Unless noted otherwise, all differences described in the text are statistically significant at the .05 level. The means and adjusted means (actual numerical values) for all three analyses are given in Appendix B. Because adolescent work experiences may have different meaning for boys and girls, and therefore different effects on contemporaneous mental health and adjustment outcomes, transition markers, and early occupational attainments, we perform all analyses separately by gender.

Early employment patterns and outcomes relevant to the adult transition

As noted earlier, we previously found that hours of work, measured during each year of high school, had no consistent effect on indicators of mental health and self-concept. Does the patterning of adolescent employment during the high school years bear any relation to contemporaneous mental health and self-concept, measured in the senior year of high school, or 4 years later, when most respondents are 21 or 22 years of age? Might working be considered a risk factor with respect to early adult mental health?

We again conclude, based on the present analysis of the *pattern* of employment through high school, that key dimensions of the self-concept – self-esteem and self-efficacy – are *not* determined by the level of investment on the job for either boys or girls in Wave 4 or Wave 8. Whereas boys' depressive affect is also unrelated to the pattern of work activity, girls' depressive affect, in Wave 8 only, is highest for those in the nonworking category (Figure 13.1).

Consistent with our earlier analyses, we find that boys' alcohol use in Wave 4 is significantly related to the high school work pattern (Figure 13.2). Senior nonworking boys drink least frequently, followed

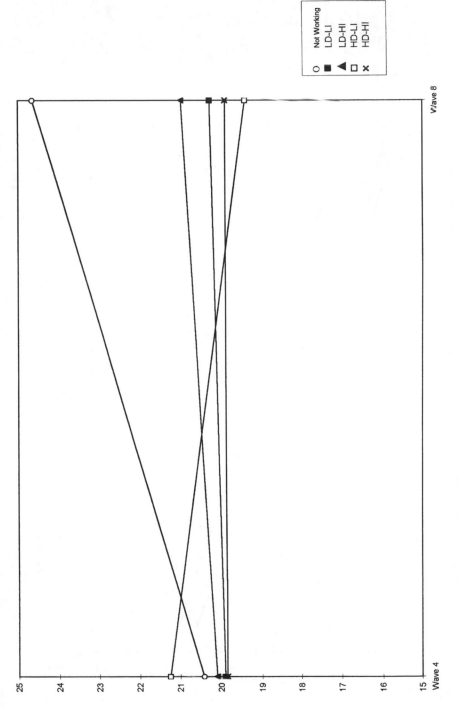

Figure 13.1 Depressive affect, girls.

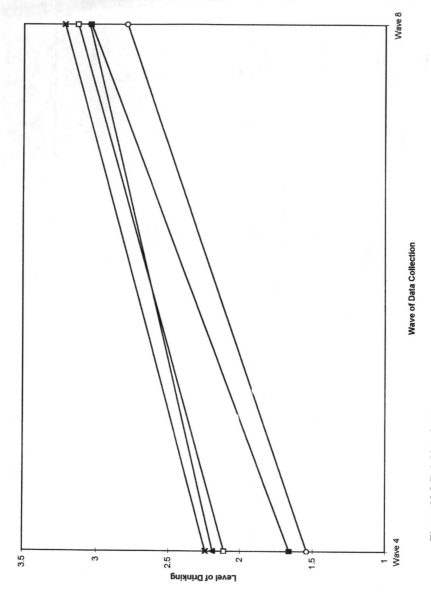

Figure 13.2 Drinking, boys.

closely by those who adhere to the low-duration, low-intensity work pattern. Those in the other three categories, who worked more during high school, drink more frequently.

Does the more frequent use of alcohol among the males who invested more time in work during high school signify the development of a pattern of greater alcohol use through the transition to adulthood? Or does it reflect only an earlier onset of an adultlike pattern of leisure behavior that other young men adopt somewhat later? It is especially interesting to find that though all categories of boys engage in more frequent alcohol use in Wave 8 than in Wave 4 (Figure 13.2), there are no longer significant differences by high school employment pattern at the latter time. This means that the male more experienced workers have increased the frequency of their alcohol use less than the other boys during this period. Furthermore, there are no significant differences in Wave 8 between the five categories of boys in binge drinking (operationalized here as the frequency of having five or more drinks in a row; findings not shown).

With respect to boys' senior-year smoking, nonworkers and low-intensity workers are less likely to smoke; high-intensity workers are more likely (see the means in Appendix B). However, the differences are reduced to statistical insignificance when we control prior problem behavior, measured in Grade 9. The same is true for smoking in Wave 8. We conclude that the association between the pattern of work and boys' smoking is spurious, resulting from earlier dispositions and behaviors.

Though we find no significant differences in boys' motivation and attitudes with respect to schoolwork in Wave 4, boys' work pattern is linked to their grade point averages and educational plans (see Appendix B). Again however, with earlier educational performance, orientations and plans controlled, differences in grades only approach significance. Differences in educational plans became insignificant when these lagged variables are included. There are no significant differences, by work pattern, in boys' school problem behavior or in the age at which the boys planned to marry.

Turning to the girls, we see relationships between the employment pattern and contemporaneous outcomes that depart from those observed among the boys. Among the girls in Wave 4, the low-duration, high-intensity pattern stands out as most deleterious with respect to

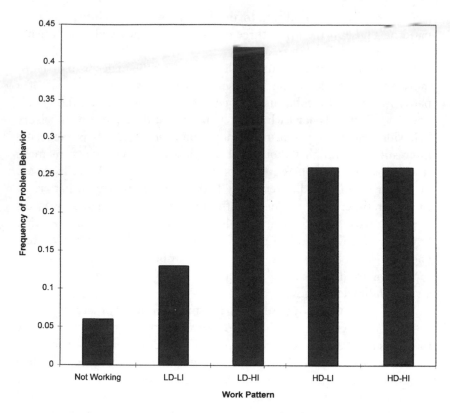

Figure 13.3 School problem behavior (Wave 4), girls.

the behavioral adjustment indicators. Those girls who pursue high-intensity employment for a relatively short period of time during high school exhibit the most school problem behavior in their senior year, drink alcohol most frequently, and smoke most frequently (Figures 13.3 and 13.4). It is particularly important to note that these differences persist even when the lagged variables are controlled. It seems most evident that short-lived or sporadic employment of high intensity is accompanied by a problematic lifestyle pattern for high school girls, involving problems in school, drinking, and smoking. Nonworking girls have the lowest levels of school problem behavior and drinking. Low-duration, low–intensity workers' scores also indicate relatively good behavioral adjustment.

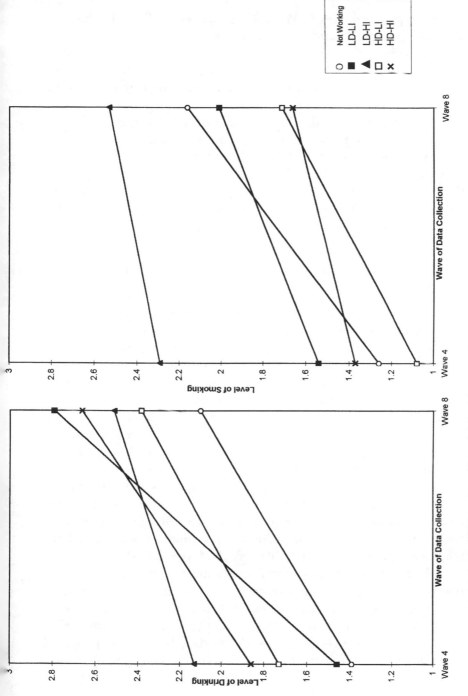

Figure 13.4 Drinking (left) and smoking (right), girls.

Among girls, drinking in Wave 8 is no longer predicted by the high school employment patterns when all controls are entered. However, girls' smoking 4 years after high school is still associated with the earlier work patterns. As in Wave 4, the most frequent Wave 8 smokers are the girls who exhibit the low-duration, high-intensity high school work pattern.

Though there are no significant differences in girls' grade point averages in the work pattern groups once prior variables are controlled, girls in the low-duration, high-intensity category have the lowest educational plans (Figure 13.5). Whereas when they were seniors girls in the two high-intensity work categories planned to marry at a relatively early age, these differential propensities can be explained by prior attitudinal and behavioral differences (see Appendix B).

Early employment patterns and subsequent transition-relevant outcomes

Let us now examine the implications of the pattern of working during high school for important status markers of the transition to adulthood. Examining the boys' data first, we find that even with the most stringent controls, the work pattern predicts the number of months of school attendance in 2 of the 4 years following high school – in Waves 6 and 7 (Figure 13.6; differences are not significant in Waves 5 and 8). Those who worked at high duration and low intensity during high school achieved the most months of schooling. It is especially interesting to observe the advantage of boys who worked at high duration but low intensity throughout high school relative to the nonworking boys. Boys in the two high-intensity employment categories also achieved less postsecondary education. These analyses indicate that high-duration, low-intensity employment for boys is an especially favorable pattern with respect to postsecondary educational attainment, with school attendance high and relatively stable over the 4-year period.

Girls' postsecondary educational achievement exhibits a similar relation to the employment categories across years (see Appendix B). Like their male counterparts, girls in the high-duration, low-intensity employment category are favored with respect to later educational attainment. Nonworking girls and those who worked for a shorter period at low intensity are similarly high achievers. The low-duration, high-

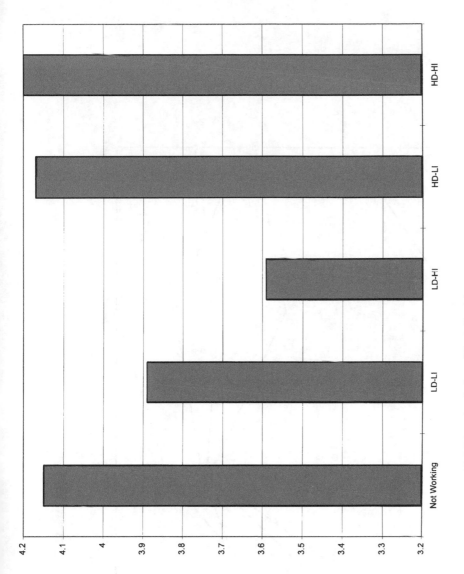

Figure 13.5 Educational plans (Wave 4), girls.

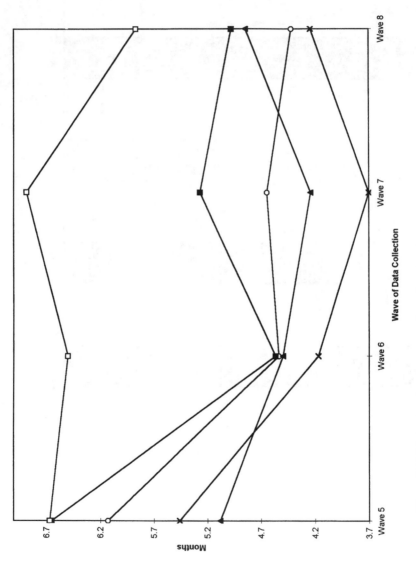

Figure 13.6 Mean months of postsecondary education, boys.

intensity workers achieve the fewest months of schooling each year. However, unlike the boys, these differences do not persist when earlier academic motivation and performance are controlled. We conclude that the relationship between the girls' work pattern and their postsecondary academic achievement is spurious, a function of earlier differences.

With regard to the second form of human capital investment, paid work experience, the boys' postsecondary part-time work, at least during the first 2 years following high school, appears to mirror their adolescent work experience (Figure 13.7). Not surprisingly, boys who worked for a longer period during high school, given that high school employment is generally part-time (part-time employment is defined in Waves 5–8 as fewer than 35 hours per week), log in more months of part-time work in Wave 5. Boys who did not work during high school are the least likely to work part-time after leaving school. However, significant differences disappear after Wave 5. Boys in the high-duration categories are especially likely to say that they obtained work in Waves 5, 6, and 7 with the same employers they had in high school (Figure 13.8). Those in the low-duration, high-intensity category follow close behind in Waves 6 and 7. Clearly, boys are capitalizing on their prior employment contacts in obtaining work in the immediate post–high school years.

Girls' part-time work exhibits the same pattern as that of boys during the first year after leaving high school in relation to high school employment, and significant differences between the work history groups persist 1 year longer beyond high school. The high-duration workers during high school are more likely to be working part-time in Waves 5 and 6; they are joined in Wave 6 by girls who worked at low intensity for a short period. Continuing the pattern established in high school, nonworkers are the least likely to subsequently hold part-time jobs (Figure 13.7). It is interesting to observe that girls who did little or no work during high school, in the low-duration, low-intensity category or the nonworking category, are less likely than other girls to be employed with the same employers they had in high school in waves 6, 7, and 8. (Figure 13.8).[3]

Turning now to full-time work, adolescent high-intensity workers, whether they were employed for a shorter or longer period of time, move earlier into full-time work roles (Figure 13.9; differences are significant for boys in Wave 5 and for girls in Waves 5, 6, and 7). The

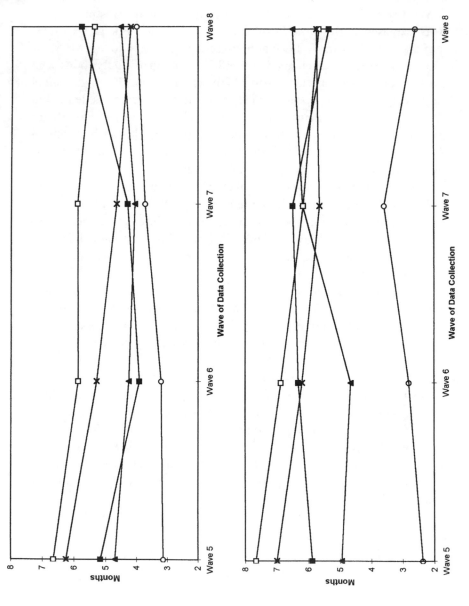

Figure 13.7 Mean months of part-time work, boys (top) and girls (bottom).

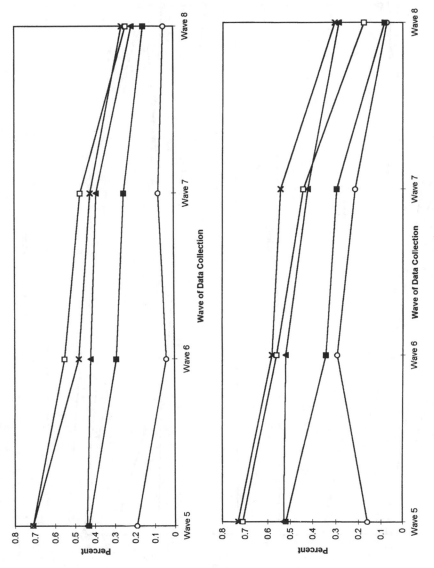

Figure 13.8 Percent worked for the same employer as in high school, boys (top) and girls (bottom).

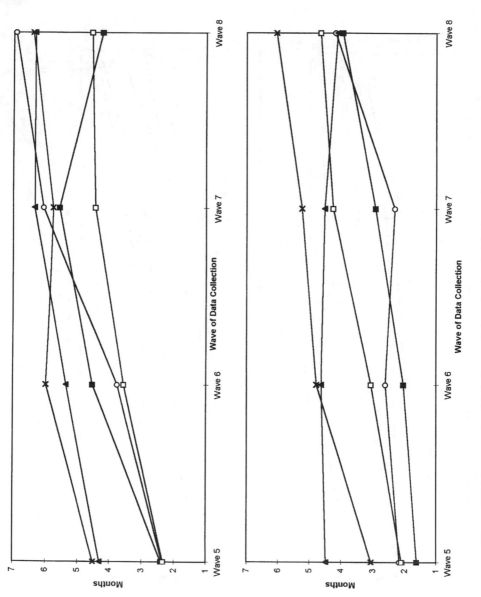

Figure 13.9 Mean months of full-time work, boys (top) and girls (bottom).

pattern is similar for boys and girls. The high-intensity workers in high school tend to have greater involvement in full-time work during the following years. By Wave 7, girls who had a high-duration, low-intensity work pattern are beginning to catch up in terms of full-time work. Furthermore, boys who invested the most time in employment during high school – the high-duration, high-intensity workers – report the highest annual earnings 4 years later (Figure 13.10). Girls' employment pattern in high school is not significantly related to their Wave 8 earnings when controls are entered.

It is interesting to observe that girls who did not work during high school, and those who worked for a relatively short period at low intensity, experience more unemployment than other girls in Waves 6 and 7 (Figure 13.11). These girls may not have acquired adequate knowledge of the job market, or sufficient social capital, to enable them to obtain jobs quickly in the years following high school. No significant relationship is found between the work pattern categories and boys' unemployment.

Turning to the indicators of males' family and living arrangements, we find that the pattern of employment during high school is not significantly predictive once background variables are taken into account. High-intensity male workers are somewhat more likely to be cohabiting only in Wave 7, but the differences between groups only approach statistical significance ($p < .10$); they become statistically insignificant ($p > .10$) when earlier problem behavior is controlled (see Appendix B).

With respect to the girls' living arrangements, we again find virtually no support for the "precocious maturity" argument. Though women who worked at greater intensity as teenagers spend more time in cohabiting relationships in Wave 8, the relationship between the employment pattern and cohabitation disappears when all controls are entered. The effects of the work investment pattern on the other residential arrangements are not statistically significant among girls. Nor does the work investment pattern predict marriage among females. Girls who worked at low duration and high intensity during high school are more likely to be parents in Wave 6, but this effect is not significant in the fully specified model. Girls in the low-duration, high-intensity group are most likely to become parents by Wave 8 – half have done

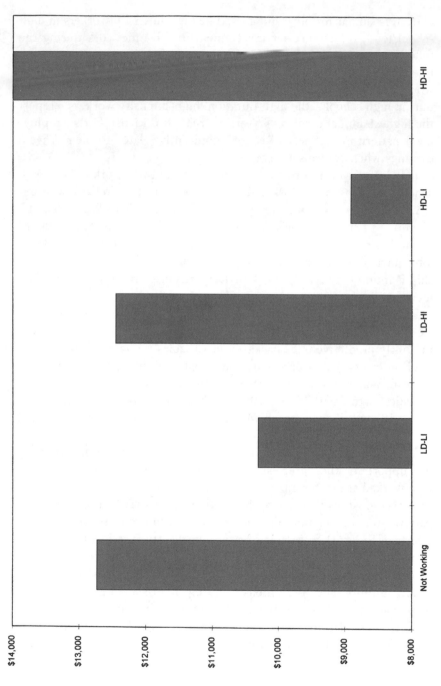

Figure 13.10 Annual income (Wave 8), boys.

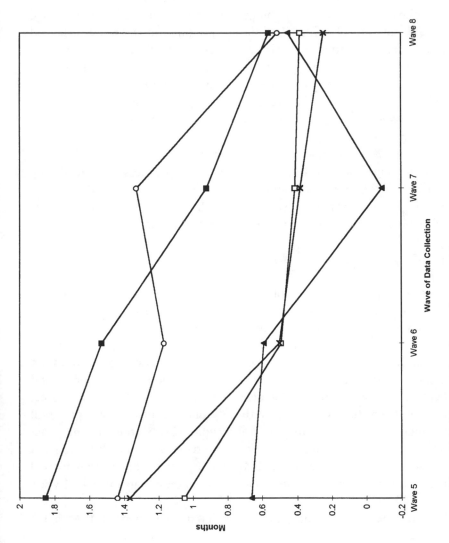

Figure 13.11 Mean months of unemployment, girls.

so – but differences between groups are again found to be spurious, accounted for by earlier behavioral differences.

It is sometimes argued that young people should limit their work as much as possible, and that ill effects may occur even at relatively low levels of intensity. If this were the case, our criterion of 20 hours, used to define the work pattern groups, could be too high. To examine this possibility, we divided the *high-duration,* low-intensity group in two, comparing those who worked 10 or fewer hours per week on average with those who worked more hours. (Because of sample size limitations, we did not control gender.) With background and the relevant lagged behavioral and attitudinal variables controlled, there were no significant differences between the two groups in grade point average or educational plans in Wave 4 or in postsecondary schooling or part-time work in Waves 5 through 8. Differences with respect to other outcomes were also statistically insignificant or, in a couple of instances, inconsistent across waves.

In the *low-duration,* low-intensity category, respondents with an average workload of 10 or fewer hours per week spent less time cohabiting in three of the four waves and were less likely to be married by Wave 8 than respondents who worked more hours. With rare exceptions, other outcomes were the same across the two groups.

Discussion

Is employment a risk or protective factor for youth? Does it compromise adolescent and early adult adjustment? This investigation, guided by new perspectives on work and adolescent risk behavior, shows that youth employment is neither wholly deleterious with respect to a range of healthy outcomes nor always protective. The answer to this question is complicated because of the multiplicity of potential outcomes and because the pattern of employment during high school does not affect each outcome the same way. With only one exception, we report null findings with respect to mental health indicators. Neither the mere fact of working, nor the hours of work at any given time, nor the pattern of employment during the entire high school period influence key mental health and self-concept dimensions either contemporaneously or 4 years after high school.

What makes this study unique is its investigation of the consequences of adolescent employment for early adult role adjustment. Whereas the enactment of adult roles is not a central focus of research on adolescent risk behavior, it is key to our concerns. There is clear evidence from this study that the patterning of youth employment does matter for important behavioral indicators of postsecondary adjustment, and that these consequences differ by gender. However, though recent commentary on adolescent work emphasizes its negative contemporaneous effects – such as undermining school performance, providing excessive discretionary income that the young person does not yet know how to handle, and exposing the youth to negative role models (often their peers) – we find that work can be protective and enhancing under some circumstances and pose clear risks in others.

For instance, though boys who work at high intensity during the high school years, and those who work for a long period at lower intensity, drink more when they are seniors, the work pattern has no predictive power 4 years after high school. With respect to alcohol use, boys who invest more in employment as adolescents exhibit an earlier onset of this behavior, but this is not a precursor of high alcohol use, relative to their peers, subsequently. Moreover, the link between boys' smoking, both before and after high school, and high-intensity teen employment is spurious.

For girls, not working at all, or working at low intensity for a short period, appears to be protective with respect to drinking in the senior year of high school. Those who work for a short duration at high intensity drink the most in the senior year. But as with the boys, girls' alcohol use is not significantly related to the work pattern groups 4 years after high school when earlier behavioral variables are controlled. In contrast, working at high intensity for a relatively short period of time is associated with significantly more school problems in Wave 4 and more frequent smoking at both times. The low-duration, high-intensity pattern also appears to be quite problematic with respect to girls' educational ambitions. However, the relation between the employment pattern and girls' actual postsecondary schooling is explained by prior differences.

Boys who work at high intensity during high school attend school fewer months each year during 2 of the 4 years after high school (Waves 6 and 7). The high-duration, low-intensity pattern, in which boys work for a relatively long time during high school but limit the intensity of their work – seems to be particularly favorable with respect to this educationally relevant outcome. Our earlier speculations about learning to manage school and work successfully during high school, so as to promote a similar mutually favorable connection thereafter, seem to be borne out by the boys' but not the girls' data.

A long period of employment during high school increases the likelihood of part-time work during the postsecondary period for both boys and girls. The fact that high school work duration is associated with subsequent employment with one of the same employers the young people had in high school suggests a mechanism through which this linkage is achieved. It should be noted that for girls only, unemployment in the postsecondary period is significantly heightened by a history of little or no employment.

We have limited evidence that entry into adultlike full-time work is hastened by highly intensive high school work experience. For both males and females, high-intensity workers are more likely to be engaging in full-time employment during the years immediately following high school. In considering high school employment in relation to both part- and full-time work, the overall stability of the pattern is most apparent. The duration of work in high school, generally of a part-time nature, predicts subsequent work of this kind thereafter; similarly, high-intensity employment in high school, averaging more than 20 hours per week, is predictive of early involvement in full-time employment. Moreover, boys who work most intensively and continuously during high school have the highest earnings 4 years thereafter. Jessor, Donovan, and Costa (1991) highlight the "stability of change": "Despite substantial change between adolescence/youth and young adulthood, the developmental process is characterized by stability and continuity across those segments of the life course" (p. 274).

What, then, is the implication of this study for the debate about whether working poses risks or benefits to youth (Finch, et al., 1997)? We conclude that there is merit in both arguments – but with respect to different features of adolescent work. That is, work of high intensity has some negative consequences for future human capital investment – through the curtailment of postsecondary schooling (for young men) – and should therefore be discouraged. Though boys who invest more time in work during high school begin to drink earlier, the earlier work pattern is not reflected in longer-term drinking behavior. However, sporadic work of high intensity seems to be especially problematic for women with respect to teenage alcohol use, and smoking both before and after high school.

However, this does not mean that working during high school has no positive consequences. The pattern of high school employment is especially relevant for the attainment indicators. Indeed, we find that young people who were employed for relatively long periods of time at low intensity during high school have quite favorable outcomes with respect to schooling (for men) and part-time work (for both genders). Male and female high-intensity high school workers move into the full-time labor force more quickly, and boys have higher earnings. For women, very restricted employment in high school (none or low-duration, low-intensity employment) is associated with more postsecondary unemployment.

It should be emphasized that earlier analyses, focused on contemporaneous outcomes while the students were still in high school, considered the effects of hours of work measured at single points in time, serially (i.e., at the time of the annual survey administrations). However, the fact that a student is employed more than 20 hours per week at the time of a particular survey may bear little relation to the employment pattern over a longer period of time. Students move in and out of work and change their hours frequently as they confront various demands and activities that lead them to change their schedules. Consistent with this line of argument, we find that work status at the time of the Wave 4 survey (working more than 20 hours per week, working 20 hours or less per week, and not employed) did not have greater predictive power, with respect to most subsequently measured dependent variables, than the work pattern considered here, despite its greater temporal proximity to the outcomes.

The findings presented in this chapter suggest that different patterns of work in high school carry quite different meanings. It could be that learning to combine school and work successfully during high school, as indicated by the maintenance of employment at low intensity over a relatively long period, sets the stage for a similar felicitous combination of postsecondary schooling (for boys) and part-time work (for both boys and girls) that provides financial support as well as continued human capital development (through what is learned on the part-time job) during the transition to adulthood.

A high level of investment in work during high school, however, as indicated by cumulative employment of more than 20 hours per week, may signify a process by which work comes to override other activities and the identity of worker comes to supersede the less adultlike student identity. A taste of some of the prerogatives of adulthood – higher earnings, more independence from parental monitoring and control, and more adultlike leisure-time activities (such as alcohol use) – may contribute to this process of identity transformation. Moreover, as work comes to consume an increasing number of hours, the combination of school and work may become ever more challenging, even stressful. It is no wonder, then, that high-intensity work during high school is associated with indicators of an accelerated transition to adulthood – a more hasty withdrawal from the student role for boys and more rapid incumbency of full-time employment (for boys and girls). Some of the findings suggest that a cumulative high-intensity work pattern may have more severe consequences for processes of psychosocial development among girls when it is of short duration. This underscores our conclusion that it is the *pattern* of work, not the mere *quantity* of investment in employment, that matters most.

In summary, this research reveals support for the working–problem behavior link, for boys and girls with respect to drinking in the senior year and for girls' smoking at both times. Consistent with our earlier analyses (Mortimer, Finch, et al., 1996), the linkage between employment and school-related outcomes, including motivation and performance, appears to be spurious during the high school period. Still, the employment pattern predicted boys' months of schooling in 2 years (out of 4) after high school. The most consistent finding, across genders, is the association between the high school employment pattern and work-related outcomes: part-time and full-time work, and employment with the same employer one had in high school. Boys with more employment in high school had higher earnings thereafter; girls experienced less unemployment. However, this investigation yielded virtually no support for the "precocious development" hypothesis with respect to family roles.

A large part of the story is still not told. We have not yet begun to assess the implications of the *quality* of work experiences in high school for the transition to adulthood. Given the importance of adolescent work quality in explaining contemporaneous psychological outcomes (such as work values, sense of competence, self-esteem, and depressive affect), it may be that the rewards, stressors, and social supports that adolescents experience in the workplace importantly influence the quality of work they obtain after high school, as well as the kinds of transition markers to adulthood that we examine here. It is of critical importance, moreover, to understand the kinds of work that are associated with the different dimensions of labor force involvement. For example, if those who engage in work of high duration and low intensity have jobs of special character – for example, jobs that are less stressful and demanding – this could explain the salutary consequences of this pattern with respect to the educational outcomes. This question, beyond the scope of the present chapter, will be addressed in our future work.

Appendix A. *Measures*

Parents' Education
1 = less than high school diploma
2 = high school graduate
3 = some college
4 = community/junior college
5 = 4 yr college degree
6 = some graduate school
7 = Masters degree
8 = Ph.D./professional
Family Income
1 = under $5,000
2 = $ 5,000– 9,999
3 = $10,000–14,999
4 = $15,000–19,999
5 = $20,000–29,999
6 = $30,000–39,999
7 = $40,000–49,999
8 = $50,000–59,999
9 = $60,000–69,999
10 = $70,000–79,999
11 = $80,000–89,999
12 = $90,000–99,999
13 = $100,000 or more
Income
What was your annual income in 1994 (before taxes)?
How much money have you earned during the past 2 weeks (before taxes, do not include benefits)?

Worked for same employer as high school
> During this past year, have you worked for any of the same employers you had in high school? (yes/no)

G.P.A.
> What is your grade point *average* so far this year? (0.00 = F, 4.00 = A)

Educational Plans
> What is the highest level of schooling you really think you will finish?
> 1 = Less than high school graduate
> 2 = high school graduate
> 3 = junior college graduate
> 4 = 4-year college degree (B.A., B.S.)
> 5 = Master's degree
> 6 = Ph.D. or professional degree

Expected Age at Marriage
> Do you expect that you will get married someday?
> If yes, about what age do you think you will be when you get married?

Smoking
> Have you ever smoked cigarettes (tobacco)? (yes/no)
> How often have you smoked cigarettes during the past 30 days?
> These two items were combined as follows:
> 0 = never (from first question)
> 1 = none in the past 30 days
> 2 = less than 1 cigarette each day
> 3 = 1 to 5 cigarettes each day
> 4 = about a half pack each day
> 5 = about 1 pack each day
> 6 = about one and a half packs each day
> 7 = about 2 packs or more each day

Drinking
> On how many occasions have you had alcoholic beverages to drink *in your lifetime?*
> How many times have you had alcoholic beverages to drink *during the past 30 days?*
> These two items were combined as follows:
> 0 = never (from first question)
> 1 = none in the past 30 days
> 2 = 1–2 times
> 3 = 3–5 times
> 4 = 6–9 times
> 5 = 10–19 times
> 6 = 20–39 times
> 7 = 40 or more times

Binge Drinking
> Think back over the last *2 weeks.* How many times have you had *five or more* drinks in a row? (a "drink" is a glass of wine, a bottle of beer, a shot glass of liquor, or a mixed drink).

1 = none
2 = once
3 = twice
4 = 3 to 5 times
5 = 6 to 9 times
6 = 10 or more times

School Problem Behavior

Since the beginning of school this year, how often have you:

Gotten into trouble for misbehaving or breaking school rules?

Been sent to the principal's office or to detention because of something you have done?

(0 = "never" to one or both of these items; 3 = more than 5 times on one or both of these items)

The following mental health variables were created using confirmatory factor analysis (unstandardized coefficients for Waves 4 and 8 in parentheses).

Self-Esteem (each indicator was measured on a 4-item scale from "strongly disagree" to "strongly agree").

I feel I have a number of good qualities. (1.000, 1.000)

I take a positive attitude toward myself. (1.774, 2.767)

On the whole, I am satisfied with myself. (1.712, 2.497)

Depressive Affect (each indicator was measured on a 4-item scale from "none of the time" to "all of the time").

Have you been under any strain, stress, or pressure? (1.000, 1.000)

Have you felt downhearted and blue? (1.505, 1.514)

Have you been moody or brooded about things? (1.303, 1.376)

Have you felt depressed? (1.814, 2.098)

Have you been in low or very low spirits? (1.735, 1.838)

Self-Efficacy (each indicator was measured on a 4-item scale from "strongly disagree" to "strongly agree").

There is really no way I can solve some of the problems I have. (1.000, 1.000) (reversed)

Sometimes I feel that I'm being pushed around in life. (.751, .945) (reversed)

I have little control over the things that happen to me. (.888, .953) (reversed)

I can do just about anything I really set my mind to do. (.458, .536)

What happens to me in the future mostly depends on me. (.271, .425)

I often feel helpless in dealing with the problems of life. (.991, 1.050) (reversed)

There is little I can do to change many of the important things in my life. (.851, .896) (reversed)

Appendix B. *Work pattern influences on outcomes*

	Boys											
	Drinking w4			Drinking w8			Smoking w4			Smoking w8		
	Mean	Socio-economic v's (SE)[a] Controlling	SE + lagged v's[b]	Mean	Socio-economic v's (SE)[a] Controlling	SE + lagged v's[b]	Mean	Socio-economic v's (SE)[a] Controlling	SE + lagged v's[b]	Mean	Socio-economic v's (SE)[a] Controlling	SE + lagged v's[b]
Nonworking	1.39	1.47	1.54	2.68	2.84	2.79	0.61	0.67	0.97	0.82	0.81	1.03
Low duration, low intensity	1.53	1.60	1.66	3.07	3.03	3.04	0.76	0.84	1.03	1.33	1.45	1.68
Low duration, high intensity	2.33	2.30	2.19	3.20	3.22	3.05	1.45	1.41	1.23	2.15	2.09	1.82
High duration, low intensity	1.99	2.00	2.11	3.05	3.04	3.13	0.74	0.74	0.96	1.07	1.11	1.27
High duration, high intensity	2.42	2.33	2.24	3.24	3.24	3.22	1.64	1.55	1.41	2.20	2.09	1.93
Overall mean	2.01			3.11			1.12			1.63		
F	5.40***	3.73**	2.47*	0.54	0.37	0.32	5.11***	3.53**	1.09	5.81***	4.30**	1.96

	GPA w4 Controlling			Educational plans w4 Controlling		
	Mean	Socio-economic v's (SE)[a]	SE + lagged v's[b]	Mean	Socio-economic v's (SE)[a]	SE + lagged v's[c]
Nonworking	2.73	2.75	2.83	3.78	3.73	3.83
Low duration, low intensity	2.73	2.66	2.70	4.12	3.94	3.94
Low duration, high intensity	2.42	2.47	2.68	3.54	3.64	3.88
High duration, low intensity	2.97	2.93	2.94	4.24	4.16	4.07
High duration, high intensity	2.51	2.58	2.67	3.53	3.69	3.73
Overall mean	2.66			3.83		
F	5.06***	3.58**	2.01†	6.74***	3.44*	1.33

Appendix B. (cont.)

	Boys											
	School w5 Controlling			School w6 Controlling			School w7 Controlling			School w8 Controlling		
	Mean	Socio-economic v's (SE)[a]	SE + lagged v's[c]	Mean	Socio-economic v's (SE)[a]	SE + lagged v's[c]	Mean	Socio-economic v's (SE)[a]	SE + lagged v's[c]	Mean	Socio-economic v's (SE)[a]	SE + lagged v's[c]
Nonworking	6.00	6.06	6.13	4.48	4.49	4.54	4.63	4.88	4.65	3.82	4.16	4.42
Low duration, low intensity	7.07	6.66	6.65	5.26	4.66	4.57	5.63	5.06	5.27	5.84	4.98	4.98
Low duration, high intensity	4.57	4.89	5.08	3.20	3.71	4.50	3.34	3.75	4.24	3.70	4.12	4.85
High duration, low intensity	7.03	6.72	6.67	6.92	6.51	6.50	6.95	6.58	6.88	6.35	5.97	5.87
High duration, high intensity	4.80	5.15	5.46	3.43	3.86	4.17	2.86	3.29	3.70	2.88	3.55	4.24
Overall mean	5.86			4.62			4.62			4.55		
F	5.82***	2.97*	1.70	7.74***	4.76**	2.94*	9.43***	5.85***	4.25**	6.18***	2.55*	0.81

	Part-time work w5 Controlling			Part time work w6 Controlling			Part time work w7 Controlling			Part time work w8 Controlling		
	Mean	Socio-economic v's (SE)[a]	SE + lagged v's[c]	Mean	Socio-economic v's (SE)[a]	SE + lagged v's[c]	Mean	Socio-economic v's (SE)[a]	SE + lagged v's[c]	Mean	Socio-economic v's (SE)[a]	SE + lagged v's[c]
Nonworking	2.92	3.04	3.14	4.13	3.86	3.20	3.52	3.57	3.71	4.59	4.87	4.00
Low duration, low intensity	4.97	4.85	5.17	4.43	4.09	3.91	4.59	4.15	4.28	6.09	5.43	5.77
Low duration, high intensity	4.52	4.75	4.70	3.77	3.95	4.25	3.62	3.90	4.05	3.67	3.97	4.51
High duration, low intensity	6.75	6.59	6.66	6.34	6.23	5.87	6.06	5.84	5.90	5.52	5.24	5.35
High duration, high intensity	6.52	6.53	6.26	4.72	5.02	5.29	4.07	4.43	4.64	3.32	3.81	4.18
Overall mean	5.48			4.74			4.47			4.61		
F	5.31***	4.50**	3.10*	2.43*	2.39†	1.90	2.66*	1.84	1.43	4.05**	1.50	1.06

Appendix B. (cont.)

	Boys											
	Full-time work w5 Controlling			Full-time work w6 Controlling			Full-time work w7 Controlling			Full-time work w8 Controlling		
	Mean	Socio-economic v's (SE)[a]	SE + lagged v's[c]	Mean	Socio-economic v's (SE)[a]	SE + lagged v's[c]	Mean	Socio-economic v's (SE)[a]	SE + lagged v's[c]	Mean	Socio-economic v's (SE)[a]	SE + lagged v's[c]
Nonworking	2.04	2.07	2.36	3.09	3.32	3.76	5.63	5.54	6.06	6.05	5.91	6.93
Low duration, low intensity	2.24	2.53	2.40	4.04	4.47	4.52	5.30	5.92	5.54	3.81	4.46	4.23
Low duration, high intensity	4.26	4.00	4.30	5.61	5.34	5.35	6.72	6.29	6.34	6.61	6.36	6.32
High duration, low intensity	2.28	2.37	2.34	3.13	3.23	3.55	3.98	4.33	4.45	4.45	4.65	4.56
High duration, high intensity	4.29	4.17	4.50	6.24	5.92	5.98	6.41	5.93	5.75	7.18	6.64	6.39
Overall mean	3.19			4.70			5.64			5.59		
F	5.09***	3.37*	3.54**	5.76***	3.77**	2.17†	3.02*	1.57	1.02	5.63***	2.58*	2.42*

	Worked for same employer as hs w5 Controlling			Worked for same employer as hs w6 Controlling			Worked for same employer as hs w7 Controlling			Worked for same employer as hs w8 Controlling		
	Mean	Socio-economic v's (SE)[a]	SE + lagged v's[c]	Mean	Socio-economic v's (SE)[a]	SE + lagged v's[c]	Mean	Socio-economic v's (SE)[a]	SE + lagged v's[c]	Mean	Socio-economic v's (SE)[a]	SE + lagged v's[c]
Nonworking	0.20	0.21	0.19	0.09	0.11	0.04	0.08	0.08	0.08	0.05	0.058	0.05
Low duration, low intensity	0.40	0.39	0.43	0.30	0.31	0.29	0.28	0.26	0.25	0.19	0.20	0.15
Low duration, high intensity	0.41	0.42	0.44	0.38	0.36	0.42	0.36	0.37	0.39	0.18	0.17	0.21
High duration, low intensity	0.70	0.69	0.71	0.58	0.58	0.55	0.49	0.47	0.47	0.27	0.27	0.24
High duration, high intensity	0.65	0.65	0.71	0.41	0.42	0.48	0.36	0.37	0.42	0.19	0.17	0.26
Overall mean	0.51			0.39			0.34			0.19		
F	8.73***	7.90***	7.24***	5.47***	4.93**	5.14***	4.17**	3.68**	3.97**	1.29	1.00	1.10

Appendix B. (cont.)

	Boys					
	Cohabiting w7 Controlling			Annual Income w8 Controlling		
	Mean	Socio-economic v's (SE)[a]	SE + lagged v's[b]	Mean	Socio-economic v's (SE)[a]	SE + lagged v's[c]
Nonworking	0.81	0.65	0.62	10,912.63	10,999.80	12,734.92
Low duration, low intensity	0.54	0.54	0.64	9,583.43	10,467.40	10,309.68
Low duration, high intensity	1.72	1.67	1.88	13,403.78	13,042.05	12,454.43
High duration, low intensity	0.63	0.77	0.67	9,174.90	9,396.38	8,906.43
High duration, high intensity	1.64	1.63	1.43	14,667.64	13,851.88	13,992.22
Overall mean	1.11			11,679.41		
F	2.35†	2.03†	1.63	6.04***	3.36*	2.85*

Girls

	School problem behavior w4			Drinking w4			Drinking w8			Smoking w4		
	Mean	Socio-economic v's (SE)[a] Controlling	SE + lagged v's[b]	Mean	Socio-economic v's (SE)[a] Controlling	SE + lagged v's[b]	Mean	Socio-economic v's (SE)[a] Controlling	SE + lagged v's[b]	Mean	Socio-economic v's (SE)[a] Controlling	SE + lagged v's[b]
Nonworking	0.00	−0.01	0.06	1.00	1.08	1.39	2.00	1.96	2.10	0.53	0.73	1.26
Low duration, low intensity	0.13	0.11	0.13	1.37	1.35	1.46	2.84	2.78	2.79	1.36	1.32	1.54
Low duration, high intensity	0.45	0.46	0.42	2.18	2.27	2.13	2.40	2.38	2.51	2.63	2.70	2.29
High duration, low intensity	0.24	0.24	0.26	1.73	1.68	1.73	2.44	2.78	2.38	0.94	0.92	1.08
High duration, high intensity	0.27	0.27	0.26	1.95	1.50	1.86	2.70	2.63	2.66	1.69	1.67	1.37
Overall mean	0.23			1.73			2.57			1.45		
F	3.63**	3.72**	2.50*	6.21***	6.86***	3.22*	2.20†	2.57*	1.71	10.87***	11.12***	7.52***

Appendix B. (cont.)

		Girls										
		Smoking w8 Controlling		Depressive affect w8 Controlling			Educational plans w4 Controlling			Planned marriage age w4 Controlling		
	Mean	Socio-economic (SE)[a] v's	SE + lagged v's[b]	Mean	Socio-economic (SE)[b] v's	SE + lagged v's[d]	Mean	Socio-economic v's (SE)[a]	SE + lagged v's[c]	Mean	Socio-economic v's (SE)[a]	SE + lagged v's[c]
Nonworking	1.39	1.60	2.16	22.93	23.55	24.65	4.17	3.95	4.15	26.75	26.49	26.07
Low duration, low intensity	1.78	1.75	2.01	20.06	20.20	20.25	3.94	3.93	3.89	24.67	24.59	24.60
Low duration, high intensity	2.98	3.00	2.53	21.71	21.01	20.96	3.23	3.31	3.59	24.08	24.23	24.54
High duration, low intensity	1.51	1.51	1.71	19.24	19.47	19.37	4.27	4.19	4.17	24.86	24.83	24.82
High duration, high intensity	2.12	2.09	1.66	20.21	20.01	19.87	3.78	3.88	4.20	23.99	24.06	24.54
Overall mean	1.90			20.16			3.92			24.54		
F	6.33***	5.97***	3.19*	2.93*	2.47*	3.96**	8.63***	5.93***	3.04*	3.62**	2.58*	0.70

	School w5 Controlling			School w6 Controlling			School w7 Controlling			School w8 Controlling		
	Mean	Socio-economic v's (SE)[a]	SE + lagged v's[c]	Mean	Socio-economic v's (SE)[a]	SE + lagged v's[c]	Mean	Socio-economic v's (SE)[a]	SE + lagged v's[c]	Mean	Socio-economic v's (SE)[a]	SE + lagged v's[c]
Nonworking	6.89	6.38	6.74	6.65	6.22	6.20	6.17	5.26	5.93	5.33	4.30	4.94
Low duration, low intensity	6.61	6.54	6.39	5.94	5.84	5.58	5.78	5.55	5.90	5.80	5.64	5.58
Low duration, high intensity	4.34	4.76	5.54	3.40	3.78	5.89	2.38	2.98	4.97	2.54	2.98	4.97
High duration, low intensity	6.97	6.58	6.69	6.50	6.17	6.10	5.77	5.39	5.49	5.64	5.35	5.49
High duration, high intensity	4.75	5.20	5.65	4.40	4.83	5.20	4.24	4.83	5.01	3.25	3.76	4.26
Overall mean	5.98			5.45			4.99			4.66		
F	6.65***	3.36*	1.10	6.34***	3.43**	0.57	6.16***	3.07*	0.48	7.45***	4.43**	1.14

Appendix B. (cont.)

	Girls											
	Part-time work w5			Part-time work w6			Part-time work w7			Part-time work w8		
	Mean	Socio-economic Controlling v's (SE)[a]	SE + lagged v's[c]	Mean	Socio-economic Controlling v's (SE)[a]	SE + lagged v's[c]	Mean	Socio-economic Controlling v's (SE)[a]	SE + lagged v's[c]	Mean	Socio-economic Controlling v's (SE)[a]	SE + lagged v's[c]
Nonworking	3.00	3.30	2.37	3.47	3.32	2.81	4.22	3.57	3.59	2.72	2.12	2.58
Low duration, low intensity	5.77	5.85	5.88	5.85	4.83	6.32	6.49	6.32	6.50	6.08	5.02	5.33
Low duration, high intensity	4.56	4.91	4.95	3.74	4.11	4.65	4.11	4.83	6.18	4.36	4.67	6.50
High duration, low intensity	7.85	7.60	7.66	7.09	6.85	6.87	6.47	6.16	6.16	5.98	5.74	5.65
High duration, high intensity	6.78	6.78	6.99	5.90	6.09	6.20	5.32	5.66	5.64	5.15	5.47	5.73
Overall mean	6.43			5.90			5.79			5.43		
F	8.12***	5.95****	5.63***	5.50***	4.14**	2.91*	3.06*	1.86	1.16	2.62*	2.62*	1.51

	Full-time work w5 Controlling			Full-time work w6 Controlling			Full-time work w7 Controlling			Full-time work w8 Controlling		
	Mean	Socio-economic v's (SE)[a]	SE + lagged v's[c]	Mean	Socio-economic v's (SE)[a]	SE + lagged v's[c]	Mean	Socio-economic v's (SE)[a]	SE + lagged v's[c]	Mean	Socio-economic v's (SE)[a]	SE + lagged v's[c]
Nonworking	1.44	1.54	2.17	1.94	2.54	2.61	1.44	2.24	2.31	3.22	3.73	4.19
Low duration, low intensity	1.55	1.54	1.62	2.63	2.57	2.04	3.47	3.52	2.92	3.79	3.77	3.95
Low duration, high intensity	3.38	3.54	4.48	4.28	4.37	4.63	4.28	4.17	4.52	5.16	5.37	4.12
High duration, low intensity	2.15	2.17	2.10	3.16	3.21	3.06	4.20	4.30	4.26	4.51	4.53	4.66
High duration, high intensity	3.40	3.31	3.06	4.98	4.79	4.78	5.46	5.16	5.24	6.52	6.29	6.05
Overall mean	2.45			3.57			4.22			4.87		
F	4.42**	4.21**	3.48**	4.76***	3.85**	4.29**	3.79**	2.23†	2.62*	4.74**	3.70**	2.03†

Appendix B. (cont.)

		Girls										
		Unemployment w5 Controlling			Unemployment w6 Controlling			Unemployment w7 Controlling			Unemployment w8 Controlling		
	Mean	Socio-economic v's (SE)[a]	SE + lagged v's[c]	Mean	Socio-economic v's (SE)[a]	SE + lagged v's[c]	Mean	Socio-economic v's (SE)[a]	SE + lagged v's[c]	Mean	Socio-economic v's (SE)[a]	SE + lagged v's[c]
Nonworking	1.56	1.40	1.44	1.29	1.28	1.17	1.33	1.34	1.33	0.39	0.44	0.51
Low duration, low intensity	1.96	1.89	1.85	1.42	1.46	1.53	0.97	0.98	0.92	0.52	0.51	0.56
Low duration, high intensity	1.50	1.30	0.66	1.24	1.13	0.59	0.47	0.44	−0.09	0.66	0.60	0.45
High duration, low intensity	0.95	1.03	1.05	0.37	0.41	0.49	0.41	0.40	0.41	0.52	0.55	0.38
High duration, high intensity	1.24	1.34	1.37	0.49	0.44	0.50	0.31	0.34	0.38	0.36	0.35	0.25
Overall mean	1.37			0.80			0.57			0.49		
F	1.72	1.20	1.23	4.42**	4.26**	3.24*	2.57*	2.46*	2.61*	0.25	0.23	0.29

	Worked for same employer as hs w5 Controlling			Worked for same employer as hs w6 Controlling			Worked for same employer as hs w7 Controlling			Worked for same employer as hs w8 Controlling		
	Mean	Socio-economic v's (SE)[a]	SE + lagged v's[c]	Mean	Socio-economic v's (SE)[a]	SE + lagged v's[c]	Mean	Socio-economic v's (SE)[a]	SE + lagged v's[c]	Mean	Socio-economic v's (SE)[a]	SE + lagged v's[c]
Nonworking	0.17	0.20	0.16	0.29	0.34	0.29	0.22	0.25	0.21	0.06	0.05	0.07
Low duration, low intensity	0.49	0.51	0.52	0.35	0.36	0.34	0.33	0.32	0.29	0.16	0.15	0.08
Low duration, high intensity	0.42	0.46	0.53	0.40	0.43	0.52	0.33	0.36	0.42	0.17	0.19	0.28
High duration, low intensity	0.75	0.72	0.71	0.59	0.58	0.56	0.47	0.46	0.44	0.19	0.18	0.17
High duration, high intensity	0.66	0.67	0.73	0.59	0.60	0.58	0.51	0.52	0.54	0.26	0.26	0.30
Overall mean	0.60			0.50			0.42			0.19		
F	10.83***	8.11***	6.54***	5.41***	4.42**	3.20*	3.11*	2.79*	2.97*	1.53	1.55	3.25*

Appendix B. (cont.)

	Girls											
	Annual income w8 Controlling			Cohabiting w8 Controlling			Parenting w6 Controlling			Parenting w8 Controlling		
	Mean	Socio-economic v's (SE)[a]	SE + lagged v's[c]	Mean	Socio-economic v's (SE)[a]	SE + lagged v's[b]	Mean	Socio-economic v's (SE)[a]	SE + lagged v's[b]	Mean	Socio-economic v's (SE)[a]	SE + lagged v's[b]
Nonworking	5,295.00	6,140.68	7,553.46	2.28	2.45	3.00	0.06	0.08	0.09	0.17	0.21	0.24
Low duration, low intensity	8,897.96	8,808.66	9,077.82	1.88	1.92	2.14	0.20	0.21	0.21	0.23	0.23	0.25
Low duration, high intensity	9,544.57	9,413.12	8,652.78	3.14	3.05	2.78	0.31	0.28	0.22	0.52	0.44	0.37
High duration, low intensity	9,868.25	10,279.34	10,533.13	1.67	1.74	2.01	0.11	0.13	0.15	0.23	0.26	0.30
High duration, high intensity	11,117.10	10,632.43	10,352.52	3.30	3.16	2.86	0.16	0.15	0.14	0.34	0.32	0.32
Overall mean	9,806.71			2.34			0.17			0.29		
F	2.76*	2.08†	1.07	2.88*	2.10†	0.77	3.56**	2.11†	1.03	5.52***	2.65*	0.86

†$p < .10$; *$p < .05$; **$p < .01$; ***$p < .001$.

[a] Race, nativity, family income, family composition, parents' education, and (for measures in w5–w8), a selection term.

[b] Socioeconomic variables (listed in a) and ninth-grade drinking, smoking, school problem behavior, and time with friends.

[c] Socioeconomic variables (listed in a) and ninth-grade grade point average, educational goals, and intrinsic motivation toward school.

[d] Socioeconomic variables (listed in a) and ninth-grade depressive affect.

Notes

1. Because the Wave 8 survey was conducted in the spring, with data collection beginning in March 1995, we are not able to determine whether a baccalaureate degree is conferred within 4 years.
2. Predictors in the selection equation were nativity, race, family income, family composition, parents' education, and academic self-esteem.
3. It is possible for girls in the nonemployed category (based on school year employment) to be "working with the same employer as in high school" because the prior employment could have been in the summer months.

References

Allen, V. L., & van de Vliert, E. (1984). A role theoretical perspective on transitional processes. In V. L. Allen & E. van de Vliert (Eds.), *Role transitions: Explorations and explanations* (pp. 3–18). New York: Plenum Press.

Aronson, P. J., Mortimer, J. T., Zierman, C., & Hacker, M. (1996). Generational differences in work experiences and evaluations. In J. T. Mortimer & M. D. Finch (Eds.), *Adolescents, work, and family: An intergenerational developmental analysis* (pp. 25 62). Newbury Park, CA: Sage.

Bachman, J. G. (1983). Premature affluence: "Do high school students earn too much?" *Economic Outlook USA, 10*(3). Ann Arbor: Survey Research Center, Institute for Social Research, University of Michigan.

Bachman, J. G., Bare, D. E., & Frankie, E. I. (1986). *Correlates of employment among high school seniors.* Ann Arbor, MI: Institute for Social Research.

Bachman, J. G., & Schulenberg, J. (1993). How part-time work intensity relates to drug use, problem behavior, time use, and satisfaction among high school seniors: Are these consequences or merely correlates? *Developmental Psychology, 29,* 220–235.

Burton, L. M., Obeidallah, D. A., & Allison, K. (1996). Ethnographic insights on social context and adolescent development among inner-city African-American teens. In R. Jessor, A. Colby, & R. A. Shweder (Eds.), *Ethnography and human development: Concept and meaning in social inquiry* (pp. 395–410). Chicago: University of Chicago Press.

Call, K. T. (1996). The implications of helpfulness for possible selves. In J. T. Mortimer & M. D. Finch (Eds.), *Adolescents, work, and family: An intergenerational developmental analysis* (pp. 63–96). Newbury Park, CA: Sage.

Call, K. T., Mortimer, J. T., & Shanahan, M. (1995). Helpfulness and the development of competence in adolescence. *Child Development, 66,* 129–138.

Carr, R. V., Wright, J. D., & Brody, C. J. (1996). Effects of high school work experience a decade later: Evidence from the National Longitudinal Study. *Sociology of Education, 69,* 66–81.

Clausen, J. A. (1991). Adolescent competence and the shaping of the life course. *American Journal of Sociology, 96,* 805–842.

Clausen, J. A. (1993). *American lives: Looking back at the children of the Great Depression.* New York: Free Press.

D'Amico, R. J. (1984). Does employment during high school impair academic progress? *Sociology of Education, 57,* 152–164.

Dreeben, R. (1968). *On what is learned in school.* Reading, MA: Addison-Wesley.

Elder, G. H., Jr. (1969). Occupational mobility, life patterns, and personality. *Journal of Health and Social Behavior, 10,* 308–323.

Elder, G. H., & Caspi, A. (1990). Studying lives in changing society: Sociological and personological explorations. In A. I. Rabin, R. A. Zucker, R. Emmons, & S. Franks (Eds.), *Studying persons and lives* (pp. 201–247). New York: Springer.

Elder, G. H., Jr., & Rockwell, R. C. (1979). Economic depression and postwar opportunity in men's lives: A study of life patterns and health. In R. G. Simmons (Ed.), *Research in community and mental health* (pp. 249–303). Greenwich, CT: JAI Press.

Erickson, E. H. (1963). *Childhood and society* (2nd ed.). New York: Norton.

Finch, M. D., & Mortimer, J. T. (1985). Adolescent work hours and the process of achievement. In A. C. Kerchkoff (Ed.), *Research in sociology of education and socialization* (Vol. 5, pp. 171–196). Greenwich, CT: JAI Press.

Finch, M. D., Mortimer, J. T., & Ryu, S. (1997). Transition into part-time work: Health risks and opportunities. In J. Schulenberg, J. Maggs, & K. Hurrelman (Eds.), *Health risks and developmental transitions during adolescence* (pp. 321–344). New York: Cambridge University Press.

Finch, M. D., Shanahan, M. J., Mortimer, J. T., & Ryu, S. (1991). Work experience and control orientation in adolescence. *American Sociological Review, 56,* 597–611.

Freedman, D., Thornton, A., Camburn, D., Alwin, D., & Young-DeMarco, L. (1988). The life history calendar: A technique for collecting retrospective data. In C. C. Clogg (Ed.), *Sociological methodology* (Vol. 18, pp. 37–68). San Francisco: Jossey-Bass.

Greenberger, E. (1984). Children, family, and work. In N. D. Reppucci,

L. A. Weithorn, E. P. Mulvey, & J. Monahan (Eds.), *Children, mental health, and the law* (pp. 103–122). Beverly Hills, CA: Sage.

Greenberger, E. (1988). Working in teenage America. In J. T. Mortimer & K. M. Borman (Eds.), *Work experience and psychological development* (pp. 21–50). Boulder, CO: Westview.

Greenberger, E., & Steinberg, L. D. (1986). *When teenagers work.* New York: Basic Books.

Heckman, J. J. (1976). The common structure of statistical models of truncation, sample selection and limited dependent variables and a sample estimator for such models. *Annals of Economic and Social Measurement, 5,* 475–492.

Heckman, J. J. (1979). Sample selection as a specification error. *Econometrica, 45,* 153–161.

Jessor, R., Donovan, J. E., & Costa, F. M. (1991). *Beyond adolescence: Problem behavior and young adult development.* New York: Cambridge University Press.

Jordan, J. P., & Super, D. E. (1974). The prediction of early adult vocational behavior. In D. F. Ricks, A. Thomas, & M. Roff (Eds.), *Life history research in psychopathology* (Vol. 3, pp. 108–130). Minneapolis: University of Minnesota Press.

Laub, H., & Sampson, R. J. (1996, March 9). *The long-term reach of adolescent competence: Socioeconomic achievement in the lives of disadvantaged men.* Paper presented at the biennial meeting of the Society for Research on Adolescence,

Lorence, J., & Mortimer, J. T. (1985). Job involvement through the life course: A panel study of three age groups. *American Sociological Review, 50,* 618–638.

Mainquist, S., & Eichorn, D. (1989). Competence in work settings. In D. Stern & D. Eichorn (Eds.), *Adolescence and work: Influences of social structure, labor markets, and culture* (pp. 327–398). Hillsdale, NJ: Erlbaum.

Manning, W. D. (1990). Parenting employed teenagers. *Youth and Society, 22,* 184–200.

Marini, M. M. (1984). Women's educational attainment and the timing of entry into parenthood. *American Sociological Review, 49,* 491–511.

Marini, M. M. (1987). Measuring the process of role change during the transition to adulthood. *Social Science Research, 16,* 1–38.

Marini, M. M., Shin, H. C., & Raymond, J. (1989). Socioeconomic consequences of the process of transition to adulthood. *Social Science Research, 13,* 89–135.

Markus, H., Cross, S., & Wurf, E. (1990). The role of the self-system in competence. In R. J. Sternberg & J. Kolligan, Jr. (Eds.), *Competence considered* (pp. 205–226). New Haven, CT: Yale University Press.

Marsh, H. W. (1991). Employment during high school: Character building or a subversion of academic goals? *Sociology of Education, 64,* 172–189.

Mihalic, S. W., & Elliott, D. (1995, November 16). *Short and long term consequences of adolescent work.* Paper presented at the annual meeting of the American Society of Criminology, Boston.

Mortimer, J. T. (1994). Individual differences as precursors of youth unemployment. In A. C. Peterson & J. T. Mortimer (Eds.), *Youth unemployment and society* (pp. 172–198). New York: Cambridge University Press.

Mortimer, J. T., & Finch, M. D. (1986). The effects of part-time work on self-concept and achievement. In K. Borman & J. Reisman (Eds.), *Becoming a worker* (pp. 66–89). Norwood, NJ: Ablex.

Mortimer, J. T., & Lorence, J. (1979). Work experience and occupational value socialization: A longitudinal study. *American Journal of Sociology, 84,* 1361–1385.

Mortimer, J. T., Finch, M. D., Dennehy, K., Lee, C. L., & Beebe, T. (1994). Work experience in adolescence. *Journal of Vocational Education Research, 19,* 39–70.

Mortimer, J. T., Finch, M. D., & Maruyama, G. (1988). Work experience and job satisfaction: Variation by age and gender. In J. T. Mortimer & K. Borman (Eds.), *Work experience and psychological development through the life span* (pp. 109–155). Boulder, CO: Westview Press.

Mortimer, J. T., Finch, M. D., Ryu, S., Shanahan, M. J., & Call, K. T. (1996). The effects of work intensity on adolescent mental health, achievement and behavioral adjustment: New evidence from a prospective study. *Child Development, 67,* 1243–1261.

Mortimer, J. T., Pimentel, E. E., Ryu, S., Nash, K., & Lee, C. (1996). Part-time work and occupational value formation in adolescence. *Social Forces, 74,* 1405–1418.

Mortimer, J. T., & Shanahan, M. J. (1991). *Adolescent work experience and relations with peers.* Paper presented at the annual meeting of the American Sociological Association, Cincinnati, OH.

Mortimer, J. T., & Shanahan, M. J. (1994). Adolescent work experience and family relationships. *Work and Occupations, 21,* 369–384.

Mortimer, J. T. Shanahan, M., & Ryu, S. (1993). The effects of adolescent employment on school-related orientation and behavior. In R. K. Silbereison & E. Todt (Eds.), *Adolescence in context: The interplay of family, schools, peers and work in adjustment* (pp. 304–326). New York: Springer-Verlag.

Mortimer, J. T., & Simmons, R. G. (1978). Adult socialization. *Annual Review of Sociology, 4,* 421–454.

Pearlin, L. I., Lieberman, M. A., Menaghan, E. G., & Mullan, J. T. (1981). The stress process. *Journal of Health and Social Behavior, 22,* 337–356.

Phillips, S., & Sandstrom, K. L. (1990). Parental attitudes towards youth work. *Youth and Society, 22,* 160–183.

Pimentel, E. E. (1996). Effects of adolescent achievement and family goals on the early adult transition. In J. T. Mortimer & M. D. Finch (Eds.), *Adolescents, work, and family: An intergenerational developmental analysis* (pp. 191–220). Newbury Park, CA: Sage.

Rosenberg, M. (1965). *Society and the adolescent self-image.* Princeton, NJ: Princeton University Press.

Sampson, R. J., & Laub, J. H. (1993). *Crime in the making: Pathways and turning points through life.* Cambridge, MA: Harvard University Press.

Schill, W. J., McCartin, R. M., & Meyer, K. (1985). Youth employment: Its relationship to academic and family variables. *Journal of Vocational Behavior, 26,* 155–163.

Schulenberg, J., & Bachman, J. G. (1993, March). *Long hours on the job? Not so bad for some adolescents in some types of jobs: The quality of work and substance use, affect, and stress.* Paper presented at the meeting of the Society for Research on Child Development, New Orleans.

Sewell, W. H., & Hauser, R. M. (1975). *Education, occupation, and earnings: Achievement in the early career.* New York: Academic Press.

Shanahan, M. J., & Elder, G. H., Jr. (1993). *Rural contexts of adolescent work experiences: Cause and consequence.* Paper presented at the meeting of the Society for Research on Child Development, New Orleans.

Shanahan, M. J., Finch, M. D., Mortimer, J. T., & Ryu, S. (1991). Adolescent work experience and depressive affect. *Social Psychology Quarterly, 54,* 299–317.

SPSS for Windows. (1993). Chicago: SPSS, Inc.

Steel, L. (1991). Early work experience among white and non-white youth. *Youth and Society, 22,* 419–447.

Steinberg, L., & Dornbusch, S. M. (1991). Negative correlates of part-time employment during adolescence: Replication and elaboration. *Developmental Psychology, 27,* 304–313.

Steinberg, L., Fegley, S., & Dornbusch, S. M. (1993). Negative impact of part-time work on adolescent adjustment: Evidence from a longitudinal study. *Developmental Psychology, 29,* 171–180.

Steinberg, L. D., Greenberger, E., Garduque, L., Ruggiero, M., & McAuliffe, S. (1982). High school students in the labor force: Some costs and benefits to schooling and learning. *Education Evaluation and Policy Analysis,* *4,* 363–372.

Steinberg, L. D., Greenberger, E., Garduque, L., Ruggiero, M., & Vaux, A. (1982). Effects of work in adolescent development. *Developmental Psychology, 18,* 385–395.

Stern, D., & Nakata, Y. F. (1989). Characteristics of high school students' paid jobs, and employment experience after graduation. In D. Stern & D. Eichorn (Eds.), *Adolescence and work: Influences of social structure, labor markets, and culture* (pp. 189–234). Hillsdale, NJ: Erlbaum.

Thoits, P. A. (1983). Dimensions of life events that influence psychological distress: An evaluation and synthesis of the literature. In H. B. Kaplan (Ed.), *Psychological stress: Trends in theory and research* (pp. 33–103). New York: Academic Press.

Thoits, P. A. (1986). Multiple identities: Examining gender and marital status differences in distress. *American Sociological Review, 51,* 259–272.

Ware, J. E., Jr., Johnson, S. A., Davies-Avery, A., & Brook, R. H. (1979). Current HIS mental health battery (r. 19879/3-Hew), Appendix E. In *Conceptualization and measurement of health for adults in the health insurance study, Vol. III, Mental Health.* Santa Monica, CA: Rand Corporation.

Part VI

Overview and integration

14

Life course capitalization and adolescent behavioral development

John Hagan

When life course development goes astray, especially in early childhood and adolescence, it frequently does so in a variety of interrelated ways. These interrelationships often unfold cross-sectionally, in clusters of high-risk problem behaviors, and longitudinally, in sequences of these involvements (Jessor & Jessor, 1977). These clusters and sequences complicate our pictures of life course development, especially when combined with the knowledge that there is no single cluster or sequence that is clearly predominate, and that the risks of youth development often coalesce and cascade into series and patterns of life events that can mutate and accumulate in highly contingent ways. This is to be expected because less problematic and more rewarding patterns of human development are similarly multifaceted, and because there is no reason to expect that the evaluation of behaviors as bad or troublesome should make them more tractable. The complexity of these patterns is a challenge to efforts to synthesize research on youth development. This chapter argues that conceptualizing youth development as a capitalization process can assist us in recognizing some advances that have been made in this field of research while simultaneously suggesting avenues for further work.

The risks and rewards of youth

At the extremes, individuals and their behaviors can be seen as coalescing in clusters that represent a polarization of possibilities in adolescent

The author wishes to acknowledge fellowship support during the period of this work from the U.S. German Marshall Fund, as well as support from the Social Sciences and Humanities Research Council of Canada and the W. T. Grant Foundation.

development. Although no single study provides a comprehensive inventory of the behavioral possibilities, this volume provides a broad picture of risk-prone in contrast with more rewarding paths of youthful development For example, in this volume Richard Udry and Peter Bearman direct our attention to youth who are more precocious and promiscuous than reserved and restricted in their sexuality. Denise Kandel and Helene White and colleagues consider youth who are experimental or abusive rather than abstinent or restrained in their use of drugs. Bruce Compas and his colleagues introduce us to adolescents who are emotionally anxious and distressed instead of calm and content. Jeylan Mortimer and Monica Johnson distinguish intermittent and erratic teenage workers from those who are more dependable and adaptable in their employment patterns. Lawrence Steinberg and Shelli Avenevoli find youth who are disengaged and alienated rather than committed and connected to school. Robert and Beverly Cairns and their colleagues explore the worlds of nonacademic and violent compared to academically competent and nonviolent young people. Rolf Loeber and his colleagues observe the significance of youth who are early and persistent rather than resistant and transitory in their delinquent involvements. And Allan Williams describes the experiences of young drivers who are at high risk of traffic accidents relative to those who are more cautious.

These depictions provide the depth and detail that only focused analyses of restricted behaviors can offer, but each also suggests that the problems considered are parts of larger pictures that include overlaps and sequences of age-graded role sets. This volume also contains a chapter by Margaret Ensminger and Hee Soon Juon, which, together with the chapter by Cairns and Cairns and their colleagues, broadens our attention to include selected clusters of problem behaviors, which they find and analyze as interrelated phenomena. The Cairns estimate that the youth involved in a distinguishable cluster of high-risk problem behaviors make up 12–18% of their North Carolina sample, and Ensminger and Juon suggest that about 20% of their Chicago sample cluster in high-risk groupings. In both cases, it seems clear that the majority of youth avoid these high-risk clusters.

Ensminger and Juon's panel research in a poor urban neighborhood in Chicago gives us a particularly striking set of comparisons that highlight the risks and rewards of youth in disadvantaged settings. At age

32, two-thirds of this urban cohort have jobs and 80% have a high school diploma. However, 3.5% also have died and more than half have had experience with the criminal justice system. Within the latter group there is a much smaller cluster, perhaps 6% of the cohort, who experience both high levels of substance use and high interpersonal aggression. Although this group is small, Ensminger and Juon note that its members conform to the stereotype portrayed in the media of African American males who grow up in the inner city. However, the implication of Ensminger and Juon's data is that youth who cross-sectionally and longitudinally share in these high-risk activities are a small, distinct, albeit important cluster in terms of the larger youth population in inner-city neighborhoods, as elsewhere.

The picture that therefore emerges is of a large plurality of youth who are developing with relatively restricted exposure to and experience with high-risk problem behaviors, even in declining urban neighborhoods, in contrast with much smaller but much higher-risk groupings. Ensminger and Juon provide evidence that the former, more successful youth are more often found in settings that are socially and personally supportive, which makes the point that these qualities of family life are found even in settings more often portrayed in opposing ways, whereas the latter, more troubled youth are more often located in more vulnerable settings characterized by limited family and community resources, a point that we further conceptualize and pursue in greater detail later in this chapter. Meanwhile, all of the chapters in this volume acknowledge, and most emphasize, a clustering of persons and behaviors. Many of the chapters further reflect a movement toward understanding the development of clusters of behaviors among individuals throughout the life course. The challenge is to find a language that can unify our analyses of the causes and consequences of these problem behaviors, as well as more rewarding behaviors, and the settings in which they develop.

Development as capitalization

A language of capitalization is one promising, although certainly not the only, useful way of synthesizing work on youth development. Although this conceptualization has well-known origins in the field of economics, its use now has broadened to include, for example, work in anthropology, sociology, social psychology, and criminology as well. So that whereas economists dwell on the empirical implications of the notion of human capital, anthropologists have joined the discussion with a wider notion of cultural capital, sociologists have introduced a further conception of social capital that is also applied in social psychological work, and criminologists are developing parallel conceptions of criminal capital. This framework may have the potential to be a powerful synthesizing force in the interdisciplinary study of human behavioral development.

Capitalization theory usefully begins with the premise that we acquire at birth and accumulate throughout our lives unequal shares of various types of capital that incrementally and interactively mediate and determine life chances. We obtain access to and begin to amass capital through a variety of processes (e.g., of genetic, biological, human, social, cultural and even criminal forms) that Dannefer (1984) usefully classifies as sociogenic and ontogenetic. The former sociogenic processes are structurally and culturally shaped, whereas ontogenetic processes are more individually and developmentally determined. Although these sociogenic and ontogenetic processes of capitalization overlap and interact, for some purposes it is useful to see them as distinct. More important for our purposes, distinct kinds of capital are involved, and it is useful to identify several of these in more detail and to consider how they interrelate.

A fundamental analogy underwrites discussions of the various forms of capital, an analogy that derives from the basic notion of physical capital and that is further represented in the economists' conception of human capital. Physical capital typically refers to tools, machinery, and other productive equipment that form the foundation of economic relations. Economists have added to this the idea of human capital. *Human capital* refers to the abilities, skills, and knowledge acquired by individuals, especially through education and training (Becker, 1964; Schultz, 1961). The capital embodied in humans is less tangible than that in tools or machinery, but both involve the accumulation of resources or power and emphasize a transformative potential. This transformative potential is a key part of the capitalization analogy, for as James Coleman (1990, p. 304) notes, "Just as physical capital is created by making changes in materials so as to form tools and facilitate production, human capital is created by changing persons so as to give them skills and capabilities that make them able to act in new ways." Thus the capitalization process can be catalytic in its productive possibilities.

Recently, anthropologists and sociologists have played important roles in expanding notions of capitalization in the behavioral sciences. Pierre Bourdieu (1986) has added the notion of cultural capital to connect the concept of human capital to the cultural conditions from which it originates. Bourdieu emphasizes a version of cultural capital that involves the unique kinds of highly valued knowledge that go beyond conventional work and occupations, involving the arts or "high culture," including music, dance, theater, and literature. Like other kinds of human capital, cultural capital can be increased through training and education, and access to and accumulation of this kind of capital is predicated on and productive of wealth and social position. Of course, if there is a high culture, then, by implication, there are "lower" cultures as well, and as we discuss later, involvement in these cultures can challenge and contravene conventional and higher cultural forms, to the point of being called criminal. These cultural forms have life course developmental consequences that can also be understood in relation to capitalization processes.

James Coleman's (1990) further notion of social capital may be even less tangible than physical, human, or even cultural capital, yet its creation and dissemination involve processes that are no less real or important. According to Coleman (1990), social capital refers not to a single entity but to a variety of social resources. These resources originate in the socially structured relations that connect individuals to families and to aggregations of other individuals in neighborhoods, churches, schools, and so on. Social capital therefore is embodied in relations between people, and it includes the knowledge and sense of obligations, expectations, trustworthiness, information channels, norms, and sanctions that these relations engender. Importantly, when it is well formed and effective, social capital facilitates purposive action. This implies that social capital unfolds in rationally planned ways, and although this may frequently be true, it is also the case that the processes involved often are adaptive without being intended or expected. And, of course, when social capital is inadequately or poorly developed, its effects are unlikely to be rational or purposive (see, for example, Hagan, MacMillan, & Wheaton, 1996; Hagan, Merkens, & Boehnke, 1995). But we are now ahead of our story because more should first be said about what exactly social capital is.

Coleman (1990, p. 305) introduces the concept of social capital with a simple triangular figure in which the end points or nodes of the triangle represent the accretion of human capital by two parents and a child. Coleman reasons that for parents to further the accumulation of human capital through the cognitive development of the child, there must be capital in the nodes and the links of the diagram. That is, the most effective means of transmitting the human capital of the parents to the child is through the social capital, represented in all the connecting links between both parents and the child. Coleman refers to this as a form of *social closure* involving the social network of the family.

The concept of closure is important, however, not just in the family, but in other aggregations and associations of individuals as well. For example, family members are connected to other families through the friendships and associations of parents and children, and these contacts extend the social capital of the family out into the community through schools, clubs, churches, and other voluntary groups. The implication is that social capital is not simply a property of individuals, but of collectivities as well. The investments of individuals and groups in these contacts and connections combine horizontally and vertically to form aggregations of social capital that can significantly shape and determine life outcomes.

Individuals therefore vary in their access to social as well as other kinds of capital, and they continually adapt to changing structures and opportunities that characterize the circumstances they inherit and inhabit. Adaptations to these conditions are expressed through various formations of capital. Parents who are well situated within secure and supportive social networks usually are inclined or driven – by their capital positions – to endow their children with forms of social, human, and cultural capital that increase their likelihood of success in school and in later life. When social capital is abundant in the community and family, cultural adaptations often include the amassing of credentials of higher education and even involvement in high culture, for example, including participation in the arts, that can significantly enhance life chances (DiMaggio, 1982, 1987).

However, in less advantaged community and family settings, parents who lack abundant social and cultural capital are less able to endow or transmit opportunities to their children. Survival itself may be a struggle, and children and families must adapt to the diminished circumstances and opportunities they encounter. Moreover, children of less advantageously positioned and less driven and controlling parents may more often drift or be driven by harsh circumstances along less promising paths of social and cultural adaptation and capital formation (Hagan, 1991). Problem or risk behaviors, such as taking cars for joy rides or expressive forms of vandalism, can be causes and consequences of unsuccessful forms and processes of conventional capitalization, as these occur and are valued in specific sociohistorical settings. Other forms and processes of problem and risk behaviors, such as drug dealing and fencing stolen property, can become sources of unconventional and, in some cases, criminal capitalization, even though, if not because, they are disvalued and criminalized sources of pleasure and profit, offering illegal opportunities for recapitalization in disadvantaged contexts.

Capitalization in context

A key aspect of the focus on youth development in terms of capitalization therefore involves a focus on individuals and the settings in which they develop. The point is that adolescent development and transitions to adulthood involve processes and contexts of capitalization in which individuals alternatively augment (e.g., through schooling) and/or deplete (e.g., through problem behaviors) their net capital positions in contexts of capital resources that have the transformative potential to alter life course trajectories. Often this transformative potential is recognized in the identification of turning points in individuals' lives, events or experiences that can alter trajectories of life course development. Graber et al., Chapter 9 of this volume, refer to these events and experiences as "transition–linked turning points."

Note that this conception of turning points and life course capitalization ultimately involves adding interaction effects to main effect models of development. For example, it is not simply that behaviors and settings add to one another in their effects, but further that the effects of behavior and setting are contingent on one another and produce unique outcomes when combined in particular ways.

The kind of interactive model we are describing is explicitly articulated in Jessor and colleagues' (1995) risk-protection paradigm for the analysis of developmental change. Jessor's formulation advances the crucial premise that the consequences of problem behaviors vary in interaction with features of the contexts in which they occur. Where Jessor's formulation does this by incorporating the useful language of risk and protection, capitalization theory adds to this framework a language of resources and investment. Nations, communities, churches, and schools, as well as families, can all invest in the improved life chances of their members. These investments are understood not only as contributions to the improved well-being of individuals and the settings in which they reside, but also as forms of insurance against the risk of declines in the well-being of these individuals and their surroundings. Investments in and by individuals help to bond them further to social institutions.

Bonds to families, schools, and other prosocial contexts can protect youth against the elaboration and extension of problem behaviors in later life (Sampson & Laub, 1993). It is in this sense that capitalization processes are protective and potentially transformative. This kind of capitalization of young people can be seen as a form of insurance against lifelong behavioral difficulties and therefore as investments in productive lives. Youth whose lives are capitalized in these ways have more to lose (e.g., a good education, entrance into college, a job) if they become involved in deviant behavior. Of course, this kind of investment and insurance is not well or evenly distributed in society.

Capital investment and disinvestment policies

One of the most important patterns apparent in research on life course development involves the interactive effects of class contexts. However, the influence of these contexts to this point often has become apparent without plan or the benefit of systematic design. This largely unnoticed and underemphasized pattern of results, which we illustrate next, often remains unrecognized and undeveloped because most longitudinal research on youth development has been done without close attention to variation in specific settings. Instead, the more common search in this work has been for generic patterns of individual life course development with broad possibilities for generalization. We need more broadly integrated work that takes into account not only the influences of covariation and trajectory in individual lives, but also of social context. In Chapter 8 of this volume, Udry and Bearman describe how the influence of these contexts can be directly measured as nested networks of peers, families, neighborhoods, schools, and so on. As Cairns et al. further note in Chapter 2, this web of social relations can provide boundaries, opportunities, and a frame of reference for actions and attitudes. The effects of these interconnected possibilities are also reflected in the influences of class-connected residential circumstances.

The results of research we briefly review next suggest that class contexts and settings are of major significance, especially when they involve variation in the seriousness of the problems explored and the resources available to the subjects examined. A brief review of some of this research is helpful in suggesting the importance of future developmental work that addresses contextualized, class-based issues of capitalization and related processes of capital investment and disinvestment in communities.

Initially, the studies we consider seemed to reveal a single relatively consistent and unvarying generic pattern of ontogenetic development. Consider first Robins's (1966) study of *Deviant Children Grown Up*. This research followed two groups into adulthood: a clinic-based sample of predominantly low-status severely antisocial children and a control group who had no adolescent behavior problems and were matched with the clinic sample on race, age, sex, IQ, and socioeconomic status. As adults the clinic sample experienced a cluster of unfolding and interrelated problems that included more unemployment for longer spells and with more frequent job changes, fewer promotions, depressed earnings, more credit problems, and greater reliance on public assistance than did the control group.

In a similarly designed study, the Gluecks (1950, 1968) applied a matched-group design to study white males from Boston who, because of their persistent delinquency, were committed to one of two correctional schools in Massachusetts. Sampson and Laub (1990, 1993) reanalyzed these data and reported that not only adult criminal behavior but also "seven adult behaviors spanning economic, educational, employment, and family domains are also strongly related to adolescent delinquency" (p. 616). These outcomes included greater adult unemployment and welfare dependency among the delinquent sample.

However, as research on the transition from adolescence to adulthood continued to accumulate, more complicated and socially contingent adult possibilities began to emerge. For example, whereas Ghodsian and Power (1987) observed continuity in drinking among a national sample of British youth followed from ages 16 to 23, a subsequent analysis of these data by Power and Estaugh (1990, p. 493) argued that teenage drinking was "generally unrelated to early adult experience of either obtaining or remaining in employment." Mixed findings also emerged from a study by Newcomb and Bentler (1988), whose sample of Los Angeles high school students demonstrated continuities in drug use and problems of job instability in early adulthood. However, the authors also noted that "early drug use did not generate a pattern of irresponsibility, laziness, and work avoidance" (p. 169). In addition, their composite measure of "social conformity" in adolescence had no effect on income, job instability, job satisfaction, collected public assistance, or amount of work in early adulthood.

These several studies exemplify a variability in results that may assume new meaning when considered in relation to an analysis by Jessor, Donovan, and Costa (1991) of Colorado high school and college students. Although these authors found continuity in problem behaviors from adolescence to adulthood, these behaviors did not affect work and status attainment. Jessor et al. (1991, pp. 268–269) argued the latter findings were made plausible by three factors:

First, our research involved normal rather than clinical samples, and the extent of their adolescent/youth involvement in problem behavior – even at its greatest – has to be seen as moderate for the most part. Second, our samples were largely middle class in socioeconomic status, and the openness of the opportunity structure for them and their access to 'second chances' have to be seen as far greater than might be the case for disadvantaged youth who had been involved in problem behavior. Third, . . . , even for samples such as ours, there can still be compromising outcomes [yet] to be manifested.

Jessor et al. (1991) combined these observations in an "interactionist perspective," asserting that the course of psychosocial development is not inexorable, that past actions do not necessarily foreclose future options, and that there can be resilience in growth and change: "at least in social contexts that are not entirely malignant, and at a time in history when the social setting itself is relatively open and undergoing change" (p. 269).

We have attempted to press the meaning of these findings further in a Canadian study. In a 13-year panel analysis of the transition of nearly 700 youth from adolescence to early adulthood, we tested the hypothesis that only relatively more serious deviant adolescent behaviors crystallize into adult deficits, and that this is more likely to occur among the adolescent sons of working-class fathers. The results of our work supported these expectations with regard to adult occupational outcomes. Sons of working-class fathers who became involved in serious forms of delinquent behavior more often were found in less rewarding occupations in early adulthood, whereas the sons of more advantaged fathers were unaffected by their adolescent involvement in serious delinquency. Again, Jessor et al. (1991) interpret such findings as indicating that more favorably positioned parents and communities are better able to absorb and protect their youth from the consequences of their problem behavior, for example, by ensuring more lenient outcomes if these youth are caught in their acts by authorities, or by accessing services and opportunities that allow the possibility of reintegration into the community.

A remaining challenge in developmental research is to set a research agenda that addresses the implications of the previously described findings and interpretations. If the line of argument developed in this section is correct, it implies a research initiative in which the *settings* of developmental studies are selected and analyzed in terms of the prospects for capitalization they offer. For example, the family and community settings in which developmental studies are undertaken vary in the levels to which they represent circumstances of capital investment and disinvestment. Families that offer strong parental support to their children, and communities that provide high levels of funding for their schools, exemplify circumstances of capital investment in youth development. Alternatively, families that can offer little parental support to their children, and communities that provide only low levels of funding for schools, are often sites of capital disinvestment in youth development. Developmental studies like those discussed earlier suggest that processes of family and community capitalization are organized in relation to class and other resource bases that establish important contexts for the understanding of youth development, both along pro- and antisocial lines of development.

Meanwhile, capital disinvestment policies associated with the slow-

down from the post–World War II economic boom that has characterized much of the last quarter of this century have resulted in unprecedented concentrations of poverty in America's ghettoized minority
communities. The nature of this process of capital disinvestment is
described by Wacquant and Wilson (1989, p. 10):

[T]he social structure of today's inner city has been radically altered by the
mass exodus of jobs and working families and by the rapid deterioration of
housing, schools, businesses, recreational facilities, and other community organizations, further exacerbated by government policies of industrial and urban laissez-faire that have channelled a disproportionate share of federal, state,
and municipal resources to the more affluent.

Wacquant and Wilson argue that these forces have transformed the
"traditional ghetto" of a half century ago into a "hyperghetto." The
effects of this process are exemplified in the description of the Woodlawn neighborhood noted by Ensminger and Juon in Chapter 11 of this
volume. Whereas in 1965 this neighborhood contained approximately
90,000 people, by 1970 that number had declined to 54,000 and in 1980
to 36,000. The majority of the residents of this poor neighborhood had
abandoned it for other settings, mostly still on the South Side of Chicago. About a quarter of the families in Woodlawn lived below the
poverty level in 1970, and in 1980 this increased to nearly one-third.
As the population of this community dropped, the concentration of
poverty increased. It is likely not an accident that Ensminger and Juon,
in turn, find weak social bonds to be strongly associated with deviant
behavioral outcomes in Woodlawn. These bonds are especially vulnerable in the Woodlawn setting, as they are in many other American
ghettoized communities of concentrated poverty.

  Weak labor force attachment in these concentrated settings is a further and increasingly common condition that William Wilson connects
directly to involvements in crime, observing that "a social context that
includes poor schools, inadequate job information networks, and a lack
of legitimate employment opportunities not only gives rise to weak
labor force attachment, but increases the probability that individuals
will be constrained to seek income derived from illegal deviant activities" (1991, p. 10). Capital disinvestment policies create concentrations
of poverty that increase these risks because individuals and families
confront the effects not only of their own difficult situations but also of

the compounding effects of the situations that surround them (Sampson & Wilson, 1994). We need to connect the meaning of these important changes more clearly to the research agenda of developmental research.

Contexts of criminal capitalization and embeddedness

In one sense, developmental and life course studies are already contributing in significant ways to the understanding of the high-risk lives of youth living in impoverished families and communities. Developmental and life course concepts are increasingly used by qualitative fieldworkers to interpret the findings of ghetto-based ethnographies, such as Joan Moore's (1991) *Going Down to the Barrio* and Mercer Sullivan's (1989) *Getting Paid.* However, there remains an unsettling gap between the focus and results of these qualitative studies and the quantitative work done in more conventional developmental research.

Quantitative developmental studies today often fail to convey a clear sense of similarities and differences in the contextualized experiences that economically disadvantaged youth confront in making transitions from adolescence to adulthood. Although the language of capitalization can be used to better understand youth developmental processes generally, some conceptual elaboration will likely be required to incorporate the influence of the special features of the disadvantaged and often criminalized settings in which many impoverished minority youth today come of age. The concepts introduced next – deviance service centers, ethnic vice industries, and criminal embeddedness – are offered as ways of elaborating our model of capitalization to incorporate the broadened research agenda we propose for developmental research.

Consider first the kinds of street settings that are seldom if ever mentioned in quantitative developmental studies, but that are central to past and especially present risks of American ghetto life. Throughout this century a great deal of law enforcement activity has been, and still is, focused on the policing of "deviance service centers" (Clairmont, 1974) that are organized around "ethnic vice industries" (Light, 1977) disproportionately located in the urban neighborhoods of the minority poor (Boritch & Hagan, 1987). The concept of a deviance service center parallels in an ironic way the economic notion of a free enterprise zone, except for the very notable fact that such centers are organized around illegal services and substances. These centers are social contexts in which activities otherwise defined as illegal (including prostitution, drugs, and alcohol) are allowed to develop and serve a clientele from within and outside the community. Such centers existed in American cities throughout this century – in areas like New Orleans' Basin Street, San Francisco's Barbary Coast, Denver's Market Street Line, and New York's Bowery and Five Points – but now are centered in Hispanic and African American inner-city ghettoes, our most ethnically and economically concentrated contemporary contexts of capital disinvestment. These are seldom if ever sites of quantitative developmental studies, even though they are essential contexts of life course development in many minority inner-city settings.

The process of recapitalization involved in the development of deviance service industries is partly indigenous to communities and partly a product of the actions of external authorities. The key to the evolution of these vice centers is that illegal markets emerge whenever and wherever desired substances and services – such as drugs, prostitution, and gambling – are made illegal. Authorities responsible for the enforcement of such laws, whether they wish to or not, have the power to regulate the location, growth, and operation of these markets because members of communities without adequate access to and involvement in legal labor markets often pursue these illegal opportunities to accumulate criminal forms of social and cultural capital, that is, criminal capital. These are the settings in which many inner-city youth, on the street and away from families and schools, experience life course development.

The linkage between deviance service industries and life course social mobility is given historical grounding in the concept of *ethnic succession,* which refers to the fact that for lack of alternatives, a series of new immigrant groups, most recently African Americans and Hispanic Americans, have sought to move up in the American social structure through organized vice (Ianni, 1972, 1974). However, although members of earlier groups did so with some success, America's changing place in the world economy, changes in local urban economies, and the dire state of America's central cities have made contemporary prospects for upward mobility through organized forms of urban vice less promising and more hazardous.

Nonetheless, lacking other sources of social and cultural capital, many youth in low-income minority communities today are drawn to the promise of deviance service industries, and the failed role of ethnic vice industries as contemporary mobility ladders therefore firmly connects the community context of these illegal enterprises to the fates of individuals. This is why a developmental theory that is relevant to America's low-income minority communities needs to trace systematically how, and with what consequences, youth in these communities often become involved in activities linked to these vice industries (Hagan & McCarthy, 1997). This can be done, for example, by tracing a process of criminal embeddedness that is closely connected to problems of labor market entry and advancement in contexts of communities that are sites of capital disinvestment.

As Mark Granovetter (1974) has demonstrated, early and sustained employment contacts can provide a source of capital that enhances the prospects of finding work and subsequent occupational mobility. Alternatively, connections to crime are likely, in a converse way, to increase the probability of unemployment. Youthful involvement in delinquency, as well as criminal involvement of friends and family, integrate adolescents and young adults into a criminal underworld, and simultaneously distance them from job contacts that initiate and sustain legitimate occupational careers. Criminal embeddedness can be a source of criminal capital, with resulting short-term benefits, but this embeddedness is a liability in terms of prospects for stable adult employment.

The costs of criminal embeddedness are compounded by the risks of becoming officially labeled and known as a criminal offender, especially in distressed community settings where few core sector jobs are available in any case. This process of separation and stigmatization can in some respects be subtle, operating through the absence rather than the presence of social ties to assist and protect minority youth. Delinquent youth run a high risk of becoming criminally embedded in contexts that isolate them from the closure of more conventional social networks and the accumulation of social capital that can derive from legitimate employment in whatever jobs are available at a particular point in time.

The special risks of criminal conviction are revealed in an analysis of youth tracked from childhood to adulthood in a London working-class neighborhood (Hagan, 1993). This study indicates that intergenerational patterns of criminal conviction make youth especially prone to subsequent delinquency and adult unemployment (Hagan, 1993; Hagan

& Palloni, 1990; 1993; see also Ward & Tittle, 1993). Other studies similarly show that working-class males with conviction records are uniquely disadvantaged in finding employment (Schwartz & Skolnick, 1964), and that a criminal arrest record can have negative effects on employment as much as 8 years later (Freeman, 1991; Grogger, 1991; Thornberry & Christenson, 1984). Sampson and Laub's (1993, p. 168) long-term study of predominantly lower socioeconomic status Boston delinquents indicates that "incarceration appears to cut off opportunities and prospects for stable employment in later life." Criminal sanctions can cause further problems by making offenders who are already disadvantaged more defiant (Sherman, 1993). This is one more way in which the social and cultural capital of such youth is further jeopardized.

It is not surprising, therefore, that recent ethnographies of poverty and crime make the point that the material gains associated with embeddedness in the drug economy usually prove to be transitory. For example, although Sullivan draws on the classic analysis of Paul Willis (1977) to argue that participation in this underground economy temporarily achieves for minority youth a "penetration of their condition," he also reports that "over time, this penetration becomes a limitation, binding them back into [the social] structure as they age out of youth crime and accept . . . low wage, unstable jobs" (1989, p. 250). Joan Moore, in *Going Down to the Barrio,* suggests a similar conclusion when she observes that "the very culture of defiance at best dooms the boys to jobs just like their fathers hold," serving in the end "to keep working-class kids in the working class" (1991, p. 42). Felix Padilla echoes this theme in his ethnography of *The Gang as an American Enterprise,* noting that "instead of functioning as a progressive and liberating agent capable of transforming and correcting the youngsters' economic plight, the gang assisted in reinforcing it" (1992, p. 163). In each of these ethnographies, and in the related studies noted earlier, it is embeddedness in crime networks, including the criminal justice system, that seals the economic fate of these youths.

We need to understand more fully the efforts at recapitalization that lead youth into urban crime networks and their consequences if we are to provide a comprehensively contextualized knowledge of adolescent development that is sensitive to the experiences of youth in unconventional and disadvantaged, as well as conventional and advantaged, family and community settings. The absence of this kind of conceptualization is reflected in a kind of distancing and detachment of quantitative, developmental studies from the high-risk urban contexts in which high-risk adolescent behaviors are prominent. A challenge for the next generation of developmental life course studies of adolescent problem behaviors is to engage these high-risk settings more fully.

References

Becker, G. (1964). *Human capital.* New York: Columbia University Press.

Bourdieu, P. (1986). The forms of capital. In J. G. Richardson (Ed.), *Handbook of theory and research for the sociology of education* (pp. 241–258). New York: Greenwood Press.

Boritch, H., & Hagan, J. (1987). Crime and the changing forms of class control: Policing public order in "Toronto the Good," 1859–1955. *Social Forces, 66,* 307–335.

Clairmont, D. (1974). The development of a deviance service center. In J. Haas & B. Shaffir (Eds.), *Decency and deviance.* Toronto: McClelland and Stewart.

Coleman, J. S. (1990). *Foundations of social theory.* Cambridge, MA: Harvard University Press.

Dannefer, D. (1984). Adult development and social theory: A paradigmatic reappraisal. *American Sociological Review, 49,* 100–116.

DiMaggio, P. (1982). Cultural capital and school success: The impact of status culture participation on the grades of U.S. high school students. *American Sociological Review, 47,* 189–201.

DiMaggio, P. (1987). Classification in art. *American Sociological Review, 52,:* 440–455.

Freeman, R. (1991). *Crime and the economic status of disadvantaged young men.* Paper presented to the Conference on Urban Labor Markets and Labor Mobility, Warrenton, Virginia.

Ghodsian, M., & Power, C. (1987). Alcohol consumption between the ages of 16 and 23 in Britain: A longitudinal study. *British Journal of Addiction, 82,* 175–180.

Glueck, S., & Glueck, E. (1950). *Unravelling juvenile delinquency.* Cambridge, MA: Harvard University Press.

Glueck., S., & Glueck, E. (1968). *Delinquents and nondelinquents in perspective.* Cambridge, MA: Harvard University Press.

Granovetter, M. (1974). *Getting a job: A study of contacts and careers.* Cambridge, MA: Harvard University Press.

Grogger, J. (1991). *The effect of arrest on the employment outcomes of young men.* Unpublished manuscript, University of California, Santa Barbara, CA.

Hagan, J. (1991). Destiny and drift: Subcultural preferences, status attainments, and the risks and rewards of youth. *American Sociological Review,56,* 567–582.

Hagan, J. (1993). The social embeddedness of crime and unemployment. *Criminology, 31,* 465–491.

Hagan, J., & McCarthy, B. (1997). *Mean streets: Youth crime and homelessness,* New York: Cambridge University Press.

Hagan, J., MacMillan, R., & Wheaton, B. (1996). New kid in town: Social capital and the life course effects of family migration on children. *American Sociological Review, 61,* 368–385.

Hagan, J., Merkens, M., & Boehnke, K. (1995). Delinquency and disdain: Social capital and the control of right-wing extremism among East and West Berlin youth. *American Journal of Sociology, 100,* 1028–1052.

Hagan, J., & Palloni, A. (1990). The social reproduction of a criminal class in working class London, circa 1950–80. *American Journal of Sociology, 96,* 265–299.

Ianni, F. (1972). *A family business.* New York: Russell Sage.

Ianni, F. (1974). *Black mafia,* New York: Simon & Schuster.

Jessor, R., Donovan, J., & Costa, F. (1991). *Beyond adolescence: Problem behavior and young adult development.* New York: Cambridge University Press.

Jessor, R., & Jessor, S. L. (1977). *Problem behavior and psychosocial development: A longitudinal study of youth.* New York: Academic Press.

Jessor, R., Van Den Bos, J., Vanderryn, J., Costa, F. M., & Turbin, M. S. (1995). Protective factors in adolescent problem behavior: Moderator effects and developmental change. *Developmental Psychology,6,* 923–933.

Light, I. (1977). The ethnic vice industry, 1880–1944. *American Sociological Review, 42,* 464–479.

Moore, J. (1991). *Going down to the barrio: Homeboys and homegirls in change.* Philadelphia: Temple University Press.

Newcomb, M. D., & Bentler, P. M. (1988). *Consequences of adolescent drug use: Impact on the lives of young adults.* Newbury Park,: CA: Sage.

Padilla, F. (1992). *The gang as an American enterprise.* New Brunswick, NJ: Rutgers University Press.

Power, C., & Estaugh, V. (1990). Employment and drinking in early adulthood: A longitudinal perspective. *British Journal of Addiction, 85,* 487–494.

Robins, L. (1966). *Deviant children grown up.* Baltimore: Williams & Wilkins.

Sampson, R. J., & Laub, J. H. (1990). Crime and deviance over the life course. *American Sociological Review, 55,* 609–627.

Sampson, R. J., & Laub, J. H. (1993). *Crime in the making*. Cambridge, MA: Harvard University Press.

Sampson, R., & Wilson, W. (1994). Toward a theory of race, crime and urban inequality. In J. Hagan & R. Peterson (Eds.), *Crime and inequality* (pp. 37–54). Stanford, CA: Stanford University Press.

Schultz, T. (1961). Investment in human capital. *American Economic Review, 51,* 1–17.

Schwartz, R., & Skolnick, J. (1964). Two studies of legal stigma." In H. Becker (Ed.), *The other side: Perspectives on deviance*. New York: Free Press.

Sherman, L. (1993). Defiance, deterrence and irrelevance: A theory of the criminal sanction. *Journal of Research in Crime and Delinquency, 30,* 445–4730.

Sullivan, M. (1989). *Getting paid: Youth crime and work in the inner city*. Ithaca, NY: Cornell University Press.

Thornberry, T., & Christenson, R. L. (1984). Unemployment and criminal involvement: An investigation of reciprocal causal structures. *American Sociological Review, 49,* 398–411.

Wacquant, L. D., & Wilson, W. J. (1989). The costs of racial and class exclusion in the inner city. *Annals of the American Academy of Political and Social Science, 501,* 8–25.

Ward, D., & Tittle, C. (1993). Deterrence or labelling: The effects of informal sanctions. *Deviant Behavior, 14,* 43–64.

Willis, P. (1977). *Learning to labour*. London: Gower.

Wilson, W. J. (1991). Studying inner-city social dislocations: The challenge of public agenda research. *American Sociological Review, 56,* 1–14.

15

Lessons we learned – problems still to be solved

Rainer K. Silbereisen

The chapters in this book represent a unique selection of current research on adolescent risk behaviors. The behaviors addressed no longer include the "usual suspects," such as alcohol and drug use or delinquency, and show that many advances have been made in this area of research. In addition to these, other externalizing behaviors, such as sexual behavior and the widely overlooked risky driving, are dealt with. Internalizing behaviors such as depression are also discussed.

It is also clear, from the age span covered in the chapters, that the study of risk behaviors in adolescence includes their childhood precursors and young adult consequences. Although it does not yet have a true life-span perspective, the research looks much more developmental than in the past and overcomes the preponderance of approaches concentrating on individual differences rather than intraindividual change.

Moreover, contexts from family to school to work really seem to matter. This was not always true in a field that for decades was characterized by research concentrating either on individuals without contexts or on contexts without individuals (Bronfenbrenner, 1986).

And yet, important as these advances are, the new perspectives offered actually go further. I see four main areas: a new emphasis on the person of the adolescents, that is, the organized, unique pattern of adaptive and maladaptive behaviors rather than the concentration on a single risk behavior; the distinction between various developmental trajectories that lead to risk behaviors characterized by different persistence across the life span, lending itself to new approaches in intervention; the growing awareness that the biological underpinnings of risk behaviors and their interplay with other levels of behavioral organization deserve more attention; and a new interest in psychologically relevant dimensions of contexts. Before I discuss the theoretical frames and empirical data illuminating the new perspectives, the background of the four perspectives themselves needs to be discussed. The point of departure is a well-known regularity in the changing prevalence of risk behaviors across the life span.

Emphasis on the person

Drug use, delinquency, and many other risk behaviors peak in adolescence and young adulthood. This association between a class of behaviors and a particular period of the life span is interpreted by most researchers as revealing more than incidental co-occurrence. Rather, the biopsychosocial changes taking place during adolescence are seen as playing a part in the emergence of risk behaviors. A widely accepted view claims, for instance, that at least some risk behaviors jointly represent adolescents' enactment of adultlike behaviors at an unduly early time, probably driven by the desire to experience the attractive and often immediate consequences, such as a reputation for popularity among friends (Jessor & Jessor, 1977). The implication that such behaviors may be problematic, due more to their timing than to their nature per se, leads to an interest in the role of risk behaviors within normative, adaptive development during adolescence (Baumrind, 1991; Silbereisen, Noack, & Schönpflug, 1994).

Moreover, if the boundaries between classes of behaviors are more fluid than previously was thought, then it is clear that addressing behaviors in isolation is inadequate. Consequently, the recent plea for a more personological orientation in research on human development in general (Magnusson & Stattin, 1998) was well received in the field of risk behavior. Central to this approach are the assumptions, first, that processes at all levels, whether physiological or behavioral, interact in a complex manner and, second, that the person is involved in a permanent interaction with the environment. Depending on the processes and capacities of the individual, this interaction can entail goal-oriented actions aimed at the achievement of life tasks and personal projects (Brandtstädter, 1998).

Whether individuals are seen as agents of their own development, or whether the course and outcome of development are shaped by forces and constraints that are not under their control, a personological approach requires the study of the ensemble of behaviors and their interplay rather than of single behaviors in isolation. With regard to risk behavior in adolescence, such an agenda would, at least, require the characterization of adolescents by a profile of behaviors and their motivational basis. In other words, rather than restricting analyses to alcohol use, for example, other youthful behaviors such as sexual activities or school absenteeism would have to be included. It is here that Jessor's idea of problem behaviors forming a syndrome of functionally equivalent behaviors has a direct link to personological approaches.

Differential trajectories

However conceptualized, human development can be seen as involving a lifelong series of complex biopsychosocial processes that lead to changes in adaptation. Adaptation to what? In a general sense, adaptation is accomplished with regard to challenges presented by three main systems of development, namely, age-graded systems, history-graded systems, and nonnormative life events (Baltes, 1987).

In the usual description of adolescence, age-graded systems are represented by a series of more or less coordinated and interwoven life tasks that have biological underpinnings, such as the growth of mature romantic relationships or the gradual establishment of an occupational identity. According to differences in the timing and sequencing of the tasks achieved or failed, the ensemble of these life tasks forms a number of trajectories into adulthood. Whereas some young people may start their own family before they have become firmly established occupationally, others may stick to the more traditional model of first establishing economic independence.

Which trajectories prevail as a result of navigating the transition to adulthood depends largely on historical and cultural constraints beyond the influence of individuals. The "ecological experiment" of German unification is a case in point. Whereas in the former East Germany many young couples had their first child before they finished their vocational training or academic studies, in the former West Germany the age at marriage and the age at first parenthood were considerably greater, implying that a higher percentage of future young parents had completed their vocational training or academic studies. In addition to factors such as housing and other financial benefits, one of the causes of this difference in trajectories was that the East German government wanted to protect the state-owned industries from the economic and organizational strains related to maternal leave (Hormuth, Heinz, Kornadt, Sydow, & Trommsdorff, 1996).

Adolescence is a time of major challenges to attitudes and behaviors that served the individual well in earlier years but that have to be recalibrated or redesigned in the face of new life tasks. This may overtax an individual's abilities, implying the risk of maladaptive behaviors. However, not all risk behaviors revealed during adolescence are established during this period. Rather, problems of adaptation that emerge at this time are rooted in childhood.

Most adolescents who show risk behaviors do so in a nonescalating fashion (e.g., stop short of problem use or drug addiction), and they refrain from the behavior or reduce its intensity after making the transition to adult life (Donovan & Jessor, 1985). On closer examination, the great majority of adolescents reveal no particular propensity toward or early precursors of risk behaviors during childhood. Moreover, unless additional risk factors such as a broken home emerge, even periods of serious risk behavior during adolescence are unlikely to result in permanent adaptation problems in adulthood.

Such observations led Moffitt (1993) to assume that the ubiquity of risk behaviors among this group is rooted in transitional difficulties shared by virtually all adolescents during the negotiation of new life tasks. The notorious discrepancy between early sexual maturity and prolonged economic dependency in adolescence is but one example of such problems. Hence, Moffitt addressed this majority as revealing adolescence-limited patterns of maladaptation.

The other, much smaller group of individuals who show life course–persistent problems may not differ from the majority in the level of risk behaviors during adolescence. Below this surface similarity, however, the roots of the adaptation problems are totally different. These adolescents share a history of difficulties such as hyperactivity, low impulse control, and problems with normative peers.

Biopsychosocial processes

Thus far, I have not addressed the nature of the biopsychosocial processes that drive developmental changes. Obviously, this topic includes a multitude of processes, of which puberty may be taken as an example (for a review, see Silbereisen & Kracke, 1993). Research has revealed that the timing of menarche plays a role in the emergence of adolescent problem behavior. More specifically, early-maturing girls, particularly if they establish contacts with older male friends, show higher levels of alcohol and marijuana use in midadolescence. Although on-time–maturing girls catch up, their early-maturing age-mates show long-term effects, such as earlier motherhood and lower educational attainment (Stattin & Magnusson, 1990). This interaction between biological factors, personal strivings, and ecological constraints is far from fully understood. Recently, Graber (Brooks-Gunn, Graber, & Paikoff, 1994) presented an elaborated model of the endocrinological, neurological, psychological, and social processes involved that shows the complexities awaiting testing.

I have used the interplay between the timing of puberty and adolescent problem behavior to make the point that in the past, research on risk behavior widely overlooked physiological and other biological processes. Except for particular fields, such as neurophysiological mechanisms of substance addiction, this is still true of current research. In the near future, new insights are likely to emerge concerning genetic liability to certain risk behaviors or their more general precursors, such as temperamental instability. The combination of socialization-oriented research with thoughts inspired by genetic studies is particularly useful (Rowe, 1994).

Psychologically relevant dimensions of contexts

No one who has ever undertaken systematic field observations in leisure localities frequented by the young would ever doubt that adolescents shape and are shaped by contexts. The relevance of physical props and social settings in helping them negotiate their new developmental tasks is well known, and recent reviews have shown how the multitude of distal and proximal contexts are relevant in the development of risk behaviors (Petraitis, Flay, & Miller, 1995). In most cases, however, contexts are treated like empty "social addresses," without specifying the psychologically relevant dimensions. Adolescents' work is a case in point. Superficially, one would certainly expect positive effects, particularly concerning the development of basic professional skills or commitment to achievement. Furthermore, thinking about occupational perspectives is a pivot of identity development (Vondracek, Lerner, & Schulenberg, 1986). However, not all work is alike and, as is well known, dimensions such as decision latitude or substantive complexity can have a positive impact on intellectual flexibility and other features of personality (Kohn & Schooler, 1983). It should also be remembered that aspects beyond the immediate quality of work are likely to be important for young people and that many jobs increase adolescents' social outreach, as well as adding new facets to their identity.

In the remainder of this chapter, I discuss the results and conclusions drawn in the various chapters of this volume, organized along the four new perspectives on adolescent risk behavior. I begin with the plea for a focus on the person rather than on isolated single risk variables.

Emphasis on the person

Until now, the emphasis on person-oriented research concerning adolescent risk behavior has been reflected primarily in a preference for certain methodologies rather than particular theoretical models. I begin, however, with some remarks concerning the notion of the problem behavior syndrome, which can be seen as an instance of a personological approach.

Problem behavior syndrome

If various problem behaviors represent manifestations of a common underlying construct, this should be revealed not only by high correlations among the respective behaviors, but also by shared risk factors, in spite of the differences in the manifestation of the syndrome. Although cross-sectional, the data set analyzed in Chapter 4 by Loeber and his colleagues offers probably the most comprehensive test of Jessor's claim that various maladaptive behaviors form a syndrome (Jessor & Jessor, 1977). In comparative analyses of three age cohorts covering childhood and early adolescence, they first confirmed that the eight behaviors studied indeed showed a strong common factor (with stronger loadings for externalizing than for other maladaptive behaviors).

Second, they demonstrated some variation with age in the personal, familial, and contextual risk factors, mainly to the effect that those factors were associated with a larger variety of problem behaviors at younger ages. In spite of this gradual specialization of risk factors, however, a few general risks relevant to various problem behaviors at various ages were prevalent, namely, attention deficit/impulsivity and hyperactivity, lack of guilt, and poor communication between parent and adolescent. Compared to these effects, the contextual factors, which range from low socioeconomic status (SES) and being on welfare, to single parenthood and coming from a broken home, to living in a crime-ridden neighborhood, seemed to exert little influence. Presumably this result is due to the fact that contextual effects were diluted in competition with more proximal variables, such as parental stress or poor parent–adolescent communication.

Although confirming a major prediction of Jessor's approach, the data do not reveal whether the association of behaviors is due to a common motivation, such as adolescents' striving for pseudoadult privileges. The fact that even such enormous data sets are silent on adolescents' thoughts and plans should give rise to complementary qualitative research.

Methodological considerations

Cairns and Cairns and their colleagues (Chapter 2, this volume) begin their chapter with a plea for developmental studies that start with the functioning of the person as a whole, rather than with a number of variables analyzed in isolation. In practical terms, the person actually is "persons," namely, groups characterized by a relatively homogeneous profile on a number of variables. The advantage is that subjects can be organized into homogeneous groups by a large number of descriptive agglomerate techniques (with various versions of cluster analysis being a prominent approach), whereas the identification of variables that form the person is a theoretical issue and depends on the aims of the research and knowledge of the substantive area. Dealing instead with a few homogeneous groups of subjects automatically catches the intricacies of higher-order relationships among aspects of psychological functioning in context. However, there is a risk implied in such an approach. It could encourage the breakdown of samples into subgroups on pragmatic grounds, using arbitrarily chosen collections of variables.

The main contribution of Cairns and Cairns and their colleagues is their delineation of four possible ways to apply the person-oriented (methodological) approach to longitudinal data. First, groups character-ized by similar individual profiles can be formed at Time 1. Individuals who deviate from the prevalent outcome of the group deserve attention; depending on the question and the design, they may represent espe-cially vulnerable or resilient cases.

Second, groups may be formed at the last wave of assessments. Whereas the first method clustered subjects according to antecedent conditions, this one categorizes individuals in terms of their develop-mental outcomes. Again, discrepancies between a high-risk load during earlier periods of development and normative outcomes may point to mechanisms of resilience.

Third, groups of individuals may be formed for each consecutive wave of measurement separately. Following this procedure, flowcharts of changes in cluster membership can be drawn, assuming that the clusters themselves are stable across time. In this way one would learn, for instance, whether repeatedly belonging to a particular cluster char-acterized by unemployment can be traced back to particular risk factors. Such data provide an insight into trajectories across time, albeit on an aggregated level.

Fourth, the individual trajectories over time may be subjected to appropriate methods of clustering. This procedure would result in ho-mogeneous sets of persons who share similar change patterns. I am not sure, however, whether this is indeed an instance of a person-oriented approach in the strict sense. Certainly an individual can be character-ized by a typical pathway through life, but this seems to be different from the notion that one is interested in catching the unique interplay of various aspects and levels of functioning within a person.

The following example from my own research group shows how one can combine theoretical notions about the processes driving individuals' trajectories with an approach compatible with the fourth option, as suggested by Cairns and Cairns et al. The basic question, asked by Labouvie (Labouvie, Pandina, & Johnson, 1991), was whether changes in risk factors immediately correspond to respective changes in the developmental outcome or whether risk factors produce lasting, cumu-lative effects. The latter conclusion would apply, for example, if reduc-tions in the level of risk factors result in preservation, not reduction, of

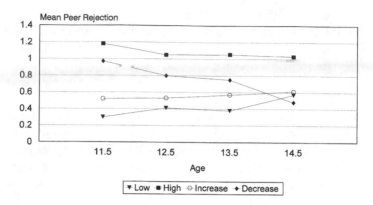

Figure 15.1 Change in peer rejection in four trajectories of external control beliefs.

the already accumulated adjustment problems. In order to distinguish these effects, different patterns of risk factors were formed and analyzed.

Utilizing data drawn from the Berlin Youth Longitudinal Study, Albrecht (1992) distinguished four trajectories of external control beliefs, assessed across three annual waves between ages 11 and 14 and ages 14 and 17. Externality could either stay high or low throughout; or externality scores could increase or decrease over time. The four outcome variables were levels of (low) self-esteem, peer rejection, transgression proneness, and contacts with deviant peers. Figure 15.1 shows the results for peer rejection in the younger sample.

As one can see, peer rejection was much more pronounced among those permanently high in externality than among those permanently low in externality. Furthermore, declining externality corresponded to a reduction in peer rejection, and vice versa. In other words, change in adjustment followed the change patterns of risk rather closely. Similar results were found for the older sample and for the other adjustment variables.

In sum, the results on externality reveal a pronounced plasticity of the adjustment indicators during the time span observed. Cumulative risk effects did not appear. In other words, there was no indication that adjustment was insensitive to a reduction in externality, nor did a constantly high level of externality result in a buildup of ever-increasing maladjustment. These results contribute to our understanding of the nature of the mechanism by which beliefs about oneself as an agent (or a pawn) influence social behavior.

Pathways of risk and opportunity

In a study following Cairns and Cairns et al.'s second way of utilizing typological approaches (Chapter 2, this volume), Ensminger and Juon (Chapter 11, this volume) relied on the longitudinal data set of the Woodlawn Study covering for almost 30 years an economically disadvantaged group of children and their mothers. The authors first grouped subjects in their adult years by patterns of variables indicating their social standing and psychosocial adjustment, and then looked for differences in childhood and adolescence risk factors that are seen as pathways of risk opportunity. The cluster-analytic patterns entail assessments of poverty status, SES, number of children, substance use, interpersonal aggression, and anxiety.

As all participants shared impoverished living conditions and other risk factors for maladjustment, such as high interpersonal aggression, at least during childhood, the fact that some groups do not show elevated scores in substance use or aggression is interesting. Comparing their profiles of risk (or protective) factors during childhood and adolescence with those of other groups can shed light on pathways of risk or opportunity.

It is important to note, however, that the pathways at the heart of the research program are merely indicated by the size of differences in childhood and adolescence variables among the clusters. Based on the empirical analyses, we do not know whether there are indeed relationships among these variables across time that would, in my view, be required in order to legitimate the use of the pathway metaphor.

The results are interesting and can be interpreted within well-known theoretical frameworks. For instance, weak social bonds to family and school represented a risk factor for later problem behaviors as adults, and premature social transitions, such as early home leaving, corresponded to heightened levels of problem behaviors in adulthood. We do not know, however, whether these two sets of experience were related to each other.

Moreover, parental involvement in children's lives was revealed as a protective factor. Two of the clusters showed relatively low levels of substance use and thus could be deemed equivalent in terms of the adult outcomes. However, on closer scrutiny, the adults in one of the clusters showed high rates of incarceration, their marriage rate was low, and their childhood and adolescence were characterized by high levels of maladjustment symptoms. In addition, low parental supervision and weak social bonding were reported for the first two decades of life. The other group, in contrast, had gained in social status and was virtually free of all indications of failure in adulthood. Not surprisingly, they showed that high social bonding and parental supervision, among other conditions, provided protection and helped to build up resources.

Differential trajectories and intervention

The effects of Moffit's (1993) distinction between adolescence-limited and life course–persistent problem behaviors can be seen throughout this volume. Beyond the general notion that studying groups of individuals rather than investigating variables in isolation gives a better grasp of the interplay between adolescents and their environment, her approach offers a substantive explanation about what is driving the two different types of pathways. Among the many possible research questions stimulated by this approach, the present volume mainly represents interesting propositions concerning the design of interventions. Before turning to this topic, however, I discuss a less spectacular but nevertheless crucial test of whether the shape of substance use trajectories during adolescence and beyond plays a role in adaptation.

Do trajectories matter?

White, Bates, and Labouvie (Chapter 5, this volume) tackle a problem relevant to all approaches that claim differential pathways of risk behaviors. Specifically, they set out to demonstrate that the shape of the growth curve in substance use makes a difference with regard to psychosocial outcomes, namely, dependent drug use, physical and psychological health, and adult role functioning. The level and shape of substance use were assessed over a considerable period during adolescence and young adulthood (15 to 31 years: four waves at intervals of 3 to 7 years).

At first glance, the authors' expectation that the use of the growth curve components (average trend, linear trend, etc.) would allow a better prediction than an alternative approach was confirmed. Whereas using measures of substance use assessed at Time 3 to predict outcomes at Time 4 resulted in few significant results, taking the entire trajectory from Time 1 to Time 4 into consideration led to many more significant results. Thus, status in mental health seems not only to be associated with individual differences in previous recent substance use, but also to differ as a function of the average level of substance use and the form of the age-related decline over many years of life.

On closer scrutiny, however, the results were seen to be virtually identical if Time 4 measures alone were used. That the level and shape of past trajectories did not play a role was further corroborated by the fact that data characterizing the Time 1 to Time 3 course of substance use revealed no significant prediction.

Does this mean that the history of substance use is irrelevant, thus giving a blow to costly long-term longitudinal research? In my view the answer, due to peculiarities of White et al.'s design, must be no. First of all, the intervals between measurements were rather large; for instance, between Time 3 and Time 4, 7 years elapsed, representing a time window from postadolescence to about age 30, depending on the cohort studied. In other words, in their normal population sample important transitions, such as the transition from college to work, were not covered by assessments. Given that dramatic changes in identity development can take place during this period (Fend, 1991), this certainly would have had an impact on at least some of the outcomes.

Moreover, given the plasticity of human development in general and the natural history of declining substance use among those whom Moffitt (1993) called "adolescence-limited users," it is obvious that disregarding change within the 7-year span should end in the view that past substance use trajectories are irrelevant.

New ideas for intervention

It is presumably fair to say that intervention methods in the past were not very successful (Hawkins, Catalano, & Miller, 1992). Many reasons have been cited in the literature, among them the idea that prevention efforts start too late and the fact that adolescents have difficulty using the threat of long-term negative consequences to control their behavior. The notion of different pathways that may require different times and means for interventions is likely to give this field a fresh impetus.

According to Baer et al. (Chapter 6, this volume), levels of adolescent substance use (mainly alcohol and marijuana), concurrently as well as longitudinally, are best predicted by peer factors, such as affiliation with friends who encourage drinking. Levels of use, even at the higher end, however, cannot be equated with problem use. This is underscored by the fact that the patterns of concurrent and longitudinal risk factors for alcohol-related impairments of social functioning, such as school absenteeism, are best predicted by family adversities and childhood problems ranging from hyperactivity to low frustration tolerance and the experience of negative affects. Given the fact that only a small minority of adolescents show such problem drinking, it is plausible to assume that similar alcohol consumption figures may actually be rooted in different developmental processes or pathways.

Although Zucker, Fitzgerald, and Moses (1995) presented a typology of pathways to alcohol abuse, the idea that different developmental trajectories may lead to similar adolescent behaviors, but entail different outlooks later in adulthood, was actually promoted by Moffitt's (1993) distinction between adolescence-limited and life course–persistent problem behaviors.

Concerning the design of prevention and treatment programs, the most striking aspect of such a view is the claim that the seriousness of the behaviors during adolescence alone does not allow the likely trajectory to be identified. Baer and colleagues' general idea is to provide an optimal match between intervention design and substance-related developmental trajectory. For example, programs aimed at reducing the harm associated with substance use would suffice in the case of adolescence-limited use. Their aim is to avoid negative labeling, minimize health risks, and offer safe contexts. On the other hand, adolescents on a life course–persistent trajectory would require prevention efforts that ideally would have already started in childhood. The aims are to reduce conduct problems, improve social skills and academic competence, strengthen parenting, and so forth.

Obviously, a reliable and cost-effective identification of an individual's particular substance-related trajectory is a prerequisite for any matching between problem and cure. Assuming that the life course–

persistent type is shown by about 10% of adolescents, unknowingly treating them with a harm reduction program may be dangerous because it could carry the message that the problems are transitory and do not require firm action.

At first glance, the major contribution by Williams (Chapter 7, this volume) is to demonstrate that risky driving by young people is another, often overlooked, instance of a behavior addressed by Jessor's problem behavior theory (Jessor & Jessor, 1977). Adolescents low in conventionality at ages 13–14 (assessed by whether they had been in trouble with the law, thus using a rather strict criterion) not only showed higher rates of various other problem behaviors during their senior year in high school, but also were much higher on reckless and dangerous driving, including car crashes.

On closer scrutiny, however, Williams's report on recent research and program development in the field of reckless driving once more illuminates the advantage of thinking in terms of developmental pathways. It would be most interesting to find out, for instance, whether the life course–persistent youth at risk Moffitt (1993) had in mind are indeed overrepresented in the group of dangerous drivers. As revealed by discouraging experiences with interventions, attempts to improve driving skills are of very limited use here. Rather, early risk factors need to be addressed, such as impulsivity and low frustration tolerance, which persist into adolescence and have ramifications for behavioral styles. In the following paragraphs, I discuss a recent German approach that addresses the developmental roots of adolescents' risky driving.

In Germany about 20% of all fatal car crashes caused by young drivers (from 18, the legal licensing age, to 24) happen in a total of 12 hours dispersed across Friday and Saturday nights. These so-called discotheque crashes typically occur on the way home from a discotheque while driving under the influence of alcohol and further handicapped by fatigue (Schulze & Berninghaus, 1990).

Results such as these led Schulze (1996) to search for lifestyle subgroups and to compare their traffic behavior. Based on representative samples from (West) Germany, comprehensive information was gathered on variables such as leisure-time activities, music and TV preferences, youthful clothing styles, and respondents' affinity to particular crowds. Utilizing cluster analysis techniques, Schulze found that the groups had remarkably different profiles of traffic-related risk-taking behavior. Three out of seven clusters showed particularly high mileage per year. Members rated high on driving-related "extra motives," such as thrill-seeking on the road or the need to show off through driving style. Their alcohol consumption was far higher than that of other groups; between 10% and 20% drank daily, and their weekly consumption was about one-third higher than that of most other groups. These groups consisted mainly of males with a low educational level, with one-third or more working in stereotypically male jobs such as construction worker. Studies conducted in Sweden (Berg & Gregerson, 1993) utilized similar approaches and found similar differences in traffic-related behavior and motives.

Against this backdrop, the prevention design is focused on the risky drivers' belief that their behavior is attractive to their (female) peers and friends. Although, according to Hoppe and Tekaat (1994), this view is not at all shared by these significant others, especially female peers, they lack the skills to resist or change the attitude of their companions. A recently developed program therefore utilizes peer messages (risky driving is not cool, alcohol is not good for sex, etc.), embedded in attractive live music shows, to influence risky young drivers. One such campaign (Schulze & Berninghaus, 1990) brought the program to 40 major discotheques all over Germany, organized in the same way as a tour of a professional pop band. Formal evaluation data are not yet available, but anecdotal reports are very encouraging.

Biopsychosocial processes

Several chapters in this volume explicitly address the interplay between biological and psychosocial processes. Bearing in mind the fact that adolescents continuously negotiate their development through transactions with their physical surroundings and social environment, in shopping malls and in discotheques, at school and at work, it is clear that advanced research programs require designs that allow such processes to be captured at all levels, including those that take place in close relationships with others, whether family or peers.

Presumably, readers will agree that "bread-and-butter" research is quite different. We almost never get a full representation of the processes by which adolescents shape their environment, and even behaviors that are almost dyadic in nature are rarely gathered from all proponents involved. In contrast, Udry and Bearman (Chapter 8, this volume) inform us about the design of a new study on adolescent health that sets new standards in this regard. By collecting data on students and their environment, whether friends or the physical props they share, all the influences, from social groups to individuals to the biological bases of their behavior and vice versa, can be analyzed. Utilizing multiple informants helps to minimize bias resulting from shared measurement variance. The very large number of cases (100,000) and the fact that natural units are investigated (schools) allow the researchers to assess networks of peers, friends, and romantic partners, enabling the roles of collectives as well as those of individuals to be studied.

Another advanced research opportunity exists because many individuals with shared genetic variance have been identified, such as identical and fraternal twins, siblings, and biologically unrelated children within the same family. Such designs are a must if one is interested in teasing apart genetic and environmental influences on interindividual differences. Moreover, an assessment of shared versus nonshared environmental factors is possible that goes beyond the usual emphasis of behavior genetics on the family (Rowe, 1994).

Graber et al. (Chapter 9, this volume) deal with adolescent sexuality in particular. In contrast to earlier research, however, and thus nicely fitting the overall framework of this book, in this chapter sexual development is seen as part of normative development. Moreover, rather than limiting analyses to single behaviors, which in past research mainly concerned intercourse, here the development of sexual identity is characterized by many transitions in modes and quality of behavior. Various aspects of problem behavior are involved, such as unprotected sexual contact. Another aspect of problem sexual behavior is precocious transitions to sexual behaviors that, according to cultural norms or functional norms of health and adaptive development, are age inadequate. In other words, the timing of transitions, their antecedents, and their consequences are important issues.

There is a large body of research on the timing of puberty (for a review, see Silbereisen & Kracke, 1993). Much less is known, however, about the timing of "firsts" with regard to sexual activities in the broader sense. The initiation of intercourse and other sexual behaviors seems to be particularly influenced by social factors (e.g., peer group norms), and biological changes seem to result from, rather than precede, some sexual behaviors. The sad case of prepubertal sexual abuse that accelerates pubertal development is an example (Trickett & Putnam, 1993).

Another important message in Chapter 9 concerns the interplay between hormonal and other factors in the emergence of sexual behaviors. Obviously, previous models, which assumed direct links between hormones and sexual activity, at least for boys, were inadequate. Rather, it appears that the timing of puberty, indicated by interindividual differences in testosterone levels, drives earlier sexual behavior in boys by motivating them to engage in relevant activities, putting them on a self-perpetuating trajectory. In contrast, girls' more advanced sexual behavior tends to occur in response to boys' attention to their advanced level of physical maturation.

It is obvious that much more research is necessary to elucidate these intricate relationships. The timing of sexual transitions may do more than influence the timing of later transitions, such as childbearing. One could even ask whether constraints on the timing of later transitions have an anticipatory impact on earlier transitions. In our own research (Silbereisen & Schwarz, in press), we used the opportunity of German unification to investigate whether the timing of first sexual encounters differed between samples from the former East Germany and West Germany. In spite of shared cultural traditions, marriage and first pregnancy formerly occurred considerably earlier in the East; thus, earlier aspects of sexual development might have been accelerated as well (Hormuth et al., 1996). Furthermore, the question was whether the same variables of biological (pubertal timing) or psychological origin would predict the onset of sexual activities. In order to comply with research ethics, the latter were described to the adolescent subjects (aged 13 to 19 years) as "first real sexual experience." Additional data reported by Silbereisen and Schwarz (in press) make it highly likely that the wording was interpreted as meaning intercourse.

Concerning experiences during adolescence in both East and West Germany, subjects who were less closely monitored by their mothers, and who had more frequent contacts within peer cliques, underwent the transition to first sexual activities earlier. This was also the case with early-maturing adolescents (self-perceived timing of pubertal maturation in comparison to age-mates) and with adolescents who had faced many family adversities during childhood (e.g. divorce, illness).

However, there was a striking East–West difference with regard to social activities during childhood. In the West those adolescents, both male and female, who preferred role-play activities during childhood that complied more with the masculine stereotype began sexual relationships earlier. According to research on gender-differential socialization, such play activities provide more opportunities for manipulation, inventiveness, and agency (Lytton & Romney, 1991). The same role-play activities were irrelevant in the East. Because we found similar differences in the timing of other transitions, such as first vocational interests, the present results support the view that the timing of psychosocial transitions in the East was less influenced by individuals' own actions (Silbereisen, Vondracek, & Berg, 1997).

Kandel's research (Chapter 3, this volume) is another example of the cross-fertilization between socialization-oriented and biologically inspired research. As the participants of her well-known New York State cohort approached middle adulthood, the opportunity arose to investigate the transmission of substance use from the former adolescents to their offspring, who themselves had grown to adolescence. Kandel found a relationship between current smoking by parents and children, but the association was particularly strong between mothers and daughters. All attempts failed to explain the difference between parents by differential modeling opportunities for smoking and role-specific socialization practices.

These observations led Kandel and her colleagues to assume that mothers may have induced a liability to smoking by exposing their offspring prenatally to nicotine by their own smoking during pregnancy. Indeed, she demonstrated a dose-related association between smoking during pregnancy and daughters' smoking in early adolescence, net of mothers' current smoking. This relationship was not attenuated by alternative predictors, such as maternal education and socialization practices. Parallel results obtained with data from the National Longitudinal Survey of Youth lend further support to the notion of a direct biological relation between prenatal maternal smoking and smoking among offspring.

Rather than assuming a direct genetic liability to smoking, Kandel points to the possibility of a latent dependency on nicotine, induced by in utero exposure and perhaps reinforced by passive smoking during childhood, which becomes manifest a decade or so later when opportunities to smoke arise due to the greater freedom granted during adolescence.

Although recent research on the role of nicotine in changing the properties and thresholds of the dopaminergic system, and on functional properties of the developing brain in general, lend plausibility to this presumption, a number of issues remain. First, if the predicted chain of events is true, one should expect a higher liability to persistent smoking among adolescents exposed to passive smoking more frequently during childhood. Moreover, the effect of smoking during pregnancy may be attenuated among mothers who stopped smoking later on or whose live-in partners did not smoke. Perhaps it is possible to use existing data on past substance use to test such predictions.

Second, the fact that the results pertained to girls but not to boys seems to be the most problematic aspect for validation of the model. Kandel seems to focus on early differences in the brain and reports that females are more liable to become dependent on psychoactive substances than males during adolescence (however, not cigarettes so far). Alternatively, one may see her results as a manifestation of a gender differential in psychological vulnerability in a more general sense (Werner & Smith, 1982).

Judged by the results of Compas et al. (Chapter 10, this volume), gender differences are not well understood in other risk behaviors either. The material presented on depression sheds new light on the question of whether the often reported higher levels of affective problems in girls compared to boys are real. A major advance in knowledge is the view that one has to distinguish between types of samples. Within samples of the normal population, gender differences seem to develop in early adolescence. However, these differences are very small. In particular, the proposed gender-differential increase with age is difficult to detect at all, even with large samples. In clinical samples of referrals, however, gender effects are much larger, with girls revealing higher levels of disturbance; still, these effects do not seem to increase with age. In comparing these trends, Compas and his colleagues do not rule out the possibility that the effect found in normal population samples is due mainly to the (small) proportion of high-risk cases (referrals).

Unfortunately, Compas et al. do not discuss whether the results require any of the established explanations to be corrected. For instance, in the normal population, gender differences in depression emerge at about ages 11 to 13. Is this fact compatible with the proposed role of gender stereotypes? At any rate, a major issue for future research is to describe the processes leading to the differences in gender effects.

Results of our own research may help to clarify the gender differences in vulnerability. Gloth (1996) analyzed a sample of about 500 adolescents, aged 10 to 13 years, from former West and East Germany, utilizing the items for affective symptoms of the German version of the CES-D (Radloff, 1977), published by Hautzinger and Bailer (1993). Controlled for parental depressive affect, family harmony, and pubertal status, peer problems (rejection by peers) and (low) school-related self-efficacy corresponded to depressive affect in both girls and boys. The roots of the peer problems, however, seem to differ between the genders. Among boys, those low in family harmony were also affected by peer problems, whereas such problems among girls were related to indicators of a difficult temperament. The latter, assessed according to Windle's procedure (1992), encompassed difficulties such as great restlessness and rigidity, low task orientation, and little openness to change. Such difficulties are certainly more far-reaching when challenged by new developmental tasks than by low family harmony. Thus, it could well be that depressive affect is a gender-typical manifestation of difficulties in coping with the new challenges of adolescence.

Psychologically relevant dimensions of contexts

This section focuses on the impact of adolescents' work history on the development of risk behavior. Although the psychological quality of the job was not assessed, in contrast to previous research the effect of the duration of work was studied across specified periods of time. The advantage is that the equivalent of a dose–response relation can be estimated to assess how much work in addition to normal school activities is beneficial or detrimental.

Mortimer and Johnson (Chapter 13, this volume) formed an a priori classification that basically distinguished combinations of high (20 hours or more per week) versus low work intensity, and long (18 months or more) versus short duration of work. Results in general showed that high-intensity work pursued over long periods of time corresponded to the most pronounced effects, both positive and negative.

Concerning outcomes, a clear advantage of work was revealed. Those who engaged in more employment (intensity and/or duration) during high school were more likely to find full-time work during the following years. Concerning the use of alcohol and nicotine, those who worked longer hours initiated and increased their use earlier than age-mates. However, a few years after high school, others had caught up. Because other manifestations of psychosocial precocity, such as an earlier transition to parenting, did not happen either, the risks facing working adolescents seem to be rather small.

The report did not address the quality of work. Thus, it cannot be ruled out that earlier full-time work comes at the expense of long-term accumulation of human capital and well-being. Further, it is unclear whether the reasons for longer or shorter duration, and higher or lower work intensity, were related to labor market opportunities or whether they actually represented the realization of adolescents' future-oriented goals. Unfortunately, as is so often the case in this research field, no assessments of adolescents' plans and future perspectives were provided.

In the chapter by Steinberg and Avenevoli (Chapter 12, this volume) a new approach to the analysis of over-time relations between problem behaviors and problem contexts during the high school years is presented. Problem behaviors are indicated by low school engagement and substance use/delinquency, and problem contexts are indicated by parental permissiveness and working long hours on a part-time job. The main result concerns the role of school disengagement in increased substance use and delinquency. The relationship is both direct and mediated by higher work intensity and, surprisingly, by greater parental permissiveness. Concerning the latter, the authors seem to favor the view that parents' increased permissiveness is an indication of "giving in" as a consequence of their children's low school engagement. Bearing in mind that only a few variables were investigated in a normal population sample, some more mundane alternative interpretations should be considered. For instance, the results could be due to other potentially important variables that were left out. Further, it is unclear how many adolescents actually represented the postulated pathway, leaving open the possibility that only a few were responsible for the effect.

When the variable-oriented analyses are amended by using a person-centered approach, additional results show that adolescents who differed at the outset in school engagement (low, medium, high) differed correspondingly in problem behavior levels across grades. Moreover, those low in school engagement revealed a disproportionately greater increase in problem behavior than the two remaining groups.

The authors give no interpretation for this phenomenon. In my view, the key issue is that school engagement (or disengagement) is very stable across time, meaning that those high in disengagement at the beginning will have accumulated a fair amount of such experience. As disengagement is a manifestation of weak conventional bonds, according to Hirschi's (1969) control theory, what the data seem to show is that consistently low engagement in school results in an accelerated increase in minor delinquency and other problem behaviors. Low and medium school disengagement, in contrast, do not reveal such devastating consequences, thus demonstrating a threshold effect. In other words, the mechanisms resulting in the outcome are likely to be different.

Outlook

At the beginning of this chapter, I distinguished four areas where the present volume offers advances and new insights, namely, the emphasis on the person, the distinction of risk behavior trajectories, the focus on biological underpinnings, and the interest in developmentally relevant dimensions of context.

In my view, the concepts and data offered are impressive, particularly with regard to a better understanding of intraindividual change processes, thus opening up new opportunities for intervention in the development of adolescent risk behaviors. In this regard, the notion of risk behavior trajectories is pivotal. Although more empirical validation is certainly required, concepts such as the distinction between adolescence-limited and life course–persistent problem behaviors allow the design of optimally timed, individually tailored interventions. If these are combined with the other advances mentioned, a true developmental-contextualist approach can be established.

Bearing all the advances in mind, I nevertheless see various issues that will need attention in future work. It is clear that until now, emphasis on the person (rather than on single variables) has been greater on the level of design and analysis than with regard to concepts and aspects of functioning. It is obvious, for instance, that motivational and cognitive processes, such as goal–setting and beliefs related to one's efficacy in pursuing goals, did not play the role they deserve in a personological approach. Phenomena such as "niche–picking" by individuals were not central to the analyses. Concerning contexts, in particular, it is still the case that developmentally instigative properties (e.g., the degree to which the intention of a context, concerning the means it provides for the attainment of a life task, is clear, see Noack, 1990, for an extensive study of such properties) are, at best, indirectly assessed.

There is a final issue that, in my view, requires more attention. The world of the adolescents sampled and represented in this volume was relatively stable, in spite of some remarkable changes and declines in the quality of life, as addressed in certain chapters. Stable, that is, at least when compared to the tremendous political transformations and societal changes that took place in Eastern Europe and that in many countries were accompanied by a rise in the rates of risk behaviors among adolescents. The reasons may be manifold but generally are not well understood.

Concerning the German situation, for instance, a core element seems to be that the entire system of government–sponsored institutions for adolescents in the East closed down before a new infrastructure for community–based leisure activities could be built. This problem was exacerbated by the economic downturn, which resulted in a lack of vocational opportunities (apprenticeships) and a high unemployment rate. In addition, self–organized activities with peers were less prevalent in the East compared to the West even before unification. Thus the demise of institutional leisure activities resulted in an even larger so-cialization gap.

I am not arguing that impoverished contexts have not been studied in the past; some of the contributions in this volume are testimony to such approaches. Nevertheless, the scale and breadth of the changes in many societies were unprecedented and, as such, provide opportu-nities for research that would help to clarify the causes of historical trends in the prevalence of risk behaviors (Silbereisen, Robins, & Rut-ter, 1995).

References

Albrecht, H. (1992). *Über den Zusammenhang von Kontrollüberzeugungen und psychosozialer Anpassung im Jugendalter* [*On the relation between control beliefs and psychosocial adaptation in adolescence*]. Unpublished Ph.D thesis, University of Giessen, Germany.

Baltes, P. B. (1987). Theoretical propositions of life-span developmental psychology: On the dynamics between growth and decline. *Developmental Psychology, 23,* 611–626.

Baumrind, D. (1991). The influence of parenting style on adolescent competence and substance use. *Journal of Early Adolescence, 11,* 56–95.

Berg, H. Y., & Gregersen, N. P. (1993). Samband mellan unga bilförares livstil och deras olychsrisk i trafiken. *VTIrapport, 60,* 37–43.

Brandtstädter, J. (1998). Action perspectives on human development. In R. M. Lerner (Ed.), *Theoretical models of human development:* Volume 1 of the *Handbook of child psychology* (5th ed., pp. 807–863). New York: Wiley.

Bronfenbrenner, U. (1986). Recent advances in research on the ecology of human development. In R. K. Silbereisen, K. Eyferth, & G. Rudinger (Eds.), *Development as action in context* (pp. 287–310). Berlin: Springer.

Brooks-Gunn, J., Graber, J. A., & Paikoff, R. L. (1994). Studying links between hormones and negative affect: Models and measures. *Journal of Research on Adolescence, 4,* 469–486.

Donovan, J., & Jessor, R. (1985). Structure of problem behavior in adolescence and young adulthood. *Journal of Consulting and Clinical Psychology, 53,* 890–904.

Fend, H. (1991). *Identitätsentwicklung in der Adoleszenz. Lebensentwürfe, Selbstfindung und Weltaneignung in beruflichen, familiären und politisch-weltanschaulichen Bereichen,* Volume 2 [*Identity development in adolescence*]. Bern: Hans Huber.

Gloth, I. (1996). *Risiken für die Entstehung depressiver Verstimmungen bei 10-bis 13jährigen Kindern und Jugendlichen* [*Risk factor for depressive affect among 10- to 13-year-olds*]. Unpublished M.A. thesis, Department of Psychology, University of Jena, Germany.

Hautzinger, M., & Bailer, M. (1993). *Allgemeine Depressionsskala (AIDS)* [*General Depression Scale*]. Weinheim: Beltz Test.

Hawkins, J. D., Catalano, R. F., & Miller, J. Y. (1992). Risk and protective factors for alcohol and other drug problems in adolescence and early adulthood: Implications for substance abuse prevention. *Psychological Bulletin, 112,* 64–105.

Hirschi, T. (1969). *Causes of delinquency.* Berkeley: University of California Press.

Hoppe, R., & Tekaat, A. (1994). *Abschlußbericht zum FP 2.8937 "Sicherheitsbeitrag spezieller nächtlicher Reförderungsangebote" [Special public transportation offers and their contribution to traffic safety].* Unpublished paper, Federal Highway Research Institute, Cologne, Germany.

Hormuth, S. E., Heinz, W. R., Kornadt, H.-J., Sydow, H., & Trommsdorff, G. (1996). *Individuelle Entwicklung, Bildung und Berufsverläufe [Individual development, education, and occupational careers].* Opladen: Leske & Budrich.

Jessor, R., & Jessor, S. L. (1977). *Problem behavior and psychosocial development: A longitudinal study of youth.* New York: Academic Press.

Kohn, M. L., & Schooler, C. (1983). *Work and personality. An inquiry into the impact of social stratification.* Norwood, NJ: Ablex.

Labouvie, E. W., Pandina, R. J., & Johnson, V. (1991). Developmental trajectories of substance use in adolescence: Differences and predictors. *International Journal of Behavioral Development, 14,* 305–328.

Lytton, H., & Romney, D. M. (1991). Parents' differential socialization of boys and girls: A meta-analysis. *Psychological Bulletin, 109,* 267–296.

Magnusson, D., & Stattin, H. (1998). Person–context interaction theories. In R. M. Lerner (Ed.), *Theoretical models of human development:* Volume 1 of the *Handbook of child psychology* (5th ed., pp. 685–759). New York: Wiley.

Moffitt, T. E. (1993). Adolescence-limited and life-course-persistent antisocial behavior: A developmental taxonomy. *Psychological Review, 100,* 674–701.

Noack, P. (1990). *Jugendentwicklung im Kontext [Adolescent development in context].* Munich: Psychologie Verlags Union.

Petraitis, J., Flay, B. R., & Miller, T. Q. (1995). Reviewing theories of adolescent substance use: Organizing pieces in the puzzle. *Psychological Bulletin, 117,* 67–86.

Radloff, L. S. (1977). The CES-D scale: A self-report depression scale for research in general population. *Applied Psychological Measurement, 3,* 385–401.

Rowe, D. C. (1994). *The limits of family influence.* New York: Guilford Press.

Schulze, H. (1996). *Lebensstil und Verkehrsverhalten junger Fahrer und Fahrerinnen [Life style and traffic behavior of young male and female drivers].* Berichte der Bundesanstalt für Straßenwesen. Mensch und Sicherheit, Heft 56. Bremerhaven: Verlag für neue Wissenschaft.

Schulze, H., & Berninghaus, P. (1990). *Damit sie die Kurve Kriegen – Fakten und Vorschläge zur Reduzierung nächtlicher Freizeitunfälle junger Leute*

[*Facts and suggestions to reduce night time traffic accidents among young people*]. Bonn: Deutscher Verkehrssicherheitsrat.

Silbereisen, R. K., & Kracke, B. (1993). Variation in maturational timing and adjustment in adolescence. In S. Jackson & H. Rodriguez-Tomé (Eds.), *Adolescence and its social worlds* (pp. 67–94). East Sussex, U.K.: Erlbaum.

Silbereisen, R. K., Noack, P., & Schöenpflug, U. (1994). Comparative analyses of beliefs, leisure contexts, and substance use in West Berlin and Warsaw. In R. K. Silbereisen & E. Todt (Eds.), *Adolescence in context: The interplay of family, school, peers, and work in adjustment* (pp. 176–198). New York: Springer.

Silbereisen, R. K., Robins, L., & Rutter, M. (1995). Secular trends in substance use: Concepts and data on the impact of social change on alcohol and drug abuse. In M. Rutter & D. J. Smith (Eds.), *Psychosocial disorders in young people: Time trends and their origins* (pp. 490–543). Chichester, U.K.: Wiley.

Silbereisen, R. K., & Schwarz, B. (in press). Predicting the timing of first romantic involvement: Commonalities and differences in the former Germanys. In J. E. Nurmi (Ed.), *Adolescents, cultures, and conflicts: Growing up in contemporary Europe*. New York: Garland.

Silbereisen, R. K., Vondracek, F. W., & Berg, L. A. (1997). Differential timing of initial vocational choice: The influence of early childhood family relocation and parental support behaviors in two cultures. *Journal of Vocational Behavior, 50*, 41–59.

Stattin, H., & Magnusson, D. (1990). *Pubertal maturation in female development. Path through life* (Volume 2). Hillsdale, NJ: Erlbaum.

Trickett, P. K., & Putnam, F. W. (1993). Impact of child sexual abuse on females: Toward a developmental, psychobiological integration. *Psychological Science, 4*, 81–87.

Vondracek, F. W., Lerner, R. M., & Schulenberg, J. E. (Eds.). (1986). *Career development: A life-span developmental approach*. Hillsdale, NJ: Erlbaum.

Werner, E. E., & Smith, R. S. (1982). *Vulnerable but invincible. A study of resilient children*. New York: McGraw-Hill.

Windle, M. (1992). Temperament and social support in adolescence: Interrelations with depressive symptoms and delinquent behavior. *Journal of Youth and Adolescence, 21*, 1–21.

Zucker, R. A., Fitzgerald, H. E., & Moses, H. D. (1995). Emergence of alcohol problems and the several alcoholisms: A developmental perspective on etiologic theory and life course trajectory. In: D. Cicchetti & D. J. Cohen (Eds.), *Developmental psychopathology* (Vol. 2, pp. 677–711). New York: Wiley.

Author index

Subject index